GRAND MANOR
HOMES

120 Distinguished Home Designs

hanley▲wood
HomePlanners

GRAND MANOR HOMES

Published by Home Planners, LLC
Wholly owned by Hanley-Wood, LLC

Senior Vice President, Andy Schultz
Chief Financial Officer, Joe Carroll
Vice President, Publishing, Jennifer Pearce
Executive Editor, Linda Bellamy
National Sales Manager, Book Division, Julie Marshall
Managing Editor, Jason D. Vaughan
Special Projects Editor, Kristin Schneidler
Editor, Nate Ewell
Lead Plans Associate, Morenci C. Clark
Plans Associates, Elizabeth Landry, Nick Nieskes
Proofreader, Douglas Jenness
Technical Specialist, Jay C. Walsh
Lead Data Coordinator, Fran Altemose
Data Coordinators, Misty Boler, Melissa Siewert
Production Manager, Brenda McClary

Big Designs, Inc.
President, Creative Director, Anthony D'Elia
Vice President, Business Manager, Megan D'Elia
Vice President, Design Director, Chris Bonavita
Editorial Director, John Roach
Assistant Editor, Tricia Starkey
Director of Design and Production, Stephen Reinfurt
Group Art Director, Kevin Limongelli
Photo Editor, Christine DiVuolo
Managing Art Director, Jessica Hagenbuch
Graphic Designer, Mary Ellen Mulshine
Graphic Designer, Lindsey O'Neill-Myers
Graphic Designer, Jacque Young
Assistant Photo Editor, Mark Storch
Project Director, David Barbella
Assistant Production Manager, Rich Fuentes

Photo Credits

Front Cover: Plan HPT920002; for details see page 22.
Photo: ©Laurence Taylor Photography

Previous Page: Plan HPT920012, for details see page 56.
Photo by Laurence Taylor

Back Cover: Plan HPT920001; for details see page 13.
Photo: ©Laurence Taylor Photography

Home Planners Corporate Headquarters
1 Thomas Circle, NW, Suite 600
Washington, DC 20005

Distribution Center
29333 Lorie Lane
Wixom, Michigan 48393

© 2003

10 9 8 7 6 5 4 3 2

Printed in the United States of America

Library of Congress Catalog Control Number: 2003105315

ISBN: 1-931131-17-1

22

GRAND MANOR HOMES

58

ON THE COVER: See page 56 for more details on this
exquisite three-bedroom Mediterranean home. The stunning
dining room is defined by the detailed architectural elements,
such as the tray ceiling, a component found throughout the
home. The room also enjoys natural light and sweeping views.

Personal Touch

Dan Sater designs every home as though it were for his own family, combining function with the ultimate in luxury.

DAN F. SATER II, AIBD, PRESIDENT OF THE SATER DESIGN COLLECTION, INC., HAS SERVED THE residential construction industry since 1983, designing countless distinctive homes throughout Florida and the United States. The Sater Design Collection, Inc. is southwest Florida's most recognized design firm and has received over 250 local and national design awards.

Dan Sater has served as a national officer and has spoken on behalf of the American Institute of Building Design on a national level in addition to serving on a state level. Sater has also been retained by some of America's most prominent business leaders and entertainers, and he has designed homes for clients all over the world.

The Designs

Sater's vast experience with designing custom homes has given him many advantages in creating his predesigned plans, and these predrawn homes have a personal touch as well; Sater designs each home as though it were for his own family. Because he wants his homes to fit their eventual owners like well-made custom gloves, he gives great attention to detail—whether the home he's designing is a family-sized 2,500 square feet or a lavish 5,000 square feet. In addition to having exteriors designed to be viewed from all angles, Sater's predrawn plans incorporate elements of his luxurious custom designs and boast striking interior architectural elements: columns, art niches, gallery halls, and a range of ceiling treatments. Sater gives careful thought to how visitors will experience each home, and he strives to give guests something new and attractive to view at every turn. Each Sater blueprint arrives with extra sheets that include information on interior details and electrical placement.

Sater's homes maximize indoor/outdoor relationships, with plenty of

© The Sater Design Collection, Inc.

porches, terraces, and decks; often, gathering areas feature several entrances to the outdoors. New glass technologies allow him to incorporate numerous windows into his designs, including his signature "vanishing wall"— a wall composed of a series of sliding glass doors that roll back so there are no barriers between the room and the outdoors. Many of Sater's classic Floridian designs, such as Plan HPT920017 on page 69, incorporate this unique design element.

Cabins, Cottages, and Villas

Sater's first themed collection consisted of cabins, cottages, and villa-style homes designed for waterfront properties; here, these designs are displayed in the "Homes for All Seasons" section, beginning on page 141. Intended to serve as vacation or second homes, these plans are somewhat larger than the usual vacation cottages; Sater's experiences with clients have taught him that people enjoy using their vacation homes as gathering spots for large groups of family and friends. Consequently, homes in this collection often include multiple bedrooms—most with private baths, and some with private decks and patios—and spacious casual gathering areas like great rooms and leisure rooms. This collection began with a series of charming beach cabins like HPT920101 on page 153—its siding exterior, standing-seam roof, and multitude of windows make it an ideal oceanfront home. After receiving some feedback from clients, Sater created a more rustic series of homes, with stone accents and Craftsman flair, for

mountain and lakefront lots. Sater's own travels, where he observed a number of vacation homes in elegant Mediterranean styles, inspired him to design his own villa-style vacation homes, with tiled roofs and smooth stucco exteriors.

Country Comfort

Sater's next themed collection focused on efficient, family-oriented plans; view these in the "Country Estates" section, which begins on page 126. These homes are Sater's interpretations of classic farmhouse-style plans. They still include his signature features—open, flowing floor plans, lots of outdoor space, and a variety of ceiling treatments—but offer extra "homelike" touches like expansive country kitchens and walk-in pantries. Plans in this collection appear in three different styles. Rural-style country homes, like Plan

HPT920088 on page 140, feature welcoming front porches and whimsical flower boxes; other designs, like Plan HPT920084 on page 136, announce their romantic Victorian character through bay windows, fishscale shingles, and asymmetrical exteriors. And homes like HPT920086, on page 138, display their French country heritage with stucco-and-stone exteriors and hipped rooflines.

European Romantics

Sater's most recent, and perhaps most luxurious, themed collection is showcased in the "European Style" section, beginning on page 81. To create these homes, Sater found inspiration in four very different design styles: sprawling British estate homes, French country chateaus, Italian Renaissance villas, and Spanish and Moorish homes. Elements of these designs are readily apparent in this collection: Plan HPT920040, on page 92, blends the earth-toned stucco exterior and tiled roof of a grand Spanish estate with the soaring arches and multiple windows of an Italian villa. European estate elements—courtyards, sweeping staircases, and formal libraries—fill the interiors of these homes as well. ■

Modern Elegance

Light abounds in this spacious mansion. Every area in the house is illuminated by natural light that serves to accentuate the home's interior.

A MAJESTIC ENTRANCE PROVIDES A STUNNING INTRODUCTION TO THIS ITALIAN Renaissance design. Once inside, the foyer—defined by columns—opens to a trio of stunning formal rooms. To the right, the dining room boasts a stepped ceiling and a bay window; to the left, the study, accessed by double doors, features a vaulted ceiling and built-in shelves and cabinetry. The centrally located living room, also with a stepped ceiling, includes a fireplace and two walls of sliding glass doors that open to the rear lanai.

Above: Elegant, rounded stairs lead gracefully up to the magnificent entry of this Italian Renaissance design.
Opposite page: The covered lanai, refreshing pool, and raised patio create the picturesque backyard.

FEATURE HOME

Above: A coffered ceiling lends a formal atmosphere to the study, where built-in shelves and cabinets line the walls. **Right:** Informal furnishings surrounding the entertainment center create a relaxed mood in the leisure room; to the right, note the view of the courtyard fireplace.

Informal spaces—the leisure room, kitchen, and breakfast nook—reside in the right wing of the home. The kitchen, with a central island, a walk-in pantry, and a convenient butler's pantry that leads to the dining room, is a gourmet's dream. The nearby nook features a curved wall of glass that overlooks the lanai. The leisure room offers a built-in entertainment center, a vaulted ceiling, and a wall of sliding glass doors that give access to an expansive side courtyard with an outdoor kitchen and a fireplace. Also found in the right wing are two front bedrooms, each with a walk-in

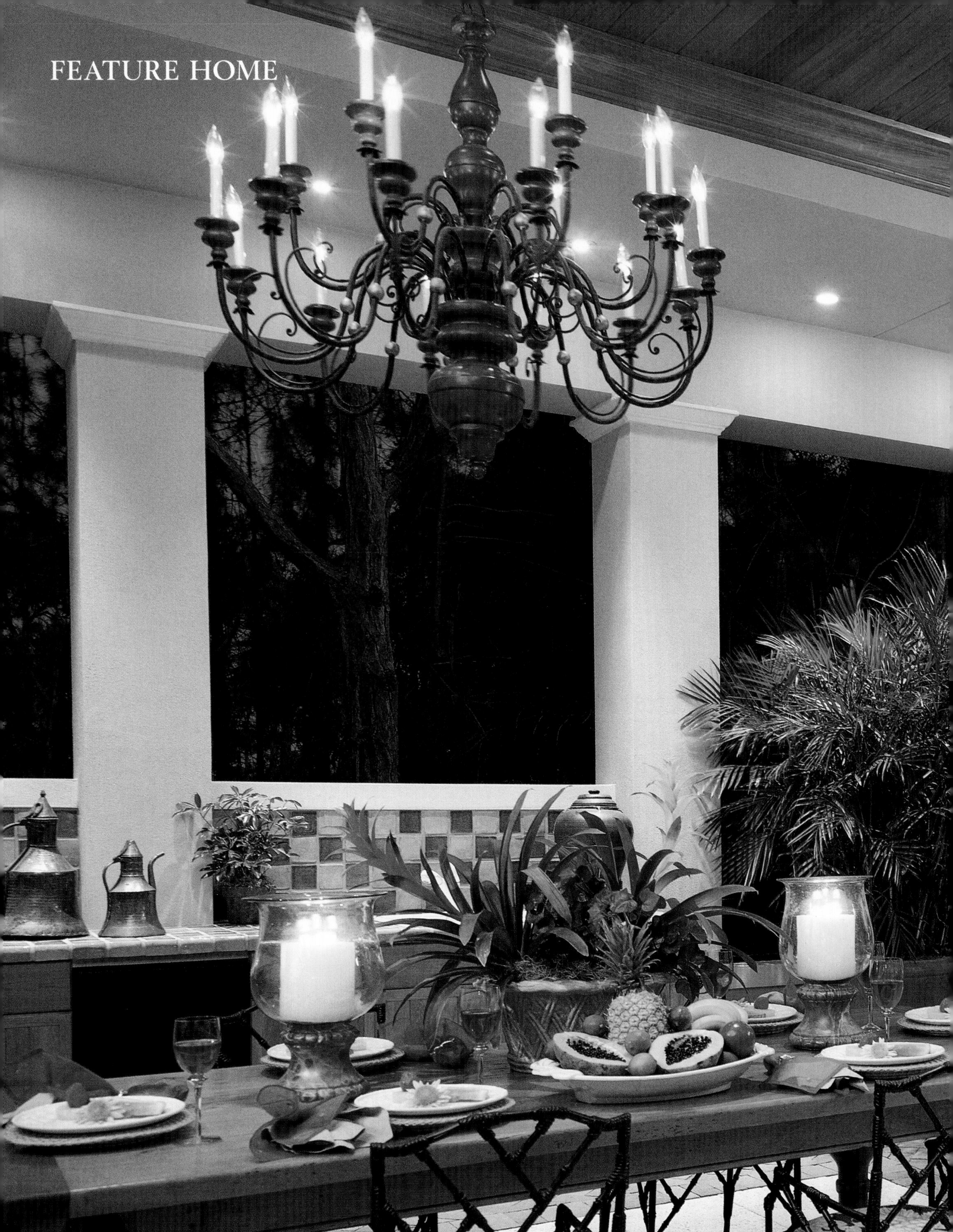

An outdoor kitchen and a stunning fireplace allow the courtyard to serve as the perfect exterior gathering spot.

FEATURE HOME

Truly the lap of luxury, the sprawling master bedroom boasts a high ceiling, sitting area, and enlarged windows that bathe the room with natural light.

plan# HPT920128

- **STYLE: ITALIAN RENAISSANCE**
- **SQUARE FOOTAGE: 4,534**
- **BEDROOMS: 3**
- **BATHROOMS: 4½**
- **WIDTH: 98'-5"**
- **DEPTH: 126'-11"**
- **FOUNDATION: SLAB**

SEARCH ONLINE @ EPLANS.COM

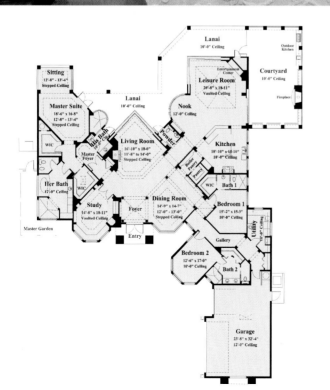

closet and a private bath, and a discreet utility room with built-in shelves.

The resplendent master suite dominates the left wing of the plan. This suite, with its own private foyer just off the living room, contains two full baths—one a simple bath with a compartmented toilet and a spacious shower, and the other a lavish retreat with a spa tub that overlooks a private garden. A cozy sitting area showcases a stepped ceiling, and double doors in the bedroom open to the lanai. Two walk-in closets in this suite ensure that the homeowners will never run out of storage space. ■

TO ORDER BLUEPRINTS CALL TOLL FREE 1-800-521-6797

Inside Outstanding

Romantic arches and fine lines define this Italianate facade, but it's the fabulous layout that makes it a great place to live…

BEAUTIFUL AND SPACIOUS, THE ARTFUL DISPOSITION OF THIS LUXURIOUS VILLA owns a distinctly Mediterranean flavor, warmed by eclectic country elements. Dramatic and inspiring, the vaulted entry is set off by a dashing arch framed by columns, a barrel ceiling, and double doors that open to an expansive interior. The octagonal living room provides a fireplace and opens through two sets of lovely doors to the rear lanai.

Below: Grand columns and distinct archways define the luxurious facade of this four-bedroom estate. The stunning design boasts a spacious interior, high ceilings, and a romantic Italian renaissance theme.

The grand fireplace is accented by the detailed architecture and two-story ceiling.

The master wing is a sumptuous retreat with double doors that open from a private vaulted foyer. The bedroom provides a tray ceiling and a bay window overlooking the backyard. The rear lanai wraps around the back of the home and features direct access to a cabana-style powder room.

The breakfast bay opens to an indoor lanai with a hearth, wet bar, and glass walls that retreat, exposing the living area to nature. The kitchen and lanai overlook a side courtyard warmed by its own fireplace. French doors open the interior to the sprawling lanai, creating a perfect entertainment arrangement.

One of the spacious guest suites can easily convert to quarters for a live-in relative. Another guest suite boasts a full bath, a bay window, and a walk-in closet. This suite is conveniently located near a rear stairway that ascends to an upper-level loft, leading to a third guest suite. This very private retreat grants exclusive access to a deck—a quiet place to view the night sky or wish upon a star. ∎

The master bath boasts a ribbon of windows, a soaking tub, and soaring ceilings.

FEATURE HOME

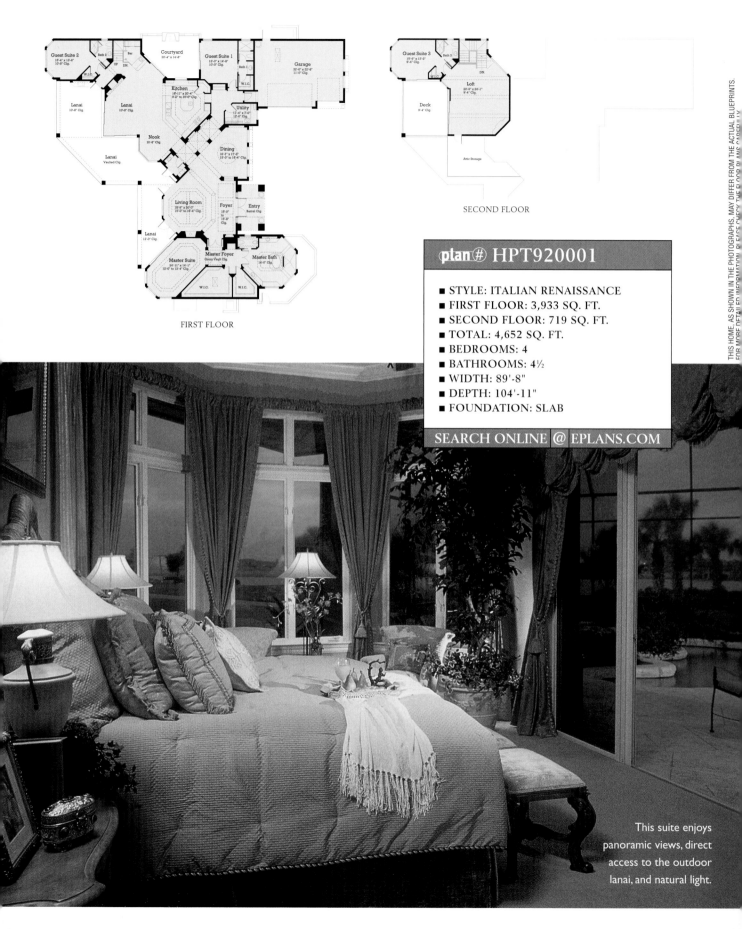

FIRST FLOOR

SECOND FLOOR

plan# HPT920001

- STYLE: ITALIAN RENAISSANCE
- FIRST FLOOR: 3,933 SQ. FT.
- SECOND FLOOR: 719 SQ. FT.
- TOTAL: 4,652 SQ. FT.
- BEDROOMS: 4
- BATHROOMS: 4½
- WIDTH: 89'-8"
- DEPTH: 104'-11"
- FOUNDATION: SLAB

SEARCH ONLINE @ EPLANS.COM

This suite enjoys panoramic views, direct access to the outdoor lanai, and natural light.

TO ORDER BLUEPRINTS CALL TOLL FREE 1-800-521-6797

Open Invitation

A unique facade rich with turrets, transoms, and tall windows announces a comfortable arrangement of interior space

CAPTIVATING AND MAGNIFICENT, THIS THOROUGHLY MODERN MEDITERRANEAN home demands the attention of even casual passersby. Form follows function inside, where every room of the plan offers the perfect equation for combining high style with a deep level of comfort.

Above: With its ornate exterior, this illuminated home would easily captivate any neighborhood.

The formal dining room, defined by decorative columns and a tray ceiling, has an expansive bay window overlooking the front yard. A butler's pantry connects the dining room to the well-planned gourmet kitchen. Complete with both an island and a snack bar, the kitchen provides the family chef with ample preparation space. The snack bar also serves as a natural buffer between the kitchen and the breakfast nook.

Adjacent to the kitchen and the nook is the family room, which features an entertainment center and built-ins. Accessible from the family room, the courtyard is prepared for entertaining with a fireplace and an outdoor kitchen.

At the heart of the home, the salon links the east and west wings and creates a perfect place for formal gatherings.

Left: High ceilings, patterned tiles, tall windows, and a cozy fireplace make this room ideal for quiet conversations and intimate gatherings.
Below: The elegant living room—accented by an intricate tray ceiling—offers an alternative spot for family and friends to gather.

The spacious study enjoys natural light, great views, and a soaring ceiling.

Directly beyond the foyer, the living room truly serves as the home's epicenter; it boasts a fireplace and retreating doors that open out to the lanai. The tray ceiling caps off the space with an air of distinction.

Across the hall, the study provides homeowners with additional space to set up the computer or to read in private. Since it's a bit removed from the main gathering areas, the study is more conducive to peace and quiet.

The master suite, which constitutes most of the home's right wing, features an extravagant master bath (complete with a walk-in shower, a whirlpool tub, and a compartmented toilet and bidet) and a separate pool bath, which has direct access to the rear lanai. A spacious sitting area is also included to provide homeowners with their own relaxing retreat.

Accommodating live-in relatives or planning for company is simple with two guest suites that have private baths and walk-in closets. The nearby laundry room offers ample workspace. Features such as storage near the lanai, a master garden, and a three-car garage add a touch of brilliance to this fabulous floor plan. ■

Truly the house for entertainers, the sprawling outdoor lanai is the perfect setting for formal gatherings or family barbecues.

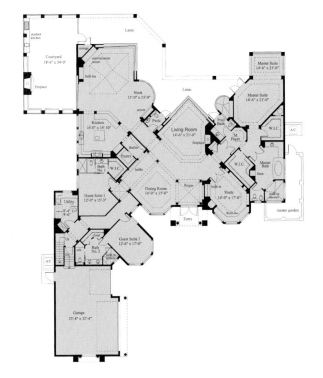

plan# HPT920005

- STYLE: MEDITERRANEAN
- SQUARE FOOTAGE: 4,604
- BONUS SPACE: 565 SQ. FT
- BEDROOMS: 3
- BATHROOMS: 4½
- WIDTH: 98'-5"
- DEPTH: 126'-11"
- FOUNDATION: SLAB

SEARCH ONLINE @ EPLANS.COM

Pillar of Strength

Bold Italianate details charge up the Mediterranean flavor of this dream house—with wide views and deeply comfortable rooms

THIS EUROPEAN STUCCO EXTERIOR PROVIDES GREAT CURB APPEAL AND CONCEALS a thoroughly modern arrangement of public and private rooms. A dramatic arched entry announces an open foyer that offers interior vistas and outdoor views through the formal rooms. A mitered wall of glass and a vaulted ceiling in the living room provide a spectacular introduction to this grand manor. Comfortable rooms and clustered secondary sleeping quarters reside to the right of the plan.

Above: Simple, sturdy wooden doors topped by a radius window accent this home's stucco exterior.
Opposite page: Serenity presides in the dining room, arranged for intimate occasions.

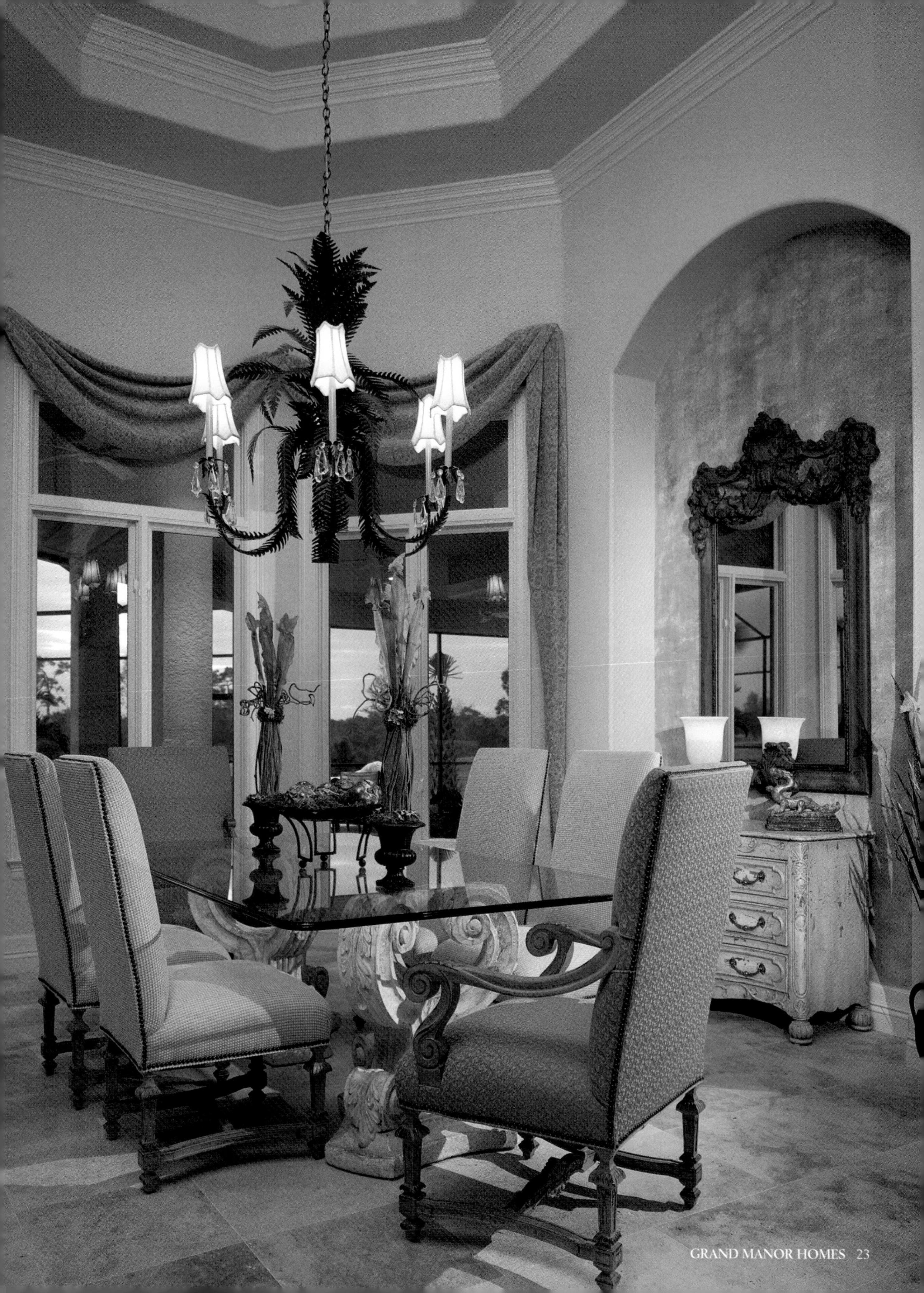

Stunning architectural details—such as columns, an arched entry, and a tray ceiling—highlight the living room.

plan# HPT920002

- **STYLE: MEDITERRANEAN**
- **SQUARE FOOTAGE: 4,255**
- **BEDROOMS: 3**
- **BATHROOMS: 3½**
- **WIDTH: 91'-6"**
- **DEPTH: 116'-11"**
- **FOUNDATION: SLAB**

SEARCH ONLINE @ EPLANS.COM

French doors lead from a central gallery hall to the master wing. The master bath provides a soaking tub, a separate shower, two vanities, and a compartmented toilet. The suite features two walk-in closets, a sitting bay, and access to a lanai. Nearby, French doors lead to a study that converts to a library or office.

Retreating glass walls connect the formal rooms to an area of the lanai that serves as an entertainment terrace. Living space leads out to a patio with an outdoor kitchen. A hallway leads past a grotto and powder bath to the private realm, which includes a leisure room with a pyramid ceiling. The kitchen connects to the dining room through a butler's pantry. ■

TO ORDER BLUEPRINTS CALL TOLL FREE 1-800-521-6797

Mediterranean Inspiration

An expansive rear lanai with a summer kitchen allows easy indoor/outdoor movement in this Mediterranean manor

TWO CHARMING TURRETS FLANK THE ENTRY OF THIS MEDITERRANEAN DESIGN. THE front door, topped by a radius window, opens to a foyer with a soaring 14-foot ceiling. Directly ahead, columns outline the entry to the living room, which features a coffered ceiling and opens to the expansive rear lanai. The study, housed in one of the turrets, is accessed by double doors and features a wall lined with built-in shelves. A tray ceiling further enhances the study. A spacious bedroom, with a private bath and walk-in closet, resides in the other turret.

Above: Designed to impress even those with the most discriminating tastes, this three-bedroom Mediterranean retreat combines luxury and elegance to meet the needs of today's homeowners.

Stylish furnishings and a soaring coffered ceiling create an elegant ambiance in this luxurious living room.

The dining room, enhanced by elegant columns and brightened by a bay window, sits just beyond the living room, conveniently close to the kitchen and charming breakfast nook. A petite butler's pantry with a sink allows easy service from the kitchen to the dining room, and the kitchen's snack-bar counter overlooks the breakfast nook. Perfect for casual meals, this cozy nook boasts a bay window that views the lanai. For extra convenience, the kitchen also enjoys a central island and access to a walk-in pantry.

A fireplace is the focal point of the nearby leisure room, which also boasts built-in shelves and long sliding glass doors that open the room to the lanai and its outdoor kitchen. Another nearby bedroom includes a private bath and walk-in closet. The utility area, sensibly placed near the secondary bedrooms, features a storage closet as well as a long counter with a sink. An additional storage closet can be found in the skylit garage, which provides enough space for three cars.

In the left wing, the master suite

Above: Special touches, including the tiled backsplash, detailed central work island, and textured cabinets, add a classic feel to the amenity-filled kitchen. The breakfast nook is perfect for sit-down meals while the kitchen offers convenient bar-style seating.

FEATURE HOME

reigns supreme; this suite showcases a bay window, two walk-in closets, and a splendid bath with two vanities, a corner spa tub, and a compartmented toilet and bidet. Double doors in the master bedroom open to the lanai, and a large soaking tub in the master bath overlooks a private garden area. Upstairs, a loft area with a walk-in closet, private bath, and access to a deck can serve as a guest or in-law suite. ■

Below: A bay window brightens the master bedroom and offers enough space for a cozy sitting area. **Right:** Built-in shelves, a comfortable vanity area, and a corner tub set near the window highlight the spacious master bath.

This private oasis is visible from almost every space in the house. Soaring columns polished with detailed architecture flank the enchanting pool.

plan# HPT920003

- **STYLE: MEDITERRANEAN**
- **FIRST FLOOR: 3,734 SQ. FT**
- **SECOND FLOOR: 418 SQ. FT.**
- **TOTAL: 4,152 SQ. FT**
- **BEDROOMS: 3**
- **BATHROOMS: 4½**
- **WIDTH: 82'-0"**
- **DEPTH: 107'-0"**
- **FOUNDATION: SLAB**

SEARCH ONLINE @ EPLANS.COM

FIRST FLOOR

Leisure Room
Open to Above

Lanai
Vaulted Clg.

Kitchen
15'-4" x 17'-11"
9'-8" x 10'-0" Clg.

Bedroom 3
14'-0" x 11'-8"
10'-0" Clg.

Bath 3

Utility

Garage
32'-8" x 21'-8"
11'-0" Clg.

Lanai
10'-0"

Nook
10'-0" Clg.

W.I.C.

Lanai
10'-0" Clg.

Dining Room
12'-8" x 13'-0"

Bath 2

Bedroom 2
12'-6" x 16'-3"
12'-0" Clg.

Living Room
12'-1" x 23'-4"
13'-0" to 14'-0" Clg.

Foyer
14'-0" Clg.

Entry
Barrel Clg.

Lanai
12'-0" Clg.

Study
15'-6" x 13'-6"
12'-0" to 14'-0" Clg.

Powder
Bath

Master Suite
23'-5" x 14'-8"
12'-0" to 14'-0" Clg.

Master Foyer

W.I.C.

Master Bath
12'-0" Clg.

W.I.C.

SECOND FLOOR

Open to Below

W.I.C.

Loft
21'-11" x 16'-3"
9'-0" Clg.

Bath

Deck

A glass double-door entry topped by two transom windows fills the entry of this striking home with natural light.

Styled Classic

Strong, clean lines lend a sensuous twist to Old-World style with this Mediterranean manor

CLASSIC DETAILS MIX IT UP WITH CONTEMPORARY FEATURES TO CREATE A THOROUGHLY MODERN look with this bold facade. Beautiful interior columns in the foyer offer a fine introduction to open, spacious rooms. A turret-shaped study provides built-in cabinetry and a bay window. The formal living room offers an enchanting fireplace and extends inner space to the lanai, providing a link with nature and a golden opportunity for entertaining outdoors.

Columns frame the formal dining room—a flex room that opens to the gallery hall and easily converts to a secondary bedroom or guest suite. To the rear of the plan, a massive corner fireplace anchors the casual living space, which includes an open leisure room, a breakfast bay, and a snack area served by the gourmet kitchen. The well-organized kitchen provides an

The living room, warmed by a fireplace, boasts a vanishing wall that rolls back to seamlessly open the room to the lanai.

island counter, an ample walk-in pantry, a spacious breakfast nook, and a vaulted leisure room that opens out to the lanai. A powder room connects the butler's pantry with an entertainment area of the lanai.

Nearby, double doors open into the master foyer, which is flanked by His and Hers baths. His bath offers a shower and direct access to the lanai. Her bath offers an indulging whirlpool tub, a separate shower, and a compartmented toilet. Individual walk-in closets provide ample dressing and wardrobe space. The master bedroom features a lovely sitting area overlooking the rear grounds.

Upstairs, the media room provides a spacious entertainment area with a vaulted ceiling. This bonus room features a shower bath and second-floor privacy—great for a home theater. ■

With a large soaking tub overlooking a private garden, this bath is a relaxing sanctuary.

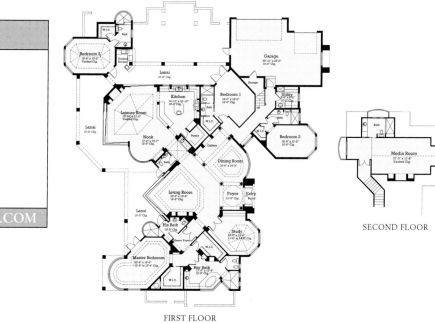

plan # HPT920004

- STYLE: MEDITERRANEAN
- FIRST FLOOR: 4,784 SQ. FT
- SECOND FLOOR: 481 SQ. FT.
- TOTAL: 5,265 SQ. FT
- BEDROOMS: 4
- BATHROOMS: 6½
- WIDTH: 106'-6"
- DEPTH: 106'-0"
- FOUNDATION: SLAB

SEARCH ONLINE @ EPLANS.COM

FIRST FLOOR

SECOND FLOOR

TO ORDER BLUEPRINTS CALL TOLL FREE 1-800-521-6797

Perfect Symmetry

Architecture and soul come together in a unifying theme that's softly stylish and strictly comfortable

Simple yet stunning arches speak volumes about the importance of beauty in an at-home environment. Massive decorative columns help to create a voluminous entry at this lovely Mediterranean home. Also at the entry are arched transoms that allow sunlight into the foyer and the living room. To the left of the living room is the dining area with a tray ceiling and French doors that open to the veranda. To the right, a see-through fireplace is shared with the study.

Above: Elegant columns frame the etched-glass, double-entry of this luxurious Floridian design, creating a memorable first impression.

FEATURE HOME

Wrapping counters, a corner pantry, and a food-preparation island in the gourmet kitchen allow stress-free meal preparation—even for planned events. The leisure room opens to the spacious morning nook, displays a pyramid ceiling, and includes a warming fireplace.

The master suite greets homeowners with lovely French doors and provides access to a master bath with a whirlpool tub, separate shower, two vanities, and a walk-in closet. Two guest suites can be found at the end of the gallery—each suite contains its own bath and a walk-in closet. The laundry is near the service entrance of the three-car garage. The outdoor kitchen and the extended veranda complete this remarkable plan. ■

Below: Marble flooring, heavy silk curtains, and brocade pillows add to the living room's elegance. **Left:** French doors allow quick and easy access to the veranda from this stately study.

The master bath boasts extravagent detail from the marble countertops to the dramatic arches.

plan# HPT920006

- STYLE: FLORIDIAN
- SQUARE FOOTAGE: 3,877
- BEDROOMS: 3
- BATHROOMS: 3½
- WIDTH: 102'-4"
- DEPTH: 98'-10"
- FOUNDATION: SLAB

SEARCH ONLINE @ EPLANS.COM

Grand Entrance

Plush gardens and pristine views define the outdoor spaces of this home and offer sweet repose

ASYMMETRICAL ROOFLINES AND STUNNING STUCCO WALLS ANNOUNCE an unrestrained interior that encourages the good life and provides privacy for the homeowners. The entry opens to the grand hall—an open, light-filled retreat defined by massive columns and wide views. Nearby, a private sitting area complements a gallery hall with an art niche. The heart of the plan is a living room set off by spectacular views of the veranda and luxurious pool area.

Above: A rotunda surrounded by a graceful colonnade opens to both formal and casual spaces.
Opposite page: A quatrefoil window to the right of the entry lends a Spanish flair to this design.

A thoughtful arrangement of public and private realms allows the gourmet kitchen to overlook the formal dining room and the vaulted leisure room. Comfortable amenities, such as a fireplace and a built-in media center, encourage family gatherings in the casual living space. Mitered glass walls retreat to allow inside and outside spaces to mingle, and an outdoor kitchen invites alfresco dining.

The secluded master wing provides a separate sitting room with its own morning kitchen and access to a private area of the veranda. A rambling master bath surrounds a spectacular step-up whirlpool tub and offers a garden view with a water feature. Upstairs, a spacious sitting loft leads outdoors to a wide deck. Each of two spacious guest suites provides a walk-in closet and luxury bath. ■

The leisure room features abundant storage space with its built-in bookcases, cabinets, and TV niche.

The veranda, accessible from all rear-facing rooms, is just steps away from the covered pool.

plan# HPT920007

- STYLE: CONTEMPORARY
- FIRST FLOOR: 4,715 SQ. FT
- SECOND FLOOR: 1,209 SQ. FT
- TOTAL: 5,924 SQ. FT
- BEDROOMS: 3
- BATHROOMS: 4
- WIDTH: 131'-7"
- DEPTH: 117'-2"
- FOUNDATION: SLAB

SEARCH ONLINE @ EPLANS.COM

FOR MORE DETAILED INFORMATION, PLEASE CHECK THE FLOOR PLANS CAREFULLY.

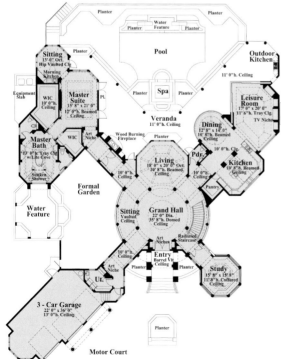

FIRST FLOOR

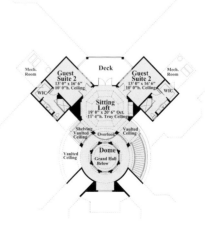

SECOND FLOOR

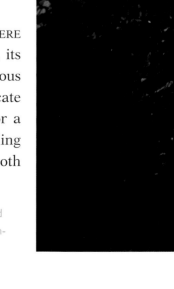

Slice of Heaven

*Savory comfort hugs a sun-kissed coastal classic that boasts
modern open space and dreamy views*

A ROMANTIC AIR FLIRTS WITH THE CLEAN SIMPLE LINES OF THIS SEASIDE HOME, WHERE
ocean breezes travel freely from front to back. Open and sophisticated, its
broad interior is made cozy by a refined decor that's also sweetly unpretentious
and downright comfortable. An enchanting mix of exotic textiles and delicate
but durable European furnishings exalts a muted palette well suited for a
coastal retreat. Soaring ceilings add a sense of spaciousness, while a sprawling
lanai blurs the line between outdoors and in—a perfect arrangement for both
traditional events as well as intimate gatherings.

Above: The arched entrance of this Mediterranean home is a stunning contrast to the sleek lines found
throughout. **Opposite:** The sprawling design takes full advantage of the outdoors with its elaborate windows, decks, and lanai.

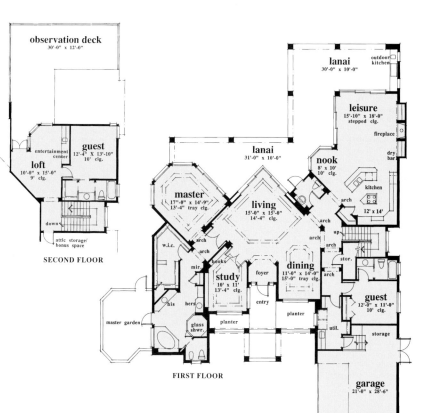

This gourmet kitchen has a food-prep island counter. The plan provides a corner cooktop and an angled counter with a double sink.

plan# HPT920008

- STYLE: MEDITERRANEAN
- FIRST FLOOR: 2,894 SQ. FT.
- SECOND FLOOR: 568 SQ. FT.
- TOTAL: 3,462 SQ. FT.
- BEDROOMS: 3
- BATHROOMS: 3½
- WIDTH: 67'-0"
- DEPTH: 102'-0"
- FOUNDATION: SLAB

SEARCH ONLINE @ EPLANS.COM

The entry's fanlight brightens the two-story foyer, which enjoys engaging views through the living area's two full walls of windows. French doors open to a quiet study with built-in bookshelves and a tall window, which looks out to the front property. A planter outside the window encourages the growth of foliage to frame the view. This room features an elegant tray ceiling and provides space for reading, relaxing, and quiet conversation with guests.

A sunlit leisure room with its own fireplace allows sights of nature and helps bring in a sense of the outdoors. The living and dining rooms are open to one another, defined by coffered ceilings. The well-appointed kitchen overlooks an island counter with a

SECOND FLOOR

observation deck
30'-0" x 12'-0"

entertainment center

guest
12'-4" X 13'-10"
10' clg.

loft
10'-0" x 15'-0"
9' clg.

down

attic storage/
bonus space

FIRST FLOOR

lanai
30'-0" x 10'-0"

outdoor kitchen

leisure
15'-10" x 18'-0"
stepped clg.

fireplace

lanai
31'-0" x 10'-0"

nook
8' x 10'
10' clg.

dry bar

kitchen

12' x 14'

master
17'-0" x 14'-9"
13'-4" tray clg.

living
15'-0" x 15'-0"
14'-4" clg.

arch

arch

up

w.i.c.

arch

arch

stor.

mir

books

dining
11'-0" x 14'-0"
15'-0" tray clg.

arch

study
10' x 11'
13'-4" clg.

foyer

guest
12'-0" x 11'-0"
10' clg.

his

hers

entry

planter

util.

master garden

glass shwr.

planter

planter

storage

garage
21'-0" x 28'-6"

TO ORDER BLUEPRINTS CALL TOLL FREE 1-800-521-6797

double sink and shares a view of the lanai with the breakfast nook. An outdoor kitchen allows easy meals and invites a "lose the shoes" attitude beyond the leisure room.

An angled wing harbors a rambling master suite with a bay window and a wall of glass that opens through sliding doors to the lanai. A private vestibule leads from the master bedroom to a dressing area with a three-way mirror and a walk-in closet designed for two. ∎

Right: The living room's two walls of windows provide panoramic views of the lanai and backyard. **Below:** Indoor and outdoor living blend together effortlessly at this coastal retreat.

PHOTOGRAPHY ©LAURENCE TAYLOR PHOTOGRAPHY

Tropical Oasis

Luxury meets functionality in this Mediterranean-styled home. An open floor plan provides sweeping views of the backyard pool and lanai

THIS ELEGANT MEDITERRANEAN RETREAT IS FILLED WITH LUXURIES THAT CATER TO THE MOST COMFORTable lifestyle. The stucco facade, topped with a Castilian-shingled roof, is designed to impress, and the sprawling home takes advantage of stunning outdoor views. Double doors lead inside to a covered portico, introducing an exotic lanai. The ultimate in luxury, there is even a secluded guest house complete with an outdoor grill for entertaining.

An evening view of the pool showcases elegant lighting and beautiful landscaping. The rear of the home conveniently opens to an outdoor oasis—perfect for entertaining, whether hosting a black-tie affair or enjoying a poolside barbeque.

Both houses are designed to take advantage of the outdoors, each accessing the lagoon-style pool and jacuzzi. The outdoor fireplace offers warmth and elegance, promising outdoor get-togethers even on breezy nights. The separation between the outdoors and the indoors is blurred as the rear of the home opens to the covered lanai.

Left: The moonlit dining room offers access to the rear lanai. **Below:** Elliptical windows, offering a magnificent water view, and a two-story coffered ceiling highlight the grand salon.

Above: The master bath is the ultimate oasis, boasting separate vanities and a scenic retreat

Upon entering the main house into a two-story grand salon, guests will enjoy the generous array of windows that illuminate every room. To the right of the grand salon, the formal dining room offers a built-in server or buffet table nearby. Leading to the casual areas of the home there is exquisite cabinetry throughout and a gourmet kitchen with a center island. A bayed alcove of glass enhances the breakfast nook, and the leisure room—which features a built-in entertainment center—opens to the lanai for easy entertaining. The octagonal shape of the study accents the contemporary design of the layout and offers tranquil

views of the family pool and backyard.

The homeowners will be pampered in the lavish master quarters. The master wing boasts a 14-foot ceiling, His and Hers walk-in closets, and private access to the rear lanai. The master bath includes a corner whirlpool tub, a separate shower, His and Hers vanities, linen storage, and a compartmented toilet. Two family bedrooms, located upstairs, share a hall bath and each boasts an observation deck. ■

Above: Grand 14-foot windows illuminate interior spaces in the master suite. **Left:** The home's sprawling, island-inspired entryway embraces its natural surroundings. Complete with a tray ceiling, this room defines luxury.

The lanai offers a private oasis highlighted by a lagoon-style pool.

plan# HPT920009

- **STYLE:** FLORIDIAN
- **FIRST FLOOR:** 2,853 SQ. FT.
- **SECOND FLOOR:** 627 SQ. FT.
- **TOTAL:** 3,480 SQ. FT.
- **BEDROOMS:** 3
- **BATHROOMS:** 3½
- **WIDTH:** 80'-0"
- **DEPTH:** 96'-0"
- **FOUNDATION:** SLAB

L

SEARCH ONLINE @ EPLANS.COM

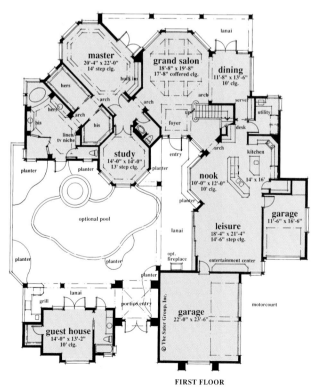

FIRST FLOOR

SECOND FLOOR

THIS HOME, AS SHOWN IN THE PHOTOGRAPHS, MAY DIFFER FROM THE ACTUAL BLUEPRINTS. FOR MORE DETAILED INFORMATION, PLEASE CHECK THE FLOOR PLANS CAREFULLY.

TO ORDER BLUEPRINTS CALL TOLL FREE 1-800-521-6797

Subtle Luxury

The richly detailed angles, curves, and arches of this captivating facade provide a warm welcome to waterfront living

THIS MEDITERRANEAN-STYLE HOME STARTS WITH A MAGNIFICENT STUCCO EXTERIOR, SPANISH-tile roof, palm-tree landscaping, and Old-World details such as arches and accent niches, which frame the spectacular entry. Double French doors lead to the tiled foyer, which is brightened with natural light brought in by the fanlight above, as well as the warm glow of a centered chandelier. To the right of the foyer, the formal dining room overlooks the front property through a wide, curved wall of glass. An archway supported by decorative columns separates the dining room from the living room, which boasts a fireplace and a tray ceiling with recessed lighting.

Above: An entry with Mediterranean flair provides a wonderful introduction to this design and its sprawling floor plan. This home is perfect for those who dream of pampering amenities and high-style architectural details.

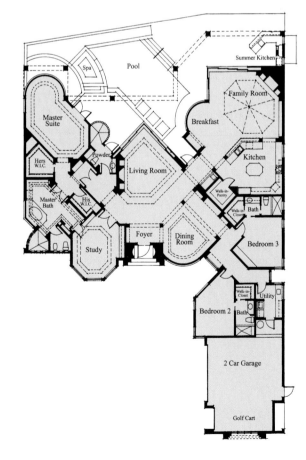

plan# HPT920010

- ■ STYLE: MEDITERRANEAN
- ■ SQUARE FOOTAGE: 4,009
- ■ BEDROOMS: 3
- ■ BATHROOMS: 4
- ■ WIDTH: 79'-0"
- ■ DEPTH: 117'-2"
- ■ FOUNDATION: SLAB

SEARCH ONLINE @ EPLANS.COM

The pocket sliding glass doors open to the covered back patio, pool, and spa. Six transom windows line the top of the doors, providing elegant definition to the room. The gourmet kitchen includes a corner walk-in pantry, wrapping counters, an island counter with a food-prep sink, and an adjoining breakfast room.

The family room features a fireplace, vaulted ceiling, and pocket sliding glass doors to a patio with a summer kitchen. A lanai wraps around a pool and spa area.

The lavish master suite and study occupy the opposite wing of the plan. A soaking tub enjoys views of a side garden while the step-up shower boasts glazed glass-block windows.

French doors open from the foyer to the quiet study. Each of two secondary bedrooms has a walk-in closet and full bath with shower. ■

TO ORDER BLUEPRINTS CALL TOLL FREE 1-800-521-6797

Similar squared columns unify this home's facade with it's interior.

PHOTOGRAPHY BY LAURENCE TAYLOR PHOTOGRAPHY

Palatial Paradise

Soaring windows and spacious architecture create an interplay of light and shadow

INDOORS MELDS WITH OUTDOORS IN THIS LUXURIOUS FOUR-BEDROOM HOME WHERE SUITES AND LIVING AREAS wrap around a series of lanais, atriums, and other outdoor destinations. The home's relaxing embrace begins with a palatial entry portico topped by a dramatic Roman arch that welcomes you to step out of the sun and into the shade. Large windows with transoms frame the entry and herald the importance of generous glazing in the 1½-story design.

Sliding glass doors in the guest and master suites lead to two separate covered lanais with 12-foot ceilings that flank the pool. The lines between indoor and outdoor spaces are further dissolved by a trio of floor-to-ceiling windows in the living room and by ingeniously angled zero-corner sliding glass doors in the leisure room. In the study, a refined octagonal floor plan harkens back to Early American library designs, and three contiguous ceiling-height transom windows shed light on your labors. A spa tub in the master bath overlooks a private garden through a dramatic window wall.

With so much light streaming in, a tropically-inspired house still knows how to keep its cool. Architecturally masterful ceiling treatments fill the home with soaring spaces that balance depth of shadow with natural light. The leisure room and second-floor bonus room have vaulted ceilings, while stepped ceilings bring sophistication to the dining room, living room, study, and other bedrooms.

The home's kitchen offers easy access to the dining and lanai areas, including a seated bar counter fronting the leisure room. Kitchen comforts include a large center island and a menu desk for planning gourmet meals. Near the kitchen are two bed-and-bath suites that open onto a charming private atrium. A summer kitchen in one of the lanais rounds out the roster of deluxe outdoor amenities. ■

The diamond orientation of the living and dining rooms gives them a spacious sense of movement and a relaxed formality. Squared columns and arches lead the eye up to the architecturally impressive stepped ceilings.

Kick back! Two covered lanais open onto the pool area, allowing for open-air relaxation while providing shade.

plan# HPT920011

- STYLE: MEDITERRANEAN
- SQUARE FOOTAGE: 3,145
- BONUS SPACE: 308 SQ. FT.
- BEDROOMS: 3
- BATHROOMS: 3
- WIDTH: 89'-9"
- DEPTH: 104'-0"
- FOUNDATION: SLAB

SEARCH ONLINE @ EPLANS.COM

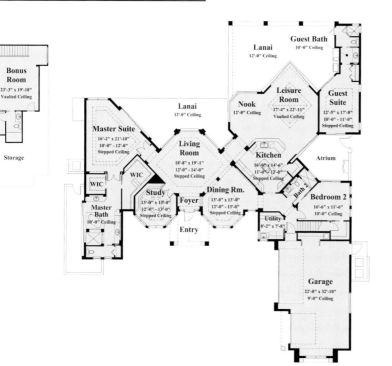

Bonus Room
23'-3" x 19'-10"
Vaulted Ceiling

WIC

Storage

Master Suite
16'-2" x 21'-10"
10'-0" - 12'-0"
Stepped Ceiling

Lanai
12'-0" Ceiling

Nook
12'-0" Ceiling

Leisure Room
17'-4" x 22'-11"
Vaulted Ceiling

Lanai
12'-0" Ceiling

Guest Bath
10'-0" Ceiling

Guest Suite
12'-5" x 17'-8"
10'-0" - 11'-0"
Stepped Ceiling

WIC

WIC

Living Room
18'-8" x 19'-1"
12'-0" - 14'-0"
Stepped Ceiling

Kitchen
16'-0" x 14'-6"
11'-0" - 12'-0"
Stepped Ceiling

Atrium

Master Bath
10'-0" Ceiling

Study
13'-0" x 13'-0"
12'-0" - 13'-0"
Stepped Ceiling

Foyer

Dining Rm.
13'-0" x 13'-0"
12'-0" - 13'-0"
Stepped Ceiling

Bath 2

Bedroom 2
16'-6" x 11'-6"
10'-0" Ceiling

Entry

Utility
8'-2" x 7'-8"

Garage
22'-8" x 32'-10"
9'-0" Ceiling

THIS HOME, AS SHOWN IN THE PHOTOGRAPHS, MAY DIFFER FROM THE ACTUAL BLUEPRINTS. FOR MORE DETAILED INFORMATION, PLEASE CHECK THE FLOOR PLANS CAREFULLY.

TO ORDER BLUEPRINTS CALL TOLL FREE 1-800-521-6797

Rich, heavy curtains add a dramatic air to the living room, which boasts a sweeping view of the lanai and pool.

The High Life

Dressed with crafted touches, this spectacular Sun Country plan is, quite simply, one in a million

A TOWERING ENTRY FLANKED BY COLUMNS AND TOPPED BY AN ARCH AND DECORATIVE IRON RAILINGS GREETS guests and sets off this sensational facade. Interesting rooflines and plenty of windows enhance a stucco exterior that's a gentle mix of European past and present. The rear grounds, accessible from the master suite, living room, and leisure room include a sprawling veranda, pool, and spa. A fireplace and outdoor kitchen further accent the veranda.

This luxurious home's multitude of windows offers picturesque views. A wall of windows in the living room allows an unobstructed view of the rear property from the front entry.

The spacious living room boasts artful window treatments. The fireplace surround is carved Mexican stone.

The foyer opens to the living room, complete with outdoor vistas and a fireplace. Columns define the dining room, which overlooks the front courtyard.

The gourmet kitchen is equipped with a butcher-block island, food-prep sink, walk-in pantry, cooktop counter, and a snack bar that separates the kitchen from the leisure room and breakfast area. The morning nook boasts views of the veranda, which includes a summer kitchen.

To the left of the foyer is a study that easily converts to a home office.

Double doors open to the master suite, which features walk-in closets and a sitting area with its own access to the veranda. The bath boasts natural stone floors, custom cabinets, granite countertops, a garden tub, a dressing area and a separate shower. An additional full bath with a circular shower off the master foyer doubles as a pool bath or ancillary master bath.

Two spacious guest suites are on the right side of the plan. One suite has a walk-in closet and full bath while the other includes a bay window and dual-sink vanity.

The three-car garage completes the luxurious plan. ■

plan# HPT920012

- STYLE: MEDITERRANEAN
- SQUARE FOOTAGE: 4,534
- BEDROOMS: 3
- BATHROOMS: 4½
- WIDTH: 87'-2"
- DEPTH: 127'-11"
- FOUNDATION: SLAB

SEARCH ONLINE @ EPLANS.COM

The Great Outdoors

This sprawling villa easily extends beyond its walls, taking full advantage of the sweeping views and natural light

A TILED ROOF AND A DECORATIVE WROUGHT-IRON BALCONY HIGHLIGHT THE bright exterior of this Italian Renaissance design, created to move easily between indoors and outdoors. The wide variety of window treatments adds excitement to the exterior and assures that all rooms are bathed in natural light. The dramatic barrel-vaulted entry opens to reveal an interior with a splendid floor plan. Columns define the entry to the dining room, which includes a stepped ceiling, a lavish triple window, and an art niche.

Above: An eye-catching roofline, a decorative balcony, and a multitude of arched windows bring Italian Renaissance flair to this stunning design. **Right:** Sturdy columns separate the living and dining rooms; a coffered ceiling adorns the living room.

Just beyond the dining room, a powder room offers convenience for guests. A triple window and a stepped ceiling also enhance the study. The living room, boasting a stepped ceiling and sharing a decorative column with the dining room, provides three large windows that overlook the rear veranda.

An art niche with a door to the veranda connects the formal gathering spaces to the more casual family living areas. The gourmet kitchen, with a central island and another separate countertop that overlooks the leisure room, easily serves a breakfast bay. Spacious enough for multiple cooks, the kitchen also features two sinks—a double sink on the counter, and a single sink on the central island—allowing for easy cleanup. The diamond-shaped leisure room, which boasts a vaulted ceiling, includes two window walls that slide back to open the room to the veranda, where an outdoor kitchen awaits casual gatherings. The leisure room also opens to a side garden.

This design's split-bedroom plan, with the master suite placed in the right wing and two guest suites in the left wing, assures privacy for everyone. All

Above: Marble countertops, weathered wood, and a simple tiled backsplash create an Italian Country look in the kitchen.
Right: Dramatic lighting and an ornate lacquered cabinet add style to this bath.

Though the entertainment center is the focal point of the casually decorated leisure room, a small recreation area with a pool table is visible to the side.

plan# HPT920127

- **STYLE: ITALIAN RENAISSANCE**
- **FIRST FLOOR: 3,745 SQ. FT.**
- **SECOND FLOOR: 747 SQ. FT.**
- **TOTAL: 4,492 SQ. FT.**
- **BEDROOMS: 4**
- **BATHROOMS: 4½**
- **WIDTH: 94'-10"**
- **DEPTH: 103'-5"**
- **FOUNDATION: SLAB**

SEARCH ONLINE @ EPLANS.COM

A sitting area, placed on the rear veranda near the outdoor kitchen, overlooks the covered pool.

SECOND FLOOR

FIRST FLOOR

three bedrooms feature lavish amenities. A bay window brightens the master bedroom, where a small hallway ornamented by columns and an art niche leads past two spacious walk-in closets to the luxurious bath; here, dual vanities, a walk-in shower, and a whirlpool tub overlooking the garden combine to create a soothing sanctuary. The guest suites also view a private garden area; one guest suite includes a built-in closet and entertainment center and shares a bath with the pool area, and the other suite contains a walk-in closet and private bath.

A third guest suite, suitable for an extra apartment or in-law suite, resides above the garage. Its adjoining private bath includes dual vanities and a walk-in closet. Also found above the garage: a cozy loft area with its own bath. ■

plan# HPT920013

- STYLE: FLORIDIAN
- SQUARE FOOTAGE: 3,477
- BEDROOMS: 3
- BATHROOMS: 2½
- WIDTH: 95'-0"
- DEPTH: 88'-8"
- FOUNDATION: SLAB

L

SEARCH ONLINE @ EPLANS.COM

QUOTE ONE®
Cost to build? See page 187
to order complete cost estimate
to build this house in your area!

Make dreams come true with this fine sunny design. An octagonal study provides a nice focal point both inside and outside. The living areas remain open to each other and access outdoor areas. A wet bar makes entertaining a breeze, especially with a window pass-through to a grill area on the lanai. The kitchen enjoys shared space with a lovely breakfast nook and a bright leisure room. Two bedrooms are located near the family living center. In the master bedroom suite, luxury abounds with a two-way fireplace, a morning kitchen, two walk-in closets and a compartmented bath. Another full bath accommodates a pool area.

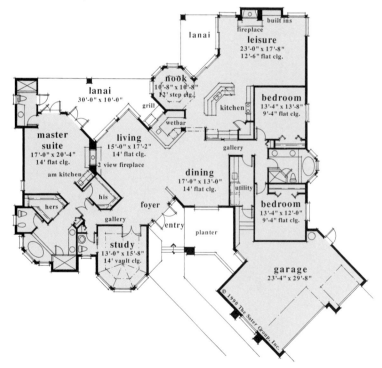

plan# HPT920014

- **STYLE: FLORIDIAN**
- **SQUARE FOOTAGE: 2,794**
- **BEDROOMS: 3**
- **BATHROOMS: 3**
- **WIDTH: 70'-0"**
- **DEPTH: 98'-0"**
- **FOUNDATION: SLAB**

L

SEARCH ONLINE @ EPLANS.COM

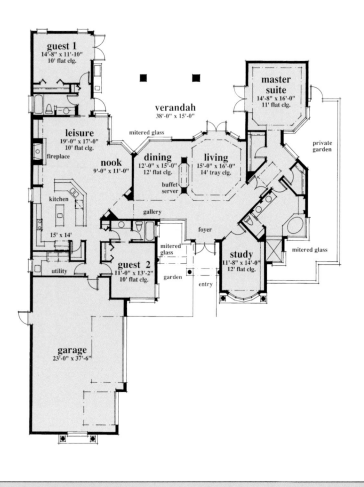

Classic columns, circle-head windows and a bay-windowed study give this stucco home a wonderful street presence. The foyer leads to the formal living and dining areas. An arched buffet server separates these rooms and contributes an open feeling. The kitchen, nook and leisure room are grouped for informal living. A desk/message center in the island kitchen, art niches in the nook and a fireplace with an entertainment center and shelves add custom touches. Two secondary suites have guest baths and offer full privacy from the master wing. The master suite hosts a private garden area, while the bath features a walk-in shower that overlooks the garden, and a compartmented toilet with space for books or a television. Large His and Hers walk-in closets complete these private quarters.

TO ORDER BLUEPRINTS CALL TOLL FREE 1-800-521-6797

© 1989 The Sater Group, Inc.

plan# HPT920015

- **STYLE:** FLORIDIAN
- **SQUARE FOOTAGE:** 3,896
- **BONUS SPACE:** 356 SQ. FT.
- **BEDROOMS:** 3
- **BATHROOMS:** 4½
- **WIDTH:** 90'-0"
- **DEPTH:** 120'-8"
- **FOUNDATION:** SLAB

L

SEARCH ONLINE @ EPLANS.COM

This elegant exterior blends a classical look with a contemporary feel. The formal living room, complete with a fireplace and a wet bar, and the formal dining room access the lanai through three pairs of French doors. The well-appointed kitchen features an island prep sink, a walk-in pantry and a desk. The secondary bedrooms are full guest suites, located away from the master suite. This suite enjoys enormous His and Hers closets, built-ins, a wet bar and a three-sided fireplace that separates the sitting room and the bedroom. The luxurious bath features a stunning rounded glass-block shower and a whirlpool tub.

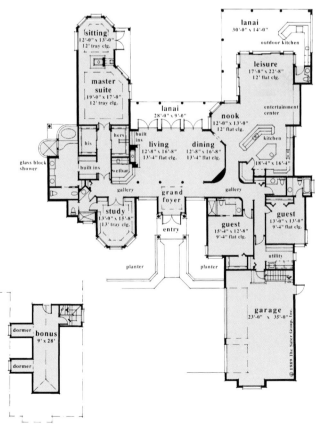

plan# HPT920016

- **STYLE: FLORIDIAN**
- **SQUARE FOOTAGE: 4,565**
- **BEDROOMS: 3**
- **BATHROOMS: 3½**
- **WIDTH: 88'-0"**
- **DEPTH: 95'-0"**
- **FOUNDATION: SLAB**

L

SEARCH ONLINE @ EPLANS.COM

A free-standing entryway is the focal point of this luxurious residence. It has an arch motif that is carried through to the rear using a gabled roof and a vaulted ceiling from the foyer out to the lanai. The kitchen, which features a cooktop island and plenty of counter space, opens to the leisure area with a handy snack bar. Two guest suites with private baths are just off this casual living area. The master wing is truly pampering, stretching the entire length of the home. The suite has a large sitting area, a corner fireplace and a morning kitchen. The bath features an island vanity, a raised tub with a curved glass wall overlooking a private garden, a sauna and separate closets. An exercise room has a curved glass wall and a pocket door to the study, where a wet bar is ready to serve up refreshments.

© 1992 The Sater Group, Inc.

Jenkins

plan# HPT920017

- STYLE: FLORIDIAN
- SQUARE FOOTAGE: 3,866
- BEDROOMS: 3
- BATHROOMS: 3½
- WIDTH: 120'-0"
- DEPTH: 89'-0"
- FOUNDATION: CRAWLSPACE

LD

SEARCH ONLINE @ EPLANS.COM

This modern home adds a contemporary twist to the typical ranch-style plan. The turret study and bayed dining room add a sensuous look from the streetscape. The main living areas open up to the lanai and offer broad views to the rear through large expanses of glass and doors. The family kitchen, nook and leisure room focus on the lanai, the entertainment center and an ale bar. The guest suites have separate baths and also access the lanai. The master bath features a curved-glass shower, whirlpool tub, and private toilet and bidet room. Dual walk-in closets and an abundance of light further the appeal of this suite.

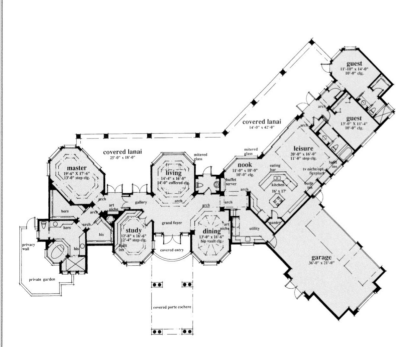

plan# HPT920018

- **STYLE: MEDITERRANEAN**
- **SQUARE FOOTAGE: 3,398**
- **BEDROOMS: 3**
- **BATHROOMS: 3½**
- **WIDTH: 121'-5"**
- **DEPTH: 96'-2"**
- **FOUNDATION: SLAB**

SEARCH ONLINE @ EPLANS.COM

Bringing the outdoors in through a multitude of bay windows is what this design is all about. The grand foyer opens to the living room with a magnificent view to the covered lanai. The study and dining room flank the foyer. The master suite is found on the left with an opulent private bath and views of the private garden. To the right, the kitchen adjoins the nook that boasts a mitered-glass bay window overlooking the lanai. Beyond the leisure room are two guest rooms, each with a private bath.

plan# HPT920019

- STYLE: FLORIDIAN
- SQUARE FOOTAGE: 3,265
- BEDROOMS: 4
- BATHROOMS: 3½
- WIDTH: 80'-0"
- DEPTH: 103'-8"
- FOUNDATION: SLAB

SEARCH ONLINE @ EPLANS.COM

A turret study and a raised entry add elegance to this marvelous stucco home. A guest suite includes a full bath, porch access and a private garden entry, making it perfect for use as an in-law suite. Secondary bedrooms share a full bath. The master suite has a foyer with a window seat overlooking another private garden and fountain area; the private master bath holds dual closets, a garden tub and a curved-glass shower.

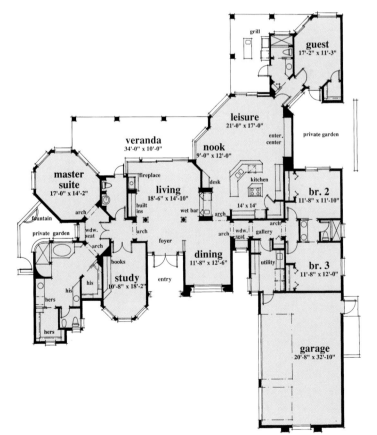

HOLZHALER INC. 94

plan# HPT920020

- STYLE: FLORIDIAN
- FIRST FLOOR: 3,092 SQ. FT.
- SECOND FLOOR: 656 SQ. FT.
- TOTAL: 3,748 SQ. FT.
- BEDROOMS: 4
- BATHROOMS: 4
- WIDTH: 82'-4"
- DEPTH: 103'-4"
- FOUNDATION: SLAB

SEARCH ONLINE @ EPLANS.COM

SECOND FLOOR

FIRST FLOOR

Luxury is paramount in this four-bedroom traditional home. A columned entry leads to the grand foyer. The exclusive master suite is split from the two secondary bedrooms, residing to the right of the plan, and has a private entrance to the lanai. An arched entry provides access to large His and Hers closets and an extravagant master bath featuring a whirlpool tub and a separate shower. The central portion of the first floor contains the living area. The living room and adjacent dining room provide space for formal entertaining. For the best in casual living, the spacious kitchen, multi-windowed nook and leisure room are combined. The second floor contains a comfortable guest suite with a full bath and a bay-windowed study. Both enjoy private decks.

plan# HPT920021

- STYLE: FLORIDIAN
- SQUARE FOOTAGE: 2,978
- BEDROOMS: 3
- BATHROOMS: 3½
- WIDTH: 84'-0"
- DEPTH: 90'-0"
- FOUNDATION: SLAB

SEARCH ONLINE @ EPLANS.COM

This home is designed to be a dream come true. A formal living area opens from the gallery foyer through graceful arches and looks out to the veranda. The veranda hosts an outdoor grill and service counter—perfect for outdoor entertaining. The leisure room offers a private veranda, a cabana bath and a wet bar just off the gourmet kitchen. Walls of windows and a bayed breakfast nook let in natural light and set a bright tone for this area. The master suite opens to the rear property through French doors and boasts a lavish bath with a corner whirlpool tub that overlooks a private garden. An art niche off the gallery hall, a private dressing area and a secluded study complement the master suite. Two family bedrooms occupy the opposite wing of the plan and share a full bath and private hall.

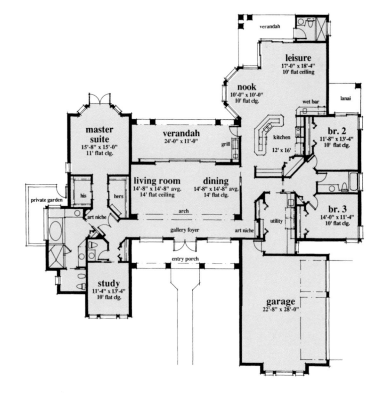

© 1991 The Sater Group, Inc.

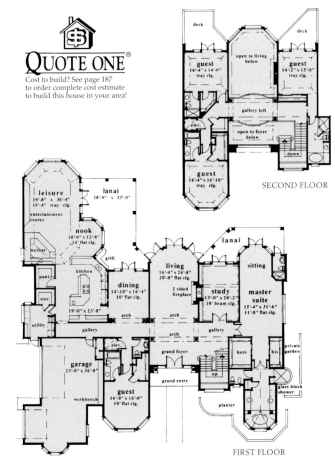

QUOTE ONE®

Cost to build? See page 187
to order complete cost estimate
to build this house in your area!

SECOND FLOOR

FIRST FLOOR

plan# HPT920022

- **STYLE: MEDITERRANEAN** **L**
- **FIRST FLOOR: 4,760 SQ. FT.**
- **SECOND FLOOR: 1,552 SQ. FT.**
- **TOTAL: 6,312 SQ. FT.**
- **BEDROOMS: 5**
- **BATHROOMS: 5½ + ½**
- **WIDTH: 98'-0"**
- **DEPTH: 103'-8"**
- **FOUNDATION: SLAB**

SEARCH ONLINE @ EPLANS.COM

This home features a spectacular blend of arch-top windows, French doors and balusters. An impressive informal leisure room has a sixteen-foot tray ceiling, an entertainment center and a grand ale bar. The large gourmet kitchen is well appointed and easily serves the nook and formal dining room. The master suite has a large bedroom and a bayed sitting area. His and Hers vanities and walk-in closets, and a curved glass-block shower are highlights in the bath. The staircase leads to the deluxe secondary guest suites, two of which have observation decks to the rear and each with their own full bath.

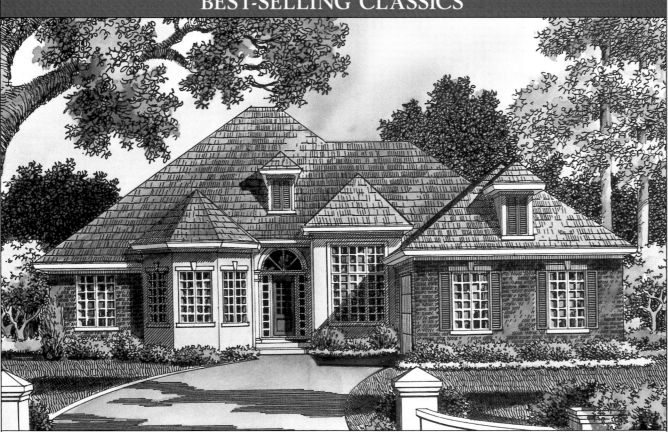

plan# HPT920023

- STYLE: TRADITIONAL
- SQUARE FOOTAGE: 2,431
- BEDROOMS: 3
- BATHROOMS: 2
- WIDTH: 65'-0"
- DEPTH: 74'-6"
- FOUNDATION: CRAWLSPACE

SEARCH ONLINE @ EPLANS.COM

Hipped rooflines, a projecting bay window and muntin windows are the key structural elements of this stunning home. Inside, the foyer opens to a great room with a built-in entertainment center surrounding a fireplace. An elegant tray ceiling and arches define the formal dining room. The study looks out through a bay window and includes a built-in bookshelf. Arched doorways lead into the island kitchen with a walk-in pantry. Two family bedrooms share a full bath to the right of the plan, while the master suite enjoys many luxuries to the left.

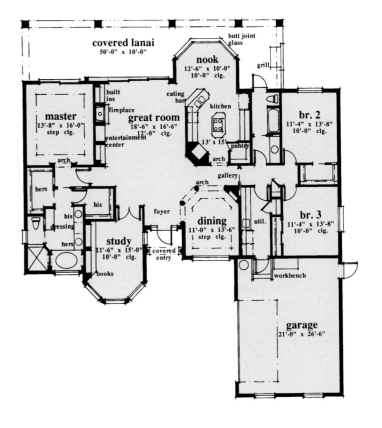

SECOND FLOOR

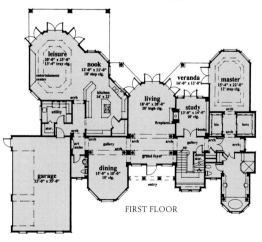

FIRST FLOOR

plan# HPT920024

- STYLE: MEDITERRANEAN
- FIRST FLOOR: 3,546 SQ. FT.
- SECOND FLOOR: 1,213 SQ. FT.
- TOTAL: 4,759 SQ. FT.
- BEDROOMS: 4
- BATHROOMS: 3½
- WIDTH: 96'-0"
- DEPTH: 83'-0"
- FOUNDATION: BASEMENT

SEARCH ONLINE @ EPLANS.COM

This grand traditional home offers an elegant, welcoming residence. Beyond the grand foyer, the spacious living room provides views of the rear grounds and opens to the veranda and rear yard through three pairs of French doors. An arched galley hall leads past the formal dining room to the family areas. Here, an ample gourmet kitchen easily serves the nook and the leisure room. The master wing includes a study or home office. Upstairs, each of three secondary bedrooms features a walk-in closet, and two bedrooms offer private balconies.

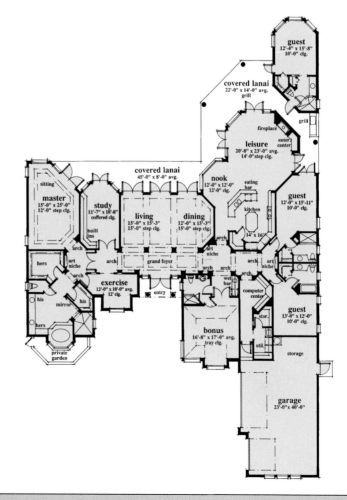

plan# HPT920025

- STYLE: ITALIANATE
- SQUARE FOOTAGE: 4,282
- BEDROOMS: 3
- BATHROOMS: 4
- WIDTH: 88'-0"
- DEPTH: 119'-0"
- FOUNDATION: SLAB

SEARCH ONLINE @ EPLANS.COM

This exciting exterior invites you in through its columned entry. Inside, the living room and dining room open to a covered rear lanai; built-ins line one wall of the adjacent study, which also opens to the lanai. A resplendent master suite occupies the left wing and provides a private garden, raised whirlpool tub, two walk-in closets and a sitting area. A leisure room to the rear of the plan features a fireplace and a built-in entertainment center. The gourmet kitchen shares an eating bar with the breakfast nook. Other special amenities include art display niches, a wet bar and a computer center.

SECOND FLOOR

deck
20'-0" x 10'-0"

br. 2
12'-6" x 15'-8"
9'-4" clg.

br. 3
11'-4" x 16'-0"
9'-4" clg.

wdw. seat

down

storage

opt. bonus room over garage

FIRST FLOOR

sitting

master
13'-10" x 21'-0"
13' step clg.

veranda
23'-0" x 7'-6"

veranda
21'-0" x 10'-0"

nook
12'-4" x 11'-0"
10' clg.

enter. center fireplace

his

hers

grand room
24'-0" x 15'-0"
14'-8" clg.

kitchen
14' x 14'

wdw. seat

arch

up

study
11'-4" x 13'-8"
14'-8" clg.

foyer

dining
11'-4" x 15'-8"
10' step clg.

util.

storage

garden

garage
21'-0" x 31'-0"

plan # HPT920026

- **STYLE: MEDITERRANEAN**
- **FIRST FLOOR: 2,181 SQ. FT.**
- **SECOND FLOOR: 710 SQ. FT.**
- **TOTAL: 2,891 SQ. FT.**
- **BONUS SPACE: 240 SQ. FT.**
- **BEDROOMS: 3**
- **BATHROOMS: 3**
- **WIDTH: 66'-4"**
- **DEPTH: 79'-0"**
- **FOUNDATION: BASEMENT, SLAB**

SEARCH ONLINE @ EPLANS.COM

An arched, covered porch presents fine double doors leading to a spacious foyer in this decidedly European home. A two-story tower contains an elegant formal dining room on the first floor and a spacious bedroom on the second floor. The grand room is aptly named with a fireplace, a built-in entertainment center and three sets of doors opening onto the veranda. A large kitchen is ready to please the gourmet of the family with a big walk-in pantry and a sunny, bay-windowed eating nook. The secluded master suite is luxury in itself. A bay-windowed sitting area, access to the rear veranda, His and Hers walk-in closets and a lavish bath are all set to pamper you. Upstairs, two bedrooms, both with walk-in closets, share a full hall bath that includes twin vanities.

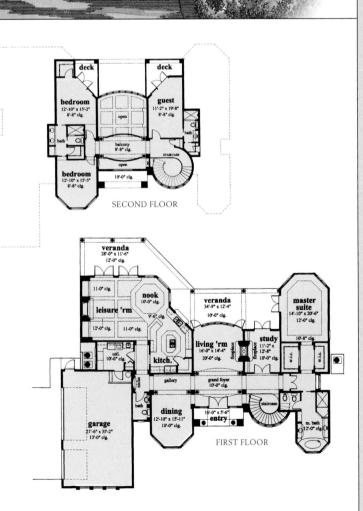

plan# HPT920027

- STYLE: MEDITERRANEAN
- FIRST FLOOR: 2,841 SQ. FT.
- SECOND FLOOR: 1,052 SQ. FT.
- TOTAL: 3,893 SQ. FT.
- BEDROOMS: 4
- BATHROOMS: 3½
- WIDTH: 85'-0"
- DEPTH: 76'-8"
- FOUNDATION: CRAWLSPACE

SEARCH ONLINE @ EPLANS.COM

Ensure an elegant lifestyle with this luxurious plan. A turret, two-story bay windows and plenty of arched glass impart a graceful style to the exterior, while rich amenities inside furnish contentment. A grand foyer decked with columns introduces the living room with curved-glass windows viewing the rear gardens. The study and living room share a through-fireplace. The master suite enjoys a tray ceiling, two walk-in closets, a separate shower and a garden tub set in a bay window. Informal entertainment will be a breeze with a rich leisure room adjoining the kitchen and breakfast nook and opening to a rear veranda. Upstairs, two family bedrooms and a guest suite with a private deck complete the plan.

SECOND FLOOR

FIRST FLOOR

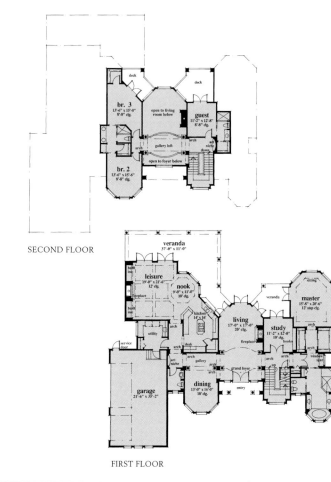

SECOND FLOOR

FIRST FLOOR

plan# HPT920028

- **STYLE: MEDITERRANEAN**
- **FIRST FLOOR: 3,027 SQ. FT.**
- **SECOND FLOOR: 1,079 SQ. FT.**
- **TOTAL: 4,106 SQ. FT.**
- **BEDROOMS: 4**
- **BATHROOMS: 3½**
- **WIDTH: 87'-4"**
- **DEPTH: 80'-4"**
- **FOUNDATION: BASEMENT**

SEARCH ONLINE @ EPLANS.COM

The inside of this design is just as majestic as the outside. The grand foyer opens to a two-story living room with a fireplace and magnificent views. Dining in the bayed formal dining room will be a memorable experience. A well-designed kitchen is near a sunny nook and a leisure room with a fireplace and outdoor access. The master wing includes a separate study and an elegant private bath. The second level features a guest suite with its own bath and deck, two family bedrooms (Bedroom 3 also has its own deck) and a gallery loft with views to the living room below.

EUROPEAN STYLE

© The Sater Design Collection, Inc.

plan# HPT920029

- STYLE: CHATEAU
- SQUARE FOOTAGE: 3,790
- BEDROOMS: 3
- BATHROOMS: 3½
- WIDTH: 80'-8"
- DEPTH: 107'-8"
- FOUNDATION: SLAB

SEARCH ONLINE @ EPLANS.COM

Grand chateau elegance was the inspiration for this magnificent European manor. Stone accents and detailed window treatments make this facade a masterpiece; inside, this family floor plan affords convenience and luxury. The living room greets you, with a coffered ceiling, fireplace and rear property access. A study and dining room are on either side of the foyer, both brightly lit with natural light. In the gourmet kitchen, meal preparation is a breeze; ample counter space and a center island allow efficient culinary expression. The leisure room is defined by an entertainment center. The game room (with extra storage) can be finished for a third family bedroom. A guest suite is great for in-laws or live-in help. The master suite is a luxurious retreat, with a sitting room and gorgeous bath.

OPTIONAL LAYOUT

plan# HPT920030

- **STYLE: EUROPEAN COTTAGE**
- **SQUARE FOOTAGE: 2,191**
- **BEDROOMS: 3**
- **BATHROOMS: 2½**
- **WIDTH: 62'-10"**
- **DEPTH: 73'-6"**
- **FOUNDATION: SLAB**

SEARCH ONLINE @ EPLANS.COM

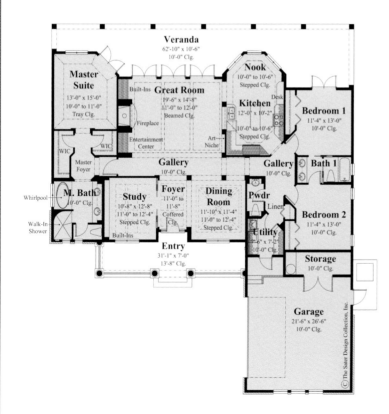

The exterior of this beautiful brick and stucco home is a lovely European rendition; inside, this plan is modern and sophisticated, designed for today's family. The entry presents a study and a dining room on either side of the foyer. The great room warms with an extended-hearth fireplace and lets in lots of natural light through three sets of French doors. An exposed-beam ceiling adds a touch of vintage elegance. The U-shaped island kitchen opens to a deep-set bayed nook. Two family bedrooms share a full bath with dual vanities. On the far left, the master suite revels in a tray ceiling, veranda access, twin walk-in closets and a luxurious bath with a walk-in shower and whirlpool tub. Don't miss the ample storage space and utility room off the two-car, side-loading garage.

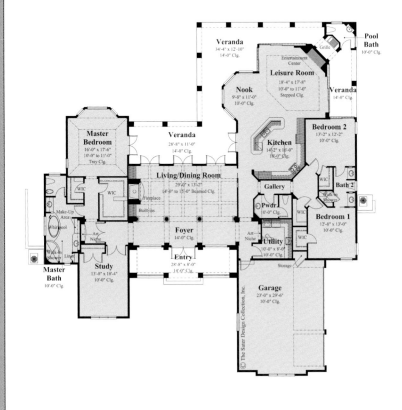

© The Sater Design Collection, Inc.

plan# HPT920031

- STYLE: EUROPEAN COTTAGE
- SQUARE FOOTAGE: 3,351
- BEDROOMS: 3
- BATHROOMS: 2½ + ½
- WIDTH: 84'-0"
- DEPTH: 92'-0"
- FOUNDATION: SLAB

SEARCH ONLINE @ EPLANS.COM

This stately European stucco manor is accented with brick, quoins and fanlight windows for a majestic facade. The striking entry and foyer present a living room/dining room, revered for its infinite interior design possibilities. Here, a vintage exposed-beam ceiling, warming fireplace and French doors to the veranda welcome family and guests. To the right, a wonderful country kitchen allows space to prepare gourmet meals with ease, courtesy of expansive workspace and cabinetry. The bayed nook could serve as a breakfast nook or sitting area. In the leisure room, a built-in entertainment center and veranda access (don't miss the outdoor grill!) are sure to make this room a family favorite. Two bedrooms share a full bath and hall storage on the far right. The left wing houses the master suite, separated for privacy and brimming with luxurious amenities.

© The Sater Design Collection, Inc.

plan # HPT920032

- STYLE: EUROPEAN COTTAGE
- SQUARE FOOTAGE: 3,351
- BEDROOMS: 3
- BATHROOMS: 2½ + ½
- WIDTH: 84'-0"
- DEPTH: 92'-0"
- FOUNDATION: SLAB

SEARCH ONLINE @ EPLANS.COM

Magnificent brick and a Colonial-inspired facade make this home a new favorite. Inside, the foyer opens to the living room/dining room combination, which allows flexibility in interior arrangement. The country kitchen serves the dining areas with ease and provides plenty of workspace for gourmet meal preparation. The leisure room entertains with a built-in media center and access to the rear veranda. Two family bedrooms share a full bath and extra hall storage. On the far left, the master suite is a dream, with a bayed window, oversized walk-in closets, and a grand spa bath with a whirlpool tub.

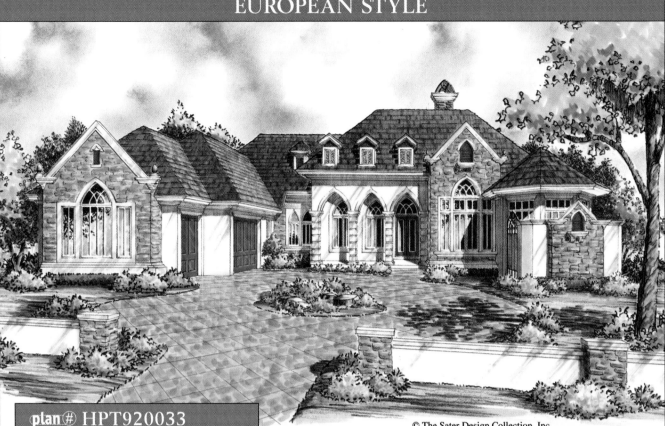

© The Sater Design Collection, Inc.

plan# HPT920033

- STYLE: ITALIAN RENAISSANCE
- SQUARE FOOTAGE: 3,942
- BEDROOMS: 3
- BATHROOMS: 4
- WIDTH: 83'-10"
- DEPTH: 106'-0"
- FOUNDATION: SLAB

SEARCH ONLINE @ EPLANS.COM

Welcome home to a country manor with Renaissance flair. Full-length, squint-style windows and brick accents bring Old World charm to a modern plan. Designed for flexibility, the open foyer, living room and dining room have infinite decor options. Down a gallery with art niches, two bedroom suites enjoy private baths. The island kitchen is introduced with a wet bar and pool bath. In the leisure room, family and friends will revel in expansive views of the rear property. An outdoor kitchen on the lanai invites alfresco dining. Separated for ultimate privacy, the master suite is an exercise in luxurious living. Past the morning kitchen and into the grand bedroom, an octagonal sitting area is bathed in light. The bath is gracefully set in the turret, with a whirlpool tub and views of the master garden.

© The Sater Design Collection, Inc.

plan# HPT920034

- **STYLE: EUROPEAN COTTAGE**
- **SQUARE FOOTAGE: 3,640**
- **BEDROOMS: 3**
- **BATHROOMS: 3½**
- **WIDTH: 106'-4"**
- **DEPTH: 102'-4"**
- **FOUNDATION: SLAB**

SEARCH ONLINE @ EPLANS.COM

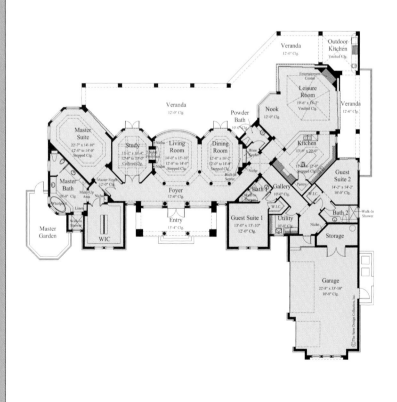

No matter how long your wish list is, you're in luck—this French Colonial home has it all! An unassuming facade is accented by a columned portico entry and a box-bay window. An elongated foyer leads to the elegant living areas: the octagonal study and dining room. Each has a distinctive ceiling treatment; both lead to the rear veranda through French doors. Between them, the living room, with a bowed window wall, shares a two-way fireplace with the study. Don't miss the built-in serving area and wine cooler in the dining room. The unique leisure room includes a bayed nook, perfect for a reading area, and a built-in entertainment center. An outdoor kitchen is a remarkable addition. The left wing is devoted to the comfort of the master suite, where a luxurious bath with a corner whirlpool tub, an unbelievable walk-in closet and a private garden provide sanctuary.

© The Sater Design Collection, Inc.

OPTIONAL LAYOUT

plan# HPT920035

- **STYLE:** EUROPEAN COTTAGE
- **SQUARE FOOTAGE:** 3,764
- **BEDROOMS:** 3
- **BATHROOMS:** 3½
- **WIDTH:** 80'-6"
- **DEPTH:** 111'-0"
- **FOUNDATION:** SLAB

SEARCH ONLINE @ EPLANS.COM

This exquisite manor will be the showpiece of any neighborhood. Classic brick and stately columns add grandeur to the facade; personal touches and exciting features make the interior a design to call home. The study and dining room border the foyer. Ahead, the living room welcomes guests with a fireplace, rear veranda access and a coffered ceiling. The step-saving kitchen provides room for more than one chef, and easily serves the dining room and sunny breakfast nook. An entertainment center separates the leisure room from the game room— or make it a bedroom—with extra storage space. The guest suite includes a private bath. Down the gallery (with a window seat) two bedrooms share a full bath. The master suite is resplendent with a defined sitting area, massive walk-in closets and a soothing spa bath with a whirlpool tub and walk-in shower.

© The Sater Design Collection, Inc.

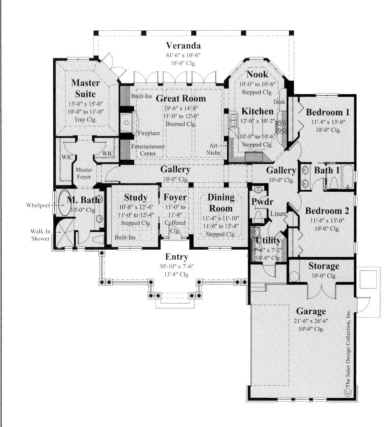

plan# HPT920036

- **STYLE: CHATEAU**
- **SQUARE FOOTAGE: 2,194**
- **BEDROOMS: 3**
- **BATHROOMS: 2½**
- **WIDTH: 62'-10"**
- **DEPTH: 73'-6"**
- **FOUNDATION: SLAB**

SEARCH ONLINE @ EPLANS.COM

A squared portico and stone accents lend European charm to any neighborhood. Intriguing and unique, this beautiful chateau would look great from the California coast to the farmlands of New Hampshire. Inside, ten-foot ceilings with distinctive treatments set the tone for luxury. The great room is the heart of the home, offering cozy nights by the fireplace and sunny days through a triplet of French doors to the veranda. The kitchen is designed for efficiency and elegance, with an island and a bayed breakfast nook. Split-bedroom planning situates two bedrooms to the right; the master suite resides on the far left. Here, a pampering bath and veranda access are a welcome indulgence.

© The Sater Design Collection, Inc.

plan# HPT920037

- **STYLE: ITALIANATE**
- **SQUARE FOOTAGE: 3,351**
- **BEDROOMS: 3**
- **BATHROOMS: 2½ + ½**
- **WIDTH: 84'-0"**
- **DEPTH: 92'-2"**
- **FOUNDATION: SLAB**

SEARCH ONLINE @ EPLANS.COM

A Spanish Colonial beauty, this stucco estate is striking with its red roof tiles and grand entry. Inside, an expansive living room/dining room combination features a rustic exposed-beam ceiling, fireplace and built-in shelving. An angled country kitchen allows plenty of workspace and an open design. The bayed nook would be a bright breakfast area or reading spot. The leisure room will be a family favorite with a built-in entertainment center and access to the rear veranda and outdoor grill. Secluded for ultimate privacy, the master suite will elate; a bay window, walk-in closets and a pampering spa bath are thoughtful touches.

© The Sater Design Collection, Inc.

plan# HPT920038

- **STYLE:** MEDITERRANEAN
- **SQUARE FOOTAGE:** 3,640
- **BEDROOMS:** 3
- **BATHROOMS:** 3½
- **WIDTH:** 106'-4"
- **DEPTH:** 102'-4"
- **FOUNDATION:** SLAB

SEARCH ONLINE @ EPLANS.COM

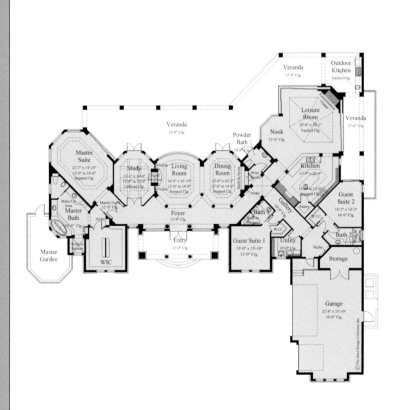

An elegant columned entry provides a fine welcome to this home. The expansive foyer introduces the formal rooms—the study and living room, which share a fireplace, and the dining room, which opens to the rear veranda. The less-formal leisure room, with a fireplace and access to a side veranda, resides to the rear of the plan. Entertain guests in style with two luxurious guest suites that are conveniently near living spaces; each suite features a walk-in closet and a private bath. The gallery hall that leads to the suites provides even more privacy. The master suite, located to the left of the plan, boasts sliding glass doors that open to the veranda.

© The Sater Design Collection, Inc.

ptan# HPT920039

- STYLE: ITALIANATE
- SQUARE FOOTAGE: 3,743
- BEDROOMS: 3
- BATHROOMS: 3½
- WIDTH: 80'-0"
- DEPTH: 103'-8"
- FOUNDATION: SLAB

SEARCH ONLINE @ EPLANS.COM

OPTIONAL LAYOUT

With California style and Mediterranean good looks, this striking stucco manor is sure to delight. The portico and foyer open to reveal a smart plan with convenience and flexibility in mind. The columned living room has a warming fireplace and access to the rear property. In the gourmet kitchen, an open design with an island and walk-in pantry will please any chef. From here, the elegant dining room and sunny nook are easily served. The leisure room is separated from the game room by a built-in entertainment center. The game area can also be finished off as a bedroom. To the rear, a guest room is perfect for frequent visitors or as an in-law suite. The master suite features a bright sitting area, oversized walk-in closets and a pampering bath with a whirlpool tub. Extra features not to be missed: the outdoor grill, game-room storage and gallery window seat.

© The Sater Design Collection, Inc.

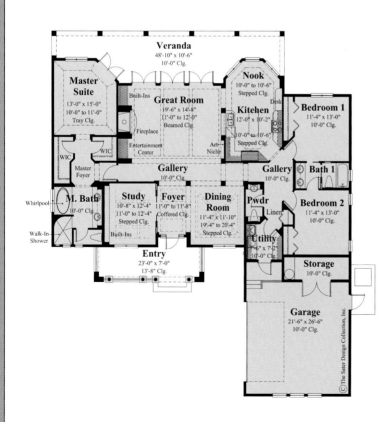

plan# HPT920040

- **STYLE: MEDITERRANEAN**
- **SQUARE FOOTAGE: 2,191**
- **BEDROOMS: 3**
- **BATHROOMS: 2½**
- **WIDTH: 62'-10"**
- **DEPTH: 73'-6"**
- **FOUNDATION: SLAB**

SEARCH ONLINE @ EPLANS.COM

Perfect for a corner lot, this Mediterranean villa is a beautiful addition to any neighborhood. Low and unassuming on the outside, this plan brings modern amenities and classic stylings together for a great family home. The study and two-story dining room border the foyer; an elongated gallery introduces the great room. Here, a rustic beamed ceiling, fireplace and art niche are thoughtful touches. The step-saving U-shaped kitchen flows into a sunny bayed breakfast nook. To the far right, two bedrooms share a full bath. The master suite is separated for privacy, situated to the far left. French door access to the veranda, and a sumptuous bath make this a pleasurable retreat.

© The Sater Design Collection, Inc.

plan# HPT920041

- STYLE: ITALIAN RENAISSANCE
- SQUARE FOOTAGE: 3,942
- BEDROOMS: 3
- BATHROOMS: 4
- WIDTH: 83'-10"
- DEPTH: 106'-0"
- FOUNDATION: SLAB

SEARCH ONLINE @ EPLANS.COM

Italian Renaissance flair sets the tone for this majestic Old World estate. An impressive entrance reveals an open floor plan; the foyer, living room and dining room are all defined by distinctive ceiling treatments for endless interior design possibilities. A wet bar and pool bath announce the gourmet kitchen with a pentagonal island and lots of counter space. Past a half-moon nook, the leisure room will be a family favorite. On the lanai, an outdoor kitchen is an easy way to cook up all-weather fun. To the far right, the master suite will amaze; an octagonal sitting area and morning kitchen are only the beginning. Two enormous walk-in closets beckon with built-in shelving. The master bath, set in a turret, will soothe and pamper with a central whirlpool tub, walk-in shower and views to the garden.

© The Sater Design Collection, Inc.

- **STYLE: MEDITERRANEAN**
- **SQUARE FOOTAGE: 3,640**
- **BEDROOMS: 3**
- **BATHROOMS: 3½**
- **WIDTH: 106'-4"**
- **DEPTH: 102'-4"**
- **FOUNDATION: SLAB**

SEARCH ONLINE @ EPLANS.COM

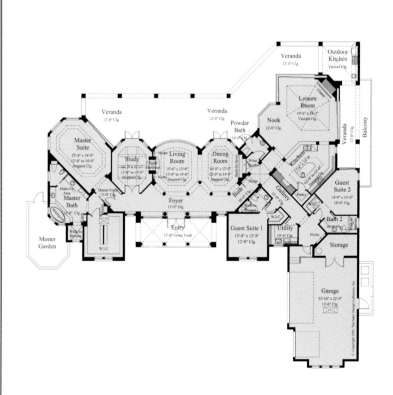

Come home to luxurious living—all on one level—with this striking Mediterranean plan. Unique ceiling treatments highlight the living areas—the living and dining rooms, as well as the study, feature stepped ceilings, while the leisure room includes a vaulted ceiling. The gourmet kitchen includes a spacious center island; another kitchen, this one outdoors, can be accessed from the leisure room. The master suite boasts plenty of amenities: a large, skylit walk-in closet, a bath with a whirlpool tub and walk-in shower, and private access to a charming garden area. Two suites, both with private baths, sit to the right of the plan.

© The Sater Design Collection, Inc.

plan# HPT920043

- STYLE: ITALIANATE
- SQUARE FOOTAGE: 3,942
- BEDROOMS: 3
- BATHROOMS: 4
- WIDTH: 83'-10"
- DEPTH: 106'-0"
- FOUNDATION: SLAB

SEARCH ONLINE @ EPLANS.COM

This sprawling Italian design will surprise you at every turn. The foyer opens to the living and dining rooms, each defined by an elegant ceiling treatment. A corner fireplace in the living room offers warmth, while an angled wall of windows presents uninhibited views of the rear property. Pass the wet bar and the pool bath to enter the angled kitchen, breakfast nook set in a half-moon bow, and diamond-shaped leisure room with fantastic views. On the lanai, an outdoor kitchen invites alfresco dining. The entire right wing is devoted to the master suite. A bayed sitting area and morning kitchen are everyday luxuries; of special note are the walk-in shower and decadent whirlpool tub set in a turret. A master garden completes this opulent escape.

© The Sater Design Collection, Inc.

plan# HPT920044

- **STYLE: EUROPEAN COTTAGE**
- **FIRST FLOOR: 2,117 SQ. FT.**
- **SECOND FLOOR: 652 SQ. FT.**
- **TOTAL: 2,769 SQ. FT.**
- **BONUS SPACE: 375 SQ. FT.**
- **BEDROOMS: 3**
- **BATHROOMS: 2½**
- **WIDTH: 60'-6"**
- **DEPTH: 94'-0"**
- **FOUNDATION: SLAB**

SEARCH ONLINE @ EPLANS.COM

SECOND FLOOR

FIRST FLOOR

The stone facade of this luxurious mountain retreat is beautifully accented with a shallow-peaked roof and a bay window with copper flashing above, making it a plan you will be delighted to come home to. The heart of the home is the great room, with a fireplace, built-in entertainment center and stately columns. The vintage exposed-beam ceiling here is echoed in the country kitchen, a chef's dream with an extended island, room for a six-burner range and plenty of counter and cabinet space. An outdoor grill in the loggia is great for entertaining; from here, enjoy the resplendent courtyard. The master suite is full of natural light, stunning with a pampering bath and bumped-out whirlpool tub. Two upstairs bedrooms share a full bath. The bonus space is easily accessed from garage stairs or the outer deck from Bedroom 3.

© The Sater Design Collection, Inc.

plan# HPT920045

- **STYLE:** MEDITERRANEAN
- **FIRST FLOOR:** 2,227 SQ. FT.
- **SECOND FLOOR:** 1,278 SQ. FT.
- **TOTAL:** 3,505 SQ. FT.
- **BEDROOMS:** 4
- **BATHROOMS:** 4½
- **WIDTH:** 63'-9"
- **DEPTH:** 80'-0"
- **FOUNDATION:** SLAB

SEARCH ONLINE @ EPLANS.COM

SECOND FLOOR

FIRST FLOOR

Whether an extravagant waterfront vacation home or an everyday residence, this luxury villa will delight at every turn. Almost 900 square feet of outdoor living areas surround the plan; inside, generous room sizes allow space for family and friends. At the heart of the home, the great room offers a coffered ceiling, warming fireplace, built-in entertainment center and French-door access to the veranda. On the right, the country kitchen features a walk-in pantry and convenient utility room and mudroom. An art niche announces the master suite, a treasure with a large bay window, ample walk-in closets and a lovely bath with a corner tub. Upstairs, each bedroom enjoys a private bath and an added feature: Bedroom 1 is in a charming turret, Bedroom 2 opens to the sun deck and the guest suite has a private deck.

© The Sater Design Collection, Inc.

plan# HPT920046

- **STYLE: ITALIAN RENAISSANCE**
- **FIRST FLOOR: 2,084 SQ. FT.**
- **SECOND FLOOR: 652 SQ. FT.**
- **TOTAL: 2,736 SQ. FT.**
- **BONUS SPACE: 375 SQ. FT.**
- **BEDROOMS: 3**
- **BATHROOMS: 2½**
- **WIDTH: 60'-6"**
- **DEPTH: 94'-0"**
- **FOUNDATION: SLAB**

SEARCH ONLINE @ EPLANS.COM

With striking Mediterranean affluence, this Renaissance estate invites family and guests with triplet arches and a dramatic vaulted portico. Upon entering, the bayed dining room is to the left; a study resides in the turret, bright with circumambient light courtesy of intricate full-length windows. The great room soars with a vintage exposed-beam ceiling and offers a fireplace and three sets of French doors to the veranda. Don't miss the country kitchen, a tribute to gourmet cooking. The master suite has an extended-bow window, access to the courtyard and a luxurious bath with a Roman tub. An elegant staircase leads to two generous bedrooms; the vaulted bonus room is accessible from garage stairs or the outdoor deck off of Bedroom 3.

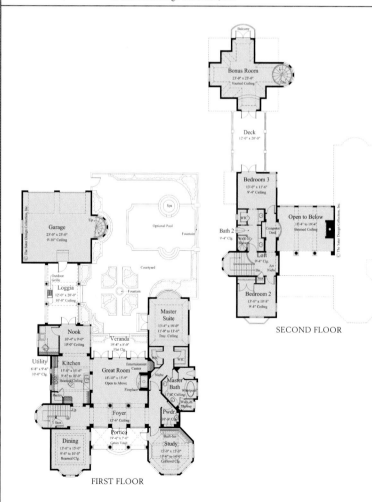

SECOND FLOOR

FIRST FLOOR

plan# HPT920047

- **STYLE: ITALIANATE**
- **FIRST FLOOR: 1,995 SQ. FT.**
- **SECOND FLOOR: 2,165 SQ. FT.**
- **TOTAL: 4,160 SQ. FT.**
- **BEDROOMS: 5**
- **BATHROOMS: 5½**
- **WIDTH: 58'-0"**
- **DEPTH: 65'-0"**
- **FOUNDATION: SLAB**

SEARCH ONLINE @ EPLANS.COM

With a Spanish-tile roof and Italian Renaissance detailing, this estate home holds the best of the Mediterranean. Upon entry, the foyer opens up to the living room/dining room combination, a highly requested feature in today's homes. A two-sided fireplace here shares its warmth with the study/library. The gourmet kitchen maximizes work space with wraparound countertops and an oversize island. The leisure room will be a family favorite, with a built-in entertainment center and outdoor access. Don't miss the outdoor grill and cabana suite on the far right. The master retreat is aptly named; a unique shape allows for an angled bath with a whirlpool tub and twin walk-in closets. Three additional bedrooms with private baths share two sun porches and convenient utility space.

SECOND FLOOR

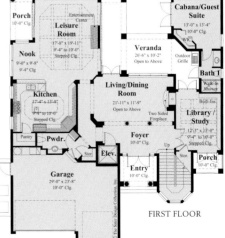

FIRST FLOOR

© The Sater Design Collection, Inc.

SECOND FLOOR

FIRST FLOOR

plan# HPT920048

- STYLE: ITALIAN RENAISSANCE
- FIRST FLOOR: 2,232 SQ. FT.
- SECOND FLOOR: 1,269 SQ. FT.
- TOTAL: 3,501 SQ. FT.
- BEDROOMS: 4
- BATHROOMS: 4½
- WIDTH: 63'-9"
- DEPTH: 80'-0"
- FOUNDATION: SLAB

SEARCH ONLINE @ EPLANS.COM

An impressive Italian Renaissance manor, this stone and stucco home is stunning from the curb and pure rapture inside. Twin bays at the front of the plan hold a study with a star-stepped ceiling and a dining room with coffer accents and decorative columns. The great room offers a warming fireplace and a soaring coffered ceiling. Not to be missed: an outdoor kitchen in addition to the modern country kitchen and bayed breakfast nook inside. The master suite is a dream come true; a large bay window, oversize walk-in closets and a pampering bath with a corner tub will delight. Upstairs, three bedrooms all have private baths and large walk-in closets. Two bedrooms enjoy deck access.

© The Sater Design Collection, Inc.

plan# HPT920049

- STYLE: ITALIAN RENAISSANCE
- FIRST FLOOR: 2,815 SQ. FT.
- SECOND FLOOR: 1,130 SQ. FT.
- TOTAL: 3,945 SQ. FT.
- BEDROOMS: 4
- BATHROOMS: 3½
- WIDTH: 85'-0"
- DEPTH: 76'-8"
- FOUNDATION: SLAB

SEARCH ONLINE @ EPLANS.COM

Stone, stucco, beautiful windows and a tile roof all combine to give this home plenty of classy curb appeal. An elegant entry leads to the grand foyer, which introduces the formal living room. Here, a bowed wall of windows shows off the rear veranda, while a two-sided fireplace warms cool evenings. A cozy study shares the fireplace and offers access to the rear veranda. Providing privacy as well as pampering, the first-floor master suite is complete with two walk-in closets, a deluxe bath, a stepped ceiling and private access outdoors. For casual times, the leisure room features a fireplace, built-ins, a coffered ceiling and outdoor access. Upstairs, Bedrooms 2 and 3 share a bath, while the guest suite has a private bath.

SECOND FLOOR

FIRST FLOOR

© Copyright 2001, The Sater Design Collection, Inc.

SECOND FLOOR

- Bedroom 2 — 13'-0" x 12'-0", 9'-4" Clg.
- Open to Below — 21'-0" to 21'-8", Coffered Clg.
- Bonus Room — 13'-8" x 14'-0", Vault to 9'-10" Clg.
- Bath 2 — 9'-0" Clg.
- Bath 1 — 9'-0" Clg.
- Computer Loft — 9'-0" Clg.
- Bonus Bath — 8'-0" Clg.
- Bedroom 1 — 13'-0" x 12'-6", 12'-0" Clg.
- Guest Suite — 13'-0" x 11'-8", 9'-0" Clg.
- Deck

plan # HPT920050

- **STYLE:** MEDITERRANEAN
- **FIRST FLOOR:** 2,219 SQ. FT.
- **SECOND FLOOR:** 1,085 SQ. FT.
- **TOTAL:** 3,304 SQ. FT.
- **BONUS SPACE:** 404 SQ. FT.
- **BEDROOMS:** 4
- **BATHROOMS:** 3½
- **WIDTH:** 91'-0"
- **DEPTH:** 52'-8"
- **FOUNDATION:** SLAB

SEARCH ONLINE @ EPLANS.COM

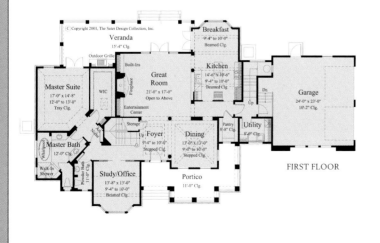

© Copyright 2001, The Sater Design Collection, Inc.

FIRST FLOOR

- Veranda — 15'-4" Clg.
- Breakfast — 9'-4" x 10'-0", Beamed Clg.
- Kitchen — 14'-6" x 10'-6", 9'-4" to 10'-0", Beamed Clg.
- Great Room — 21'-0" x 17'-0", Open to Above
- Garage — 24'-0" x 23'-0", 10'-2" Clg.
- Master Suite — 17'-0" x 14'-8", 12'-0" to 13'-0", Tray Clg.
- Master Bath — 12'-0" Clg.
- Foyer — 9'-4" to 10'-4", Stepped Clg.
- Dining — 13'-0" x 13'-0", 9'-4" to 10'-0", Stepped Clg.
- Utility — 8'-0" Clg.
- Pantry — 8'-8" Clg.
- Study/Office — 13'-8" x 13'-0", 9'-4" to 10'-0", Beamed Clg.
- Portico — 11'-0" Clg.

This home features two levels of pampering luxury filled with the most up-to-date amenities. Touches of Mediterranean detail add to the striking facade. A wrapping front porch welcomes you inside to a formal dining room and two-story great room warmed by a fireplace. Double doors from the master suite, great room and breakfast nook access the rear veranda. The first-floor master suite enjoys a luxury bath, roomy walk-in closet and close access to the front-facing office/study. Three additional bedrooms reside upstairs. The bonus room above the garage is great for an apartment or storage space.

© The Sater Design Collection, Inc.

plan# HPT920051

- **STYLE: FRENCH COUNTRY**
- **FIRST FLOOR: 2,794 SQ. FT.**
- **SECOND FLOOR: 1,127 SQ. FT.**
- **TOTAL: 3,921 SQ. FT.**
- **BEDROOMS: 4**
- **BATHROOMS: 3½**
- **WIDTH: 85'-0"**
- **DEPTH: 76'-8"**
- **FOUNDATION: SLAB**

SEARCH ONLINE @ EPLANS.COM

Elegance is showcased on this European manor by its stone and stucco facade, multi-pane windows, grand entrance and varied rooflines. The foyer introduces the formal dining room on the left and a spacious formal living room directly ahead. The study and living room share a through-fireplace, and both have access to the backyard. The kitchen features a walk-in pantry, a cooktop island, a pass-through to the rear veranda and an adjacent octagonal breakfast nook. Nearby, the leisure room is complete with a coffered ceiling, built-ins and another fireplace. The master suite resides on the right side of the home and pro-vides two walk-in closets and a lavish bath.

SECOND FLOOR

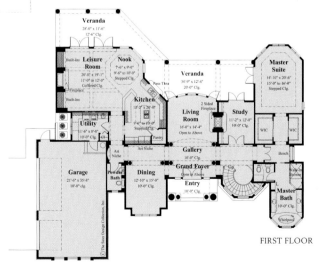

FIRST FLOOR

© The Sater Design Collection, Inc.

FIRST FLOOR

SECOND FLOOR

Stone, stucco and soaring rooflines combine to give this elegant Mediterranean design a stunning exterior. The interior is packed with luxurious amenities, from the wall of glass in the living room to the whirlpool tub in the master bath. A dining room and study serve as formal areas, while a leisure room with a fireplace offers a relaxing retreat. The first-floor master suite boasts a private bayed sitting area. Upstairs, all three bedrooms include private baths; Bedroom 2 and the guest suite also provide walk-in closets.

© The Sater Design Collection, Inc.

plan# HPT920053

- **STYLE: ITALIAN RENAISSANCE**
- **FIRST FLOOR: 3,025 SQ. FT.**
- **SECOND FLOOR: 1,639 SQ. FT.**
- **TOTAL: 4,664 SQ. FT.**
- **BONUS SPACE: 294 SQ. FT.**
- **BEDROOMS: 4**
- **BATHROOMS: 4½**
- **WIDTH: 70'-0"**
- **DEPTH: 100'-0"**
- **FOUNDATION: SLAB**

SEARCH ONLINE @ EPLANS.COM

An Italian Renaissance masterpiece, this family-oriented design is ideal for entertaining. Double doors reveal a foyer, with a columned dining room to the right and a spiral staircase enclosed in a turret to the left. Ahead, the great room opens above to a soaring coffered ceiling. A bowed window wall and a two-sided fireplace (shared with the study) make an elegant impression. The country-style kitchen is a host's dream, with an adjacent wet bar, preparation island and space for a six-burner cooktop. Near the leisure room, a bayed nook could serve as a breakfast or reading area. The master suite is a pampering sanctuary, with no rooms directly above and personal touches you will surely appreciate. Upstairs, two bedrooms, one with a window seat, and a guest suite with a balcony, all enjoy private baths and walk-in closets.

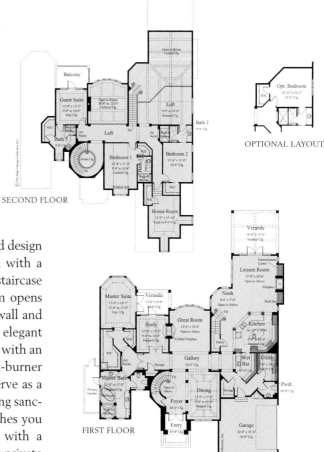

SECOND FLOOR

OPTIONAL LAYOUT

FIRST FLOOR

© The Sater Design Collection, Inc.

plan# HPT920054

- **STYLE: FRENCH COUNTRY**
- **FIRST FLOOR: 2,084 SQ. FT.**
- **SECOND FLOOR: 652 SQ. FT.**
- **TOTAL: 2,736 SQ. FT.**
- **BONUS SPACE: 365 SQ. FT.**
- **BEDROOMS: 3**
- **BATHROOMS: 2½**
- **WIDTH: 60'-6"**
- **DEPTH: 94'-0"**
- **FOUNDATION: SLAB**

SEARCH ONLINE @ EPLANS.COM

FIRST FLOOR

SECOND FLOOR

Warm brick and Mediterranean stucco accents create a beautiful facade for this French Country manor. A turret with arched keystone windows holds a bright study; the bay window brings natural light into the dining room. The great room is graced with a two-story exposed-beam ceiling, triplet French doors leading to the veranda and courtyard, and a fireplace. The country-style kitchen features beamed ceilings and tons of space for preparing gourmet meals. In the master suite, homeowners can relax in a bayed bedroom with courtyard access and wash away the day in the luxurious bath, complete with a bumped-out whirlpool tub. Two upstairs bedrooms share a full bath; from Bedroom 3, the outdoor deck leads to bonus space (also accessible from the garage).

© The Sater Design Collection, Inc.

© The Sater Design Collection, Inc.

Deck
26'-0" x 15'-10"

Bedroom 1
13'-0" x 14'-6"
9'-4" to 10'-4"
Tray Clg.

Bedroom 2
12'-2" x 14'-4"
10'-0" Clg.

Bath 2
10'-0" Clg.

W/c Walk-In Shower

Linen

Loft
9'-0" Clg.

Dn. Desk 10'-0" Clg. Niche

Bonus Bath
9'-8" Clg.

Walk-In Shower

Bonus Room
16'-6" x 19'-2"
Vaulted to
9'-8" Clg.

SECOND FLOOR

Bath 1
10'-0" Clg.

Lanai
26'-0" x 15'-10"
10'-0" Clg.

Master Suite
13'-2" x 21'-2"
12'-0" to 13'-0"
Stepped Clg.

Walk-In Shower Linen

Great Room
21'-3" x 17'-8"
Vaulted w/
Beamed Clg.
Fireplace
Entertainment Center
Built-In Shelves

Nook
9'-0" to 10'-0"
Stepped Clg.

Dining Room
11'-0" x 17'-8"
9'-0" to 10'-0"
Coffered Clg.

Kitchen
13'-0" x 13'-9"
9'-0" to 9'-6"
Stepped Clg.

WIC WIC Walk-In Shower

Master Bath
12'-0" Clg.
Whirlpool

Study
11'-0" x 15'-4"
16'-4" to 17'-4"
Beamed Clg.

Foyer
18'-8" to 19'-8"
Stepped Clg.

Entry
18'-3" Clg.

Dn. Storage

Gallery
10'-0" Clg.

Pwdr.
10'-0" Clg.

Utility
6'-8" x 12'-0"
10'-0" Clg.

Garage
21'-0" x 25'-4"
10'-0" Clg.

© The Sater Design Collection, Inc.

FIRST FLOOR

plan# HPT920055

- STYLE: MEDITERRANEAN
- FIRST FLOOR: 2,250 SQ. FT.
- SECOND FLOOR: 663 SQ. FT.
- TOTAL: 2,913 SQ. FT.
- BONUS SPACE: 351 SQ. FT.
- BEDROOMS: 3
- BATHROOMS: 3½
- WIDTH: 72'-0"
- DEPTH: 68'-3"
- FOUNDATION: SLAB

SEARCH ONLINE @ EPLANS.COM

European stylings and beautiful windows present a lovely facade. Inside, a grand entry reveals a modern floor plan that fits today's family and your busy lifestyle. Elegant ceiling treatments throughout bring splendor to every room in the home. The great room soars with a vaulted beamed ceiling for vintage appeal. A lateral fireplace allows for sweeping rear views; French doors provide access to the lanai. The open dining room leads to a spacious country kitchen, adorned with a charming bayed nook. The first-floor master suite is a dream come true; a bayed window and a whirlpool tub set in a turret are exquisite touches. French doors lead to a private lanai. Upstairs, two generous bedrooms share a full bath and deck access. A bonus room with a full bath can be finished as your needs change.

© The Sater Design Collection, Inc.

plan# HPT920056

- **STYLE: EUROPEAN COTTAGE**
- **FIRST FLOOR: 2,250 SQ. FT.**
- **SECOND FLOOR: 663 SQ. FT.**
- **TOTAL: 2,913 SQ. FT.**
- **BONUS SPACE: 351 SQ. FT.**
- **BEDROOMS: 3**
- **BATHROOMS: 3½**
- **WIDTH: 72'-0"**
- **DEPTH: 68'-3"**
- **FOUNDATION: SLAB**

SEARCH ONLINE @ EPLANS.COM

SECOND FLOOR

FIRST FLOOR

While this beautiful manor may appear to be a traditional neighborhood home, the interior reveals a unique plan, designed to inspire. Multi-pane and bay windows flood the home with natural light, and an open plan brings this European estate to life. From the grand entry, the great room is an impressive sight: a vaulted, beamed ceiling adds grandeur while the fireplace lends a cozy touch. Rear views are breathtaking through a wall of windows. The dining room leads to the gourmet country kitchen and an extended-bay nook. A study, with French doors, would make a beautiful guest room. The master suite shines with today's most-desired amenities. Raised ceilings and a rear bay bring in light, and His and Hers walk-in closets are sure to please. The bayed whirlpool tub and the walk-in shower are wonderful luxuries. Two upstairs bedrooms share a full bath, deck access and a bonus room.

© The Sater Design Collection, Inc.

plan# HPT920057

- **STYLE:** FRENCH COUNTRY
- **FIRST FLOOR:** 1,996 SQ. FT.
- **SECOND FLOOR:** 2,171 SQ. FT.
- **TOTAL:** 4,167 SQ. FT.
- **BEDROOMS:** 5
- **BATHROOMS:** 5½
- **WIDTH:** 58'-0"
- **DEPTH:** 65'-0"
- **FOUNDATION:** SLAB

SEARCH ONLINE @ EPLANS.COM

Striking on the outside, extraordinary on the inside, this French country manor is no cookie-cutter home! Sloping rooflines, a flower-box window and a two-story turret encased in multi-pane glass give great curb appeal; step inside to voluminous ten-foot ceilings and a stylish floor plan designed for family living. A living room/dining room combination allows endless possibilities in interior design. Here, the two-sided fireplace shares its warmth with the library/study. The kitchen invites gourmet cooking with space for a six-burner range and tons of preparation area (including an oversized island). The second-floor master retreat is anything but ordinary; a unique shape highlights the expansive rear windows. Private porch access and a soothing spa bath are engaging. Three additional bedrooms enjoy two sun porches and great views.

SECOND FLOOR

FIRST FLOOR

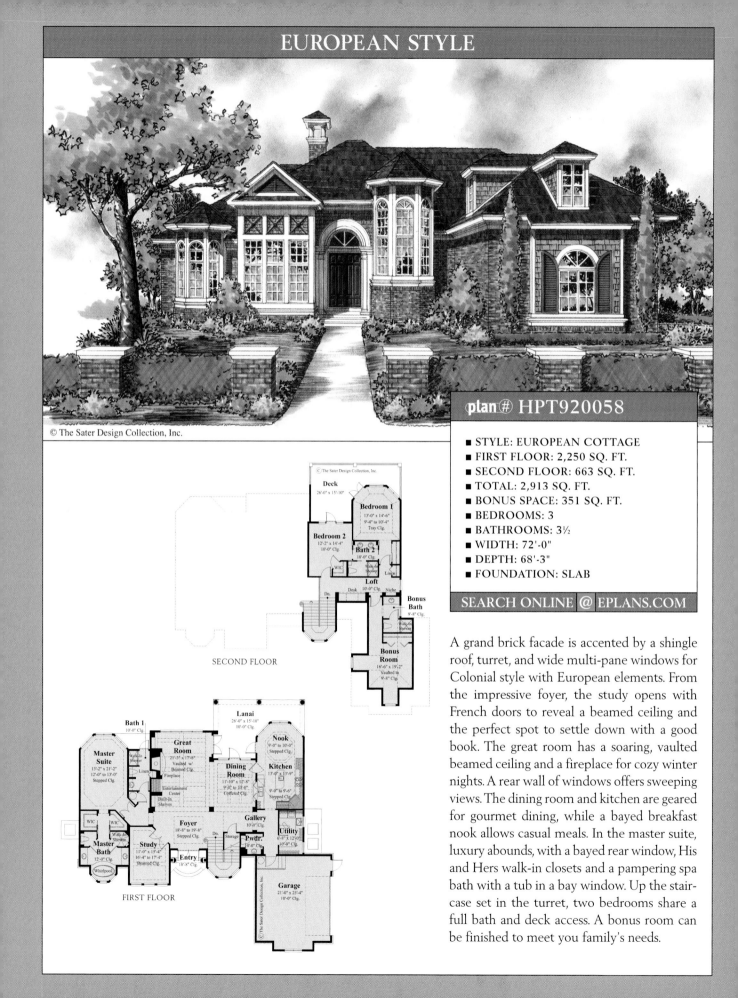

© The Sater Design Collection, Inc.

ptan# HPT920058

- STYLE: EUROPEAN COTTAGE
- FIRST FLOOR: 2,250 SQ. FT.
- SECOND FLOOR: 663 SQ. FT.
- TOTAL: 2,913 SQ. FT.
- BONUS SPACE: 351 SQ. FT.
- BEDROOMS: 3
- BATHROOMS: 3½
- WIDTH: 72'-0"
- DEPTH: 68'-3"
- FOUNDATION: SLAB

SEARCH ONLINE @ EPLANS.COM

A grand brick facade is accented by a shingle roof, turret, and wide multi-pane windows for Colonial style with European elements. From the impressive foyer, the study opens with French doors to reveal a beamed ceiling and the perfect spot to settle down with a good book. The great room has a soaring, vaulted beamed ceiling and a fireplace for cozy winter nights. A rear wall of windows offers sweeping views. The dining room and kitchen are geared for gourmet dining, while a bayed breakfast nook allows casual meals. In the master suite, luxury abounds, with a bayed rear window, His and Hers walk-in closets and a pampering spa bath with a tub in a bay window. Up the staircase set in the turret, two bedrooms share a full bath and deck access. A bonus room can be finished to meet you family's needs.

SECOND FLOOR

FIRST FLOOR

© The Sater Design Collection, Inc.

plan# HPT920059

- **STYLE: ITALIANATE**
- **FIRST FLOOR: 1,996 SQ. FT.**
- **SECOND FLOOR: 2,171 SQ. FT.**
- **TOTAL: 4,167 SQ. FT.**
- **BEDROOMS: 5**
- **BATHROOMS: 5½**
- **WIDTH: 58'-0"**
- **DEPTH: 65'-0"**
- **FOUNDATION: SLAB**

SEARCH ONLINE @ EPLANS.COM

Beautiful stone accents add warmth to this Italianate stucco home. Porches front and rear enhance the bright, airy sensation of natural light from expansive windows throughout. From the entry, the foyer opens to a living room/dining room combination, desired for its unlimited design potential. French doors to the right present a library/study with a two-way fireplace. In the kitchen, gourmet meals are a snap; abundant counter and cabinet space, an island and room for professional-grade appliances will please the family chef. Between the kitchen and the comfortable leisure room, a nook could be a breakfast area or cozy reading spot. Upstairs, an angled master retreat lives up to its name, with lots of light, a fantastic spa bath and two enormous walk-in closets. Three more bedrooms include private baths—Bedroom 1 has a romantic balcony.

SECOND FLOOR

FIRST FLOOR

© Sater Design Collection, Inc.

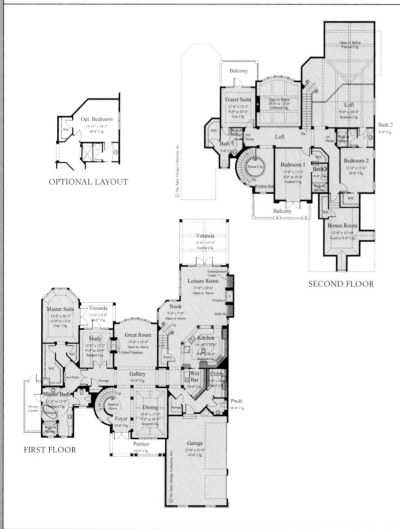

OPTIONAL LAYOUT

Opt. Bedroom
13'-11" x 14'-2"
10'-0" Clg.
WIC

SECOND FLOOR

FIRST FLOOR

plan# HPT920060

- STYLE: EUROPEAN COTTAGE
- FIRST FLOOR: 3,018 SQ. FT.
- SECOND FLOOR: 1,646 SQ. FT.
- TOTAL: 4,664 SQ. FT.
- BONUS SPACE: 294 SQ. FT.
- BEDROOMS: 4
- BATHROOMS: 4½
- WIDTH: 70'-0"
- DEPTH: 100'-0"
- FOUNDATION: SLAB

SEARCH ONLINE @ EPLANS.COM

European accents and intriguing details make this stone-and-stucco home a unique addition to any neighborhood. The Juliet balcony is a romantic touch, complementing the vintage two-story turret, which houses a spiral staircase topped with Palladian windows for circumambient light. From the foyer, the dining room is defined by columns. The two-story great room is graced with a bowed window wall for excellent views, and a two-sided fireplace, shared with the study. The hexagonal kitchen includes a wet bar and looks over the bayed breakfast nook and family-friendly leisure room. The master suite is designed to pamper with His and Hers walk-in closets, an elegant bath and a private garden. Upstairs, two bedrooms and a guest suite all enjoy private baths and walk-in closets.

plan# HPT920061

- **STYLE:** EUROPEAN COTTAGE
- **FIRST FLOOR:** 2,834 SQ. FT.
- **SECOND FLOOR:** 1,143 SQ. FT.
- **TOTAL:** 3,977 SQ. FT.
- **BEDROOMS:** 4
- **BATHROOMS:** 3½
- **WIDTH:** 85'-0"
- **DEPTH:** 76'-8"
- **FOUNDATION:** SLAB

SEARCH ONLINE @ EPLANS.COM

Mediterranean accents enhance the facade of this contemporary estate home. Two fanciful turret bays add a sense of grandeur to the exterior. Double doors open inside to a grand two-story foyer. A two-sided fireplace warms the study and living room, with a two-story coffered ceiling. To the right, the master suite includes a private bath, two walk-in closets and double-door access to the sweeping rear veranda. Casual areas of the home include the gourmet island kitchen, breakfast nook and leisure room warmed by a fireplace. A spiral staircase leads upstairs, where a second-floor balcony separates two family bedrooms from the luxurious guest suite.

SECOND FLOOR

FIRST FLOOR

© The Sater Design Collection, Inc.

SECOND FLOOR

FIRST FLOOR

plan# HPT920062

- **STYLE: CHATEAU**
- **FIRST FLOOR: 2,850 SQ. FT.**
- **SECOND FLOOR: 1,155 SQ. FT.**
- **TOTAL: 4,005 SQ. FT.**
- **BONUS SPACE: 371 SQ. FT.**
- **BEDROOMS: 4**
- **BATHROOMS: 4½**
- **WIDTH: 71'-6"**
- **DEPTH: 83'-0"**
- **FOUNDATION: SLAB**

SEARCH ONLINE @ EPLANS.COM

Sparkling expanses of glass—a window wall in the living room, a triple window in the dining room and bay windows in the breakfast nook and master-suite sitting area—ensure plenty of natural illumination for this lofty Mediterranean design. Other special amenities include fireplaces in the leisure and living rooms, a walk-in pantry in the kitchen and a private garden accessible from the master suite. Three lanai areas provide outdoor living and entertaining space. Upstairs, two bedrooms—one with a walk-in closet and bay window—share easy access to a bonus room, and the guest suite provides a walk-in closet and private baths.

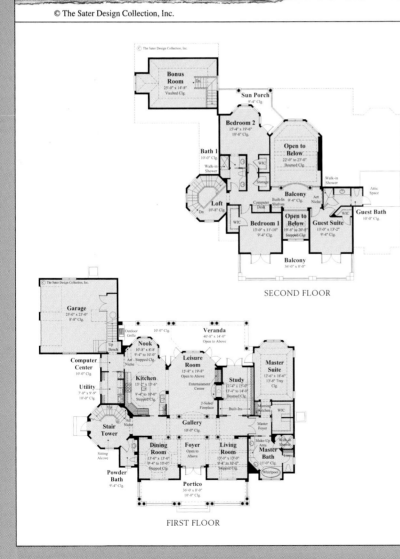

© The Sater Design Collection, Inc.

BONUS
Room
25'-0" x 14'-6"
Vaulted Clg.

Sun Porch
9'-4"

Bedroom 2
15'-4" x 19'-6"
10'-8" Clg.

Bath 1
10'-0" Clg.
Walk-in
Shower

Open to
Below
22'-0" to 23'-0"
Beamed Clg.

Loft
10'-8" Clg.

Balcony
9'-4" Clg.

Bedroom 1
13'-0" x 11'-10"
9'-4" Clg.

Open to
Below
10'-8" to 20'-8"
Stepped Clg.

Guest Suite
13'-0" x 13'-2"
9'-4" Clg.

Guest Bath
10'-0" Clg.

Balcony
36'-0" x 8'-0"

SECOND FLOOR

© The Sater Design Collection, Inc.

Garage
25'-0" x 23'-0"
8'-8" Clg.

Computer
Center
10'-0" Clg.

Utility
7'-0" x 9'-9"
10'-0" Clg.

Nook
10'-8" x 8'-8"
9'-4" to 10'-0"

Veranda
40'-8" x 14'-0"
Open to Above

Leisure
Room
15'-4" x 19'-8"
Open to Above

Kitchen
13'-2" x 13'-6"
9'-4" to 10'-0"
Stepped Clg.

Study
13'-4" x 15'-0"
13'-4" to 14'-0"
Beamed Clg.

Master
Suite
12'-6" x 18'-6"
13'-4" Tray Clg.

Entertainment
Center

2-Sided
Fireplace

Stair
Tower

Gallery
10'-0" Clg.

Dining
Room
13'-0" x 13'-0"
9'-4" to 10'-0"
Stepped Clg.

Foyer
Open to Above

Living
Room
13'-0" x 15'-0"
9'-4" to 10'-0"

Master
Bath
11'-0" Clg.

Powder
Bath
9'-4" Clg.

Portico
36'-0" x 8'-0"
10'-0" Clg.

FIRST FLOOR

plan# HPT920063

- **STYLE:** FRENCH
- **FIRST FLOOR:** 2,483 SQ. FT.
- **SECOND FLOOR:** 1,127 SQ. FT.
- **TOTAL:** 3,610 SQ. FT.
- **BONUS SPACE:** 332 SQ. FT.
- **BEDROOMS:** 4
- **BATHROOMS:** 3½
- **WIDTH:** 83'-0"
- **DEPTH:** 71'-8"
- **FOUNDATION:** SLAB

SEARCH ONLINE @ EPLANS.COM

For a family desiring lots of outdoor living areas and an elegant interior, this French stucco manor is a place to call home. Formal areas at the front of the home welcome guests; ahead, the leisure room is bathed in light, an effect enhanced by the two-story ceiling. A two-sided fireplace here adds a cozy element. To the right, the study is stunning, with a beamed ceiling, built-in shelving and shared heat from the fireplace. The country kitchen will please every member of the family, with plenty of counter space, room for a six-burner range and an outdoor grill. The master suite is a resort on its own, featuring a bayed window, morning kitchen, enormous walk-in closet and a sumptuous bath with a bumped-out whirlpool tub. Up the spiral staircase, three generous bedrooms—one with a private sun deck—share a bonus room.

© The Sater Design Collection, Inc.

SECOND FLOOR

FIRST FLOOR

plan# HPT920064

- STYLE: CHATEAU
- FIRST FLOOR: 2,163 SQ. FT.
- SECOND FLOOR: 2,302 SQ. FT.
- TOTAL: 4,465 SQ. FT.
- BEDROOMS: 5
- BATHROOMS: 5½
- WIDTH: 58'-0"
- DEPTH: 65'-0"
- FOUNDATION: SLAB

SEARCH ONLINE @ EPLANS.COM

Capturing the best of New England Colonial architecture, this stately brick manor includes appealing features, both classic and modern. Formal rooms toward the front are sure to impress, but the heart of the home is the kitchen and leisure room area. The country kitchen has an island and plenty of counter space to accommodate most any appliance. A bayed nook adds charm. The leisure room has a warming fireplace, built-in entertainment center and sweeping rear views. Don't miss the built-in wine cellar, just outside the kitchen. Rear outdoor living areas include an open-air kitchen for exciting alfresco dining. The upper level includes three family suites (each with private baths and porch access) and a beautiful master retreat with a refreshing bath and soothing whirlpool tub.

© The Sater Design Collection, Inc.

plan# HPT920065

- **STYLE: FRENCH**
- **FIRST FLOOR: 2,232 SQ. FT.**
- **SECOND FLOOR: 1,269 SQ. FT.**
- **TOTAL: 3,501 SQ. FT.**
- **BEDROOMS: 4**
- **BATHROOMS: 4½**
- **WIDTH: 63'-9"**
- **DEPTH: 80'-0"**
- **FOUNDATION: SLAB**

SEARCH ONLINE @ EPLANS.COM

This stately brick manor features large, bright windows, impressive columns and stucco accents. Three entrances—a grand main portico, a side "friends'" porch and a mudroom—cater to any occasion, welcoming family and guests. Encased in twin bay windows, a study and dining room enjoy elegant ceiling treatments. The two-story grand room is warmed by abundant sunlight and a fireplace framed by built-ins. The large family kitchen is joined by a bayed breakfast nook and an all-weather outdoor kitchen. In the master suite, a stepped ceiling and bay window embellish the bedroom; the bath has a walk-in shower and a corner whirlpool tub. Three upstairs bedrooms have private baths—Bedroom 2 and the guest suite offer private decks.

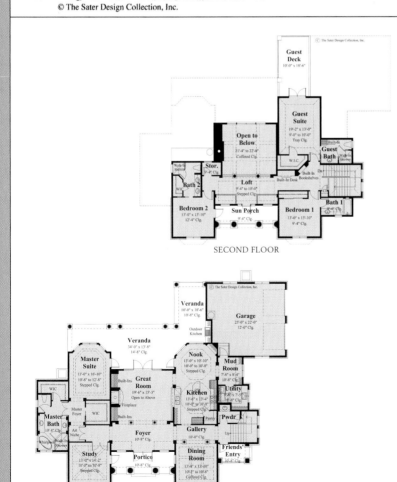

SECOND FLOOR

FIRST FLOOR

© The Sater Design Collection, Inc.

plan # HPT920066

- **STYLE: EUROPEAN COTTAGE**
- **FIRST FLOOR: 2,163 SQ. FT.**
- **SECOND FLOOR: 2,302 SQ. FT.**
- **TOTAL: 4,465 SQ. FT.**
- **BEDROOMS: 5**
- **BATHROOMS: 5½**
- **WIDTH: 58'-0"**
- **DEPTH: 65'-0"**
- **FOUNDATION: SLAB**

SEARCH ONLINE @ EPLANS.COM

In true European style, this stunning brick-and-stucco manor combines elegance and functionality for a perfect family home. Double doors open to reveal a foyer encircled by formal living areas. To the left, a library/study and formal dining room enjoy vintage beamed ceilings. Ahead, the living room, defined by decorative columns, displays expansive views of the rear property. A full guest suite is great for frequent visitors. The country kitchen lies to the far right; here, an island and a bayed nook create a charming and efficient workspace. The leisure room is sure to be a family favorite. Not to be missed: the wine cellar, located behind the staircase. Upstairs, the master suite enjoys privacy and luxury. Three additional suites have private baths. All four generous bedrooms open to porches and balconies.

SECOND FLOOR

FIRST FLOOR

© The Sater Design Collection, Inc.

plan# HPT920067

- **STYLE: CHATEAU**
- **FIRST FLOOR: 2,867 SQ. FT.**
- **SECOND FLOOR: 1,155 SQ. FT.**
- **TOTAL: 4,022 SQ. FT.**
- **BONUS SPACE: 371 SQ. FT.**
- **BEDROOMS: 4**
- **BATHROOMS: 4½**
- **WIDTH: 71'-6"**
- **DEPTH: 82'-2"**
- **FOUNDATION: SLAB**

SEARCH ONLINE @ EPLANS.COM

SECOND FLOOR

FIRST FLOOR

With a stucco facade and copper-flashing bay window, this estate gives the impression of a traditional neighborhood home. Inside, however, it is instantly clear that it is so much more. From the barrel-vault entry, the two-story foyer leads to the living room, sure to be a family favorite. An exposed-beam ceiling can be rustic or refined; the rear bowed window wall offers fantastic views. The country kitchen and bayed breakfast nook are designed for family living. In the leisure room, a built-in entertainment center and lanai access are inviting. The expansive master suite provides peace and relaxation, with a bayed sitting room, pampering bath with a corner tub, and a private garden. Upstairs, two family bedrooms and a guest suite all enjoy private baths and access to the bonus space and indoor balcony.

© The Sater Design Collection, Inc.

plan# HPT920068

- **STYLE: FRENCH COUNTRY**
- **FIRST FLOOR: 2,484 SQ. FT.**
- **SECOND FLOOR: 1,127 SQ. FT.**
- **TOTAL: 3,611 SQ. FT.**
- **BONUS SPACE: 332 SQ. FT.**
- **BEDROOMS: 4**
- **BATHROOMS: 3½**
- **WIDTH: 83'-0"**
- **DEPTH: 71'-8"**
- **FOUNDATION: SLAB**

SEARCH ONLINE @ EPLANS.COM

This appealing French country design emphasizes effective indoor/outdoor relationships. A wide, welcoming front porch can be viewed from the living and dining rooms; to the back of the plan, the kitchen, leisure room and study all open to the lanai. Upstairs, Bedroom 1 shares a balcony with the guest suite, while Bedroom 2 opens to a private deck. Other amenities include a fireplace shared by the living room and study, stepped ceilings in the living and dining rooms, kitchen and study, and plenty of counter and cabinet space in the utility room. A vaulted bonus room above the garage offers room to grow.

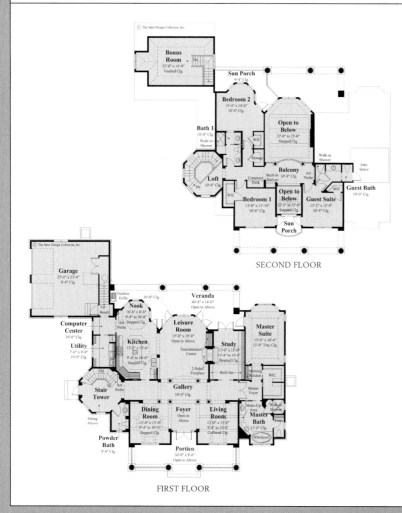

SECOND FLOOR

FIRST FLOOR

© The Sater Design Collection, Inc.

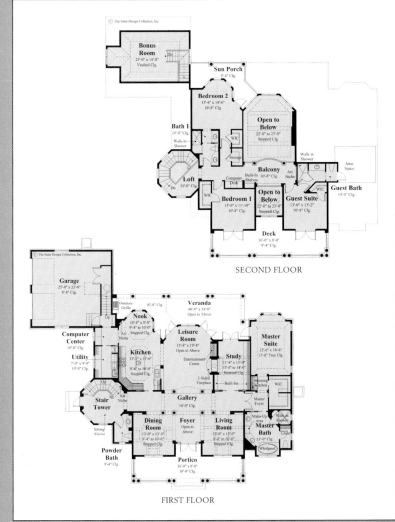

plan# HPT920069

- **STYLE: FRENCH**
- **FIRST FLOOR: 2,481 SQ. FT.**
- **SECOND FLOOR: 1,132 SQ. FT.**
- **TOTAL: 3,613 SQ. FT.**
- **BONUS SPACE: 332 SQ. FT.**
- **BEDROOMS: 4**
- **BATHROOMS: 3½**
- **WIDTH: 83'-0"**
- **DEPTH: 71'-8"**
- **FOUNDATION: SLAB**

SEARCH ONLINE @ EPLANS.COM

SECOND FLOOR

FIRST FLOOR

A classic plantation-style home with all the charm of a double-decker porch and multiple sets of twin columns, this is a family plan with elegant touches. Framing the foyer, the formal living and dining rooms have distinctive stepped ceilings. The gallery leads into the bayed two-story leisure room, magnificent with a two-way fireplace shared with the study, a built-in media center and rear-property access. The country kitchen has an oversize island and plenty of counter space. Don't miss the computer center and outdoor grill! To the far right, the master suite is an extraordinary retreat; a box-bay, morning kitchen, walk-in closet built for two and bumped-out whirlpool tub make this a relished haven. In an octagonal turret, the spiral staircase presents two upstairs bedrooms, a guest suite, storage space, a bonus room and a private sun deck off Bedroom 2.

© The Sater Design Collection, Inc.

- **STYLE: ITALIAN RENAISSANCE**
- **FIRST FLOOR: 3,023 SQ. FT.**
- **SECOND FLOOR: 1,623 SQ. FT.**
- **TOTAL: 4,646 SQ. FT.**
- **BONUS SPACE: 294 SQ. FT.**
- **BEDROOMS: 4**
- **BATHROOMS: 4½**
- **WIDTH: 70'-0"**
- **DEPTH: 100'-0"**
- **FOUNDATION: SLAB**

SEARCH ONLINE @ EPLANS.COM

This stunning Italian Renaissance estate will be the showpiece of your neighborhood. Beautiful brickwork sets off Palladian-style windows and a two-story turret for a romantic treasure you will be glad to call home. Enter past the columned dining room to the great room, with a bowed wall of windows that offers spectacular views, and a two-way fireplace shared with the study. The island kitchen allows plenty of room for two cooks, making meal preparations a joy. The leisure room features a fireplace, built-in entertainment center and French doors to the veranda. The master suite is an archetype for luxury with a bayed nook, perfect for a sitting area, a spa bath with a corner whirlpool tub, and a secluded master garden. Three upstairs suites enjoy private baths and walk-in closets.

OPTIONAL LAYOUTS

SECOND FLOOR

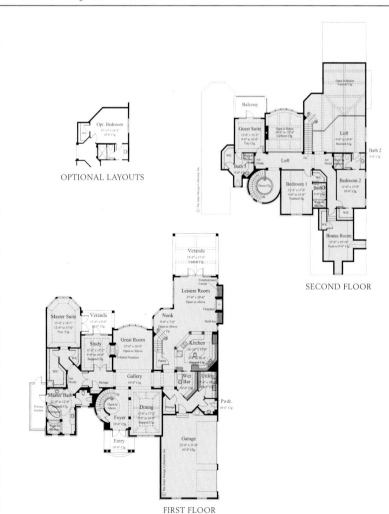

FIRST FLOOR

© The Sater Design Collection, Inc.

plan# HPT920071

- **STYLE: EUROPEAN COTTAGE**
- **FIRST FLOOR: 2,219 SQ. FT.**
- **SECOND FLOOR: 1,088 SQ. FT.**
- **TOTAL: 3,307 SQ. FT.**
- **BONUS SPACE: 446 SQ. FT.**
- **BEDROOMS: 4**
- **BATHROOMS: 3½**
- **WIDTH: 91'-0"**
- **DEPTH: 52'-8"**
- **FOUNDATION: SLAB**

SEARCH ONLINE @ EPLANS.COM

This English manor is sure to please, with its attractive facade and accommodating interior. The wraparound portico leads to the graceful foyer. Here, a formal dining room opens to the right and offers a refined ceiling treatment. The spacious great room provides a fireplace, built-ins, an entertainment center and access to the rear veranda. The sumptuous kitchen provides a worktop island, a beamed ceiling and a nearby bayed breakfast nook. The lavish, first-floor master suite is complete with a large, skylit walk-in closet, deluxe bath and private access to the rear veranda. Upstairs, a computer loft separates the guest suite from the family bedrooms. Note the bonus room over the garage—perfect for another guest suite or maid's quarters.

SECOND FLOOR

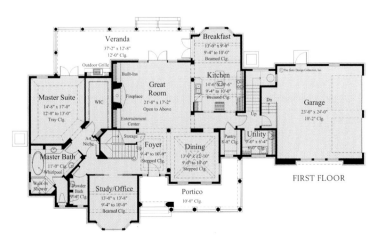

FIRST FLOOR

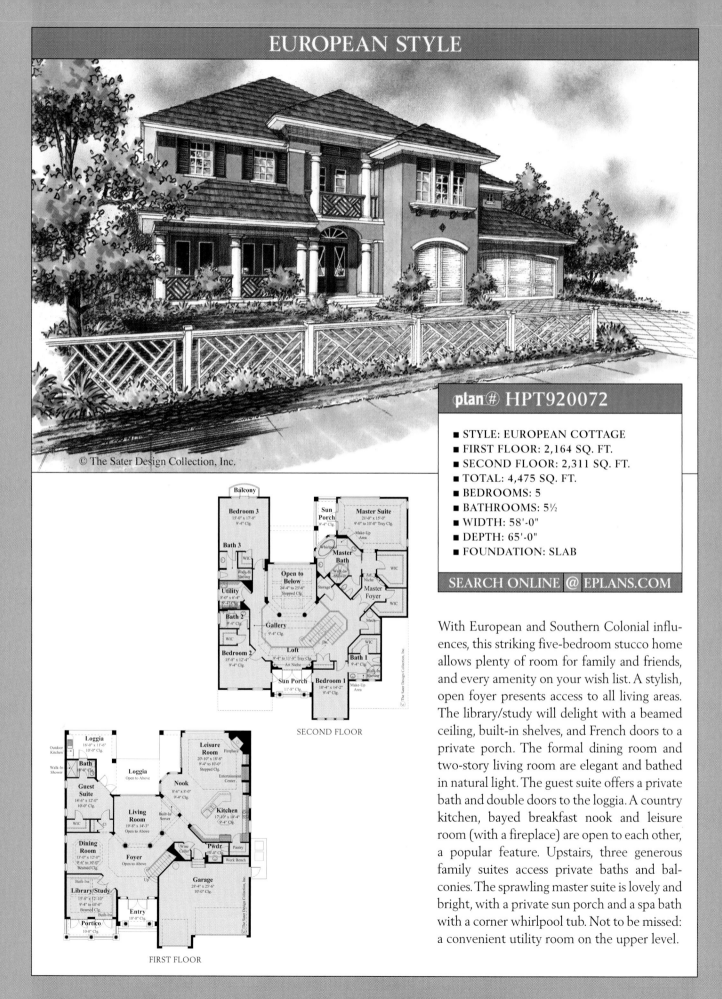

© The Sater Design Collection, Inc.

plan# HPT920072

- **STYLE: EUROPEAN COTTAGE**
- **FIRST FLOOR: 2,164 SQ. FT.**
- **SECOND FLOOR: 2,311 SQ. FT.**
- **TOTAL: 4,475 SQ. FT.**
- **BEDROOMS: 5**
- **BATHROOMS: 5½**
- **WIDTH: 58'-0"**
- **DEPTH: 65'-0"**
- **FOUNDATION: SLAB**

SEARCH ONLINE @ EPLANS.COM

SECOND FLOOR

FIRST FLOOR

With European and Southern Colonial influences, this striking five-bedroom stucco home allows plenty of room for family and friends, and every amenity on your wish list. A stylish, open foyer presents access to all living areas. The library/study will delight with a beamed ceiling, built-in shelves, and French doors to a private porch. The formal dining room and two-story living room are elegant and bathed in natural light. The guest suite offers a private bath and double doors to the loggia. A country kitchen, bayed breakfast nook and leisure room (with a fireplace) are open to each other, a popular feature. Upstairs, three generous family suites access private baths and balconies. The sprawling master suite is lovely and bright, with a private sun porch and a spa bath with a corner whirlpool tub. Not to be missed: a convenient utility room on the upper level.

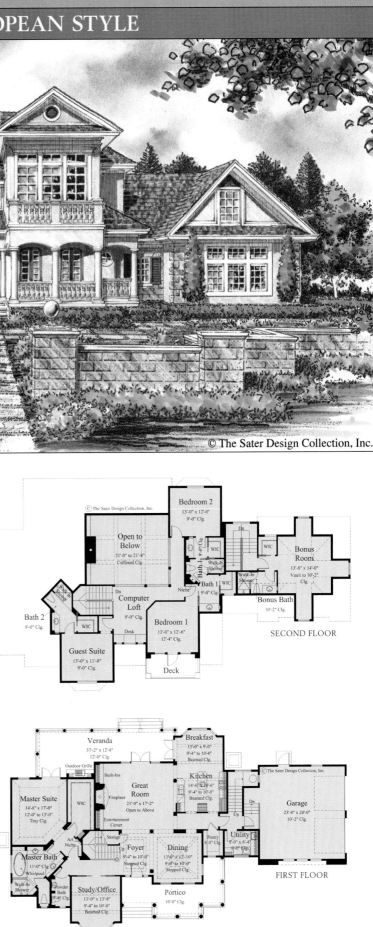

plan# HPT920073

- STYLE: FRENCH COUNTRY
- FIRST FLOOR: 2,219 SQ. FT.
- SECOND FLOOR: 1,085 SQ. FT.
- TOTAL: 3,304 SQ. FT.
- BONUS SPACE: 404 SQ. FT.
- BEDROOMS: 4
- BATHROOMS: 3½
- WIDTH: 91'-0"
- DEPTH: 52'-8"
- FOUNDATION: SLAB

SEARCH ONLINE @ EPLANS.COM

© The Sater Design Collection, Inc.

Stucco and stone combine with graceful details on this four-bedroom home. A covered front porch welcomes friends and family alike, and ushers you into the elegant foyer. A formal dining room is to your right, defined by columns and a grand ceiling treatment. Convenient to the front door, as well as to the lavish master suite, a study/office provides a bay window and lots of privacy. The spacious great room offers a warming fireplace, built-ins and a pass-through to the efficient kitchen. Here, the gourmet of the family will be well pleased with a worktop island, plenty of wrapping counters and a huge pantry nearby. A sunny bayed breakfast area will be perfect for early morning coffee. Separated on the first floor for privacy, the master suite is full of tempting amenities. Upstairs, two family bedrooms share a bath, while a guest suite revels in privacy.

Porch
54'-0" x 12'-0"

Master Bedroom
15'-2" x 15'-6"
Tray Clg.

built-in

Great Room
21'-6" x 15'-6"
Coffered Clg.

fireplace

built-in

Nook
11'-0" x 8'-6"

Desk

Kitchen

glass
hutch

Island

13'-0" x 11'-8"

art niche

P

CL

Bedroom 2
13'-2" x 11'-10"

Her
WIC

His
WIC

M.
Bath

make-up

Study
12'-10" x 14'-10"
Beamed Clg.

built-in

Foyer

Dining
12'-0" x 14'-6"
Stepped Clg.

art niche

Pwdr.

Utility

Linen

Bath

Bedroom 1
13'-6" x 12'-0"

CL

Porch
36'-6" x 8'-0"

workbench

Storage

Garage
23'-0" x 24'-0"

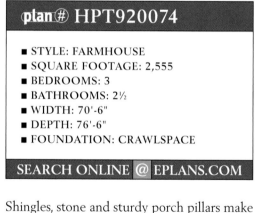

plan# HPT920074

- STYLE: FARMHOUSE
- SQUARE FOOTAGE: 2,555
- BEDROOMS: 3
- BATHROOMS: 2½
- WIDTH: 70'-6"
- DEPTH: 76'-6"
- FOUNDATION: CRAWLSPACE

SEARCH ONLINE @ EPLANS.COM

Shingles, stone and sturdy porch pillars make this farmhouse an eye-catching retreat. Inside, the foyer is flanked by formal rooms—a dining room with a stepped ceiling and a study with a beamed ceiling and built-in bookshelves. Family living space is to the center of the plan—the kitchen includes a built-in planning desk and an adjoining breakfast nook, while the great room features a coffered ceiling, a fireplace, built-in shelves and three sets of French doors that open to the rear porch. The split-bedroom plan—family bedrooms to the right, and the master suite to the left—allows everyone plenty of privacy.

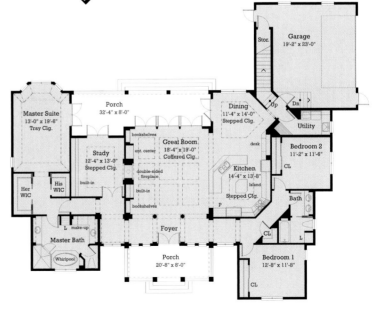

plan# HPT920075

- **STYLE: COUNTRY COTTAGE**
- **SQUARE FOOTAGE: 2,454**
- **BONUS SPACE: 256 SQ. FT.**
- **BEDROOMS: 3**
- **BATHROOMS: 2**
- **WIDTH: 80'-6"**
- **DEPTH: 66'-0"**
- **FOUNDATION: CRAWLSPACE**

SEARCH ONLINE @ EPLANS.COM

This traditional home offers a wide variety of modern amenities. The spacious foyer opens to the great room, which boasts built-in book-shelves, a wall of double doors to the rear porch and a double-sided fireplace shared with the study. To the far left, the master suite is enhanced by a bay window, His and Hers walk-in closets and a luxury whirlpool bath. The island cooktop kitchen serves the dining area with ease. Two additional family bedrooms share a hall bath. The bonus room above the garage is perfect for a home office or guest suite.

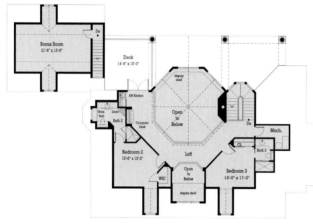

SECOND FLOOR

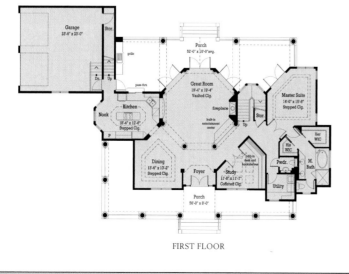

FIRST FLOOR

ptan# HPT920076

- **STYLE: COUNTRY COTTAGE**
- **FIRST FLOOR: 1,874 SQ. FT.**
- **SECOND FLOOR: 901 SQ. FT.**
- **TOTAL: 2,775 SQ. FT.**
- **BONUS SPACE: 382 SQ. FT.**
- **BEDROOMS: 3**
- **BATHROOMS: 3½**
- **WIDTH: 90'-0"**
- **DEPTH: 58'-6"**
- **FOUNDATION: CRAWLSPACE**

SEARCH ONLINE @ EPLANS.COM

From the wraparound porch to the gabled dormer windows, this sweet cottage is pure country. Inside, an open floor plan lends a spacious appeal. The formal dining room is defined by a pentagonal stepped ceiling. To the right, the study has unique angles and a sophisticated coffered ceiling. The two-story vaulted octagonal great room is brimming with architectural interest. Three sets of French doors extend to the rear porch; a fireplace can be viewed from the gourmet kitchen with a cooktop island. An outdoor grill invites dining alfresco. The master suite is designed to pamper, with French doors and a plush bath. Two bedroom suites and bonus space reside on the second level and enjoy upper-deck access.

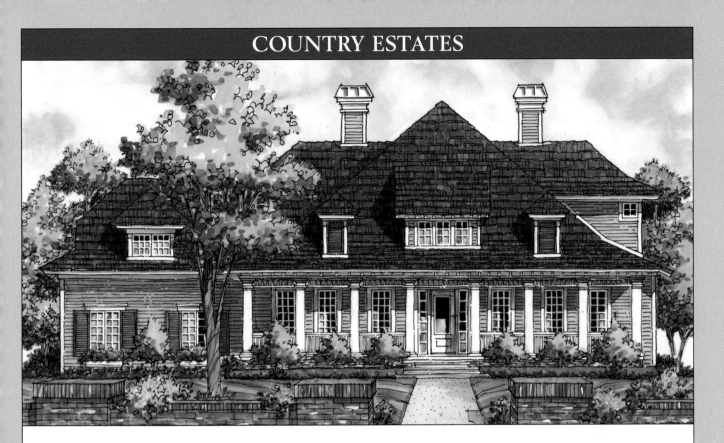

plan# HPT920077

- **STYLE: COUNTRY COTTAGE**
- **FIRST FLOOR: 2,138 SQ. FT.**
- **SECOND FLOOR: 944 SQ. FT.**
- **TOTAL: 3,082 SQ. FT.**
- **BONUS SPACE: 427 SQ. FT.**
- **BEDROOMS: 3**
- **BATHROOMS: 3½**
- **WIDTH: 76'-8"**
- **DEPTH: 64'-0"**
- **FOUNDATION: CRAWLSPACE**

SEARCH ONLINE @ EPLANS.COM

An elegant porch colonnade accentuates the classic good looks of this home. The foyer is flanked by formal rooms featuring ornate ceilings that add to those special gatherings. The great room is set off by three French doors opening to the spacious rear porch, which provides an extended family space. The kitchen and breakfast nook combination is ideal for casual meals. The master bedroom sits to the right of the plan and offers an abundance of privacy and luxury. The second floor reveals two family bedrooms—each with a private bath and entrance to the shared upper deck. The bonus room is a great space for a future media or game room.

FIRST FLOOR

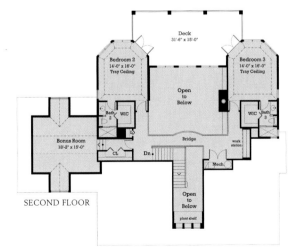

SECOND FLOOR

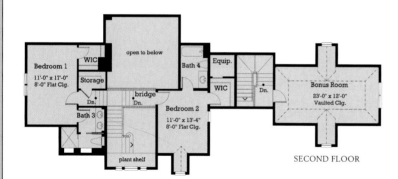

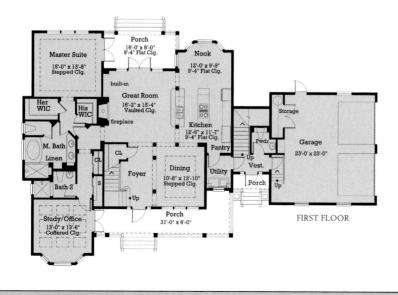

SECOND FLOOR

FIRST FLOOR

plan# HPT920078

- STYLE: COUNTRY COTTAGE
- FIRST FLOOR: 1,842 SQ. FT.
- SECOND FLOOR: 739 SQ. FT.
- TOTAL: 2,581 SQ. FT.
- BONUS SPACE: 379 SQ. FT.
- BEDROOMS: 3
- BATHROOMS: 4½
- WIDTH: 79'-0"
- DEPTH: 50'-0"
- FOUNDATION: CRAWLSPACE

SEARCH ONLINE @ EPLANS.COM

Vaguely Victorian, this home is a modern antique with a layout purely out of the twenty-first century. This home takes formal and casual living to the next level. With open, flowing spaces, rooms connect without feeling undefined. The great room features a fireplace and rear-porch access. The dining room is accented by columns and a stepped ceiling. The galley-style kitchen works hard to serve the dining room and adjoining breakfast nook. A private study can be used as a guest room. Private luxury rests in the master suite. Upstairs, two family bedrooms—each with a private bath—feature walk-in closets. A bonus room is found above the garage.

plan# HPT920079

- **STYLE:** FARMHOUSE
- **FIRST FLOOR:** 1,627 SQ. FT.
- **SECOND FLOOR:** 1,024 SQ. FT.
- **TOTAL:** 2,651 SQ. FT.
- **BEDROOMS:** 3
- **BATHROOMS:** 3½
- **WIDTH:** 78'-6"
- **DEPTH:** 80'-6"
- **FOUNDATION:** CRAWLSPACE

SEARCH ONLINE @ EPLANS.COM

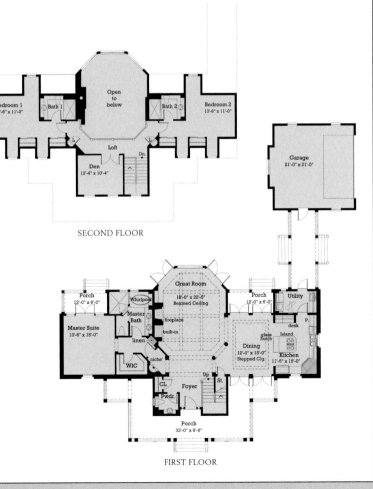

The symmetry of this home indicates Colonial roots. Double pediments sit above the porch entry. The octagonal-shaped great room is the heart of the home, separating the master quarters from the living zones. The open dining room enjoys a stepped ceiling and convenience to the island kitchen. Access to the rear porch is found just off the dining room. Two bedrooms with private baths, a loft and a den complete the second level of this home.

plan# HPT920080

Clean simple lines define this Victorian-style home, which opens through double doors to a spacious grand room. Adornments here include a coffered ceiling and triple French doors to the covered porch at the back. Both the dining room and the master bedroom feature stepped ceilings. Two walk-in closets and a fine bath with a separate tub and shower further enhance the master suite. Both family bedrooms upstairs have walk-in closets and built-ins. A bonus room can become an additional bedroom later, with space for a full bath.

- STYLE: FARMHOUSE
- FIRST FLOOR: 2,215 SQ. FT.
- SECOND FLOOR: 708 SQ. FT.
- TOTAL: 2,923 SQ. FT.
- BONUS SPACE: 420 SQ. FT.
- BEDROOMS: 3
- BATHROOMS: 3
- WIDTH: 76'-4"
- DEPTH: 69'-10"
- FOUNDATION: CRAWLSPACE

SEARCH ONLINE @ EPLANS.COM

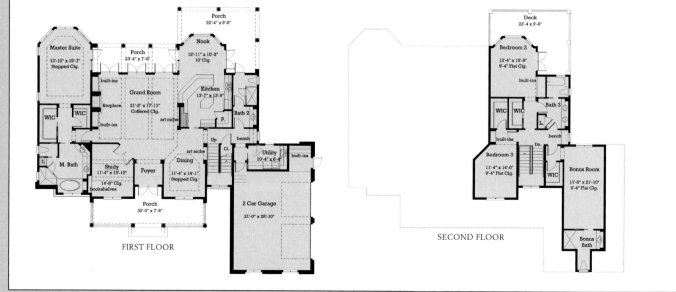

FIRST FLOOR

SECOND FLOOR

TO ORDER BLUEPRINTS CALL TOLL FREE 1-800-521-6797

plan# HPT920081

- **STYLE:** FARMHOUSE
- **FIRST FLOOR:** 1,387 SQ. FT.
- **SECOND FLOOR:** 1,175 SQ. FT.
- **TOTAL:** 2,562 SQ. FT.
- **BONUS SPACE:** 362 SQ. FT.
- **BEDROOMS:** 3
- **BATHROOMS:** 2½
- **WIDTH:** 54'-0"
- **DEPTH:** 78'-0"
- **FOUNDATION:** CRAWLSPACE

SEARCH ONLINE @ EPLANS.COM

This elegant two-story farmhouse features a floor plan that's perfect for today's active families. A spacious leisure room, with built-ins and a coffered ceiling, sits to the left of the foyer; to the right, the living room boasts a fireplace. Outdoor access and a beamed ceiling enhance the dining room, which adjoins a breakfast nook with a wall of windows. The kitchen opens to an outdoor grilling area. Upstairs, two family bedrooms join the master suite, which includes deck access and a private sitting area. A bonus room above the garage offers a full bath.

SECOND FLOOR

FIRST FLOOR

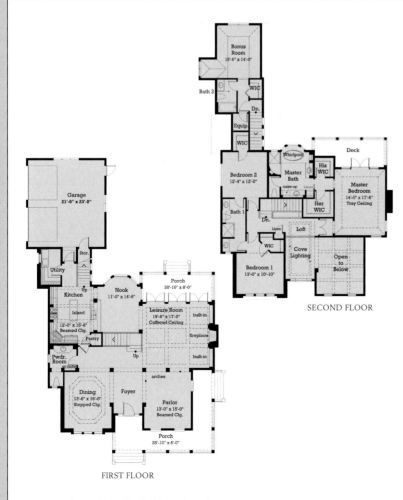

FIRST FLOOR

SECOND FLOOR

plan# HPT920082

- **STYLE: FARMHOUSE**
- **FIRST FLOOR: 1,642 SQ. FT.**
- **SECOND FLOOR: 1,205 SQ. FT.**
- **TOTAL: 2,847 SQ. FT.**
- **BONUS SPACE: 340 SQ. FT.**
- **BEDROOMS: 3**
- **BATHROOMS: 3½**
- **WIDTH: 53'-7"**
- **DEPTH: 72'-6"**
- **FOUNDATION: CRAWLSPACE**

SEARCH ONLINE @ EPLANS.COM

This impressive two-story farmhouse is a family delight. A wraparound front porch welcomes you inside to a foyer flanked on either side by a formal dining room and parlor. The leisure room is enhanced by a fireplace flanked by built-ins and a wall of double doors opening to the rear porch. The island kitchen overlooks the bayed nook. The second floor features a pampering master bedroom with a private second-floor deck, His and Hers walk-in closets and a whirlpool master bath. Two additional bedrooms share a Jack-and-Jill bath. The bonus room above the garage is perfect for a guest suite or home office.

plan# HPT920083

- STYLE: COUNTRY COTTAGE
- FIRST FLOOR: 1,664 SQ. FT.
- SECOND FLOOR: 1,463 SQ. FT.
- TOTAL: 3,127 SQ. FT.
- BEDROOMS: 3
- BATHROOMS: 2½
- WIDTH: 59'-10"
- DEPTH: 62'-0"
- FOUNDATION: CRAWLSPACE

SEARCH ONLINE @ EPLANS.COM

Perfect for a rustic landscape, this two-story home offers a dazzling, spacious interior punctuated with multiple ceiling treatments. The foyer opens to the living and dining rooms on the left with a nearby island kitchen that does double duty serving the sunny nook. The leisure room and nook enjoy a fireplace with built-ins and an assortment of windows with wonderful views. The study at the front boasts French doors and access to a powder room. The second floor holds the master suite—complete with sitting room, deck and private bath—and two bedrooms that share a full bath.

FIRST FLOOR

SECOND FLOOR

plan# HPT920084

- **STYLE: VICTORIAN**
- **FIRST FLOOR: 2,073 SQ. FT.**
- **SECOND FLOOR: 682 SQ. FT.**
- **TOTAL: 2,755 SQ. FT.**
- **BEDROOMS: 3**
- **BATHROOMS: 2½**
- **WIDTH: 64'-0"**
- **DEPTH: 76'-2"**
- **FOUNDATION: CRAWLSPACE**

SEARCH ONLINE @ EPLANS.COM

Fishscales, circle-top windows and ornate railings make this home decidedly Victorian. A double-door entry is a formal welcome into this home. The foyer is offset by columns forming a gallery between the entrance and the dining room, great room and private study. The great room is highlighted by three sets of French doors opening to the rear porch. The kitchen features an island, stepped ceiling, walk-in pantry and adjoining breakfast nook. Double French doors open from the master suite to the porch. On the second floor, two family bedrooms, a computer nook and a full bath complete this design.

SECOND FLOOR

FIRST FLOOR

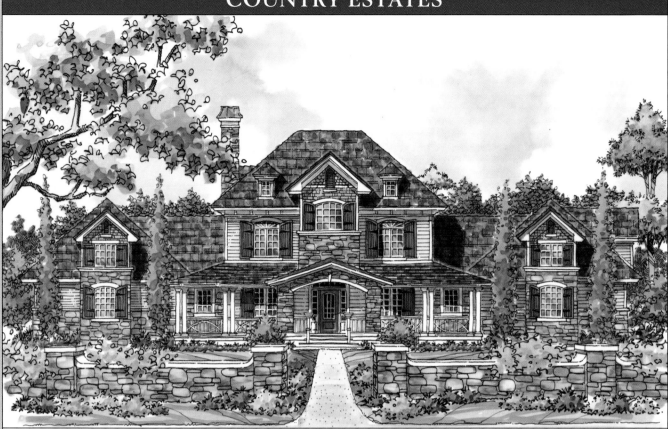

plan# HPT920085

- **STYLE: FARMHOUSE**
- **FIRST FLOOR: 2,151 SQ. FT.**
- **SECOND FLOOR: 738 SQ. FT.**
- **TOTAL: 2,889 SQ. FT.**
- **BONUS SPACE: 534 SQ. FT.**
- **BEDROOMS: 3**
- **BATHROOMS: 2½**
- **WIDTH: 99'-0"**
- **DEPTH: 56'-0"**
- **FOUNDATION: CRAWLSPACE**

SECOND FLOOR

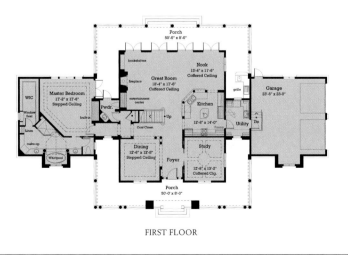

FIRST FLOOR

A wide, welcoming porch and plenty of stone accents highlight the facade of this charming symmetrical design. Inside, coffered ceilings enhance the study, great room and breakfast nook; the dining room and master suite both boast stepped ceilings. From the great room, four sets of French doors open to a wraparound rear porch with a grilling area. The master bedroom, also with porch access, includes built-in shelves, a walk-in closet with a window seat, and a luxurious bath with a whirlpool tub. On the second floor, two family bedrooms share a full bath with a whirlpool tub; a loft area and a bonus room offer extra space.

COUNTRY ESTATES

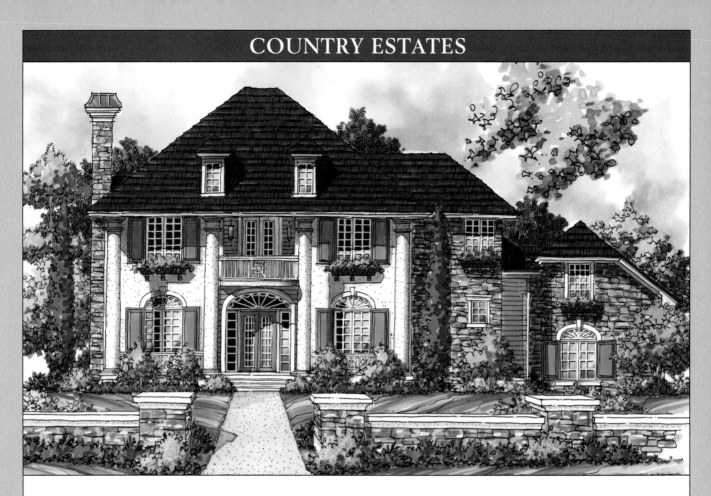

SECOND FLOOR

FIRST FLOOR

plan# HPT920086

- STYLE: COUNTRY COTTAGE
- FIRST FLOOR: 1,865 SQ. FT.
- SECOND FLOOR: 1,477 SQ. FT.
- TOTAL: 3,342 SQ. FT.
- BONUS SPACE: 584 SQ. FT.
- BEDROOMS: 4
- BATHROOMS: 2½
- WIDTH: 79'-0"
- DEPTH: 79'-2"
- FOUNDATION: CRAWLSPACE

SEARCH ONLINE @ EPLANS.COM

This eloquent French cottage design features an enchanting country layout. Double doors open inside to a formal welcoming foyer. To the left, a living room is warmed by a fireplace, which connects to a bay-windowed study. A formal dining room is found to the right. The island kitchen opens to a nook and leisure room with built-ins. Three sets of double doors open onto the rear porch. Upstairs, the study hall opens to a romantic front balcony. Three family bedrooms share a hall bath. The master suite is an impressive retreat with a large sitting area accessing the master deck, a private whirlpool bath and a huge walk-in closet.

plan# HPT920087

- **STYLE: FARMHOUSE**
- **FIRST FLOOR: 1,373 SQ. FT.**
- **SECOND FLOOR: 1,552 SQ. FT.**
- **TOTAL: 2,925 SQ. FT.**
- **BEDROOMS: 4**
- **BATHROOMS: 2½**
- **WIDTH: 64'-6"**
- **DEPTH: 51'-2"**
- **FOUNDATION: CRAWLSPACE**

SEARCH ONLINE @ EPLANS.COM

SECOND FLOOR

This luxurious farmhouse is a historic plantation filled with modern-day amenities. Classic columns add drama to the facade, while the wide front porch welcomes you inside. Double doors open into a foyer flanked by formal living and dining rooms. The leisure room is a cozy retreat offering a warm fireplace flanked by built-ins and topped by a stepped ceiling. From here, two sets of double doors open to the rear porch. The gourmet island kitchen opens to a nook and provides a storage pantry. A utility room, powder room and garage complete the first floor. Upstairs, a loft overlooks the foyer and two-story living room. The master suite offers a private whirlpool bath and two walk-in closets. Three additional bedrooms share a hall bath.

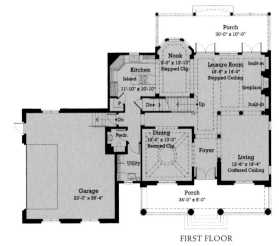

FIRST FLOOR

COUNTRY ESTATES

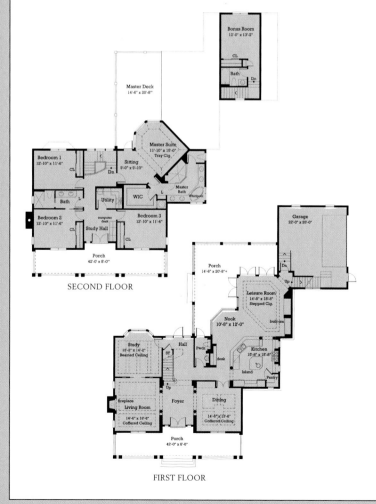

SECOND FLOOR

FIRST FLOOR

plan# HPT920088

- STYLE: FARMHOUSE
- FIRST FLOOR: 1,865 SQ. FT.
- SECOND FLOOR: 1,477 SQ. FT.
- TOTAL: 3,342 SQ. FT.
- BONUS SPACE: 282 SQ. FT.
- BEDROOMS: 4
- BATHROOMS: 3½
- WIDTH: 78'-0"
- DEPTH: 78'-8"
- FOUNDATION: CRAWLSPACE

SEARCH ONLINE @ EPLANS.COM

Double columns and porches on both levels give this farmhouse a touch of Southern Colonial charm. The living room includes a fireplace, and opens to a study that features a bay window. The kitchen boasts a walk-in pantry and a central island; nearby, the leisure room offers three sets of French doors that open to the expansive rear porch. Upstairs, three family bedrooms share a full bath and a study area that opens to a porch. The master suite features a private deck, a sitting area, and a private bath with a walk-in closet and a whirlpool tub. A bonus area above the garage includes another full bath.

plan# HPT920089

L

- STYLE: FLORIDIAN
- FIRST FLOOR: 2,066 SQ. FT.
- SECOND FLOOR: 810 SQ. FT.
- TOTAL: 2,876 SQ. FT.
- BONUS SPACE: 1,260 SQ. FT.
- BEDROOMS: 3
- BATHROOMS: 3½
- WIDTH: 64'-0"
- DEPTH: 45'-0"
- FOUNDATION: PIER

SEARCH ONLINE @ EPLANS.COM

If entertaining is your passion, then this is the design for you. With a large, open floor plan and an array of amenities, every gathering will be a success. The foyer embraces living areas accented by a glass fireplace and a wet bar. The grand room and dining room each access a screened veranda for outside enjoyments. The gourmet kitchen delights with its openness to the rest of the house. A morning nook here also adds a nice touch. Two bedrooms and a study radiate from the first-floor living areas. Upstairs—or use the elevator—is a stunning master suite. It contains a huge walk-in closet, a whirlpool tub and a private sun deck with a spa.

BASEMENT

FIRST FLOOR

SECOND FLOOR

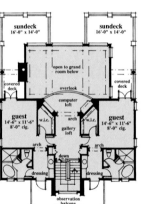

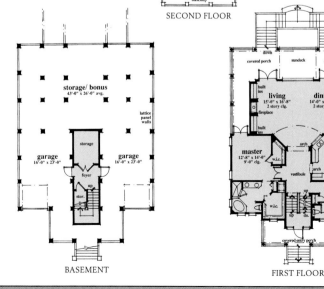

SECOND FLOOR

BASEMENT

FIRST FLOOR

plan# HPT920090

- **STYLE: TIDEWATER**
- **FIRST FLOOR: 1,642 SQ. FT.**
- **SECOND FLOOR: 1,165 SQ. FT.**
- **TOTAL: 2,807 SQ. FT.**
- **BEDROOMS: 3**
- **BATHROOMS: 3½**
- **WIDTH: 44'-6"**
- **DEPTH: 58'-0"**
- **FOUNDATION: PIER**

SEARCH ONLINE @ EPLANS.COM

Hurricane shutters let fresh air in, while five decks make the outside easily accessible. Inside, the open living and dining areas are defined by two pairs of French doors that frame a two-story wall of glass, while built-ins flank the living room fireplace. The efficient kitchen features a walk-in pantry, a work island and a door to the covered porch. Split sleeping quarters offer privacy to the first-floor master suite. Upstairs, a gallery loft leads to a computer area with a built-in desk and a balcony overlook.

plan# HPT920091

- **STYLE: TIDEWATER**
- **FIRST FLOOR: 1,642 SQ. FT.**
- **SECOND FLOOR: 1,165 SQ. FT.**
- **TOTAL: 2,807 SQ. FT.**
- **BEDROOMS: 5**
- **BATHROOMS: 3½**
- **WIDTH: 44'-6"**
- **DEPTH: 58'-0"**
- **FOUNDATION: PIER**

SEARCH ONLINE @ EPLANS.COM

Inspired by 19th-Century Key West designs, the exterior of this plan is in the Neoclassical Revival tradition. Inside, the mid-level foyer eases the trip from ground level to the living and dining areas. Two sets of French doors lead out to the gallery and the sun deck. The kitchen offers a large central island and a walk-in pantry. The master bedroom is on the first floor, with four family bedrooms and a computer loft upstairs. Bedrooms 2 and 3 open to sun decks.

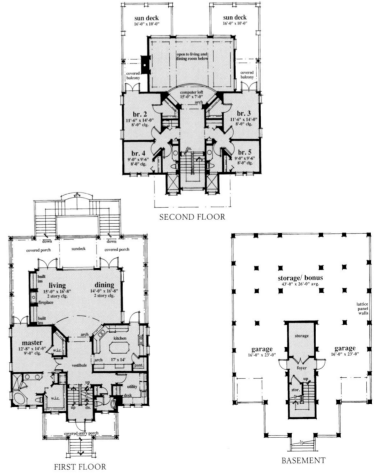

SECOND FLOOR

FIRST FLOOR

BASEMENT

This home comprises symmetry and the perfect blend of past and future. A steeply pitched roof caps a collection of Prairie-style windows and elegant columns. The portico leads to a mid-level foyer, which rises to the grand salon. A wide-open leisure room hosts a corner fireplace that's ultra cozy. The master wing sprawls from the front portico to the rear covered porch, rich with luxury amenities and plenty of secluded space.

plan# HPT920092

- **STYLE: TIDEWATER**
- **SQUARE FOOTAGE: 3,074**
- **BEDROOMS: 3**
- **BATHROOMS: 3½**
- **WIDTH: 77'-0"**
- **DEPTH: 66'-8"**
- **FOUNDATION: ISLAND BASEMENT**

SEARCH ONLINE @ EPLANS.COM

FIRST FLOOR

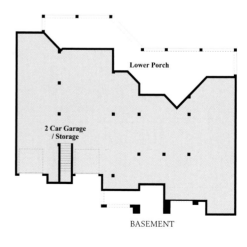

BASEMENT

plan# HPT920093

- STYLE: SEASIDE
- FIRST FLOOR: 1,637 SQ. FT.
- SECOND FLOOR: 1,022 SQ. FT.
- TOTAL: 2,659 SQ. FT.
- BONUS SPACE: 532 SQ. FT.
- BEDROOMS: 3
- BATHROOMS: 3½
- WIDTH: 50'-0"
- DEPTH: 53'-0"
- FOUNDATION: PIER

SEARCH ONLINE @ EPLANS.COM

Variable rooflines, a tower and a covered front porch all combine to give this home a wonderful ambiance. Enter through the mid-level foyer and head either up to the main living level or down to the garage. On the main level, find a spacious light-filled great room sharing a fireplace with the dining room. A study offers access to the rear covered veranda. The efficient island kitchen is open to the dining room, offering ease in entertaining. A guest suite with a private full bath completes this level. Upstairs, a second guest suite with its own bath and a deluxe master suite with a covered balcony, sun deck, walk-in closet and lavish bath are sure to please.

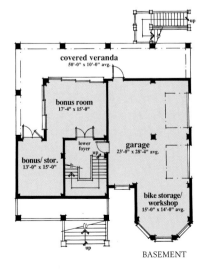

BASEMENT

FIRST FLOOR

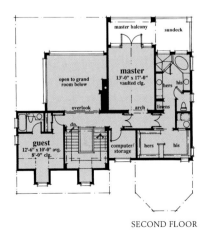

SECOND FLOOR

plan# HPT920094

- **STYLE: TIDEWATER**
- **FIRST FLOOR: 2,039 SQ. FT.**
- **SECOND FLOOR: 1,426 SQ. FT.**
- **TOTAL: 3,465 SQ. FT.**
- **BEDROOMS: 3**
- **BATHROOMS: 4**
- **WIDTH: 56'-0"**
- **DEPTH: 54'-0"**
- **FOUNDATION: ISLAND BASEMENT**

SEARCH ONLINE @ EPLANS.COM

Outside living spaces extend the interior of this sensational Bahamian-style home, bringing the outdoors in with three sets of sliding glass doors. The grand foyer leads to a winding staircase and opens to the great room. An open arrangement of the spacious great room and formal dining room is partially defined by a three-sided fireplace and a wet bar, and the entire space boasts a nine-foot ceiling. The wide veranda is home to an outdoor kitchen. A utility room and two bedrooms, each with a full bath, complete the main level. The upper level is dedicated to a lavish master suite. A three-sided fireplace warms the master bedroom and a sitting area, which open to an upper deck.

plan# HPT920095

- **STYLE: TIDEWATER**
- **FIRST FLOOR: 2,096 SQ. FT.**
- **SECOND FLOOR: 892 SQ. FT.**
- **TOTAL: 2,988 SQ. FT.**
- **BEDROOMS: 3**
- **BATHROOMS: 3½**
- **WIDTH: 58'-0"**
- **DEPTH: 54'-0"**
- **FOUNDATION: BASEMENT**

SEARCH ONLINE @ EPLANS.COM

The variety in the rooflines of this striking waterfront home will certainly make it the envy of the neighborhood. The two-story great room, with its fireplace and built-ins, is a short flight down from the foyer. The three sets of French doors give access to the covered lanai. The huge well-equipped kitchen will easily serve the gourmet who loves to entertain. The stepped ceiling and bay window of the dining room will add style to every meal. The master suite completes the first level. Two bedrooms and two full baths, along with an expansive loft, constitute the second level. Bedroom 3 has an attached sun deck.

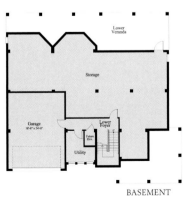

BASEMENT

FIRST FLOOR

SECOND FLOOR

plan# HPT920096

- **STYLE: TIDEWATER**
- **FIRST FLOOR: 2,491 SQ. FT.**
- **SECOND FLOOR: 1,290 SQ. FT.**
- **TOTAL: 3,781 SQ. FT.**
- **BEDROOMS: 5**
- **BATHROOMS: 4½**
- **WIDTH: 62'-0"**
- **DEPTH: 67'-0"**
- **FOUNDATION: ISLAND BASEMENT**

SEARCH ONLINE @ EPLANS.COM

Elements from the Victorian era create this wonderful facade, all decked out with a square tower loft, two-story turret and charming stickwork. Grand amenities dress the interior with splendor as cottage charm becomes urbane comfort in the living space. Three sets of sliding glass doors open the interior to the wraparound veranda, where the outdoor kitchen provides a pass-through to the gourmet kitchen. On the main level, Bedroom 4 boasts a private veranda, built-in desk, and a fireplace shared with the great room. To the front of the plan, a spacious guest suite surrounds live-in relatives or extended-stay visitors with a sense of comfort. A very private secondary suite resides on the upper level with two wardrobes and a private deck. Nearby, a mitered window highlights the master bedroom, which has its own deck.

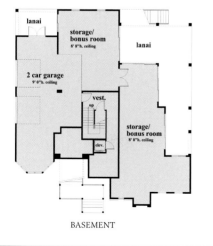

BASEMENT

FIRST FLOOR

SECOND FLOOR

plan # HPT920097

- STYLE: TIDEWATER
- FIRST FLOOR: 1,855 SQ. FT.
- SECOND FLOOR: 901 SQ. FT.
- TOTAL: 2,756 SQ. FT.
- BEDROOMS: 3
- BATHROOMS: 3½
- WIDTH: 66'-0"
- DEPTH: 50'-0"
- FOUNDATION: ISLAND BASEMENT

SEARCH ONLINE @ EPLANS.COM

This Southern tidewater cottage is the perfect vacation hideaway. An octagonal great room with a multi-faceted vaulted ceiling illuminates the interior. The island kitchen is brightened by a bumped-out window and a pass-through to the lanai. Two walk-in closets and a whirlpool bath await to indulge the homeowner in the master suite. A set of double doors opens to the vaulted master lanai for quiet comfort. The U-shaped staircase leads to a loft, which overlooks the great room and the foyer. Two additional family bedrooms offer private baths. A computer center and a morning kitchen complete the upper level.

BASEMENT

FIRST FLOOR

SECOND FLOOR

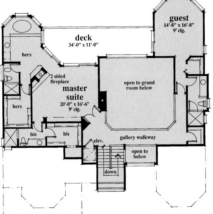

SECOND FLOOR

QUOTE ONE®

Cost to build? See page 187
to order complete cost estimate
to build this house in your area!

plan# HPT920098

- STYLE: FLORIDIAN
- FIRST FLOOR: 2,725 SQ. FT.
- SECOND FLOOR: 1,418 SQ. FT.
- TOTAL: 4,143 SQ. FT.
- BEDROOMS: 4
- BATHROOMS: 5½
- WIDTH: 61'-4"
- DEPTH: 62'-0"
- FOUNDATION: SLAB

L

SEARCH ONLINE @ EPLANS.COM

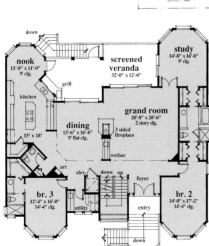

FIRST FLOOR

Florida living takes off in this inventive design. A grand room gains attention as a superb entertaining area. A see-through fireplace here connects this room to the dining room. In the study, quiet time is assured—or slip out the doors and onto the veranda for a breather. A full bath connects the study and Bedroom 2. Bedroom 3 sits on the opposite side of the house and enjoys its own bath. The kitchen features a large work island and a connecting breakfast nook. Upstairs, the master bedroom suite contains His and Hers baths, a see-through fireplace and access to an upper deck. A guest bedroom suite is located on the other side of the upper floor.

plan# HPT920099

- **STYLE: KEY WEST**
- **FIRST FLOOR: 1,542 SQ. FT.**
- **SECOND FLOOR: 971 SQ. FT.**
- **TOTAL: 2,513 SQ. FT.**
- **BEDROOMS: 4**
- **BATHROOMS: 3**
- **WIDTH: 46'-0"**
- **DEPTH: 51'-0"**
- **FOUNDATION: ISLAND BASEMENT**

SEARCH ONLINE @ EPLANS.COM

Arches, columns and French doors pay homage to a captivating Key West style that's light and airy. French doors lead to a study or parlor, which features a wall of built-in shelves and a view of the front property through an arch-topped window. Built-ins frame the fireplace in the great room too, providing an anchor for a wall of glass that brings in a sense of the outdoors. The main level includes a secluded secondary bedroom that's thoughtfully placed near a full bath, coat closet and linen storage. Upstairs, a balcony hall allows interior vistas of the living area below, and connects a secondary bedroom and bath with the master suite. French doors open from both bedrooms to a wrapping deck. The master bath provides a bumped-out garden tub and a walk-in closet designed for two.

SECOND FLOOR

BASEMENT

FIRST FLOOR

plan# HPT920100

- **STYLE: FLORIDIAN**
- **FIRST FLOOR: 1,684 SQ. FT.**
- **SECOND FLOOR: 1,195 SQ. FT.**
- **TOTAL: 2,879 SQ. FT.**
- **BONUS SPACE: 674 SQ. FT.**
- **BEDROOMS: 3**
- **BATHROOMS: 3**
- **WIDTH: 45'-0"**
- **DEPTH: 52'-0"**
- **FOUNDATION: PIER**

SEARCH ONLINE @ EPLANS.COM

Asymmetrical rooflines set off a grand turret and a two-story bay that allow glorious views from the front of this home. Arch-top clerestory windows bring natural light into the great room, which shares a corner fireplace and a wet bar with the dining room. Two guest suites are located on this floor. A winding staircase leads to a luxurious master suite that shares a fireplace with the bath and includes a morning kitchen, French doors to the balcony, and a double walk-in closet. Down the hall, a study and a balcony overlooking the great room complete the plan.

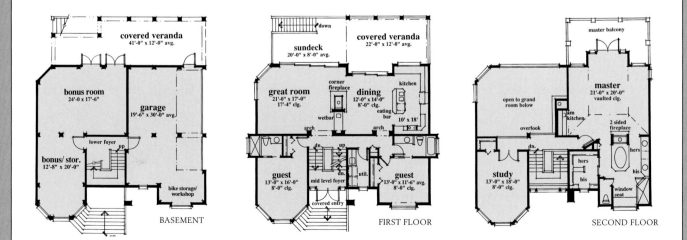

TO ORDER BLUEPRINTS CALL TOLL FREE 1-800-521-6797

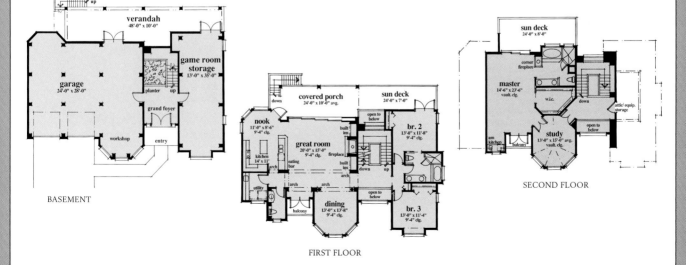

plan# HPT920101

- **STYLE:** FLORIDIAN
- **FIRST FLOOR:** 1,642 SQ. FT.
- **SECOND FLOOR:** 927 SQ. FT.
- **TOTAL:** 2,569 SQ. FT.
- **BONUS SPACE:** 849 SQ. FT.
- **BEDROOMS:** 3
- **BATHROOMS:** 2½
- **WIDTH:** 60'-0"
- **DEPTH:** 44'-6"
- **FOUNDATION:** SLAB

SEARCH ONLINE @ EPLANS.COM

This stunning Gulf Coast cottage features wide windows to take in gorgeous views, while cool outdoor spaces invite festive gatherings, or just a little light reading. The staircase from the ground-level foyer to the raised living area enjoys elaborate views that make a powerful "welcome home" statement. Sliding glass doors open the great room to the covered porch and sun deck, while a fireplace lends coziness. A columned archway announces the elegant dining room, while French doors open to a front balcony nearby. The gourmet kitchen is open to the bay-windowed morning nook and a single French door leads out to the covered porch. The upper level is dedicated to a spacious master suite and a bayed private study.

BASEMENT

FIRST FLOOR

SECOND FLOOR

plan# HPT920102

Victorian detailing in the gables, transom windows, and heavy columns at the front porch add a touch of country elegance to this beautiful home. Inside, a two-story great room at the center of the plan adds air and space. Tray ceilings adorn all the bedrooms, which also have their own baths, walk-in closets and porch access. The master suite, with a private location on the first floor, has access to the rear porch, a luxurious garden tub and extra-large shower. A loft on the second floor provides a great location for quiet contemplation. The basement has a two-car garage conveniently tucked under the house, as well as plenty of additional space for storage and a bonus room.

- **STYLE: LAKEFRONT**
- **FIRST FLOOR: 1,492 SQ. FT.**
- **SECOND FLOOR: 854 SQ. FT.**
- **TOTAL: 2,346 SQ. FT.**
- **BEDROOMS: 3**
- **BATHROOMS: 3½**
- **WIDTH: 44'-0"**
- **DEPTH: 48'-0"**
- **FOUNDATION: BASEMENT**

SEARCH ONLINE @ EPLANS.COM

BASEMENT

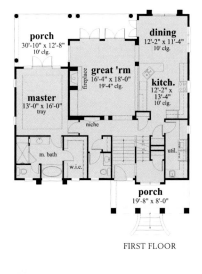

FIRST FLOOR

SECOND FLOOR

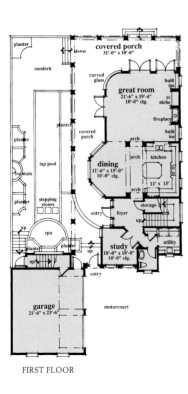

FIRST FLOOR

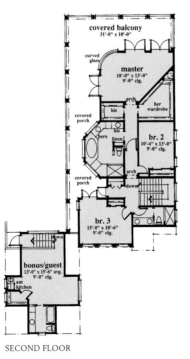

SECOND FLOOR

plan# HPT920103

- STYLE: LAKEFRONT
- FIRST FLOOR: 1,293 SQ. FT.
- SECOND FLOOR: 1,154 SQ. FT.
- TOTAL: 2,447 SQ. FT.
- BONUS SPACE: 426 SQ. FT.
- BEDROOMS: 3
- BATHROOMS: 2½
- WIDTH: 50'-0"
- DEPTH: 90'-0"
- FOUNDATION: SLAB

SEARCH ONLINE @ EPLANS.COM

Louvered shutters, circle-head windows and a courtyard are images from the Charleston Row past brought up-to-date in a floor plan for today's lifestyles. From the great room, three sets of French doors open to the covered porch and sun deck. The U-shaped kitchen includes a central island and adjoins the dining bay. The second floor includes two family bedrooms, a master suite, and a bonus room with a private bath, walk-in closet and morning kitchen. A covered balcony is accessible from the master suite and Bedroom 3.

plan# HPT920104

- **STYLE: MEDITERRANEAN**
- **SQUARE FOOTAGE: 2,385**
- **BEDROOMS: 3**
- **BATHROOMS: 3**
- **WIDTH: 60'-0"**
- **DEPTH: 52'-0"**
- **FOUNDATION: ISLAND BASEMENT**

SEARCH ONLINE @ EPLANS.COM

This enticing European Villa boasts an Italian charm and a distinct Mediterranean feel. The foyer steps lead up to the formal living areas. To the left, a study is expanded by a vaulted ceiling and double doors that open to the front balcony. The island kitchen is conveniently open to a breakfast nook. The guest quarters reside on the right side of the plan—one boasts a private bath; the second suite uses a full hall bath. The secluded master suite features two walk-in closets and a pampering whirlpool master bath. The home is completed by a basement-level garage.

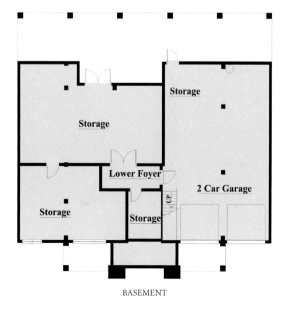

BASEMENT

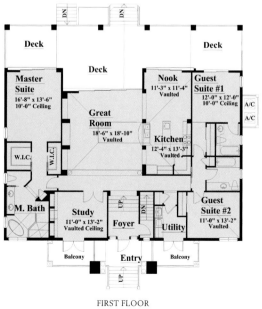

FIRST FLOOR

plan# HPT920105

- **STYLE:** MEDITERRANEAN
- **FIRST FLOOR:** 1,671 SQ. FT.
- **SECOND FLOOR:** 846 SQ. FT.
- **TOTAL:** 2,517 SQ. FT.
- **BEDROOMS:** 3
- **BATHROOMS:** 2
- **WIDTH:** 44'-0"
- **DEPTH:** 55'-0"
- **FOUNDATION:** ISLAND BASEMENT

SEARCH ONLINE @ EPLANS.COM

This magnificent villa boasts a beautiful stucco exterior framing a spectacular entry. The heart of the home is served by a well-crafted kitchen with wrapping counter space and an island cooktop counter. The breakfast nook enjoys a view of the veranda and beyond, and brings natural light to the casual eating space. Archways supported by columns separate the dining room from the great room, which boasts a fireplace and built-in cabinetry. On the upper level, the master suite features a sitting area and a private veranda. The master bath provides a knee-space vanity, whirlpool tub and walk-in closet.

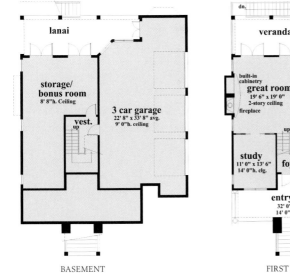

BASEMENT

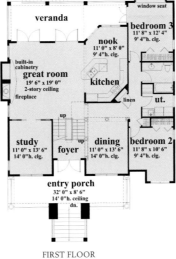

FIRST FLOOR

SECOND FLOOR

plan# HPT920106

- STYLE: TIDEWATER
- FIRST FLOOR: 1,305 SQ. FT.
- SECOND FLOOR: 1,215 SQ. FT.
- TOTAL: 2,520 SQ. FT.
- BONUS SPACE: 935 SQ. FT.
- BEDROOMS: 3
- BATHROOMS: 3
- WIDTH: 30'-6"
- DEPTH: 72'-2"
- FOUNDATION: SLAB

SEARCH ONLINE @ EPLANS.COM

This elegant Old Charleston Row design blends high vogue with a restful character that says shoes are optional. A flexible interior enjoys modern space that welcomes sunlight. Wraparound porches on two levels offer views to the living areas, while a "sit and watch the stars" observation deck opens from the master suite. Four sets of French doors bring the outside in to the great room. The second-floor master suite features a spacious bath and three sets of doors that open to the observation deck. A guest bedroom on this level leads to a gallery hall with its own access to the deck. Bonus space awaits development on the lower level, which—true to its Old Charleston roots—opens gloriously to a garden courtyard.

SECOND FLOOR

BASEMENT

FIRST FLOOR

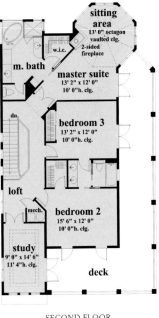

plan# HPT920107

- **STYLE:** MEDITERRANEAN
- **FIRST FLOOR:** 1,266 SQ. FT.
- **SECOND FLOOR:** 1,324 SQ. FT.
- **TOTAL:** 2,590 SQ. FT.
- **BEDROOMS:** 3
- **BATHROOMS:** 2½
- **WIDTH:** 34'-0"
- **DEPTH:** 63'-2"
- **FOUNDATION:** SLAB

SEARCH ONLINE @ EPLANS.COM

This lovely contemporary home boasts plenty of indoor/outdoor flow. Four sets of double doors wrap around the great room and dining area and open to the stunning veranda. The great room is enhanced by a coffered ceiling and built-in cabinetry, while the entire first floor is bathed in sunlight from a wall of glass doors overlooking the veranda. The dining room connects to a gourmet island kitchen. Upstairs, a beautiful deck wraps gracefully around the family bedrooms. The master suite is a skylit haven enhanced by a sitting bay, which features a vaulted octagonal ceiling and a cozy two-sided fireplace. Private double doors access the sun deck from the master suite, the secondary bedrooms and the study.

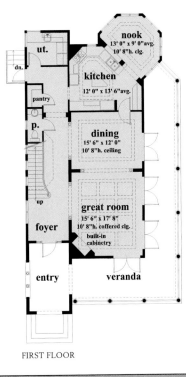

FIRST FLOOR

SECOND FLOOR

plan# HPT920108

- **STYLE: MEDITERRANEAN**
- **FIRST FLOOR: 1,798 SQ. FT.**
- **SECOND FLOOR: 900 SQ. FT.**
- **TOTAL: 2,698 SQ. FT.**
- **BEDROOMS: 3**
- **BATHROOMS: 3**
- **WIDTH: 54'-0"**
- **DEPTH: 57'-0"**
- **FOUNDATION: CRAWLSPACE**

SEARCH ONLINE @ EPLANS.COM

This lovely Mediterranean-style home combines a luxurious floor plan with lots of outdoor living space. Tray ceilings augment the master bedroom, study and dining room, while the central great room offers a two-story ceiling and shares a fireplace with the dining room. Built-in cabinetry and three sets of French doors leading to the veranda further accent the great room. The lavish master suite includes a sitting bay, two walk-in closets, a private bath and access to the veranda. Two family bedrooms, two baths and a balcony overlook reside upstairs.

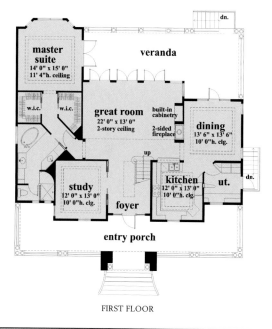

FIRST FLOOR

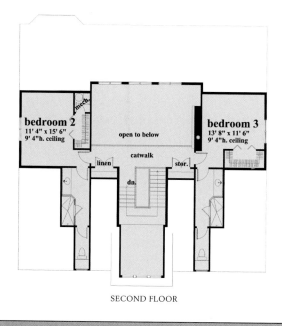

SECOND FLOOR

plan# HPT920109

- **STYLE: ITALIANATE**
- **FIRST FLOOR: 2,391 SQ. FT.**
- **SECOND FLOOR: 1,539 SQ. FT.**
- **TOTAL: 3,930 SQ. FT.**
- **BEDROOMS: 3**
- **BATHROOMS: 3½**
- **WIDTH: 71'-0"**
- **DEPTH: 69'-0"**
- **FOUNDATION: ISLAND BASEMENT**

SEARCH ONLINE @ EPLANS.COM

Impressive pillars, keystone lintel arches, a covered carport, an abundance of windows and an alluring fountain are just a few of the decorative touches on this elegant design. The two-story foyer leads to a two-story great room, which enjoys built-in cabinetry, a two-sided fireplace and spectacular views to the rear property. To the left of the great room is the dining area, with a wet bar, island kitchen and nearby bayed breakfast nook. Bedroom 2 boasts a semi-circular wall of windows, a full bath and a walk-in closet. The second-floor master suite is filled with amenities, including a two-sided fireplace.

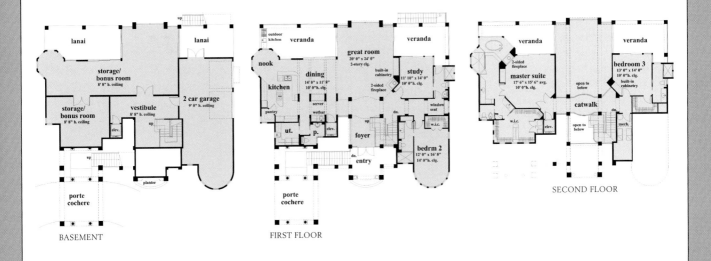

BASEMENT

FIRST FLOOR

SECOND FLOOR

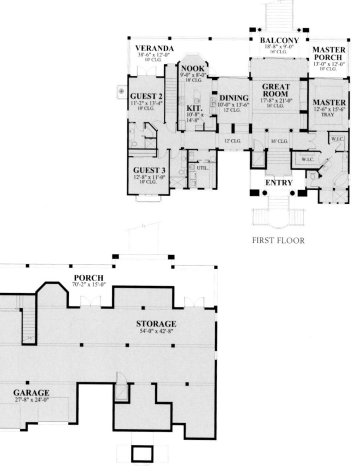

FIRST FLOOR

BASEMENT

plan # HPT920110

- **STYLE:** ITALIANATE
- **SQUARE FOOTAGE:** 2,430
- **BEDROOMS:** 3
- **BATHROOMS:** 3
- **WIDTH:** 70'-2"
- **DEPTH:** 53'-0"
- **FOUNDATION:** ISLAND BASEMENT

SEARCH ONLINE @ EPLANS.COM

With a row of pretty windows, this gentle Mediterranean home offers plenty of views and outdoor spaces for mingling with nature. High ceilings in the great room and dining room extend the sense of spaciousness and propose planned events that spill out to the outdoor spaces. The formal dining room opens through a colonnade from the central gallery hall and shares the comfort of the central fireplace. A food-preparation island and service counter allow easy meals or fabulous dinners. Of course, the best part of the eating area is the morning nook—a bright reprieve from daily cares surrounded with the beauty of sunshine and trees.

TO ORDER BLUEPRINTS CALL TOLL FREE 1-800-521-6797

plan# HPT920111

- **STYLE:** MEDITERRANEAN
- **SQUARE FOOTAGE:** 3,074
- **BEDROOMS:** 3
- **BATHROOMS:** 3½
- **WIDTH:** 77'-0"
- **DEPTH:** 66'-8"
- **FOUNDATION:** ISLAND BASEMENT

SEARCH ONLINE @ EPLANS.COM

This stunning paradise achieves its casual European character by mixing Spanish and French influences. A fanlight transom caps the stately entry. The dazzling portico leads to a mid-level foyer and to the grand salon. Two guest suites provide accommodations for visiting relatives and friends. Each of the suites offers a private bath and walk-in closet. A gallery hall connects the suites and leads to a convenient laundry and lower-level staircase. The master wing opens to a private area of the rear covered porch. Nearby, a cabana-style powder room opens to the porch and to the homeowner's private hall. Pocket doors to the study provide a quiet place for reading and quiet conversations.

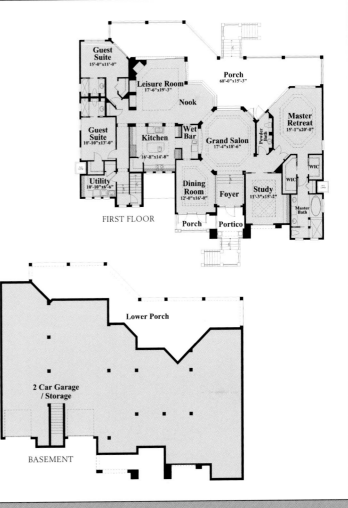

Chic and glamorous, this Mediterranean facade pairs ancient shapes, such as square columns, with a refined disposition set off by radius windows. A magnificent entry leads to an interior gallery and the great room. This extraordinary space is warmed by a two-sided fireplace and defined by extended views of the rear property. Sliding glass doors to a wraparound veranda create great indoor/outdoor flow. The gourmet kitchen easily serves any occasion and provides a pass-through to the outdoor kitchen. A powder room accommodates visitors, while an elevator leads to the sleeping quarters upstairs. Double doors open to the master suite, which features a walk-in closet, two-sided fireplace and angled whirlpool bath. The master bedroom boasts a tray ceiling and doors to a spacious deck. The upper-level catwalk leads to a bedroom suite that can easily accommodate a guest or live-in relative.

plan# HPT920112

- STYLE: MEDITERRANEAN
- FIRST FLOOR: 2,491 SQ. FT.
- SECOND FLOOR: 1,290 SQ. FT.
- TOTAL: 3,781 SQ. FT.
- BEDROOMS: 5
- BATHROOMS: 4½
- WIDTH: 62'-0"
- DEPTH: 67'-0"
- FOUNDATION: ISLAND BASEMENT

SEARCH ONLINE @ EPLANS.COM

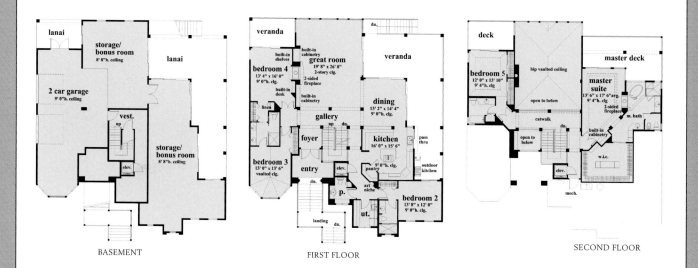

BASEMENT

FIRST FLOOR

SECOND FLOOR

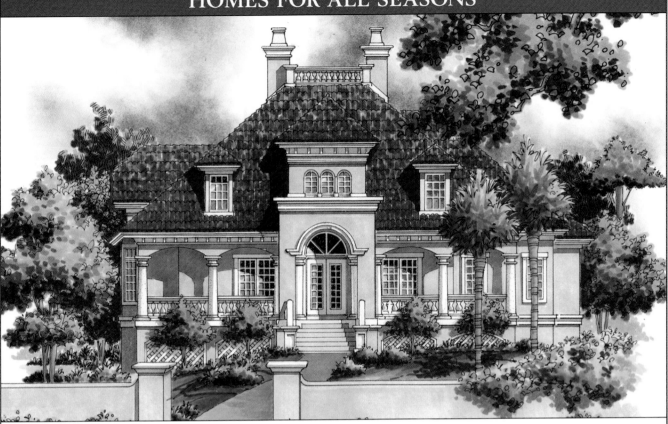

Villa enchantment is romantically enhanced by the facade of this Italianate design. The wraparound entry porch is majestically inviting. Enter through double doors into the two-story foyer—notice the study with built-in cabinetry to the right and the formal dining room to the left. Straight ahead, an octagonal great room with a multi-faceted vaulted ceiling illuminates the entire plan. The island kitchen is brightened by a bayed window and a pass-through to the lanai. Two spacious walk-in closets and a whirlpool bath await to pamper the homeowner in the master suite. A set of double doors open to the vaulted master lanai for relaxing comfort. Two additional family bedrooms each feature a private bath. A computer center and a morning kitchen are located at the end of the hallway, before opening onto the outer deck.

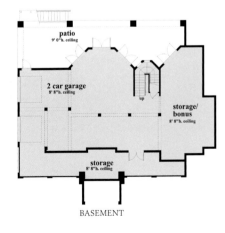

BASEMENT

FIRST FLOOR

SECOND FLOOR

plan# HPT920114

- STYLE: MEDITERRANEAN
- FIRST FLOOR: 1,492 SQ. FT.
- SECOND FLOOR: 854 SQ. FT.
- TOTAL: 2,346 SQ. FT.
- BONUS SPACE: 810 SQ. FT.
- BEDROOMS: 3
- BATHROOMS: 3½
- WIDTH: 44'-0"
- DEPTH: 48'-0"
- FOUNDATION: ISLAND BASEMENT

SEARCH ONLINE @ EPLANS.COM

This lovely pier home is the picture of island living. Space on the lower level is devoted to the garage, but allows for a storage area if needed. The first floor holds the great room, with access to a rear porch. The dining room and kitchen are nearby for easy access. The master suite is also on this floor and features porch access and a stunning bath. Two family bedrooms with private baths and a loft area are found on the second floor. A porch can be accessed from each of the bedrooms.

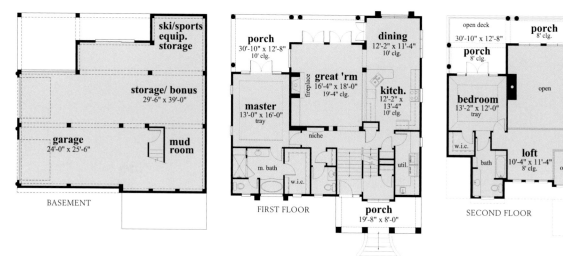

plan# HPT920115

- **STYLE: TRADITIONAL**
- **FIRST FLOOR: 2,096 SQ. FT.**
- **SECOND FLOOR: 892 SQ. FT.**
- **TOTAL: 2,988 SQ. FT.**
- **BEDROOMS: 3**
- **BATHROOMS: 3½**
- **WIDTH: 56'-0"**
- **DEPTH: 54'-0"**
- **FOUNDATION: ISLAND BASEMENT**

SEARCH ONLINE @ EPLANS.COM

Multiple windows bring natural light to this beautiful home, which offers a floor plan filled with special amenities. Arches provide a grand entry to the beam-ceilinged great room, where built-ins flank the fireplace and three sets of French doors open to a veranda. Step ceilings grace the master suite and the dining room. The master suite provides two walk-in closets and a resplendent bath, while dazzling windows in the dining room allow enjoyment of the outdoors. Two second-floor bedrooms, one with a sun deck, feature walk-in closets and private baths.

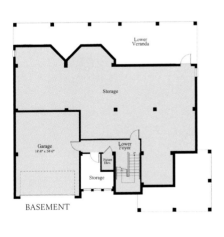

BASEMENT

FIRST FLOOR

SECOND FLOOR

plan# HPT920116

- **STYLE: FLORIDIAN**
- **MAIN LEVEL: 2,385 SQ. FT.**
- **LOWER-LEVEL ENTRY: 80 SQ. FT.**
- **TOTAL: 2,465 SQ. FT.**
- **BONUS SPACE: 1,271 SQ. FT.**
- **BEDROOMS: 3**
- **BATHROOMS: 2½**
- **WIDTH: 60'-4"**
- **DEPTH: 59'-4"**
- **FOUNDATION: PIER, BLOCK**

SEARCH ONLINE @ EPLANS.COM

A classic pediment and low-pitched roof are topped by a cupola on this gorgeous coastal design, influenced by 19th-Century Caribbean plantation houses. Savory style blended with a contemporary seaside spirit invites entertaining as well as year-round living—plus room to grow. The beauty and warmth of natural light splash the spacious living area with a sense of the outdoors and a touch of joie de vivre. The great room features a wall of built-ins designed for even the most technology-savvy entertainment buff. Dazzling views through walls of glass are enlivened by the presence of a breezy porch. The master suite features a luxurious bath, a dressing area and two walk-in closets. Glass doors open to the porch and provide generous views of the seascape; a nearby study offers an indoor retreat.

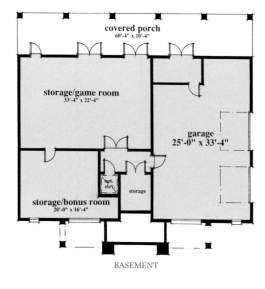

BASEMENT

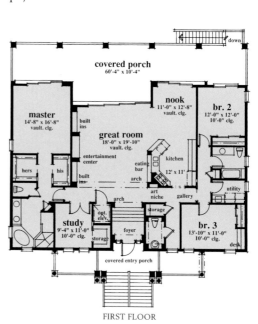

FIRST FLOOR

plan# HPT920117

This country villa design is accented by a gazebo-style front porch and an abundance of arched windows. Most of the rooms in this house are graced with tray, stepped or vaulted ceilings, enhancing the entire plan. The first-floor master suite boasts multiple amenities, including a private lanai, His and Hers walk-in closets and a bayed whirlpool tub. Other highlights on this floor include a study with a window seat and built-in cabinetry, a bayed breakfast nook, a butler's pantry in the island kitchen, a utility room and an outdoor kitchen on the lanai. Three secondary bedrooms reside upstairs, along with two full baths.

- **STYLE: ITALIANATE**
- **FIRST FLOOR: 2,083 SQ. FT.**
- **SECOND FLOOR: 1,013 SQ. FT.**
- **TOTAL: 3,096 SQ. FT.**
- **BEDROOMS: 4**
- **BATHROOMS: 3½**
- **WIDTH: 74'-0"**
- **DEPTH: 88'-0"**
- **FOUNDATION: SLAB**

SEARCH ONLINE @ EPLANS.COM

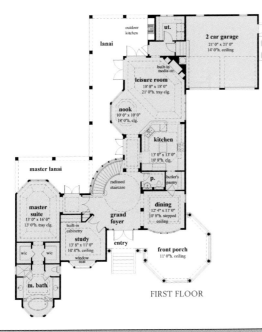

FIRST FLOOR

SECOND FLOOR

This dream cabin captures the finest historic details in rooms furnished with comfort and style. A grand foyer features a radius staircase that decks out the entry hall and defines the wide-open interior. A formal dining room is served through a butler's pantry by a well-equipped kitchen. Casual space includes a leisure room that sports a corner fireplace, tray ceiling and built-in media center. An outdoor kitchen makes it easy to enjoy life outside on the wraparound porch. The main-level master suite is suited with a spacious bedroom, two walk-in closets, and a lavish bath with separate vanities and a bumped-out whirlpool tub. Upstairs, two family bedrooms share a compartmented bath, and a guest suite boasts a roomy bath.

plan# HPT920118

- **STYLE: MOUNTAIN**
- **FIRST FLOOR: 2,083 SQ. FT.**
- **SECOND FLOOR: 1,013 SQ. FT.**
- **TOTAL: 3,096 SQ. FT.**
- **BEDROOMS: 4**
- **BATHROOMS: 3½**
- **WIDTH: 59'-6"**
- **DEPTH: 88'-0"**
- **FOUNDATION: SLAB**

SEARCH ONLINE @ EPLANS.COM

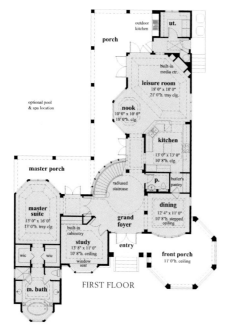

FIRST FLOOR

SECOND FLOOR

plan # HPT920119

- **STYLE:** MOUNTAIN
- **FIRST FLOOR:** 2,391 SQ. FT.
- **SECOND FLOOR:** 1,539 SQ. FT.
- **TOTAL:** 3,930 SQ. FT.
- **BEDROOMS:** 3
- **BATHROOMS:** 3½
- **WIDTH:** 71'-0"
- **DEPTH:** 69'-0"
- **FOUNDATION:** ISLAND BASEMENT

SEARCH ONLINE @ EPLANS.COM

Climate is a key component of any mountain retreat, and outdoor living is an integral part of its design. This superior cabin features open and covered porches. A mix of matchstick details and rugged stone set off this lodge-house facade, concealing a well-defined interior. Windows line the breakfast bay and brighten the kitchen, which features a center cooktop island. A door leads out to a covered porch, a summer kitchen with a built-in grill and another porch with a cabana bath. The upper level features a secluded master suite with a spacious bath beginning with a double walk-in closet and ending with a garden view of the porch. A two-sided fireplace extends warmth to the whirlpool tub.

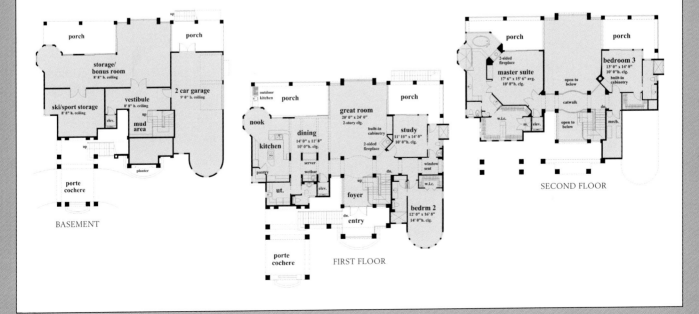

plan# HPT920120

- **STYLE: MOUNTAIN**
- **SQUARE FOOTAGE: 2,430**
- **BEDROOMS: 3**
- **BATHROOMS: 3**
- **WIDTH: 70'-2"**
- **DEPTH: 53'-0"**
- **FOUNDATION: BASEMENT**

SEARCH ONLINE @ EPLANS.COM

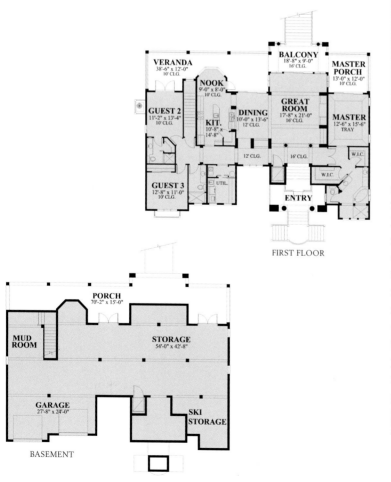

FIRST FLOOR

BASEMENT

With a rugged blend of stone and siding, an inviting mix of details creates the kind of comfortable beauty that every homeowner craves. Massive stone columns support a striking pediment entry. A spacious formal dining room complements a gourmet kitchen designed to serve any occasion and equipped with a walk-in pantry and a nearby powder room. The morning nook boasts a wall of glass that allows casual diners to kick back and be at one with nature. Separate sleeping quarters thoughtfully place the master suite to the right of the plan, in a wing of the home that includes a private porch. Guest suites on the opposite side of the plan share a hall and a staircase that leads to a lower-level mudroom, porch and ski storage.

plan# HPT920121

- **STYLE: MOUNTAIN**
- **FIRST FLOOR: 1,798 SQ. FT.**
- **SECOND FLOOR: 900 SQ. FT.**
- **TOTAL: 2,698 SQ. FT.**
- **BEDROOMS: 3**
- **BATHROOMS: 3**
- **WIDTH: 54'-0"**
- **DEPTH: 57'-0"**
- **FOUNDATION: CRAWLSPACE**

SEARCH ONLINE @ EPLANS.COM

This rustic stone and siding exterior with Craftsman influences includes a multitude of windows flooding the interior with natural light. The foyer opens to the great room, which is complete with three sets of French doors and a two-sided fireplace. The master suite offers an expansive private bath, two large walk-in closets, a bay window and a tray ceiling. The dining room, kitchen and utility room make an efficient trio.

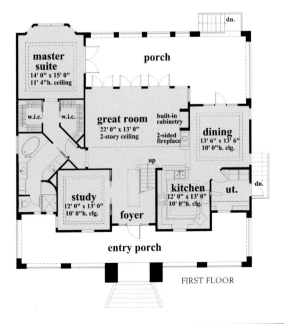

FIRST FLOOR

SECOND FLOOR

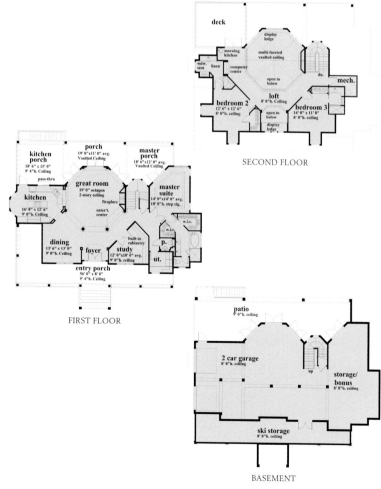

SECOND FLOOR

FIRST FLOOR

BASEMENT

ptan# HPT920122

- STYLE: MOUNTAIN
- FIRST FLOOR: 1,855 SQ. FT.
- SECOND FLOOR: 901 SQ. FT.
- TOTAL: 2,756 SQ. FT.
- BEDROOMS: 3
- BATHROOMS: 3½
- WIDTH: 66'-0"
- DEPTH: 50'-0"
- FOUNDATION: BASEMENT

SEARCH ONLINE @ EPLANS.COM

This luxurious vacation cabin is the perfect rustic paradise, whether set by a lake or in a mountain scene. The wraparound entry porch is friendly and inviting. Double doors open to the foyer, which is flanked on either side by the study with built-in cabinetry and the formal dining room. The octagonal great room features a multi-faceted vaulted ceiling, fireplace, built-in entertainment center and three sets of double doors leading to a vaulted lanai. The gourmet island kitchen is brightened by a bay window and a pass-through to the lanai.

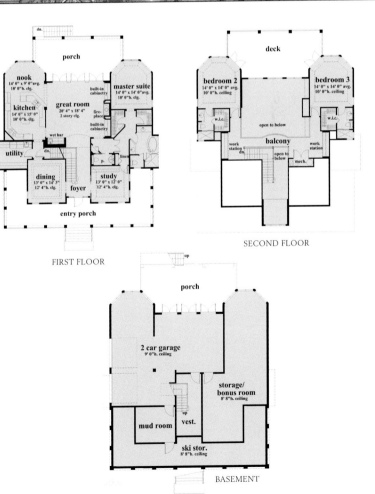

plan# HPT920123

- **STYLE: MOUNTAIN**
- **FIRST FLOOR: 2,146 SQ. FT.**
- **SECOND FLOOR: 952 SQ. FT.**
- **TOTAL: 3,098 SQ. FT.**
- **BEDROOMS: 3**
- **BATHROOMS: 3½**
- **WIDTH: 52'-0"**
- **DEPTH: 65'-4"**
- **FOUNDATION: BASEMENT**

SEARCH ONLINE @ EPLANS.COM

Tall windows wrap this noble exterior with dazzling details and allow plenty of natural light inside. A wraparound porch sets a casual but elegant pace for the home, with space for rockers and swings. Well-defined formal rooms are placed just off the foyer. A host of French doors opens the great room to an entertainment porch and, of course, inspiring views. Even formal meals take on the ease and comfort of a mountain region in the stunning open dining room. Nearby, a gourmet kitchen packed with amenities serves any occasion.

FIRST FLOOR

SECOND FLOOR

BASEMENT

Siding and shingles give this home a Craftsman look while columns and gables suggest a more traditional style. The foyer opens to a short flight of stairs that leads to the great room, which features a lovely coffered ceiling, a fireplace, built-ins and French doors to the rear veranda. To the left, the open island kitchen enjoys a pass-through to the great room and easy service to the dining bay. The secluded master suite has two walk-in closets, a luxurious bath and veranda access. Upstairs, two family bedrooms enjoy their own full baths and share a loft area.

plan# HPT920124

- **STYLE: MOUNTAIN**
- **FIRST FLOOR: 2,096 SQ. FT.**
- **SECOND FLOOR: 892 SQ. FT.**
- **TOTAL: 2,988 SQ. FT.**
- **BEDROOMS: 3**
- **BATHROOMS: 3½**
- **WIDTH: 56'-0"**
- **DEPTH: 54'-0"**
- **FOUNDATION: BASEMENT**

SEARCH ONLINE @ EPLANS.COM

BASEMENT

FIRST FLOOR

SECOND FLOOR

plan# HPT920125

- **STYLE:** MOUNTAIN
- **FIRST FLOOR:** 2,039 SQ. FT.
- **SECOND FLOOR:** 1,426 SQ. FT.
- **TOTAL:** 3,465 SQ. FT.
- **BEDROOMS:** 3
- **BATHROOMS:** 4
- **WIDTH:** 56'-0"
- **DEPTH:** 54'-0"
- **FOUNDATION:** BASEMENT

SEARCH ONLINE @ EPLANS.COM

This fabulous mountain home begins with a stunning transom, which tops a classic paneled door and sets off a host of windows brightening the facade. Inside, a three-sided fireplace and wet bar invites entertaining on any scale, grand or cozy. The gourmet of the family will easily prepare meals in a well-equipped kitchen. A wide window overlooks the outdoor kitchen area of the patio, which includes a rinsing sink and outdoor grill. An upper level dedicated to the master retreat boasts a wide deck where, on a clear day, the beauty of natural light splashes this room with a sense of the outdoors and mingles with the crackle of the fireplace. Private baths for two provide separate amenities, including an exercise area and a knee-space vanity. Separate garages on the lower level lead to an entry vestibule with both an elevator and stairs.

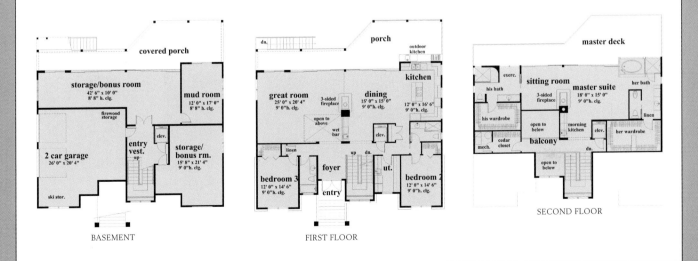

BASEMENT

FIRST FLOOR

SECOND FLOOR

An engaging blend of comfort and architectural style creates a high-spirited home. The foyer provides a magnificent view through the great room, where a two-story glass wall allows the vista to extend to the rear property. Amenities such as two-sided fireplaces, built-in shelves and cabinetry, wide decks and verandas are perfectly suited to a casual yet elegant lifestyle. Bedroom 4 shares a fireplace with the great room, while Bedroom 3 provides a beautiful bay window. The wraparound veranda includes an outdoor kitchen with a grill, rinsing sink and pass-through to the main kitchen. The upper-level master suite offers its own observation deck and a private bath loaded with amenities.

plan⊕ HPT920126

- **STYLE: MOUNTAIN**
- **FIRST FLOOR: 2,491 SQ. FT.**
- **SECOND FLOOR: 1,290 SQ. FT.**
- **TOTAL: 3,781 SQ. FT.**
- **BEDROOMS: 5**
- **BATHROOMS: 4½**
- **WIDTH: 62'-0"**
- **DEPTH: 67'-0"**
- **FOUNDATION: ISLAND BASEMENT**

SEARCH ONLINE @ EPLANS.COM

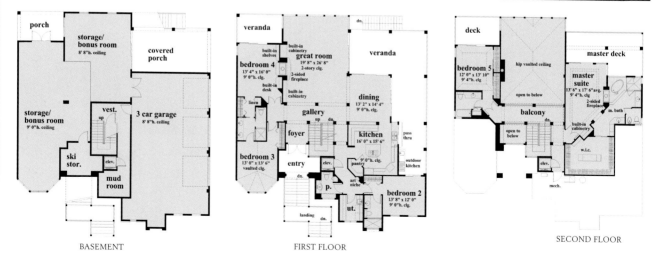

BASEMENT

FIRST FLOOR

SECOND FLOOR

plan # HPT9220001

- STYLE: TIDEWATER
- FIRST FLOOR: 2,391 SQ. FT.
- SECOND FLOOR: 1,539 SQ. FT.
- TOTAL: 3,930 SQ. FT.
- BEDROOMS: 3
- BATHROOMS: 3½
- WIDTH: 71' - 0"
- DEPTH: 69' - 0"
- FOUNDATION: ISLAND BASEMENT

SEARCH ONLINE @ EPLANS.COM

Classic columns, beautiful windows, and a grand porte cochere set off this dramatic entry. An abundance of windows invite the best views, plenty of sunlight, and cool breezes that will open the mind and soothe the spirit. Decorative columns announce the great room, which enjoys a wall of glass and two sets of sliding doors to separate verandas.

SECOND FLOOR

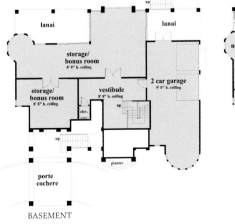

BASEMENT

FIRST FLOOR

Dramatic rooflines cap a host of asymmetrical gables and complement a variety of windows on this visually stunning coastal cottage. A mid-level foyer leads up to the main-level great room, which opens to the rear porch through grand French doors, providing views and easing the transition to the outside space. In the heart of the home, the gourmet kitchen serves a stunning formal dining room. To the left of the plan, a secluded master suite boasts a coffered ceiling, walk-in closet and private access to one of the rear porches. A grand central staircase leads to the upper-level sleeping quarters and offers a splendid window that brings sunlight indoors. Generous sitting space at the head of the stairs can convert to a computer loft.

plan # HPT9220002

- **STYLE: TIDEWATER**
- **FIRST FLOOR: 1,537 SQ. FT.**
- **SECOND FLOOR: 812 SQ. FT.**
- **TOTAL: 2,349 SQ. FT.**
- **BONUS SPACE: 702 SQ. FT.**
- **BEDROOMS: 3**
- **BATHROOMS: 2½**
- **WIDTH: 45' - 4"**
- **DEPTH: 50' - 0"**
- **FOUNDATION: ISLAND BASEMENT**

SEARCH ONLINE @ EPLANS.COM

BASEMENT

FIRST FLOOR

SECOND FLOOR

eplans.com

THE GATEWAY
TO YOUR NEW HOME

Looking for more plans? Got questions?
Try our one-stop home plans resource—eplans.com.

We'll help you streamline the plan selection process, so your dreams can become reality faster than you ever imagined. From choosing your home plan and ideal location to finding an experienced contractor, eplans.com will guide you every step of the way.

Mix and match! Explore! At eplans.com you can combine all your top criteria to find your perfect match. Search for your ideal home plan by any or all of the following:

> Number of bedrooms or baths
> Total square feet
> House style
> Designer
> Cost

With over 10,000 plans, the options are endless. Colonial, ranch, country, and Victorian are just a few of the house styles offered. Keep in mind your essential lifestyle features—whether to include a porch, fireplace, bonus room, or main floor laundry room. And the garage—how many cars must it accommodate, if any? By filling out the preference page on eplans.com, we'll help you narrow your search. And, don't forget to enjoy a virtual home tour before any decisions are set in stone.

At eplans.com we'll make the building process a snap to understand. At the click of a button you'll find a complete building guide. And our eplan task planner will create a construction calendar just for you. Here you'll find links to tips and other valuable information to help you every step of the way—from choosing a site to moving day.

For your added convenience, our home plans experts are available for live, one-on-one chats at eplans.com. Building a home may seem like a complicated project, but it doesn't have to be—particularly if you'll let us help you from start to finish.

COPYRIGHT DOS & DON'TS

Blueprints for residential construction (or working drawings, as they are often called in the industry) are copyrighted intellectual property, protected under the terms of United States Copyright Law and, therefore, cannot be copied legally for use in building. However, we've made it easy for you to get what you need to build your home, without violating copyright law. Following are some guidelines to help you obtain the right number of copies for your chosen blueprint design.

COPYRIGHT DO

■ Do purchase enough copies of the blueprints to satisfy building requirements. As a rule for a home or project plan, you will need a set for yourself, two or three for your builder and subcontractors, two for the local building department, and one to three for your mortgage lender. You may want to check with your local building department or your builder to see how many they need before you purchase. You may need to buy eight to 10 sets; note that some areas of the country require purchase of vellums (also called reproducibles) instead of blueprints. Vellums can be written on and changed more easily than blueprints. Also, remember, plans are only good for one-time construction.

■ Do consider reverse blueprints if you want to flop the plan. Lettering and numbering will appear backward, but the reversed sets will help you and your builder better visualize the design.

■ Do take advantage of multiple-set discounts at the time you place your order. Usually, purchasing additional sets after you receive your initial order is not as cost-effective.

■ Do take advantage of vellums. Though they are a little more expensive, they can be changed, copied, and used for one-time construction of a home. You will receive a copyright release letter with your vellums that will allow you to have them copied.

■ Do talk with one of our professional service representatives before placing your order. They can give you great advice about what packages are available for your chosen design and what will work best for your particular situation.

COPYRIGHT DON'T

■ Don't think you should purchase only one set of blueprints for a building project. One is fine if you want to study the plan closely, but will not be enough for actual building.

■ Don't expect your builder or a copy center to make copies of standard blueprints. They cannot legally—most copy centers are aware of this.

■ Don't purchase standard blueprints if you know you'll want to make changes to the plans; vellums are a better value.

■ Don't use blueprints or vellums more than one time. Additional fees apply if you want to build more than one time from a set of drawings. ■

hanley wood
HomePlanners
ORDERING IS EASY

HANLEY WOOD HOMEPLANNERS HAS EVERYTHING YOU NEED to build the home of your dreams, and with more than 50 years of experience in the industry, we make it as easy as possible for you to reach those goals. Just follow the steps on these pages and you'll receive a high-quality, ready-to-build set of home blueprints, plus everything else you need to make your home-building effort a success.

WHERE TO BEGIN?
1. CHOOSE YOUR PLAN

■ Browsing magazines, books, and eplans.com can be an exciting and rewarding part of the home-building process. As you search, make a list of the things you want in your dream home—everything from number of bedrooms and baths to details like fireplaces or a home office.

■ Take the time to consider your lot and your neighborhood, and how the home you choose will fit with both. And think about the future—how might your needs change if you plan to live in this house for five, 10, or 20 years?

■ With thousands of plans available, chances are that you'll have no trouble discovering your dream home. If you find something that's almost perfect, our Customization Program can help make it exactly what you want.

■ Most important, be sure to enjoy the process of picking out your new home!

WHAT YOU'LL GET WITH YOUR ORDER

Each designer's blueprint set is unique, but they all provide everything you'll need to build your home. Here are some standard elements you can expect to find in your plans:

1. FRONT PERSPECTIVE
This artist's sketch of the exterior of the house gives you an idea of how the house will look when built and landscaped.

2. FOUNDATION PLANS
This sheet shows the foundation layout including support walls, excavated and unexcavated areas, if any, and foundation notes. If your plan features slab construction rather than a basement, the plan shows footings and details for a monolithic slab. This page, or another in the set, may include a sample plot plan for locating your house on a building site.

3. DETAILED FLOOR PLANS
These plans show the layout of each floor of the house. Rooms and interior spaces are carefully dimensioned and keys are given for cross-section details provided later in the plans. The positions of electrical outlets and switches are shown.

4. HOUSE CROSS-SECTIONS
Large-scale views show sections or cutaways of the foundation, interior walls, exterior walls, floors, stairways, and roof details. Additional cross-sections may show important changes in floor, ceiling, or roof heights, or the relationship of one level to another. Extremely valuable during construction, these sections show exactly how the various parts of the house fit together.

5. INTERIOR ELEVATIONS
These elevations, or drawings, show the design and placement of kitchen and bathroom cabinets, laundry areas, fireplaces, bookcases, and other built-ins. Little extras, such as mantelpiece and wainscoting drawings, plus molding sections, provide details that give your home that custom touch.

6. EXTERIOR ELEVATIONS
Every blueprint set comes with drawings of the front exterior, and may include the rear and sides of your house as well. These drawings give necessary notes on exterior materials and finishes. Particular attention is given to cornice detail, brick, and stone accents or other finish items that make your home unique.

GETTY IMAGES

ORDERING IS EASY

GETTING DOWN TO BUSINESS

2. PRICE YOUR PLAN

HANLEY WOOD
HOMEPLANNERS
ADVANTAGE
ORDER 24 HOURS!
1-800-521-6797

BLUEPRINT PRICE SCHEDULE

PRICE TIERS	1-SET STUDY PACKAGE	4-SET BUILDING PACKAGE	8-SET BUILDING PACKAGE	1-SET REPRODUCIBLE*
P1	$20	$50	$90	$140
P2	$40	$70	$110	$160
P3	$70	$100	$140	$190
P4	$100	$130	$170	$220
P5	$140	$170	$210	$270
P6	$180	$210	$250	$310
A1	$440	$490	$540	$660
A2	$480	$530	$580	$720
A3	$530	$590	$650	$800
A4	$575	$645	$705	$870
C1	$625	$695	$755	$935
C2	$670	$740	$800	$1000
C3	$715	$790	$855	$1075
C4	$765	$840	$905	$1150
L1	$870	$965	$1050	$1300
L2	$945	$1040	$1125	$1420
L3	$1050	$1150	$1240	$1575
L4	$1155	$1260	$1355	$1735
SQ1				.35/SQ. FT.
SQ3				.50/SQ. FT.

PRICES SUBJECT TO CHANGE

* REQUIRES A FAX NUMBER

plan #

READY TO ORDER

Once you've found your plan, get your plan number and turn to the following pages to find its price tier. Use the corresponding code and the Blueprint Price Schedule above to determine your price for a variety of blueprint packages.

Keep in mind that you'll need multiple sets to fulfill building requirements, and only reproducible sets may be altered or duplicated.

To the right you'll find prices for additional and reverse blueprint sets. Also note in the following pages whether your home has a corresponding Deck or Landscape Plan, and whether you can order our Quote One® cost-to-build information or a Materials List for your plan.

**IT'S EASY TO ORDER
JUST VISIT
EPLANS.COM OR CALL
TOLL-FREE
1-800-521-6797**

PRICE SCHEDULE FOR ADDITIONAL OPTIONS

OPTIONS FOR PLANS IN TIERS P1-P6	COSTS
ADDITIONAL IDENTICAL BLUEPRINTS FOR "P1-P6" PLANS	$10 PER SET
REVERSE BLUEPRINTS (MIRROR IMAGE) FOR "P1-P6" PLANS	$10 FEE PER ORDER
1 SET OF DECK CONSTRUCTION DETAILS	$14.95 EACH
DECK CONSTRUCTION PACKAGE (INCLUDES 1 SET OF "P1-P6" PLANS, PLUS 1 SET STANDARD DECK CONSTRUCTION DETAILS)	ADD $10 TO BUILDING PACKAGE PRICE

OPTIONS FOR PLANS IN TIERS A1-SQ3	COSTS
ADDITIONAL IDENTICAL BLUEPRINTS IN SAME ORDER FOR "A1-L4" PLANS	$50 PER SET
REVERSE BLUEPRINTS (MIRROR IMAGE) WITH 4- OR 8-SET ORDER FOR "A1-L4" PLANS	$50 FEE PER ORDER
SPECIFICATION OUTLINES	$10 EACH
MATERIALS LISTS FOR "A1-C3" PLANS	$70 EACH
MATERIALS LISTS FOR "C4-SQ3" PLANS	$70 EACH

IMPORTANT EXTRAS	COSTS
ELECTRICAL, PLUMBING, CONSTRUCTION, AND MECHANICAL DETAIL SETS	$14.95 EACH; ANY TWO $22.95; ANY THREE $29.95; ALL FOUR $39.95
HOME FURNITURE PLANNER	$15.95 EACH
REAR ELEVATION	$10 EACH
QUOTE ONE® SUMMARY COST REPORT	$29.95
QUOTE ONE® DETAILED COST ESTIMATE (FOR MORE DETAILS ABOUT QUOTE ONE®, SEE STEP 3.)	$60

IMPORTANT NOTE

■ THE 1-SET STUDY PACKAGE IS MARKED "NOT FOR CONSTRUCTION."

Source Key

HPT922

PLAN #	PRICE TIER	PAGE	MATERIALS LIST	QUOTE ONE®	DECK	DECK PRICE	LANDSCAPE	LANDSCAPE PRICE	REGIONS
HPT920001	SQ3	13							
HPT920002	SQ3	22							
HPT920003	SQ1	25							
HPT920004	SQ3	30							
HPT920005	SQ3	17							
HPT920006	SQ3	6							
HPT920007	SQ3	36							
HPT920008	SQ1	40	Y						
HPT920009	SQ1	44	Y				OLA008	P4	1234568
HPT920010	SQ3	49	Y						
HPT920011	SQ3	51							
HPT920012	SQ3	56							
HPT920013	SQ1	65	Y	Y			OLA001	P3	123568
HPT920014	C2	66					OLA004	P3	123568
HPT920015	SQ1	67	Y				OLA017	P3	123568
HPT920016	C4	68	Y				OLA008	P4	1234568
HPT920017	SQ1	69	Y	ODA011	P2	OLA012	P3	12345678	
HPT920018	SQ1	70							
HPT920019	SQ1	71	Y						
HPT920020	C3	72	Y						
HPT920021	C2	73	Y						
HPT920022	SQ1	74	Y	Y			OLA008	P4	1234568
HPT920023	C1	75							
HPT920024	SQ1	76	Y						
HPT920025	SQ1	77							
HPT920026	C2	78	Y						
HPT920027	SQ1	79							
HPT920028	SQ1	80	Y						
HPT920029	L1	81							
HPT920030	C2	82							
HPT920031	C4	83							
HPT920032	C2	84							
HPT920033	L1	85							
HPT920034	L1	86							
HPT920035	SQ1	87							
HPT920036	C2	88							
HPT920037	C4	89							
HPT920038	L2	90							
HPT920039	L1	91							
HPT920040	C2	92							
HPT920041	SQ1	93							
HPT920042	SQ1	94							
HPT920043	L1	95							
HPT920044	C3	96							
HPT920045	L1	97							
HPT920046	SQ1	98							
HPT920047	SQ1	99							
HPT920048	L1	100							
HPT920049	L1	101							
HPT920050	C4	102							
HPT920051	L1	103							
HPT920052	SQ1	104							
HPT920053	SQ1	105							
HPT920054	C3	106							
HPT920055	C3	107							
HPT920056	C3	108							
HPT920057	L2	109							
HPT920058	C3	110							
HPT920059	L2	111							
HPT920060	L2	112							
HPT920061	L1	113							
HPT920062	L1	114							
HPT920063	L1	115							
HPT920064	L2	116							
HPT920065	SQ1	117							
HPT920066	SQ1	118							
HPT920067	L2	119							
HPT920068	SQ1	120							
HPT920069	L1	121							
HPT920070	L2	122							
HPT920071	C4	123							
HPT920072	L2	124							
HPT920073	C4	125							
HPT920074	C2	126							
HPT920075	C2	127							
HPT920076	C3	128							
HPT920077	C4	129							
HPT920078	C3	130							

PLAN #	PRICE TIER	PAGE	MATERIALS LIST	QUOTE ONE®	DECK	DECK PRICE	LANDSCAPE	LANDSCAPE PRICE	REGIONS
HPT920079	C3	131							
HPT920080	C3	132							
HPT920081	C3	133							
HPT920082	C3	134							
HPT920083	C4	135							
HPT920084	C3	136							
HPT920085	C3	137							
HPT920086	C4	138							
HPT920087	C3	139							
HPT920088	C4	140							
HPT920089	C4	141				OLA004	P3	123568	
HPT920090	C1	142							
HPT920091	C1	143	Y						
HPT920092	C4	144							
HPT920093	C1	145	Y						
HPT920094	L1	146							
HPT920095	C3	147							
HPT920096	L1	148							
HPT920097	C1	149							
HPT920098	C4	150	Y	Y		OLA024	P4	123568	
HPT920099	C3	151							
HPT920100	C1	152	Y						
HPT920101	C1	153							
HPT920102	C2	154							
HPT920103	C1	155							
HPT920104	A4	156							
HPT920105	C3	157							
HPT920106	C1	158	Y						
HPT920107	C3	159							
HPT920108	C3	160							
HPT920109	SQ1	161							
HPT920110	C1	162							
HPT920111	C4	163							
HPT920112	L2	164							
HPT920113	C1	165							
HPT920114	C2	166							
HPT920115	C3	167							
HPT920116	C1	168	Y						
HPT920117	C1	169							

PLAN #	PRICE TIER	PAGE	MATERIALS LIST	QUOTE ONE®	DECK	DECK PRICE	LANDSCAPE	LANDSCAPE PRICE	REGIONS
HPT920118	C1	170							
HPT920119	L2	171							
HPT920120	C1	172							
HPT920121	C3	173							
HPT920122	C1	174							
HPT920123	C4	175							
HPT920124	C3	176							
HPT920125	L1	177							
HPT920126	SQ1	178							
HPT920127	SQ3	58							
HPT920128	SQ3	6							
HPT9220001	L2	179							
HPT9220002	C2	180							

ORDER ONLINE AT EPLANS.COM

MORE TOOLS FOR SUCCESS
3. GET GREAT EXTRAS

WE OFFER A VARIETY OF USEFUL TOOLS THAT CAN HELP YOU THROUGH EVERY STEP OF THE home-building process. From our Materials List to our Customization Program, these items let you put our experience to work for you to ensure that you get exactly what you want out of your dream house.

MATERIALS LIST

For many of the designs in our portfolio, we offer a customized list of materials that helps you plan and estimate the cost of your new home. The Materials List outlines the quantity, type, and size of materials needed to build your house (with the exception of mechanical system items). Included are framing lumber, windows and doors, kitchen and bath cabinetry, rough and finished hardware, and much more. This handy list helps you or your builder cost out materials and serves as a reference sheet when you're compiling bids.

SPECIFICATION OUTLINE

This valuable 16-page document can play an important role in the construction of your house. Fill it in with your builder, and you'll have a step-by-step chronicle of 166 stages or items crucial to the building process. It provides a comprehensive review of the construction process and helps you choose materials.

QUOTE ONE®

The Quote One® system, which helps estimate the cost of building select designs in your zip code, is available in two parts: the Summary Cost Report and the Material Cost Report.

The Summary Cost Report, the first element in the package, breaks down the cost of your home into various categories based on building materials, labor, and installation, and includes three grades of construction: Budget, Standard, and Custom. Make even more informed decisions about your project with the second element of our package, the Material Cost Report. The material and installation cost is shown for each of more than 1,000 line items provided in the standard-grade Materials List, which is included with this tool. Additional space is included for estimates from contractors and subcontractors, such as for mechanical materials, which are not included in our packages.

If you are interested in a plan that does not indicate the availability of Quote One®, please call and ask our sales representatives, who can verify the status for you.

CUSTOMIZATION PROGRAM

If the plan you love needs something changed to make it perfect, our customization experts will ensure that you get nothing less than your dream home. Purchase a reproducible set of plans for the home you choose, and we'll send you our easy-to-use customization request form via e-mail or fax. For just $50, our customization experts will provide an estimate for your requested revisions, and once it's approved, that charge will be applied to your changes. You'll receive either five sets or a reproducible master of your modified design and any other options you select.

BUILDING BASICS

If you want to know more about building techniques—and deal more confidently with your subcontractors—we offer four useful detail sheets. These sheets provide non-plan-specific general information, but are excellent tools that will add to your understanding of Plumbing Details, Electrical Details, Construction Details, and Mechanical Details. These fact-filled sheets will help answer many of your building questions, and help you learn what questions to ask your builder and subcontractors.

HANDS-ON HOME FURNITURE PLANNER

Effectively plan the space in your home using our Hands-On Home Furniture Planner. It's fun and easy—no more moving heavy pieces of furniture to see how the room will go together. The kit includes reusable peel-and-stick furniture templates that fit on a 12"x18" laminated layout board—enough space to lay out every room in your house.

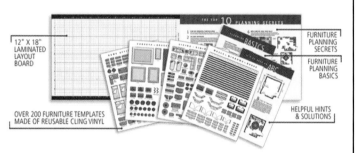

12" X 18" LAMINATED LAYOUT BOARD

OVER 200 FURNITURE TEMPLATES MADE OF REUSABLE CLING VINYL

FURNITURE PLANNING SECRETS

FURNITURE PLANNING BASICS

HELPFUL HINTS & SOLUTIONS

DECK BLUEPRINT PACKAGE

Many of the homes in this book can be enhanced with a professionally designed Home Planners Deck Plan. Those plans marked with a **D** have a corresponding deck plan, sold separately, which includes a Deck Plan Frontal Sheet, Deck Framing and Floor Plans, Deck Elevations, and a Deck Materials List. A Standard Deck Details Package, also available, provides all the how-to information necessary for building any deck. Get both the Deck Plan and the Standard Deck Details Package for one low price in our Complete Deck Building Package.

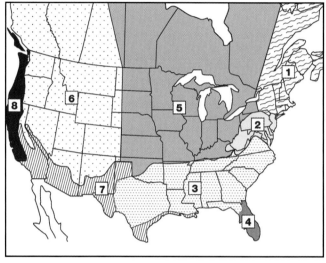

LANDSCAPE BLUEPRINT PACKAGE

Homes marked with an **L** in this book have a front-yard Landscape Plan that is complementary in design to the house plan. These comprehensive Landscape Blueprint Packages include a Frontal Sheet, Plan View, Regionalized Plant & Materials List, a sheet on Planting and Maintaining Your Landscape, Zone Maps, and a Plant Size and Description Guide. Each set of blueprints is a full 18" x 24" with clear, complete instructions in easy-to-read type.

Our Landscape Plans are available with a Plant & Materials List adapted by horticultural experts to eight regions of the country. Please specify from the following regions when ordering your plan:

Region 1: Northeast
Region 2: Mid-Atlantic
Region 3: Deep South
Region 4: Florida & Gulf Coast
Region 5: Midwest
Region 6: Rocky Mountains
Region 7: Southern California & Desert Southwest
Region 8: Northern California & Pacific Northwest

OUR EXCHANGE POLICY

With the exception of reproducible plan orders, we will exchange your entire first order for an equal or greater number of blueprints within our plan collection within **60 days** of the original order. The entire content of your original order must be returned before an exchange will be processed. Please call our customer service department at 1-888-690-1116 for your return authorization number and shipping instructions. If the returned blueprints look used, redlined, or copied, we will not honor your exchange. Fees for exchanging your blueprints are as follows: 20% of the amount of the original order, plus the difference in cost if exchanging for a design in a higher price bracket or less the difference in cost if exchanging for a design in a lower price bracket. (Reproducible blueprints are not exchangeable or refundable.) Please call for current postage and handling prices. Shipping and handling charges are not refundable.

ABOUT REPRODUCIBLES

Reproducibles (often called "vellums") are the most convenient way to order your blueprints. In any building process, you will need multiple copies of your blueprints for your builder, subcontractors, lenders, and the local building department. In addition, you may want or need to make changes to the original design. Such changes should be made only by a licensed architect or engineer. When you purchase reproducibles, you will receive a copyright release letter that allows you to have them altered and copied. You will want to purchase a reproducible plan if you plan to make any changes, whether by using our convenient Customization Program or going to a local architect.

ABOUT REVERSE BLUEPRINTS

Although lettering and dimensions will appear backward, reverses will be a useful aid if you decide to flop the plan. See Price Schedule and Plans Index for pricing.

ARCHITECTURAL AND ENGINEERING SEALS

Some cities and states now require that a licensed architect or engineer review and "seal" a blueprint, or officially approve it, prior to construction. Prior to application for a building permit or the start of actual construction, we strongly advise that you consult your local building official who can tell you if such a review is required.

ABOUT THE DESIGNS

The architects and designers whose work appears in this publication are among America's leading residential designers. Each plan was designed to meet the requirements of a nationally recognized model building code in effect at the time and place the plan was drawn. Because national building codes change from time to time, plans may not fully comply with any such code at the time they are sold to a customer. In addition, building officials may not accept these plans as final construction documents of record as the plans may need to be modified and additional drawings and details added to suit local conditions and requirements. Purchasers should consult a licensed architect or engineer, and their local building official, before starting any construction related to these plans.

LOCAL BUILDING CODES AND ZONING REQUIREMENTS

At the time of creation, these plans are drawn to specifications published by the Building Officials and Code Administrators (BOCA) International, Inc.; the Southern Building Code Congress International, (SBCCI) Inc.; the International Conference of Building Officials (ICBO); or the Council of American Building Officials (CABO). These plans are designed to meet or exceed national building standards. Because of the great differences in geography and climate throughout the United States and Canada, each state, county, and municipality has its own building codes, zone requirements, ordinances, and building regulations. Your plan may need to be modified to comply with local requirements. In addition, you may need to obtain permits or inspections from local governments before and in the course of construction. We authorize the use of the blueprints on the express condition that you consult a local licensed architect or engineer of your choice prior to beginning construction and strictly comply with all local building codes, zoning requirements, and other applicable laws, regulations, ordinances, and requirements. Notice: Plans for homes to be built in Nevada must be redrawn by a Nevada-registered professional. Consult your building official for more information on this subject.

TERMS AND CONDITIONS

These designs are protected under the terms of United States Copyright Law and may not be copied or reproduced in any way, by any means, unless you have purchased reproducibles which clearly indicate your right to copy or reproduce. We authorize the use of your chosen design as an aid in the construction of one single- or multi-family home only. You may not use this design to build a second or multiple dwellings without purchasing another blueprint or blueprints or paying additional design fees.

HOW MANY BLUEPRINTS DO YOU NEED?

Although a four-set building package may satisfy many states, cities, and counties, some plans may require certain changes. For your convenience, we have developed a reproducible plan, which allows you to take advantage of our Customization Program, or to have a local professional modify and make up to 10 copies of your revised plan. As our plans are all copyright protected, with your purchase of the reproducible, we will supply you with a copyright release letter. The number of copies you may need: 1 for owner, 3 for builder, 2 for local building department, and 1-3 sets for your mortgage lender.

DISCLAIMER

The designers we work with have put substantial care and effort into the creation of their blueprints. However, because we cannot provide on-site consultation, supervision, and control over actual construction, and because of the great variance in local building requirements, building practices, and soil, seismic, weather, and other conditions, **WE MAKE NO WARRANTY OF ANY KIND, EXPRESS OR IMPLIED, WITH RESPECT TO THE CONTENT OR USE OF THE BLUEPRINTS, INCLUDING BUT NOT LIMITED TO ANY WARRANTY OF MERCHANTABILITY OR OF FITNESS FOR A PARTICULAR PURPOSE. ITEMS, PRICES, TERMS, AND CONDITIONS ARE SUBJECT TO CHANGE WITHOUT NOTICE.**

IT'S EASY TO ORDER JUST VISIT EPLANS.COM OR CALL TOLL-FREE 1-800-521-6797

OPEN 24 HOURS, 7 DAYS A WEEK
If we receive your order by 3:00 p.m. EST, Monday-Friday, we'll process it and ship within two business days. When ordering by phone, please have your credit card or check information ready.

CANADIAN CUSTOMERS
Order Toll Free 1-877-223-6389

ONLINE ORDERING
Go to: **www.eplans.com**

After you have received your order, call our customer service experts at 1-888-690-1116 if you have any questions.

1 BIGGEST & BEST

1001 of our Best-Selling Plans in One Volume. 1,074 to 7,275 square feet. 704 pgs. $12.95 1K1

2 ONE-STORY

450 designs for all lifestyles. 810 to 5,400 square feet. 448 pgs. $9.95 OS2

3 MORE ONE-STORY

475 Superb One-Level Plans from 800 to 5,000 square feet. 448 pgs. $9.95 MO2

4 TWO-STORY

450 Best-Selling Designs for 1½ and 2-stories. 448 pgs. $9.95 TS2

5 VACATION

450 designs for Recreation, Retirement, and Leisure. 448 pgs. $9.95 VS3

6 HILLSIDE

208 designs for Split-Levels, Bi-Levels, Multi-Levels, and Walkouts. 224 pgs. $9.95 HH

7 FARMHOUSE

300 fresh designs from Classic to Modern. 320 pgs. $10.95 FCP

8 COUNTRY HOUSES

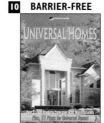

208 unique home plans that combine Traditional Style and Modern Livability. 224 pgs. $9.95 CN

9 BUDGET-SMART

200 Efficient Plans from 7 Top Designers, that you can really afford to build! 224 pgs. $8.95 BS

10 BARRIER-FREE

Over 1,700 products and 51 plans for Accessible Living. 128 pgs. $15.95 UH

11 ENCYCLOPEDIA

500 exceptional plans for all styles and budgets— The Best Book of its Kind! 528 pgs. $9.95 ENC3

12 SUN COUNTRY

175 Designs from Coastal Cottages to Stunning Southwesterns. 192 pgs. $9.95 SUN

13 AFFORDABLE

300 modest plans for savvy homebuyers. 256 pgs. $9.95 AH2

14 VICTORIAN

210 striking Victorian and Farmhouse designs from today's top designers. 224 pgs. $15.95 VDH2

15 ESTATE

Dream big! Eighteen designers showcase their biggest and best plans. 224 pgs. $16.95 EDH3

16 LUXURY

170 lavish designs, over 50% brand-new plans added to a most elegant collection. 192 pgs. $12.95 LD3

17 WILLIAM E. POOLE

100 classic house plans from William E. Poole. 224 pgs. $17.95 WP2

18 HUGE SELECTION

650 home plans— from Cottages to Mansions 464 pgs. $8.95 650

19 SOUTHWEST

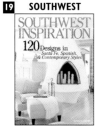

120 designs in Santa Fe, Spanish, and Contemporary Styles. 192 pgs. $14.95 SI

20 COUNTRY CLASSICS

130 Best-Selling Home Plans from Donald A. Gardner. 192 pgs. $17.95 DAG2

21 COTTAGES

245 Delightful retreats from 825 to 3,500 square feet. 256 pgs. $10.95 COOL

22 CONTEMPORARY

The most complete and imaginative collection of contemporary designs available. 256 pgs. $10.95 CM2

23 FRENCH COUNTRY

Live every day in the French countryside using these plans, landscapes and interiors. 192 pgs. $14.95 PN

24 SOUTHWESTERN

138 designs that capture the spirit of the Southwest. 144 pgs. $10.95 SW

25 SHINGLE-STYLE

155 home plans from Classic Colonials to Breezy Bungalows. 192 pgs. $12.95 SNG

26 NEIGHBORHOOD

170 designs with the feel of main street America. 192 pgs. $12.95 TND

27 CRAFTSMAN

170 Home plans in the Craftsman and Bungalow style. 192 pgs. $12.95 CC

28 GRAND VISTAS

200 Homes with a View. 224 pgs. $10.95 GV

29 MULTI-FAMILY

115 Duplex, Multiplex & Townhome Designs. 128 pgs. $17.95 MFH

30 WATERFRONT

200 designs perfect for your Waterside Wonderland. 208 pgs. $10.95 WF

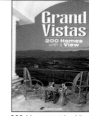

Essentials of Ultrasound Physics

Essentials of Ultrasound Physics

James A. Zagzebski, PhD

Professor
Department of Medical Physics,
  Human Oncology, and Radiology,
University of Wisconsin
Madison, Wisconsin

with 369 illustrations

St. Louis Baltimore Boston Carlsbad Chicago Naples New York Philadelphia Portland
London Madrid Mexico City Singapore Sydney Tokyo Toronto Wiesbaden

Mosby
Dedicated to Publishing Excellence

A Times Mirror
Company

Publisher: Don E. Ladig
Senior Editor: Jeanne Rowland
Senior Developmental Editor: Lisa Potts
Project Manager: John Rogers
Project Specialist: Kathleen L. Teal
Composition Specialist: Joan Herron
Designer: Yael Kats
Manufacturing Supervisor: Linda Ierardi
Cover Art: Combined gray scale and color flow image of a 22-week old fetus, providing visualization of hepatic flow. (Courtesy of Acuson Corporation, Mountain View, CA)

Printed in the United States of America

Composition by Mosby Electronic Production–St. Louis
Lithography/color film by Top Graphics
Printing/binding by Maple-Vail Book Manufacturing Group

Mosby–Year Book, Inc.
11830 Westline Industrial Drive
St. Louis, Missouri 63146

International Standard Book Number: 0-8151-9852-3

97 98 99 00 / 9 8 7 6 5 4 3 2

To Henrietta,

who walked many miles around the campus of old Central State College

one early August morning.

Preface

What an exciting time to be in the field of medical ultrasound! Technical innovations are rapidly producing dramatic improvements in the performance capabilities of clinical instruments. Although basic ultrasound imaging has not changed substantially over the past 25 years, today's ultrasound devices provide image quality and diagnostic capabilities that go way, way beyond what was even thought possible in earlier ultrasound days. Linear and phased arrays, for example, certainly were available in commercial instruments during the early 1970's. But today's "1 1/2 D" linear and phased arrays, made of "composite piezoelectric materials" produce images with vastly improved spatial resolution compared to images produced by their older cousins. The newer transducers also are much more sensitive to weak echoes and are much more versatile than their predecessors, even enabling the same transducer to be used at multiple imaging frequencies. Similar stories are emerging for most major components of a diagnostic ultrasound instrument. "Leaner and meaner" ultrasound imaging devices are emerging as manufacturers take advantage of modern digital technology, new fabrication techniques and an ever expanding knowledge base of bioacoustics and digital signal processing. More accurate and more cost-effective patient care will be the beneficial outcome of this equipment and scientific evolution, and most of you will play important roles in its application.

Essentials of Ultrasound Physics is about ultrasound technology and ultrasound instrumentation. This textbook is intended for students, sonographers, and technologists who need a thorough understanding of physics and instrumentation in this field. Therefore, the book starts with the basics, covering all topics usually found in beginning courses and board exams. There are multiple choice questions and problems at the end of each chapter to help you evaluate your level of understanding. An additional set of questions in the form of a "certification exam" is provided at the end of the book. This practice exam allows you to evaluate your strengths and weaknesses before taking the physics portion of the certification exam given by the American Registry of Diagnositc Medical Sonographers. Answers and explanations to questions can be found in the appendices. A comprehensive glossary of technical terms is also found in the appendix.

Earlier versions of some of the chapters in this book were part of Sandra Hagen-Ansert's third edition of the *Textbook of Diagnostic Ultrasonography*, also published by Mosby–Year Book. Compiling these newly updated and expanded chapters plus several new ones into the *Essentials of Ultrasound Physics* permits a complete presentation of ultrasound physics.

Acknowledgements

I am indebted to John Parks, Director of the University of Wisconsin School of Diagnostic Medical Sonography, for his help and encouragement during the production of this book. John also assisted in designing figures and reviewing early versions of some of the chapters. Chris Labinsky, Jackie Cassiday, Rhonda Arbogast, Dana Walker, Tim Heyser, Patty Kiel, and Nancy Bell all were very generous with their time by assisting with scanners and image archiving equipment, allowing interruptions during busy clinical ultrasound imaging schedules, and supplying interesting ultrasound images. I am grateful to them as well as to Drs. Myron Pozniak, Fred Lee Jr., Kathy Scanlan, and Peter Rahko who staff the ultrasound clinics at University of Wisconsin Hospital and provided helpful discussions and interesting cases. I am also thankful to Betsy True and Irene Golembiewski for expert help in producing the illustrations and to Lisa Potts and Kathy Teal from Mosby who helped immensely with editing. Finally, thanks to Ann Marie Zagzebski, Kathy Zagzebski, and Lynn Zagzebski for their enduring support and encouragement.

Contents

Essentials of Ultrasound Physics

Chapter 1

Physics of Diagnostic Ultrasound

Sound is mechanical energy transmitted by pressure waves in a medium. . . . Sound waves whose frequency is greater than 20 kilohertz is termed ultrasound. Diagnostic ultrasound involves frequencies in the 1 MHz to 20 MHZ range.

NATURE OF SOUND

Definition of sound

Nearly all of us have an idea of what sound is because of our ability to hear. However, familiar definitions such as "sound is the sensation perceived by the sense of hearing"[1] are too limited in describing medical ultrasound, in which frequencies much higher than those we can hear are used. At a fundamental level, sound is *mechanical energy transmitted by pressure waves in a material medium.*[1] This general definition encompasses all types of sound, including audible sound, low-frequency seismic waves, and ultrasound used in diagnostic imaging.

Let's examine this definition more closely. First, it describes sound as a form of **energy.** Energy is the capacity to do work, whether by moving an object, heating a room, or lighting electrically. When sound travels from one location to another it carries energy; that is, it can cause slight back-and-forth displacements of objects in its path. Sound striking an ear, for example, causes the eardrum to vibrate, producing the sensation of audible sound (Figure 1-1).

Sound energy is said to be *mechanical,* meaning it exists in the form of physical movements of the molecules and particles in the medium. This distinguishes sound energy from other forms of energy, such as electromagnetic. Sound waves always involve rapid back-and-forth displacements, or vibrations, of molecules in the medium.

Another important idea in the definition of sound is that it involves propagation through a *material medium.* Sound waves only exist in media containing molecules or particles, including air, water, tissues in the body, and many other examples. Sound waves cannot travel through a vacuum, as in outer space or in an experimental vacuum chamber where there is no medium in which to propagate.

Sources of sound

Sound production requires a vibrating object. A tuning fork in air is a good example (Figure 1-2, *A*). It vibrates when struck by a hammer. As the tuning fork vibrates it pushes and pulls against adjacent air molecules, causing them to vibrate as well (Figure 1-2, *B*). These vibrations cause still further molecules to vibrate, and so forth. Thus this disturbance spreads through the air as a wave. Other examples of sources of sound include the reed of a musi-

Figure 1-1. Sound is transmitted through air by molecules vibrating against one another. A person can hear audible sounds when energy in these vibrations is transmitted to the ear. The eardrum's vibrations result in the sensation of sound.

cal instrument, an audio speaker system, and a person's voice box. All sources involve some type of vibration to produce a sound wave.

The source of sound waves in medical ultrasound is a piezoelectric transducer (Figure 1-3). In response to an electrical impulse, it vibrates somewhat like a piston, producing sound waves in the tissue with which it is placed in contact. Piezoelectric transducers can be made to vibrate at the very high frequencies needed in an ultrasound examination.

Wave motion

Our definition indicated that sound travels in the form of a **wave**. A wave is a coordinated disturbance moving at a fixed speed through a medium. Sound waves move very fast and generally do not produce visible changes in a medium, so it is difficult to "visualize" them. Therefore we often revert to examples such as ripple patterns in water (Figure 1-4) to help illustrate properties of wave motion. A wave may be produced by dropping an object into a quiet pond. The wave spreads outward at a speed determined by the water surface and density. "People-waves" in the stadium at a football or soccer game travel around the stadium at a speed that depends on the make-up (and enthusiasm) of the crowd. Sound waves in air travel at a speed that depends on the pressure and temperature of the air. Typically the speed of sound in air is about 330 m/s (Figure 1-5), or a little over 1000 ft/s.

A wave carries energy through a medium without actual passage of the molecules and particles of the medium. After the wave moves through the medium, the particles return to their normal positions. A familiar example that helps illustrate this is when a small floating object is "struck" by waves in water. The wave motion carries the object up and down as the wave travels by. However, after the wave passes, the object is in the same spot as before the wave arrived.

Several types of waves exist; the box on p. 3 gives two general categories. Sound is an example of a mechanical wave, requiring a molecular medium for transmission. Other examples of mechanical waves include ocean waves, vibrations of a string, and seismic waves. The second type listed in the box is electromagnetics waves,

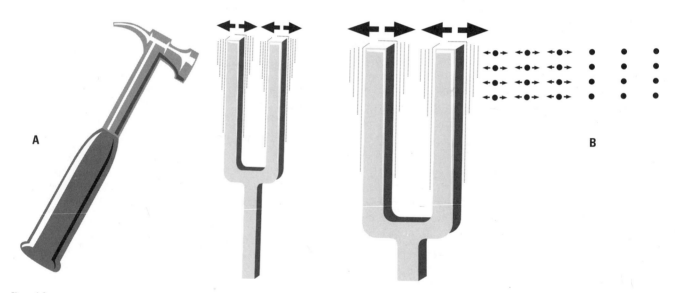

Figure 1-2. Sound generated by a tuning fork. **A,** The tuning fork vibrates when struck by the hammer. **B,** Vibrations of the tuning fork cause air molecules to vibrate. The vibration disturbance travels away from the tuning fork as a wave.

Figure 1-3. Ultrasound transducer element. It vibrates when an electrical signal of the correct form is applied.

Figure 1-4. Ripple pattern in a quiet pond after an object is dropped into the water.

which include radio waves, x-rays, and light. Electromagnetic waves do not require a molecular medium for propagation. In fact, they travel through the vacuum of outer space. Electromagnetic waves have much higher propagation speeds than mechanical waves.

Longitudinal versus transverse waves

Sound waves that travel through tissue are **longitudinal waves.** The sound source acts like a piston, vibrating back and forth (Figure 1-6). The wave travels away from the source more or less parallel to the direction the particles vibrate. Other types of mechanical waves are possible in some media. For example, **transverse vibrations** or shear waves may be transmitted through solid materials. These are characterized by particle vibrations perpendicular to the direction of propagation (Figure 1-6). Transverse waves can propagate easily through some solid materials, such as steel and bone. However, transverse waves do not travel effectively through soft tissue. Only longitudinal sound waves are important in diagnostic ultrasound imaging.

Box 1-1. Two general types of waves	
Mechanical	**Electromagnetic**
Ocean waves	Radio waves
Seismic waves	X-rays
Sound waves	Light

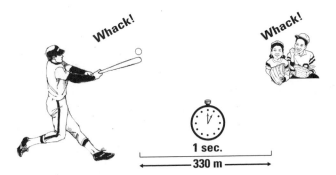

Figure 1-5. Sound waves travel in air at a speed of 330 m/s. In this cartoon depiction, a stopwatch measures the time from when a sound is produced (the bat striking a baseball) to when the sound reaches a listener's ear. It takes 1 second for sound waves to travel 330 m (about 1000 feet; about $1/5$ mile) in air.

Compressions and rarefactions

A sound wave travels away from the source, filling the affected medium with vibrational energy. If we could view a "snapshot" of the molecules in the medium at an instant when a sound wave is present, the results might be as shown in Figure 1-7. The back-and-forth displacement of the source squeezes and pulls on the particles in the medium, which push and pull on neighboring molecules, etc. Places where the molecules are pushed together when our snapshot is taken are called regions of *compression*. Here the density of the medium (i.e., the mass per unit volume, in g/cm^3) is slightly greater than it would be if the wave were absent. Areas where the molecules are drawn apart at the instant of our snapshot are called regions of *rarefaction*. The density is slightly lower in these regions.

Acoustic pressure

An acoustic quantity used frequently by engineers and physicists to quantify the strength of a wave is the **acoustic pressure.** We are all familiar with the concept of "atmospheric pressure," the steady pressure due to the weight of air at a point on earth. Atmospheric pressure is about 14.7 psi. The pressure in an automobile tire can be increased by pumping air into the tire. We often elevate the pressure in a tire to about 32 psi above atmospheric pressure. In a sound wave, the regions of compression are accompanied by elevations in the pressure compared to atmospheric pressure; the regions of rarefaction correspond to spots where the pressure is lower than atmospheric pressure.

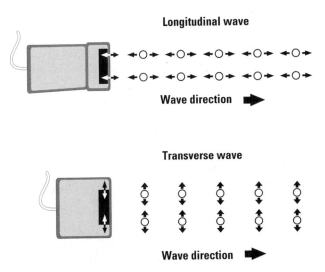
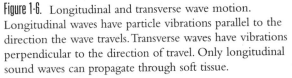

Figure 1-6. Longitudinal and transverse wave motion. Longitudinal waves have particle vibrations parallel to the direction the wave travels. Transverse waves have vibrations perpendicular to the direction of travel. Only longitudinal sound waves can propagate through soft tissue.

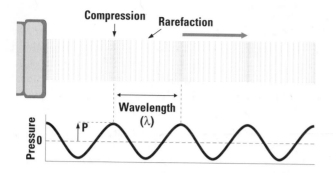

Figure 1-7. "Snapshot" of the medium at an instant in the presence of a sound wave. Compressions are regions where the density and pressure are elevated with respect to the background; rarefactions are regions where these quantities are less that those of the background. The lower trace is the acoustic pressure vs. distance. The acoustic wavelength is given by λ and the pressure amplitude by P.

If it were possible to measure the pressure at different points in a sound wave at the instant corresponding to the schematic diagram, the results would appear as in the lower part of Figure 1-7. Here *0* refers to atmospheric pressure, and we see the increased and decreased pressure at regions of compression and rarefaction. The maximum pressure elevation is called the *pressure amplitude, P.* The higher the magnitude of the wave, the greater the pressure amplitude. In ultrasonics, pressure is expressed in pascals, abbreviated Pa. For reference, the 14.7 psi of atmospheric pressure is equal to about 10^5 (100,000) Pa. Some diagnostic ultrasound beams have been "clocked" with pressure amplitudes exceeding 1 MPa (1,000,000 Pa), or 10 times atmospheric pressure.

Acoustic PRESSURE is measured in PASCALS.

As the sound source vibrates, the pressure wave travels (to the right in the diagram). Thus the pattern illustrated in Figure 1-7 changes with time. Figure 1-8 compares the original pressure distribution with what might be found at a slightly later time. The pattern is similar, but shifted, with the compressions and rarefactions appearing in slightly different places. As the sound wave travels, the pressure distribution continuously changes.

Period and frequency

A useful way of expressing the temporal behavior of a sound wave is to plot the pressure versus time at a single point in the medium. The resultant curve traces out a **sine wave** (Figure 1-9). The number of times per second the disturbance is repeated at any point is called the **frequency.** The frequency of a sound wave is determined by the number of oscillations per second made by the sound source.★

★For a review of math concepts see Appendix A on p. 179.

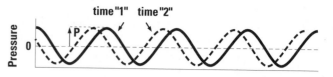

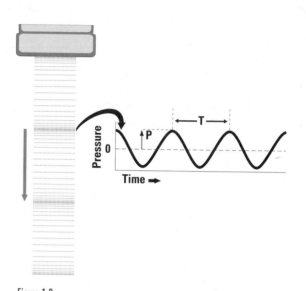

Figure 1-8. Comparison of two pressure vs. distance curves at slightly different times.

Figure 1-9. Change in pressure vs. time in the presence of a sound wave. Such a curve would be obtained at a fixed point in space when the sound source vibrates continuously. The period, that is, the time for 1 cycle of oscillation to occur, is labeled T.

The time it takes for the disturbance to repeat itself, that is, to go through one complete cycle, is the **period.** Period is labeled T in Figure 1-9. Frequency, f, and period, T, are inversely related; that is,

$$T = \frac{1}{f}$$

(1-1)

Example: Suppose the frequency of a wave is 10 cycles/s. Calculate the period.

Solution: Using the above equation, we find:

$$T = \frac{1}{f} = \frac{1}{10 \text{ cycles/s}} = 0.1 \text{ s}$$

Example: Suppose the period is 1 μs (0.000001 s). What is the frequency?

You can rearrange Equation 1-1 by multiplying both sides of the equation by f and dividing both sides by T. The result is

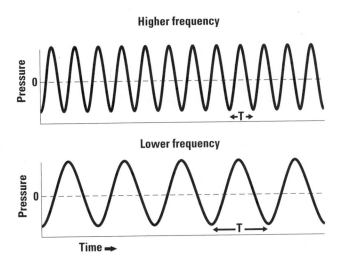

Figure 1-10. Pressure vs. time representation for two different frequencies. The higher frequency has a shorter period, T.

$$f = \frac{1}{T}$$

Substituting gives

$$f = \frac{1}{0.000001 \text{ s}} = 1,000,000 \text{ cycles/s}$$

In other words, if the period is 1 μs, the frequency is 1 million cycles/s (1 MHz).

The important relationship expressed here is that frequency and period are inversely related (Figure 1-10). As the frequency increases, the period decreases, and vice versa. If the frequency doubles, the period halves; if it quadruples, period is reduced to $\frac{1}{4}$ the original value, and so forth.

PERIOD is the INVERSE of the FREQUENCY.

ULTRASOUND

The frequency is the number of oscillations per second that the particles in the medium make as they vibrate about their resting position. Frequency is determined by the sound source, that is, by the number of oscillations per second it makes. The unit for frequency is *cycles per second* (cycles/s) or *hertz* (Hz). Commonly used multiples of 1 hertz are as follows:

1 cycles/s = 1 hertz = 1 Hz
1000 cycles/s = 1000 hertz = 1 kilohertz = 1 kHz
1,000,000 cycles/s = 1,000,000 hertz = 1 megahertz = 1 MHz

(Appendix A gives common metric prefixes and their decimal equivalents.)

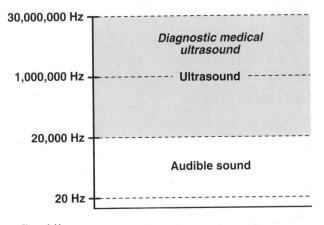

Figure 1-11. Classification of sounds according to frequency.

A classification scheme for acoustic waves according to their frequency is given in Figure 1-11. Most humans can hear sound if it has a frequency in the range of 20 Hz to approximately 20 kHz. This range is referred to as the *audible frequency range*. Sound whose frequency is greater than 20 kHz is termed *ultrasonic*. Mechanical vibrations whose frequencies are below the audible range are termed *infrasonic*. Examples of infrasonic transmissions include vibrations introduced by air ducts, ocean waves, and seismic waves.

The ultrasonic frequency range is used extensively, both in different types of instruments and by animals. Diagnostic ultrasound involves mainly frequencies in the 1-MHz to 20-MHz range.

SPEED OF SOUND

What determines the speed?

The speed of sound in any medium is determined primarily by the characteristics of the medium. (There are slight dependencies on other factors, such as the ultrasonic frequency, but these are so small that they can generally be ignored.) Specifically, for longitudinal sound waves in either liquids or body tissues, an expression for the speed of sound, *c*, is:

$$c = \sqrt{\frac{B}{\rho}} \tag{1-2}$$

In this equation *B* is a property of the medium called the *bulk modulus*. It is a measure of the stiffness of the material, that is, the resistance of the material to being compressed. The symbol ρ is the density, given in grams per cubic centimeter (g/cm³) or kilograms per cubic meter (kg/m³). Equation 1-2 tells us that the speed of sound in a medium depends both on the "stiffness" of the medium and on its density.

Speeds in nonbiological media

Appropriate units for speed are meters per second (m/s) or centimeters per second (cm/s). The speed of sound in some nonbiological materials is given in Table 1-1.[2]

Sound speed in tissue

The speed of sound in biological tissues is an important parameter in imaging applications. Values that have been measured in different human tissues are given in Table 1-2.[2-5]

The lowest sound speed shown is that for lung tissue; the low value is due to air-filled alveoli in this tissue. Most tissues of concern to us (i.e., those through which sound can be readily propagated in the megahertz frequency range) have speed-of-sound values in the neighborhood of 1500 to 1600 m/s. Fat is on the low end of the range for soft tissue and muscle tissue on the high end. Measurements of the speed of sound in bone tissue result in values two to three times those recorded in most soft tissues.

The average speed of sound in soft tissues (excluding the lung) is 1540 m/s, and range-measuring circuits on most diagnostic ultrasound instruments are calibrated on this basis. Close inspection of the biological tissue list above reveals that the propagation speed in every soft tissue of concern to us in diagnostic ultrasound is within a few percentage points of 1540 m/s.

Table 1-1. Speed of sound in some nonbiological materials*

Material	Sound speed (m/s)
Air	330
Water	1480
Lead	2400
Aluminum	6400

*From Wells PNT: *Biomedical ultrasonics,* New York, 1977, Academic Press.

Table 1-2. Speed of sound in selected tissues[2-5]

Material	Sound speed (m/s)
Lung	600
Fat	1460
Aqueous humor	1510
Liver	1555
Blood	1560
Kidney	1565
Muscle	1600
Lens of eye	1620
Skull bone	4080

The following are equivalent designations for the average speed of sound in soft tissue:

Average speed of sound in soft tissue
1540 m/s
154,000 cm/s
1.54 mm/μs = 0.154 cm/μs

WAVELENGTH

The wavelength is the distance between two peaks, valleys, or other corresponding points on the wave (Figure 1-7). It is the distance the sound wave travels during one complete cycle of the wave. Wavelength is usually designated by the symbol λ.

The acoustic wavelength depends on the frequency, f, and the speed of sound in the medium, c. It is given by the following relationship:

$$\lambda = \frac{c}{f} \tag{1-3}$$

Thus the wavelength is simply the speed of sound divided by the ultrasonic frequency. The important relationship to keep in mind here is the inverse relationship between the wavelength and the ultrasound frequency. The higher the ultrasonic frequency, the smaller will be the wavelength.

Example: Calculate the wavelength for a 2-MHz ultrasound beam in soft tissue. Assume the speed of sound is 1540 m/s.

Solution: The wavelength can be calculated directly using Equation 1-3, with c = 1540 m/s and f = 2 MHz = 2×10^6 cycles/s. Thus

$$\lambda = \frac{1540 \text{ m/s}}{2 \times 10^6 \text{ s}} = 0.00077 \text{ m} = 0.77 \text{ mm}$$

Appendix A reviews metric conversions. It also contains examples of addition, subtraction, multiplication, and division in which numbers are expressed as exponentials (i.e., 2,000,000 cycles/s = 2×10^6 cycles/s).

There is a simple way to calculate the wavelength in soft tissue, assuming the speed of sound is 1540 m/s. Call the soft tissue wavelength λ_{st}. If we express the speed of sound in mm/μs and the frequency in MHz:

$$\lambda_{st} = \frac{1.54 \text{ mm}}{f(\text{MH}_z)} \tag{1-4}$$

This means that the wavelength (in millimeters) equals 1.54 divided by the frequency (in Megahertz).

Example: Calculate the wavelength in soft tissue if the frequency is 10 MHz.

Solution: Using Equation 1-4,

$$\lambda_{st} = \frac{1.54 \text{ mm}}{f(\text{MHz})} = \frac{1.54 \text{ mm}}{10} = 0.154 \text{ mm}$$

Ultrasonographers routinely select the ultrasound frequency when they choose a transducer or a probe control setting. When you change frequencies, the wavelength also changes. As the frequency increases, the wavelength decreases. Doubling the frequency halves the wavelength, halving the frequency doubles the wavelength, and so forth.

The wavelength is important in ultrasound physics because it is related to imaging factors such as **spatial resolution** (see Chapter 2). In addition, the physical size of an object (e.g., a reflecting surface or a transducer surface) is significant only when we compare it to the ultrasonic wavelength. For example, an element in an array transducer produces a beam that spreads out if the element is about the size of the wavelength; a transducer element whose dimensions are much larger than the wavelength produces a well-defined, directed beam. It might be said then that the wavelength is our "acoustic yardstick" (Figure 1-12). Objects are large or small relative to the wavelength. In soft tissue, wavelengths for diagnostic ultrasound are on the order of 1 mm or less, with 0.77 mm wavelengths for 2-MHz beams and proportionally smaller ones for higher frequencies.

AMPLITUDE AND INTENSITY

When discussing reflection, attenuation, and scatter, we often must make a quantitative statement regarding the magnitude or strength of a sound wave. One variable that can be used here is the **pressure amplitude.** The acoustic pressure amplitude was illustrated in Figure 1-7 and was defined as the maximum increase (or decrease) in the pressure relative to ambient conditions in the absence of the sound wave. A wave of higher magnitude is accompanied by a greater pressure amplitude than one of a lower magnitude. For audible sounds, amplitude is associated with the "loudness" of the sound.

In some applications, particularly when discussing biological effects of ultrasound (see Chapter 9), it is useful to specify the acoustic intensity. The intensity at a location in an ultrasound beam, I, is proportional to the square of the pressure amplitude, P. The actual relationship is:

$$I = \frac{P^2}{2\rho c} \tag{1-5}$$

Again, ρ is the density of the medium and c the speed of sound. Thus, if the amplitude were to double, the intensity at that location would quadruple; if it were to

Figure 1-12. The wavelength is our "acoustic yardstick." Objects are measured in terms of their size compared to the wavelength.

increase by three, the intensity would increase by nine, etc. Acoustic intensity will be discussed in greater detail in Chapter 9.

REFLECTION AND TRANSMISSION AT INTERFACES

Acoustic impedance

An important property of tissues that influences the strength or amplitude of reflected echoes is a quantity called the **acoustic impedance.** It is defined in advanced ultrasound texts as the acoustic pressure divided by the resultant particle velocity. For our purposes, the acoustic impedance (or the *characteristic impedance*) of a material, Z, is equal to the product of the medium's density (ρ) and its speed of sound (c). That is,

$$Z = \rho c \tag{1-6}$$

Table 1-3 shows a compilation of acoustic impedance values for both nonbiological and biological tissues. The units for expressing these are kilograms per square meter per second (kg/m²/s), which result after multiplying density times speed. Sometimes we find impedance given in **rayls.** One rayl is the same as 1 kg/m²/s.

Air or an air-filled structure, such as the lung, has a very low acoustic impedance compared to tissue. For other tissues, except for bone, the range of acoustic impedances is relatively narrow.

Reflection—perpendicular incidence

Whenever an ultrasound beam is incident on an interface formed by two materials having different acoustic impedances, some of the energy in the beam will be reflected and the remainder transmitted. The amplitude of the reflected wave depends on the difference between

Table 1-3. Acoustic impedances of selected tissues

Tissue	Impedance (rayls)
Air	0.0004×10^6
Lung	0.18×10^6
Fat	1.34×10^6
Water	1.48×10^6
Liver	1.65×10^6
Blood	1.65×10^6
Kidney	1.63×10^6
Muscle	1.71×10^6
Skull bone	7.8×10^6

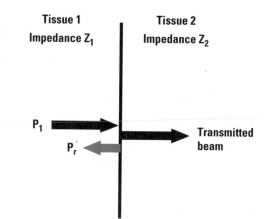

Figure 1-13. Specular reflection at a smooth interface. The incident wave amplitude is P_i and the reflected wave amplitude is P_r. Z_1 is the impedance of the material on the proximal side of the interface while Z_2 is the impedance on the distal side of the interface.

the acoustic impedances of the two materials forming the interface.

Consider first the case of normal or perpendicular beam incidence on a large flat interface (Figure 1-13). A large smooth interface such as depicted here is termed a *specular reflector*. It has dimensions that are much greater than the ultrasonic wavelength. The ratio of the reflected pressure amplitude, P_r, to the incident pressure amplitude, P_i, is called the *amplitude reflection coefficient, R*. R is given by:

$$R = \frac{P_r}{P_i} = \frac{Z_2 - Z_1}{Z_2 + Z_1} \tag{1-7}$$

where Z_2 is the acoustic impedance on the distal side of the interface and Z_1 is the impedance on the proximal side. Equation 1-7 emphasizes that the reflected wave amplitude depends on the difference in impedances of the two materials forming the interface.

Some authors use the intensity reflection coefficient rather than the amplitude reflection coefficient to quantify the reflection process. The mathematical expression for the reflection looks similar to Equation 1-7, except that the quantity involving the acoustic impedances is squared. In other words, if I_r is the reflected intensity and I_i is the incident intensity, then:

$$\frac{I_r}{I_i} = \left(\frac{Z_2 - Z_1}{Z_2 + Z_1} \right)^2 \tag{1-8}$$

The ratio of the reflected intensity to the incident intensity at an interface is equal to the square of the ratio of the reflected amplitude to the incident amplitude. This follows directly from the fact that the intensity is proportional to the square of the amplitude.

Example: Using the values for acoustic impedance just given, calculate the amplitude reflection coefficient for a fat–liver interface.

Solution: The acoustic impedance of fat is 1.34×10^6 rayls, that of liver 1.65×10^6 rayls. From Equation 1-7:

$$R = \frac{1.65 \times 10^6 \text{ rayls} - 1.34 \times 10^6 \text{ rayls}}{1.65 \times 10^6 \text{ rayls} + 1.34 \times 10^6 \text{ rayls}}$$

Factoring out 10^6 rayls gives

$$R = \frac{(1.65 - 1.34) \times 10^6 \text{ rayls}}{(1.65 + 1.34) \times 10^6 \text{ rayls}} = \frac{(1.65 - 1.34)}{(1.65 + 1.34)} =$$

$$\frac{0.31}{2.99} = 0.10$$

We see from the example that the ratio of the reflected to the incident amplitude is quite small. In fact, at most soft tissue–soft tissue interfaces in the body the reflection coefficient is fairly small and most of the sound is transmitted through the interface. If this were not the case, it would be difficult to use diagnostic ultrasound for examining anatomical structures at significant tissue depths.

Example: Calculate the reflection coefficient for a muscle-air interface.

Solution: From the acoustic impedances given in Table 1-3, calculate:

$$R = \frac{0.0004 \times 10^6 - 1.7 \times 10^6}{0.0004 \times 10^6 + 1.7 \times 10^6} =$$

$$\frac{0.0004 - 1.7}{0.0004 + 1.7} = -0.99$$

In this case the beam is almost completely reflected, as the magnitude of the reflection coefficient is nearly 1! (The minus sign has to do with the phase of the reflection, but has no bearing on the size of the reflection.) This example illustrates the difficulty in transmitting ultrasound beyond any tissue-to-air interface (Figure 1-

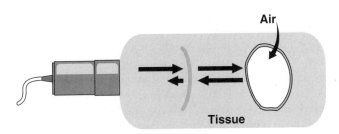

Figure 1-14. Reflection at a tissue-tissue interface and at a tissue-air interface. No sound travels beyond the tissue-air interface because of complete reflection.

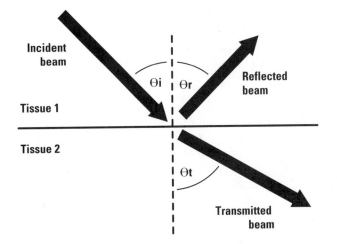

Figure 1-15. Reflection and transmission at a specular interface when the beam is incident at an angle. The reflected beam travels off at an angle, as shown. The transmitted beam undergoes refraction if the speeds of sound in the media forming the interface differ.

Table 1-4. Reflected amplitude ratios and intensity ratios for various interfaces

Interface	P_r/P_i	I_r/I_i
Kidney-liver	0.006	0.00004
Liver-muscle	0.018	0.0003
Fat-liver	0.10	0.01
Muscle-bone	0.64	0.41
Muscle-air	−0.99	0.98

14). The complete reflection at air interfaces also explains the need for a coupling medium, such as gel or oil, between the ultrasound transducer and the patient during ultrasound examinations. The coupling material ensures that no air is trapped between the transducer and the skin surface, thereby providing good sound transmission into the patient.

Examples of amplitude reflection coefficients (P_r/P_i) and intensity reflection coefficients (I_r/I_i) for specular reflecting interfaces are given in Table 1-4.

The data presented here show that a soft tissue–to–bone interface also is a fairly strong reflector. Because of this, whenever possible, transmission through bone is avoided in diagnostic ultrasound. (Another difficulty with bone is that it distorts ultrasound beams, spreading them out and decreasing spatial resolution.) Most soft tissue interfaces of importance are fairly weakly reflecting, just as we calculated in the first example.

In summary, reflection of a sound beam occurs whenever the beam is incident on an interface formed by two tissues having different acoustic impedances. The acoustic impedance difference could be caused by a change in speeds of sound, a change in densities, or both. The magnitude of the reflected wave and the percentage of the beam energy that is reflected depend on the acoustic impedance difference at the interface. Interfaces where there is a large difference in acoustic impedance reflect more of the incident beam than do interfaces where the acoustic impedance difference (mismatch) is small. For interfaces formed by two soft tissues, the impedance mismatch is small and the reflection coefficient is almost always much less than 0.1.

Nonperpendicular sound beam incidence

For nonperpendicular beam incidence on a specular reflector the situation changes somewhat. First, the reflected beam does not travel back toward the source (Figure 1-15) but instead travels off at an angle, θ_r, which is equal to the incident angle, θ_i, only in the opposite direction. This has an effect on echo detection from interfaces. As we shall see in Chapter 3, in most applications of ultrasound a single

transducer serves both as the source of the sound beam and the detector of echoes from reflectors in the beam. Therefore the amplitude of a detected echo depends on the orientation of the interface relative to the incident beam (Figure 1-16). Because of this significant angular dependence on the detection of an echo, specular reflectors are sometimes difficult to visualize because their orientation usually is not perpendicular to the ultrasound beam.

A second factor that arises when the incident beam is not perpendicular to an interface is the possibility of refraction of the transmitted beam. **Refraction** refers to a "bending" of the sound beam, that is, a change in the direction of the transmitted beam, at the interface. This results in the transmitted beam emerging in a different direction from the incident beam (compare the incident and transmitted beam directions in Figure 1-15).

Most of us are familiar with the effects of refraction of light waves; for example, due to refraction a swimming pool appears shallower than it actually is and the location of objects may be somewhat distorted when viewed from

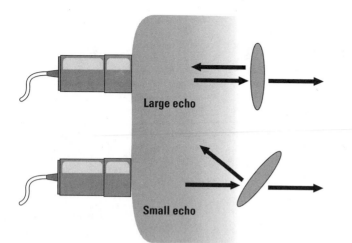

Figure 1-16. The reflected wave from a specular interface travels back to the source transducer for perpendicular incidence, producing a large echo signal. When the beam is not perpendicular, most of the echo does not return to the transducer.

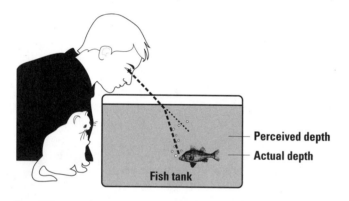

Figure 1-17. Objects and distances in a pool of water seen from above the surface appear distorted because of refraction of light at the water-air interface. Because of refraction, light coming from a certain depth, such as from the location of the fish or from the bottom of the container, appears to the observer to come from a shallower depth.

above the water (Figure 1-17). Light wave refraction occurs because the velocity of light is significantly greater in air than in water.

Two conditions are required for refraction of a sound wave to occur:

1. The sound beam must be incident on the interface at an angle that is not perpendicular.
2. The speeds of sound must be different on the two sides of the interface.

Both conditions must be met. If the incident beam is perpendicular to the interface, no matter what the sound speed difference is between the two materials forming

the interface, no refraction will occur. Likewise, even for a very oblique angle of incidence, if the sound speed does not change across the interface, no refraction will occur.

The amount of refraction is predicted by **Snell's law.** Snell's law relates the transmitted beam direction to the incident beam direction and the speeds of sound in the two materials forming the interface. Let c_1 be the speed of sound on the incident beam side of the interface and c_2 the speed of sound on the transmitted beam side, θ_i be the incident beam angle in Figure 1-15 and θ_t the transmitted beam angle. Snell's law states that:

$$\frac{\sin \theta_t}{\sin \theta_i} = \frac{c_2}{c_1} \qquad (1\text{-}9)$$

The angle θ_t is also shown in Figure 1-15. Equation 1-9 is a statement of Snell's law.

Engineers sometimes use Snell's law to calculate exactly the transmitted beam direction given the direction of the incident beam and the propagation speeds on either side of the interface.

We can gain insight into refraction and Snell's law without detailed computations. The relationship between an angle and its trigonometric sine (sin) is discussed in Appendix A. For angles between 0 and 90 degrees, as the angle increases, its sine also increases. With this in mind, inspection of Equation 1-9 reveals the following: if c_2 is greater than c_1, the transmitted beam angle will be greater than the incident beam angle; if c_2 is less than c_1, the transmitted beam angle will be less than the incident beam angle. These two conditions are illustrated in Figure 1-18.

How much refraction (or, how big a change in beam direction) might be anticipated in ultrasonography? Let's apply Equation 1-9 for several hypothetical interfaces. We'll assume the ultrasound beam is incident at a 30 degree angle with the interface. First, consider what we might expect to be a fairly extreme situation, one where the incident beam is traveling through bone and encounters a bone–soft tissue interface. Assuming the speed of sound in bone is 4080 m/s and in soft tissue is 1540 m/s, if the incident beam angle is 30 degrees, the large speed of sound change results in a transmitted beam angle of just 10.9 degrees, a 19.1-degree shift!

Table 1-5 lists results for some soft tissue interfaces, where refraction effects are not as drastic as in bone–soft tissue interfaces. For the three soft tissue–soft tissue interfaces, muscle-to-fat presents the severest refraction. This is because this interface has the greatest change in speeds of sound at the interface. In fact, fat and adipose tissue often pose difficulty to ultrasound imaging; some of this difficulty is believed to be from refraction that occurs at adipose tissue interfaces.

An automobile traveling from a smooth ("fast") surface to a rough ("slow") surface, or vice versa, can provide

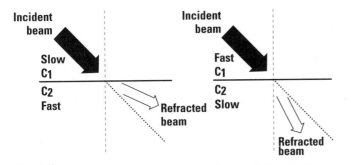

Figure 1-18. Refraction when c_2 is greater than c_1 (*left*) and when c_2 is less than c_1 (*right*).

Table 1-5 Change in beam direction for a 30 degree angle of incidence

Interface	Transmitted beam angle (degrees)	Change
Bone–soft tissue	10.9	19.1
Muscle–fat	27.1	2.9
Muscle–fluid	28.8	1.2
Muscle–blood	29.2	0.8

an analogy to help remember the direction of refraction. In Figure 1-19 a car is moving from the fast to the slow surface at an angle. The wheel passing the interface first would move more slowly than the one still on pavement, forcing the car to turn. The direction it turns is slightly to the car's right in the diagram. Once both front wheels are in the "slower" material they both turn at the same speed and the automobile moves straight ahead; however, the path has changed from the original direction. This is analogous to a wave entering a medium having a lower wave speed. (Compare with Figure 1-18.) If the automobile were traveling from the slower surface to the faster surface, the opposite effect would occur, again analogous to sound wave refraction.

Diffuse reflection

Many times echo signals are produced in the body from interfaces that are not perfectly specular. For example, small vessels whose dimensions are on the order of the acoustic wavelength fall into this category. So do many larger interfaces, such as the collecting system of the kidney, the walls of the heart chambers, and some organ boundaries, which are generally not perfectly smooth. Interfaces that possess a degree of roughness, as illustrated schematically on the right in Figure 1-20, are referred to as **diffuse reflectors.** An echo from a dif-

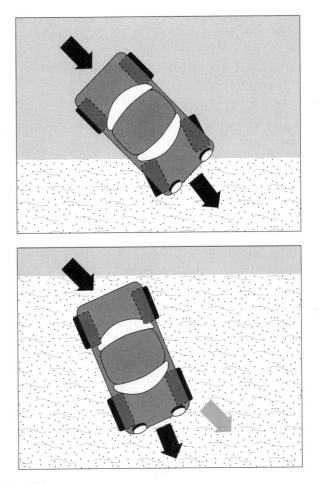

Figure 1-19. Analogy to help remember the direction a beam will be refracted. An automobile traveling from a "fast" region (e.g., solid pavement) into a "slow" region (e.g., a plowed field) would be changed in its direction, as shown. Moving from a slow to a fast medium has the opposite effect. If the automobile approaches the interface perpendicularly, no diversion occurs.

fuse reflector detected with a single pulse-echo transducer, though perhaps weaker, is not as sensitive to the orientation of the reflector as an echo from a smooth, specular reflector.

Evidence of specular and diffuse reflectors

Diffuse and specular reflections are most closely associated with echoes from boundaries of objects, such as the diaphragm and the kidney surface shown in Figure 1-21. The dependence of the echo signal strength on the angle the ultrasound wave makes with the reflecting interface can be appreciated. The scan in Figure 1-21 was obtained with a sector transducer, which transmits and receives from the location shown in the diagram. When the sound beam from the transducer is nearly perpendicular to the kidney-to-liver interface, a strong echo signal is detected. This is evident from the brightness of the display. The echo from this same interface is not detected from the upper margins of the kidney because of the unfavorable beam angle.

Echoes from scattering

Perhaps the most important sources of echo signals in the body are those arising from a process called *acoustic scattering*. Acoustic scattering is a term used for reflections from small objects, the size of the wavelength or smaller. The parenchyma of most organs seems to be loaded with such reflectors, as gray scale images usually exhibit numerous echoes from the interior of an organ (Figure 1-22). More will be said in Chapter 7 on the appearance of the echo pattern.

Waves that are scattered tend to travel off in all directions, as suggested in Figure 1-22. This has both good and bad effects. The bad effect is that echoes from scattering tend to be weaker than echoes from reflections at organ boundaries. Fortunately, modern ultrasound imagers have enough sensitivity to detect and display these weak echo signals, enabling us to make heavy use of them in imaging and Doppler applications. The good effect of having scattered waves travel off in various directions is that there is little orientation dependence of the echo signal strength. No matter what the direction of the incident ultrasound beam on a region of an organ, usually the scattered echo signals are of about the same amplitude. The exception to this is if the organ interior varies in echogenicity from one location to another. Therefore an organ's interior will appear homogeneous on an ultrasound image. The echo signals from the liver in Figure 1-23 tend to be of about the same magnitude regardless of the incident beam direction. This is in contrast to the strong orientation dependence seen for specular reflectors.

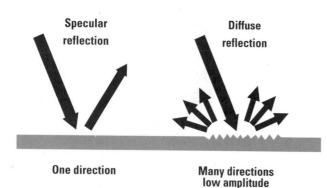

Figure 1-20. Comparison of specular and diffuse reflection. For a diffuse reflector, waves travel in various directions away from the interface so an echo would not be as dependent on interface orientation as for a specular reflector.

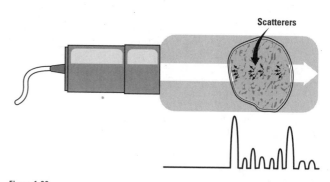

Figure 1-22. Scattering by small reflectors. Echoes travel in all directions from each interface. Therefore the incident beam direction has little effect on the strength of the detected echo signal.

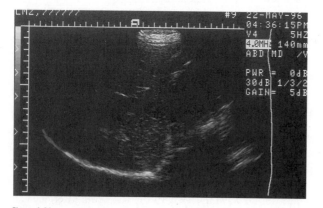

Figure 1-21. An ultrasound image of the liver and kidney area taken with a low receiver gain and displaying only strong echoes. The image emphasizes specular and diffusely reflecting interfaces.

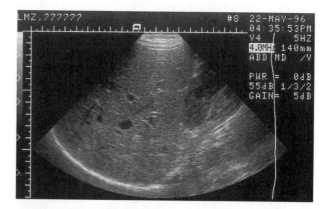

Figure 1-23. Same region imaged as in Figure 1-21, only now the gain and the echo display range are such that weaker echo signals resulting from scattering are displayed. The liver appears uniform, partially because the scattering does not depend on the direction of the incident beam.

Ultrasonic scattering gives rise to much of the diagnostic information seen in ultrasound imaging. In our earlier example in Figure 1-23, much of the detail of the liver, fat pad surrounding the kidney, and kidney results from changes in the scattering from one entity to another. On an image of a fairly mature fetus the lungs are delineated from liver because the fetal lungs are hyperechoic compared to fetal liver (Figure 1-24). Countless other examples are generated daily in ultrasound imaging centers.

Changes in scattering amplitude from one region to another result in brightness changes on an ultrasound image and therefore are useful in delineating abnormal structures. The terms **hyperechoic** and **hypoechoic** are used often in clinical imaging to describe structures on B-mode images. Hyperechoic regions result from increases in the ultrasound scattering level compared to the surrounding tissue. Hypoechoic refers to the opposite condition, where the scattering level is lower than in the surrounding tissue. For example, a liver hemangioma (Figure 1-25) is visualized because of the increased echogenicity that resulted from higher scattering of this tumor.

For very small scatterers, echo signals depend on the following:

1. The number of scatterers per unit volume.
2. The acoustic impedance changes at the scatterer interfaces.
3. The size of the scatterer. (Scattering usually increases with increasing radius for very small scatterers.)

4. The ultrasonic frequency. (Scattering usually increases with increasing frequency for very small scatterers.)

The dependence on frequency can sometimes be used to an advantage in ultrasound imaging. Since specular reflection is frequency independent but scattering increases with frequency, it is often possible to enhance scattered signals over specular echo signals by using higher ultrasonic frequencies.

Rayleigh scatterers. Scattering from red blood cells (Figure 1-26) gives rise to echo signals from blood for Doppler and color flow imaging applications. Red blood cells are sometimes called **Rayleigh scatterers.** This term is used when the dimensions of scattering objects are much less than the ultrasonic wavelength. (Recall, a 5 MHz ultrasound beam has a wavelength of 0.3 mm, or 300 μm, which is much larger than the 8-μm sized red blood cell.) Scattering from Rayleigh scatterers increases with frequency, the intensity being proportional to frequency raised to the fourth power! This means that doubling the frequency, for example, switching from 2 to 4 MHz, increases the scattered intensity by 16 times. Of course other factors, including attenuation, also influence the strength of scattered waves. Sound beam attenuation, which also increases with frequency (see section on attenuation) can more than offset the increased echo signal strength from blood if the vessel is a long distance from the transducer.

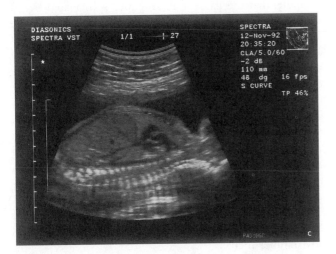

Figure 1-24. Ultrasound scan showing a fetal thorax, abdomen, and spine. The lung appears brighter (or more "echogenic") than the liver because of its higher scattering level. (Courtesy of Diasonics Ultrasound, Milpitas, CA.)

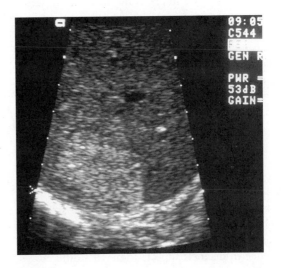

Figure 1-25. Ultrasound image of the liver where a tumor (brighter region) is visualized because of its elevated scatter level. (Courtesy of Acuson Corporation, Mountain View, CA.)

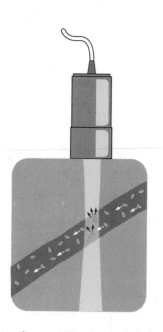

Figure 1-26. Scattering from red blood cells. Although the echoes are weak, they are responsible for Doppler signals. Because red blood cells are very small compared to the wavelength, they are called *Rayleigh scatterers.*

DECIBEL NOTATION

Let us digress at this point and discuss a fairly standard method for quantifying intensities, or power levels in medical ultrasound. The decibel notation provides a comparison of two signal levels, such as two amplitudes or two intensities. It is used primarily to express changes in these quantities resulting, for example, from attenuation, signal amplification, signal compression to vary dynamic range, and instrument power control variations.

Suppose we have two echo signals, the amplitude of one designated by A_2 and of the other by A_1. If we want to describe the relative amplitudes of these signals, we simply take the ratio of one to the other. However, using decibels, the relationship between A_2 and A_1 is expressed as follows:

$$\text{Relative signal level (dB)} = 20 \log \frac{A_2}{A_1} \quad (1\text{-}10)$$

Sometimes decibels are used to compare two signal intensities; for example, the output power control of many scanners is calibrated in decibels. If the power or intensity is given rather than the amplitude, the expression for the relative difference in decibels appears somewhat different:

$$\text{Relative intensity level (dB)} = 10 \log \frac{I_2}{I_1} \quad (1\text{-}11)$$

where I refers to an intensity.

In fact, Equation 1-11 can be shown to be equivalent to Equation 1-10. To do this we make use of the fact that the logarithm of a number raised to any power (e.g., log 10^2) is equal to that power times the logarithm of the number alone:

$$\log 10^2 = 2 \times \log 10$$

If we use the expression for decibels employing the intensities (Equation 1-11):

$$\text{Signal level (dB)} = 10 \log \frac{I_2}{I_1}$$

and note from Equation 1-5 that the intensity is proportional to the amplitude squared, we can write

$$\text{Signal level (dB)} = 10 \log \left(\frac{A_2}{A_1} \right)^2 = 20 \log \frac{A_2}{A_1}$$

which is identical to Equation 1-10. Authors usually present the decibel notation in either of these two forms. This exercise shows that both forms are essentially the same.

The amplitude and intensity ratios corresponding to a given decibel level can be calculated fairly easily. Some examples are presented in Table 1-6.

Column one in this table presents selected amplitude ratios, and column two gives the computed logarithm for each ratio. Multiplying the logarithm of the ratio by 20 yields the decibel relation between the two amplitudes, shown in column three. Intensity ratios corresponding to each amplitude and each decibel value are shown in column four.

Here are a couple of examples where the decibel notation is used on ultrasound instruments. Suppose, for example, that the gain of an amplifier is increased by 20 dB. (Gain is discussed in Chapter 3.) Inspection of Table 1-6 shows that 20 dB corresponds to an amplitude ratio of 10. Therefore, a 20 dB increase is equivalent to increasing the amplification by 10. The displayed echo dynamic range of an imager is usually given in decibels. If the dynamic range is 40 dB, the ratio of the largest to the smallest echo signals that are displayed without distortion is 100. (Dynamic range also is defined in Chapter 3.)

It often happens that when we are comparing signal amplitudes or intensities, the ratio (column one or column four) is a fraction. This is generally the case when considering effects of attenuation, discussed in the next section. The decibel notation allows us to account for such changes conveniently—simply by using the fact that if n is any number then:

$$\log \frac{1}{n} = -\log n$$

Let's say the amplitude is reduced to $1/10$ its original value because of attenuation. The log $1/10$ is equal to $-\log 10$.

Table 1-6. Amplitude and intensity ratios, their logarithms and their equivalent values expressed in decibels

Amplitude ratio A_2/A_1	Log A_2/A_1	dB	Intensity ratio I_2/I_1	Log I_2/I_1
1	0	0	1	0
1.414	0.15	3	2	0.3
2	0.3	6	4	0.6
4	0.6	12	16	1.2
10	1	20	100	2
100	2	40	10,000	4
1000	3	60	1,000,000	6
1/2	−0.3	−6	1/4	−0.6
1/10	−1	−20	1/100	−2
1/100	−2	−40	1/10,000	−4

This corresponds to a −20 dB signal change. If the amplitude is reduced to 1/2 its original value, this is the same as a −6 dB change, etc. Table 1-6 is expanded in the lower rows to provide decibel levels corresponding to fractional amplitude and intensity ratios.

One of the conveniences of decibel notation is that it compresses the range of numbers that must be used when large differences in amplitude or intensity are found. This compression of the number scale should be apparent in Table 1-6.

The 3-dB rule

Another noteworthy fact from the table: whenever the intensity changes by 3 dB, this corresponds to a doubling of the intensity. If the original intensity produced at some point in the beam of a transducer is 20 mW/cm², a 3-dB increase in the output of the machine results in a new intensity of 40 mW/cm²; another 3-dB increase results in an intensity of 80 mW/cm², etc. Conversely, whenever the intensity or the power decreases by 3 dB, this halves the quantity. If the original intensity were 20 mW/cm², a 3-dB decrease results in an intensity of 10 mW/cm², another 3-dB decrease halves the intensity again, this time to 5 mW/cm², etc.

> A 3-dB increase (decrease) in the intensity and the power multiplies (divides) the intensity and power by 2.

In summary, decibels do not represent absolute signal levels but quantitatively describe the *ratio* of two amplitudes or intensities. The decibel notation is used to express the amplification or gain of an amplifier. Decibels are also used to calibrate output power controls on instruments and to express ultrasonic attenuation in tissue.

ATTENUATION OF ULTRASOUND BEAMS IN TISSUE

As a sound beam traverses tissue, its amplitude and intensity are reduced as a function of distance (Figure 1-27). The general term for this decrease in amplitude with increasing distance traveled is **attenuation.**

Sources of attenuation

There are two sources of sound beam attenuation in body tissues: (1) reflection and scatter at interfaces, and (2) absorption.

Reflection and scatter of sound at tissue interfaces can contribute to attenuation. In some situations (e.g., in the presence of small calcifications or stones) reflective losses may contribute substantially. For large organs, however, reflection and scatter apparently contribute less significantly, although their exact contribution to the total attenuation has not yet been determined exactly.

An important source of attenuation in tissue is **absorption,** whereby acoustic energy is converted to heat energy. (Under ordinary circumstances with diagnostic ultrasound, the amount of heat produced is too small to cause a measurable temperature change.) This means the sound energy is lost and cannot be recovered.

Attenuation coefficient

The degree of sound beam attenuation in a tissue is usually given in decibels per centimeter (dB/cm). This is illustrated in Figure 1-28. Echoes from two reflectors separated by a distance of 1 cm are shown. A sound beam would travel twice this distance, or 2 cm, in its back-and-forth journey between the reflectors. If the reflectors are "equal," that is, if they are of equal size, have the same orientation, and have the same reflection coefficient, they would produce about the same sized echo in the absence of attenuation. However, attenuation has caused the echo from reflector 2 to be a certain dB level smaller than the echo from reflector 1. The attenuation coefficient for a tissue, expressed in dB/cm, quantifies this change in signal amplitude.

Typical values reported for the ultrasonic attenuation coefficients in soft tissues are given in Table 1-7.[2-5]

More complete compilations are provided by Goss, Johnston, and Dunn.[3] The values in Table 1-7 are for a frequency of 1 MHz. At this frequency the attenuation coefficient of water is very low, that of organ parenchyma (e.g., the liver) is intermediate, and that of muscle is somewhat higher.

Much of the present information on attenuation in tissues is based on measurements of excised organs. Techniques are being developed to allow measurements in vivo. Results obtained with these techniques suggest that in vivo attenuation coefficients may be somewhat lower than the above values.[4]

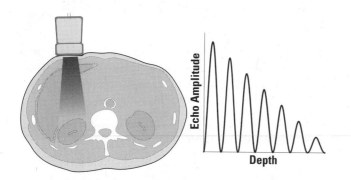

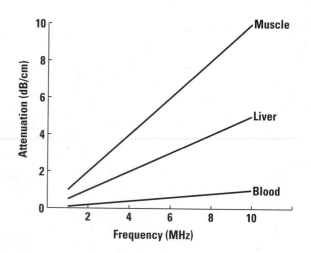

Figure 1-27. Reduction of echoes with increasing depth in tissue due to attenuation.

Figure 1-29. Ultrasound attenuation vs. frequency for several tissues. Attenuation is approximately proportional to frequency, meaning the attenuation coefficient at 5 MHz is two times the attenuation coefficient at 2.5 MHz, that at 7 MHz is two times the attenuation coefficient at 3.5 MHz, etc.

Table 1-7. Ultrasound attenuation coefficient of various tissues

Tissue	Attenuation at 1 MHz (dB/cm)
Water	0.0002
Blood	0.18
Liver	0.5
Muscle	1.2

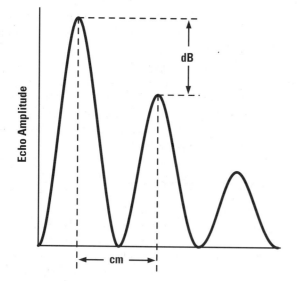

Figure 1-28. The attenuation coefficient is specified in dB/cm.

As a rough guide, we find that for most soft tissues the attenuation coefficient is near 0.5 to 1 dB/cm at 1 MHz.[3-5]

Frequency dependence of attenuation

Attenuation in soft tissues is highly dependent on the ultrasonic frequency. In most cases attenuation is nearly *proportional* to the frequency, tracing out curves as shown in Figure 1-29. Thus if the attenuation coefficient for a tissue is given at a frequency of 1 MHz, it doubles at 2 MHz, quintuples at 5 MHz, and so on.

Figure 1-30 presents two images of the same region in an adult liver; one image is obtained using a 5-MHz transducer, the other using a 3.5-MHz probe. The increased attenuation with increasing frequency results in poorer "penetration" into tissues with the higher frequency. This dependence of ultrasonic attenuation on frequency represents one of the limitations imposed on diagnostic ultrasound. We shall see in Chapter 2 that the best

spatial detail (spatial resolution) in ultrasound is obtained when imaging is done at high ultrasound frequencies. However, it has just been pointed out that high ultrasound frequencies are accompanied by high attenuation losses. This prohibits their use at anything but very superficial tissue levels. The frequency range used in most scanning applications is a compromise between attenuation losses in tissue and spatial resolution requirements.

Calculating attenuation

To determine the amount of attenuation occurring when a sound beam passes through a given thickness of tissue, simply multiply the attenuation coefficient (in dB/cm) by the distance traveled (cm). Thus

$$\text{Attenuation (dB)} = \alpha(\text{dB/cm}) \times d(\text{cm}) \quad (1\text{-}12)$$

where α is the attenuation coefficient and d the distance.

Example: Calculate the attenuation for a 1-MHz beam traversing 10 cm of water.

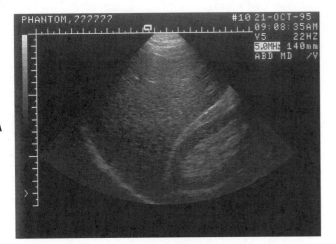
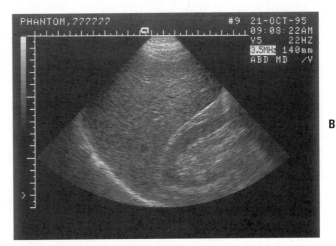

Figure 1-30. B-mode images of the liver taken with a 5-MHz transducer (A), and a 3.5-MHz transducer (B). Much better penetration is found at 3.5 than 5 MHz because of the higher attenuation at 5 MHz.

Solution:

Attenuation = 0.0002 dB/cm × 10 cm = 0.002 dB
(a very small attenuation)

Example: Calculate the attenuation for a 1-MHz beam traversing 10 cm of muscle.
Solution:

Attenuation = 1.2 dB/cm × 10 cm = 12 dB

Example: If the frequency were raised to 5 MHz, what would the attenuation in the previous example be?
Solution: The attenuation coefficient at 5 MHz is 5 times that at 1 MHz, so

Attenuation = (1.2 dB/cm) × 5 × 10 cm = 60 dB

It is left as an exercise for you to use Table 1-6 to compare the amplitude ratios for the two circumstances. The problem of beam penetration at higher frequencies should be apparent when considering the last two examples.

WAVE INTERFERENCE

When waves are produced by more than one source, they may overlap and produce **interference.** The effect at any point is a wave whose amplitude may be greater or less than that of either wave alone, depending on the relative **phase** of the two waves.

To see how this applies, consider the two sine waves of the same frequency depicted in Figure 1-31. On the left, the waves are exactly in phase, although their ampli-

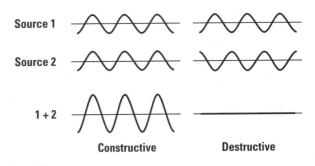
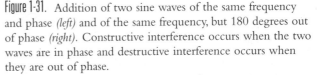

Figure 1-31. Addition of two sine waves of the same frequency and phase *(left)* and of the same frequency, but 180 degrees out of phase *(right).* Constructive interference occurs when the two waves are in phase and destructive interference occurs when they are out of phase.

tudes are slightly different. Their net effect at the point shown is just the sum of the individual waves, added point by point. On the right part of the diagram the waves are completely out of phase. The positive part of one wave occurs exactly during the negative part of the other. This method by which waves add together is termed *interference.* Interference may be *constructive* or *destructive,* depending on the relative phase of the individual waves. Completely destructive interference occurs on the right of Figure 1-31.

References

1. *Webster's ninth new collegiate dictionary,* Springfield, MA, 1986, Merriam Webster.
2. Wells PNT: *Biomedical ultrasonics,* New York, 1977, Academic Press.

3. Goss S, Johnston R, Dunn F: Comprehensive compilation of empirical ultrasonic properties of mammalian tissue, *J Acoust Soc Am* 64:423, 1978.
4. Ophir J: Measurements of ultrasound attenuation in human liver tissue, *Ultrasonic Imaging* 1986.
5. Robinson D, Wilson L, Kossoff G: Shadowing and enhancement in ultrasonic echograms by reflection and refraction, *J Clin Ultrasound* 9:181, 1981.

Questions for Review

1. "Mechanical energy transmitted by pressure waves in a medium" is an accurate description for:

   A. Audible sound only
   B. All types of sound
   C. Ultrasound waves only
   D. High-energy sound waves only

2. Sound waves can travel through each of the following except:

   A. Air
   B. Water
   C. Vacuum
   D. Steel

3. Which of the following properties are common to all sound sources?

   A. They are larger than the wavelength
   B. They cause vibrations in the medium
   C. They produce transverse waves
   D. They cannot move back and forth

4. The speed of sound depends on which one of the following?

   A. Wavelength
   B. Frequency
   C. Medium
   D. Amplitude

5. In a sound wave, regions where the pressure is higher than normal are called regions of:

   A. Rarefaction
   B. Attenuation
   C. Compression
   D. Constructive interference

6. Which of the following is a type of sound wave that can propagate through soft tissue?

   A. Transverse wave
   B. Longitudinal wave
   C. Shear wave
   D. Radio wave

7. Units for pressure are:

   A. Joules
   B. Newtons
   C. Pascals
   D. None of these; pressure is unitless

8. The time for one cycle of a wave is the:

   A. Duty factor
   B. Period
   C. Wave duration
   D. Phase

9. If the frequency is 1 MHz, the period is:

   A. 1,000,000 s
   B. 100 s
   C. 0.01 s
   D. 0.000001 s

10. Deci-, centi-, milli-, and micro- mean:

    A. 100, 1,000, 0.1, and 0.000001
    B. 0.1, 100, 0.001, and 0.000001
    C. 0.1, 0.01, 0.001, and 0.000001
    D. 10, 100, 0.001, and 0.000001

11. Which of the following lists correctly arranges the materials according to their speeds of sound, from lowest to highest?

    A. Water, tissue, bone, air
    B. Bone, air, tissue, water
    C. Air, bone, water, tissue
    D. Air, water, tissue, bone

12. The average speed of sound in soft tissue is taken to be:

    A. 1300 m/s
    B. 1460 m/s
    C. 1540 m/s
    D. 450 m/s

13. The distance a wave travels during one period of oscillation of the source is the:

    A. Period
    B. Wavelength
    C. Speed of sound
    D. Depth of penetration

14. The wavelength for a 5 MHz sound wave in tissue is about:

    A. 0.3 mm
    B. 3 mm
    C. 1.54 m
    D. 1.54 mm

15. If the frequency doubles, the wavelength

    A. Doubles
    B. Halves
    C. Increases by four times
    D. Does not change

16. The acoustic impedance is found by multiplying the:

    A. Attenuation by the speed of sound
    B. Density by the speed of sound
    C. Density by the wave amplitude
    D. Speed of sound by the particle displacement

17. If the density of Material B is 10% greater than that of Material A, and they have equal speeds of sound and attenuation values, the impedance of B is _____ that of A.

    A. The same as
    B. 1% higher than
    C. 10% lower than
    D. 20% higher than

18. If the impedance on one side of an interface is two times the impedance on the other, the amplitude reflection coefficient is:

    A. 1
    B. 0.33
    C. 0.1
    D. 0.033

19. About what percent of the incident intensity is reflected at a soft tissue–bone interface?

    A. 2% or less
    B. Between 10% and 60%
    C. 100%
    D. 200%

20. About what percent of the incident intensity is reflected at a soft tissue–soft tissue interface?

    A. 2% or less
    B. Between 10% and 60%
    C. 100%
    D. 200%

21. About what percent of the incident intensity is reflected at a soft tissue–air interface?

    A. 2% or less
    B. Between 10% and 60%
    C. 100%
    D. 200%

22. In order to produce refraction what condition(s) must be met at an interface?

    A. Perpendicular incidence, different sound speeds
    B. Perpendicular incidence, same sound speeds
    C. Nonperpendicular incidence, different acoustic impedances
    D. Nonperpendicular incidence, different sound speeds
    E. Perpendicular incidence, different acoustic impedances

23. Snell's law predicts:

    A. The direction of the reflected beam
    B. The amplitude of the incident beam
    C. The direction of the transmitted beam
    D. The amplitude of the transmitted beam

24. For angles between 0 degrees and 90 degrees, as the angle increases, the sine of that angle:

    A. Does not change
    B. Increases
    C. Decreases

25. The best way to describe the role of ultrasonic scattering in diagnostic imaging is it:

    A. Gives rise to diagnostic information
    B. Is responsible for echo enhancement
    C. Must be eliminated to provide clear detail
    D. Results in greater acoustic exposure to the patient

26. Interfaces that scatter ultrasonic energy are usually considered those that:

    A. Are much larger than the ultrasound beam
    B. Are much larger than the wavelength
    C. Are the size of or smaller than the wavelength
    D. Surround soft tissue–bone interfaces

27. One advantage a diffuse reflector provides over a specular reflector is it:

    A. Exhibits less angular dependence of the reflection
    B. Does not attenuate the ultrasound beam
    C. Exhibits a greater acoustic impedance change
    D. Intersects only a small fraction of the beam

28. Decibels provide a convenient way to express the _____ two amplitudes or intensities.

    A. Sum of
    B. Difference between
    C. Product of
    D. Ratio of

29. Which statement is INCORRECT regarding ultrasound absorption?

    A. It is part of attenuation
    B. Sound energy is converted to heat
    C. It increases when the frequency increases
    D. It is greater in fluid cavities than in soft tissue

30. The rate of attenuation, or the attenuation coefficient, is expressed in:

    A. $\mu W/cm^2$
    B. μW
    C. dB/cm
    D. dB/cm^2

31. If the attenuation coefficient of a tissue is 0.5 dB/cm at 1 MHz, it is probably about _____ at 5 MHz.

    A. 0.1 dB/cm
    B. 0.5 dB/cm
    C. 2.5 dB/cm
    D. 12.25 dB/cm

32. Echo "enhancement" results from a structure having a:

    A. Higher speed of sound than adjacent material
    B. Higher acoustical impedance than adjacent material
    C. Lower attenuation than surrounding material
    D. Greater absorption rate than surrounding tissue

33. The attenuation of an ultrasound pulse traveling 12 cm in a tissue that has an attenuation coefficient of 1 dB/cm is:

    A. $1/12$ dB
    B. 1 dB
    C. 12 dB
    D. 13 dB

34. Which of the following conditions are MINIMAL REQUIREMENTS for a sound wave to be classified as ultrasound?

    A. Frequency above 10 kHz
    B. Frequency above 20 kHz
    C. Frequency above 10 kHz; intensity greater than 1 W/m^2
    D. A frequency above 20 kHz; longitudinal waves
    E. Frequency above 20 kHz; underwater propagation

Chapter 2

Properties of Ultrasound Transducers

Spatial resolution refers to how closely positioned two reflectors or echogenic regions can be and still be identified as separate reflectors on an image . . . The design and operation of the ultrasound transducer is the most important factor in determining the spatial resolution.

The general term **transducer** refers to any device that is used to convert signals or energy from one form to another. In medicine many different types of transducers are used to measure patient or laboratory data. Most of these respond to the parameter of interest (e.g., pressure, electrolyte levels, or movement) by converting detected values into electrical signals, which can be applied to electronic instruments for processing and display. **Ultrasonic transducers** convert acoustic energy to electrical signals (Figure 2-1, *A*) and electrical energy to acoustic energy (Figure 2-1, *B*) They are used both as detectors and as transmitters of ultrasonic waves.

PIEZOELECTRIC TRANSDUCERS

The piezoelectric effect

Transducers used in medical ultrasound employ the *piezoelectric effect* to generate sound waves and detect echo signals. The piezoelectric effect was discovered in the 1880s by Pierre and Jacques Curie. They found that when a force is applied perpendicular to the faces of a quartz crystal, an electrical charge results. This charge can be detected and amplified, producing a useful electrical signal (Figure 2-2). Conversely, if an electrical signal is applied to the crystal (Figure 2-3), the crystal vibrates, sending a sound wave into the medium. Hence the dual action of piezoelectric transducers as detectors and transmitters of acoustic signals.

A number of naturally occurring materials, including quartz and a substance called *tourmaline,* are piezoelectric. These were used for transducers in the early days of med-

ical ultrasound. Quartz is still found in transducers that are used for precision acoustic measurements in the laboratory and occasionally in transducers intended for high-power applications. However, in diagnostic ultrasound quartz has been superseded by *piezoelectric ceramic* transducer elements.[1]

Ceramic elements

Ceramic elements, such as **lead zirconate titanate** (PZT), consist of mixtures of microscopic crystals randomly oriented throughout the volume of the element (Figure 2-4). Mechanically these materials are somewhat brittle and may be damaged if dropped or pounded. During manufacturing they can be shaped into various configurations, such as rectangular slabs, planar disks, or concave disks. The shape can be optimized for the scan-head frequency, size, and type.

To be useful for transmitting and receiving ultrasound waves, these ceramics must first be polarized. This is done by heating the material above what is called the *Curie temperature* (365° C for PZT), which frees the microscopic crystals, allowing them to move. A high voltage is then applied across the element, producing partial alignment, or **polarization,** of the microscopic crystals, as shown in Figure 2-4. The element is then cooled with the voltage still applied. It will now remain polarized and exhibit the desired piezoelectric properties.

The element can lose its piezoelectric properties (become depolarized) if it is inadvertently heated above the Curie temperature. (See section on damage to transducers later in this chapter.)

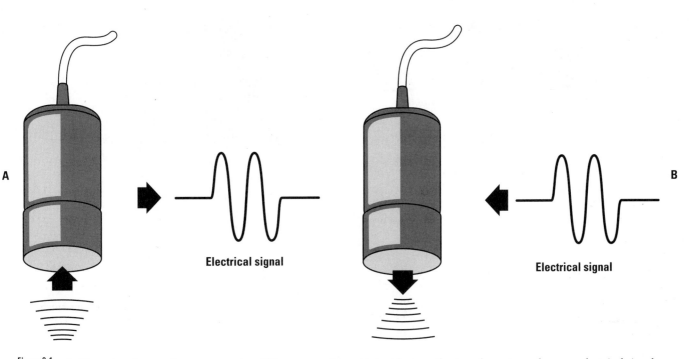

Figure 2-1. **A,** Piezoelectric transducer as a receiver. When a sound wave is incident on the transducer, it produces an electrical signal. **B,** Piezoelectric transducer as a transmitter. When an electrical signal is applied to the transducer, it vibrates, producing sound waves.

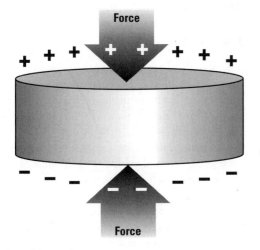

Figure 2-2. The piezoelectric effect; a force applied to a piezoelectric element produces an electrical signal.

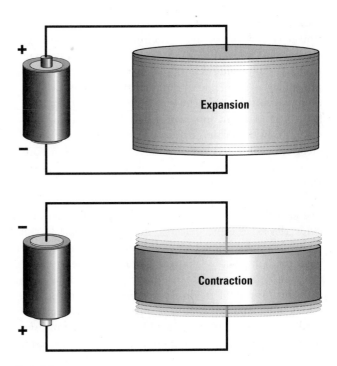

Figure 2-3. Reverse piezoelectric effect; an electrical signal applied to the piezoelectric crystal causes it to vibrate.

Unpolarized **Polarized**

Figure 2-4. Cartoon depiction of a piezoelectric ceramic transducer element before polarization *(left)* and after polarization *(right)*. Polarization produces partial alignment of the microscopic crystals. (The size of the crystals is exaggerated in this depiction.)

Composite piezoelectric materials

A new type of transducer element, a "composite ceramic," is now used in many transducers and ultrasound scanheads.[2] The composite is a mixture of a piezoelectric ceramic and another material, such as epoxy. It is formed by grinding grooves into the face of a standard piezoelectric element, leaving behind rods or posts. The space between the rods is then filled with epoxy (Figure 2-5). The resulting element is lighter in weight than the original ceramic. Ceramic-epoxy composites appear to have several advantages over ordinary piezoelectric ceramics. First, they have a lower acoustic impedance than ordinary ceramic (Table 2-1). This makes it easier to match the impedance of the transducer to that of tissue, which is important for efficient transmission of sound waves into tissue. (See later section regarding impedance matching.) Second, transducers with piezoelectric composite elements can be made to have very wide frequency bandwidths; the same transducer can operate at different frequencies, or it can be made to emit pulses that have a very short duration. So-called matched impedance, broad bandwidth transducers now available commercially usually have piezoelectric composite elements. Third, in many cases composites appear to be more sensitive than standard piezoelectric ceramic materials.[2]

One other type of piezoelectric material is important in medical ultrasound engineering. Polyvinylidene difluoride (PVF₂) is a piezoelectric material available in thin membranes that look like plastic wrap. This material is used for constructing miniature **hydrophones,**[3] which are small ultrasound transducers for measuring the acoustic output of medical ultrasound equipment (see Chapter 9). The advantage of this material is that very small transducer detectors, useful for probing and measuring the beam of diagnostic transducers, can be made from it. Until now only limited use has been made of PVF₂ as an actual transmit-receive transducer, apparently because of its suboptimal sensitivity.[3]

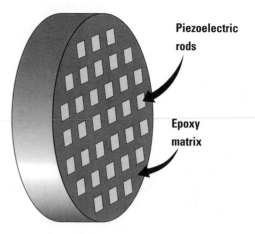

Piezoelectric rods

Epoxy matrix

Figure 2-5. Composite piezoelectric element, consisting of grooves cut into the face of a piezoelectric element, leaving piezoelectric rods. The space between the rods is filled with epoxy. (The size of and distance between the rods are much smaller and the rods are more numerous than in this cartoon depiction.)

Table 2-1. Acoustic impedances of materials relevant to transducer design

Material	Impedance (rayls)
Piezoelectric ceramic (PZT)	30×10^6
Backing material (without impedance-matching layers on transducer face)	Matched to that of the ceramic element
Matching layers for PZT★	7×10^6
Typical soft tissue	1.7×10^6
Piezoelectric composite material★	10×10^6

★Actual values may differ depending on manufacturing techniques.

TRANSDUCER CONSTRUCTION

Basic components

Some general properties of transducer design transducer used in pulse-echo work, a single-element, nonfocused probe. In later sections focusing techniques, transducer arrays, and transducer designs for continuous wave Doppler applications will be brought out.

Single-element transducers are used in some M-mode, ophthalmological, and pulsed Doppler applications. A few are shown in Figure 2-6, *A*. A sketch of a single-element nonfocused transducer is presented in Figure 2-6, *B*. The piezoelectric element for this application is a flat circular disk. The element is mounted coaxially in a cylindrical case, and the ultrasound beam travels to the right in the diagram. Acoustic insulation such as rubber or cork is necessary to avoid coupling ultrasonic energy to the case. A metal elec-

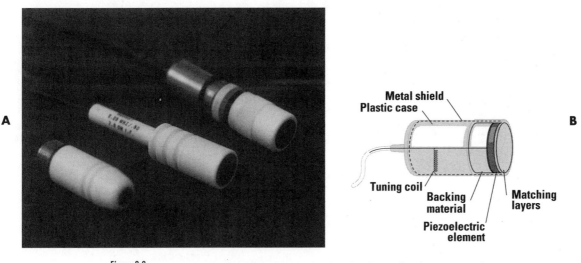

Figure 2-6. **A,** Single-element transducers; **B,** sketch of a single-element transducer.

trical shield prevents pickup of extraneous electrical noise signals by the transducer leads. Such signals are undesirable because they contribute to excessive noise on a display during echo detection. Wires that connect to a tuning coil and then to the external connectors provide electrical contact between the transducer element and the instrument.

Resonance frequency

A piezoelectric transducer has a resonance frequency at which it is most efficient in converting electrical energy to acoustic energy and vice versa. The resonance frequency is determined mainly by the *thickness* of the piezoelectric element. Analogous to strings on a guitar, thin elements have high resonance frequencies, and thick elements have lower resonance frequencies (Figure 2-7). Transducers usually are operated at or near the resonance frequency of the element. Thus the elements contained within a high-frequency transducer must be thinner than those in low-frequency transducers.

Some broadbandwidth transducers are designed to be operated at more than one frequency. With these transducers, the ultrasound instrument itself (Figure 2-8) determines the sound wave frequency emitted. The operator chooses the examination frequency by selecting a control on the instrument. This causes the instrument's transmitter to shape the electrical pulse applied to the transducer for the frequency selected; the amplifiers in the receiver (see Chapter 3) also may be tuned to this frequency.

Backing material

Pulse-echo transducers are excited by short bursts of electrical energy from a pulse transmitter in the ultrasound instrument. In response to this excitation pulse, the transducer element "rings," vibrating at its resonance fre-

quency. This sends a "pulse" of sound into the medium. For most applications it is desirable to produce pulses of very short duration. This optimizes the axial resolving capabilities of the transducer.

The pulse duration may be minimized by **damping** the vibration of the transducer as quickly as possible following each excitation. The backing material of some transducers plays a major role in damping out the transducer element's vibrations. Just as when you place your hand on a bell its ringing is quickly dampened, the backing material stops the ringing of the transducer after excitation. To facilitate this role, the backing material needs to have two properties. First, its acoustic impedance must be comparable to the impedance of the piezoelectric element (Table 2-1). This reduces reflections at the transducer–backing material interface so that any energy propagated in the backward direction is transmitted out of the element. Second, it must absorb the sound waves transmitted into it. A heavy, sound-absorbing backing material serves to damp the vibrations of the piezoelectric element, resulting in short-duration acoustic pulses transmitted into the medium.

Figure 2-9 illustrates transducer pulses following light and heavy damping. We will see later that for imaging applications, the "best" approaches are those that result in short duration pulses, such as shown here with heavy damping.

Quarter-wave impedance-matching layers

Most transducers have **impedance-matching layers** to improve their sensitivity, that is, their ability to detect very weak echoes. Impedance-matching layers provide efficient transmission of sound waves from the transducer element to soft tissue and vice versa. They do this by reducing reflections at the transducer-tissue interface.

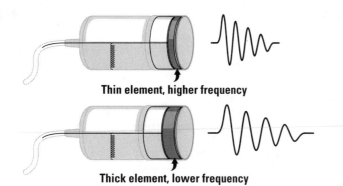

Figure 2-7. Resonance frequency and thickness of the transducer element.

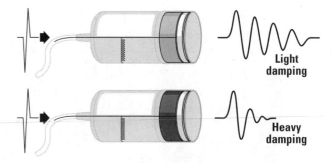

Figure 2-9. Role of damping material (or the *backing layer*) in producing short-duration ultrasound pulses.

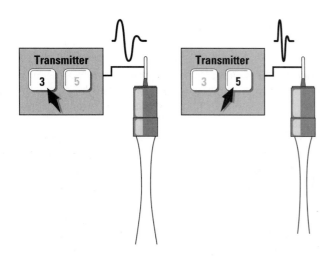

Figure 2-8. Multifrequency operation for a broadbandwidth transducer. The frequency of the beam is determined by the frequency of the transmit pulse. Tuning of the receiver (see Chapter 3) also helps select the frequency.

Inspection of Table 2-1 shows that the acoustic impedance of piezoelectric ceramics, such as PZT, is about 20 times the impedance of soft tissue. This is a significant mismatch, producing a reflection coefficient of 0.82 if an element were used in contact with the skin surface. Thus the large acoustic impedance difference between transducer element and skin would result in much of the energy produced by the transducer reflected back into the element. A plastic protective layer covered the element in some older transducer designs. This improved the transmission somewhat but did not provide the best results possible.

Transmission of sound into soft tissue is optimized when impedance-matching layers are attached to the transducer element. A typical matching layer design for a solid PZT element is shown in Figure 2-10. As shown in the diagram, the layer is $1/4$ the wavelength of the ultrasound beam. The layer makes it "appear" to the trans-

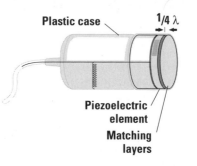

Figure 2-10. Design of matching layers on the face of a transducer.

ducer that the tissue has the same impedance as the piezoelectric element (hence the term *impedance matching*). A single quarter-wave matching layer has the following properties:

1. Its acoustic impedance, Z_m, is intermediate between the impedance of the transducer element, Z_t, and the impedance of soft tissue, Z_{st}. (Actually $Z_m = \sqrt{Z_{st} \times Z_t}$ is the appropriate value. But just remember that the matching layer impedance should be between the impedances of the element and the tissue.)
2. Its thickness exactly equals one fourth of the ultrasonic wavelength in the layer.

If these properties are present, there is no reflection at a soft tissue–transducer interface; hence sound transmission is very efficient.

As will be seen later in this chapter, a pulsed transducer emits not a single ultrasonic frequency but rather a *spectrum* of frequencies. A single quarter-wave matching layer is exactly one-quarter wavelength only for one frequency. Thus all frequencies in a pulsed waveform are not efficiently transmitted with a single matching layer. Transducer manufacturers overcome this problem by designing transducers with *multiple* matching layers adhered to the face of the element. Multiple matching layers provide efficient sound transmission between the piezoelectric element and soft tissue for a range, or spectrum, of ultrasound frequencies.

Because the acoustic impedance of composite piezoelectric elements is closer to that of soft tissue, impedance matching is said to be carried out much more efficiently with these newer elements.[2] This is one of the significant advantages of composite transducer material.

Well-designed matching layers can ease the requirements mentioned above for the backing layers. Heavy damping was said to be important for a transducer to provide short-duration pulses. The backing layer does this by removing ultrasonic, vibrational energy from the transducer element. Matching layers actually help here also, because they efficiently transmit sound energy out of the transducer as well. Unlike the backing layer, which must absorb the energy removed from the element, thereby wasting it, the matching layers provide very efficient use of the ultrasonic energy; the energy transmitted out the front of the transducer contributes to the useful ultrasound beam. Transducer engineers vary the properties of both the backing layer and the matching layers in optimizing their probe designs.

TRANSDUCER FREQUENCY CHARACTERISTICS

The damping material in a pulsed transducer is somewhat analogous to having your hand on a bell after you ring it in order to stop the vibrations of the bell. Without your hand on the bell, its ringing produces a long, clean tone.

However, with your hand on it, (Figure 2-11) the sound loses its tonal qualities and you hear only a short, dull "click" when the bell is rung. The sound tonal qualities, that is, the frequencies produced by the bell when it is heavily dampened, are very different from those produced when it is allowed to ring steadily.

A dampened ultrasound transducer produces a short pulse (Figure 2-12, *A*) or burst of sound each time it is driven electrically. Analogous to the dampened bell's sound, the resultant sound pulse is more like an ultrasonic "click" than a steady sound at a single frequency. This means the pulse of ultrasound energy does not contain one pure frequency, but is composed of a range, or spectrum, of frequencies. For example, the sound pulse transmitted by a 5 MHz pulsed transducer contains energy not only at 5 MHz, but at frequencies both above and below the nominal frequency of the transducer, covering a fairly wide spectrum.

The frequency range represented in the pulse is described in terms of the **frequency bandwidth** of the ultrasound transducer. The bandwidth may be determined by **spectral analysis** of the sound pulse. Figure 2-12, *B* shows a typical spectral plot. The spectral display represents a plot of the fraction of signal within a given frequency interval versus the frequency. The curve usually peaks out at the resonance frequency of the transducer, with a gradual decline on either side of the maximum value.

The frequency bandwidth is a measure of the spread of frequencies in the plot. Another important measure of

Figure 2-11. When you dampen the ringing of a bell, for example, by holding your hand on it as shown, you hear an indistinct "click" rather than a pure tone.

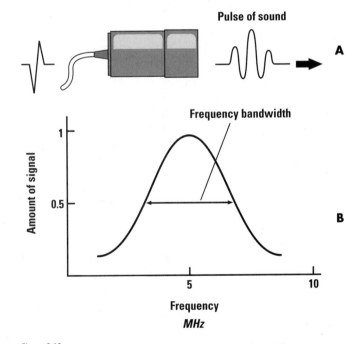

Figure 2-12. **A,** Short-duration acoustic pulse produced by a transducer. **B,** Spectral analysis of signal in **A,** showing distribution of ultrasound frequencies in the pulse. The degree of spread is described by the frequency bandwidth.

a pulse is its duration, the length of time from its beginning to its end. Figure 2-13 depicts three different pulse durations. It turns out that for a given resonance frequency, the shorter the pulse duration, the wider the frequency bandwidth. Conversely, the longer the pulse duration, the narrower the frequency bandwidth. This is also depicted in Figure 2-13 for the three pulse durations.

Another measure of the frequency bandwidth is the transducer Q, or quality factor. The Q is defined as the ratio of the transducer center frequency to its bandwidth. For a fixed center frequency, the wider the frequency bandwidth, the lower the Q. The narrower the bandwidth, the higher the Q. Low Q transducers are used in pulse-echo ultrasound applications, such as ultrasound imaging.

TRANSDUCERS AND SPATIAL RESOLUTION

Spatial detail in ultrasound

A pulse of ultrasound emitted by a transducer travels through the medium in a well-directed beam (Figure 2-14). In ultrasound imaging, echo signals are received from reflectors throughout the beam path and displayed on a monitor. The time it takes for an echo to return to the transducer fol-

lowing emission of the pulse depends on the reflector depth. Reflectors at different depths are distinguished from one another because of their different echo arrival times.

To produce an image, the ultrasound beam is swept across the region to be scanned, sort of like a searchlight scanning the night sky, as shown by the large arrow in Figure 2-14. The image is constructed using echo arrival times to determine reflector depths and beam axis positions to determine lateral locations of reflectors. This process is discussed more completely in Chapter 3.

Spatial resolution or *reflector resolution* refers to how closely positioned two reflectors or scattering regions can be to one another and still be identified as separate reflectors on an image or other display. We consider initially the axial resolution and the lateral resolution, and show that they depend on different aspects of the imaging process. Later we will consider the elevational resolution, or "slice thickness," yet another important measure of spatial resolution. In each case the design and operation of the ultrasound transducer are the most important factors in determining the spatial resolution.

Choice of ultrasound frequency

Spatial resolution is closely related to the ultrasound frequency; it improves as the frequency is increased. On the other hand, sound beam attenuation also increases when

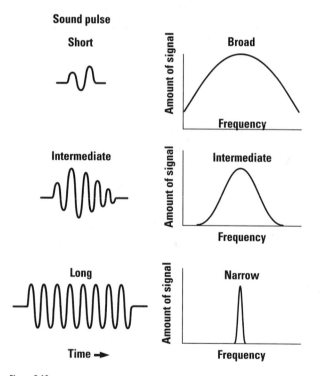

Figure 2-13. Relationship between frequency bandwidth and pulse duration. A short-duration pulse is almost indescript in terms of its frequency; it is represented by a large frequency bandwidth. A long-duration pulse is a purer "tone" with most of the sound at or near a well-defined frequency. An intermediate sized pulse has characteristics between these two extremes.

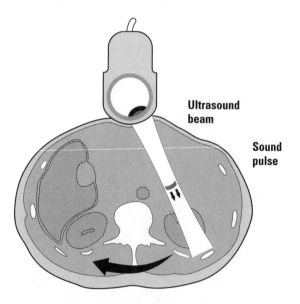

Figure 2-14. Echo data acquisition during production of an ultrasound image. A pulse of ultrasound from a transducer travels in a well-defined beam and echoes are received from its path. During imaging, the sound beam is swept (*big arrow*) across the region being imaged. Echoes appear as dots on the display. This method of ultrasound image generation is followed with all current real-time ultrasound imagers, although the example specifically involves a mechanically scanned beam.

the frequency is increased, so beam penetration decreases. The choice of ultrasound frequency for any examination is the result of a compromise between resolution requirements (where higher frequencies are better) and the ability to obtain satisfactory sound beam penetration (where lower frequencies are better) to image all the tissues of interest.

Axial resolution

Axial resolution refers to the *minimum* reflector spacing *along the axis of an ultrasound sound beam* that results in separate, distinguishable echoes on the display. This is illustrated in Figure 2-15. The top two reflectors can be distinguished on the display. However, echoes from the bottom two merge together; these reflectors are too closely spaced to be resolved. They are closer than the axial resolution limits of the scanner.

Axial resolution is determined by the pulse duration, that is, the duration of the ultrasonic pulses transmitted into the medium by the transducer. The pulse duration, illustrated in Figure 2-16, is simply the time required for the transducer "ringing" to decrease to a negligible level following each excitation. It is equal to the number of cycles in the pulse multiplied by the ultrasound wave period, that is, the amount of time for each cycle. This is expressed as:

$$PD = N_c \times T \qquad (2\text{-}1)$$

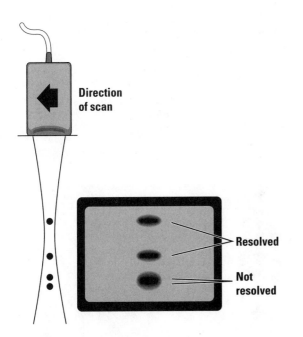

Figure 2-15. Illustration of axial resolution. Axial resolution is the minimum distance between two reflectors positioned along the axis of an ultrasound beam that allows both reflectors to be visualized as separate objects. The two bottom reflectors are not resolved on the image.

where N_c is the number of cycles and T is the wave period. The period in μs is equal to 1 over the frequency when expressed in MHz. Therefore, we can also write:

$$PD = \frac{N_c}{f(\text{MHz})} \ \mu s \qquad (2\text{-}2)$$

where f is the frequency in MHz.

As an example, if N_c is 3 cycles, as in Figure 2-16, and if the frequency is 3 MHz, the pulse duration is 1 μs. On the other hand, if the frequency is 7.5 MHz, the pulse duration is 0.4 μs for a 3-cycle pulse. Generally higher frequencies result in shorter pulse durations than lower frequencies.

If the time-gap between when echo signals arrive from two reflectors at different positions along the beam axis is greater than the pulse duration, the two echoes are distinguished on the display. Figure 2-17 illustrates this. The top panel depicts echo pulses from the two reflectors (dark circles) approaching the transducer. The length of each echo pulse (sometimes called the *spatial pulse length*) is determined by the pulse duration. For this situation the two echo pulses are spaced far enough apart so they will arrive separately and be resolved. The middle panel represents a situation where the reflectors are more closely spaced. With the same pulse duration as for the top panel, these echo pulses overlap and the reflectors cannot be resolved. However, if the pulse duration is smaller (lower panel), echo pulses even for this reflector spacing can be distinguished.

Whatever the manufacturer can do to reduce the pulse duration leads to an improvement in the axial resolution. For a given transducer frequency, short pulses are obtained by rapidly damping the "ringing" of the transducer after it is excited, making N_c, the number of cycles in the pulse, small. This is illustrated in Figure 2-18. The axial resolution for a 3-cycle pulse is better than that of a 6-cycle pulse of the same frequency.

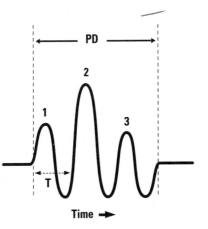

Figure 2-16. Pulse duration, PD. The pulse duration equals the number of cycles in the pulse (three in this case) times T, the time for each cycle. T is also the wave period.

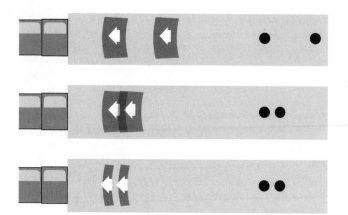

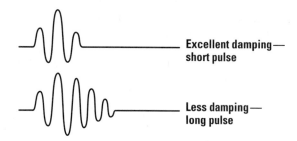

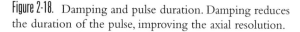

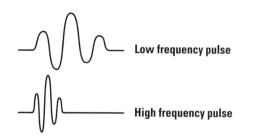

Figure 2-17. Axial resolution and pulse duration. Each panel represents echo pulses arriving from two reflectors *(dark circles)*. The length of each echo pulse depends on the pulse duration. In the top panel the echo pulses are well separated; however, in the middle panel the two reflectors are closely positioned and the echo pulses overlap. If a shorter pulse duration is used *(bottom panel),* even this closer spacing between reflectors can be resolved.

Excellent damping— short pulse

Less damping— long pulse

Figure 2-18. Damping and pulse duration. Damping reduces the duration of the pulse, improving the axial resolution.

Low frequency pulse

High frequency pulse

Figure 2-19. Frequency and pulse duration. Increasing the frequency leads to shorter pulse durations and better axial resolution.

Because the pulse duration is inversely proportional to the frequency, increasing the ultrasound frequency shortens the pulse duration, as demonstrated in Figure 2-19. This also improves the axial resolution.

The dependence of axial resolution on frequency is easily demonstrated in a test phantom. Figure 2-20, *A* illustrates a target arrangement available in some phan-

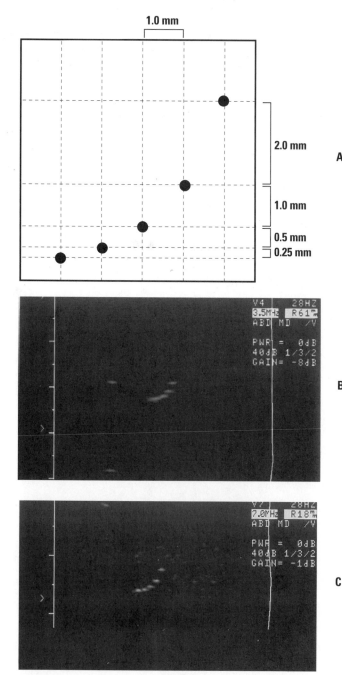

Figure 2-20. **A,** Reflectors in a test object for studying axial resolution. **B,** Image using a 3.5 MHz transducer. **C,** Image using a 7.0-MHz transducer.

toms for estimating resolution. Figure 2-20, *B* shows an ultrasound image of this group of targets scanned using a 3.5-MHz transducer, while Figure 2-20, *C* is for a 7.0-MHz probe. The improved clarity with the 7.0-MHz transducer is evident.

The best axial resolution is obtained with a short-duration pulse. However, we also have learned that the shorter the pulse duration, the wider the frequency bandwidth of the pulse. Therefore, we can summarize a relationship between pulse duration, axial resolution, and frequency bandwidth as follows:

Pulse duration	Axial resolution	Frequency bandwidth
Long	Poorer	Narrow
Short	Better	Wide

Lateral resolution

Lateral resolution refers to the ability to distinguish two closely spaced reflectors that are positioned *perpendicular* to the axis of the ultrasound beam. Lateral resolution is most closely related to the transducer *beam width*.

The relationship between lateral resolution and beam width is illustrated in Figure 2-21. Three small reflectors are being imaged. Each traces out a line on the display, the length of the line equals the width of the ultrasound beam.

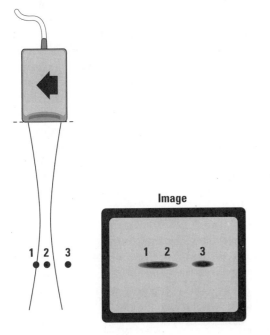

Figure 2-21. Illustration of lateral resolution and its dependence on beam width. Lateral resolution refers to how closely positioned two reflectors can be perpendicular to the beam axis and be seen as separate objects on an ultrasound image. Echoes from reflectors 1 and 2 blend together and the reflectors are not resolved. Reflectors 2 and 3 are resolved.

If the reflectors are far enough apart, that is, if they are separated more laterally than the beam width, then they are resolved on the display. This is the case for the two reflectors on the right. On the other hand, the two reflectors on the left are closer than the beam width; their images merge together on the display and the reflectors are not resolved.

TRANSDUCER BEAM CHARACTERISTICS

Beam directivity

We saw in the previous section that the beam width affects the lateral resolution in an ultrasound image. In this section we will examine the sound beam pattern for single-element, unfocused transducers and study how the width of the beam at different depths depends on the frequency and diameter of the ultrasound transducer. Single-element, unfocused transducers were used in many early scanners, though they are seldom used today. However, the general properties of ultrasound beams studied in this section set the stage for understanding beams from focused transducers and beams from transducer arrays, discussed later.

Many sources of audible sound appear as "point sources"; the sound energy emitted radiates outward in all directions (Figure 2-22). Bells, loudspeakers, the ringer in a telephone, and human voices all have this character. An ultrasound beam produced by a medical transducer, on the other hand, is very *directional*. With a single-element transducer, for example, most of the acoustic energy in the beam is confined to a region close to the transducer axis, as suggested in the diagram in Figure 2-21, in the search

Figure 2-22. Audible source of sound (telephone ringer), where the sound waves spread out in all directions. You can hear the sound at any angle because the waves radiate out in all directions.

light analogy mentioned earlier and in Figure 2-14. This is fortunate because it allows ultrasound images to be built up by sweeping the beam across the region to be imaged.

Huygen wavelets

Engineers and physicists sometimes describe an ultrasound beam by conceptually dividing the transducer face into a large collection of point sources (Figure 2-23). A diverging wave emanates from each source. The strength of the beam at any position in the transducer field is found by mathematically adding together the contributions from each point source on the transducer surface. The point sources are referred to as *Huygen sources,* and the individual diverging waves as *Huygen wavelets.*

Near the end of Chapter 1 the phenomenon of interference of waves produced by two different sources was discussed. It was mentioned that whenever two waves of the same frequency are in phase when they reach a spot, the amplitude at that spot is the sum of the individual wave amplitudes. If the waves are out of phase, destructive interference occurs, with the signals partially or totally canceling each other, depending on their relative amplitudes and phases.

Interference among waves from different points on the surface of the transducer plays a major role in shaping the resultant beam. In some locations the field varies significantly from one point to another; in other areas, the beam is smooth and well behaved. The point-to-point variations in the field are most important in the near field, that is, up close to the transducer, whereas the far-field beam is smoother and better behaved. These regions of a sound beam are discussed in more detail in the next section.

Near field versus far field

The sketch in Figure 2-24 illustrates two zones in the beam of a single-element, unfocused ultrasound trans-

ducer. The near field is also called the *Fresnel zone.* It is characterized by fluctuations in the amplitude and intensity from one point in the beam to another. (The fluctuations are represented in the figure by the wavy lines in the near field.) The beam remains well collimated in the near field, even narrowing down a bit for axial points approaching the NFL, the near-field length.

The region of the beam beyond the near field of a single-element transducer is called the *far-field,* or *Fraunhofer, zone.* Here the beam is smooth, as indicated by the smooth lines in the figure. The beam in the far field also diverges. Divergence is depicted here by the gradual widening of the beam with increasing distance from the transducer.

The length of the near field (NFL) depends on the diameter of the transducer element, d, and on λ, the ultrasound wavelength. The NFL is given by:

$$NFL = \frac{d^2}{4\lambda} \qquad (2\text{-}3)$$

Thus if you have two transducers of the same frequency but different diameters, the larger diameter one will have a longer near-field length. If you have two transducers of the same diameter but different frequencies, the higher frequency transducer, with its shorter wavelength, will have a longer near-field length.

Ultrasound beam characterization is important to the equipment design engineer. One test these individuals do frequently is to probe the ultrasound beam with a reflector and evaluate the distribution of energy in the beam. Experimentally the process is fairly straightforward: a tiny reflector attached to a translation device is positioned a given distance from the transducer, as in Figure 2-25. Starting outside the confines of the beam, the reflector is slowly translated perpendicular to the ultrasound beam axis. At different positions the transducer transmits a sound pulse, an echo signal from the reflector is received, and a measure is obtained of the echo amplitude from this reflector. The experiment is often done with the reflector close to the transducer and then repeated with it placed at various distances.

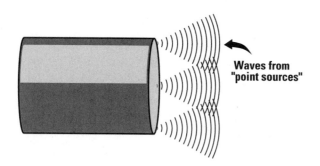

Figure 2-23. Conceptual method used for calculating the properties of a beam from an ultrasound transducer. According to Huygen's principle the beam at any location in the field can be calculated by adding up wavelets from point sources distributed all across the transducer surface. Only three of these sources are included in the diagram.

Figure 2-24. Beam pattern from a single-element, unfocused transducer. The near field is also called the *Fresnel zone,* and the far field is also known as the *Fraunhofer zone.* NFL is the near field length.

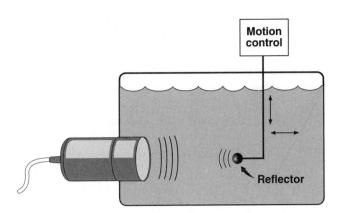

Figure 2-25. Method used by transducer manufacturers to study the field of a transducer. A small reflector is translated perpendicular to the beam axis, and the strength of an echo from the reflector is measured. This usually is done for various axial distances.

You might expect the echo from the reflector to be strongest when the reflector is directly on the axis of the beam. Surprisingly this is not always the case, particularly in the near field! Figure 2-26 illustrates this. Each of the graphs results from one of the reflector passes through the beam. The point *0* on each graph represents the center of the beam and the transducer axis. The first plot within the near field exhibits minima and maxima for different positions of the reflector. This is a manifestation of the roughness of the beam within the near field. At distances approaching the NFL, the beam becomes narrower and smoother. Here the echo from the reflector is strongest when it is in the center of the beam and gradually gets weaker and weaker as the reflector is moved further and further off axis. For an unfocused transducer the best spatial detail, that is, the narrowest beam, is obtained in the region corresponding to the NFL.

Beam profiles obtained in the far field also exhibit smooth curves, as illustrated in Figure 2-26. However, the central peak gets weaker as you look further along the transducer beam axis. The beam also diverges with increasing distance from the transducer, shown by the profile widening out.

The far-field divergence angle, shown by the angle θ in Figure 2-27, also depends on the wavelength and transducer size. It is given by the relationship

$$\sin\theta = \frac{1.2\lambda}{d} \qquad (2\text{-}4)$$

where λ is the wavelength and d the diameter of the transducer. Thus the divergence angle is less severe at higher frequencies, where the wavelength is smaller. Also the divergence angle is less when large diameter transducers are used rather than small diameter probes.

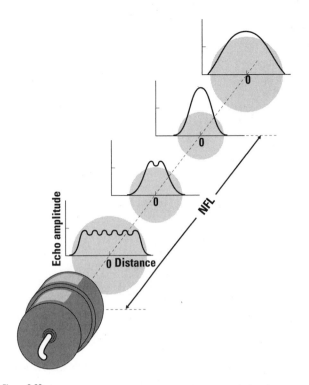

Figure 2-26. Series of beam plots obtained at several depths using the method outlined in Figure 2-25. Each graph depicts the echo amplitude from the reflector versus the distance the reflector is from the beam axis. The narrowest profile occurs at the NFL. (The gray-shaded regions depict the projection of the ultrasound beam at the depth of the plot.)

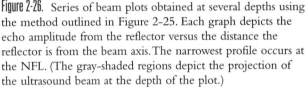

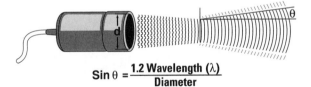

$$\text{Sin } \theta = \frac{1.2 \text{ Wavelength } (\lambda)}{\text{Diameter}}$$

Figure 2-27. Far-field divergence of an unfocused transducer beam. The divergence angle, θ, depends on the wavelength, λ, and the diameter of the transducer, d.

Dependencies on transducer frequency and size

We will illustrate important properties of the transducer beam parameters with some examples.

Example: What is the near field length for a 2.25-MHz 13-mm diameter unfocused transducer?

Solution: You are given the diameter and hence the transducer radius. You need to know the wavelength, λ, before computing the NFL. From Chapter 1, Equation 1-3:

$$\lambda = \frac{c}{f}$$

where c is the speed of sound and f the frequency. First, find

$$\lambda = \frac{1540 \text{ m/s}}{2.25 \times 10^6 \text{ c/s}}$$

$$= 6.8 \times 10^{-4} \text{ m}$$

$$= 0.68 \text{ mm}$$

Then, from Equation 2-3,

$$\text{NFL} = \frac{d^2}{4\lambda}$$

$$= \frac{(13 \text{ mm})^2}{4 \times 0.68 \text{ mm}}$$

$$= 62 \text{ mm}$$

$$= 6.2 \text{ cm}$$

The near field for this transducer extends out to a distance of 6.2 cm. Now consider a similar situation, in which the ultrasound frequency is greater.

Example: What is the near field length for a 5-MHz 13-mm diameter transducer?

Solution: First, compute the wavelength.

$$\lambda = \frac{1540 \text{ m/s}}{5.0 \times 10^6 \text{ c/s}}$$

$$= 3 \times 10^{-4} \text{ m}$$

$$= 0.3 \text{ mm}$$

Again, from Equation 2-3,

$$\text{NFL} = \frac{(13 \text{ mm})^3}{4 \times 0.3 \text{ mm}}$$

$$= 140 \text{ mm}$$

$$= 14 \text{ cm}$$

From these two examples we see that for transducers of the same size, the NFL increases with increasing frequency.

Equation 2-4 above illustrates that the divergence angle also depends on the transducer frequency. The sine of the divergence angle is inversely proportional to the frequency. Since the sine of an angle *increases* with increasing angle (if the angle is between 0 and 90 degrees), as frequency *increases,* the divergence angle *decreases.*

Thus for a given transducer size

1. The NFL increases with increasing frequency.
2. Beam divergence is less for higher frequencies.

The dependence of these two beam characteristics on transducer frequency is illustrated in Figure 2-28.

Perhaps it is counterintuitive that the near field length should extend further for higher frequencies, because higher frequencies do not penetrate into tissue as readily as lower frequencies. Is there an error somewhere in our thought process? Actually these discussions on beam patterns only account for dependencies of the beam on the size of the transducer and on the wavelength, which depends on the frequency. They illustrate that one would like to use as high a frequency as possible in any examination because of the better beam definition at higher frequencies. They vividly point out why abdominal ultrasound examinations are done using 3.5 MHz rather than, say, 100 kHz, because beams from 100-kHz transducers would be very divergent if these transducers were of the standard sizes with which we are acquainted. Nevertheless, the basic discussions on single-element, nonfocused beams do not take attenuation into account; in the real world, attenuation ultimately limits the frequency at which the design engineer—as well as the ultrasonographer—can expect to conduct an ultrasound examination.

The near field length also increases with increasing transducer size. This is seen very readily upon inspection of Equation 2-3 above. Since NFL is proportional to the square of the diameter, doubling the transducer diameter quadruples the NFL. The divergence angle in the far field, on the other hand, *decreases* with increasing transducer diameter, as shown in Equation 2-4. The dependence on transducer diameter may be summarized as follows:

1. For a given frequency the NFL extends farther for larger diameter transducers.
2. For a given frequency, beam divergence in the far field decreases with increasing transducer size.

This behavior is illustrated in Figure 2-29.

The beam patterns shown in Figures 2-28 and 2-29 give some hints about how the lateral resolution behaves with frequency and transducer size. The smaller divergence angle with higher frequencies indicates that lateral resolution is generally improved if higher frequencies are used. Also, at large distances from the transducer (Figure 2-29) a larger-diameter transducer results in better lateral resolution than does a smaller-diameter transducer.

Side lobes

A side lobe is energy in the far field or focal region of an ultrasound transducer that is not part of the main beam. In the beam sketch in Figure 2-24 **side lobes** are shown in the far field. If they are strong, side lobes degrade lateral resolution.

A standard single-element transducer producing continuous sound has side lobes that are about 14% of the main beam. Side lobes of this strength are not good in most ultrasound studies because they significantly degrade resolution. Fortunately side lobes are suppressed significantly below this level. One reason they are suppressed is that we use pulsed transducers rather than continuous wave ones. When a transducer is pulsed rather than operated continuously, side lobes for different frequencies in the pulse spectrum appear at different angles; they literally smear one another out, nearly eliminating them. Thus under normal circumstances they are probably inconsequential to the image.

In applications where additional side lobe reduction is desirable, the manufacturer can choose to apply **apodization.** This is a process whereby the strength of the signal applied to the transducer face is not uniform over the whole surface of the piezoelectric element, but is made to get progressively weaker from the center of the element outward. With single-element transducers special electrical contacts (electrodes) make this possible. With transducer arrays, any needed side lobe reduction through

apodization can be done quite readily during the beam-forming process.

FOCUSED TRANSDUCERS

Having established a basis for how an ultrasound beam is affected by frequency and transducer diameter, we now turn our attention to transducer designs used more frequently by ultrasonographers. The first to be considered are single-element, focused transducers. These are used in nonimaging echocardiography applications; in addition, many mechanically scanned transducers contain one or more single-element, focused transducers.

Single-element transducers are focused by an acoustic lens attached to a planar piezoelectric element or by using an element that is curved. Both techniques are illustrated in Figure 2-30. The curved element is the more common approach.

Focusing has the effect of narrowing the beam profile and increasing the amplitude of echoes from reflectors over a limited axial range in comparison to an equivalent (one with the same frequency and diameter) but unfocused transducer (Figure 2-31). The **focal distance** corre-

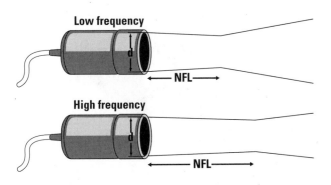

Figure 2-28. Sketches illustrating the dependence of the near field length and the divergence angle on transducer frequency. For a given diameter, *d,* higher frequencies have beams with longer near field lengths, but smaller divergence angles.

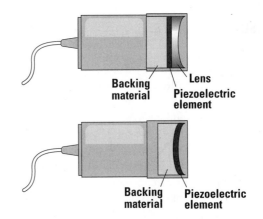

Figure 2-30. Focusing for single-element transducers. The top diagram illustrates a flat disk element with an attached lens. The bottom diagram shows a curved element.

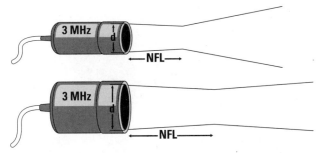

Figure 2-29. Sketches illustrating the dependence of the near field length and the divergence angle on the transducer diameter. For a fixed frequency a larger diameter transducer exhibits a beam that has a longer near field length and less divergence.

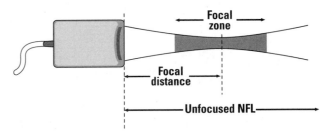

Figure 2-31. Beam pattern for a single-element, focused transducer. The beam is narrowest at the focal distance. The best lateral resolution is of reflectors that are in the focal zone.

sponds to the plane where the beam width is narrowest. The **focal zone** corresponds to the region over which the width of the beam is less than two times the width at the focal distance. Obviously the lateral resolution is best for reflectors that fall within the focal zone of the transducer.

If d is the diameter of the transducer and F the focal distance, the beam width at the focal distance can be approximated as

$$W = \frac{1.22\lambda}{d} \qquad (2\text{-}5)$$

For identically shaped transducers (same diameter, same focus) of different frequencies, higher frequency transducers have narrower beams in the focal region than lower frequency probes[4] (Figure 2-32).

With a single-element, focused transducer, the focal distance is fixed during the manufacturing process. Therefore in a clinical situation a transducer's frequency and dimensions should be chosen to optimize the resolution over the region of interest. In the next section we will see that transducer arrays can provide much more flexibility in focusing characteristics of transducers.

TRANSDUCER ARRAYS

General properties of arrays

In most of today's ultrasound instruments, transducer arrays are used rather than single-element transducers. An array transducer assembly consists of a group of closely spaced piezoelectric elements, each with its own electrical connection to the ultrasound instrument. This enables elements to be excited individually or in groups to produce ultrasound beams; echo signals detected by individual elements are amplified separately before being combined into one signal for each reflector.

Types of arrays

Four types of arrays are shown in Figures 2-33 to 2-36. Linear and curvilinear (or *curved*) arrays consist of groups

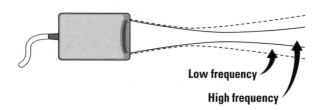

Figure 2-32. Effect of frequency on a focused beam pattern. Higher frequency transducers produce narrower beams in the focal region than lower frequency probes of the same diameter and curvature.

of rectangularly shaped piezoelectric elements arranged side by side as shown in the figures. An entire array might consist of 120 to 250 or more separate elements. Individual sound beams are produced by activating groups of, say, 20 or more of these elements to produce a pulse and collect echo signals from along the beam line. The pulse travels along a beam line that is perpendicular to the face of the array. Consequently, the linear array produces a rectangular imaged field, while the curved array produces a trapezoid-shaped image field.

Modern phased array transducers typically have 128 separate elements. However, the phased array is usually smaller than the linear and curved arrays, so the elements are narrower than in those arrays. Individual sound pulses are produced by activating all elements in the array. The pulse travels along a beam line that can be "steered" in different directions using time-delay methods discussed in Chapter 3.

Annular arrays consist of a circular target and bull's eye arrangement of elements, shown in Figure 2-36. Sound pulses travel along a beam line that is perpendicu-

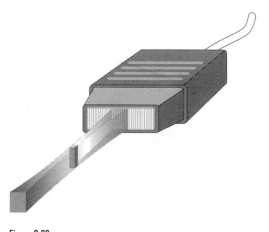

Figure 2-33. Linear array, with an ultrasound pulse emerging along one beam line.

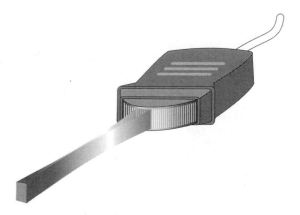

Figure 2-34. Curvilinear array, with an ultrasound pulse traveling along a beam line.

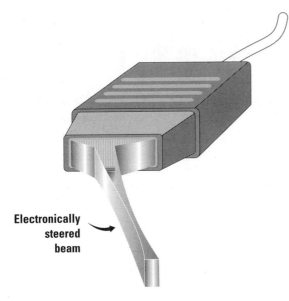

Electronically steered beam

Figure 2-35. Phased array, with an ultrasound pulse traveling off at an angle.

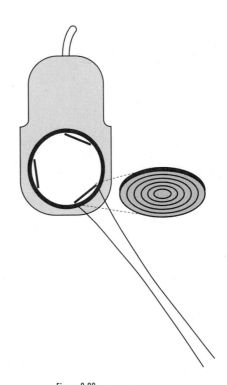

Figure 2-36. Annular array.

lar to the surface of the array. The beam line is swept mechanically across the region to be imaged by translating the array using an arrangement such as that shown in the figure.

Advantages of arrays

Arrays provide two advantages:

1. They enable electronic beam steering; beams are swept across the imaged field with no mechanical motion of parts in the scanhead. (This applies only to linear, curved, and phased arrays.)
2. They enable electronic focusing and beam forming, providing very effective control of the focal distance and the beam width throughout the imaged field. (This applies to all four array types, linear, curved, phased, and annular).

Beam formation with an array

A sound beam is produced by a transducer array by applying electrical signals to each element used to form the beam. With linear and curvilinear arrays a group of elements is involved for each beam; with sectored and annular arrays all elements usually are activated for transmitting and detecting echoes for every beam. The emerging sound beam is the sum of individual beams from each of the elements. Since the individual elements are quite small, often less than a half wavelength, the transmitted pattern from a single element by itself is very broad and not very useful (Figure 2-37). However, when a group of elements transmits simultaneously, the transmitted pat-

terns reinforce one another along the common beam direction and cancel one another in other directions, yielding a well-defined, narrow ultrasound beam (Figure 2-37). Furthermore, this beam may be focused by manipulation of individual signals applied to different elements.

Transmit focus

When all elements in an array cluster are excited precisely at the same time, the effect is analogous to the situation in which a planar, unfocused transducer element is pulsed. The resultant beam is directional but unfocused. Electronic focusing is achieved by introducing time delays in the application of the excitation pulses to the separate elements (Figure 2-38). In this case the wavefronts emerging from the transducer converge toward the focal position, producing a narrow sound beam over the focal region. With the time delays in action, the situation is as though a focusing lens or a curved piezoelectric element were producing the beam.

Unlike the focal distance of a single-element transducer, the focal distance of an array may be varied electronically, by changing the electronic delay sequence. Thus arrays allow the selection of the **transmit focal distance** by the operator. When you vary the focus on an array instrument, you are actually changing the position of the transmit focal distance, moving it closer to or farther from the transducer. Usually some type of focus indicator is placed on the display to help the operator to know where the transmit focus is set.

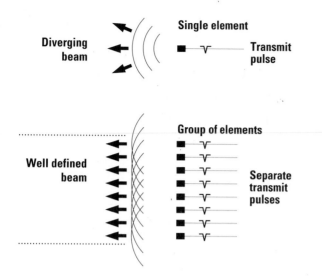

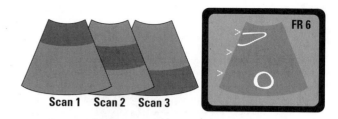

Figure 2-39. Schematic of an image with three simultaneous transmit focal zones. An image is shown built up in three passes, each pass with the transmit focal distance at a different depth; during each pass echo signals are only accepted from the zone corresponding to the transmit focus depth. The frame rate (FR) is low (e.g., six per second here) because of the multiple passes needed for the image.

Figure 2-37. Side view of array elements, showing the sound pattern that emerges from an individual element *(top)* and a group of elements *(bottom)*. In the top part of the diagram, because the element is very narrow, the pattern from an individual element diverges. For the group of elements *(lower part),* sound waves from individual elements reinforce in the beam direction and cancel one another at other directions. This results in a well-defined ultrasound beam.

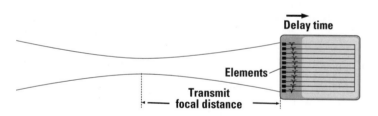

Figure 2-38. Transmit focusing of the beam from a group of elements in an array. The focal distance is controlled by the operator by adjusting the "transmit focal distance."

Another feature provided by array transducers is simultaneous **multiple transmit focal zones,** greatly expanding the focal region of the instrument. The process becomes a bit complicated because of an important limitation when transmitting: a sound beam launched by the array can be focused during transmission at only one depth at a time. If multiple transmit focal zones are used, this requires multiple sound pulses, each focused at a different depth along the beam line. Say we have three transmit focal zones set up (Figure 2-39). One method to acquire the image data is to combine echo data for three "scans" or "passes" of the beam, each pass done with a different

transmit focal depth. During each pass, echoes are accepted only from the zone corresponding to the transmit focal depth for that pass. The resultant image has optimal lateral resolution at each depth, but takes longer to produce than an image using only a single transmit focal zone.

Manufacturers may choose other pulse-echo sequences to acquire data. For example, it may be desirable to acquire all the echo data along one beam line before moving to the next, rather than sweeping through the entire field with one focal distance, then sweeping with the second focal distance, etc. Thus for the first beam line a pulse is launched with the focal depth set at the middle of the first transmit zone, and echo signals are accepted from within that zone only. Then a second sound pulse is launched along the same beam line; this time the transmit focal distance is within zone two, and echo signals are accepted only from zone two. Finally, an ultrasound pulse is launched along the same beam line, this time with the transmit focal distance within zone three, and echo signals accepted from this zone. Once this is done, the beam line is shifted slightly and the entire process repeated along a second beam line, and so forth. Again, the result is an extended focal zone for the transmitted beam, but at the expense of extra time to acquire image data and lower image frame rates.

Dynamic receive focus

Instruments with array transducers also focus the received echo signals electronically. The group of elements involved in forming the transmitted beam also detects echoes from reflectors in the body. As echoes arrive at the various elements in the active group they are amplified and then combined together in the "beam former" (see Chapter 3), producing a single signal for each reflector. However, before combining, something must be done to correct for the fact that the echoes from a reflector arrive at the elements at slightly different times due to differences in the distance the returning pulses must travel (Figure 2-40). Thus the individual signals from the reflector are not in phase and partially cancel one another if combined directly. (For example, if the positive going part of the signal from one element occurs at the time of the negative part of the signal from another, these two signals cancel each other completely when summed.) A large-amplitude signal can be recovered if the individual signals are first brought back into phase before summing. This is done once again with electronic delays set up properly for the reflector depth. Figure 2-40 shows the signals from the various elements all in phase after they emerge from the time delay section. The required delay time depends on the reflector depth.

In contrast to the transmitted beam of an array, during reception, focusing is done dynamically. When a sound pulse is launched, the receiving focal distance of the array is set initially shallow. As the time after the transmitted pulse increases and echoes arrive from deeper and deeper structures, the receive focus changes automatically, keeping up with, or tracking, the position of the sound pulse as it encounters deeper reflectors. It is almost like viewing a receding object through a pair of binoculars, changing the binocular focus as the object gets farther and farther away. With dynamic receive focus, however, the tracking happens very fast, all taking place within the 100 to 200 μs needed for echoes to return from all depths. The result of using dynamic focus is an extended focal depth that is considerably greater than that achievable with a single element transducer or with a single focal distance applied to an array.

In summary, for array transducers, the transmit focal distance is selected by the operator. The focusing is done by applying slight time delays among individual transmit pulses applied to elements in the array. Multiple transmit focal zones may be selected, but this usually slows down the image rate. Receive focusing also is applied, but this is not controlled by the operator. It is done dynamically, the focus changing rapidly as echoes arrive from deeper and deeper reflectors. Dynamic receive focusing is applied at all depths, but it does not slow down the frame rate.

Dynamic aperture

To minimize variations of beam width with depth, most array systems also provide **dynamic aperture.** The aperture refers to the size of the transducer surface involved in producing the ultrasound beam and detecting echoes for each beam line. With an array transducer, the aperture size can be controlled in the instrument by varying the number of elements that are active for producing echo data (Figure 2-41). For a fixed aperture size the "effective" sound beam width, that is, the combined pattern during transmission and reception, varies with depth. Variations are minimized by changing the aperture size as echoes arrive from deeper and deeper reflectors. A small receiving aperture is applied shortly after the ultrasound pulse is launched into the tissue. This may be done by accepting the echoes from only a few of the elements in the array. As echoes return from deeper and deeper structures, the number of elements used to pick up echo signals and hence the aperture is increased. This keeps lateral resolution nearly constant over the entire image region.[5]

Apodization of arrays

It was mentioned earlier that side lobes in a transducer beam degrade lateral resolution, but using a broadband pulse decreases the side lobe strength. Another method for reducing side lobes, apodization, apparently is built into some transducer array instrumentation. *Apodization* means that the transducer's vibration amplitude during transmission and its echo sensitivity during reception are not uniform across the surface, but fall off gradually with increasing distance from the center of the transducer. An array may be apodized by varying the size of the excitation

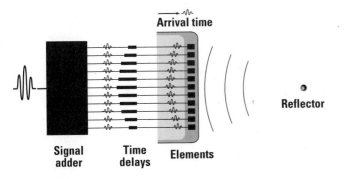

Figure 2-40. Focusing during echo reception. Because of slightly different distances from the reflector to individual elements, echo signals arrive at slightly different times. Receive focusing is done by applying time delays of different durations to the individual signals so the signals will be in phase when summed.

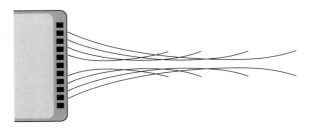

Figure 2-41. Dynamic aperture; by using fewer elements during echo reception from shallow reflectors, the effective beam pattern is narrow. The active aperture is expanded as echoes arrive from deeper structures, keeping the effective beam narrow at all depths.

pulse applied to various elements when a sound beam is produced, with the innermost elements getting a greater excitation than the outer elements (Figure 2-42).

Additional off-axis radiation from arrays

With arrays, additional off-axis radiation resulting, for example, from the presence of **grating lobes** and **clutter** may be present. If significant, this also can degrade the lateral resolution.

Grating lobes (Figure 2-43) result from the division of the transducer into small individual elements that are regularly spaced across the aperture. They are quite well understood and predictable, as the angle they emerge from the transducer face depends on the wavelength and the element spacing. Grating lobes may be reduced in amplitude and directed further away from the main beam axis (where their effects are less important) if narrow closely spaced elements are used. For many applications this means cutting the elements so their spacing is $1/2$

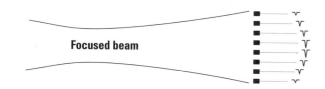

Focused beam

Figure 2-42. Apodization during transmission. Varying the size of the signal applied to individual elements when a pulse is transmitted is one method to help reduce side lobes. *This is called apodization.*

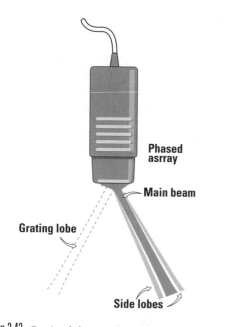

Phased asrray

Main beam

Grating lobe

Side lobes

Figure 2-43. Grating lobes produced by a phased array scanner. Grating lobes are eliminated using very closely spaced elements, typically less than $1/2$ wavelength apart.

wavelength or less. For example, this means element spacings of $1/2$ of 0.3 mm/2, or 0.15 mm for a 5-MHz array.

The additional clutter level in the beam pattern of an array apparently arises from a number of factors, including failure to isolate completely the various elements in the array from one another and other modes of oscillation of the elements besides their thickness mode. The importance of both factors varies with the design of the array. Apparently these factors are reduced using the composite piezoelectric element designs[2] mentioned at the beginning of the chapter.

The channel horsepower race: Is more better?

The term *channel* refers to a transducer element in the array and the pulser-receiver circuit to which it is connected in the instrument. The number of channels available in the instrument dictates the number of array elements that can be simultaneously activated to transmit a pulse and receive echo signals along any one beam line. Systems with 48, 64, and 128 channels are available, and new beam formers are being developed with even higher channel counts.

Are more channels better? The answer basically is "yes," although it may not always be possible to take full advantage of huge numbers of channels. The law of diminishing returns must be considered.

There are two important physics principles that lead to the conclusion that higher channel numbers are better:

1. The larger the aperture, the better the lateral resolution, particularly at large distances from the transducer. Equation 2-5 helps here, even though it applies to a circular transducer. It indicates that as the width of the transducer increases (larger *d*), the beam width at the focal distance decreases. Likewise, as the aperture size increases, the beam width from an array decreases; hence, lateral resolution improves. This is especially important at larger depths.
2. Individual elements in an array generally are designed to be only $1/2$ wavelength in width to reduce grating lobes.

Therefore to obtain the necessary aperture size to optimize lateral resolution at large depths, higher channel number systems are required. Figure 2-44 shows an image of a test phantom taken using a system that has both 128 channel and 256 channel capability on the same phased array transducer. It is evident that the 256 channel system, where the aperture size is essentially doubled, provides smaller spot sizes of the deeper point-like targets in the phantom than the 128 channel system. This means the 256 channel system has better lateral resolution for this test.

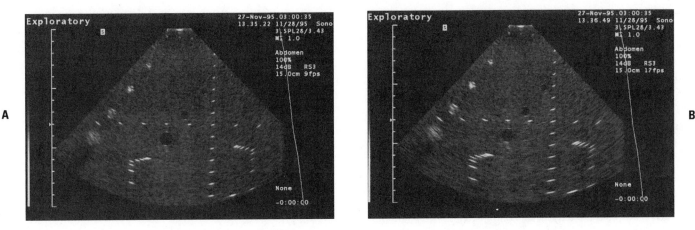

Figure 2-44. Image of a tissue phantom using 128 channels to both transmit and receive (**A**) and 128 channels to transmit, but only 64 channels to receive (**B**) in the same phased array instrument. The improved resolution when all 128 channels are active in both transmit and receive can be appreciated by the smaller sizes of the point targets on the image, particularly at large depths. (Courtesy of Siemens Medical Systems, Issaqua, WA.)

It may not always be practical, however, to apply large apertures on the body. The patient surface contact area available, bone and air pockets, and even distortions of the waves received by elements separated at large distances may pose limitations for present day systems. Nevertheless, remarkable progress towards improving image quality continues to be made by array transducer manufacturers.

SLICE THICKNESS, ELEVATIONAL RESOLUTION

In ultrasound imaging we attempt to define and display echo information from anatomical structures located in a specific plane, called the *image plane* or the *scanning plane*. This is the plane visualized on the B-mode image; it contains the centers of all of the ultrasound beams that form the image. The image plane is defined by the operator when the scanhead is positioned on the patient.

Relationship between slice thickness and lateral and axial resolution

Earlier in this chapter we discussed reflector resolution, a measure of how closely positioned two reflectors can be and still be distinguished from each other on an ultrasound image. One component, lateral resolution, indicates how close the reflectors can be along a line perpendicular to the beam and remain distinguishable; it depends on the beam width in the image plane. Axial resolution, on the other hand, indicates how close the reflectors can be to one another along the beam axis and still be resolved; axial resolution depends on the pulse duration.

A third measure of resolution, the elevational resolution, also termed the *slice thickness,* is equally important. Slice thickness works in a direction perpendicular to the image plane. It dictates the thickness of the section of tissue that contributes to echoes visualized on the image. Slice thickness depends on beam size, analogous to lateral resolution. However, it is the size of the beam **perpendicular** to the image plane—rather than in the image plane as in lateral resolution—that establishes slice thickness (Figure 2-45).

What determines slice thickness?

For circular disk transducers and annular array transducers, the slice thickness is essentially the same as the lateral resolution because the beams from the transducers are symmetrical about the beam axis; that is, the size of the beam perpendicular to the image plane is the same as the size in the image plane. This is particularly important for annular arrays, in that the electronic focusing during transmission and reception not only reduces the in-plane beam width at all depths, but also improves the width of the beam in the slice thickness direction.

However, for most linear, curved, and phased arrays the slice thickness and the lateral resolution are very different. This is because the electronic focusing just discussed for these transducers only reduces the in-plane width of the beam; that is, it improves lateral resolution, but it has no effect on slice thickness. Beam width in the slice thickness direction is determined by a fixed focal length lens attached to the entire array (Figure 2-46). The slice thickness usually is approximately the size of the scanhead up close to the array, narrows down to a few millimeters (depending on the size, frequency, and focal length of the lens) at the lens focal distance, and then broadens out considerably at points beyond the focal distance. At the present time the slice thickness is the worst measure of resolution for array scanners (with the exception, of course, of annular arrays).

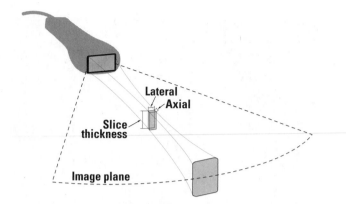

Figure 2-45. Sound pulse traveling along a beam line. Dimensions related to the axial and lateral resolution as well as the slice thickness are shown.

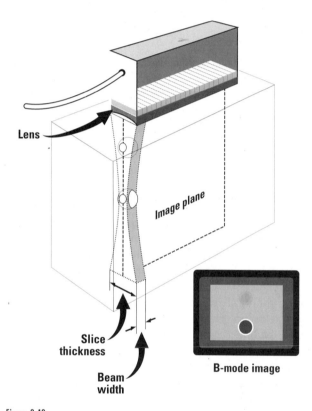

B-mode image

Figure 2-46. Linear array scanhead imaging phantom with low scatter spherical objects. The beam width in the slice thickness direction is determined by the element size in this direction, the frequency, and the focal length of a mechanical lens.

Results of large slice thickness

We usually think of an ultrasound image as depicting an anatomical plane in the body. Because of the slice thickness, however, our images actually are built up from a tissue volume, depicted in Figure 2-47. The volume is thick up close to the transducer, narrower at the focal depth of the elevational focus, and broad at distances beyond the slice thickness focus.

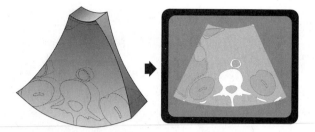

Figure 2-47. Schematic depiction of the volume of tissue contributing to the echoes on a typical B-mode scan done with a phased array. The slice thickness varies from wide up near the transducer, narrower near the focal length of the slice thickness lens, and wider beyond the lens focal distance.

The effects of slice thickness may be observed by scanning a phantom containing spherical, cystlike targets. Figure 2-48 was produced using a 3.5-MHZ phased array scanner. The phantom contains 4-mm low scatter objects randomly distributed throughout the volume. These objects are not visible up close to the scanhead, near the top of the phantom, although they are present in the phantom. They are obliterated because of the slice thickness of this imager. They are quite visible at depth ranges from approximately 5.0 cm through approximately 12 cm, but disappear into the background beyond this depth.

Advantage of annular arrays

Both annular arrays and rectangularly shaped linear arrays offer the features of multiple transmit focus, dynamic receiver focus, and dynamic aperture. However, with the annular, the slice thickness at any axial distance is the same as the lateral (in-plane) resolution (Figure 2-49). Therefore these arrays appear to have some advantages over rectangular arrays, particularly for imaging small focal masses. Their main disadvantage, of course, is that the beam must be swept mechanically, by translating the array within the scanhead, for example. This makes them more difficult to use in Doppler and color flow imaging applications than the linear, curved, and phased arrays, which scan electronically. There also may be reliability differences, since the mechanically scanned probe has moving parts that wear.

Summary of array focusing

We should emphasize here that electronic beam focusing and electronic beam steering are two different functions. Beam focusing is applied to individual ultrasound beams to improve the lateral resolution and the slice thickness. Beam steering, on the other hand, is done to sweep ultrasound beams over a scanned volume during imaging; for beam steering, think of the searchlight

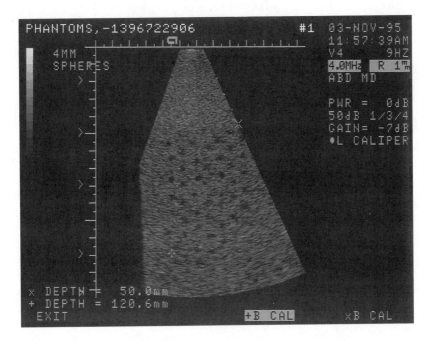

Figure 2-48. Image of 4-mm diameter, low-scatter, spherical objects in a test phantom. These objects are not visualized until a depth of 5 cm with this transducer; beyond a depth of 12 cm they also are hardly seen. The slice thickness is the main factor that limits their detection to 5 to 12 cm.

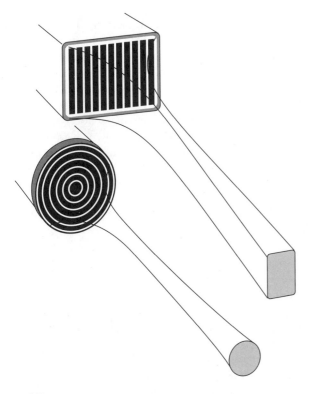

Figure 2-49. Comparison of typical beam shapes, in three dimensions, for a phased array and an annular array. With the annular array, electronic focusing narrows the beam in the slice thickness direction as well as in the image plane. Only the in-plane beam width is affected by electronic focusing for the phased array.

analogy mentioned earlier. Table 2-2 summarizes the beam focusing and beam steering methods for various transducer types.

Two-dimensional (or 1½-SD) linear, curvilinear, and phased arrays

Some transducer manufacturers are developing another approach to fixing the poor slice thickness performance of these arrays: the two-dimensional array. These consist of a two-dimensional matrix of elements (Figure 2-50), rather than the single row of elements in standard (one-dimensional) arrays. With a two-dimensional array, electronic focusing methods done to enhance resolution within the scanning plane of one-dimensional arrays are also done in the slice thickness direction. There are several manufacturers of array instruments who offer this technology. It is usually referred to as "1½-D" rather than full two-dimensional array technology because the number of elements in the elevational direction (say five or seven) is much less than the number in the lateral direction (say 100 to 200).

Other proposed uses of two-dimensional arrays include doing three-dimensional, volumetric imaging and correcting for distortions of ultrasound beams in tissue.[6] These advances may be incorporated into some future ultrasound imagers.

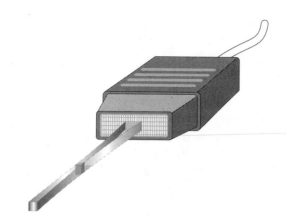

Figure 2-50. 1¹/₂-dimensional array, permitting dynamic electronic focusing in the elevational, or slice thickness direction, as well as in the image plane. Such arrays are being evaluated by ultrasound equipment manufacturers to improve slice thickness.

Table 2-2. Methods of beam steering and beam focusing in current medical ultrasound transducers*

Type of transducer	Method used for beam focusing	Method used for beam steering
Linear array	Electronic†	Electronic
Curved array	Electronic†	Electronic
Phased array	Electronic†	Electronic
Annular array	Electronic‡	Mechanical
Single-element	Mechanical lens	Mechanical

*Does not include new, 1-¹/₂-D array technology discussed.
†Electronic focusing is applied in the scanning plane, affecting the lateral resolution; the slice thickness focus with current linear, curved, and phased array systems is with a mechanical lens.
‡The annular array's electronic focus affects both the lateral resolution and the slice thickness.

EFFECTS OF THE FREQUENCY SPECTRUM

For pulsed transducers a spectrum of frequencies is emitted, and this adds some complexity to our simple beam models. The different components of the frequency spectrum of a pulsed transducer have slightly different beam-forming characteristics. This follows from reasoning presented earlier for single frequencies. The resultant beam is the sum total of all frequencies available in each pulse. We know that the higher frequency components of a pulse result in narrower beams than the lower frequencies, so if the pulse is dominated by high frequencies, these will also dominate the beam shape.

During clinical scanning, attenuation in soft tissues modifies the frequency spectrum since higher frequencies in the pulse are attenuated to a greater degree than are lower frequencies. This leads to a loss of resolution in tissue during clinical scanning.[7]

DAMAGE TO TRANSDUCERS

Ultrasound transducers should not be heat sterilized, since this can damage the probe severely. One manifestation of heat damage is depolarization if the transducer is heated above its Curie temperature. Actually, transducer damage due to heat occurs at elevated temperatures that are lower than the Curie temperature, for the different bonding joints and cements in the probe are susceptible to thermal damage. Cleaning and sterilization of the transducer is an important task of operators of ultrasound equipment. The preferred agents depend on the transducer materials, so the operator's manual should be consulted for the preferred method.

If a transducer is dropped or sustains an impact, the interior of the probe may be damaged. A cracked transducer surface can lead to a dangerous situation, even involving possible electrical shock. This is especially true with the use of acoustic coupling materials since they also tend to be good electrical conductors. A transducer that has a cracked scanning surface should be replaced immediately.

Partial delaminations of the transducer scanning surface have been said to result in excessive surface heating of some transducers, causing discomfort to the patient. To the best of the author's knowledge, however, reports of patient discomfort have not been documented or verified. It is well known, however, that some transducer surface heating occurs, especially in higher output power modes, as can be verified by manual inspection. Some intercavitary transducers are equipped with thermal sensors to interrupt power to the probe when the temperature exceeds predetermined limits.

A frequent source of transducer malfunction, especially in probes with built-in cables, is damage to the cable assembly. Twisting and bending that take place quite naturally during handling may cause cable damage and lead to loss of sensitivity, intermittent operation, and/or excessive electrical noise on the display. Worse yet, many scanning instruments must be transported to the patient bedside, another lab, the operating room or the ICU, or even other hospitals. During these transports the possibility exists that cables will be rolled over by the instrument or suffer some other damage. Most sonographers are acutely aware of the high costs to replace or repair probes and take special care of these units during all operations.

References

1. Wells PNT: *Biomedical ultrasonics,* New York, 1977, Academic Press.
2. Smith WA: *The role of piezocomposites in ultrasonic transducers,* 1989, IEEE Ultrasonics Symposium Proceedings, Catalog No 89CH2791-2, IEEE, Piscataway, NJ.
3. Lewin P: Miniature piezoelectric polymer ultrasonic hydrophone probes, *Ultrasonics* 19:213, 1981.
4. Kossoff G: Analysis of focusing action of spherically curved transducers, *Ultrasound Med Biol* 5:359, 1979.
5. Maslak S: Computed sonography. In Sanders R, Hill M, editors: *Ultrasound annual,* New York, 1985, Raven Press.
6. Nock L, Trahey, G, Smith S: Phase aberration correction in medical ultrasound using speckle brightness as a quality factor, *JASA* 85:1819, 1989.
7. Zagzebski J et al: Focused transducer beams in tissue-mimicking material, *J Clin Ultrasound* 10:159, 1982.

Questions for Review

1. Which statement is INCORRECT for piezoelectric transducers?

   A. Convert sound waves to electrical signals
   B. Respond equally to most frequencies
   C. Convert electrical signals to sound waves
   D. Vibrate when an electrical signal is applied

2. The resonance frequency of a transducer depends on:

   A. The strength of the pulser
   B. The diameter of the piezoelectric element
   C. The acoustic wavelength
   D. The thickness of the piezoelectric element

3. Which of the following will not change if you change the transducer to one having a different frequency?

   A. Amount of attenuation
   B. Amount of scatter
   C. Speed of sound
   D. Axial resolution
   E. Lateral resolution

4. Before a ceramic transducer element, such as lead zirconate titanate, is suitable as an ultrasonic transducer, it must be:

   A. Polarized
   B. Pressurized
   C. Electrified
   D. Homogenized

5. The advantage of composite transducer materials over solid PZT is they:

   A. Are easier to manufacture
   B. Produce lower intensity ultrasound beams
   C. Have a lower impedance and wider bandwidth
   D. Produce ultrasound beams that undergo less attenuation
   E. Have better lateral resolution and smaller slice thickness

6. To produce a sound beam a pulsed transducer is caused to oscillate by:

   A. Applying a pressure pulse
   B. Applying a magnetic impulse
   C. Applying an electrical pulse
   D. Applying a continuous electrical signal

7. The backing layer:

   A. Dampens the transducer
   B. Provides electrical shielding
   C. Tunes the crystal
   D. Excites the transducer

8. The purpose of quarter-wave matching layers on the transducer surface is to:

   A. Help the transducer glide smoothly over the patient
   B. Retain coupling gel between the transducer and patient
   C. Reduce the ultrasonic wavelength in the medium
   D. Improve the sensitivity of the transducer

9. A manufacturer is selecting a material to use as a matching layer on a transducer. The piezoelectric element has an impedance of 30×10^6 rayls. The impedance of soft tissue is 1.6×10^6 rayls. The best material for the matching layer likely has an impedance of about:

   A. 1.0×10^6 rayls
   B. 6.9×10^6 rayls
   C. 32×10^6 rayls
   D. 121×10^6 rayls

10. Multiple frequency operation with a single scanhead is possible on those transducer systems that have:

    A. Very narrow elements
    B. Very thin elements
    C. Very short elements
    D. Very large bandwidths

11. Axial resolution is most closely associated with:

    A. Transducer size
    B. Transducer focusing
    C. Beam width
    D. Pulse duration

12. For a fixed frequency, increasing the pulse duration does what to the frequency bandwidth?

    A. Increases it
    B. Decreases it
    C. Does not change it
    D. Increases or decreases, depending on the center frequency

13. Ultrasound imaging transducers typically generate pulses of how many cycles?

    A. 0
    B. 2 to 3
    C. 20 to 30
    D. 200 to 300

14. As the number of cycles in the pulse increases, the axial resolution:

    A. Improves
    B. Stays the same
    C. Gets worse
    D. Either improves or gets worse, depending on the frequency

15. If the frequency increases but the number of cycles in the pulse stays the same, the axial resolution:

    A. Improves
    B. Stays the same
    C. Gets worse

16. Short pulses are associated with _____ spatial burst lengths.

    A. Long
    B. Short
    C. Any (spatial burst length is independent of pulse duration.)

17. Lateral resolution is most closely associated with:

    A. Transducer size
    B. Transducer shielding
    C. Beam width
    D. Pulse duration

18. The principle that says that the intensity at any point in a sound beam is determined by summing up sound wavelets from all points on the transducer surface is known as:

    A. Newton's law
    B. The Bernoulli principle
    C. Snell's law
    D. Huygen's principle

19. The region in an unfocused beam that extends from the transducer surface to an axial distance where the field is smooth, is called the:

    A. Near field
    B. Fraunhofer zone
    C. Focal zone
    D. Far field

20. The beam of an unfocused transducer diverges:

    A. Because of inadequate damping
    B. In the Fresnel zone
    C. When the pulse duration is long
    D. In the Fraunhofer zone
    E. More for higher frequencies

21. Greater beam divergence in the far field results in:

    A. Better axial resolution
    B. Poorer axial resolution
    C. Better lateral resolution
    D. Poorer lateral resolution

22. The near field length of a 2-MHz, 10-mm diameter unfocused transducer is:

    A. 1.6 cm
    B. 3.2 cm
    C. 4.8 cm
    D. 9.4 cm
    E. 16.2 cm

23. If the frequency doubles but the diameter remains the same for single-element unfocused transducers, the near field length:

    A. Doubles
    B. Does not change
    C. Halves
    D. Quadruples
    E. Is reduced to $1/4$ the original

24. Which of the following is most closely associated with large beam widths and poor lateral resolution?

    A. Poor penetration into tissue
    B. Uneven gray levels on a B-mode image
    C. Significant echo enhancement distal to fluid-filled structures
    D. Apparent echoes detected within small, fluid-filled structures
    E. Excessive electronic noise because of electrical interference

25. The distance from a focused transducer to the center of its focal region (or to the location of the spatial peak intensity) is called the:

    A. Incidence angle
    B. Focal zone
    C. Effective reflecting area
    D. Focal distance

26. A transducer that consists of many small elements is called:

    A. An array
    B. A hydrophone
    C. An oscillator
    D. A beam former
    E. A Huygen source

27. The type of transducer that uses time delays to steer the beam at an angle for imaging is called _____ array.

    A. A phased
    B. An annular
    C. A curved
    D. A linear

28. The type of transducer that does not allow the operator to vary the focus is:

    A. A linear array
    B. An annular array
    C. A single-element transducer
    D. A phased array

29. The type of array transducer that images by transmitting many ultrasound beams in parallel directions is:

    A. An annular array
    B. A linear array
    C. A mechanical sector scanner
    D. A phased array

30. When you use the instrument console control to vary the focal depth on a linear array transducer, you are actually varying:

    A. The position of the focus of the transmitted beam only
    B. The position of the focus of the received signal only
    C. The position of the focus in the slice thickness direction
    D. Both the transmitted beam focus and the received beam focus

31. Which of the following types of current transducer assemblies applies electronic focusing to the slice thickness direction as well as the lateral resolution?

    A. 1-D phased (sectored) array
    B. 1-D linear sequential array
    C. 1-D convex sequential array
    D. Annular array

32. Apodization helps reduce:

    A. The pulse duration
    B. Attenuation in tissue
    C. Slice thickness
    D. Side lobes

33. Dynamic aperture:

    A. Guards the transducer from noise
    B. Reduces beam width changes with depth
    C. Provides a diverging image field
    D. Expands the focal region of single-element transducers

34. With current linear, curved, and phased arrays, slice thickness is determined by the size of the element and:

    A. A fixed lens
    B. A lens that has variable focal distance
    C. An electronically set lens
    D. The speed of sound in tissue

35. A narrow slice thickness helps visualize:

    A. Vessels running perpendicular to the image plane
    B. Small focal lesions
    C. Large, specular interfaces
    D. Large, low-contrast objects

Chapter 3
Pulse-Echo Ultrasound Instrumentation

Today's ultrasound imager is a very sophisticated medical device, often supporting a number of different transducers, operating modes, and image display devices.

PULSE-ECHO ULTRASOUND: THE RANGE EQUATION

This chapter describes instrumentation that utilizes pulse-echo ultrasound to produce images of structures in the body. In this technique an ultrasound transducer transmits short-duration acoustic pulses into the body. Each pulse travels in a narrow, well-defined beam. As the pulse travels through the tissues it undergoes partial reflection at interfaces. This gives rise to echo signals returning to the transducer. The time delay between transmitting a pulse and detecting an echo signal is used to determine the transducer-to-interface distance.

The principle is illustrated in Figure 3-1. A reflector is positioned a distance, D, from the transducer. Let T be the time it takes for a pulse of sound to travel to the interface and an echo to return to the transducer; T is given by:

$$T = \frac{2D}{c}$$

(3-1)

where c is the speed of sound in the medium. The time is just the total distance the pulse must travel to the reflector and back, $2D$, divided by the sound speed.

Example: If the speed of sound is 1540 m/s and a reflector is positioned 1 cm from the transducer, how long does it take a pulse of sound to travel to the reflector and an echo to return to the transducer?

Solution: 1540 m/s is the same as 0.154 cm/μs, so we have:

$$T = \frac{2D}{c}$$

$$= \frac{2 \times 1 \text{ cm}}{0.154 \text{ cm}/\mu\text{s}}$$

$$= 13 \ \mu\text{s}$$

In soft tissue, where the speed of sound is about 1540 m/s, each centimeter of round-trip distance takes 13 μs. If a reflector is 5 cm from the transducer, the echo returns 65 μs after the transmit pulse; if it is 10 cm, the return time is 130 μs, etc. Table 3-1 summarizes this relationship.

You can also compute the reflector distance if the pulse-echo travel time, T, and the sound speed, c, are known.

Example: If the echo return time is 100 μs after pulse transmission, and the speed of sound is 0.154 cm/μs, what is the reflector distance?

Solution: First, isolate D on one side of Equation 3-1 by multiplying both sides of the equation by c and dividing both sides by 2. This gives:

$$D = \frac{cT}{2}$$

Then

$$D = \frac{0.154 \text{ cm}/\mu\text{s} \times 100 \ \mu\text{s}}{2}$$

$$= 7.7 \text{ cm}$$

The expression given in Equation 3-1 is often referred to as the **range equation.**[1] This relationship between echo transit time, T, and reflector depth, D, is implicitly built into pulse-echo imaging instruments. The distance from the transducer to a reflector is inferred from the echo return time, using knowledge of the speed of sound in soft tissue. Except for special instruments used in ophthalmology,[2] a speed of sound of 1540 m/s is always assumed.

PULSING CHARACTERISTICS AND DUTY FACTOR

It is important to realize that when an ultrasound machine operates in a pulse-echo mode, the transducer transmits sound waves for only a small fraction of the total time an examination is taking place. When the transducer is applied to the patient, most of the time is spent "listening" for echoes that result from reflections of the sound waves by the tissue.

The fraction of time the transducer actively transmits sound is called the **duty factor.** In ultrasound imaging and other pulse-echo applications the duty factor is typically less than 0.01 (1%). Figure 3-2 helps illustrate this more clearly. Shown are waveforms that correspond to two successive ultrasound pulses emitted by a transducer. Pulsing parameters illustrated are the pulse duration, *PD*, and the pulse repetition period, *PP*. Notice the pulse duration is the time from the *beginning* of a pulse to the *end* of the *same pulse*. The pulse repetition period, on the other hand, is the time from the *beginning* of a pulse to the *beginning* of the *next one*.

The pulse duration usually is less than 1 μs to enhance axial resolution, as discussed in Chapter 2. Pulse repetition periods, however, are much greater than this. Thus the time between pulses, when the transducer is listening for echoes, is much greater than the duration of an individual transmit pulse, and so the duty factor is small.

Table 3-2, column two, gives approximate values for the pulse-repetition frequency, that is, the number of pulses emitted per second, for various operating modes. Column four presents ballpark values for the duty factor. Exact values for both parameters are quite variable, and depend on the instrument and operator settings, but the table helps illustrate typical conditions.

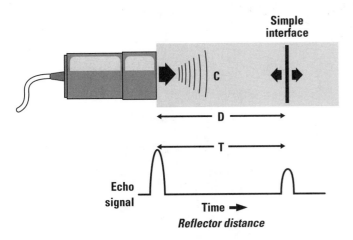

Figure 3-1. The range equation in medical ultrasound. *T*, the time delay between transmitting a pulse into the tissue and receiving an echo signal from a reflector, indicates the reflector-to-transducer distance, *D*.

Table 3-1. Pulse-echo travel time for various reflector distances in soft tissue (speed of sound = 1540 m/s)

Distance to reflector	Pulse-echo travel time
1 cm	13 μs
5 cm	65 μs
10 cm	130 μs
20 cm	260 μs

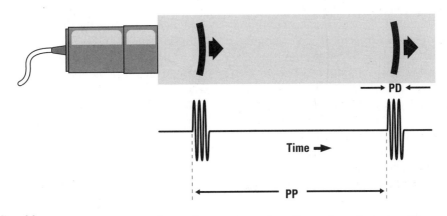

Figure 3-2. Pulsing characteristics for an ultrasound transducer in a pulse-echo system. The signals represent two successive transmit pulses. The pulse repetition period *(PP)* and the pulse duration *(PD)* are shown. Because the pulse duration, *PD*, is much shorter than the pulse repetition period, *PP*, the duty factor is low.

Table 3-2. Typical pulse-repetition frequencies (PRFs), pulse repetition periods (PP), and duty factors in ultrasound

Mode of operation	PRF	PP	Duty Factor (assume 1 μs PD)
M-mode	500/s	2 ms	0.0005
Real-time imaging	2000-4000/s	500-250 μs	0.002-0.004
Pulsed Doppler	4000-12,000/s	250-83 μs	0.004-0.012

INSTRUMENTATION

Today's ultrasound imager is a very sophisticated medical device, often supporting a number of different transducers, operating modes, and image display devices (Figure 3-3). A simplified block diagram showing principal components of an ultrasound scanning instrument is presented in Figure 3-4. Identified are a pulse transmitter, a receiver, a scan converter, and various methods for displaying and recording images. The role of each of these components is discussed in the next few pages. Modern systems that use array transducers also have a separate component called a *beam former,* used to provide beam steering and electronic focusing.

Beam former

The role of the beam former is best understood by considering the material on array transducers in Chapter 2. We mentioned that array transducers can be focused electronically at different depths. The beam former provides the pulse-delay sequences applied to individual elements to achieve transmit focusing. It also controls dynamic focusing of the received echoes and controls the beam direction for electronically scanned arrays.

The receive focus and the scanning part of a beam former traditionally have been an analog device (see discussion later on analog vs. digital systems), operating on echo signal waveforms from each element and combining these into a single signal for later stages of processing. In Figure 3-5, *A*, the analog delay circuit serves both as the source of time delays for focusing the received echo signals and adds signals from all elements to produce a single echo signal for each reflector. Technical documents refer, for example, to "summing delay lines" to carry out this function.[3] The echo signal is sent on to later stages of the instrument, and eventually to a digitizing device to convert the signal into a digital format for image storage (see Chapter 4).

There is a growing tendency among ultrasound equipment manufacturers to incorporate digital beam formers (Figure 3-5, *B*) into their scanners. Individual echo signals from the array elements are first digitized, converting each signal to sequences of zeroes and ones.

Figure 3-3. A modern ultrasound scanner (Courtesy of Siemens Medical Systems, Issaqua, WA).

Digital electronic components then introduce the delays necessary for focusing and other beam-forming functions and finally combine the digitized signals from all elements into one signal. This signal goes on to form the image.

The advantages of digital beam formers include their stability, their programmability, and their acceptance of a very wide range of signal frequencies; that is, they are broadband. The programmability feature expedites use of new transducer types and new beam-forming functions as they are developed. When a manufacturer develops a new transducer, computer programs loaded into the system adapt the digital beam former to the new probe. The acceptance of a wide frequency range means that digital beam formers can take full advantage of new broadband transducers, with the short-pulse, wide-frequency bandwidth of which these transducers are capable.

Disadvantages of digital beam formers in the past have included the complexity of producing a beam former digitally that provides adequate focus control while

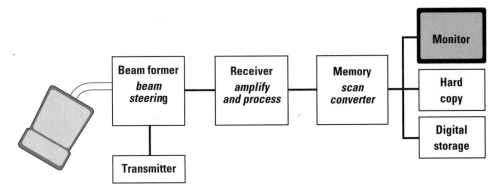

Figure 3-4. Simplified block diagram highlighting principal components of an ultrasound imager.

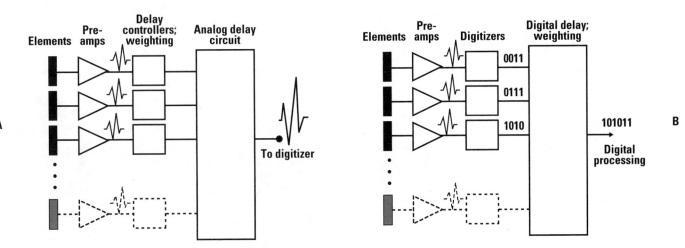

Figure 3-5. A, Analog beam former. The echo signal remains in analog format when time delays for focusing are applied and summation of signals from individual channels is done. **B,** Digital beam former. Time delays and summation are done on echo signals after they are digitized.

accepting and processing a sufficient range of echo signal amplitudes; however, this disadvantage is gradually diminishing as technical advancements continue and more experience is obtained with the digital variety. We likely will see many instruments utilizing digital beam formers in the near future.

Pulse transmitter

The function of the pulse transmitter, or pulser, is to provide electrical signals for exciting the piezoelectric transducer. In response to each signal the transducer vibrates, producing an ultrasound pulse that travels through the tissue. The pulsing signals are provided at a rate called the **pulse–repetition frequency (PRF).** The PRF varies with operating mode and other settings on the machine; typical conditions are indicated in the second column of Table 3-2 above.

Some instruments provide an operator-adjustable control of the output power to vary the sensitivity of the scanner (Figure 3-6). Sensitivity refers to the weakest echo signals that the instrument is capable of detecting and displaying. By increasing the output power to the transducer we produce higher-intensity ultrasound pulses traveling into the tissue. This results in larger-amplitude echo signals from all reflectors, and allows echoes from weaker reflectors to be visualized on the display.

Thus when the transmit power is increased (Figure 3-6),

1. The amplitude of the electrical signal applied to the transducer increases;
2. The transducer produces higher intensity sound waves;
3. Echo signals from structures throughout the field have higher amplitudes and appear brighter (Figures 3-7 and 3-8);

4. Echo signals from weaker reflectors appear on the display;
5. Acoustical exposure to the patient increases.

Different instruments label the output power control differently, calling it names such as *output, power, dB,* or *transmit*. Some provide an indication of the time average intensity, such as the spatial peak time average (see Figures 3-7 and 3-8). Currently there appears to be no preferred label among different manufacturers. However, a new output labeling standard has recently been adopted by manufacturers, regulatory agencies, and scientific bodies,[4] and some manufacturers are following this standard.

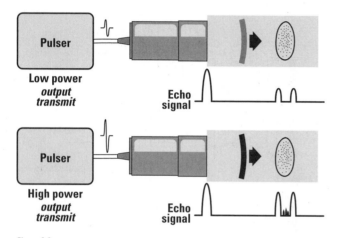

Figure 3-6. Function of the output power control. Increasing the pulser power increases the amplitude of the transmit pulse *(darker pulse in the lower diagram)*, increasing the amplitudes of all echo signals. This results in weaker echoes being picked up.

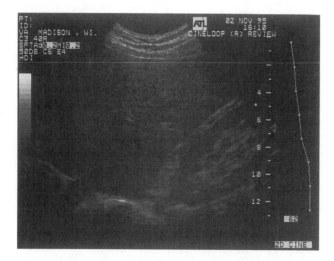

Figure 3-7. 2-D ultrasound image of the liver obtained using a relatively low-output power setting. (On this scanner, the transmit level is indicated by both the spatial peak time average intensity [SPTA] and the mechanical index [MI] values in the upper left-hand corner. Here the MI is 0.2.)

Under it, the acoustical energy produced by the transducer is labeled in terms of a mechanical index (MI) and a thermal index (TI). These terms are discussed in more detail in Chapter 9. The instrument used for obtaining Figures 3-7 and 3-8 employs the MI label, which can be seen on the top left side of these images.

Receiver

Echo signals detected by the transducer are applied to the receiver, where they are processed for display. The first part of this processing involves echo signal amplification and **compensation** for attenuation losses.

Signal amplification is necessary since the amplitudes of echo signals at the transducer are generally too low to allow visualization on a display. The degree of amplification is called the **gain** of the receiver. The gain is the ratio of the output signal amplitude to the input signal amplitude (Figure 3-9). The gain may be expressed as a simple

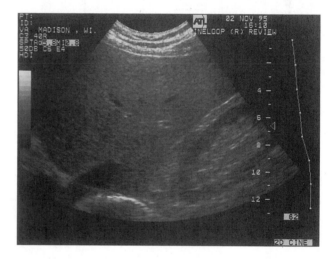

Figure 3-8. Scan of the same region as in Figure 3-7, but with higher transmit power. When the power is increased, echoes are of greater magnitude and appear brighter throughout the imaged field. The transmit level is indicated by the SPTA value and the MI value in the top left of the image. Here the MI is 1.

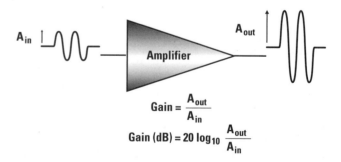

$$\text{Gain} = \frac{A_{out}}{A_{in}}$$

$$\text{Gain (dB)} = 20 \log_{10} \frac{A_{out}}{A_{in}}$$

Figure 3-9. Definition of the gain of an amplifier. The gain may be expressed as a ratio of the output to input amplitudes; sometimes it is given in dB.

ratio (say 100). More commonly it is expressed in decibels. For example, a gain of 40 dB is the same as an amplification ratio of 100.

The preamplifier. Most instruments carry out the amplification in different stages. The first stage often is identified separately as a *preamplifier;* the preamplifier must be as close to the transducer as practical. It boosts weak echo signals so they are large enough to be amplified by the main amplifier. It also has special circuit components that protect the amplifier from the high-voltage transmit pulse applied to the transducer (Figure 3-10). One problem with all amplifiers is that besides amplifying the desired signals, they also generate low-level, spurious electrical signals, called *noise.* The preamplifier must generate as little noise as possible because later amplification stages in the receiver amplify the noise as well as the echo signals.

Gain adjustments. All instruments provide for operator adjustment of the receiver gain. This is done to increase or decrease the sensitivity of the instrument. Operator-adjustable gain controls usually are in two parts: an overall gain control and TGC.

Overall gain control. This is a single gain control that increases amplification at all depths. It is found on most, but not all, instruments operating in pulse-echo mode. Increasing the overall gain can have a similar effect as increasing the transmit power: echo signals from throughout the field are increased in amplitude, and the entire image appears brighter (Figure 3-11). However, it is important to keep in mind that changing the receiver gain simply changes the amount of amplification of echo signals detected by the transducer. In contrast, varying the transmit power varies the magnitude of the pulse emitted by the transducer and, therefore, the size of echoes returning to the transducer. Increasing the transmit power increases acoustical exposure to the patient; increasing receiver amplification does not! (Overall gain should not

be confused with compression or dynamic range control, which may appear to have a similar effect. Compression is discussed later.)

Swept gain, or TGC. Echoes returning to the transducer from structures situated at large distances from the transducer generally are weaker than echoes returning from nearby structures. This is a result of sound beam attenuation in the medium. The situation is depicted schematically in Figure 3-12. If the reflectors all are the same, a gradual weakening of the echo signals with increasing reflector distance results from attenuation.

Sound beam attenuation is compensated for using swept gain (also called *TGC,* for **time gain compensation,** and *DGC,* for *depth gain compensation*) in the receiver (bottom signal trace in Figure 3-12). In this process, the receiver amplification is increased with time following each transmit pulse, so that echo signals origi-

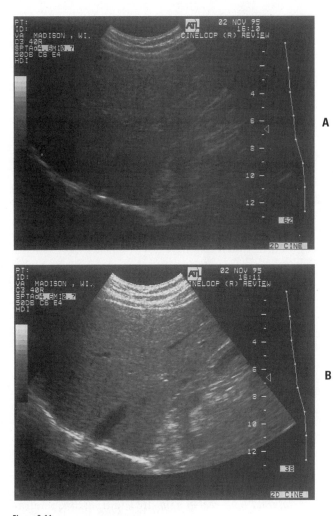

A

B

Figure 3-11. **A,** Scan of the liver obtained with low gain. **B,** Scan of the same region as in **A,** but with a higher gain. Echo signals from throughout the field of view are stronger, producing a brighter image.

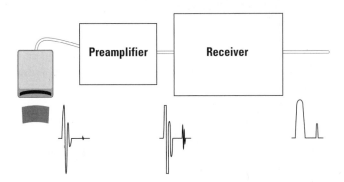

Figure 3-10. Function of the preamplifier. It provides the initial stages of amplification of echo signals. It also protects the later stages of the receiver from large echo signals.

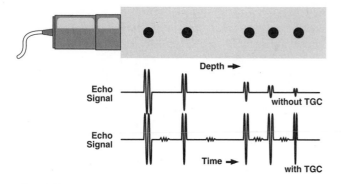

Figure 3-12. The TGC function in the receiver of a pulse-echo system. The top signal trace represents echoes from equal reflectors, where attenuation decreases the amplitude as the distance to the reflector increases. TGC compensates for attenuation in tissue by increasing the receiver gain as a function of time following each transmit pulse.

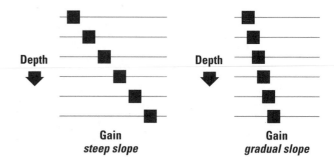

Figure 3-13. Slider bar TGC controls. Each bar adjusts the gain at one depth range. The farther any one control is pushed to the right, the higher the gain at the corresponding depth.

nating from distal reflectors are amplified more than echo signals originating close to the transducer. Proper application of the swept gain function has the effect of equalizing echo signals from similar reflectors.

Slider bar TGC control. The most common TGC controls consist of a series of slider knobs, each providing adjustment of the receiver gain at a specific depth range (Figure 3-13). The slider knob arrangement traces a pattern sometimes called a *gain curve*. The "slope" of the gain curve needed to effectively compensate for attenuation and produce a uniform image of tissue structures depends on the tissue's attenuation and on the frequency. More highly attenuating tissues require steeper-sloped gain curves than tissues that have low attenuation coefficients. When higher frequency transducers are used, the higher attenuation also dictates steeper slopes to provide adequate compensation.

3-Knob TGC control. Another TGC method available in some instruments consists of a limited number of gain controls, each controlling a different aspect of the gain curve. Controls for the "initial gain," the "slope," and the "far gain" are common (Figure 3-14). The actions of these controls on the gain curve are illustrated in the figure. The initial setting regulates the receiver gain at the time of the transmit pulse by the transducer. The slope adjusts the rate of compensation with depth. The far gain control adjusts the maximum receiver gain following each transmit pulse.

Internal time-varied gain. In addition to operator-adjusted gain controls, some instruments provide an internal, automatically set swept gain. This feature can both correct for changes in sensitivity versus depth for transducers and can provide an average swept gain compensa-

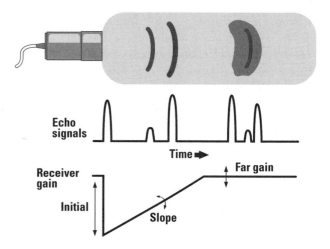

Figure 3-14. Effect of 3-knob TGC controls. One control adjusts the initial gain, a second the slope, and a third the far gain. These are shown on the "gain curve," the lower trace in the figure.

tion rate. The instrument can be made to sense whatever transducer assembly is connected to the pulser-receiver and make an initial setting of the swept gain. Operator adjustments, though still necessary, are minimized somewhat by this feature.

Lateral gain. Some instruments have a function called *lateral gain*. It is found useful, for example, in echo cardiography to compensate for side-to-side nonuniformities in image brightness caused by different amounts of attenuation for different pathways through which individual beams travel (Figure 3-15).

In contrast to TGC, which increases receiver gain with increasing echo arrival time along each beam line,

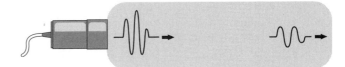

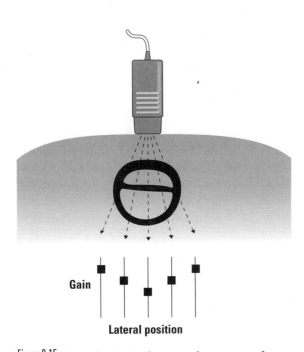

Figure 3-15. Lateral gain, used to vary the amount of amplification from one side of the image to the other.

Figure 3-16. Pulse shape changes resulting from attenuation in tissues. Attenuation reduces the amplitude of the pulse as it travels more deeply into the tissue. It also changes the pulse shape, preferentially eliminating higher frequencies.

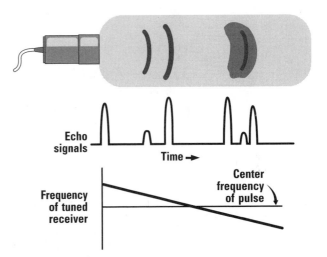

Figure 3-17. Dynamic frequency tracking feature. The center frequency of the receiver is varied with time after each transmit pulse, giving emphasis to high frequencies for shallow structures and low frequencies for greater depths.

lateral gain controls affect echo data from individual beam lines differently. Many applications where it is used require higher amounts of amplification from lateral margins of the image than along the central part of the image, as in Figure 3-15.

Dynamic frequency tuning. Most receivers are broadband, that is, they amplify and process echo signals for all frequencies contained in the ultrasound pulse. For example, a 5-MHz center frequency pulse may contain a range of frequencies between 3 and 7 MHz, and all frequencies are processed equally by a broadbandwidth amplifier. It is also possible to tune the receiver to amplify a more limited range of frequencies. Sometimes this can help reduce spurious electrical noise.

Some instruments provide a **dynamic frequency tracking** feature. Its use has to do with the fact that not all ultrasound frequencies contained in the sound pulse emitted by a transducer are attenuated at the same rate in tissue. As mentioned in Chapter 1, higher frequency sound waves are attenuated more rapidly and penetrate less deeply than lower frequencies. Because a brief pulse of ultrasound contains a range of frequencies (see Chapter 2), the preferential attenuation of high frequencies results in a change in the pulse shape, and in the frequency content, as it interrogates deeper and deeper structures. This is shown in Figure 3-16, where the pulse of sound emitted by the transducer gradually loses more of the higher frequency components with increasing distance traveled.

The receiver can be set up so that, for echo signals arriving from shallow regions, it responds most effectively to the higher frequencies in the pulse bandwidth. Then the response can be shifted gradually to favor the lower frequencies for signals from deeper structures (Figure 3-17). This makes most efficient use of the ultrasound frequencies available from the transducer. Dynamic frequency tracking is available on some, though not all, ultrasound instruments.

Reject. Some instruments also provide a reject control. The term *reject* stems from its use with older radar and ultrasound instruments, in which the operator adjusted an electronic noise rejection control to "clean up" the radar or sonar signal. In ultrasound, reject eliminates both low-level electronic noise and low-level echoes from the display (Figure 3-18). Large-amplitude echo signals are affected very little.

Dynamic range and compression. Most electronic devices have a limited input signal amplitude range over which they will respond effectively. This is called the *dynamic range* of the device and is often is given in decibels. If the incoming signal is too low, the device will not respond to the signal at all. An example here might be a weak radio or television signal from a distant transmitting station, where all that can be identified is noise on the speaker or "snow" on the television screen. If the input is too large, the output of the device "peaks out" and it can no longer respond to variations in the input; we say "saturation" has occurred. Input signals between these two extremes—threshold and saturation—are within the dynamic range of the device.

Different components of an ultrasound scanner have different dynamic range capabilities. This is illustrated in Figure 3-19. The transducer and the receiver must be capable of responding to a tremendous range of echo signal amplitudes, usually in excess of 100 dB. This large amplitude range represents echoes from highly reflecting interfaces positioned close to the transducer down to very

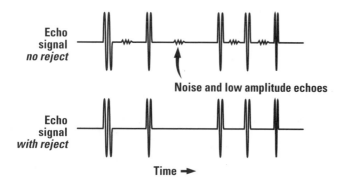

Figure 3-18. Reject function in the receiver of a pulse-echo instrument. Reject eliminates low-level signals and low-level electronic noise from the display.

weak signals from scatterers, which may have lost additional strength because of ultrasound attenuation. Image memories are generally more limited; a typical one has a dynamic range capability of 40 to 45 dB. Display devices tend to have even more limited dynamic range capabilities, usually only about 20 to 30 dB.

The "gray scale," or dot brightness, of an ultrasound image is related to the echo signal amplitude (see Figure 3-26). Clinically it is useful to display dot brightness changes for echo signal amplitude variations of at least 60 dB. However, this echo range significantly exceeds the dynamic range of the display device. To overcome this problem the echo signals are "compressed" within the receiver (Figure 3-20). Compression takes a large dynamic range, say 60 dB, and squeezes the amplitudes of these echo signals into a range to which the display can respond. A special form of compression, known as *logarithmic amplification,* compresses the larger amplitude signals while actually boosting the lower amplitudes. This gives emphasis on the display to echo signal changes among the lower amplitude signals. It makes sense to do this because this emphasizes variations in signal amplitude among scattered echoes, the source of the majority of the echoes seen on current ultrasound imagers.

Most ultrasound scanners allow the operator to vary the dynamic range of the echo signals compressed into the display. This control affects the range of echo signals appearing as shades of gray on the image monitor. On different scanners, the control for this comes under diverse names such as *compression, log compression,* or *dynamic range.* Figure 3-21, *A* is an image of the liver in an adult taken with a 60-dB dynamic range. Figure 3-21, *B* is with a 40-dB dynamic range. The 40-dB dynamic range image clearly has a higher contrast than the 60-dB dynamic range image. The reason is that for the lower dynamic range a smaller change in echo signal amplitude is needed

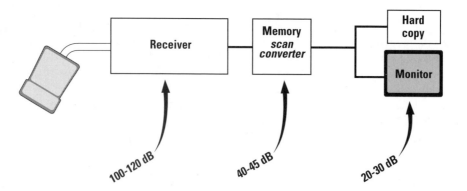

Figure 3-19 Dynamic range of various components of an ultrasound device. Notice the dynamic range capabilities at the transducer are much greater than those of the display devices. By applying logarithmic compression to the echo signals, the manufacturer can display echo signals covering a wide dynamic range, say 50 or 60 dB, on the image display, even though the latter's dynamic range is more limited.

to cover the black-to-white transition on the image monitor than for a high dynamic range. Consequently the image appears to be of higher contrast at the low dynamic range setting than at the higher setting. Table 3-3 summarizes this feature of compression.

On some scanners, reducing the dynamic range preferentially cuts out the low-level echo signals, producing similar effects as reducing the overall gain. This is the case for the 40-dB dynamic range setting in an image of objects in a gray scale phantom in Figure 3-22. However, keep in mind the different roles played by the two functions, overall gain and dynamic range. Overall gain reductions reduce all echo signals equally; the dynamic range reduction on these machines cuts out the lower echo signals, but has only a small effect on the higher level echo signals, as shown in Figure 3-23.

Demodulation. Demodulation is done in the receiver to convert the amplified echo signal burst into a single pulse, or "spike," for each reflector. Steps in a simple demodu-

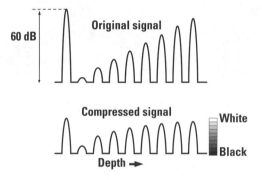

Figure 3-20. Echo signal compression. The echo signal amplitudes for a given dynamic range, say 60 dB, are reduced or compressed so they can be accommodated by the display. Logarithmic compression boosts the low-level echo signals, allowing echo variations among them to be seen, while reducing the size of higher level signals.

lation process are illustrated in Figure 3-24. The oscillating type of echo signal waveforms in the top trace of Figure 3-24 are referred to as *radio frequency (rf) signals.* The rf signal is rectified (inversion of negative components, shown in the middle trace) and then smoothed. Thus demodulation changes the form of the signal, converting it from the rf waveform to a signal that is suitable for display devices.

In summary, the receiver carries out several functions, and the principal ones are summarized in Figure 3-25. Amplification is necessary because echo signals detected by the transducer are initially too weak for display. TGC compensates for echo signal reduction with depth caused by attenuation, and log compression enables a large echo signal dynamic range to be viewed on a display monitor. Demodulation and rejection are further processes involved in conditioning echo signals before they are displayed.

Principal echo display modes

A-mode (amplitude mode). Two well-known echo signal display modes in pulse-echo ultrasonography are illustrated in Figure 3-26. The first, the A-mode, or amplitude mode display, is a trace that shows the instantaneous echo signal amplitude versus time after transmission of the acoustic pulse. In pulse-echo ultrasound, the echo return time is proportional to the reflector depth, so the A-mode display shows echo amplitude (spike height) versus reflector distance. Recall, a pulse propagation speed of 1540 m/s is assumed in the instrument's calibration for determining reflector distance from the transit time.

Table 3-3. Displayed dynamic range and image contrast

| Low dynamic range | High contrast |
| High dynamic range | Low contrast |

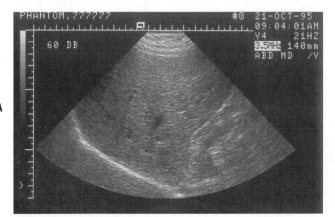

A

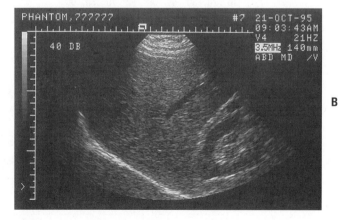

B

Figure 3-21. **A,** Image of an adult liver obtained using a 60-dB dynamic range. **B,** Same image as **A,** but taken using a 40-dB dynamic range.

The A-mode enables precise transducer-to-reflector distance measurements; therefore it is used in some ophthalmological applications, where accurate measurements of ocular dimensions are needed[5] (Figure 3-27). Stand-alone A-mode instruments are commonly found in ophthalmology laboratories. The A-mode also allows studies of the relative echogenicity of structures within the transducer beam, as shown in Figure 3-28. Spike height indicates echo amplitude, so the overall echogenicity of masses can be estimated from the distribution of spikes on the display. However, the A-mode by itself is very limited because it only presents echo data from a single beam line. In most ultrasound imaging instruments, if an A-mode trace is present, it is only as an ancillary display used by the operator to assist the setting of the gain controls and other operating conditions. In fact, many sonographers never encounter an A-mode on any of their instruments.

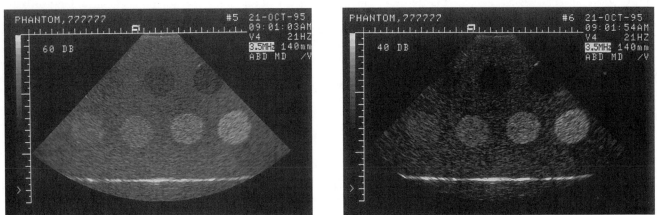

A **B**

Figure 3-22. **A,** Image of a gray scale phantom using a 60-dB dynamic range. **B,** Image of the same phantom using a 40-dB dynamic range. Notice, besides the image having higher contrast, the weaker echoes visualized in A are lost using the smaller dynamic range.

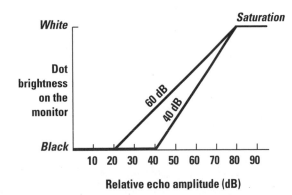

Figure 3-23. Brightness vs. relative echo signal level for the two images in Figure 3-22. The higher dynamic range setting also brings weaker echo signals into the display for this type of dynamic range variation.

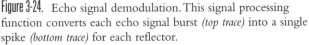

Figure 3-24. Echo signal demodulation. This signal processing function converts each echo signal burst *(top trace)* into a single spike *(bottom trace)* for each reflector.

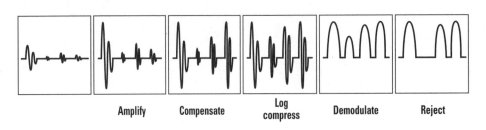

Figure 3-25. Summary of functions of the receiver.

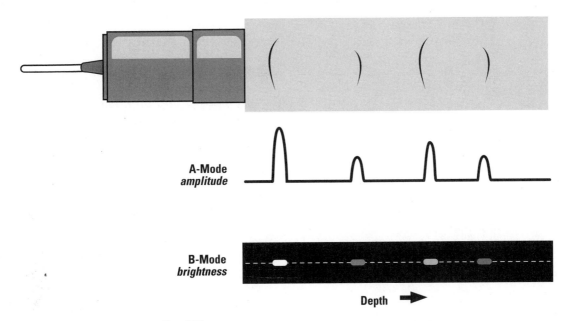

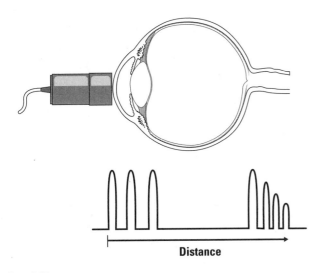

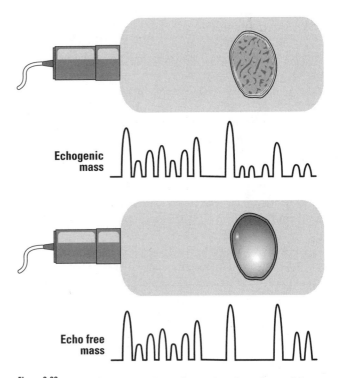

Figure 3-26. Illustration of the A-mode and B-mode displays.

Figure 3-27. Schematic illustration of the A-mode display for measuring ocular dimensions.

Figure 3-28. Use of the A-mode to determine the echogenicity of objects. An echogenic mass *(top)* has A-mode signal spikes corresponding to the reflectors and scatterers within the mass. An echo-free mass, such as a cyst *(lower)*, produces no A-mode spikes within.

B-mode (brightness mode). In a B-mode, or brightness mode, display echo signals are electronically converted to intensity-modulated dots on the screen. The brightness of the dot is proportional to the echo signal amplitude (see Figure 3-26). The B-mode display is used both in generating M-mode traces and in gray scale, two-dimensional imaging.

M-mode (motion mode). A basic M-mode display is shown in Figure 3-29. The *M* in M-mode stands for *motion,* as this echo display frequently is used to display the moving walls of the heart and the heart valves. (It is also known as *T-M mode* for *time motion mode.*) The M-mode display, very rich in information, is simple to produce; it is gen-

erated by slowly sweeping a B-mode trace across a screen, as shown. The resultant display illustrates reflector depth on one axis and time on an orthogonal axis. (Note "time" in this context is generally on the order of seconds; it should not be confused with echo return time,

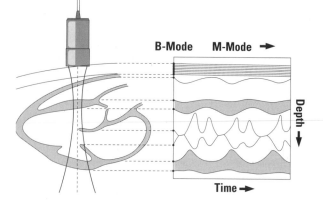

Figure 3-29. An M-mode display, obtained by sweeping the B-mode trace across the display while the ultrasound beam is stationary. The M-mode display presents reflector distance from the transducer versus time.

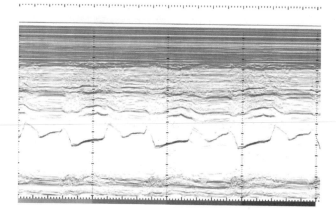

Figure 3-30. M-mode display of the heart, emphasizing the trace from the mitral valve. The M-mode trace usually provides excellent temporal detail of rapidly moving structures.

already discussed.) Stationary reflectors trace out a straight line on an M-mode display, whereas moving reflectors trace out curved lines.

The M-mode is applied most frequently in echo cardiography, where the movement patterns of walls and valves of the heart may be recorded and studied. Reflector displacement patterns, vessel linear dimensions, and echogenicity of objects are part of the basic information content of this modality. For a very long time in the history of echo cardiography, M-mode was the primary display technique. M-mode can provide excellent temporal resolution of motion patterns. The M-mode trace in Figure 3-30 is of a normal mitral valve and displays excellent detail of the mitral valve position over time. Even rapid movements of heart structures, such as the flutter pattern of the mitral valve accompanying aortic valve regurgitation, are easily recorded with this technology.[6]

Most M-mode instruments have a variable sweep speed, allowing the time representation to be magnified or compressed. The time calibration is usually achieved by internal markers multiplexed on the echo display line at prescribed intervals, such as every $1/2$ second. The markers also provide echo depth information by being produced to correspond to, say, 1-cm distance intervals. Since the velocity is the displacement per unit time, the velocity of a reflector is estimated from the slope of the M-mode trace. The slope is given by $\Delta d/\Delta t$, where Δd and Δt are as shown in Figure 3-31. (Do not confuse this method of computing a reflector velocity with the Doppler effect discussed in Chapter 5.)

The main disadvantage of M-mode is that only one anatomical dimension (distance from the transducer) is represented. M-mode displays are sometimes referred to as *ice pick* views of the internal anatomy. The view on a standard M-mode is along a single axis, established by the

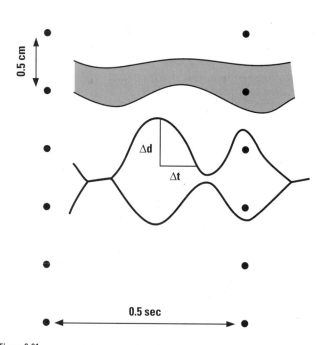

Figure 3-31. Use of the slope, $\Delta d/\Delta t$, of an M-mode trace to estimate reflector velocity. Depth marker dots on the display are generated at fixed time intervals, such as every $1/2$ s shown here, so they provide both depth (cm) and time (s) calibration information for the M-mode trace.

location of a stationary ultrasound beam. Most current echo cardiography examinations are done using real-time 2-D imaging, Doppler, and color flow, gradually relegating M-mode to a display of lesser importance in cardiography than it was just a few years ago.

ULTRASOUND B-MODE SCANNING

Image build-up

Both real-time and static ultrasound B-mode scanning are done by sweeping a pulsed ultrasound beam over the volume of interest and displaying echo signals using the B-mode as shown in Figure 3-32. With modern real-time imagers, beam sweep is rapid and a continuous image appears, so the operator has little appreciation of this sweep even taking place. Nevertheless, the image is progressively built up or updated as the beam is swept, as indicated in this figure.

Echo signals are positioned on the display in a location that corresponds to the reflector position in the body. The location of each reflector is obtained from:

1. The position and orientation of the sound beam axis; as the ultrasound beam is swept over the region being scanned, detected echo signals are placed along a line on the display that corresponds to the axis of the sound beam.
2. The delay time between launching of the acoustic pulse by the transducer and reception of an echo signal; from the delay time and the assumed sound propagation speed (1540 m/s) the distance from the reflector to the transducer is known by applying the range equation.

Scanning technology: the first generation

Ultrasound B-mode imaging was once done in most clinics using manual scanners. With these instruments, a single element transducer was attached to a mechanical arm (Figure 3-33). Sound pulses were transmitted along the axis of the transducer. To produce an image, the sonographer swept the beam manually by moving the transducer across the skin of the patient and tilting it in various directions. The mechanical arm constrained the motion of the transducer to a plane, so the resultant image depicted an anatomical slice. The arm also contained sensors at each of its pivot points; these sensors tracked the position and orientation of the transducer face, and hence the ultrasound beam axis. This information was, of course, necessary for placing echo signals in their proper location on the display, as illustrated in Figure 3-32.

One advantage of manual scanners was the large fields of view obtained. The images produced views we now associate with CT and MRI imaging (Figure 3-34). Significant disadvantages of manual scanners, however, resulted in their virtual elimination from most departments. For example:

1. It took several seconds to produce each image; These devices became known as "static" imagers because they worked best on stationary structures.

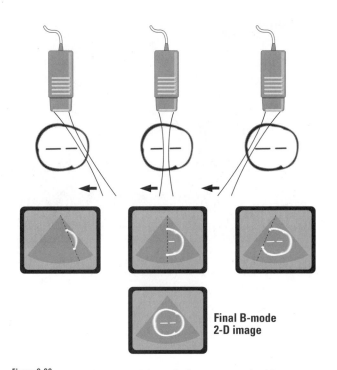

Final B-mode 2-D image

Figure 3-32. B-mode image (also called *2-D image*) build-up. Ultrasound pulses are sent into the body along different beam paths, three of which are shown. Echo signals are displayed using the B-mode display. Echoes are positioned along a line on the display that corresponds to the beam axis when they are detected; the echo arrival time indicates the reflector depth.

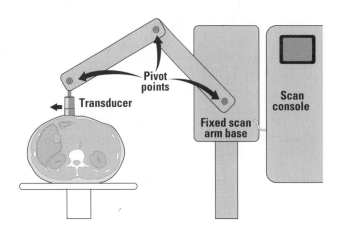

Figure 3-33. Manual (static) scanner, formerly used to produce ultrasound B-mode images.

2. The scan arm was cumbersome and limited the available anatomical views.
3. There was a higher dependence of image quality on the skill of the sonographer than with modern scanners.

Another type of large anatomical scanner also appeared at various times in the history of ultrasound

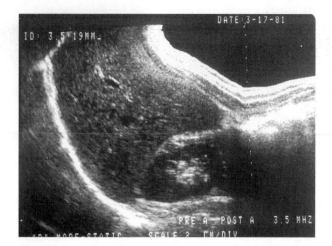

Figure 3-34. B-mode image of the liver and kidney obtained using a static scanner.

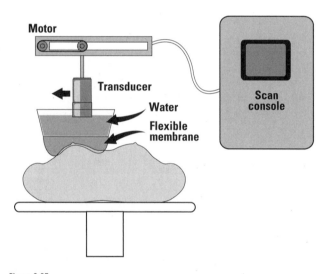

Figure 3-35. Water path scanner; this arrangement was used commonly for ultrasound breast imaging.

imaging. So-called water path scanners (Figure 3-35) still exist in some departments. In these instruments, the transducer is offset from the patient's skin surface by a water path. The structure to be imaged can be immersed in water or coupled to a water-filled bag. The scan is done by mechanically translating the transducer across the region to be imaged, thus sweeping the sound beam axis through the tissue. Water path scanners have two advantages over static scanners: the automated scanning operation provides more uniform imaging; and the offset between the transducer and the skin surface results in better detail of superficial structures.

Real-time scanners

Manual and water path scanners have for the most part been replaced by automated real-time scanners. Their use provides performance capabilities not attainable with manual scanners—including the ability to visualize rapidly moving structures such as heart valves and the ease in locating and following internal anatomical landmarks and organs. The common types of automated real-time scanners are linear arrays, convex (or curvilinear) arrays, phased arrays, and mechanical scanners.

Linear array transducers. Linear array transducers consist of small rectangular elements lined up side by side, as shown in Figure 3-36. Imaging is done by sequentially transmitting and receiving along parallel beam lines starting at one end of the array, as shown in Figure 3-36, *A*. Echo signals arriving at individual elements in the group are applied to the beam former, where they are electronically focused and then added, producing a single echo signal for each beam line. After echoes arrive at the transducer from the maximum depth for the first beam line, a second beam is transmitted along a slightly different, but parallel, line (Figure 3-36, *B*) and echoes are received. Then a third beam is transmitted, and so forth, continuing to the end of the array. A single scan takes typically $1/30$ s, more or less depending on the number of beam lines and the image depth. Then the process is repeated. Scanning is continuously repeated and the image updated until the operator "freezes" the image. Individual acoustic lines forming the B-mode image are separated by one element width. (Even closer positioning of beam lines is possible if different element groupings are adopted.)

In Chapter 2 we mentioned that individual beams from linear arrays are produced using a group of elements rather than a single element. The reasons for this are (1) a beam from an individual element quickly diverges, so an individual element's beam is broad and lateral resolution is poor; (2) the sensitivity is also very poor if just one element is used; and (3) multiple elements enable electronic focusing. Electronic transmit focusing as well as focusing during reception, also discussed in Chapter 2, are crucial to the image quality achieved with these systems. Other features mentioned in Chapter 2, including dynamic aperture size and dynamic apodization, are also applied.

Curvilinear arrays. A curvilinear, or convex, array operates on the same principles as a linear array (Figure 3-37). The array is made up of small rectangular elements arranged side by side. However, because the elements are laid out on a convex surface, beam lines are not parallel, but emerge at different angles—like the spokes of a wheel (Figure 3-38). The scan format traces out a section of a sector; the exact shape of the sector varies with the radius of the array and the angle over which elements are placed.

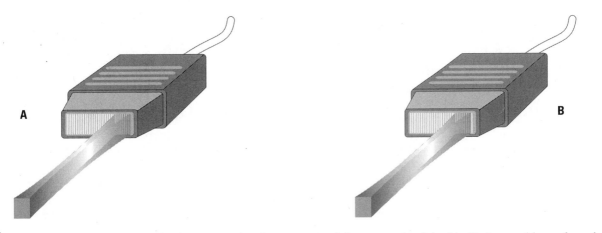

Figure 3-36. **A,** Linear array transducer with a beam emerging from a group of elements at the right side. **B,** A second beam from the linear array; the center axis of this beam is shifted by one element compared to the situation in A. This was done by dropping the right-most element from the previous group and picking up the next element to the left.

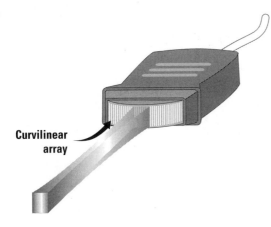

Figure 3-37. Convex (curvilinear) array.

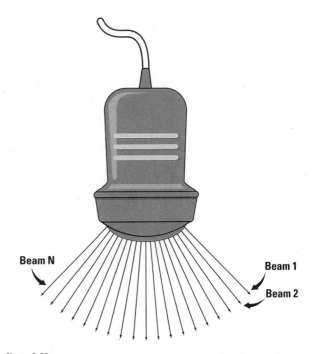

Figure 3-38. Typical beam line arrangement for the curvilinear array. Echo data are obtained first from beam 1, then beam 2, etc.

The region of a transducer assembly through which sound is coupled to the patient is sometimes referred to as the *entrance window*. For many regions the convex shape of this array provides better transducer-to-patient coupling along the entrance window than is provided by the simple linear array. The styles range from very tightly curved arrays to larger arrays with a gradual curvature. The sector scan format enables larger imaged fields from a smaller entrance beam area than the linear array. Multiple transmit focusing and dynamic focus of received echo signals are important design features in these arrays as well.

In comparison to a phased array, which also produces a sector image (see below), a curvilinear array requires a larger entrance window. However, a possible advantage over the phased array is that the beams emerge perpendicular to the surface of the active elements of the curvilinear array. In other words, the convex array elements always direct their sound beams forward; in contrast, a phased array must steer beams off to the side to pick up

echoes from structures near the edges of the imaged field, and in so doing there often is some fall off in the sensitivity of the elements and some degradation of lateral resolution near the edges of the field.

Phased-array scanners. The transducer assembly of a phased array sector scanner consists of a tightly grouped array of elements. Unlike the previous two types of arrays, all elements are involved in producing the sound beam and receiving echoes for each acoustic line. Sound beams produced by a phased array are electronically steered at various angles with respect to the array surface (Figure 3-39). Steering for each beam is achieved by introducing appropriate time delays in the excitation pulses applied to individual elements in the array. The direction in which the sound beam is steered is dependent on the exact time delay settings and is varied from one transmit pulse to the next, steering the beam in different directions. Beam steering is also applied during echo reception by varying the "directivity" of the array. Echo signals from a reflector received by the different elements are delayed in an appropriate sequence, depending on the beam direction, then added together forming one signal for that reflector. This is carried out within the beam former circuitry of the scanner.

Besides beam steering, electronic focusing also is done. Delay settings for focusing, similar to those described in Chapter 2, are programmed along with the beam-steering delays. Both single and multiple transmit focal zones and dynamic receive focusing are used in phased arrays.

An advantage of phased arrays over linear and curvilinear arrays is their relatively small entrance window, permitting coupling through the intercostal space. Phased arrays may have 120 or more individual piezoelectric elements packed into a 1- to 2-cm row. Thus they may be used effectively in pediatric and adult cardiac imaging.

An advantage of phased arrays over mechanical scanners (see below) is the flexibility introduced in the scanning format. It is easy to share a scanning beam with one or more static M-mode lines, for example, enabling multiple-trace M-mode displays to be produced along with a two-dimensional image. Also, since there are no mechanical movements involved in producing the scan, it is easy to synchronize scanning movements to external triggers, such as derived from ECG signals. Both these features have been employed in some electronic sector scanning instruments. Finally, Doppler and color flow imaging, discussed later in this book, are easier to do using phased arrays than using mechanically scanned transducers.

Mechanically scanned real-time instruments. Conceptually the simplest type of rapid autoscanners are mechanical systems. These usually employ one or more focused, single-element transducers to transmit and receive ultrasound signals. A common arrangement is shown in Figure 3-40. This system employs from two to four separate transducers positioned in different locations on the rim of a rotating wheel. Transducers are pulsed only during the time they sweep past the scanning window, as shown. The transducer assembly housing must be filled with a fluid to ensure acoustic coupling between the transducer element and the window. (The type of fluid used and whether it is user replenishable if, for example, air bubbles are formed should be explained in the accompanying operator's manual.)

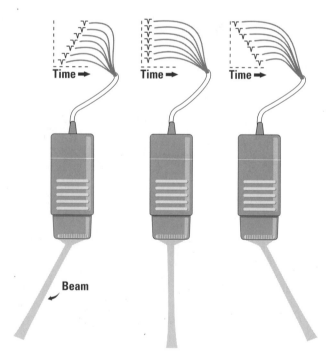

Figure 3-39. Phased array transducer. Successive beams are steered in different directions by varying time delay sequences among the transmit pulses. Three different beam directions are shown, but typically 100 to 200 separate beams sent in different directions are used for each image.

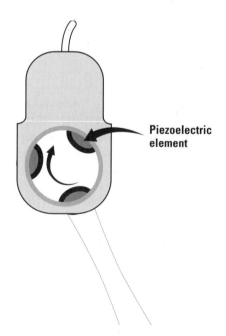

Figure 3-40. Mechanical scanning transducer. Focused, single-element transducers are mechanically swept over the region to be scanned. This method of scanning also is done with annular array transducers.

Some mechanical scanners incorporate annular array transducers rather than single-element transducers. When this is the case, multiple transmit focusing, dynamic receiving focusing, and dynamic aperture control are possible with these units as well. Of course, beam sweeping for scanning still is done mechanically by translating the elements within the transducer assembly.

Unlike sequential linear arrays and electronically sectored arrays, mechanical scanners contain moving parts to generate the scan. The parts may consist of gears, pulleys, wheels, or oscillating shafts, depending on the design. Normal wear and tear on the drive mechanism can be reduced by placing the transducer assembly in a nonscanning mode when not in use. Again, consult the operator's manual for the recommended transducer assembly standby mode between patient scans.

Special purpose automatic scanners

Most of the real-time scanning arrangements just described have also been used in various special purpose scanners. Special purpose transducer assemblies or scanning instruments are those designed mainly for a single imaging application. For example, transrectal scanners are used effectively for imaging the prostate and sometimes the colon. Linear, curvilinear, and phased arrays, as well as mechanically scanned probes, are used in this application. Some configurations provide simultaneous scanning of two planes perpendicular to each other. This is referred to as *biplane imaging* and has been found advantageous for determining the extent of disease in the prostate.

Transvaginal scanners commonly are of the curvilinear design, although mechanical and phased array probes are also used in this application. Just as is the case with transrectal probes, distinct advantages provided with use of such transducer assemblies include use of higher frequencies for better spatial resolution, since the attenuating path to the scanned region is reduced significantly, and avoidance of any beam distorting attenuating tissue layers making up the abdominal wall.

Intraoperative and laparoscopic transducer assemblies are also becoming available. These enable the sonographer to place the probe in direct contact with the organ to be imaged, so higher frequencies, with their inherently better spatial resolution, than are used for transcutaneous imaging are common. The higher frequency also is advantageous in enabling miniaturization of the probe, necessary to provide accessibility through the available windows. Many laparoscopic and intraoperative transducers are linear, curvilinear, and phased array designs.

Finally, various designs for intravascular transducers are also available. A common configuration is a mechanical probe, shown in Figure 3-41, *A*. The transducer typically is 12 to 20 MHz, although 30 MHz or higher are being used for coronary artery imaging. The transducer is mounted on the end of a catheter that can be inserted into the vessel. In the schematic in Figure 3-41, *A*, a single-element piezoelectric element is mounted radially on a shaft within the flexible protective sheath of the catheter. The shaft is rotated by an external drive mechanism. The high-frequency miniature element provides excellent spatial detail (Figure 3-41, *B*), but imaging is done only over short distances.

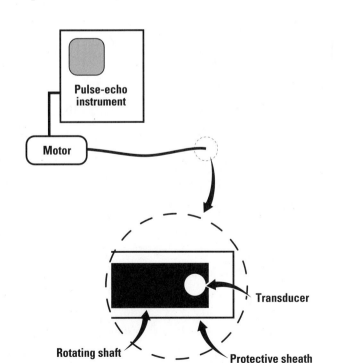

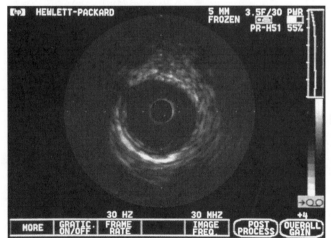

Figure 3-41. **A,** Intravascular transducer and scanning system. **B,** B-mode image showing the lumen and walls of an LAD (left anterior descending) artery in an adult heart; the image was obtained using a 30-MHz intravascular scanner. (Courtesy of Hewlett Packard Company, Andover, MA.)

FRAME RATE AND SCANNING SPEED LIMITATIONS

Scanning speed, expressed as the *image frame rate,* or the number of times per second a sweep of the ultrasound beam is done by the transducer, is an important performance characteristic of real-time scanners. This aspect of imaging performance is closely related to temporal resolution characteristics. The higher the frame rate, the better is the ability to image rapidly moving structures, to overcome patient motion artifacts, and to do rapid survey scans of a region. As it turns out, the maximum speed with which a real-time instrument can build up images is limited by the finite travel time of sound pulses in tissue (Figure 3-42).

The principle behind this limitation is straightforward: the separate transducer beam lines used to form an image (see, for example, Figure 3-38) each require a small time interval to collect all echoes emerging from that line. After each transmit pulse, the instrument waits to collect all echo signals down to the maximum depth setting before a subsequent transmit pulse is launched along an adjacent beam line. The time delay required between pulses depends on the speed of sound in the medium and the maximum visualization depth (Figure 3-42).

Consider the sector scan arrangement in Figure 3-43. An image is produced by separate ultrasound beams distributed evenly over the sector angle. For simple scanning arrangements such as shown here, it might be useful to employ 120 or more individual lines to form the image. Fewer lines could be used, but only at the cost of larger gaps between individual lines, which might be undesirable. If the field of view (i.e., the depth setting) in Figure 3-43 results in a visualization depth of D, the delay time, T_{line}, needed to collect all echoes from any single line is given by

$$T_{line} = 13 \ \mu s \times D \ (cm) \qquad (3-3)$$

where D (cm) is the distance D expressed in cm. We used the information in Table 3-1 that the pulse-echo travel time is 13 μs for each cm when the speed of sound is 1540 m/s.

The time required to produce a complete image or "frame" consisting of N such lines is simply N times T_{line} or

$$T_{frame} = NT_{line} = N \times 13 \ \mu s \times D \ (cm) \qquad (3-4)$$

The maximum allowable frame rate, FR_{max} is the reciprocal of the time needed for a single complete image. For example, if it takes 0.1 s to do 1 scan, the maximum rate is 10/s; if it takes 0.5 s, the maximum rate is 2/s, and so forth. Taking the reciprocal of T_{frame}, we get,

$$FR_{max} = \frac{1}{T_{frame}}$$

$$= \frac{1}{13 \mu s \times N \times D \ (cm)}$$

or,

$$FR_{max} = \frac{77,000 \ /s}{N \times D \ (cm)} \qquad (3-5)$$

This equation tells us that the maximum frame rate (in units of frames per second) equals a constant (77,000) divided by the number of lines used to form the image frame, and divided by the depth setting (in units of cm). The constant, 77,000/s, is approximately what you get when you take the ratio 1/13 μs; this may be verified easily with a calculator.

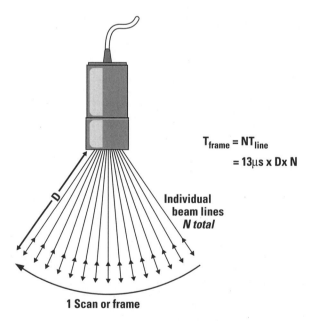

Figure 3-43. The speed of sound dictates that each beam line requires 13 μs × D to acquire echo data, where D is the depth setting in cm. Therefore the total time required for one frame is 13 μs × D × N, where N is the number of beam lines used to form the image.

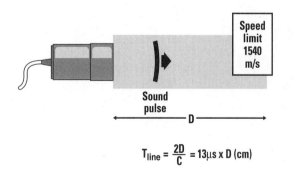

Figure 3-42. The scanning speed in ultrasound imaging ultimately is limited by the speed of sound in tissue, 1540 m/s, or 0.154 cm/μs.

Example: Suppose the field of view of a sector scanner is set for a maximum depth of 20 cm, and N is 120 lines. Calculate the maximum frame rate.

Solution:

Using Equation 3-5,

$$FR_{max} = \frac{77,000/s}{N \times D \ (cm)}$$

$$= \frac{77,000 \ /s}{120 \times 20}$$

$$= 32/s$$

Equation 3-5 tells us that the maximum possible frame rate is dictated by the depth setting, D, and N, the number of beam lines used to form the image. Higher frame rates are possible if the depth setting is lower (Figure 3-44), which a sonographer can quickly verify with any scanner. Higher frame rates also are possible if the number of beam lines used to form the image is smaller. The number of beam lines can be reduced using greater spacing between beam lines (Figure 3-45). This, however, could compromise image quality, as the ultrasound image may look coarser and grainier when the line density is low. Another way to reduce N is to reduce the imaged field size (Figure 3-46). This is done quite frequently in color flow imaging, where image acquisition times are quite long. Field sizes sometimes are reduced in B-mode imaging as well when higher frame rates are required.

Results calculated using Equation 3-5 are for imaging with a single transmit focal zone. Instruments that allow simultaneous multiple transmit focal zones must decrease the image frame rate when these conditions are present; this is because of the longer time required to form each acoustic line with multiple transmit focal zones. (Note, multiple receive focal zones do not decrease the frame rate since receive focusing happens dynamically as the echo signals arrive from deeper and deeper structures.)

Manufacturers are continuously attempting to push scanners beyond the limits implied by Equation 3-5. For example, confocal imaging[2] uses optimized pulsing and receiving parameters to attempt to obtain high frame rates when large numbers of multiple transmit focal zones are applied. Parallel processing, in which image data from more than one beam line are acquired simultaneously, is another of these methods. As these techniques improve, we can expect instruments with higher spatial resolution, superior image quality, and better temporal resolution than current scanners to be available.

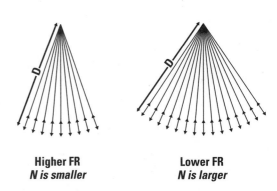

Higher FR
N is smaller

Lower FR
N is larger

Figure 3-45. Dependence of frame rate on N, the number of beam lines used to form the image. Here N is varied by varying the spacing between beam lines.

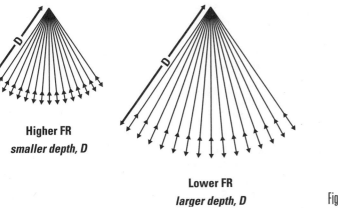

Higher FR
smaller depth, D

Lower FR
larger depth, D

Figure 3-44. Dependence of frame rate on the depth setting.

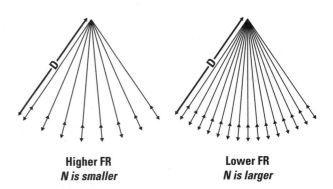

Higher FR
N is smaller

Lower FR
N is larger

Figure 3-46. Dependence of frame rate on N, the number of beam lines used to form the image. In this example N is changed by varying the size of the imaged sector.

References

1. Kremkau F: *Diagnostic ultrasound principles, instrumentation and exercises,* ed 4, Orlando, 1993, Grune & Stratton.
2. Diasonics VST Master Series Product literature, Milpitas, CA, 1994, Diasonics.
3. McKnight RN: A mixing scheme to focus a transducer array dynamically, *Hewlett Packard Journal,* p 16, December 1993.
4. American Institute of Ultrasound in Medicine: *Standard for real time display of thermal and mechanical indices of diagnostic ultrasound equipment,* Laurel, MD, 1992.
5. Kendall CJ: *Ophthalmic echography,* Thorofare, NJ, 1990, Slack.
6. Hagen-Ansert L: *Textbook of diagnostic ultrasonography,* ed 4, St. Louis, 1995, Mosby.

Questions for Review

1. The range equation relates:

   A. Reflector distance to speed of sound
   B. Reflector distance to echo arrival time
   C. Reflector distance to echo amplitude
   D. Echo frequency to speed of sound

2. Reflector B is three times the distance from the transducer as reflector A. It takes _____ times as long for an echo to arrive from reflector B as from reflector A.

   A. 1.5
   B. 3
   C. 4.5
   D. 6

3. If the distance to a reflector is 10 cm, the time between transmitting a pulse and receiving an echo from that reflector is about:

   A. 55 μs
   B. 130 μs
   C. 650 μs
   D. 1000 μs

4. The speed of sound assumed in time versus distance calibrations of most scanners is:

   A. 1.54 mm/μs
   B. 1540 mm/s
   C. 2630 m/s
   D. 1.54 m/s

5. Duty factor is:

   A. The fraction of time the transducer emits sound
   B. The fraction of time the transducer receives echoes
   C. The fraction of time transmitting and receiving
   D. The amount of energy consumed by the pulser
   E. The amount of energy consumed by the pulser and receiver

6. Pulse repetition period is the inverse of:

   A. Ultrasound frequency
   B. Pulse repetition frequency
   C. Pulse duration
   D. Doppler frequency

7. The pulse duration is the time from the beginning of a pulse to:

   A. The beginning of the next pulse
   B. The end of the same pulse
   C. The end of the first cycle in the pulse
   D. The end of the next pulse

8. Typical duty factors in pulse-echo ultrasound are:

   A. Between 0.1% and 1%
   B. Between 1% and 10%
   C. Between 20% and 50%
   D. Between 50% and 100%

9. Which of the following will increase the duty factor?

   A. Increasing the pulse repetition frequency
   B. Increasing the transmit amplitude
   C. Increasing the receiver gain
   D. Decreasing the reject control
   E. Increasing the examination time

10. If the original acoustic power is 50 mW and the power control is changed to increase it by 3 dB, the new power is:

    A. 53 mW
    B. 60 mW
    C. 100 mW
    D. 150 mW
    E. 200 mW

11. Which *one* of the following *does not* increase when the output (transmit) power control is increased?

    A. Amplitude of acoustic pulses transmitted into tissue
    B. Number of transmit pulses per second
    C. Amplitude of echoes returning to the transducer
    D. Patient exposure
    E. Dot brightness on a gray scale echo display

12. In ultrasound, receiver gain is the ratio of:

    A. Input signal amplitude to output signal amplitude
    B. Input frequency to output frequency
    C. Output bandwidth to input bandwidth
    D. Output dynamic range to input dynamic range
    E. Output signal amplitude to input signal amplitude

13. From the standpoint of minimizing exposure to patients, it's best to use:

    A. Low power, high gain
    B. High power, low gain
    C. Intermediate power, intermediate gain
    D. High power, high gain

14. TGC or swept gain compensates for sound:

    A. Propagation speed
    B. Attenuation
    C. Reflection
    D. Refraction

15. To which component of an ultrasound scanner is TGC applied?

    A. The pulser
    B. The receiver
    C. The scan converter
    D. The image monitor

16. Reject eliminates:

    A. Electronic noise only
    B. Electronic noise and low-level echo signals
    C. Electronic noise and high-frequency echo signals
    D. Artifactual echo signals

17. A measure of the echo signal amplitude range over which a noticeable change in display dot brightness occurs is the:

    A. TGC slope
    B. Gain
    C. Echo range
    D. Dynamic range

18. Which of the following components of an ultrasound imaging instrument has the severest limitations in terms of dynamic range?

    A. Transducer
    B. Preamplifier
    C. Amplifier
    D. Memory
    E. Monitor

19. Compared to when a low dynamic range setting is present, a high dynamic range setting yields:

    A. Lower image contrast
    B. Larger frequency bandwidth
    C. Less electronic noise on the display
    D. Greater rejection of low-amplitude echoes
    E. Ability to visualize more rapidly moving interfaces

20. The process of converting the amplified echo signal burst into a single pulse for each reflector is called:

    A. Rejection
    B. Demodulation
    C. Compensation
    D. Amplification
    E. Scan conversion

21. Data presented on an A-mode display are:

    A. Echo return time versus reflector depth
    B. Echo amplitude versus reflector depth
    C. Reflector depth versus time
    D. Dot brightness versus reflector depth
    E. Reflector position versus reflector impedance

22. Information conveyed on A-mode includes all of the following *except:*

    A. Whether a structure is echogenic
    B. Relative amplitudes of echo signals
    C. Reflector distance from the transducer
    D. Organ cross-sectional information
    E. Distances between reflectors

23. The axes of an M-mode display are:

    A. Dot brightness versus reflector depth
    B. Reflector depth versus time
    C. Reflector velocity versus time
    D. Reflector impedance versus time
    E. Reflector position versus reflector impedance

24. Information conveyed on M-mode include *all of the following except:*

    A. Reflector movement patterns
    B. Reflector distance from the transducer
    C. Echo amplitude
    D. Organ cross-sectional information
    E. Distance between reflectors

25. A B-mode image generally is formed using _____ individual ultrasound beam(s).

    A. 1
    B. About 10 to 20
    C. About 100 to 200
    D. About 10,000

26. The *B* in B-mode stands for:

    A. Beam lines
    B. Lesser grade than *A*
    C. Basic
    D. Brightness
    E. Broadcast

27. Assumptions implicitly built into an ultrasound scanner to construct images include *all of the following except:*

    A. Pulses and echoes travel at 1.54 mm/μs
    B. Reflectors are positioned as though they originate along the beam axis
    C. The brighter the display, the greater the echo amplitude
    D. Scattered energy is eliminated by the transducer

28. Information used to LOCATE reflectors in their proper position on a B-mode image display includes *all of the following except:*

    A. Echo signal amplitude
    B. Speed of sound in the medium
    C. Echo arrival time
    D. Beam position/orientation

29. An advantage of manual static scanners over real-time scanners is:

    A. Faster scanning times
    B. Larger imaged fields
    C. Combined Doppler and B-mode imaging
    D. Higher frame rates
    E. Depiction of motion

30. An advantage of a water path scanner is:

    A. Better imaging of superficial structures
    B. Better imaging of deep structures
    C. Higher scanning speeds
    D. Keeps the tissue warm
    E. Keeps the transducer warm

31. The general term for a transducer assembly consisting of a number of small, separate piezoelectric elements is:

    A. A sector scanner
    B. An annulus
    C. A hybrid system
    D. An array

32. Which of the following that can be done with array transducer assemblies can't be done with single-element transducer assemblies?

    A. Transmission through air and bone can be done.
    B. The focal distance can be changed electronically.
    C. The axial resolution can be changed electronically.
    D. Reverberation artifacts can be eliminated.
    E. Coupling oil or gel can be eliminated.

33. The scanning speed and frame rate in a pulse-echo instrument are limited mainly by:

    A. Pulser heating
    B. Patient heating
    C. Amplifier heating
    D. Sound travel time
    E. Sound attenuation

34. The pulse-echo transit time is 13 μs per cm of tissue path. The amount of time needed to acquire echo data on an image made from 100 acoustic lines using a depth setting (image field of view) of 10 cm is:

    A. 13 μs
    B. 13 ms
    C. 1.3 s
    D. 7.6 s

35. If the depth setting in the previous problem is halved, the maximum possible frame rate will:

    A. Halve
    B. Remain unchanged
    C. Double
    D. Triple
    E. Quadruple

36. In the above problem, if three transmit focal zones are applied rather than one zone, the maximum frame rate will (roughly):

    A. Decrease to $^1/_3$
    B. Remain unchanged
    C. Double
    D. Triple
    E. Quadruple

37. By increasing the number of acoustic beam lines per frame, the manufacturer can:

    A. Increase the frame rate
    B. Reduce the acoustic exposure to the patient
    C. Reduce the slice thickness
    D. Decrease the examination time
    E. Improve the spatial detail in the image

38. Reducing the sector angle of a phased array could provide:

    A. An increase in the frame rate
    B. A larger imaged field
    C. More beam lines in the image
    D. Better axial resolution

39. An advantage of a phased array over a curvilinear array in some applications is the phased array's:

    A. Higher frequency
    B. Smaller "footprint"
    C. Wider field of view
    D. Greater sensitivity

40. The type of transducer for which the method of scanning is most similar to that of a linear array is:

    A. An annular array
    B. A phased array
    C. A curvilinear array
    D. Any two-dimensional array

Chapter 4
Image Storage and Display

The scanner and the image monitor are like a couple dancing, but each doing a different step and following different musical beats. The "scan converter memory" serves as the buffer between the two different formats for echo data acquisition and image display.

In this chapter we will look at components of the ultrasound imager involved with storing and displaying ultrasound echo information. We also will consider the various methods used to obtain hard copy records. The first topic is the scan converter, the memory device in which images are formed and then presented to monitors and hard copy devices.

SCAN CONVERTER MEMORY

Role of the scan converter

Most ultrasound scanners write image data to a memory device called a *scan converter*. The scan converter plays two important roles during imaging:

1. It stores images during scan build-up, for viewing and recording.
2. It performs scan conversion, enabling image data to be viewed on video monitors.

Temporary image storage is an obvious role of the scan converter. The device accepts echo signal data from the ultrasonic scanner, stores this information in an internal memory, and reads out the data to a TV monitor (Figure 4-1). In addition to B-mode image data, this may include M-mode records, Doppler signal, and color flow information. When the scan converter is "unfrozen," it operates in a continuously refreshed state; that is, echo information is updated in real time at the same time that it is displayed. In "freeze" mode, scanning operations are suspended and only the readout function is active.

"Scan conversion" is necessary because the display and the image acquisition occur in different formats. Ultrasound images are displayed on a video monitor. Video monitors require image data to be ordered in a raster scanned format, as suggested in Figure 4-1. However, the echo image signals produced by the scanner arrive at the memory in a completely different order and at different data rates than those required by monitors. The example in Figure 4-1 is for a sector imager, and the arrows to the left of the scan converter correspond to individual beam lines. Echoes arrive at the scan converter from along these individual beam lines. Usually they arrive from locations in the scanned field at the instant the monitor is "painting" a totally different part of the image. The scanner and the monitor are like a couple dancing, but each doing a different step and following different musical beats.

The scan converter memory is the buffer between the two very different data formats during the writing and reading operations. The scan converter accepts echo image data in the format and at the data speeds presented by the scanner; it writes these data into its memory as an image. It must do this for any transducer type—that is, linear, curved, and phased arrays, and mechanical scanners—supported by the scanner. Data are read out of the memory for viewing on a video monitor, synchronized to the horizontal raster sweeps of the video device.

Early scan converters were of an analog design, using a kind of cathode ray tube as the image storage matrix. Image storage could be quite good, at least for brief periods during a given day; however, analog storage tubes were subject to instability and drift. Images frequently became fuzzy and defocused, sometimes even after only a few hours of scanning. Gray levels drifted so that cameras and image-recording devices needed frequent readjustments to compensate.

Current instruments use digital technology for storage and manipulation of data. Digital devices are extremely stable. Furthermore, when images are stored in a digital format, they can be readily manipulated and processed using different mathematical functions. Characteristics of digital devices are discussed in the next section.

Digital devices

Bits and bytes. Most modern ultrasound instruments have digital computers and computer hardware for signal processing and system control. On-board computers provide a readout of the current operational status of the instrument (such as the display magnification, transducer assembly identification, power and gain settings, and acoustic output indexes) and adjust the operating conditions of the instrument in response to operator control adjustments. Digital signal processors are involved in many of the functions of the receiver, both in the pulse-echo modes discussed in the previous chapter and in Doppler and color flow imaging modes, which will be discussed later. Another important role of digital circuitry in an ultrasound scanner is that of image formation and storage in the scan converter. The emphasis in this section is on concepts regarding storage of digital image data.

Most signals may be represented and displayed in either an analog or a digital format. In an analog format values of the signal vary continuously between a minimum and a maximum level, and the representation of the signal is continuous in time. In digital format, on the other hand, the values are represented in discrete levels, with fixed steps between the levels. Some of the differences between the two types of representations can be appreciated if we consider a speedometer on an automobile; analog and digital types are both available (Figure 4-2). The analog device uses a pointer to indicate the speed, and the pointer's position changes continuously as the driver accelerates. The digital speedometer presents a meter reading consisting of discrete values for the automobile speed. The reading changes in discrete steps as the driver accelerates.

Digital systems offer advantages over analog devices in stability and immunity to electronic noise. These properties stem from the fact that all digital systems employ as a basic unit a stable electronic circuit, which we will refer to as a **bit**, for *binary digit*. The circuit comprising a single bit can be electronically switched into either of two states: high or low, as in Figure 4-3. It cannot be at any other level! The output signal level of the circuit indicates which state it is in. Typically the two states are used to represent the binary digits 1 and 0, respectively. Thus a bit is the smallest piece of information that a digital device can store and manipulate. A single bit can represent a quantity as being either of two different levels.

Figure 4-2. Analog and digital speedometers used in automobiles. The digital values are discrete (79, 80, 81, etc.) whereas the analog unit presents a continuous variation in speed as a driver accelerates.

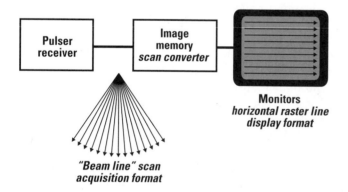

Figure 4-1. Function of the scan converter memory. Scan and other echo information is written to the scan converter as it arrives from the receiver of the ultrasound instrument. The data are read out to a video monitor. Usually echoes arrive from specific locations in the body at a slightly different time than when the video monitor is "painting" that area. The scan converter serves as the go-between for the two data formats.

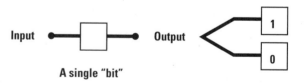

Figure 4-3. Digital "bit" (for "binary digit"). The bit has two possible states, expressed as 0 and 1. By forming multibit storage units, computer designers form units that can store many different values even though 0 and 1 are the only values available for each bit.

Digital devices are made much more sophisticated than single bit devices. Additional signal level representations for quantities are obtained by stringing a number of bits together to form a *multibit storage unit*. The number of bits used to represent the storage unit determines the amount of information that can be represented or stored in the unit.

Consider the very simple situation of a storage unit that consists of just two bits. How many discrete values could that unit represent? If we allow each bit to be in its 0 or its 1 state, there are four different possibilities for the storage unit configuration, all shown in Figure 4-4. It could have both bits in the 1 state; it could have the first bit 0 and the second 1 or the first 1 and the second 0; finally, both bits could be 0. Thus each of these four states could represent a different signal level, and there are four levels possible. A "2-bit" speedometer, for example, might let one level represent the speed range 0 to 24 mph, a second level could indicate the speed is somewhere between 25 and 49 mph, level three could indicate the 50 to 74 mph range, and level four could be 75 mph or greater.

The hypothetical 2-bit speedometer probably would not serve us very well because of the limited amount of information presented. Motorists need finer resolution of their speed than the gross representation the 2-bit system provides in order to keep within posted speed limits. Better resolution would be provided if the digital speedometer used more bits. If we add one additional bit, giving us a 3-bit storage unit, it can readily be seen that now eight different combinations are possible (Figure 4-4) and eight levels represented. Four bits would yield 16

combinations, five bits 32 combinations, etc. Table 4-1 shows a longer list of possibilities.

The number of levels grows exponentially with the number of bits. The number of discrete levels, *L,* for a multibit storage unit consisting of *n* bits is equal to two raised to the power of the number of bits. That is,

$$L = 2^n \qquad (4\text{-}1)$$

The more bits available in a single storage unit, the larger the integer number that can be represented. A common unit is an 8-bit storage unit, called a *byte*. Bytes usually are used to store values representing the characters of the alphabet, as well as other symbols. Often personal computers have 4 to 8 megabytes (Mbytes) or more of internal, volatile (i.e., erased if the computer is powered down) memory, and internal fixed disk storage capacities of hundreds of megabytes.

Binary numbers. Multibit storage units can become quite large, and the values or levels they represent complex. Perhaps you have seen references to 32-bit machines, now becoming common even in personal computers. A 32-bit storage unit has over 4 billion unique combinations of zeroes and ones, so the possible number of levels seems almost endless. Appropriate coding applied to the string of bits forming any multibit storage unit permits these "words" to represent meaningful numbers.

Computers employ the **binary number** system as a basis for representing numbers and carrying out mathematical computations. Analogous to the decimal number system, employing 10 as a base and using the digits 0 through 9 in the representation, the binary number system employs 2 as a base and uses only the digits 0 and 1 to represent numbers. For example, the string of digits 1011001 is a binary number; its decimal equivalent is 89, as we will see in a moment.

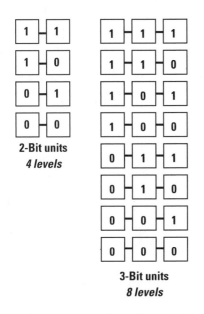

2-Bit units
4 levels

3-Bit units
8 levels

Figure 4-4. Digital storage units of two bits and three bits and their possible bit configurations. Four unique combinations are possible with the two-bit unit, while eight combinations are possible with the three-bit system.

Table 4-1. Number of discrete levels available in a digital storage unit versus the number of bits

Number of bits	Number of levels
1	2
2	4
3	8
4	16
5	32
6	64
7	128
8	256
9	512
10	1024
12	4096

Conversion from a binary number to its decimal equivalent isn't too difficult once you know the basic rules. Binary numbers follow the same logical pattern as decimal numbers, only as mentioned earlier, they utilize a more limited set of digits and a different "base." Consider first the meaning of numbers we write in decimal format, say 748. This really is

$$7 \times 100 + 4 \times 10 + 8 \times 1$$

or

$$7 \times 10^2 + 4 \times 10^1 + 8 \times 10^0$$

The base of the decimal number system is 10, and each place in a decimal number represents taking the digit in that place and multiplying by a power of 10, starting with 10^0 at the decimal point and increasing by one power of 10 for every place you move left. The numeral 7 is in the second power of 10 (100) position, 4 the first power of 10, and 8 the zeroth power (any number to the zeroth power is 1). Hence we have 748 is "seven hundred forty-eight."

Binary numbers are similar, only the base is 2 rather than 10. Thus the number 1011001 written earlier is

$$1 \times 2^6 + 0 \times 2^5 + 1 \times 2^4 + 1 \times 2^3 + 0 \times 2^2 + 0 \times 2^1 + 1 \times 2^0$$

Raising 2 to the various powers indicated, we can find the decimal equivalent of this number. It is easy to calculate that 2^6 is 64, 2^5 is 32, 2^4 is 16, 2^3 is 8, 2^2 is 4, and 2^1 is 2. Thus, we have for 1011001,

$$1 \times 64 + 0 \times 32 + 1 \times 16 + 1 \times 8 + 0 \times 4 + 0 \times 2 + 1 \times 1$$

the result of which is $64 + 16 + 8 + 1 = 89$.

Sonographers probably do not have to worry about doing such conversions. Most digital devices do a conversion automatically, so the number or value represented can be easily understood. Take the digital speedometer example from earlier in this chapter. Even though the internal representation of speed in this device is in true binary digital form, a string of 0s and 1s, the device actually reads out the digitized value as a decimal number.

Similarly, all of the functions of a sophisticated ultrasound scanner, even though they may be represented internally as binary values, are generally presented in the form of alphabetical characters, standard decimal numbers, or characteristics on an image. It is useful to be aware, however, of the difference between representing values in the decimal and the binary system and that binary numbers can be manipulated and processed as meaningfully as decimal numbers.

The analog-to-digital converter

Echo signals emerging from the ultrasonic transducer are in an analog format, that is, they are a continuous voltage signal pattern. They must be translated into digital signals before they can be utilized by the scan converter. This translation, or conversion, takes place in an analog-to-digital (A/D) converter. The A/D converter forms a pattern of 0s and 1s from the original analog signal, producing the digital representation of the signal (Figure 4-5), which computer systems and digital hardware processors can manipulate. Once in binary digital format, the signals can be manipulated by computer hardware or stored in the scan converter memory.

The A/D converter provides only an approximate translation of the original signal. Rather than providing a continuous representation, it digitizes at fixed time intervals, sort of like a strobe light applied to the signal. If it does not digitize frequently enough, that is, if the intervals between points are too far apart, sharp changes in the signal between digitized points could be lost. This is an important design consideration that equipment manufacturers take into account when applying A/D converters. They must match the digitization rate to the frequency content of the signal. Higher rates are needed for unprocessed echo signals emerging from the transducer than are required for the echo signal following demodulation, for example. (The digitization rate must exceed the Nyquist rate, discussed in Chapter 5.)

Another approximation in the A/D conversion is the signal is quantized into discrete steps in amplitude, the size of the steps depending on the number of bits to which the signal is digitized. Obviously a 10-bit digitization (providing 1024 discrete levels according to Table

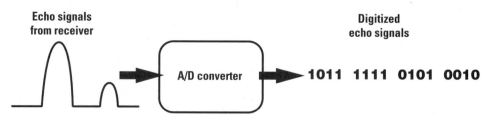

Figure 4-5. Analog-to-digital conversion. Continuously varying echo signals are formed into a string of 0s and 1s.

4-1) would follow the contour of the signal better than a 3-bit digitization, with only eight different levels. It is sort of like a student grading system used in a classroom. A pass-fail grade provides only a little differentiation between student performance in a class, not distinguishing, for example, between individuals just barely passing and those doing work that far exceeds the minimum. The familiar "letter grade" (A, B, C, D, F) provides more discrimination in student achievement; even greater differentiation is provided by a numeric score (such as a percent).

Typically the higher the bit count in a digitizer, the better the amplitude resolution; the higher the digitization rate, the better the time resolution of the signal. In both cases, however, a limit is reached beyond which no additional useful information is gained by higher digitization rates or higher bit counts.

Instruments differ in precisely where in the receiver the echo signal digitization occurs. Some array instruments employ digital beam formers, requiring echo signals to be digitized from each element before they are combined into a single signal for reflectors along each beam line (see Figure 3-5, B). A 128 channel digital beam former requires 128 A/D converters to produce digital representations of echo signals received from each element. The digitization rate must be fast enough to follow the high-frequency wave pattern that transducer elements produce. Other instruments digitize the echo signals at late stages in the receiver, for example, either just before demodulation or just after. In the example in Figure 4-5, we assume the digitization is done just after the demodulation process, just before signals are sent to the scan converter memory. Future machines will probably have more of a tendency to digitize the echo signals closer to the "front end," that is, the ultrasound transducer.

The scan converter matrix

The digital scan converter memory may be thought of as a matrix of elements, each element consisting of a multibit storage unit for ultrasound image data from a given location. The discrete elements are referred to as *picture elements* or **pixels.** The memory is a matrix of such pixels (Figure 4-6). The memory size often is about 500 pixels wide by 500 pixels high. (In the example in Figure 4-6 we show a 525 × 525 pixel memory.) Any ultrasound image that we view on the monitor of a scanning instrument actually exists in the form of a matrix of digital numbers inside the scan converter memory.

During scan build-up, echo signals are inserted into the memory at pixel locations (addresses) corresponding to reflector positions in the body. The machine uses the echo delay time and the transducer beam coordinates to compute the correct *pixel address.* Most instruments use at least 8 bits to represent the echo value in each pixel location. Examination of Table 4-1 shows that 8 bits provides 256 amplitude levels at each location.

The memory is continuously refreshed with new echo data as the ultrasound beam is swept over the volume being scanned. Simultaneously the ultrasound B-mode information is read out to a monitor, providing real-time visualization of the scanned plane. Buffer registers allow transfer of data in and out of the memory at a rate not visible on the display. An **image freeze** enables the echo data to be stored in memory for examination and/or photography as well as video recording and digital archiving. The digital memory is read by transference of pixel values to a digital-to-analog (D/A) converter, providing signals for intensity modulating a screen or a TV monitor. The signal is transferred in raster scanned television format to multiimage cameras and other image recording devices.

Writing, reading, and image freeze

In scan converter jargon, the term *write* refers to placing image data into the scan converter matrix. (The echoes are written into the scan converter memory.) Echo data stored in the memory are "read" by applying the data to a monitor.

Most instrument provide an image freeze stage. When you apply freeze, the scanner stops acquiring image data, and the last values written in memory are "frozen." The scanning mechanism of mechanically scanned transducers is turned off and most machines even turn the transducer pulser off during freeze, so the probe no longer emits

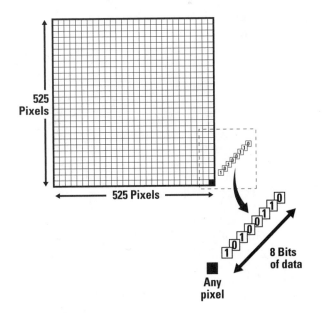

Figure 4-6. The scan converter matrix. This sketch is for a 525 × 525 pixel matrix, with image values at each pixel represented by an 8-bit storage unit. Other matrix sizes and bits/pixel are also possible.

ultrasound energy. The image data continue to be read out, however, so you can see the frozen image on the viewing monitor.

Gray scale and echo amplitude resolution: bits/pixel

The number of bits available to represent the echo data at each pixel location determines the number of useful shades of gray in the image and affects the ability to discriminate slight variations in echogenicity from one loca-

A

B

Figure 4-7. Image recorded using 8 bits (256 shades of gray) **(A)**, and **(B)** 3 bits (8 shades of gray). The loss of information in image **(B)** is apparent. (From Gonzalez RC, Wintz P: *Digital image processing,* Reading, MA, 1977, Addison Wesley.)

tion to the next. The effect of changing the number of bits per pixel is demonstrated using the portrait image in Figure 4-7. When the number of gray levels is reduced from 256 to 8, the loss of detail in the image is evident.

Some early digital memories had as few as 3 bits, with only 8 possible levels. Today's ultrasound imager stores with at least 8-bit—or 256 discrete level—resolution.

Interpolation during write operations

In writing image data to the scan converter memory, the pixel address is established from the beam orientation and the echo arrival time. Those pixels situated along the path corresponding to an ultrasound beam line are written during each pulse-echo sequence done by the scanner. As Figure 4-8 illustrates, some image pixels may be missed in the write operation, particularly at larger depths within sectored scan formats, where beam lines do not cross through all pixel locations. What happens to the empty pixels? Here it is necessary to interpolate the echo data from filled pixels to obtain data for missing pixels. Interpolation means that image data for "missed" pixels are calculated from the image data in nearby pixels that are situated along a beam line. The results between two filled pixels might simply be averaged for a single empty pixel lying between two filled ones. The process becomes a little more complex than simple averaging, however, particularly for echo signals arriving from large depths where several adjacent pixels need to be filled by interpolation. Interpolation schemes are a topic of research interest because of the potential influence on image quality.[1]

We saw in the previous chapter that beam line density can be "traded" for scanning speed if it becomes necessary to increase the frame rate. If this is done in the machine, when the beam line density is decreased, more interpola-

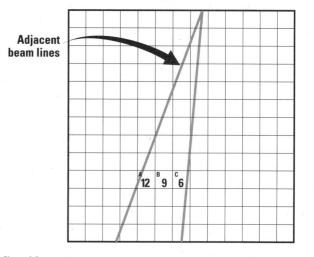

Adjacent beam lines

Figure 4-8. Writing data to the scan converter matrix; sometimes interpolation is necessary to fill in all pixels.

tion between pixels becomes necessary. In fact in some color flow imaging modes the image data can become severely "pixelated" when operating conditions are set for high image frame rates, because these may require reduced beam line densities. Evident pixelation in some color images is an extreme example of interpolation.

Dependence of image quality on pixel density. The number of pixels horizontally and vertically determines the scan converter's spatial resolution. Generally, the more pixels, the better the resolution, although at some point a limit is reached beyond which no additional information can be obtained by using more pixels.

The effects of different pixel densities can be visualized quite readily. Figure 4-9 presents images of an astronaut. Figure 4-9*A* is done on a 500 × 500 pixel matrix, 4-9*B* on a 64 × 64 matrix. The decrease in image resolution and poorer image quality are readily apparent for the low pixel numbers. The lower pixel density matrix leads to excessive "pixelation" of the image, that is, the forming of rectangular blobs that smear out the image data from higher resolution pixels within.

Most of us have seen the pixelation process on television news broadcasts, or better yet, tabloid presentations. On these transmissions it frequently is desirable to hide the identity of individuals, or perhaps cover parts of an image. The image can be heavily pixelated on those regions for which identity is undesirable or good taste dictates privacy.

Read zoom versus write zoom

Magnification, or "zooming," of regions of an image can be a great help in closely visualizing certain anatomical details. The general area in the patient can be scanned using a large image field; from this image the anatomical region of interest is selected and expanded on the monitor.

Both write zoom and read zoom features are available on different machines. The difference between them is explained with the help of Figure 4-10. The top part of the diagram illustrates read zoom, that is, magnifying the image data already existing within the scan converter memory as these data are read out to the video monitor. The stored image data from pixels within the region of interest are expanded to fill the whole screen on the viewing monitor. The advantage of read zoom is that it may be done on a frozen image, so the patient does not have to be rescanned. The disadvantage is that there is potential for the data to appear coarse (pixelation) because the memory pixels themselves are enlarged.

Another approach is write zoom. Instruments that have this feature allow the operator to first select the region to be enlarged by applying cursors to the original image. When write zoom is enabled, the transducer rescans the region. Only echo data arising from within the zoomed region are written to the memory, and all pixels in the memory are used to represent this region. Thus the image should not lose the detail that it might when using read zoom.

The two zoom methods are compared in Figures 4-11 and 4-12. The images are of a gray scale test phantom, and the region to be enlarged contains closely spaced line targets. Part *B* of Figure 4-11 was obtained using a write zoom feature, while part *B* of Figure 4-12 was obtained with read zoom. For the magnification settings on the original image and the degree of zoom, there seems to be slightly better resolution of the write zoom set. Usually with modern systems the differences between the two zoom methods are subtle at best, as the case here illustrates.

Figure 4-9. Image acquired with 500 × 500 pixel matrix and displayed with **(A)** 500 × 500 pixels; **(B)** 64 × 64 pixels. Decrease in image detail with the lower pixel density is evident. (From Gonzalez RC, Wintz P: *Digital image processing,* Reading, MA, 1977, Addison Wesley.)

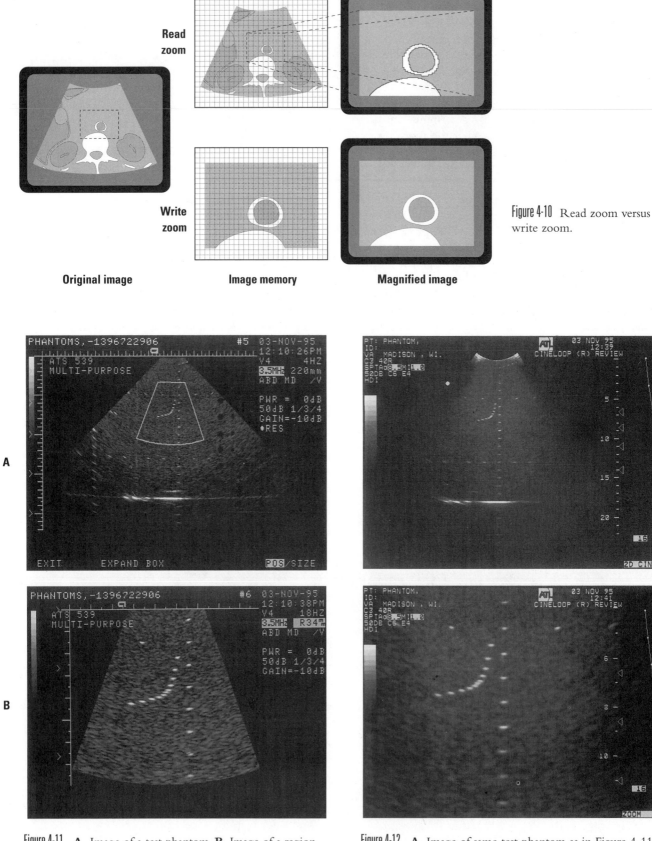

Read zoom

Write zoom

Original image   **Image memory**   **Magnified image**

Figure 4-10 Read zoom versus write zoom.

Figure 4-11. **A,** Image of a test phantom. **B,** Image of a region in the phantom, zoomed up using write zoom.

Figure 4-12. **A,** Image of same test phantom as in Figure 4-11. **B,** Image of a region in the phantom, zoomed up using read zoom.

A sonographer can determine whether read zoom or write zoom is available by freezing the image and attempting to apply zoom. As mentioned above, read zoom can be done on a frozen image, whereas write zoom requires a rescanning of the field to view the effects. You must have a "live" image to visualize instantaneously the effects of write zoom.

PREPROCESSING AND POSTPROCESSING

Preprocessing

It was mentioned earlier that one of the steps involved in signal processing consists of compression of the echo amplitudes. At that point only reduction of the amplified echo signal amplitude range corresponding to a given echo level range was discussed. Whereas echo signals spanning a 60-dB dynamic range might have amplitudes of, say 0.005 to 5 V in the receiver before compression, this same echo range might have a signal amplitude range of 0.1 to 1 V after compression.

Additional signal processing is provided in some instruments. Depending on whether this processing occurs before or after echo data storage in memory, the signal processing is referred to as **preprocessing** or **postprocessing** (Figure 4-13).

Examples of preprocessing functions carried out by various instruments include the following:

1. Selection of different forms of echo signal compression to enhance echo signals within a particular amplitude range.
2. Echo signal edge enhancement, producing sharper echo signals on a B-mode display.
3. Persistence; as data are written to the scan converter, signals for each pixel location can be combined with previous signals from the same location acquired during earlier sweeps of the beam.

Postprocessing

The assignment of stored digital echo values to brightness levels on the TV monitor can be varied if postprocessing control options are provided. Postprocessing refers to manipulation of ultrasound data stored in the memory. Whereas preprocessing can apply only to image data being written to memory, effects of different postprocessing settings can be viewed on both a live image and an image already frozen in memory. Figure 4-14 is an example of such manipulation of echo signal data by postprocessing. The same B-mode image of a carotid artery with bifurcation was photographed using two different postprocessing settings. The relationship between image brightness and signal level in the image memory is shown graphically by the insert in the lower right of each image. (The horizontal axis of the inserted graphs represents the level stored in memory, and the vertical axis depicts dot brightness.)

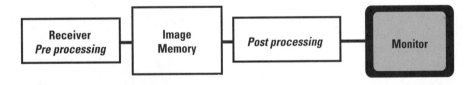

Figure 4-13. Preprocessing versus postprocessing.

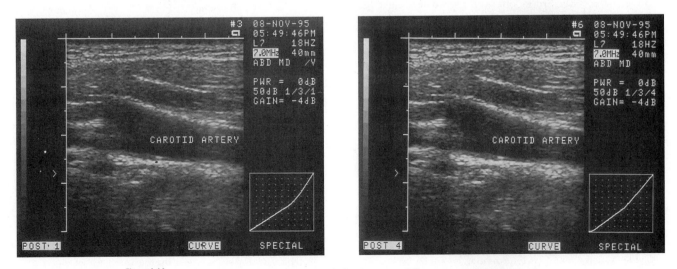

Figure 4-14. Image of the same region recorded using two different postprocessing settings.

DISPLAY DEVICES

Oscilloscope (CRT) displays

An old type of echo signal display device, seldom used in modern scanners except in some stand-alone A-mode instruments, is an oscilloscope. The operation of a standard cathode ray tube (CRT) oscilloscope is illustrated in Figure 4-15. Electrons (or "cathode rays") are produced in an electron gun by heating a filament. The electrons are focused into a beam and accelerated toward a phosphor screen. Upon striking the phosphor they cause the phosphor to emit light, which is visible to anyone observing the screen from the outside.

The usefulness of the device lies in the fact that the electron beam can be swept or steered across the screen by applying electrical signals to horizontal and vertical deflection plates inside the tube. For example, it may be swept from left to right on the screen, tracing out a straight line. An A-mode signal can be displayed by synchronizing the start of the left-to-right sweep with the excitation pulse applied to the transducer. As echo signals are received and processed, they are applied to the vertical deflection plates. This produces the characteristic "spikes" associated with this display. The horizontal sweep speed is calibrated so reflector depths can be determined from the echo arrival time.

In early ultrasound scanners the oscilloscope was also used for displaying M-mode data and ultrasound B-mode images. The oscilloscope was useful in these applications because its electron beam can be deflected in any direction and brightened at any spot on the phosphor screen. In imaging, this permits actual tracking of the sound pulse position as it is reflected from interfaces at different depths. The sweep of the electron beam on the screen can be made to follow the sound beam for any scan motion. A special-purpose memory oscilloscope, or storage oscilloscope, allowed the image to be viewed directly during and after image build-up. Ultrasound images built up on storage oscilloscopes most often employed leading-edge signal processing along with a *bistable* storage screen. This produces a very high contrast image on which each sec-

tion of the display is either white or black, depending on whether an echo signal happens to be detected from the corresponding point in the patient.

In gray scale processing, echo signal amplitudes are encoded in display intensity. Early gray scale scanning consisted of building up the image on photographic film, which was continuously exposed by the oscilloscope screen during scanning. This has been superseded by television monitor displays and digital memory scan converters.

Television (video) monitors

TV screens, or more precisely, video monitors also function somewhat like oscilloscopes, having an electron beam that is accelerated and directed toward a phosphor screen. The screen emits light in response to the electron beam. The brightness of the light is controlled by the intensity of the electron beam current.

In contrast to an oscilloscope display, the electron beam scanning arrangement of most TV monitors is *fixed* in a repeating, horizontal raster format (Figure 4-16). The scan begins at the top left corner of the screen, moving horizontally to the right tracing out a line, rapidly returning to the left side and tracing out a second line, etc. The video signal sent to the monitor controls the brightness at every spot by modulating the electron beam current. Synchronization (sync) pulses are also available to make sure the start of each horizontal trace is precisely in step

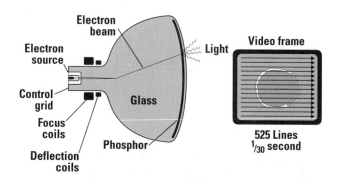

Figure 4-16. Video monitor CRT display.

Figure 4-15. Oscilloscope (CRT, or cathode ray tube) display.

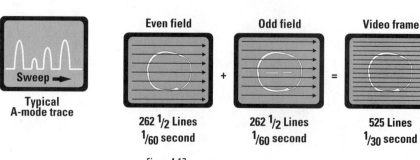

Figure 4-17. Interlacing of fields for one frame of video.

with the data emerging from the scan converter or other video source.

A complete 525 line image is read in $1/30$ s. However, human observers can detect individual flashes of light occurring this rapidly, and this was considered bothersome during the development of television. To overcome effects of flicker, ordinary 525-line monitors sweep the electron beam over the screen in two passes, referred to as *fields*. This is illustrated in Figure 4-17. In the first field the raster scan arrangement traces out $262^1/2$ lines on the screen, the process taking $1/60$ of a second. In the second field the electron beam is swept so that it fills in between the lines of the first field, again taking $1/60$ of a second. A completed frame consists of both interlaced fields and requires $1/30$ of a second, but the flashes from a resolvable region on the image are occurring at 60 times per second and are hardly perceptible.

Television monitors are advantageous for gray scale imaging because they can produce a large number of distinct brightness levels or gray levels. This is done with very good spatial detail or resolution. (Even higher resolution monitors, with more than 525 raster scanned TV lines, are available and are used in some areas of medical imaging.)

Color monitors have three electron guns, each producing image signals that activate either red, green, or blue. Each addressable spot on the screen surface has three elements, one for red, one for green, and another for blue. Different mixtures of the primary colors red, green, and blue are used to produce the desired display color.

IMAGE RECORDING

Photographic film

The most common method of obtaining hard copy of ultrasound images is to photograph a monitor that is continuously viewing the image stored in the scan converter. This can be done with any type of photographic negative film, Polaroid positive film, or image-recording transparency film. In addition, special copying techniques such as thermal printing and ultraviolet-sensitive paper are sometimes used; these are especially handy in systems designed for M-mode recording because they can provide long, continuous records. No matter what the image-recording process, the hard copy materials and camera settings all require proper matching to optimize the end results. A basic comprehension of the principles of these recording techniques is especially useful in understanding the trade-offs in this matching process and helping to pinpoint problems in image recording when they exist.

The following discussion deals with the principles underlying recording images on photographic film, since many of these also apply in the other recording media mentioned. Photographic film contains small grains of sil-

ver bromide crystals suspended in a gelatin emulsion (Figure 4-18). The emulsion is supported on a cellulose acetate sheet. When light strikes the silver bromide crystals in the emulsion, they form a latent image and are very susceptible to chemical change upon development. During the development process the crystals that absorbed light are converted to silver grains. Any unexposed crystals are removed from the film during the fixing stage, leaving behind the exposed silver grains, which form an image.

Several types of film are used in medical image recording. General properties can be compared with the aid of characteristic curves such as in Figure 4-19. Such curves are obtained by exposing patches of a film and then determining the optical density (or film density), a measurement of the opacity of the exposed part of the film. The film density is plotted against the relative exposure, the latter being the product of the intensity of the light and the exposure time. In Figure 4-19 we compare films of different contrast and films of different speed.

The base plus fog in Figure 4-19, *A* refers to a slight opacity of the film found upon developing without any exposure. There is a threshold exposure required before any additional film darkening occurs. This threshold level varies for different films. There also is a maximum exposure, above which no additional exposure can cause film darkening. The useful exposure range is situated between these extremes; in the useful range, any change in the light level is recorded as a change in the developed film density.

The curves in Figure 4-19, *A* are for two films having different speeds. The higher-speed film requires less light exposure to cause film darkening than does the low-speed film. The curves in Figure 4-19, *B* represent films with different contrast. The steeper curve is for a high-contrast film, which takes only a small exposure variation to go from minimum to maximum optical density. Low-contrast film has a wider latitude, accommodating a much wider light exposure range.

For optimal results the monitors used for exposing film must be matched in brightness, contrast, and expo-

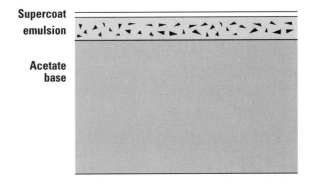

Figure 4-18. Schematic showing the make-up of photographic film.

sure time, so the particular film used is exposed to a level corresponding to its useful range on its characteristic curve. Ideally exposure settings should be such that variations in image brightness caused by amplitude changes among high-level echo signals are successfully recorded at the same time that the weakest echo signals (e.g., recorded from organ parenchyma) are detected on the film image. This can usually be achieved with proper exposure and camera monitor control settings. It often requires an experienced service technician or sonographer to determine the correct settings.

The results of the developing process are highly dependent on the developing time and the temperature of the processor and the condition of the processing chemicals. Most medical imaging facilities regularly test the photography performance and maintain quality assurance notebooks in which important processing parameters are logged daily. In addition, it is important to keep in mind that photographic films can be adversely affected by storage conditions of high temperature and humidity. To ensure consistent clinical results, the film manufacturer's instructions for film handling and processing should always be followed.

Multiimage cameras

These have long been the mainstay in radiology applications. The camera contains a high-quality video monitor on which images from the scan converter are displayed internally and recorded on film (Figure 4-20). Large sheet (e.g., 8½ by 11 inch) films are loaded into the camera from a cassette. A mechanical device within the camera aligns the film or the monitor to expose one section of the film. By transporting either the film or the lens system, or by activating different lenses in sequence (Figure 4-20), images are produced on different sections of the film. Typically, six to nine images are recorded separately. The film is developed in a darkroom, usually using automatic processors.

Laser imagers

Laser imagers are capable of higher resolution, better gray level uniformity, and greater freedom from image distortion than video monitors within multiimage cameras. Although significantly more expensive than stand-alone image recorders, these devices are becoming common in large departments. Laser cameras can service several scanners and/or digital imaging devices simultaneously.

The laser imaging system contains an internal laser that exposes the film, a film drive mechanism, a control computer with image memory, and, optionally, a dedi-

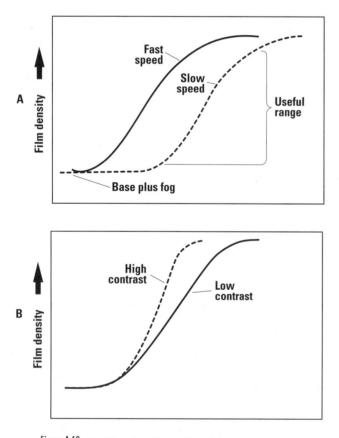

Figure 4-19. **A,** Sketches illustrating characteristic exposure curves for films that have different speeds. **B,** Sketches of characteristic curves for films that have different gammas, or contrasts.

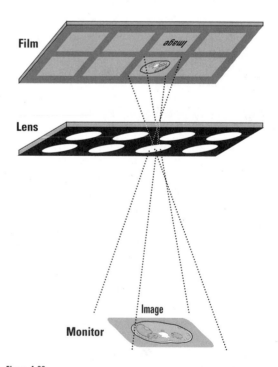

Figure 4-20. One type of multiimage camera. The monitor exposes different sections of the film by sequencing different lens-shutter systems, each pointing to a different region of the film.

cated film processor. Both gallium arsenide and helium neon lasers with mainly red light beams are used. The laser light can be focused to a very small spot on the film. On its way to the film it passes through a modulator that controls the light intensity. The laser beam may be steered using light-deflecting mirrors.

In operation, each image from the scanner is stored in the memory of the laser imager. The image data are applied to the modulator as the laser light is deflected across the film, exposing a single horizontal line on a section of the film. The beam is then returned to its original position and the film advanced a minute amount; then a second line is scanned, etc. The process continues line-by-line until the entire image is written to the film. Several such images are recorded, after which the film is processed. In most systems, wet film processing is used.

Most laser imagers have on-board film handling systems, both to transport the sheets of film during exposures and then to develop the films. The operator loads a magazine with several dozen sheets, each sheet large enough to hold 15 or so ultrasound images. After each patient exam is complete, the films for that patient are exposed and developed.

Thus although laser cameras are costly, the advantages, especially for busy imaging departments are:

1. Automated film handling and developing, saving sonographer time
2. Excellent gray scale on images
3. No image distortion, even near the edges of images, unlike that seen on video monitors that are generally found in multiformat cameras (Multiformat cameras minimize this problem with high-quality monitors.)

Color thermal printers

Many of the flow images generated by today's color flow imaging systems are printed on color thermal printers. The process produces very vivid colors of quite high quality.

A color thermal printer feeds a sheet of specially coated paper from a bin into the print engine, where the paper is pressed against a wide ribbon coated with colored inks. The ribbon contains a band of each of the composite printing colors, cyan, magenta, yellow, and black (Figure 4-21). As the paper passes through the print engine, it first presses against the cyan band of the ribbon. Heating elements on a thermal print head are activated by the image data and melt small dots of the cyan dye. The melted dots are pressed against the paper. The paper continues moving through the print system until it is almost ejected. The unmelted (unexposed) cyan ink remains on the ribbon and the melted dye sticks to the paper. The color ribbon then turns to expose the magenta band,

repeating the thermal process, etc. The process is repeated for all colors in the band, and then the printed paper is finally ejected.[2]

Fiber-optic recorders

M-mode records are often obtained on a fiber-optic recorder. The ultrasound signals for the trace are applied to a CRT screen, producing a single line of dots corresponding to reflectors in the beam. Movement of the recording paper across the screen, in a direction perpendicular to the line of dots, results in the M-mode display on the paper (Figure 4-22). One process uses a CRT emitting ultraviolet light to expose the paper, forming a latent image. The paper is developed by exposure to visible light. Another type of recorder uses dry silver paper as the recording medium. The latent image is developed in a thermal processor housed in the recorder. The chief advantage of the latter technique is that better gray scale can be obtained on hard copy records.

Video thermal printers

Video copy thermal printers produce reasonably high resolution hard copy with sufficient gray scale to yield acceptable quality B-mode image and M-mode records for some applications. They are used for recording gray scale images in some scanning facilities, though the image quality is not considered as good as that obtained from multiimage cameras or laser printers. They also are frequently used for M-mode recording (Figure 4-23).

Figure 4-21. A color thermal printer with the ribbon system opened, exposing the printing ribbon.

Thermal printers accept standard video signals from the image memory of the ultrasound instrument and store the image in their own internal digital memory. The information is transferred to a thermal printing mechanism that exposes the paper. The paper is heat sensitive, so the thermal print heads just heat up spots on the paper surface differentially to create a gray scale image. The paper is "exposed" as it is drawn past the thermal printhead. Image and M-mode records are viewed instantaneously.

Video tape recording

Video cassette recorder (VCR) tapes play an important role in many ultrasound imaging departments, especially in echo labs. They are used commonly in cardiology studies and other applications of real-time scanners. The basic operation of a VCR is illustrated in Figure 4-24.[3] The recording medium itself is a continuous acetate tape that has microscopic magnetic oxide particles deposited. These magnetic particles behave like tiny dipole magnets and may be aligned in a preferential direction if the tape is placed in a magnetic field. The degree of alignment is directly related to the strength of the magnetic field. Any such magnetized regions retain this magnetization until they are placed in a different magnetic field.

A video image may be stored on magnetic tape by transporting the tape past magnetic recording *heads,* which align the magnetic dipoles in the tape as it flies by.

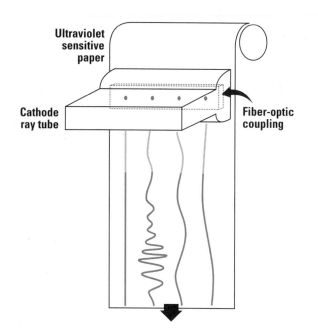

Figure 4-22. Sketch of a fiber-optic strip chart recorder.

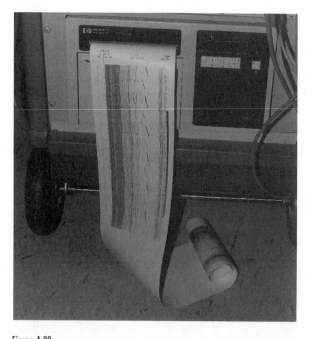

Figure 4-23. Gray scale thermal printer on an echo cardiology machine. The device can feed out single images or it can feed continuous strips of M-mode data.

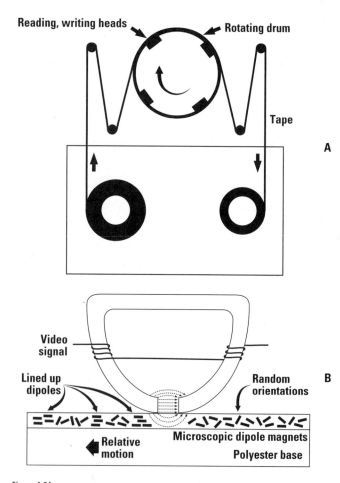

Figure 4-24. Operation of a video cassette recorder (VCR). **A,** The tape transport system. **B,** The read/write heads and tape.

The heads consist of small electromagnets, which convert an electric signal into a fluctuating magnetic field when the unit is in record mode. The magnetic field strength is made proportional to the signal strength corresponding to pixels in the image. Thus the recorded image consists of *tracks* of varying amounts of magnetization. To record signals at a fast enough speed both the read/write heads and the tape move. Head movement is done by placing them on a rotating drum, against which the video tape travels.

The recorded image is played back by transporting the tape past the read/write heads, which now act as pickup coils. As the tape moves past the heads, the induced signal in the reading head is amplified and routed to a video monitor. Because the heads reside on a spinning drum, it is possible to stop the motion of the tape and continuously read the signal from a single track (called *pause*). Most tape machines have protection mechanisms that stop the reading process and disengage the stationary tape from the spinning head if the pause feature is activated for more than a few minutes.

Sonographers should follow recommended procedures when handling and storing video tapes. In addition, the VCR recording and playback heads should be cleaned at intervals recommended by the manufacturer.

VHS, super VHS, and RGB

The most common video recorder format is called VHS (for *video home system*).[4] In this format, the video signal (i.e., the signals that eventually modulate the intensity of the monitor) and synchronizing pulses are combined to form what is termed a *composite video* signal. Most of our home VCRs utilize this format. A single cable connection is all that is needed between the source of video signals (such as the ultrasound imager's "video" port) and the VCR in this format. The format is somewhat limited in resolution and compared to other video formats is subject to some distortion, particularly if color signals are applied.

Super VHS (S-VHS) systems have inherently better spatial resolution, and consequently are preferred in some medical imaging applications, particularly when color images are recorded. Whereas the composite video signal in the VHS recorder is limited to an effective resolution of around 240 horizontal lines on the monitor, the S-VHS provides approximately 400 horizontal lines.[4] Part of this is due to use of higher signal bandwidths in the S-VHS device, enabling its amplifiers to respond more rapidly to changes in the video signal than ordinary VHS systems' amplifiers. It also is because the S-VHS video signal utilizes two separate signals: a brightness signal (also called *luminance*) and a color signal (also called *chrominance*). There is less distortion of colors and brightnesses using the two separate signals. A third factor in S-VHS is the use of specially coated cassette film capable of storing more

minute signal details than standard VHS cassettes. The S-VHS cassettes have an extra notch (Figure 4-25) that the recorder/playback machine can recognize and go into the S-VHS mode.

VCRs are in common use in both VHS and S-VHS formats in medical ultrasound. Unfortunately this situation leads to frequent incompatible recording-playback paths, even in the hands of experienced users. Super VHS recorders can be set to record video cassettes in either format; they also can play cassettes that have been recorded in either format. However, VHS recorders can only play back tapes recorded in VHS format. It sometimes happens that a conference speaker arrives for a presentation carrying a tape recorded in Super VHS, only to find the audio-visual equipment in the auditorium is a VHS system. (One advantage is that this sometimes leads to shorter presentations!) Table 4-2 lists a few possibilities for tapes, recording devices (or settings), and playback devices; the list from top to bottom is in the order of decreasing image quality.[5]

RGB. The RGB format breaks video signals down into signals separately representing three image colors, red, green, and blue; it also provides a separate video synchronization pulse. RGB format is considered the most effective method of transmitting video signals, particularly those containing color. Many scanners incorporating color signals utilize RGB format for the internal transmission between devices and provide RGB signals for accessory devices that support this format, such as color printers.

Computer storage

Digital archiving and image storage is gradually replacing at least some of the film recording in departments. This trend is now accelerating as digital hardware becomes more accessible, even at remote sites through networking, and as information storage media become more compact.

The amount of computer storage for a typical radiology examination can be approximated roughly. Let's

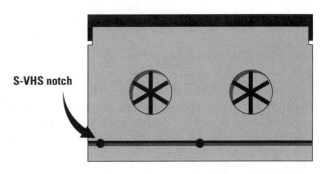

Figure 4-25. Identification of Super VHS (S-VHS) cassettes by the special notch on the case.

Table 4-2 Combinations of tape type, VCR recorder type, and VCR playback machine that will work successfully

Tape format	Recording machine	Playback machine
S-VHS	S-VHS	S-VHS
VHS	S-VHS (set to record in VHS)	S-VHS, VHS
VHS	VHS	S-VHS, VHS

assume that a single image consists of 500 × 500 pixels, with 8 bits equal 1 byte for each pixel location. With no "data compression," the storage space required for a single image is roughly 500 × 500 = 250 kbytes. An examination in which 20 images are acquired therefore requires about 5 Mbytes of storage. Significantly more space is required if color signals are recorded. Data compression schemes can reduce the storage requirements, perhaps to $1/2$ or $1/3$ of this. In spite of this, massive image storage devices are required to obtain appreciable amounts of storage.

Fixed storage disks in computers consist of metal oxide–coated plates containing minute magnetic media distributed throughout (Figure 4-26). The plate is formatted into tracks and sectors. Data are written to the disk while it spins, translating different sectors and tracks past the read/write heads. During write operations the digital 0s and 1s are applied to the disk by changing the magnetization at microscopic spots. Readout simply detects the state of magnetization of each spot. Fixed disks with capacities of around 1 gigabyte (Gbyte, 1 thousand megabytes) are now becoming available. Some information management systems with huge storage facilities use units that incorporate several large capacity fixed disks. Removable disks (or diskettes) with capacities of 1.4 Mbytes are useful for limited transference of images and for storing programs to be transferred.

Digital archiving and storage of images has become practical as massive data storage devices are now available. One of the devices commonly used is digital tape (e.g., DAT tape). Small, inexpensive cassettes can reliably store 2 to 4 Gbytes of information.

Tape is considered a reliable backup medium, but is fairly slow when it comes to retrieving specific image sets. There are several alternative methods. For example, WORM drives (for write once, read many times) use a laser to inscribe digitally encoded spots on the surface of a disk. A lower intensity laser then reads the data at a later time. CD-ROM technology is similar; digital data are encoded in the form of microscopic pits on the surface of the medium. The advantage of optically writing data is that the beam of light from a laser can be focused to a

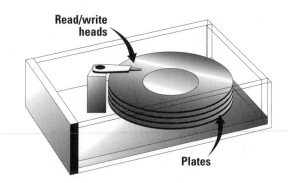

Figure 4-26. Sketch showing the internal components of a fixed disk, such as those found in intermediate-sized and large computer workstations.

much much smaller point than the magnetic field from the read/write heads of a disk or diskette. Therefore much more data can be incorporated into an optically encoded disk than a magnetic disk or diskette of the same size.

MO disks

A popular option being explored very heavily in the mid-1990s is magneto-optical, also referred to as *optical* technology. This technology seems to combine the best of both the optical and the magnetic technologies:

1. Magneto-optical (MO) can pack lots of information onto a disk (optical part)
2. MO drives can be rewritten and erased (magnetic part)

Two magneto-optical disk drives and their media are pictured in Figure 4-27.

During writing of information to the MO disk, an intense laser beam is focused on a spot on the disk. The beam heats tiny spots in the alloy material on the disk as it spins by. The spots are heated to a temperature above the Curie point for the alloy. This loosens magnetic crystals within the alloy so they can be moved by the magnetic field of a magnetic write head. Data are written by the magnetic head, but now the area written to is defined by the spot from the laser, which as mentioned before is much smaller than the spot affected by the magnetic write head alone. The resultant disk can hold hundreds of megabytes of information. Reading is done by a weaker laser beam scattering off the magnetic crystals as the disk spins. A detector measures the amount of light scattered, which is proportional to the magnetization applied during the write process.

Another advantage of magneto-optic technology is the information is relatively safe compared to other forms of magnetic storage because it is not as susceptible to magnetic fields as regular diskettes or digital tape.

Figure 4-27. 1.2-Gbyte *(left)* and 128-Mbyte magneto-optical disk drives, along with a removable diskette from each.

References

1. Richard WD, Martin RM: Real-time ultrasonic scan conversion via linear interpolation of oversampled vectors, *Ultrasonic Imaging* 16:87, 1994.
2. White R: *How computers work,* Emeryville, CA, 1994, Ziff-Davis.
3. Curry T, Dowdey J, Murray, R: *Christensian's introduction to the physics of diagnostic radiology,* Philadelphia, 1984, Lea & Febiger.
4. McComb G: *Troubleshooting and repairing VCRs,* ed 2, Blue Ridge Summit, PA, 1991, Tab Books.
5. *Acuson 128XP10 operator's manual,* Mountain View, CA, 1994, Acuson Corp.
6. Gonzales RC, Wintz P: *Digital image processing,* Reading, MA, 1977, Addison Wesley.

Questions for Review

1. When an image is "frozen," the echo data are stored in the:

    A. Transducer
    B. Receiver
    C. Scan converter
    D. Video monitor

2. Scan conversion is necessary in order to _____.

    A. View ultrasound data on a video monitor
    B. View ultrasound data on an oscilloscope
    C. Switch from a curved array to a phased array
    D. Switch the scanner to another operating mode

3. Advantages of digital devices over analog circuitry include all but which ONE of the following?

    A. Freedom from drift
    B. Greater immunity to electrical noise
    C. Better spatial resolution
    D. Data are accessible to computers

4. Digital devices represent signals in _____.

    A. Discrete levels; at discrete time intervals
    B. Continuous levels; at discrete time intervals
    C. Discrete levels; continuously over time
    D. Continuous levels; continuously over time

5. The term *bit* stands for:

    A. Small byte
    B. Discrete piece
    C. Binary digit
    D. $1/8$ Mbyte

6. The ordinary decimal number system uses 10 as its base. The binary number system used in computers uses _____ as the base.

    A. 0 and 1
    B. 2
    C. 3
    D. 4

7. The term *pixel* is an acronym for:

    A. Picture element
    B. Element location
    C. Picture accelerator
    D. Pie-shaped Excel chart

8. The number of pixels horizontally and vertically in the memory is most closely associated with:

    A. Amplitude resolution
    B. Dynamic range
    C. Spatial resolution
    D. Depth calibration accuracy

9. The number of bits per pixel is most closely associated with:

    A. Amplitude resolution
    B. Length of time image can be frozen
    C. Spatial resolution
    D. Depth calibration accuracy

10. Which of the following could lead to resolution being limited by the image scan converter pixel size?

    A. Read zoom
    B. Write zoom
    C. High magnification, small fields of view
    D. Low-frequency transducers

11. A scan converter has 500 × 500 pixels, each eight bits deep. How many amplitude levels does it store at each pixel address?

    A. 8
    B. 256
    C. 500

D. 250,000

12. Ultrasound echo signals emerging from the transducer are converted to a digital format in the:

A. Video monitor
B. Analog-to-digital converter
C. Preamplifier
D. Preprocessing circuits

13. Image data for pixels that correspond to spots not intersected by beam lines can be acquired using:

A. Rescanning
B. Compression
C. Demodulation
D. Interpolation

14. The ability to distinguish between two digitized signals whose amplitudes before digitization vary only slightly is most closely associated with the:

A. Pixels per centimeter
B. Rate of digitization
C. Bits per pixel
D. Memory size

15. Postprocessing can be distinguished from preprocessing by freezing the image and being aware that:

A. Postprocessing and preprocessing are both disabled on a frozen image
B. Changes in postprocessing have no effect on a frozen image
C. Changes in preprocessing have no effect on a frozen image
D. Postprocessing does not work on a live image

16. An oscilloscope is useful for:

A. Displaying an image using data emerging from the scan converter
B. Displaying signals in an A-mode display
C. Enlarging images taken from photographic film
D. Looking at a microscopic view of part of an ultrasound image

17. Video monitors that are used in diagnostic ultrasound generally have:

A. About 1000 lines and image rates of 1000/s
B. About 500 lines and image rates of 1000/s
C. About 1000 lines and image rates of 100/s
D. About 500 lines and image rates of 30/s

18. Video monitors produce images in two separate fields in order to:

A. Enhance spatial resolution
B. Reduce image flicker
C. Improve gray scale contrast
D. Expand dynamic range

19. Advantages of laser imagers over multiimage cameras include all of the following except:

A. Less costly
B. Inherently better resolution
C. Better uniformity
D. Not subject to monitor distortions

20. Video recorders store ultrasound images by doing what?

A. Digitizing the echo signal before TGC is applied and recording digital values on audio tape
B. Digitizing the echo signal after TGC is applied and recording on magnetic tape
C. Analog recording the same video signal sent to the viewing monitors
D. Recording digital data from the image memory in binary format

21. Which of the following VCR record-playback scenarios does not work?

A. Record with a S-VHS unit on S-VHS tape; play back on VHS unit
B. Record with a VHS unit on VHS tape; play back on a S-VHS unit
C. Record with a S-VHS unit on VHS tape; play back on a VHS unit
D. Record with a S-VHS unit on VHS tape; play back on an S-VHS unit

22. Which of the following will cause the least damage to VCR cassettes and computer disks?

A. Exposure to magnetic fields
B. Prolonged temperatures of 50° to 75° F
C. Storage in dusty environments
D. Temperatures significantly above room temperature

Chapter 5

Doppler Instrumentation

The Doppler frequency is the difference between the frequency of the incident ultrasound beam and that of the received echoes. With ultrasound Doppler equipment, MHz-range frequencies are transmitted and detected by the transducer; Doppler frequencies, however, usually are in the audible frequency range.

The Doppler effect is used in medical ultrasound to quantify and to image blood flow and to detect fetal heart motion. A "Doppler mode" commonly is present on today's multi-modality ultrasound instruments; some laboratories and clinics use stand-alone Doppler instruments in these studies. In this chapter we will describe the Doppler effect and outline principles and limitations of Doppler instruments.

NATURE OF THE DOPPLER SHIFT

Doppler shifts for audible sounds

Whenever there is relative motion between a sound source and a listener, the frequency heard by the listener differs from that produced by the source. The perceived frequency is either greater or less than that transmitted by the source, depending on whether the source and the listener are moving toward or away from one another. This change in the perceived frequency relative to the transmitted frequency is called a *Doppler shift*. In general, a Doppler shift can occur for a moving source and stationary listener, a moving listener and stationary source, or a moving source and moving listener.

Most of us are familiar with the Doppler effect occurring when an automobile, truck, or other motor vehicle sounds its horn as it passes us. If the horn is sounding continuously, its pitch seems to drop abruptly just as the vehicle passes. As the vehicle approaches the listener, the Doppler shift results in the perceived pitch of the horn being higher than that actually transmitted.

Similarly, the perceived frequency is lower than that transmitted as the vehicle recedes. The very noticeable drop in pitch as the vehicle passes is just the transition between the two conditions.

The origin of the Doppler shift for sounds from a moving vehicle is illustrated in Figure 5-1. In Figure 5-1, *A*, a motorist in a stationary vehicle is sounding his horn. The circles represent the resultant diverging sound waves, spreading uniformly in all directions. A listener is situated at point L in the diagram. The number of wavefronts per second striking the listener's ear, that is, the frequency heard by the listener, is the same as the frequency transmitted by the horn.

In Figure 5-1, *B* the vehicle, with horn still sounding, is moving towards the right. Now the appearance of the wavefronts changes. The motion causes wavefronts in front of the sound source to be "squeezed together" somewhat. Likewise, the wavefronts in the back of the vehicle are spread apart somewhat. Now a listener in front of the vehicle at point L hears a higher frequency than the actual frequency transmitted, and a listener in back of the vehicle would hear a lower frequency.

Another way to experience a Doppler shift is to be a listener travelling towards or away from a stationary source. A listener moving towards a stationary sound source hears a higher frequency, while a listener moving away hears a lower frequency than the transmitted frequency.

Doppler shift in medical ultrasound

In medical ultrasound we get Doppler shifts when echo signals are picked up from moving reflectors. In Figure

5-2 a stationary transducer is sending sound waves to the right and receiving echoes from a reflector. The emerging echo pattern from the reflector varies, depending on whether the reflector is stationary or moving. Slightly higher frequencies are received from a reflector moving towards the transducer than from a stationary reflector, while the opposite is true for a reflector moving away from the transducer. (The Doppler effect actually is manifested twice in the production of an echo from a moving reflector. First the reflector plays the role of a moving "listener" as it travels towards or away from the ultrasound transducer. The ultrasound waves the reflector encounters are thus initially Doppler shifted. The reflector subsequently acts as a moving "source" as it sends echoes back towards the transducer. This results in an additional shift in the frequency of the waves compared to the transmitted frequency.)

The Doppler frequency is the *difference* between the frequency of the incident ultrasound beam and that of the received echoes. Suppose scatterers are moving at a speed of 1 m/s towards the transducer, as in Figure 5-3. If the incident beam frequency is 5 MHz (5,000,000 Hz), the

reflected waves have a frequency of 5,006,490 Hz, just a tiny bit higher than the incident beam. The Doppler shift frequency in this case is 6490 Hz, or 6.49 kHz. This is in the audible frequency range. With ultrasound Doppler equipment, MHz-range frequencies are transmitted and detected by the transducer; however, the Doppler frequencies usually are in the audible frequency range.

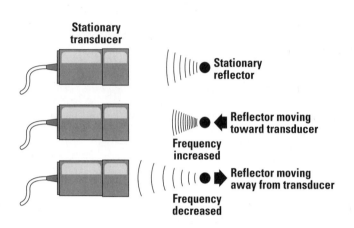

Figure 5-2. The Doppler shift in medical ultrasound. The frequency of echoes from a stationary reflector is the same as that produced by the transducer. Slightly higher frequency echoes result if the reflector moves towards the transducer and slightly lower frequencies occur for reflectors moving away.

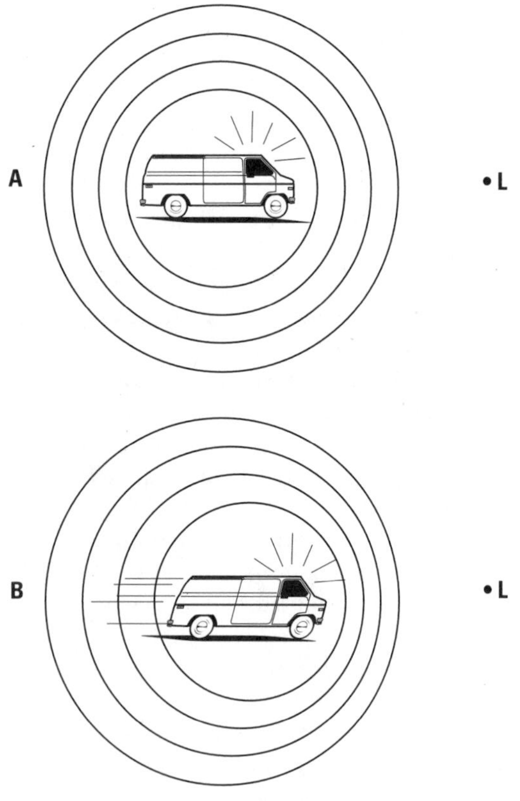

Figure 5-1. **A,** Sound waves from a stationary source. Waves spread uniformly in all directions. **B,** Waves from a moving source. Because of motion of the source, the centers of the wavefronts change, causing a higher frequency to be heard in front of the source than is heard from the side or in back.

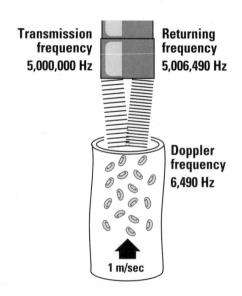

Figure 5-3. Received echo frequency for a transmitted frequency of 5 MHz and a reflector velocity of 1 m/s. The Doppler shift usually is small compared to the ultrasound frequency.

The Doppler equation

Doppler equipment is commonly used for detecting and evaluating blood flow in arteries and veins. A typical arrangement is shown in Figure 5-4. The ultrasonic transducer is placed in contact with the external skin surface and the ultrasound beam directed toward the vessel. The beam is at an angle Θ with respect to the axis of the vessel. Red blood cells flowing in the vessel scatter ultrasound waves, giving rise to echo signals. In most instruments the echo signals are detected by the same transducer used to produce the incident beam. Because the scatterers are moving, the frequency of the return echo signals is Doppler shifted. The Doppler frequency is given by:

$$f_D = \frac{2f_o v \cos\Theta}{c}$$

(5-1)

where

f_o	is the transmitted ultrasound frequency,
v	is the reflector velocity,
c	is the speed of sound, and
$\cos\Theta$	is the cosine of the angle between the transmitted beam and the reflector path.

Doppler frequency depends on reflector speed. In many situations we use Doppler ultrasound equipment to estimate reflector velocities. As Equation 5-1 indicates, the Doppler frequency is directly proportional to the reflector velocity. When the reflector velocity doubles, the Doppler frequency doubles; when it halves, the Doppler frequency halves.

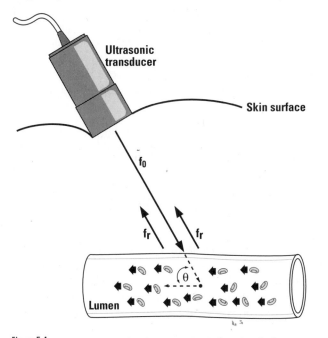

Figure 5-4. Arrangement for detecting Doppler signals from within a vessel. Θ is the Doppler angle.

Doppler frequency depends on the ultrasound frequency. Equation 5-1 also indicates that the Doppler frequency depends on the frequency of the incident ultrasound beam. The Doppler frequency obtained from red blood cells within a vessel when using a 10-MHz beam is twice that obtained when a 5-MHz beam is used for the same vessel and geometry. A 2.5-MHz beam yields a Doppler frequency that is half that obtained with a 5-MHz beam.

The Doppler angle

Description of the Doppler angle. The angle Θ in Figure 5-4 is called the *Doppler angle*. With ultrasound Doppler equipment, the Doppler frequency detected is proportional not only to the reflector velocity but also to the cosine of the Doppler angle.

The cosine function is plotted in Figure 5-5 for angles from 0 to 180 degrees. It varies from 1 for a 0-degree angle to 0 for 90 degrees to -1 at 180 degrees. Looking closely at Figure 5-4, a 0-degree Doppler angle corresponds to reflectors moving directly towards the transducer, while a 180-degree Doppler angle means the reflectors are moving directly away from the transducer. If the Doppler angle is 90 degrees, reflectors are moving perpendicular to the ultrasound beam.

The Doppler angle affects detected Doppler frequencies. Figure 5-6 illustrates the effect of Doppler angle on the Doppler frequency for a given reflector velocity. The example assumes that the reflectors are moving at a speed of 1 m/s and that the ultrasound frequency is 5 MHz. Doppler frequencies for different Doppler angles, determined by the location of the ultrasound transducer, are presented.

For a Doppler angle of 0 degrees, the Doppler signal frequency is 6.49 kHz, or if we round off, 6.5 kHz. This frequency would be detected if it were possible to "inter-

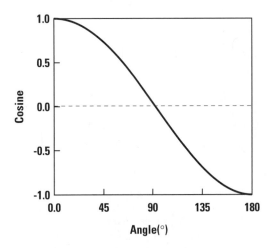

Figure 5-5. Cosine function for angles from 0 to 180 degrees.

rogate" the flow at a 0-degree angle. For other angles, the Doppler frequency is lower. Applying the cosine Θ term for the angles illustrated, we see that the Doppler frequency decreases to 5.6 kHz for a 30-degree angle and to just 3.3 kHz for a 60-degree angle. Finally, at 90 degrees, when the ultrasound beam is perpendicular to the reflector direction, the detected frequency is 0 Hz! There is no Doppler shift at this angle.

If the incident beam angle is greater than 90 degrees to the flow, the cosine of the angle is negative. This corresponds to flow directed away from the transducer; the frequency of echo signals from moving reflectors is now lower than f_o, the transmitted frequency. Most equipment detects the magnitude of the Doppler frequency, so the Doppler signals sound the same as for signals from flow directed towards the transducer. And, as we shall see later, "directional" Doppler instruments detect whether the received frequency is greater than or less than the transmitted frequency and, hence, display whether flow is directed toward or away from the transducer.

Notice, the transducer beam orientation that provides the best B-mode image detail of a vessel wall, that is, perpendicular beam incidence, results in the least favorable Doppler signals from within the vessel. In practice the transducer beam is usually oriented to make a 30- to 60-degree angle with the lumen of the vessel when the vessel runs nearly parallel to the skin surface. If the Doppler angle is greater than 60 degrees, Doppler

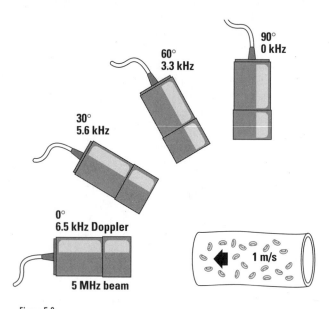

Figure 5-6. Doppler frequency from reflectors moving at a velocity of 1 m/s versus the Doppler angle. The ultrasound transducer frequency is assumed to be 5 MHz. At 0 degrees these conditions yield a Doppler frequency of 6.5 kHz, at 30 degrees 5.6 kHz, and at 60 degrees only 3.3 kHz for this reflector velocity. No Doppler frequency shift is detected when the Doppler angle is 90 degrees.

shift signals can usually be detected; however, it becomes difficult to quantify the velocity from the Doppler signal frequency because:

1. Errors in estimating the Doppler angle introduce large uncertainties in the reflector velocities as the Doppler angle approaches 90 degrees. This is discussed later.
2. Transducer-related spectral broadening results in uncertainties in the peak Doppler frequencies. The uncertainty gets worse as the Doppler angle approaches 90 degrees.

Spectral broadening caused by the transducer. Spectral analysis allows us to visualize the range of Doppler frequencies present in a signal when Doppler shifts are detected simultaneously from reflectors moving at different speeds. An interesting artifact related to the Doppler frequency spectrum and to the Doppler angle occurs, which can lead to errors in estimates of peak frequencies. When reflectors pass through the ultrasound beam at a fixed speed, there actually is a band of Doppler signal frequencies created. This results in uncertainties in the actual velocity of the reflector.

The theoretical explanation is complex,[1] but a simple diagram helps us understand. Figure 5-7, *A* shows a transducer positioned close to a vessel. A single reflector passing through the ultrasound beam actually "sees" a small range of Doppler angles because of the size of the transducer, rather than just one angle. Consequently, a reflector moving at a fixed velocity actually produces a range of Doppler shift frequencies.

One way this phenomenon is manifested is when we attempt to look at the peak frequency or peak velocity on a Doppler spectral display. In Figure 5-7, *B* the velocity in the middle of this vessel within a test phantom is around 50 cm/s. The peak velocity seen on the spectral display is 57 cm/s. The Doppler angle in this case is 62 degrees.

A Doppler spectral display for the same vessel is presented in Figure 5-7, *C* only the Doppler angle is 72 degrees. Now the peak velocity appears to be around 70 cm/s. There seems to be more fill-in of the spectrum as well. For best results when quantifying velocities, keep the Doppler angle as small (farthest from 90 degrees) as possible.[1]

Angle correction and angle error. Ultrasound devices display the velocity of reflectors, computed from the Doppler signal frequency. The spectral trace in Figure 5-8 is an example. Velocity computation requires input of the Doppler angle, which must then be accounted for to get an accurate result.

Current Doppler instruments require the operator to input the flow angle. This is done using the B-mode image. The operator positions and adjusts an angle cursor on the screen so that the cursor follows the assumed direction of flow (Figure 5-8). A determination of the Doppler angle is then made in the instrument. The cosine of the angle is applied to display the correct velocity scale.

If the operator makes a slight mistake in specifying the flow angle, as suggested in Figure 5-9, this results in errors in the estimated velocity. The magnitude of a velocity error resulting from an erroneously positioned angle cursor depends on the actual Doppler angle. Table 5-1 gives an idea of this dependence. Here it is assumed that the actual reflector velocity is 50 cm/s, and the operator makes an error of 5 degrees in positioning the angle cursor. Thus when the actual Doppler angle is 0 degrees, the cursor is positioned at an angle of 5 degrees, when it is 20 degrees the cursor is positioned at 25 degrees, etc. The estimated velocity was calculated using the assumed angle rather than the actual angle.

The results in column five of Table 5-1 indicate that when the Doppler angle is small, for example, 0 to 40 degrees, a 5-degree error has only a small effect on the estimated velocity. The error is less than 10%. On the other hand, for a Doppler angle that is near 90 degrees, a 5-degree error has a significant effect on the estimated velocity! At 80 degrees this mistake in positioning the angle cursor leads to an error of nearly 100% in the estimated velocity.

In most cases sonographers will experience some uncertainties in estimating the flow angle and positioning the angle cursor. If the Doppler angle is small, this uncertainty leads to only a small error in the estimated velocity. On the other hand, for Doppler angles of 60 degrees or greater, precise positioning of the angle cursor becomes mandatory to avoid large errors in the estimated velocity.

Doppler frequency calculations

Here are several examples to demonstrate further the Doppler equation and angle effects.

Example: Suppose f_o = 2 MHz and v = 5 cm/s. What is the Doppler frequency? Assume the Doppler angle is 0 degrees and the speed of sound is 1540 m/s.

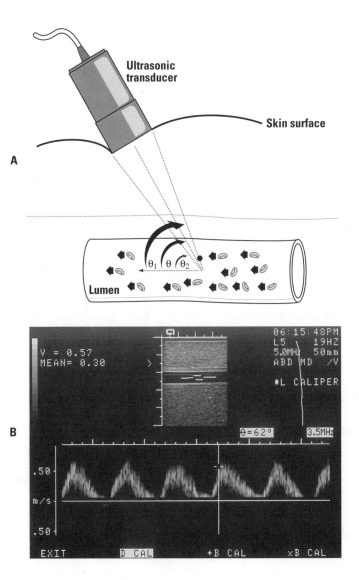

A

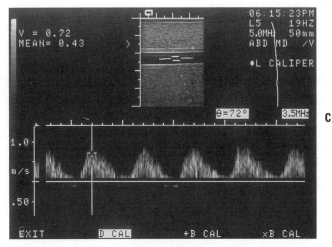

C

Figure 5-7. **A,** Origin of transducer-related spectral broadening. The Doppler angle is Θ; however, all angles between Θ_1 and Θ_2 are present. **B,** Spectral trace for a vessel in which the speed of flow is 50 cm/s. The peak velocity readout is 57 cm/s when the Doppler angle is 62 degrees. **C,** Spectral trace from the same vessel and same reflector speed, only now the Doppler angle is 72 degrees. The peak velocity readout is greater than in the previous figure. To minimize errors, use a Doppler angle that is as far from 90 degrees as possible.

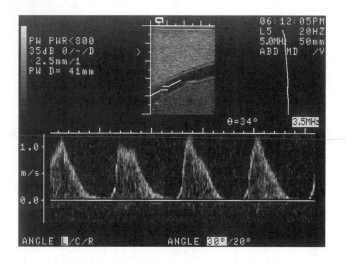

Figure 5-8. Ultrasound B-mode image of a Doppler phantom *(top)* along with a spectral Doppler trace *(bottom)*. The vertical scale in the spectral Doppler trace indicates velocity in meters per second (m/s). The operator-positioned angle cursor is located in the middle of the gated region. The cursor is aligned along the assumed axis of the vessel.

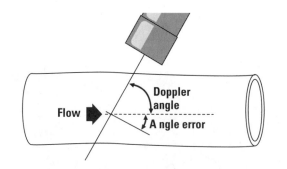

Figure 5-9. Schematic showing a setup for recording Doppler signals along a vessel axis, only with an operator error in placing the angle cursor. The "angle correct" cursor is not aligned along the axis of the vessel.

Solution: Simply substitute the given values into Equation 5-1, using the fact that the cosine of 0 degrees = 1. Notice that 2 MHz = 2×10^6 Hz.

$$f_D = \frac{2 \times 2 \times 10^6 \text{ Hz} \times 0.05 \text{ m/s} \times 1}{1540 \text{ m/s}}$$

The units m/s in the numerator and denominator cancel. Simplifying gives

$$f_D = \frac{0.2 \times 10^6 \text{ Hz}}{1.54 \times 10^3} = 1.3 \times 10^2 \text{ Hz}$$

or

$$f_D = 130 \text{ Hz}$$

For the example presented, the frequency of the transmitted wave was said to be 2.0 MHz. The received ultrasound frequency is very close to the same value, 2.00013 MHz. The Doppler frequency, the difference between the received and transmitted frequencies, is in the audible frequency range for this example.

Example: If a 2000-Hz Doppler signal is detected using a 5-MHz transducer, how fast is the reflector moving? The Doppler angle is 60 degrees.

Solution: We must solve Equation 5-1 for v. This is done by multiplying both sides of the equation by c and then dividing both sides by $2f_o \cos\Theta$. The result is

$$v = \frac{f_D c}{2f_o \cos\Theta}$$

(5-2)

The cosine of 60 degrees is 0.5. Substituting this and the rest of the parameters that were given, we have

$$v = \frac{2000/s \times 1540 \text{ m/s}}{2 \times 5,000,000/s \times 0.5} = 0.6 \text{ m/s} = 60 \text{ cm/s}$$

Equation 5-2 is used to determine the reflector velocity from the frequency of the Doppler signal.

Table 5-1. Effect of a 5-degree error in the "angle correct" setting (the actual velocity is assumed to be 50 cm/s)

Actual angle	Erroneously set angle	Actual velocity	Estimated velocity	Percent error
0 degrees	5 degrees	50 cm/s	50.2 cm/s	0.4%
20 degrees	25 degrees	50	51.8	3.6
40 degrees	45 degrees	50	54.2	8.4
60 degrees	65 degrees	50	59.2	18.3
80 degrees	85 degrees	50	99.6	99

CONTINUOUS-WAVE DOPPLER INSTRUMENTS

CW Doppler system description

Continuous-wave (CW) Doppler instruments are the simplest and often the least expensive Doppler devices available. A simplified block diagram is presented in Figure 5-10. A CW transmitter continuously excites the ultrasonic transducer with a sinusoidal electrical signal. This produces a sound wave of frequency f_o. Echo signals resulting from reflection and scattering return to the transducer, creating an electrical signal that is applied to the receiver amplifier. The signal is boosted in strength and then applied to the demodulator. Here the echo signal is multiplied with a reference signal derived from the transmitter, producing a complicated product shown in Figure 5-11. The product contains a mixture of signals, one whose frequency is equal to the *sum* of the reference frequency and the return echo signal frequency and another that is equal to the *difference* between the reference frequency and the return frequency. The "difference frequency" signal is the Doppler signal that we are after. It is isolated by electronically filtering away all of the high frequencies in the complicated product. The result is that only low-frequency Doppler shift signals—say 20 kHz and less—emerge in the output.[2]

High-frequency signals are removed in the demodulator. Further filtering is applied after this stage to remove the very low–frequency Doppler signals originating from slowly moving reflectors, such as vessel walls. This filter is usually called a *wall filter* and is adjustable by the operator.

Wall filter. Wall filters available on most Doppler instruments preferentially remove low-frequency Doppler signals from the display. This is illustrated in Figure 5-12. As the wall filter setting (or the "filter" setting) is adjusted upward, more and more of the Doppler signal from the baseline is lost.

The filtered output Doppler signal may be applied to a loudspeaker or headphones for interpretation. The signals also can be recorded on audio tape or applied to a spectral analysis system.

Instrument controls for CW Doppler. Continuous-wave Doppler instruments range in complexity from simple, pocket-type instruments to units that are part of large, "duplex" scanners (see below). Operator controls available on a continuous-wave Doppler instrument vary with the degree of complexity of the unit. Typically the following are available:

1. Transmit power control; this varies the electrical power applied to the ultrasound transducer and, hence, varies the amplitude of the transmitted beam. Higher power output settings result in

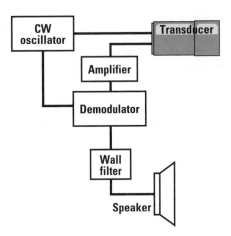

Figure 5-10. Schematic showing parts of a CW (continuous-wave) Doppler instrument.

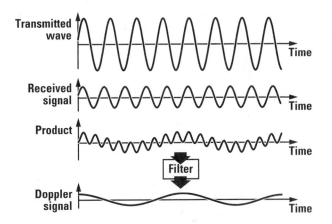

Figure 5-11. Simple Doppler signal processing. The top trace represents the wave transmitted into the tissue; the second trace represents echo signals from a reflector moving towards the transducer, with the signal frequency slightly higher than the transmitted frequency. The Doppler signal is derived by multiplying the received signal by a signal derived from the transmitter, then filtering out all the ultrasound frequencies and higher. It is shown on the bottom.

larger amplitude echo signals picked up by the transducer. Of course, they also result in greater acoustic exposure to patients.

2. Receiver sensitivity (or gain) control; this adjusts the amount of amplification or gain of the receiver amplifier.

3. Loudness or volume control; this allows adjustments of the gain of the audio amplifier section of the instrument.

4. Wall filter control; adjusts the low-frequency cutoff of the output Doppler signals. Signals whose frequencies are lower than this cutoff are eliminated from the display.

Some combination of the first three controls generally is available to allow the operator to vary the sensitivity of the Doppler instrument. Most Doppler units have a wall filter adjustment also.

Continuous-wave Doppler transducers

Most continuous-wave Doppler instruments employ separate transducer elements for transmitting and receiving. The reason for this is that since the transducer transmits sound waves continuously, weak echo signals picked up by the transducer would be overwhelmed by the transmit signal if the same element were used for both transmitting and receiving. Thus one element is used for continuous transmitting while the other is used for receiving. This could be done using separate elements in the array of a duplex (see below) scanner. More commonly, stand-alone transducers are used in continuous-wave Doppler instruments.

A typical stand-alone transducer design for continuous-wave Doppler is illustrated in Figure 5-13. Each element is cut in the shape of a semicircle and the elements are tilted slightly, as shown in the figure. The beam patterns of the transmitting and receiving transducers are thus made to cross. The region of beam overlap is the most sensitive area of this type of transducer, and scatterers that happen to be within this region yield the largest amplitude Doppler signals. Transducers may be designed to emphasize signals from any depth by appropriate choice of beam overlap or beam focal distance.

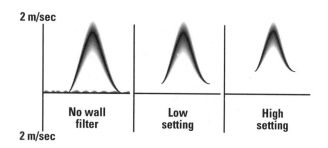

Figure 5-12. Effect of variations in the wall filter setting of a Doppler instrument. Increasing the setting cuts off a larger range of the lower frequency Doppler signals.

Since a continuous-wave Doppler transducer does not produce short duration pulses, steps taken to dampen the ringing of the element that are common to pulsed transducers do not need to be taken. It may be advantageous, however, to add quarter-wave matching layers to improve the sensitivity of the probe.

Choice of Doppler ultrasound frequency

In our discussions of pulse-echo imaging we indicated that the choice of operating frequency for that modality was the result of a trade-off between the desire to obtain high resolution (which improves with increasing frequency) and the need to obtain adequate penetration of the ultrasound beam (which decreases with increasing frequency). These trade-offs also are factors in determining the best frequency for specific applications of Doppler instruments.

However, factors in addition to attenuation play a role in the signal strength in Doppler ultrasound. Since the source of Doppler ultrasound signals is blood, the scatterers are small, Rayleigh scatterers. The intensity of scattered signals for Rayleigh scatterers increases with the frequency raised to the fourth power. It would thus seem reasonable to use a high ultrasound frequency to increase the intensity of echo signals scattered from blood.

As the frequency increases, however, the rate of beam attenuation also increases. In selecting the optimal frequency for detecting blood flow these competing processes must be balanced, and the choice is related to the depth of the vessel of interest. For small, superficial vessels, where attenuation from overlying tissues is not significant, Doppler probes operating in the 8- to 10-MHz frequency range are common. Frequencies as low as 2 MHz are sometimes used where significant ranges and large amounts of attenuation are present.

In instruments that provide combined B-mode imaging and Doppler operating modes, it is not unusual to have different ultrasound frequencies applied for each mode. For example, a 7.5-MHz B-mode image might be combined with Doppler processing done at 5 MHz to optimize the detectability of the Doppler signals from all depth of interest. The echoes originating from stationary structures displayed in B-mode are of significantly greater

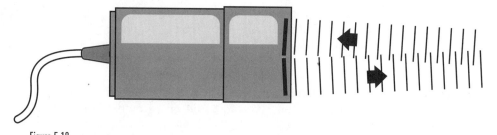

Figure 5-13. CW Doppler transducer containing two piezoelectric elements. One element continuously transmits ultrasound waves and the other continuously detects echoes.

amplitude than those from blood, so greater amounts of beam attenuation can be tolerated for their detection than for detection of signals from blood.

DIRECTIONAL DOPPLER

In a simple, "nondirectional" Doppler instrument, the output Doppler signals are identical for reflectors moving at a fixed speed, say 50 cm/s, toward the transducer or away from the transducer. In other words, a nondirectional Doppler instrument cannot distinguish whether the Doppler shift in the returning echoes is positive or negative. In some applications only the presence of flow or the relative speed of reflectors needs to be detected, and simple processing without this directional information will do. However, in many situations the direction of flow also is important, requiring directional Doppler circuitry.

Special signal processing is required in an instrument that displays the direction of flow. Ordinarily this is done in two stages: (1) Doppler signals are generated that have the directional information encoded, and (2) the directional information is displayed using loudspeakers, spectral analyzers, or velocity waveform circuits.

A commonly used signal processing method in directional Doppler instruments is known as *quadrature detection*[2-4] (Figure 5-14). After the received signal is amplified it branches into two separate demodulator circuits. In each circuit the signal is mixed with a reference signal derived from the transmitter, similar to nondirec-

tional processing outlined earlier. Filtering out the high-frequency signals, leaving only the audible Doppler signals for each branch, yields two nearly identical Doppler signals, V_a and V_b, from the separate demodulators. Processing in the two demodulators is the same except for a slight difference in the reference signals. These differ in phase by exactly one fourth the period of the reference frequency, hence the term *quadrature detectors*. It turns out that the output Doppler signals, V_a and V_b, also differ in phase. Their relative phase depends on whether the received echo signal frequency is greater or less than the transmitted signal frequency. Hence the phase relationship of the output quadrature signals depends on whether the scatterers are moving toward or away from the transducer (Figure 5-15). This can be used to determine the flow direction.

The two quadrature signals sound identical when applied individually to loudspeakers. They are processed further to derive directional information. Clever schemes have been described[3] for combining the two signals into stereo-like Doppler displays, motion towards transducer producing Doppler signals in one speaker and motion away being heard in the other. The quadrature signals are also used in spectral analysis displays. This is discussed later in this chapter.

PULSED DOPPLER

With continuous-wave Doppler instruments, reflectors and scatterers anywhere in the beam of the transducer

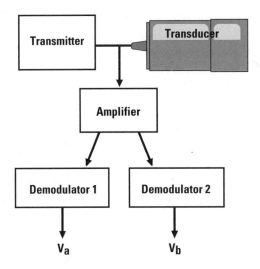

Figure 5-14. Quadrature detection to determine flow direction. The echo signals are sent to two demodulators, producing two Doppler signals, V_a and V_b. The phase relationship between these two signals can be used by the instrument to determine whether the Doppler shift is positive or negative.

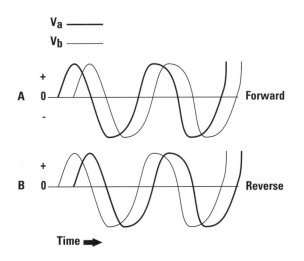

Figure 5-15. The two output Doppler signals, V_a and V_b, following quadrature demodulation. Their relative timing, or phase, depends on whether flow is towards the transducer or away from the transducer. Additional processing within the instrument takes advantage of this phase relationship in the two channels to determine reflector direction.

can contribute to the Doppler signal. Pulsed Doppler provides the ability to select Doppler signals from specific depths. The region from which the signals are selected is called the *sample volume*. When combined with steerable Doppler beams on duplex scanners, pulsed Doppler enables the precise selection of the depth and angle of the sample volume.

Pulsed Doppler circuitry

Pulsed Doppler is somewhat like pulse-echo ultrasound in that sound pulses are produced by the transducer at regular intervals. A transmitter (Figure 5-16) applies a transmit pulse to the transducer; this pulse has a well-defined frequency. Some pulsed Doppler instruments allow the operator to vary the pulse duration, that is, the number of cycles in the pulse, in order to vary the sensitivity. More cycles in the pulse results in improved sensitivity and better performance of the Doppler circuitry. This is done at the expense of somewhat greater acoustic exposure to the patient and poorer axial resolution.

Amplification and demodulation of the echo signals occur, analogous to CW Doppler. The output of a Doppler demodulator depends not only on the amplitude of echoes from reflectors, but also on the precise phase of the echo signals. An operator-adjusted "range gate" isolates signals from the desired depth. These are stored temporarily in the sample and hold unit, awaiting the outcome of another transmit pulse. If reflectors within the gated volume are moving, echoes collected during the subsequent pulse-echo sequence are of slightly different phase. This difference will show up during Doppler processing in the demodulator. By repeating this process over and over, the Doppler signal from the gated volume is built up gradually in the sample and hold unit.

The build-up of the Doppler signal

A more detailed view of the build-up of the pulsed Doppler signal is obtained with the help of Figure 5-17. In this sketch, we are assuming a single reflector is moving towards the transducer. The amplified echo signal shows only the signal from the reflector; four waveforms corresponding to four successive pulse-echo sequences are shown. Because of the motion of the reflector, the time for the echo to return shortens from one pulse to the next. The gated output of the demodulator depends on the phase of the amplified echo signal compared to that of the transmit oscillator. It is highest when the phases are the same and lowest when they differ by 180 degrees. Because the echo signal phase varies between pulses, the gated demodulator output also varies. The sample and hold unit retains the demodulator output between pulse-echo sequences. The filtered version of this retained signal is the Doppler signal!

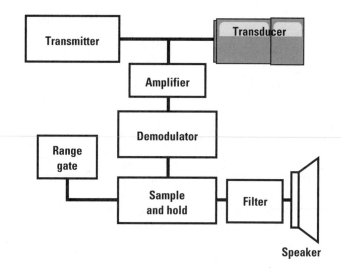

Figure 5-16. Pulsed Doppler instrument. Following each transmit pulse, echoes are amplified and Doppler processed in the demodulator, so the signal depends both on the echo amplitude and the phase. A segment of the signal from a fixed depth is selected by the range gate/sample and hold system.

Size of the pulsed Doppler sample volume

The sample volume size, indicated in Figure 5-18, is determined by two factors. The ultrasound beam width, both in the scan plane and perpendicular to the scan plane, determines the cross-sectional area of the sample volume. Thus a more tightly focused ultrasound beam results in a smaller beam area and narrower sample volume. The axial length of the sample volume is determined by the pulse duration and by the sample gate size. Most instruments provide a control so that the operator can adjust the gate size.

If you increase the gate size, you increase the volume from which Doppler signals are picked up. This is easily demonstrated using a flow phantom (Figure 5-19). When a narrow gate is used (Figure 5-19, *A*) and is centered in the middle of the vessel, a very narrow range of velocities is picked up, as shown by the velocity traces on the bottom. When a larger gate is used (Figure 5-19, *B*), a larger range of velocities is picked up.

Pulsed Doppler controls

Operator controls on pulsed Doppler instruments, in addition to those already mentioned for continuous-wave Doppler units, include the following:

1. Range gate position; the operator can place the range gate at various depths. With duplex instruments the operator can also place it at various positions in the B-mode image field.

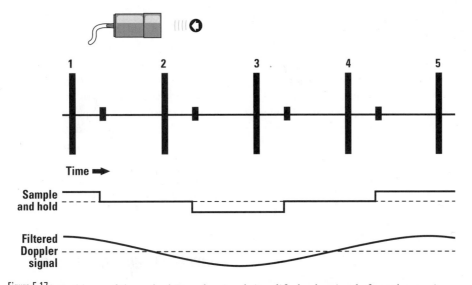

Figure 5-17. Build-up of the pulsed Doppler signal. Amplified echo signals from the moving reflector are shown for four successive pulse-echo sequences. (A fifth pulse has been launched, but the echo does not show up in this diagram.) Also shown is the output of the sample and hold device; this signal varies because the phase of the echo from the reflector changes as it moves. The bottom trace is a filtered (smoothed) version of this signal, which is the Doppler signal!

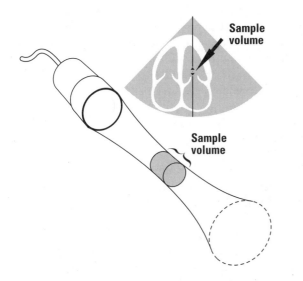

Figure 5-18. Pulsed Doppler sample volume. The beam width, both in the scan plane and perpendicular to the scan plane, determines the sample volume cross-sectional area. The gate size and pulse duration determine the axial extent of the sample volume.

2. Gate or sample volume size; increasing the range gate accepts Doppler signals from a longer axial region.
3. Pulse duration (on some instruments).
4. Flow angle cursor; (for duplex instruments); the angle cursor is positioned by the operator so that it follows the perceived direction of flow. The instrument then makes an angle correction to the velocity display.

Duplex instruments

A pulse-echo scanner and a Doppler instrument provide complementary information in that the scanner can best outline anatomical details whereas a Doppler instrument yields information regarding flow and movement patterns. "Duplex" ultrasound instruments are real-time B-mode scanners with built-in Doppler capabilities. In typical applications the pulse-echo B-mode image obtained with a duplex scanner is used to localize areas where flow will be examined using Doppler. The area to be studied in pulsed Doppler mode is selected on the B-mode image with a "sample volume" or "sample gate" indicator (Figure 5-8). The cursor position is controlled by the operator. Many duplex instruments allow the operator to indicate the direction of flow with respect to the ultrasound beam direction by adjusting an angle cursor. This is necessary to estimate the reflector velocity from the frequency of the Doppler signal. Most of the examples of Doppler records in this chapter are obtained using duplex equipment. The records include both a gray scale image of the region scanned and a Doppler display from an operator-selected sample volume.

During duplex scanning the ultrasound transducer assembly and the instrument "time-shares" between pulse-echo and Doppler mode. The extent of this time sharing is often under operator control directly or indirectly. Thus some instruments allow the operator to specify the rate at which the B-mode image is updated while in Doppler mode. This may range from 7 to 10 times per second to no updating at all. Of course, the more frequently the B-mode image is updated, the more certain the operator is of the exact location of the sample volume during a Doppler study, an important consideration especially for smaller vessels. However, as we will discuss below, pulsed Doppler sometimes is very demanding in the fraction of time the instrument must launch Doppler mode pulses into the sample volume, especially if reflectors are moving very rapidly. This usually limits the frequency of image updating.

Transducers for duplex

Both mechanical scanners and array transducer assemblies are used as duplex scanners. Mechanical sector scanners provide the ability to incorporate annular array

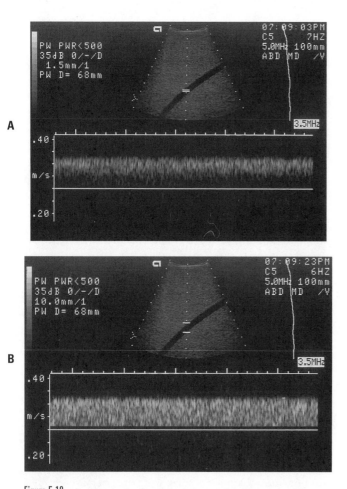

Figure 5-19. **A,** Control of sample volume size by varying the gate size of a pulsed Doppler instrument. In this flow phantom, the velocities are highest in the middle of the vessel and slowest near the edges. When a narrow gate is used and is centered in the middle of the vessel, a very narrow range of velocities is picked up, as shown by the velocity trace on the bottom. **B,** When a larger gate is used, a larger range of velocities is picked up. The spectral velocity trace is filled in from approximately 0 m/s all the way up to the maximum velocity in the vessel, about 25 m/s.

transducers (see Chapter 2) for an improved slice thickness over the image. However, phased linear and curvilinear arrays offer other advantages for duplex scanning, especially in the flexibility in switching between Doppler and real-time B-mode. Because there are no moving parts in the transducer assembly the array scanning instrument can quickly and automatically shift between steering the beam toward the sample volume in Doppler mode and then back to B-mode to build up part of the B-mode image, then back to Doppler mode, and so on. Thus B-mode image updating may be more rapid when studies are done in a combined B-mode scan and pulsed Doppler mode.

DOPPLER SPECTRAL ANALYSIS

Characteristics of flow in vessels

Doppler signals from flowing blood may be complicated because of the nature of the flow patterns encountered by the sound beam. Sometimes the flow is parabolic or laminar, as shown in *A* of Figure 5-20. Blood cells move fastest along the axis of the vessel; the velocity drops to zero at the vessel wall. Laminar flow is often considered an ideal condition that slow to moderately fast flow reaches if there are no abrupt discontinuities in the flow such as caused by turns and obstructions.

In large vessels, such as the aorta, the flow may take on a more blunt profile. Here the flow profile is nearly constant across the vessel; near the wall the flow decreases to zero again. Finally, a turbulent flow pattern as might be caused by a blockage or narrowing is shown in *C* of Figure 5-20.

The actual velocity profile across any vessel depends on a number of factors, including the diameter of the vessel, the mechanical properties of blood, the flow velocity, and the time. If echo signals are detected simultaneously from across the vessel, a range of Doppler frequencies is present in the signal. The number of different frequencies depends on the distribution of velocities present, the transducer beam width, and the size of the Doppler sample volume if pulsed Doppler is employed. A quantitative analysis showing the distribution of frequencies is done by spectral analysis.

Spectral analysis

Spectral analysis is a process by which a complex signal is broken down or analyzed into simple frequency components. In physics and engineering the most common way to do spectral analysis is to use a process called *Fourier analysis*. A commonly used device that performs the spectral analysis in ultrasound instruments is a fast Fourier transform (FFT) analyzer. The FFT instrument, along with a display screen, allows the amount of Doppler signal present at different frequencies to be displayed as a function of time.

The FFT analyzer (Figure 5-21) operates serially on small, 1- to 5-ms, segments of the Doppler signal. The signal segment is converted to digital format ("digitized") in an analog-to-digital (A/D) converter and is then sent to the spectral analyzer. The analyzer produces a record showing the relative amount of signal within each of sev-

eral discrete frequency bins. It then operates on another signal segment, and so on, producing a continuous display.

The result of the FFT's operation is illustrated schematically in Figure 5-22. In this figure the horizontal axis represents time and is broken into small intervals to correspond to the signal segments mentioned earlier. The vertical axis represents Doppler frequency, or reflector velocity, and is divided into discrete frequency bins. The higher the bin on the vertical scale, the greater the frequency. The FFT analyzer fills each frequency bin with a density or shade of gray that represents the amount of signal with that frequency during the segment. The amount of signal is related to the number of red blood cells and the Doppler frequency is proportional to their velocity; hence, we have the representation as illustrated. By operating on successive signal segments the analyzer produces a continuous spectral display.

Information on the spectral display

The Doppler spectral display provides a readout of the distribution of frequencies—and hence, reflector velocities—contributing to the signal. Velocity versus time flow patterns for arteries and many large veins have been established. Deviations of these patterns from normal are evaluated using spectral Doppler. The example in Figure 5-23 is for a normal carotid artery and one that has a stenosis, where the sample volume was placed at the distal margin of the stenotic region.

Other important characteristics of the flow pattern may also be gleaned from the spectral display. For exam-

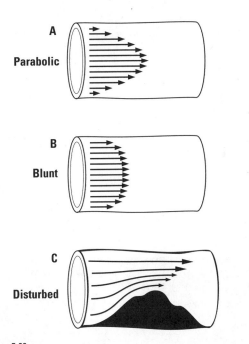

Figure 5-20. Laminar, blunt, and turbulent flow patterns.

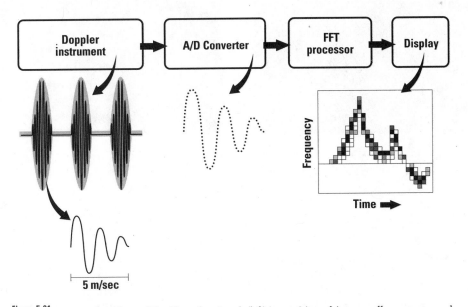

Figure 5-21. Spectral analyzer. The Doppler signal *(left)* is partitioned into small segments, and each chunk is analyzed to determine the amount of signal present at various frequencies. Each segment is represented as a column on the display, with the frequency (or velocity) appearing vertically and the amount of signal at each frequency (or velocity) indicated as a shade of gray.

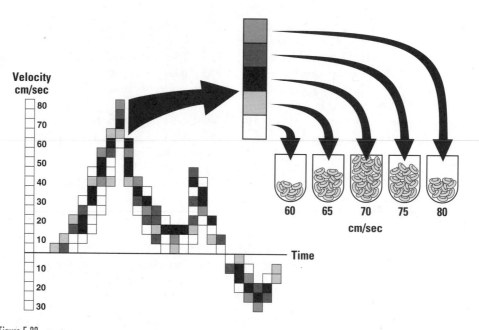

Figure 5-22. Information content on a spectral Doppler display. Velocity (or Doppler frequency is plotted versus time, with the amount of signal at specific times and velocities as a shade of gray. Because the amount of signal is related to the number of scatterers at the corresponding speed, the display represents a binning of the scatterers, as shown.

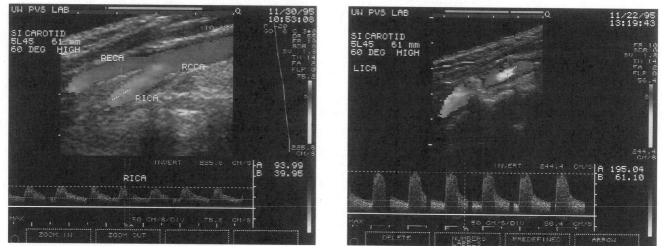

Figure 5-23. Spectral Doppler tracings for a normal right internal carotid artery (RICA), **(A)** and an internal carotid artery with a stenosis **(B)**. In the normal artery the peak velocity during systole is 94 cm/s; in the stenosis the peak systolic velocity is 195 cm/s.

ple, with pulsed Doppler and a short sample gate positioned in the center of a vessel, a narrow-band Doppler frequency spectral display is usually obtained (Figure 5-24). The area beneath the peak of the spectral trace is called the *spectral window*. Partial or total fill-in of the spectral window can occur in the presence of turbulence. These disturbances in the Doppler spectrum are also called *spectral broadening* because they are related to a wider range of Doppler frequencies from the sample volume.

The presence of obstructions may sometimes be detected from the spectrum. If the vessel is large compared

to the sample volume, a fairly narrow velocity range is sampled. This results in a narrow frequency band and the spectral window on the display. In the presence of mild or severe turbulence caused by obstructions, this spectral window is filled in partially or entirely (Figure 5-24).

Some instruments display additional information related to the instantaneous distribution of velocities in the spectrum. The "mean" (Figure 5-25) is the average value of all signals in the spectrum at any given time. An example is shown in Figure 5-26, where the mean frequency trace is superimposed on a spectral trace from the

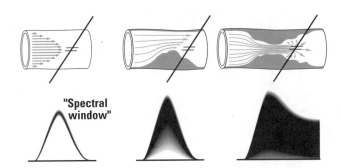

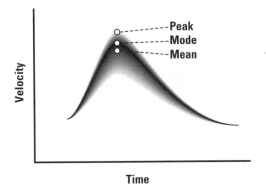

Figure 5-24. Some characteristics of the Doppler signal spectral display for different flow conditions. The left diagram presents a normal spectrum with the gate selecting a very narrow range of velocities that contribute to the signal. The open region within the spectral envelope during peak flow is called the *spectral window.* Partial or total fill-in of the spectral window occurs with turbulence, seen in the two panels on the right.

Figure 5-25. Definition of the "peak," "mode," and "mean" frequencies (or velocities) on a Doppler spectral display.

carotid artery. The "mode" is the most likely velocity, or the value in the spectrum that is the whitest shade of gray; this corresponds to the most prevalent red blood cell velocity in the sample volume. The spectral "width" indicates the range of Doppler frequencies, and hence, reflector velocities contributing to the Doppler signal, and the "peak" is the top of the spectral envelope.

Various parameters have been derived from the Doppler signal spectrum to quantify important properties of the flow. For example, the pulsatility index, PI, is defined by:

$$PI = \frac{max - min}{ave}$$

where *max* and *min* refer to the peak systolic and minimum diastolic velocities, respectively, during the cardiac cycle and *ave* is the average flow during the cycle. These quantities are obtained from the spectral display as shown in Figure 5-27. The average value during the cardiac cycle either must be obtained by the operator tracing the mean spectral waveform, or, for some instruments, by algorithms in the instrument. A simpler index, the resistivity index, does not require estimates of the mean velocity during the cardiac cycle, but only maximum and minimum values. It is defined by:

$$RI = \frac{max - min}{max}$$

An advantage of these parameters is that they provide data on the relative resistance to flow of the vascular bed; they do this without the need to quantify velocities and flow absolutely, where angle corrections must be provided. Angle correction may be impossible, especially in situations where the vessel lumen cannot be visualized, such as in the kidney.[5]

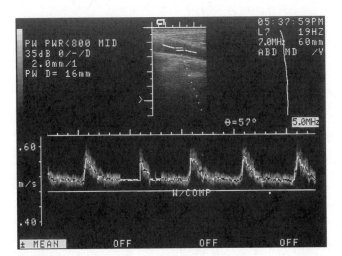

Figure 5-26. Spectral Doppler display, with the calculated "mean" velocity superimposed on the trace.

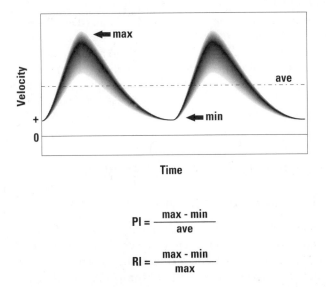

$$PI = \frac{max - min}{ave}$$

$$RI = \frac{max - min}{max}$$

Figure 5-27. Parameters used to compute the pulsatility index, PI, and the resistivity index, RI.

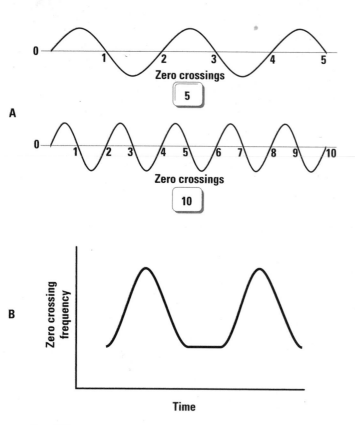

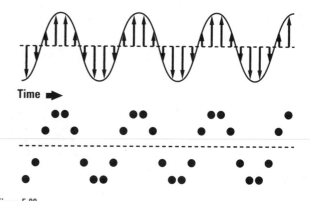

Figure 5-29. Sampling a signal. The solid line on top is a sine wave. The arrows are meant to represent times when discrete samples of the signal are taken. The dotted line on the bottom is the resultant sampled signal.

Figure 5-28. Zero-crossing detector. **A,** A rough estimation of the Doppler frequency is obtained from the number of times the signal crosses 0 volts during short time intervals. **B,** Most zero-crossing detectors present a continuous trace of the zero-crossing frequency versus time, such as shown here.

Zero-crossing detector

Many stand-alone Doppler instruments provide a "zero-crossing" detector to present a waveform displaying the Doppler frequency. The zero-crossing device simply counts the number of times the oscillating Doppler signal crosses the "zero-volts" line during small time intervals (Figure 5-28, *A*). The output often is applied to a physiological recording device, on which the zero-crossing frequency is displayed along with other traces, such as an electrocardiogram and arterial pressure signals (Figure 5-28, *B*).

ALIASING AND THE NYQUIST FREQUENCY

Sampling the Doppler signal

With a pulsed Doppler instrument the output Doppler signal is built up in discrete "pieces," one piece being added each time a pulse is launched, and echo signals are detected from the sample volume. We say that the Doppler signal is "sampled" rather than recorded contin-

uously. Sampling in this context is somewhat like a strobe light illuminating a dancer on a stage. If the strobe frequency is high enough, the movements of the dancer may be followed easily, but if the strobe flashes are too slow, the audience only sees a jerky, discontinuous movement. In pulsed Doppler, each time a pulse is launched by the transducer and an echo from moving reflectors detected, a sample of the Doppler signal is stored in the sample and hold unit. The sampling frequency of a pulsed Doppler instrument is equal to the pulse repetition frequency (PRF) in Doppler mode.

In any situation where sampling occurs, the greater the sampling frequency in comparison to the actual frequencies present, the better the rendition of that signal after it has been sampled. This is illustrated in Figure 5-29, where a sine wave signal *(solid line)* is shown sampled at a fairly high rate *(arrows)*. The lower curve is the resultant sampled version of the signal. It is fairly easy to appreciate the original signal with the sampling conditions in this example. To carry the example over to the pulsed Doppler case, the sine wave corresponds to the actual Doppler signal, the arrows to individual pulses transmitted and echoes picked up by the transducer, and the dotted line to the output Doppler signal.

In a practical ultrasound system we usually reach an upper limit on the PRF, limiting the sampling frequency. For pulsed Doppler instruments the upper limit of the PRF is established by the fact that a sound pulse takes a small but measurable amount of time to travel to the sample volume and return. Before a pulse is launched by the instrument, it is necessary to wait for echoes from all previous pulses to return from the sample volume; if the waiting time between pulses is insufficient, "range ambiguities" arise; *range ambiguities* are uncertainties in the actual range from which Doppler signals occur.

At the very least the PRF on the instrument must be great enough to sample the Doppler signal at least

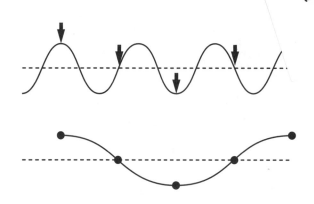

two times for each cycle of the Doppler signal. If the PRF is less than twice the frequency of the maximum Doppler signal frequency, then **aliasing** will occur. Aliasing is the production of artifactual, lower-frequency components in the signal spectrum when the pulse repetition frequency of the instrument is less than two times the maximum frequency of the Doppler signal. The condition when the PRF equals $2f_D$, known as the **Nyquist sampling rate.**[5] It defines a minimum sampling rate for a signal whose frequency is f_D; if the sampling rate is below the Nyquist rate, aliasing will occur. If it is above the Nyquist rate, the signal can be determined unambiguously.

Aliasing

The production of aliasing is illustrated in Figure 5-30. This is the same as in the previous figure, only now the signal *(top solid curve)* is sampled *(arrows)* once every cycle and a quarter, a rate that is less than two times the frequency. The solid dots illustrate the sampled signal, and a curve is drawn to assist the reader in visualizing the resulting sampled signal shape. The result of undersampling the signal is one that is lower in frequency than the frequency of the actual signal.

Aliasing is manifested in three ways on a pulsed Doppler instrument equipped with a spectral display. First, the display "wraps around," producing an apparent reversal of the flow direction (Figure 5-31). Second, the audible Doppler signal exhibits a noticeable loss of high frequencies as the frequency exceeds the maximum. Third, the audible Doppler signal also sounds as though flow reversal occurs.

Eliminating aliasing

The most straightforward way to eliminate aliasing when it occurs is to adjust the velocity or frequency scale on the Doppler spectral display (Fig 5-30, *B*). Most instruments have the PRF of the pulsed Doppler unit linked to the scale setting. As the scale setting is increased, the PRF is automatically increased to satisfy the Nyquist rate for the maximum scale setting.

If the spectral scale is at its maximum setting, another method to eliminate the appearance of aliasing is to adjust the spectral baseline (Figure 5-32). Normally the spectral scale is set to display Doppler signal frequencies ranging from −PRF/2 to +PRF/2. (Alternatively, the spectral scale displays the reflector velocities corresponding to this range.) Adjusting the spectral baseline reassigns the frequency scale, enabling Doppler signals to be displayed whose frequency is as high as the PRF on the machine. Thus the normal criteria to avoid aliasing state that the Doppler signal cannot exceed ± PRF/2; however, baseline adjustments can allocate the entire allowable fre-

Figure 5-30. Production of aliasing when the sampling rate is less than two times the frequency of the signal. The upper curve is the signal being sampled at discrete times indicated by arrows. The lower curve is a lower frequency "alias" of the real signal.

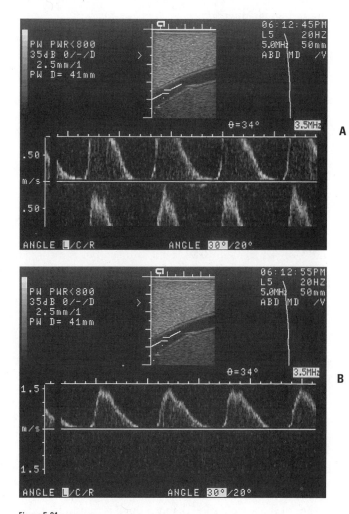

Figure 5-31. A, Manifestation of aliasing on a spectral Doppler display. The spectrum "wraps around" from the top to the bottom of the display, producing an apparent reversal of flow even though flow does not reverse itself. High frequencies are converted to low frequencies on the display. **B,** Elimination of aliasing by increasing the velocity scale. The Doppler instrument automatically increases the PRF when the operator changes the scale setting.

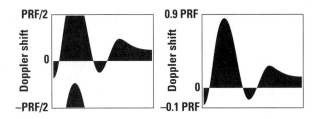

Figure 5-32. Adjustment of the spectral baseline to eliminate aliasing. Normally Doppler frequencies from -PRF/2 to +PRF/2 can be accommodated, but if the velocities detected are all in the same direction, the entire spectral scale can be assigned to them.

quency range to Doppler frequencies for reflectors moving in a single direction.

If neither of these methods succeeds, aliasing may sometimes be eliminated by using a lower frequency ultrasound transducer. A lower ultrasound frequency results in a lower frequency Doppler signal for the same velocity. Another possible method is to locate a window to the region of interest for which the incident sound beam angle is closer to 90 degrees. A Doppler angle closer to perpendicular results in a lower frequency Doppler signal; however, as mentioned earlier, larger uncertainties in velocities are introduced from angle errors.

Still further measures to get around pulsed Doppler aliasing involve using a high PRF mode (described later), if available, or even using continuous-wave rather than pulsed Doppler. CW Doppler is not subject to aliasing, as the Doppler signal in CW is not sampled but is recorded continuously. So even though the CW Doppler signal accumulates results from throughout the beam, its lack of aliasing is sometimes helpful; this modality frequently is used in echo cardiology examinations of heart valves when accurate specification of high flow velocities passing through damaged heart valves is necessary.

MAXIMUM VELOCITY DETECTABLE WITH PULSED DOPPLER

We have seen that to avoid aliasing of the Doppler signal the PRF of a pulsed Doppler instrument must be at least two times the maximum frequency in the signal. However, an upper limit to the PRF is established by the depth of the sample gate. Before a pulse is transmitted, the pulsed transmitter must wait until echoes from the previous transmit pulse return from the sample volume. If it does not, confusion may exist in the exact origin of any detected Doppler signals. Because of this need to wait between transmit pulses, an upper limit exists for the PRF, and hence, for the maximum reflector velocity that we can detect without aliasing.

Let v_{max} be this maximum reflector velocity and PRF_{max} the maximum PRF from the sample volume depth. Then, to avoid aliasing,

$$PRF_{max} = 2f_D = \frac{4f_o v_{max}}{c}$$

where we are assuming that the Doppler angle is zero, so the $\cos\Theta$ term in the Doppler equation is 1. Solving for v_{max},

$$v_{max} = \frac{cPRF_{max}}{4f_o}$$

What is PRF_{max}? We can use the range equation, Equation 3-1, to find an expression for the time needed to acquire echoes from the sample gate depth. If this depth is d, the time is $2d/c$. The maximum PRF for this echo delay time is the inverse of the echo delay time, or $c/2d$. Substituting this for PRF_{max} in the previous equation, we have

$$v_{max} = \frac{c^2}{8f_o d} \tag{5-3}$$

Example: What is the maximum detectable velocity in soft tissue if the ultrasound operating frequency is 5 MHz and the reflector depth is 5 cm?

Solution: Use 1540 m/s for the speed of sound; first convert d to meters so all units are the same. Then apply Equation 5-3.

$$v_{max} = \frac{(1540 \text{ m/s})^2}{8 \times 5 \times 10^6/\text{s} \times 0.05 \text{ m}} = 1.18 \text{ m/s} = 118 \text{ cm/s}$$

If the reflector were deeper than 5 cm, the maximum detectable velocity would decrease.

A group of curves illustrating the maximum detectable reflector velocity for several different ultrasound operating frequencies is provided in Figure 5-33. Notice that as the reflector depth increases, the maximum detectable Doppler signal frequency, and hence the maximum detectable reflector velocity, decreases. At any depth lower ultrasound frequencies permit detection of greater reflector velocities than higher operating frequencies, because lower frequencies result in lower frequency Doppler signals for the same velocity.

HIGH PRF MODE

To overcome the maximum velocity limitations some instruments provide a "high PRF" option. When high velocities need to be detected at large depths, the instrument can be placed in a mode where the Doppler PRF is higher than that allowed to avoid range ambiguity; the presence of the range ambiguities may be recognized by the existence of multiple gates on instruments displaying the Doppler sample volume position. This is illustrated in Figure 5-34. Although Doppler signals could be picked up from any of these sample volumes, this usually poses no problem since the operator usually has already isolated the vessel of interest and thus can pretty well determine that the Doppler signals are originating from the gate positioned at maximum depth.

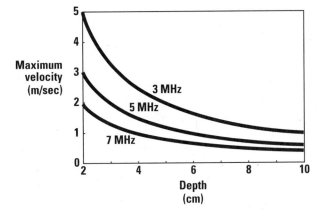

Figure 5-33. Maximum velocity detectable using pulsed Doppler versus depth of the sample volume. Curves for three different ultrasound frequencies are shown. It is assumed that the Doppler angle is zero and that the maximum Doppler frequency is PRF/2.

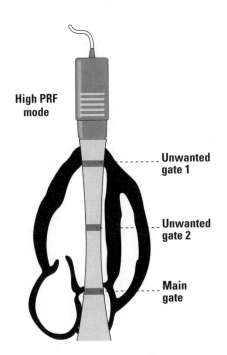

Figure 5-34. Multiple Doppler sample volumes in high PRF mode. Higher Doppler frequencies are detectable from the "main gate" than for standard, single-gate conditions. However, Doppler signals from "unwanted" gates are included in the Doppler signal.

ACOUSTIC OUTPUT LEVELS FROM DOPPLER EQUIPMENT

The topic of acoustic output levels from ultrasound equipment is considered in Chapter 9. One aspect of these data is the relatively high time average intensity from some pulsed Doppler instruments compared to intensities from real-time B-mode imaging equipment. This is due in part to the large duty factors during pulsed Doppler mode, and the effect of having the Doppler beam dwell along a single acoustic line. Users should be aware of the relative intensities produced in each of the operating modes of their instruments and how changing the operating conditions, such as varying the output power level, affects the acoustic intensities. Consult the operator's manual or contact the equipment manufacturer to find out the actual intensities produced by your equipment! If an output power control is provided in Doppler mode, use a low output power setting if practical, especially when examining potentially sensitive tissue, such as a fetus. Also, consider the guidelines presented at the end of Chapter 9.

SUMMARY

The Doppler effect is used in medical ultrasound to detect moving reflectors and to measure and characterize blood flow. The Doppler shift frequency, f_D, is the *difference* between the received and the transmitted frequencies. It is directly proportional to the reflector velocity and to the cosine of the angle at which the reflector is moving relative to the ultrasound beam. The Doppler angle must be taken into account for accurate measurements of reflector velocity.

Both CW and pulsed Doppler devices are available. Continuous wave instruments have a transmitter operating continuously and two elements in the transducer, one for transmitting and one for receiving. They provide no range discrimination of the reflector range. Pulsed Doppler provides discrimination of Doppler signals from different depths, allowing for the detection of moving interfaces and scatterers from within a well-defined sample volume. Duplex ultrasound instruments are real-time B-mode scanners with built-in Doppler capabilities.

A quantitative analysis showing the distribution of frequencies (or velocities) in a Doppler signal is done by **spectral analysis.** Aliasing is the production of artifactual, lower-frequency components in the signal spectrum when the pulse repetition frequency (PRF) of a pulsed Doppler instrument is less than two times the maximum frequency of the Doppler signal. The maximum detectable reflector velocity for a pulsed Doppler instrument is established by the need to avoid aliasing while also avoiding range ambiguities. To overcome the maximum velocity limitations some instruments provide a high PRF option. Many pulsed Doppler instruments produce spatial peak time average intensities that are significantly greater than spatial peak time average intensities for other operating modes. Users should be aware of which controls affect the power and intensity on their instrument.

References

1. Evans DH et al: *Doppler ultrasound: physics, instrumentation and clinical applications,* New York, 1989, John Wiley & Sons.
2. Smith H, Zagzebski J: *Doppler ultrasound,* Madison, WI, 1991, Medical Physics Publishing.
3. Beach K, Phillips D: Doppler instrumentation for the evaluation of arterial and venous disease. In Jaffe C, editor: *Clinics in diagnostic ultrasound,* vol 13, *Vascular and Doppler ultrasound,* New York, 1984, Churchill Livingstone.
4. Taylor KJW, Burns P, Wells PNT: *Clinical applications of Doppler ultrasound,* New York, 1988, Raven Press.
5. Marple SL Jr: *Digital spectral analysis,* Englewood Cliffs, NJ, 1987, Prentice-Hall.

Questions for Review

1. A Doppler shift is best described as a change in _____ as a result of motion.

   A. loudness of the sound source
   B. frequency of the source
   C. loudness of perceived sound
   D. perceived frequency

2. Which of the following does not result in a Doppler shift?

   A. stationary sound source, stationary listener
   B. stationary sound source, moving listener
   C. moving sound source, stationary listener
   D. moving sound source, moving listener

3. The Doppler equation in medical ultrasound relates:

   A. reflector angle to reflector speed
   B. speed of sound to reflector velocity
   C. reflector depth to received frequency
   D. reflector speed to Doppler frequency

4. If the transmitted beam is 5 MHz, echoes received by the transducer, even after Doppler shifts, are generally about:

   A. 5 Hz
   B. 500 kHz
   C. 5 MHz
   D. 10 MHz

5. When a 5-MHz ultrasound beam is used to examine a vessel, the Doppler shift frequency is 3 kHz. If a 2.5-MHz beam were used and the Doppler angle is the same, the Doppler frequency would be:

   A. 1.5 kHz
   B. 2.5 kHz
   C. 3 kHz
   D. 6 kHz

6. What is the Doppler angle?

   A. flow direction relative to the patient axis
   B. beam direction relative to the patient axis
   C. the angle that two vessels make to one another
   D. flow direction relative to the ultrasound beam

7. Suppose the original Doppler angle is 0 degrees. If the vessel direction changes and the angle is increased to 45 degrees, the frequency of the Doppler signal will be:

   A. unchanged
   B. increased
   C. decreased
   D. either increased or decreased, depending on the ultrasound frequency

8. In combined Doppler and B-mode (also called *duplex ultrasound*), how is the Doppler angle detected?

   A. automatically using quadrature detection
   B. the machine sends Doppler beams in multiple directions and detects the direction for the highest intensity signal
   C. the machine sends Doppler beams in multiple directions and detects the direction for the highest frequency signal
   D. the sonographer aligns a cursor on the B-mode image and the machine determines the cursor angle with respect to the beam direction

9. Which of the following Doppler angles would result in the lowest frequency Doppler signal?

   A. 0 degrees
   B. 25 degrees
   C. 60 degrees
   D. 85 degrees

10. Which of the following Doppler angles would result in the greatest percentage error in calculating the velocity from the Doppler shift if the sonographer made a 5-degree mistake in the angle cursor setting?

    A. 0 degrees
    B. 25 degrees
    C. 60 degrees
    D. 85 degrees

11. The Doppler signal heard on the loudspeaker of a CW Doppler unit is:

    A. the received ultrasound frequency
    B. the sum of the transmitted and received frequencies
    C. the product of the transmitted times the received frequency
    D. the difference between the transmitted and received frequencies

12. In the transducer of a very basic CW Doppler device there often are two separate piezoelectric elements. The reason for this is:

    A. one serves as a spare
    B. one is a transmitter and the other a receiver
    C. to electronically focus the beam
    D. to electronically steer the beam

13. Which of the following controls would NOT be found on a CW Doppler instrument?

    A. wall filter
    B. output power
    C. receiver gain
    D. sample volume depth

14. The wall filter of a Doppler instrument eliminates:

    A. low-frequency Doppler signals
    B. high-amplitude signals
    C. low-amplitude signals
    D. noise on the display

15. Quadrature detection indicates

    A. whether flow is towards or away from the transducer
    B. Doppler angle
    C. whether flow is through a stenosis or a normal vessel
    D. Doppler frequency

16. In "laminar flow" within a vessel, blood velocities are:

    A. turbulent, or "chaotic"
    B. equal throughout the entire vessel cross-section
    C. highest in the center of the vessel, and decrease to zero at the walls
    D. at an angle to the axis of the vessel

17. The strength of the Doppler signal from flowing blood is most closely related to:

    A. the area of the ultrasound beam
    B. the shape of the red blood cells
    C. the speed at which the blood is moving
    D. the number of red blood cells in the beam

18. The purpose of fast Fourier transform programs is to:

    A. eliminate aliasing
    B. automatically vary system gain
    C. display the Doppler frequency spectrum
    D. filter out low-frequency Doppler signals

19. The function of a zero-crossing detector is to determine the:

    A. direction of flow
    B. amplitude of the Doppler signal
    C. approximate frequency of the Doppler signal
    D. Doppler frequency spectrum

20. The Doppler signal spectral display presents Doppler frequency, or _____, on the vertical axis.

    A. time
    B. signal strength
    C. Doppler angle
    D. reflector velocity

21. On a continuous Doppler spectral display, the amount of signal for any given velocity and time is indicated by:

    A. spike height
    B. the gray level
    C. the trace sweep speed
    D. the slope of the trace

22. The pulsatility index gives an indication of:

    A. vessel diameter
    B. heart rate (pulses per second)
    C. flow resistance distal to the sample volume
    D. whether flow is towards or away from the probe

23. The term *gating* is associated primarily with:

    A. A-mode
    B. B-mode imaging
    C. pulsed Doppler
    D. continuous wave Doppler

24. Which of the following may be present in pulsed Doppler but NOT in continuous wave Doppler?

    A. aliasing
    B. a wall filter control
    C. directional detection capabilities
    D. spectral analysis of the Doppler signal

25. The production of artifactual, lower frequency signals when the sampling frequency is too low is called:

    A. spectral broadening
    B. the Nyquist criteria
    C. low-frequency generation
    D. aliasing

26. To successfully record a signal when "sampled," the sampling rate must be at least _____ the frequency of the signal.

    A. $1/4$
    B. $1/2$
    C. as great as
    D. twice

27. In pulsed Doppler, the rate at which the Doppler signal is sampled is the:

    A. image frame rate
    B. backscatter rate
    C. Doppler frequency
    D. pulse repetition frequency

28. If the PRF of an instrument in Doppler mode is 12,000/s, the maximum Doppler frequency that can be detected without aliasing and without adjusting the spectral baseline is:

    A. 6000 hz
    B. 9000 hz
    C. 12,000 hz
    D. 24,000 hz

29. Which of the following controls on a duplex ultrasound instrument has the most direct effect on the Doppler pulse repetition frequency?

    A. wall filter
    B. output power
    C. spectral sweep speed
    D. spectral velocity scale

30. Suppose the maximum velocity that can be detected at a depth of 10 cm from the transducer in pulsed Doppler is 1 m/s. If the ultrasound frequency were halved, the maximum velocity would be:
    A. 0.25 m/s
    B. 0.5 m/s
    C. 1 m/s
    D. 2 m/s

31. Suppose the maximum velocity that can be detected at a depth of 10 cm from the transducer in pulsed Doppler is 1 m/s. If the distance were reduced to 5 cm, the maximum velocity would be:
    A. 0.25 m/s
    B. 0.5 m/s
    C. 1 m/s
    D. 2 m/s

32. High PRF mode allows detection of high velocities without aliasing by introducing:
    A. ambiguities in range gate depth
    B. ambiguities in range gate angle
    C. amplitude uncertainties
    D. amplitude distortions

Chapter 6

Color Doppler and Color Flow Imaging

This remarkable technology not only provides real-time flow visualization, but can accurately delineate a wide range of flow conditions, ranging from high velocities in large vessels to minute trickles coursing through highly echogenic, stationary structures.

Our discussion of pulsed Doppler instruments in the previous chapter dealt with use of a single time gate to select Doppler signals from a specific depth range in the field of the transducer. Motion of scatterers within this gated region was detected and displayed. Color flow imaging provides complete, two-dimensional cross-sectional images depicting velocities of moving reflectors and scatterers. By combining color data with gray scale B-mode images, color flow scanners provide anatomical details along with physiological flow information. This remarkable technology not only provides real-time flow visualization, but can accurately delineate a wide range of flow conditions, ranging from high velocities in large vessels to minute trickles coursing through highly echogenic, stationary structures.

There are two different processes used by various equipment manufacturers to derive color flow images.[1] The more common method utilizes Doppler processing of echo signals, in a sense, analyzing Doppler signals as they are acquired from a continuum of depths, for beam lines distributed over a large imaged field. The reflector velocity at each depth and for each color beam is detected and displayed. An alternative method does not use Doppler processing, but derives flow information directly from echo arrival times for reflectors in the beam. Changes in the echo arrival time from one transmit pulse to the next are mathematically converted to reflector displacements, and finally, to reflector speeds. We will examine both of these methods in this chapter.

COLOR FLOW IMAGING FROM DOPPLER PROCESSED ECHO SIGNALS

Acquiring and processing the signals

Echo data acquisition for color flow imaging may be viewed as an extension of pulse-echo gray scale imaging, only now reflector velocities rather than echo amplitudes are determined. Ultrasound pulses are transmitted along beam lines distributed across the imaged field (Figure 6-1). B-mode data are acquired essentially as outlined in Chapter 3. For color imaging, a longer duration transmit pulse (Figure 6-2) than used in B-mode imaging is applied. This pulse has a narrower frequency bandwidth than the short B-mode pulse, a quality found advantageous for Doppler processing. For each color beam line, echo signals are amplified and then applied to the Doppler processing unit. After Doppler processing, the echo signal has an A-mode-like appearance. However, the instantaneous signal value depends not only on the echo amplitude, but also on the **phase** of the incoming echo signal. Because the phase is related to the exact distance from the transducer to the reflectors (Figure 6-3), it is sensitive to reflector motion.

Pulse packets. Contrary to conventional B-mode imaging, where echoes for a single transmit pulse are all that are necessary to produce the B-mode dots along each beam line, it takes multiple pulse-echo sequences to acquire the echo data along each beam line in color flow imaging (Figure 6-4). Textbooks often refer to *color pack-*

ets or *pulse packets*[2] when describing this element of color flow data acquisition. For each color beam line, echoes produced following the first pulse in a packet contain signals from both stationary and moving reflectors. A series of digital registers temporarily stores this wave train, each register retaining information for a different depth. A second transmit pulse is launched along the same beam line and echo signals again acquired. Those parts of the new echo signal that arrive from stationary reflectors are identical to corresponding parts obtained during the previous pulse-echo sequence. They can be eliminated from further processing. Those parts arriving from reflectors that are moving are different following Doppler processing. These changes are used to estimate reflector velocities. For each color beam line, the more pulses in a packet, generally, the better the estimates of the reflector velocities. The price to be paid, however, is slower image rates because the more pulses in the packet, the longer it takes to acquire the echo data for each beam line. Often 8 to 10 pulse-echo sequences make up a pulse packet for each color beam line.

Stationary echo cancelers. Signals from stationary reflectors contain no useful information for color imaging. In fact, they get in the way because frequently they are much

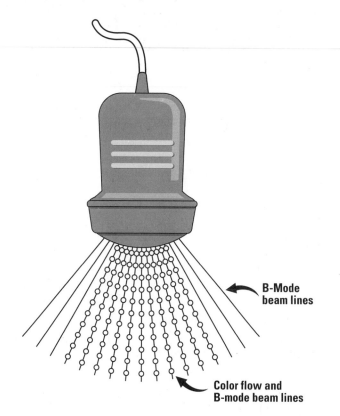

Figure 6-1. Data acquisition format for combined B-mode imaging and color flow imaging. Usually only part of the imaged field is used for color because of frame rate considerations.

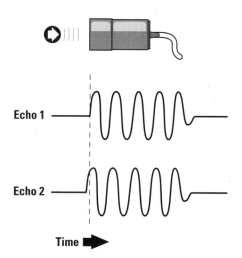

Figure 6-3. Small changes in the reflector distance from one pulse-echo sequence to the next produce changes in echo signal phase. Phase changes are easily detected in Doppler processing.

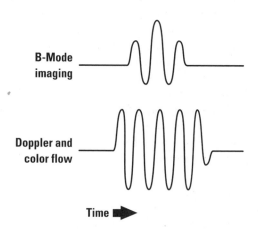

Figure 6-2. Transmit pulse shape for B-mode imaging and for pulsed Doppler and color flow imaging. The Doppler transmit pulse is of longer duration and narrower frequency bandwidth, providing better definition of the ultrasound frequency.

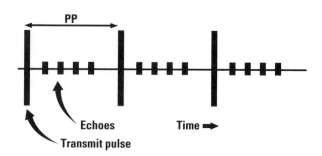

Figure 6-4. Pulse packets, or color packets in color flow imaging. The pulse packet is a series of 8 to 10 pulse-echo sequences along the same beam line; three sequences are shown.

greater in amplitude than echo signals from blood and must be eliminated before flow velocities are determined. They are gotten rid of by applying some type of tissue filter or "stationary echo canceler." Unlike wall filters in standard Doppler, the task in color flow imaging is much more difficult. Often we are displaying slowly moving flow, and the machine must deal only with a brief glimpse of the flow for each beam line forming the image; high pass wall filters that just eliminate low frequencies, as in pulsed Doppler, often are inadequate.

In its simplest form, a stationary echo canceler subtracts point-by-point one Doppler processed echo signal wave train from the previous one, eliminating those parts of the signal that do not change from one transmit pulse to the next in the pulse packet (Figure 6-5). Because Doppler processing is sensitive to the phase, parts of the echo signal that arrive from moving reflectors are different from their counterparts in the previous pulse-echo sequence. These differences are used to construct a

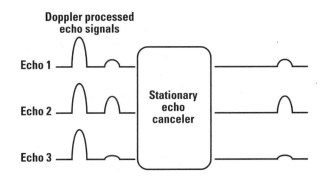

Figure 6-5. Function of the stationary echo canceler. It gets rid of those parts of the Doppler processed echo signals that do not change from one pulse-echo sequence to the next.

Doppler signal or to make direct estimates of the reflector velocity for each of the multiple registers. More sophisticated stationary echo cancelers, or "clutter rejection filters"—alluded to in sales brochures but a mystery to the average user—are present in today's color imaging applications.

Phase shift autocorrelation. Determining the flow velocity for each register requires special signal processing circuitry. A single parameter, usually the mean velocity, is to be displayed at each location. Spectral analyzers described in the previous chapter are not appropriate here, in part because of the short time spurts over which echo signal data are acquired for each register. In cases where reflectors are moving slowly, the short spurts may represent only a fraction of a cycle of the Doppler signal. Alternative techniques have been chosen by instrument manufacturers to provide estimates of flow velocity from the Doppler processed signals.

There are several techniques that are used to derive mean velocities for each depth segment in the Doppler processed echo signal.[2-4] The best known of these uses what is termed *phase shift autocorrelation*[5] to estimate the reflector velocity for each depth register (Figure 6-6). Correlation is a process for closely comparing the value of two quantities. Here correlation measures the change in the phase of the signals in each register from one transmit pulse to the next.[6] This in turn is used to compute an average Doppler frequency, and hence, an average or mean reflector velocity.

Forming the image. The pulse packets and Doppler frequency estimations mentioned so far were applied to determine reflector velocities for pixels along a single

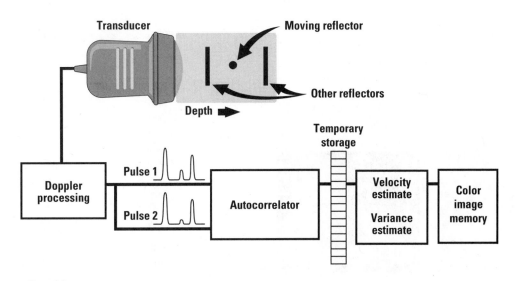

Figure 6-6. Overview of the hardware arrangement within a color flow imager. The autocorrelator computes the mean Doppler frequency and variance. The registers store the signals for different reflector depths from the beam line being interrogated.

beam line. These velocity data are placed in an image memory, and then a second color beam line is interrogated and echo data acquired and processed. The process continues until the entire area selected for color flow imaging has been interrogated. As the velocity data are being acquired, the image monitor is continuously updated by combining color data with B-mode image data. The combined color and B-mode image data are usually acquired at real-time scan rates.

To speed up the frame rate the operator usually can adjust the size of the imaged field in color mode (Figure 6-7). An entire scan can be done in a fraction of a second, allowing 10 or 15 frames per second image rates. Even higher rates are possible with reduced color image fields to accommodate, for example, cardiac applications.

Variance. Another attribute of the flow that is displayed on most color flow instruments that use Doppler processing is called *variance*. This is a measure of the variation of Doppler frequencies within each pixel on the image during the brief period associated with a pulse packet. It may be an effective method to detect turbulent flow, such as caused by obstructions, since there are many velocities present from regions when turbulence is present. If the velocity is nearly the same for each pulse in the packet, such as during laminar flow (Figure 6-8), the variance is small. Fluctuations in the velocity within the space corresponding to each pixel, however, lead to larger values for the variance. The autocorrelator provides a measure of the variance, which may be displayed on the image. Either the hue or the color saturation, described in the next section, can be used to encode the output of variance estimators for detecting the presence of turbulence (Figure 6-9).

Properties of color displays

There are several terms used to describe the attributes of a color display. It is well known that any color in the visible range of the electromagnetic spectrum may be formulated by suitable mixing of the three *primary colors:* red, blue, and green. If all three colors are added together

in equal amounts, the perceived color is white. Any single color in the visible spectrum can be produced by mixtures of two of the primary colors in the right proportion. This property of color perception is used advantageously in color television and video monitors. Each small element within the screen of a color monitor consists of three phosphors, one producing red light, one blue, and one green. Three separate electron guns provide the electron current to modulate the intensity of each phosphor, and hence of the primary colors at every addressable location on the screen. Thus different mixtures of the primary colors result in our perception of different colors on the screen.

We use the terms *hue, saturation,* and *intensity* to describe properties of an image related to the psychophysical perception of color. Hue is the attribute of colors that permits them to be classified as red, yellow, green, blue, or an intermediate between any contiguous pair of colors. The hue is associated with the wavelength of the light. In color flow instruments a red hue might be chosen to represent flow moving toward the ultrasound transducer, while a blue hue could be used to display flow signals from reflectors moving away from the probe. (Obviously, different schemes are also possible.) Color saturation has to do with the fact that mixtures involving all three primary colors turn out partially or totally white. Saturation is a measure of the chromatic purity, that is, the freedom from dilution with white

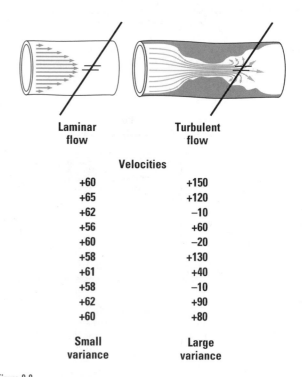

Laminar flow	Turbulent flow
Velocities	
+60	+150
+65	+120
+62	−10
+56	+60
+60	−20
+58	+130
+61	+40
+58	−10
+62	+90
+60	+80
Small variance	**Large variance**

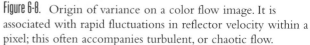

Figure 6-8. Origin of variance on a color flow image. It is associated with rapid fluctuations in reflector velocity within a pixel; this often accompanies turbulent, or chaotic flow.

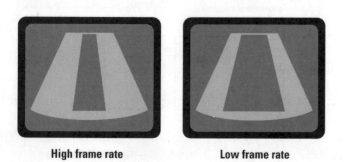

High frame rate   **Low frame rate**

Figure 6-7. Trade-off between frame rate and color sector width.

light. A completely saturated color has only one wavelength associated with it. It is a pure hue. On the other hand, white light is made up of many wavelengths, so the more white there is, the *less* saturated is the color. If we see a color flow display in which higher flow rates, for example, appear whiter than lower flow rates, we know that this is done by varying the saturation of the colors according to the detected flow rate. A third attribute used to describe color in an image is the intensity or brightness; this is similar to the corresponding property of a gray scale B-mode image. Intensity also is used in some color flow instruments to indicate flow rate, giving a range of colors from "dull" red to "bright" red, for example (Figure 6-10).

When setting up the combined color flow B-mode display, different choices are available to the manufacturer when deciding whether a particular pixel should display color flow data or B-mode data. These choices influence the sensitivity of an instrument to low flow rates and the degree of immunity to spurious motion accompanying heart beats, breathing, and probe movements. In some situations the operator can adjust a color threshold control (also referred to as *color versus echo write priority*) to favor either color information or gray scale echo information on the display.

An operator-controlled gate may be manipulated on the display of most units to allow detailed Doppler signal spectral analysis from selected regions. Signals originating from the gated region may be applied to an FFT analyzer in the manner discussed in Chapter 5.

Peculiarities associated with the flow direction

It is important to understand that a color flow instrument (as well as an ordinary directional continuous-wave or pulsed Doppler instrument) displays flow direction *with respect to the direction of the incident ultrasound beam,* and not with respect to an anatomical reference. Changing the orientation of the ultrasound beam with respect to the flow direction may change the apparent direction of flow within a vessel and hence the displayed color. This is brought out vividly by imaging a vessel using a sector imager, where the axis of the vessel is oriented as shown in Figure 6-11, *A*. When using a display scheme that depicts flow toward the transducer with a red hue and flow away from the transducer with a blue hue, the vessel image appears as in Figure 6-11, *B*. For the orientation shown, the flow within the right half of the image is directed slightly toward the ultrasound source and the direction of the incident ultrasound beam, and that on the left half of the image is directed slightly away from the ultrasound source. Hence the vessel image is divided into two regions: a red section and a blue section. Notice that the image is generated using a sector sweep of the ultrasound beam across the vessel. When the beam is perpendicular to the direction of flow, there is no detected Doppler shift; hence we see a discontinuity in the flow image.

In some applications it is desirable to obtain images of vessels running parallel to the surface of the skin using linear array transducers. The standard arrangement for linear arrays is with beams emerging perpendicular to the surface of the array, but this arrangement produces perpendicular beam incidence to the vessel. Two methods have been developed to provide a continuous color flow image of a vessel when using a linear array (Figure 6-12). In one a transducer offset cut at an angle is used so that the ultrasound beams producing the color flow image always are incident on the vessel at an angle other than 90 degrees with respect to the direction of flow. B-mode image information and Doppler flow information are obtained along the same acoustic lines. In another method (Figure 6-12, *B*) the Doppler and color flow image beams are steered at an angle with respect to the standard direction of the B-mode imaging beams. This is

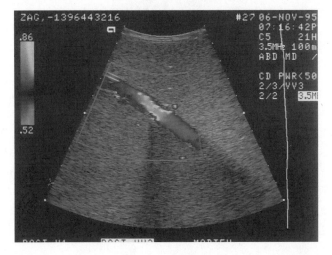

Figure 6-9. Image of a Doppler phantom with a variance display map. The variance is shown in yellow. (See Color Plate that follows p. 178.)

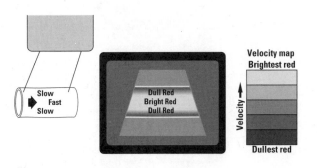

Figure 6-10. Effect of using a color map in which mean velocity is encoded in red intensity. With laminar flow, flow near the edges of the vessel would appear dull red while the more rapid flow along the axis would appear bright red.

done using phased array techniques analogous to those described in Chapter 2. The B-mode image information is still obtained in the usual manner by directing sound beams perpendicular to the surface of the transducer; however, the Doppler and color flow information is picked up with the beams that are steered off at an angle. (Of course, the color field can also be the same as the B-mode field, which is useful if the vessel is at an angle to the skin surface.)

Color aliasing

A color flow examination is subject to the effects of aliasing, just as a single-channel pulsed Doppler study is. When aliasing is present, the displayed Doppler signals tend to "wrap around," appearing as high velocities but in the wrong direction (Figure 6-13). In color flow imaging this wrap around results in an erroneous color, appearing as though the flow direction reversed (Figure 6-14). Aliased signals originating from flow toward the probe

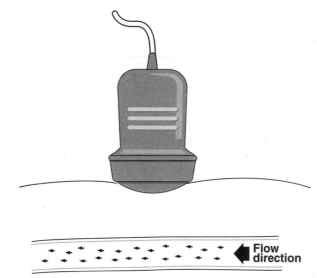

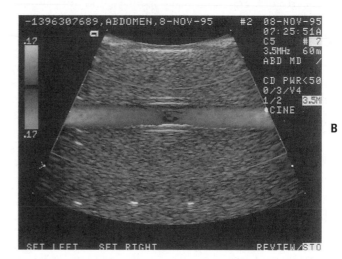

Figure 6-11. **A,** Flow within a horizontally oriented vessel imaged with a sector or curvilinear transducer. Flow on the right is towards the probe; on the left it is directed away from the probe. **B,** Color flow image for the arrangement in **A.** (See Color Plate that follows p. 178.)

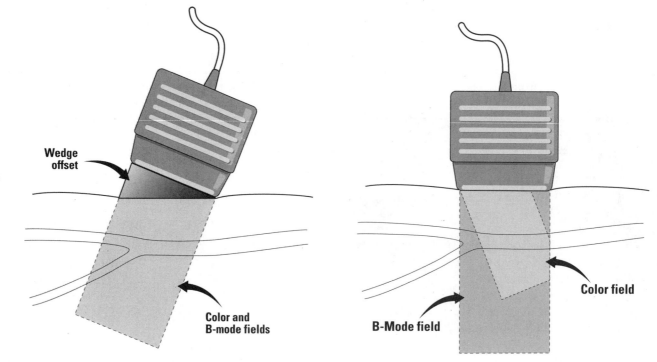

Figure 6-12. **A,** Use of a wedge offset with a linear array; **B,** beam steering with a linear array. Both methods have been used for color imaging in vessels that are parallel to the skin surface.

begin to be displayed as though originating from reflectors moving away from the probe, and vice versa. The reversal can usually be identified because it occurs first in the region of an image corresponding to the middle of the vessel, where the highest velocities are present. Most color flow instruments provide controls to adjust the displayed velocity scale. Generally the pulse repetition frequency, or PRF, of the instrument is linked to the velocity scale setting, so increasing the velocity scale increases the PRF and vice versa.

Why does the image frame rate in color appear to slow down upon shifts to very low color scales? The answer is simple: because the PRF is linked to the color scale setting. When a low color scale setting is applied, the PRF decreases and the time between transmit pulses in a pulse packet increases. Therefore, it takes longer to acquire Doppler data and do velocity estimates along each color line. Thus the color image takes longer to build, and the frame rate decreases.

Some color flow instruments allow the region from which flow signals are displayed to be either expanded or reduced (Figure 6-7). Reducing the color flow imaged region reduces the total number of acoustic lines needed to form the color flow image and allows higher PRFs. This in turn allows detection of higher flow velocities. Conversely, expanding the imaged region often is done to include a greater fraction of the total ultrasound image on the color display, but the frame rate is reduced.

Scanning speed and image quality. Since data for each scan line are acquired using multiple pulse-echo sequences, scanning frame rates in color flow imaging are lower than

frame rates in standard B-mode imaging. Often the color flow image is formed only over a fraction of the B-mode field. The operator can vary the extent of the color field, trading color field size for frame rate.

Another strategy used to speed up the scan process is to widen the spatial gap between color scan lines, thus reducing the number of scan lines in the image. Image data corresponding to regions between scan lines are obtained by interpolation. This often leads to noticeable trade-offs between color image quality and scanning speed or frame rate. Compare the two images of a flow phantom shown in Figures 6-15 and 6-16, taken with the same instrument. In Figure 6-15 the signal processing was such that the image frame rate was 10 per second, while it was 20 per second in Figure 6-16. The faster image is noticeably coarser. Evidently the higher frame rate was obtained using scan lines that were spaced longer distances apart, requiring more interpolation. Other short cuts, such as decreasing the number of pulse-echo sequences per scan line, may also increase the frame rate. Most instruments provide operator controls that allow the user to optimize imaging parameters (i.e., scan speed versus image detail) for specific applications.

Transducers for color flow imaging

Color flow imaging has been done using each of the real-time scanning transducers described in Chapter 2. When phased, linear, or curved array transducer assemblies are used, the pulses in a color packet are transmitted with the ultrasound beam dwelling along the beam line. However, with mechanical transducer assemblies the scanning motion cannot be started and stopped abruptly, so the beam is actually scanning during the process.[7,8] This

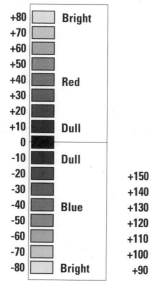

Figure 6-13. Conceptualization of color aliasing display wrap around. Aliased velocities from positive flow appear as negative flow.

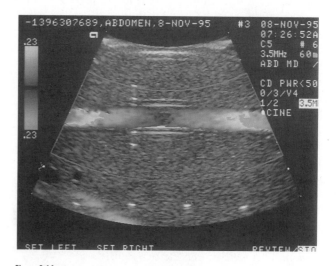

Figure 6-14. Color flow image of horizontally oriented vessel, done with a sector probe. In this example, aliasing is present. Flow is from right to left. (See Color Plate that follows p. 178.)

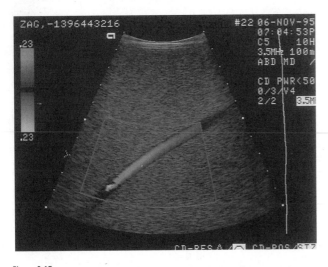

Figure 6-15. Image of a flow phantom, with signal processing yielding a frame rate of 10 images per second. (See Color Plate that follows p. 178.)

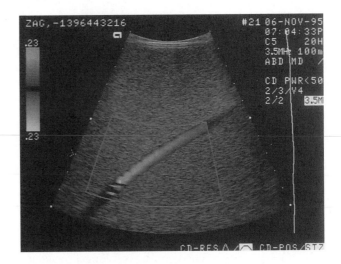

Figure 6-16. Image of the same flow phantom as in Fig. 6-15, only now the signal processing in the scanner was adjusted, yielding a frame rate of 20 per second. This image is noticeably coarser than that of Figure 6-15. (See Color Plate that follows p. 178.)

appears to be a bit of a disadvantage, especially for imaging slowly moving reflectors. Therefore electronically scanned arrays are becoming increasingly popular for color flow imaging.

Doppler power (or energy) mode

Color flow imaging displays reflector and scatterer velocities at positions throughout the field. The machine estimates Doppler frequencies during the multiple transmit-receive sequences of a color packet. It converts these into a velocity for presentation on the display.

An alternative processing method ignores the reflector velocity information, but instead estimates the total strength of the Doppler signal within each gated region.[9] Any Doppler shifted signal, regardless of the frequency of the shift, contributes to the pixel data. The net signal and the value displayed are ultimately related to the number of red blood cells moving within the gated region, regardless of the velocity. This processing is known as *power mode, energy mode,* and several other trade names.

Energy mode is compared to color flow imaging in Figures 6-17 and 6-18. In Figure 6-17 two hypothetical Doppler signals are shown; they both have the same amplitude, but have different frequencies. A color flow image pixel displaying this information varies for these two signals, the pixel value depending on the Doppler frequency (and reflector velocity). Since the amplitude of the signal is the same in both cases, an energy mode pixel does not change between the two signals.

In Figure 6-18 the frequency is the same for each Doppler signal, but the amplitude varies. Now the color flow image pixel is the same from one signal to the next.

However, the energy mode pixel changes with the signal strength.

The differences between color flow imaging and energy mode can be explored further using images generated by each modality. First, color flow imaging depends on velocity, whereas energy mode does not. Figure 6-19 shows images of a flow phantom with a vessel containing a stenosis. Flow through the stenosis produces a velocity jet. The higher velocities are easily seen with color flow imaging (Figure 6-19, *A*) but the energy mode image does not display them (Figure 6-19, *B*).

Strong angular effects seen with color flow imaging (Figure 6-20, *A*) are absent with energy mode (Figure 6-20, *B*). The energy mode image depends mainly on the strength of the Doppler signal. As long as signals are of sufficient Doppler shift to pass through the stationary echo cancelers, they produce signals for the energy mode. Even with flow nearly perpendicular to the beam, as in Figure 6-20, *B*, energy mode signals can be seen.

In energy mode, the image does not vary significantly with the direction of the flow with respect to the ultrasound beam. Remember, Doppler signal strength, not reflector velocity, is the parameter being displayed. Any variation of the image with angle of flow relative to the ultrasound beam is related to the strength of the Doppler signal for different orientations rather than the value of the velocity component.

In energy mode there is a tendency for the scanner to spend more time during image build-up. Current energy processing appears to be accompanied by slower frame rates and greater susceptibility to motion artifacts than standard color, although this may vary with the instrument manufacturer.

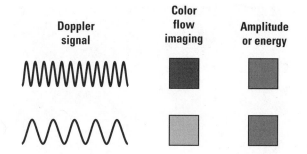

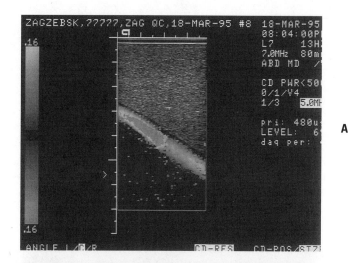

Figure 6-17. Information provided from color flow imaging vs. that from energy mode for two Doppler signals of the same amplitude but different frequencies. The color flow image pixel depends on frequency, but the energy mode signal does not.

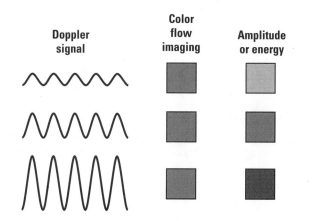

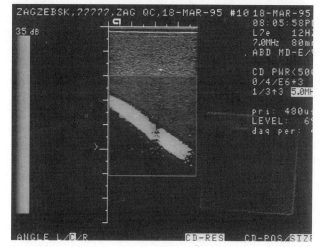

Figure 6-18. Information provided from color flow imaging versus that from energy mode for Doppler signals of the same frequency, but different amplitudes. The color flow image pixel is unchanged, but the energy mode pixel depends on the amplitude.

Figure 6-19. A, Color flow image of a phantom containing a stenosis. Higher velocities are seen in the stenosis. **B,** Energy mode image of the same region in the phantom. (See Color Plate that follows p. 178.)

Energy mode is fairly new, so whether it offers significant benefits over standard color flow is still being debated at the time of this writing. However, the modality appears to have several advantages:[9]

1. It appears to have more sensitivity than standard color imaging. The source of the increased sensitivity is not clearly stated. Some believe this is a result of a greater degree of temporal averaging. As mentioned earlier, energy mode usually is accompanied by reduced image rates compared to color.
2. Doppler angle effects are essentially ignored in this method of display. Although discarding angle effects on the image is a form of eliminating information, some believe the more continuous display of an artery or vein that results in energy mode's nondirectional display is easier to interpret.

3. If aliasing is present, it does not affect the energy mode display. This is because energy mode does not process the Doppler frequency, but only measures the strength of Doppler shifted signals.

The modality also has these disadvantages:

1. Image build-up and image rates tend to be slower and image frame rates tend to be lower than in standard color.
2. There appear to be greater amounts of flash artifact. Flash artifact is related to color signals arising from soft tissues that are moving, inadvertent patient motion, or motion of the transducer. It seems to be more prevalent in energy mode than in color mode.

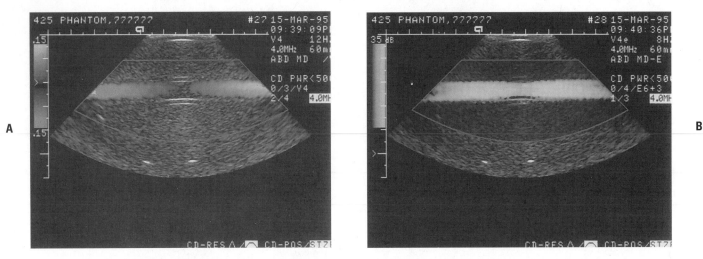

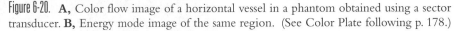

Figure 6-20. **A,** Color flow image of a horizontal vessel in a phantom obtained using a sector transducer. **B,** Energy mode image of the same region. (See Color Plate following p. 178.)

COLOR FLOW IMAGING USING TDC TO MEASURE REFLECTOR MOTION

TDC stands for *Time Domain Correlation*,[10,11] an alternative signal processing method that has been used by several manufacturers to determine reflector displacements. This method of color flow processing measures reflector displacements from changes in the echo transit times from one pulse-echo sequence to another when the transducer beam is stationary. Doppler detection and processing are not involved, although the instrument may provide a pulsed Doppler mode for close evaluation of reflector velocities from gated regions.

Reflector displacements versus reflector velocity

The time domain correlation technique employs pulse-echo ultrasound, similar to B-mode imaging. However, unlike B-mode imaging, and similar to color flow imaging based on Doppler processing, ultrasound beams are held stationary along each beam line for a long enough time to transmit and receive a series of pulse-echo sequences. Figure 6-21 shows the arrangement, along with three hypothetical pulse-echo signal waveforms acquired along a fixed beam line. Because of reflector motion, there is a shift, Δt, in the return time of echoes from these reflectors from one pulse-echo sequence to the next.

We use the range equation in Chapter 3 to calculate the corresponding scatterer displacement, Δx between pulse-echo sequences. The displacement is given by:

$$\Delta x = \frac{c\Delta t}{2} \tag{6-1}$$

where c is the speed of sound. Thus the scatter displacement between transmit pulses may be determined using the time shift in the echo.

Displacement is a distance, which can be expressed in cm or m. Velocity is distance per unit time, expressed in cm/s or m/s. The scatterer velocity v_r relative to the beam axis is simply the displacement, Δx, divided by PP, the time between transmit pulses, or the pulse repetition period. That is,

$$v_r = \frac{\Delta x}{PP} \tag{6-2}$$

As in standard Doppler, the actual reflector velocity, v, may be obtained if Θ, the angle between the beam axis and the direction of motion, is known:

$$v = \frac{v_r}{\cos\Theta}$$

The geometry is shown in Figure 6-22.

Time domain correlation

Time domain correlation is used for extracting the Δt for calculating reflector displacements. Correlation is a mathematical measure of the similarity of two quantities. In the present application the correlation processor operates on the returning echo signal. "Templates" are formed from all parts of the echo signal from echo one (Figure 6-23, *A*). These are manipulated back and forth over echo two by computer hardware in the machine. For the echo one template, the machine searches for the time shift that results in the best overlap with echo two. The overlap is measured by the correlation process.

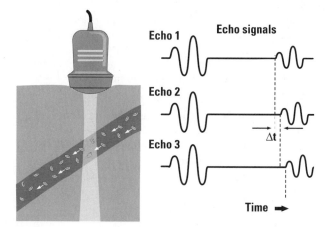

Figure 6-21. Typical arrangement for measuring flow using time domain correlation. Motion of a group of reflectors along the vessel axis results in a shift in echo arrival time from one pulse-echo sequence to the next. Three hypothetical pulse-echo sequences are shown.

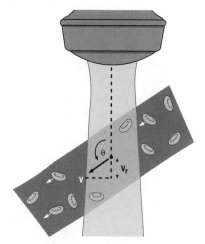

Figure 6-22. Geometry for computing reflector velocity, v. The system first determines Δx, then v_r, the velocity relative to the beam direction. The actual reflector velocity along the vessel axis, v, is determined by applying an angle correction.

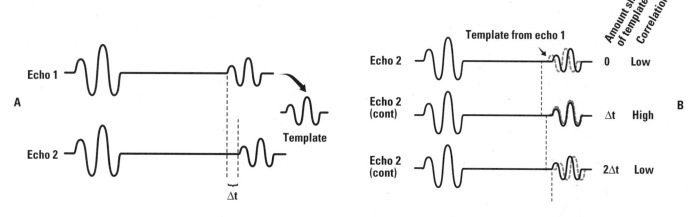

Figure 6-23. Time domain correlation for measuring Δt, the change in echo arrival time from a group of reflectors. **A,** Templates are formed by mathematically segmenting echo 1 into numerous sections. **B,** Each section is shifted in time and compared with echo 2, i.e., is "slid" over echo 2, looking for the amount of time shift resulting in the highest correlation. In this example, a time shift of Δt yields the maximum correlation.

Figure 6-23, *B* shows the degree of correlation ("low" and "high") between the template and echo two. When the template has been shifted exactly Δt relative to its original position, the correlation is best.

The above process must be done for templates throughout the entire echo one wave train so that velocities over the entire beam line may be estimated. Stationary reflectors need no time shift to provide maximum correlation, as expected. The time shift needed for high correlation in the cases of templates from moving reflectors indicates exactly how much the reflector has moved from pulse-echo sequence one to pulse echo sequence two. This time shift is the Δt used in the displacement computation in Equation 6-1 on p. 118.

Multiple pulse-echo sequences are utilized for each beam line to provide as good as estimate of reflector displacements as possible. Once sufficient data are obtained to make these estimations, a second acoustic line is interrogated, etc. The resultant color images appear essentially the same as color images obtained using Doppler processing.

There appear to be at least two advantages to the time domain correlation method compared to Doppler-based estimates of scatterer velocities. One is that short-duration transmit pulses, essentially the same as those used in B-mode imaging, may be used to acquire echo data. The shorter pulse duration means better axial resolution than that available in systems using Doppler detection, where long-duration pulses must be used to provide narrow frequency bandwidths. Second, the time domain correlation technique is less subject to aliasing than processing based on Doppler detection.[10] The former can tolerate greater time shifts in the returning echo signals from one pulse-echo sequence to the next than Doppler processing, while still providing accurate velocity estimates. This means that higher velocities can be measured with this technique.

References

1. Smith H, Zagzebski J: *Doppler ultrasound,* Madison, WI, 1991, Medical Physics Publishing.
2. Kisslo J, Adams D, Belkin R: *Doppler color flow imaging,* New York, 1988, Churchill Livingstone.
3. Loupas T, McDicken N: Low-order AR models for mean and maximum frequency estimation in the context of Doppler color flow mapping, *IEEE Trans on Ultrasonics, Ferroelectrics and Frequency Control* 37: 590, 1990.
4. van Leeuwen G, Hoeks A, Renemen R: Simulation of real-time frequency estimators for pulsed Doppler systems, *Ultrasonic Imaging* 8:252, 1986.
5. Omoto R, Kasai C: Basic principles of Doppler color flow imaging, *Echocardiography* 3:463, 1986.
6. Kasai C et al: Real-time two-dimensional blood flow imaging using an autocorrelation technique, *IEEE Transactions on Ultrasonics, Ferroelectrics and Frequency Control* 32:458, 1985.
7. Evans D, *Doppler ultrasound: physics, instrumentation and clinical applications,* New York, 1989, John Wiley & Sons.
8. Burckhardt C: The performance of mechanically scanned color flow mapping, *Ultrasonic Imaging* 11:227, 1989.
9. Rubin J et al: Power Doppler: a potentially useful alternative to mean frequency-based color Doppler US, *Radiology* 190:853, 1994.
10. Bonnefous O, Pesque D: Time domain formulation of pulse-Doppler ultrasound and blood velocity estimation by cross-correlation, *Ultrasonic Imaging* 8:73, 1986.
11. Embree P, O'Brien W: Volumetric blood flow via time-domain correlation: experimental verification, *IEEE Transactions on Ultrasonics, Ferroelectrics and Frequency Control* 37:176, 1990.

Questions for Review

1. The primary advantage of color flow over spectral Doppler is color flow's ability to display:

   A. the range of velocities
   B. high velocities without aliasing
   C. more accurate velocity measurements
   D. cross-sectional views of flow patterns

2. In color flow imaging, Doppler processing is used because the processed signals depend on:

   A. the approximate location of reflectors
   B. the phase of the echo signal
   C. the reflection coefficient of reflectors
   D. the speed of sound

3. A pulse packet refers to:

   A. a series of transmit-receive sequences along a beam line
   B. several quick transmit pulses, followed by one listening period
   C. a series of transmit pulses along multiple beam lines
   D. echoes resulting from one transmit pulse

4. More pulses in a color packet result in:

   A. more accurate distance determinations
   B. smaller spaces between color beam lines
   C. more accurate velocity determinations
   D. a larger color image field

5. The disadvantage of more pulses in a color packet is

   A. lower frame rates
   B. worse velocity estimations
   C. no calculation of the variance
   D. less acoustical exposure to the patient

6. Phase shift autocorrelation is a process used to calculate

   A. Doppler angle
   B. flow direction
   C. reflector impedances
   D. scatterer velocities

7. The pixel data displayed on the image obtained by a color flow instrument are most closely associated with the:

   A. peak Doppler frequency
   B. mean Doppler frequency
   C. lowest Doppler frequency
   D. Doppler frequency spectrum

8. A measure of the variation of reflector velocities within each gated pixel region is called:

   A. autocorrelation
   B. echo cancellation
   C. time domain correlation
   D. variance

9. Variance is used to:

   A. detect turbulence
   B. estimate direction
   C. evaluate flow rate differences between vessels
   D. detect flow variation as a function of vessel depth

10. Most color flow instruments limit the fraction of the image field on which flow information is displayed in order to:

    A. maintain adequate color frame rates
    B. avoid confusion of color and B-mode data
    C. maintain sufficiently low acoustic intensities
    D. maintain adequate gray scale imaging frame rates

11. Which one of the following is not one of the primary colors in the spectrum?

    A. red
    B. yellow
    C. blue
    D. green

12. On a color flow image done with a sector scanner, a horizontal vessel in a phantom appears completely blue on one segment of the image and completely red on another. The most probable reason for this color discontinuity is:

    A. aliasing
    B. Doppler angle effects
    C. poor temporal resolution
    D. poor directional discrimination

13. If you decrease the width of the color part of the image, what happens to the frame rate?

    A. it decreases
    B. it stays the same
    C. it increases
    D. it decreases or increases, depending on ultrasound frequency

14. The best way to eliminate "bleeding" of color outside the walls of a vessel is to:

    A. decrease the velocity scale
    B. adjust the color threshold
    C. increase the color gain
    D. increase the gate size

15. With a linear array, electronic beam steering or an angle wedge is important for imaging:

    A. flow in vessels parallel to the skin surface
    B. stationary reflectors in vessels parallel to the skin surface
    C. flow in vessels perpendicular to the skin surface
    D. stationary reflectors in vessels perpendicular to the skin surface

16. The most common manifestation of aliasing in color is:

    A. apparent flow reversal
    B. apparent flow going to zero
    C. apparent introduction of turbulence
    D. no change; the color image is not affected by aliasing

17. Which of the following would not eliminate aliasing in color flow imaging?

    A. adjust the color baseline
    B. increase the color scale
    C. lower the color threshold
    D. use a lower ultrasound frequency

18. Aliasing of the Doppler signal or display could occur in all of the following modes *except*:

    A. pulsed Doppler
    B. color flow imaging
    C. continuous wave Doppler
    D. combined color flow imaging and Doppler

19. For laminar flow in a circular vessel, at what part of the vessel diameter would color aliasing appear earliest?

    A. near the middle
    B. halfway from the middle to the edge
    C. near the edge
    D. uniformly throughout the vessel diameter

20. Which of the following will lead to higher frame rates in color?

    A. increase the spatial gap between color lines
    B. decrease the number of B-mode lines
    C. increase the image depth
    D. decrease the output

21. Which statement about use of mechanical transducers in color flow imaging is correct?

    A. they cannot be used in color flow imaging
    B. their beams do not dwell, but move during a pulse packet
    C. they are quickly replacing curved arrays for color flow imaging
    D. they are preferred in color flow imaging because of lower acoustical power

22. Doppler power mode *does not* display:

    A. flow velocity
    B. Doppler signal strength
    C. position of moving reflectors
    D. presence of flow within small vessels

23. An advantage of Doppler power mode is:

    A. higher frame rates
    B. more accurate determination of volume flow
    C. greater sensitivity to weak Doppler signals
    D. more precise determination of reflector velocities

24. Time domain correlation applied to the returning high-frequency echo signals to detect blood flow fundamentally measures:

    A. Doppler shift
    B. reflector angle
    C. reflector amplitude
    D. reflector displacement

25. The displacement per unit time is also called the:

    A. acceleration
    B. velocity
    C. vector
    D. power

26. An advantage of time domain correlation over Doppler processing for determining flow velocities is:

    A. angle independent flow imaging
    B. no need for multiple pulse–echo sequences
    C. better axial resolution because of shorter pulses
    D. better lateral resolution because of higher Doppler frequencies

27. Units for velocity are:

    A. cm/s^2
    B. m/s
    C. m^3
    D. mm/s^2

28. An appropriate unit for volume flow rate is:

    A. milliliters
    B. cm^2/s
    C. l/s
    D. cm/min

29. Which modality provides the best display of the velocities present at a selected location in the field?
    A. CW Doppler with directional capabilities
    B. pulsed Doppler with spectral analysis
    C. color flow imaging with variance
    D. power Doppler

30. Acoustic output levels are higher in Doppler and color flow than in modes such as B-mode imaging because of greater
    A. duty factors
    B. image frame rates
    C. sound beam attenuation
    D. pulse repetition periods

7

Image Characteristics and Artifacts

Assumptions implicitly made by the scanner when an image is formed are (1) reflectors giving rise to echoes lie along the transmitted beam axis and (2) the speed of sound, needed to compute the distance to each reflector, is constant along this path and equal to 1540 m/s. The scanner also assumes that the echo strength indicates organ echogenicity. The extent to which these assumptions are incorrect results in artifacts on ultrasound images.

In this chapter we will examine ultrasound images in more detail than we did in previous sections, studying the information the images convey and the artifacts they contain. The reason for the mottled appearance of ultrasound images will be discussed also. Methods for measuring structure dimensions, areas, and volumes are described near the end of the chapter.

We start by looking at differences exhibited on images between specular reflectors and scatterers.

SPECULAR VERSUS DIFFUSE REFLECTION AND SCATTERING

Longitudinal scans of the liver or spleen and kidneys contain many practical examples of the tissue–sound beam interactions that were considered earlier from a conceptual point of view. Proper scanning techniques for imaging the liver with B-mode ultrasonography are discussed in clinical texts.[1]

With a sector scanner, images depicting sagittal planes within the liver are obtained by scanning from an anterior subcostal window. The liver-to-kidney interface (Figure 7-1), seen partially as a bright, smooth surface, has characteristics of a **specular reflector.** The amplitude of an echo picked up from this interface and displayed on the monitor as a shade of gray is highly dependent on the angle between the incident sound beam and the reflector. The scanning window resulted in perpendicular beam incidence over a limited region of the liver-kidney interface. That region (Figure 7-1, *B*) is accompanied by a large-amplitude echo returning to the transducer and appears as a bright area on the image. However, other parts of the interface are not visualized clearly because the incident sound beam was not perpendicular during scan build-up. As Figure 7-1, *B* illustrates, for nonperpendicular ultrasound beam incidence the reflected wave from a specular interface travels away from the transducer.

Interfaces that reflect sound in all directions are referred to as *diffuse reflectors,* while very small reflectors distributed throughout an organ are referred to as *scatterers.* The parenchyma of most organs, including the liver and kidneys, contains a large number of acoustical scatterers. Echo signals from scattering regions are much less dependent on the transducer beam orientation than are echoes from specular reflectors. Thus the brightness of displayed echo signals from different regions of the liver does not vary greatly, no matter what transducer angle is needed to visualize that region. Thus the liver interior appears uniform on the B-mode image in Figure 7-1.

As mentioned in Chapter 1, ultrasonic scattering gives rise to much of the diagnostic information seen in ultrasound imaging. Regional variations in the scattered signal amplitude sometimes provide diagnostic informa-

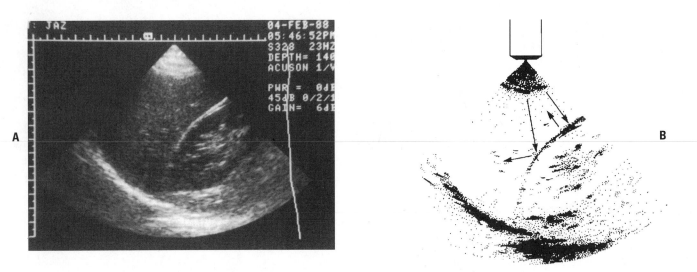

Figure 7-1. **A,** Ultrasound B-mode image of the liver and right kidney. **B,** Line drawing illustrating reflection at the liver-kidney interface for several incident beam directions that were included in the scan to obtain the image in **(A)**.

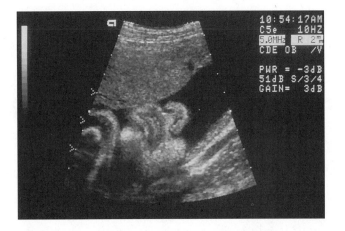

Figure 7-2. Gray scale image of a fetal face. Echoes due to ultrasound scattering, rather than from specular reflection, help delineate most of the image features. (Courtesy Acuson, Mountain View, CA.)

tion or added anatomical detail. With a gray scale display these amplitude variations are transformed into changes in displayed echo brightness, providing the image details that enable us to identify structures. The fetal face in Figure 7-2 is seen partially because of the scattered echo signals from all parts of the face. Other examples, including some abnormal structures, were given in Figures 1-23, 1-24, and 1-25 in Chapter 1.

Regions where the acoustical scattering is greater than that of the surrounding tissue are referred to as *hyperechoic*. Thus the subtle lesion in the liver in Figure 1-25 is slightly hyperechoic. Conversely, lower scattering regions are termed *hypoechoic*.

TEXTURE (SPECKLE) IN AN ULTRASOUND B-SCAN IMAGE

Why do ultrasound B-mode images appear granular, with a mottled, dot pattern rather than a continuous shade of gray? Examples are presented in Figure 7-3 for a tissue phantom. The echoes here are caused by microscopic glass beads too numerous for individual beads to be resolved by the machine. The arrangement of dots or B-mode marks on an ultrasound image of an organ or tissue phantom is referred to as image *texture*. A cursory understanding of why a region such as that imaged in Figure 7-3 appears mottled helps when interpreting the information in an ultrasound image.

Texture on an ultrasound image is a result of scattered and reflected waves from sites distributed throughout an organ. At present the interfaces and scattering sites giving rise to these scattered waves are not precisely known for many anatomical regions that are imaged. This is the subject of ongoing research studies in a number of laboratories. (In the case of the phantom in Figure 7-3, we know the scattering sites are the microscopic beads mentioned above.)

What is known about tissue scatterers is that (1) they are very numerous and (2) they are more or less randomly positioned throughout the tissues. Generally they are too close together for individual reflectors to be resolved on ultrasound images. In fact, an echo signal—and its corresponding "dot" on the ultrasound image—usually is a combined signal from a group of scatterers. This is illustrated schematically in Figure 7-4, where the ultrasonic pulse is traversing a bunch of scatterers, all of which produce a small echo.

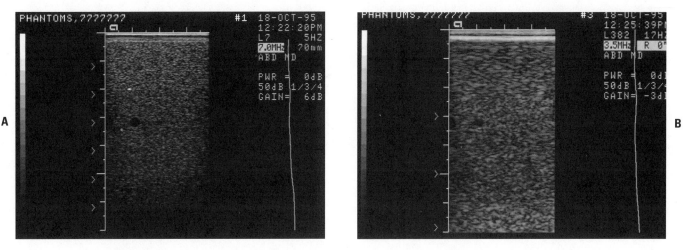

Figure 7-3. **A,** Scan of a tissue-mimicking phantom, with texture visualized to a depth of 7 cm. The image was obtained using a 7.0-MHz transducer. **B,** Image of the same location in the phantom as in **(A),** only this scan was done at 3.5 MHz.

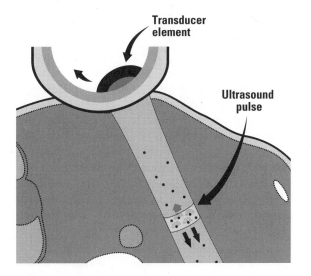

Figure 7-4. An ultrasound pulse traveling through tissue. At the instant shown, echoes are emerging from a group of scatterers. Because the echoes from all scatterers in the group arrive at the transducer at approximately the same time, the amplitude of the signal from this group depends on whether constructive or destructive interference predominates. This in turn depends on the exact positions of the scatterers.

Interference among the echo signals from these scatterers plays a major role in determining the echo strength from a given location. (See section on interference in Chapter 1.) Depending on whether the scatterers are arranged in a "favorable" way—so that the echoes at the transducer interfere constructively—or in a less favorable way so more of them interfere destructively, the echo signal (and dot brightness) from a given location is large, small, or somewhere in between. Due to the random positions of the scatterers, the echo amplitude and dot brightness fluctuate as the ultrasound beam sweeps through the tissue to form an image. Examining Figure 7-3, the bright spots correspond to locations where the echoes interfered constructively, while the darker regions are for locations where destructive interference occurred. The resultant pattern on the image display is sometimes called *speckle,* a word that seems appropriate in describing the image.

Clinically, we sometimes interpret image texture using adjectives such as "coarse echoes," "grainy echoes," and "fine echoes." However, it is interesting to observe that many characteristics of the texture pattern, such as the size of the dots and the number of dots per unit area on the image, depend also on the imaging system itself. Figure 7-3 illustrates this for an image of a tissue phantom. The dots for the 7-MHz transducer have a different appearance than the dots from the 3.5-MHz transducer, even though the same region is scanned. Figure 7-5 presents a similar comparison from the liver, where an image obtained with a 5-MHz probe is closely compared to one obtained with a 2.5-MHz transducer.

If we examine speckle dots closely from a uniform region in tissue or from a tissue phantom, we see that the dot pattern also varies with the depth from the transducer. Therefore any clinically significant variations in texture from normal must be interpreted with these instrumentation-dependent changes in mind.

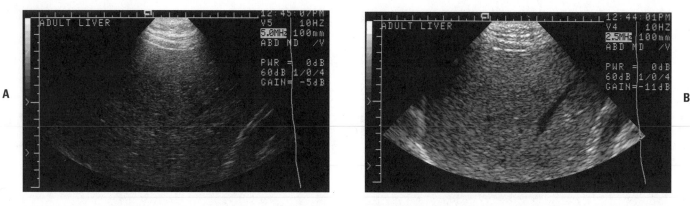

Figure 7-5. Comparison of image of an adult liver obtained using 5-MHz **(A)** and 2.5-MHz transducers **(B)**.

IMAGE ARTIFACTS

Assumptions in ultrasound scanners

Assumptions implicitly made by the scanner when an image is formed are:

1. Reflectors giving rise to echoes lie along the transmitted beam axis; each dot on a B-mode or color image is positioned along a line corresponding to the beam axis when the echo is picked up (see Figure 3-32).
2. The speed of sound, which is needed to compute the distance to each reflector, is constant along this path and equal to 1540 m/s.
3. The echo strength, displayed as a shade of gray on a B-mode image, only indicates organ echogenicity.

In reality, these assumptions are never completely met. For example, slight changes in sound propagation speed are encountered as the pulse travels through different tissues. This causes echo signals to be placed at erroneous locations on the display. Second, actual ultrasound beams have a certain beam width, so sometimes echoes are picked up from structures that are slightly off the beam axis; moreover, slight deflections and refraction of an ultrasound beam might occur, unbeknownst to the imaging machine. This causes echo signals to be displayed in the "wrong location" on the image. Finally, variations in attenuation along the beam path can cause shadowing and enhancement of echo signals from structures below.

Definition of an artifact

The extent to which the three assumptions listed above are not met results in artifacts on ultrasound images. Artifacts are structures and features on an image that do not have a one-to-one correspondence to the object being scanned. Common types of artifacts in ultrasound imaging are discussed in this section.

Reverberation artifacts

Some tissue interfaces can produce a relatively large-amplitude echo returning to the transducer. Examples include fat-fascia-muscle interfaces within the body wall and soft tissue–bone interfaces. This can lead to reverberation artifacts on an ultrasound image.

Consider the situation shown in Figure 7-6. The reflector could represent, for example, a fat-muscle interface just below the skin surface. In the figure a reflected wave (*solid arrow*) from this interface is shown directed back toward the transducer, where it is detected, amplified, and displayed (*first echo* on the image in the illustration). If the echo is of significant magnitude, it is partially reflected at the transducer surface and redirected toward the interface. Reflection of this reverberation pulse back to the transducer produces another echo, a reverberation echo signal from the reflector. The reverberation echo results from a pulse that has traveled the round trip distance between the transducer and interface twice. Thus, the "first reverb" echo is displayed in a position corresponding to twice the reflecting interface distance. Additional reverberations, as illustrated in Figure 7-6, corresponding to additional round trips of the sound pulse between the transducer and the interface, are sometimes observed. The first echo and the reverb echoes are all equidistant, as they all occur from additional journeys of sound pulses between the transducer and the reflector.

An example of a strong reverberation signal is presented in Figure 7-7. The origin of this pattern was an air pocket within the water-filled condom surrounding an intercavitary transducer. Figure 7-8 is an image of the gallbladder of a normal adult. Reverberations from the tissue layers between the transducer and the gall bladder cause artifactual echoes within this normally echo-free structure.

Reverberations produce artifactual echo signals that can partially mask actual echo signals on a display. They also contribute additional "acoustical noise" on an image.

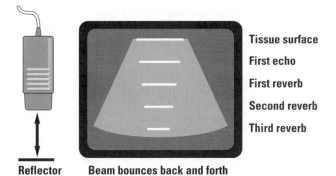

Figure 7-6. Generation of a reverberation artifact.

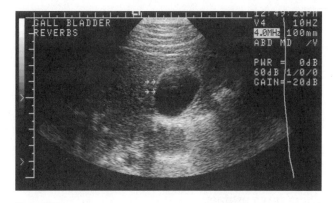

Figure 7-8. Reverberation echo signals (*arrows*) displayed within the gallbladder.

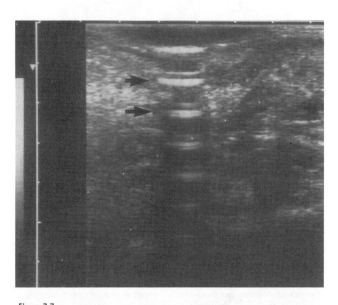

Figure 7-7. Image showing reverberation echoes (black arrows) from an air bubble within a water-filled latex condom placed on an intercavitary probe. (From Scanlan KA, Hunt KR: Ultrasound imaging: artifacts and medical devices. In Hunter T, Bragg D,editors: *Radiologic guide to medical devices and foreign bodies,* St Louis, 1994, Mosby.)

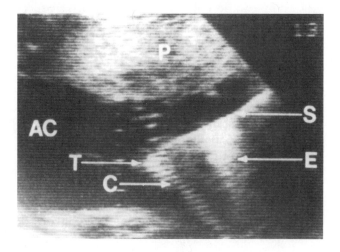

Figure 7-9. Ultrasound image of a fetoscope positioned in the uterus. A curvilinear series of short echoes, *C,* leads to the location of the fetoscope tip, *T.* Additional artifactual echoes, *E,* arise from the metal fetoscope. *P* is the placenta and *AC* the amniotic cavity. (From Schwartz D et al: The use of real-time ultrasound to enhance fetoscopic visualization, *J Clin Ultrasound* 11:161, 1983.)

This sometimes makes it difficult to view clearly an echo-free structure, such as the aorta, or abnormal fluid collections like abscesses, by contributing to artifactual fill-in of these structures.

Reverberations within metallic objects (comet-tail artifact)

Reverberation artifacts do not necessarily occur because of back-and-forth reflections between the transducer and reflecting surface. Sometimes the reverberating path can be distal to the transducer. For example, when a metallic object such as a foreign body or a biopsy needle appears in an ultrasound image, the object often leaves a clear pat-

tern that allows it to be distinguished from soft tissue interfaces.[2-4] The B-mode image in Figure 7-9 illustrates a interesting echo pattern obtained from a fetoscope shaft during a biopsy procedure.[2] Such artifacts are the result of reverberations and ringing of the sound pulse within the metallic object. In the example the reverberation pattern assists the operator because it helped identify the position of the tip of the fetoscope.

Similarly, ringing and reverberations of pulses within metallic objects, and the resultant "tail" sign, assist in identifying these objects.[3-6] The reverberation path is illustrated in Figure 7-10. Once the acoustical pulse partially enters the object, some of the energy is trapped, ringing back and forth like echoes within a silo. For each back and forth journey of the pulse within the metallic object, some of the acoustical energy escapes, returning to the transducer. This results in a dense collection of echoes emanating from the position of the object. The echo complex is known as the *comet-tail artifact* because it resembles somewhat an actual comet tail. An example is presented in Figure 7-11, showing the echographic appearance of a bullet fragment in the liver of a gunshot victim. Easily recognizable, comet-tail artifacts appear to emanate from many types of metallic objects, such as clips, staples, and sutures.

Reverberations within gas-bubbly stuff (ring-down artifact)

Another type of reverberation artifact is commonly seen at interfaces where small bubbles or partial liquids are believed to exist. So-called ring-down* artifacts are spot-

ted in many locations, including the diaphragm, the larynx and pharynx, bowels, and in the wall of the gallbladder. Their production is nearly identical to the generation of the comet-tail artifact (Figure 7-12). The ring-down artifact in Figure 7-13 was found to be related to the presence of cholesterol lipid globules.[5,7]

---

*The term *ring-down* is unfortunate, because its original and still-used meaning was to describe the ringing occurring following excitation of the transducer. Thus originally, ring-down was more closely associated with the pulse duration. In this chapter we follow conventions in the clinical literature, using the term *ring-down* to describe the artifacts shown in Figures 7-11 and 7-13.

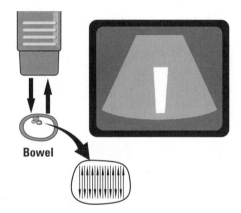

Bowel

Figure 7-12. Illustration of reverberation path within froth or lipid globules, resulting in the so-called ring-down artifact.

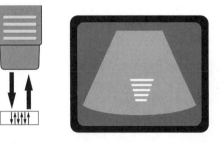

Metal

Figure 7-10. Production of a comet-tail artifact, caused by reverberations within a metallic object.

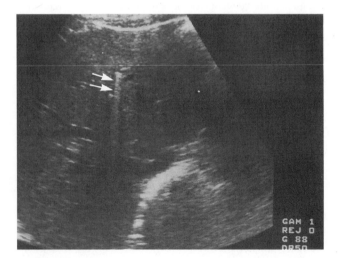

Figure 7-11. Ultrasound image of the liver of a gunshot victim, illustrating "comet-tail" (white arrows) that results from reverberations within the bullet fragment. (From Scanlan KA, Hunt KR: Ultrasound imaging : artifacts and medical devices. In Hunter T, Bragg D, editors: *Radiologic guide to medical devices and foreign bodies,* St Louis, 1994, Mosby.)

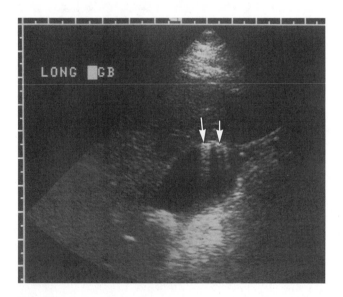

Figure 7-13. Example of a ring-down artifact from lipid globules in the gallbladder wall. (From Scanlan KA, Hunt KR: Ultrasound imaging: artifacts and medical devices. In Hunter T, Bragg D, editors: *Radiologic guide to medical devices and foreign bodies,* St Louis, 1994, Mosby.)

Mirror image artifacts

Very often echo signals appear to come from a region that is beyond a very strong reflector, such as a bone or air interface. For example, on many B-mode images of the liver echo signals appear to arise from beyond the tissue-air interface of the diaphragm (Figure 7-14). This is the result of a mirror image artifact, a phenomenon closely related to reverberations.

The generation of mirror image artifacts is illustrated in Figure 7-15. An object is situated fairly close to a highly reflecting surface, that is, the bottom of the "box" in Figure 7-15. An image of the object and of the reflecting surface is produced in the usual way, as described in Chapter 3. Because the echo from the bottom interface is strong, on its trip back to the transducer part of the echo can be rereflected by the object, returning to the interface. This smaller echo in turn is reflected at the interface and finally travels back to the transducer. Because it arrives *after* the bottom interface echo, these artifactual signals are displayed as though they originate from beyond the interface. The image is literally a mirror image of some structure or group of structures from the proximal side of the interface; the interface acts as the mirror.

The order of events that lead to this artifact is as follows:

1. A transmit pulse is produced by the transducer; the pulse is partially reflected (1) by the object, giving rise to echo signals that produce a primary image of the object.
2. Sound that is not reflected by the object continues to the bottom interface, giving rise to a strong echo (2) from the interface.

3. On its journey back to the transducer, the echo from the interface undergoes partial reflection (3) at the object.
4. This secondary echo returns to the bottom interface, where it is finally reflected, giving rise to mirror image echoes (4).

Because the mirror echoes from the mass arrive after the echo from the bottom, they are displayed as though they originate beyond the bottom interface.

Another example of a mirror image artifact is presented in Figure 7-16. This color flow image of the inferior vena cava has associated with it another "vessel" (*arrows*); the secondary vessel is a mirror image associated with reflections from the diaphragm.[8]

Doppler spectral mirroring

Mirroring of the Doppler spectral display is sometimes seen, but this is an entirely different phenomenon from the anatomical mirroring we have been discussing. Spectral mirroring (Figure 7-17) generally refers to an erroneous display of Doppler signals on the opposite side of the spectral baseline from the true spectrum.

There are two known sources of spectral mirroring. One occurs because of inadequate directional discrimination in the Doppler processor, or more commonly, because of too high a Doppler gain setting (Figure 7-18). With too high a Doppler gain, even though the directional discrimination circuits are technically flawless, the strong Doppler signals presented by the high receiver gain overwhelm the direction-sensing circuitry, producing a weak mirroring of the spectrum[8] (Figure 7-18, *B*).

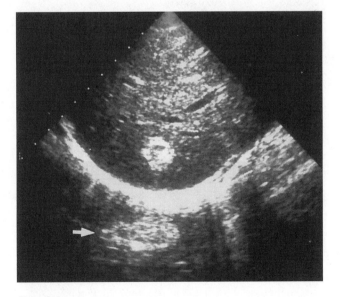

Figure 7-14. B-mode image of the liver and diaphragm. An apparent structure viewed beyond the diaphragm is actually a mirror image artifact.

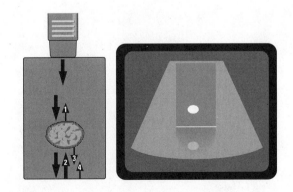

Figure 7-15. Origin of a mirror image artifact. The various echoes are labeled as follows: *(1)* first echo from the object; *(2)* echo from the bottom interface; *(3)* partial reflection of bottom echo from the object; *(4)* redirection of the partial reflection back towards the transducer. Mirrored echo *(4)* originates from the object, but arrives at the transducer after the echo from the interface. The echo signal is displayed beyond the diaphragm.

Spectral mirroring also can occur when the Doppler beam approaches a 90-degree angle with respect to the vessel axis. We saw in Chapter 5 that a 90-degree Doppler angle results in essentially no Doppler shift detected from the vessel. If transducers were extremely narrow, this would be the end of the story. However, because a transducer has a finite size, the entire beam emerging from the probe generally is not at a 90-degree angle to the flow within the sample volume. This is illustrated for an array transducer in Figure 7-19. The central elements are assumed to make up the active aperture for the Doppler beam. Parts of the beam are at an angle slightly lower than 90 degrees, while parts are incident at slightly greater than 90 degrees. Therefore even with the perpendicular incidence, Doppler signals may be obtained both above and below the spectral baseline when the measured Doppler

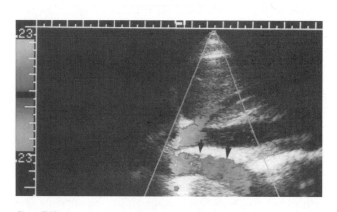

Figure 7-16. Mirror image artifact in color Doppler. This longitudinal image is of the inferior vena cava. A second "vessel" *(arrows)* is perceived deep to the true inferior vena cava. This mirror image vessel was associated with reflections from the diaphragm. (From Pozniak MA, Zagzebski JA, Scanlan KA: Spectral and color Doppler artifacts, *Radiographics* 12:35, 1992.)

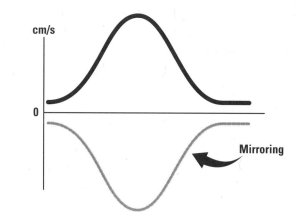

Figure 7-17. Schematic illustration of mirroring of a Doppler spectral display. The primary display shows reflector velocity above the baseline. Mirroring produces apparent velocities below the baseline.

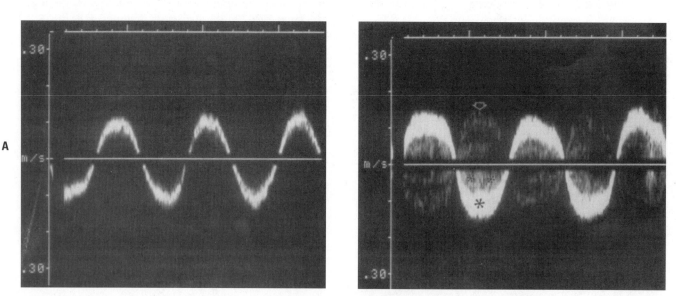

Figure 7-18. **A,** Doppler spectral trace obtained when a gray scale phantom was moved back and forth with respect to the Doppler ultrasound beam. With proper gain settings, a clear, distinct velocity pattern is displayed. **B,** Same as in **(A)**, only the Doppler gain has been increased, causing both a thickening of the velocity trace and a mirror image tracing *(arrow)*. In this case, spectral mirroring occurs because of too high a gain setting. (From Pozniak MA, Zagzebski JA, Scanlan KA: Spectral and color Doppler artifacts, *Radiographics* 12:35, 1992.)

angle is 90 degrees. Strong, pulsatile signals can enhance this effect, as illustrated in Figure 7-20, *B* for a spectral tracing from the carotid artery. The correct presentation of the Doppler spectral signal, without mirroring, is obtained when the beam is not 90 degrees to the flow direction (Figure 7-20, *A*).

Beam width effects

When an ultrasound beam is scanned over a small, point-like reflector, the resultant B-scan image of the reflector is a line. The size of the line depends on the width of the ultrasound beam at the location of the target (Figure 7-21). Images of pointlike targets are often used to make lateral resolution assessments, done by measuring the size of the image of the target or by imaging target pairs that are very closely positioned laterally (see Chapter 8). The beam width and the lateral resolution are, of course, closely linked in ultrasound.

Beam width artifacts are manifested in several ways on an ultrasound image. First, images of small discrete reflectors, such as calcifications and small specular reflectors, are broadened, appearing as small lines. This may be illustrated further by imaging a column of pointlike tar-

gets in a tissue phantom (Figures 7-22, *A* and 7-23, *A*) The width of each line is closely related to the beam width at the corresponding reflector depth. The figures contrast beam width effects for a single element transducer and for an array having electronic focusing. Beam width effects partially obliterate information related to closely positioned reflectors in the body. The narrower the beam, the sharper and crisper the echo signals displayed from any region and the better the lateral resolution. This contributes to imaging finer detailed anatomical structures.

A second way that beam width artifacts are manifested is by "smearing" of the echo information in the region scanned. Beam width effects cause partial fill-in of small anechoic objects, such as vessels, in an echogenic background. Figure 7-22, *B* and 7-23, *B* present images of a phantom containing anechoic tubes; diameters of 8 mm, 6

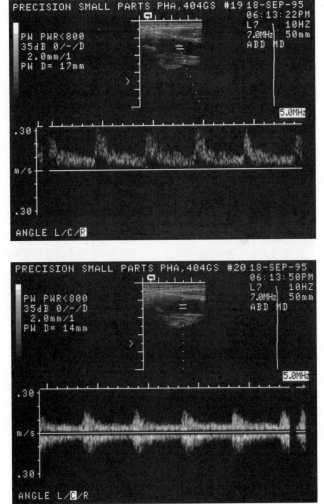

A

B

Figure 7-20. Doppler signal from a carotid artery, generated with a normal beam angle **(A)** and when the beam was nearly perpendicular to the flow direction **(B)**. Spectral mirroring occurs for the case of perpendicular beam incidence.

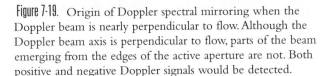

Figure 7-19. Origin of Doppler spectral mirroring when the Doppler beam is nearly perpendicular to flow. Although the Doppler beam axis is perpendicular to flow, parts of the beam emerging from the edges of the active aperture are not. Both positive and negative Doppler signals would be detected.

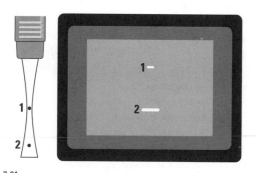

Figure 7-21. Effect of the beam width on the image of pointlike targets. The size of the line is an indication of the width of the beam at the location of the target.

mm, 4 mm, 3 mm, and 2 mm are present. With both 3.5-MHz transducers the 2 mm objects are hardly seen; visualization is more difficult with the single-element transducer than with the array. There is a close correlation between the width of the beam as presented in Figures 7-22, *A* and 7-23, *A* and the degree of fill-in of the anechoic structures in the corresponding Figures 7-22, *B* and 7-23, *B*.

Yet another manifestation of beam width artifacts occurs when two distinct signals are detected from the same apparent location in an M-mode or in a Doppler study. Figure 7-24 illustrates this on a Doppler spectral display. The spectrum shows overlap of signals from adjacent flow. Here, the left ventricular inflow signal (LVI) is superimposed with high-velocity Doppler signals from aortic regurgitation (*AR*).[9]

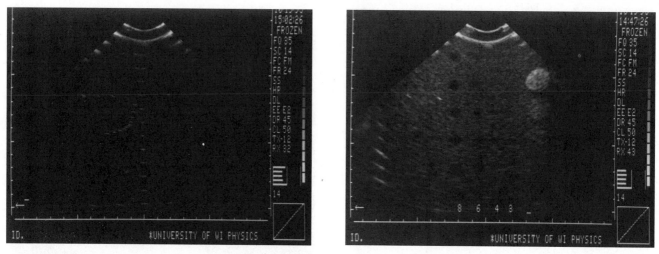

Figure 7-22. **A,** Scan of a column of pointlike targets in a tissue phantom. A single-element 3.5-MHz mechanical transducer was used. The targets appear elongated rather than like dots because of the beam width. **B,** Image of columns of hypoechoic tubes using the 3.5-MHz single-element mechanical probe from **(A).** The tube diameters in the different columns are 8 mm, 6 mm, 4 mm, 3 mm, and 2 mm.

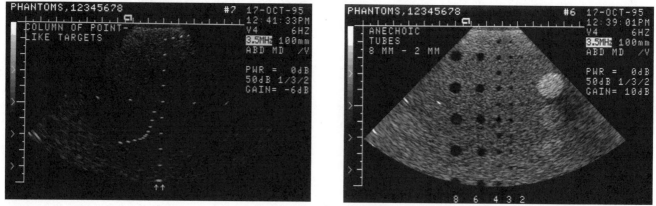

Figure 7-23. **A,** Scan of a column of point targets in a tissue phantom. This image was produced by scanning with an electronically focused array transducer resulting in smaller images of the point targets than in Figure 7-22. **B,** Image of columns of hypoechoic tubes using the 3.5-MHz electronically focused transducer **(A).**

Side lobe artifacts

In Chapter 2 side lobes were described as energy in an ultrasound beam from a single element or array transducer that falls outside the main lobe. Side lobes are reduced by pulsed rather than continuous wave transmission; sometimes manufacturers choose to further reduce side-lobe levels by "apodizing," which is not too difficult a task when array transducers are used. Apodizing is done by exciting the transducer nonuniformly over its surface. One way to achieve this is to use different amplitude excitation pulses applied to the elements forming a beam, exciting the central elements with greater voltage signals than the outer elements. Another way is to amplify echoes received by the central elements in the active aperture more than the echoes received by the outer elements before summation by the beam former.

If side lobes are still strong enough, they are manifested as extensions of the main lobe and may be visualized when scanning small, high-contrast targets. In addition to the main beam mark displayed from a point reflector, secondary marks from the side lobes striking the reflector occur (Figure 7-25; also, see Figure 7-27).

Grating lobe artifacts

We mentioned in Chapter 2 that it is possible for an array transducer to exhibit grating lobes. These are secondary lobes of beam energy that occur because the transducer is not a continuous surface, but is diced into small elements. Grating lobes, if present, "shoot" ultrasound energy off at a large angle from the main beam (Figure 7-26, *A*). Figure 7-26, *B* shows how this can add ghost images of the object; when the main beam is interrogating a section displaced from the grating lobe, the figure shows the grating lobe insonifying the target. Echoes are displayed, of course, as though they arrive along the beam axis; that is, the scanner assumes all echo signals arrive from along the main beam. Figure 7-26, *C* shows the resultant B-mode image, showing ghost images from the object resulting from grating lobes on either side of the main beam. We also mentioned in Chapter 2 that grating lobes are reduced in strength and importance by designing the array so that there is no greater than $1/2$ wavelength between the centers of individual elements.

Sometimes it is not possible to meet this design requirement, and grating lobes appear at noticeable levels. An example of an image of a high-contrast object in an echo-free background, with grating lobes in evidence, is presented in Figure 7-27. The objects off at the sides in the image of the phantom with IV needle are the result of grating lobes.

What is the difference between grating lobes and side lobes? Side lobes are possible with any type of transducer system, both single element and array. If present they are located directly alongside the main beam, as shown in Figure 7-25. Grating lobes, on the other hand, are found only with array transducers. Rather than being situated directly alongside the main beam, if present they are off at a fairly large angle, as shown in Figure 7-26. In most array transducer designs it is possible for the manufacturer to eliminate grating lobes altogether by using very thin, closely spaced elements.

Slice thickness artifacts

Slice thickness artifacts are analogous to beam width effects, only here we consider the effects of the ultrasound beam width *perpendicular* to the scanning plane. Analogous to the way in which beam width effects cause partial fill-

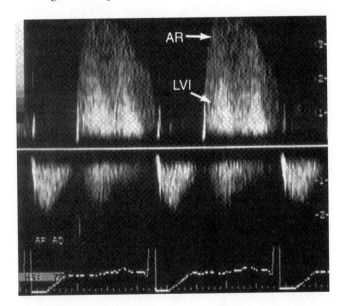

Figure 7-24. Spectral Doppler display showing overlap of signals from adjacent regions. The left ventricular inflow signal *(LVI)* is superimposed with the high-velocity Doppler signals from aortic regurgitation *(AR)*. (From Otto CM, Pearlman AS: *Textbook of clinical echocardiography,* Philadelphia, 1994, Saunders.)

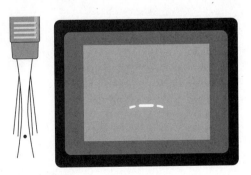

Figure 7-25. How side lobes might be manifested on an image of a point target in an anechoic background. Instead of a single mark from the small reflector, additional marks appear from the side lobes.

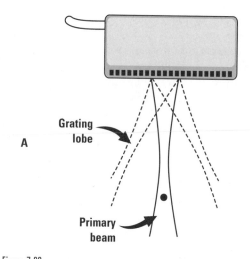

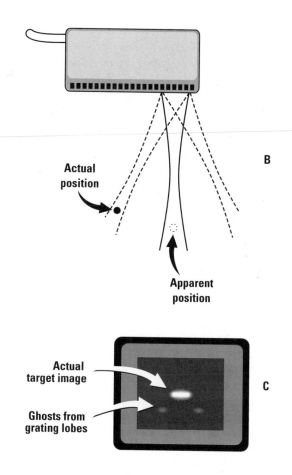

Figure 7-26. Illustration of grating lobes from a linear array transducer and their effect on the image of a point target. **A,** At this instant, the target is within one of the beams of the array during scan build-up. **B,** The beam axis has shifted to the right, but now the object is insonified by a grating lobe. Echoes are displayed as though arriving from the axis of the main beam. **C,** Resultant image of the target, including the actual image and two ghost images resulting from the grating lobes.

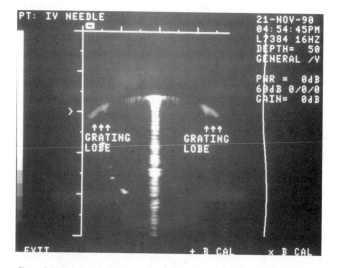

Figure 7-27. Ultrasound image of metallic object (an IV needle in a phantom) with side lobes and grating lobes contributing to ghost images of the target. A reverberation artifact from the object also is very clearly seen.

in of hypoechoic structures in an echogenic background, slice thickness effects can also lead to fill-in of echo-free structures. This is shown in Figure 7-28, where an individual beam from a linear array is schematically illustrated. Generally the beam width perpendicular to the image plane (in the slice thickness direction) is greater than the beam width in the image plane, as discussed in Chapter 2. The figure illustrates imaging two small spherical masses (such as small cysts). One is at the "elevational" focal distance, where the slice thickness is narrow; the other is farther from the transducer, where the slice thickness is larger. The B-mode image depicts the object at the slice thickness focal depth being well visualized, but the one in the broader part of the beam as being partially obliterated because of slice thickness effects. (The drawing deliberately portrays the in-plane beam width as being narrow enough to successfully visualize the object if the slice thickness is narrow enough.)

It is quite easy to demonstrate this result using tissue phantoms. Figure 7-29 presents an image of a phantom that contains 5-mm diameter, spherical, anechoic masses. A general purpose, abdominal imaging transducer was used to obtain the scan. Even though masses are present throughout the phantom, they are not visualized at shallow depths, due primarily to slice thickness effects. However, the objects are successfully visualized at depths of about 4.5 cm through 12.5 cm because of a narrower slice thickness throughout this depth range. Beyond 12.5 cm the ability to visualize the objects decreases with this transducer; this is evidently due to the slice thickness increasing and possibly to the beam width increasing also.

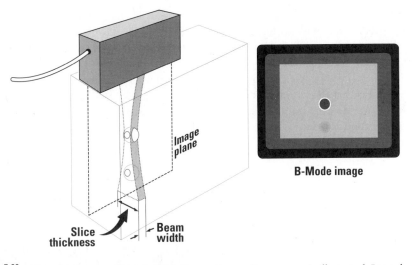

B-Mode image

Figure 7-28. Slice thickness artifact. A single beam from a linear array is illustrated. Lateral resolution is related to the width of the beam in the image plane (scanning plane). Slice thickness is related to the dimension of the beam perpendicular to the scanning plane. Because of the slice thickness, there is partial fill-in of focal objects, such as small masses. Fill-in is most severe at depths where the slice thickness is broadest.

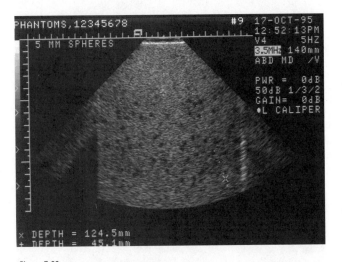

Figure 7-29. B-mode image of a phantom containing 5-mm diameter focal masses. The masses can only be viewed from a depth of 4.5 to about 12.5 cm. Detection at shallower and deeper depths than this range is limited by the slice thickness.

Note, the actual depth at which small spherical masses will be visualized depends on the transducer; the depth range differs for different transducers.

Another way to view slice thickness effects is by imaging anechoic tubes in ordinary tissue phantoms. Figure 7-30 compares images of a 6-mm diameter tube, situated at a depth of 3 cm, for a 3.5-MHz phased array and a 5-MHz, small, linear array. Slice thickness at this depth is much smaller for the 5-MHz linear array, as shown by the lack of fill-in of the tube with echoes.

The effects of slice thickness may also be viewed as in the diagram in Figure 7-31. An ultrasound image is sometimes said to represent a thin plane of tissue defined by the position of the transducer. However, slice thickness results in the image actually representing reflectors within a volume of tissue as shown in the figure. The thickness of this volume varies, being broad at the transducer surface, narrowing at a depth depending on the slice thickness focal distance, and then broadening again in the far field. At a given location on the image, all reflectors within the section contribute to the echo signal. In other forms of two-dimensional radiographic imaging, such as computerized tomography, and MRI imaging, this facet is referred to as *partial volume*. Regardless of the name, the effect is similar to that found in ultrasound: small focal objects in the scan plane can be partially (or even totally) obliterated on the image because of echoes from reflectors that are not in the scan plane, but are within the region defined by the slice thickness.

Another manifestation of slice thickness artifacts occurs when echoes appear from an object that is clearly not in the image plane. For example, in two-dimensional echo cardiography images, occasionally highly echogenic objects such as artificial valves or calcifications are partially "viewed" within one of the chambers of the heart (Figure 7-32).

Shadowing and enhancement (useful artifacts)

If output power controls and receiver sensitivity controls are properly adjusted, a uniform echo signal brightness level can be obtained on ultrasound scans of homogeneous tissue volumes. In particular, adequate setting of the swept gain controls on the receiver can result in a uniformly displayed echo level versus depth, even when sound beam attenuation takes place in the medium. The requirement for this condition is that the attenuation rate not vary significantly from one area to another. Local variations in the ultrasonic attenuation are detected on ultrasound B-mode images because of partial or total "acoustical shadowing" or because of distal echo enhancement. The resultant artifacts actually provide useful diagnostic information.[5,10]

Partial shadowing is a reduction in the amplitude of echo signals detected from regions distal to a mass whose attenuation is greater than that of the surrounding region. The origin is shown in Figure 7-33. In this drawing, a linear array transducer is used to scan an object containing several masses. We assume the operator controls on the B-mode scanner have been adjusted for a uniform texture pattern from the background region being scanned. Each mass creates its own characteristic disruption to the pattern of echoes from the background.

One mass in the diagram in Figure 7-33 has an attenuation that is higher than that of the surrounding mater-

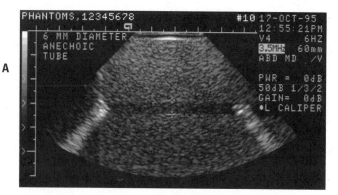

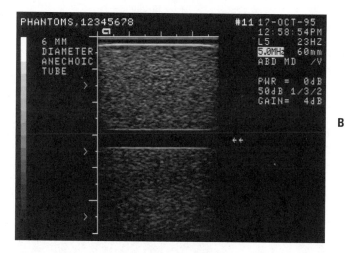

Figure 7-30. B-mode image of a 6-mm diameter anechoic tube in a phantom. The tube is oriented horizontally in these images. **A,** Image obtained using a 3.5-MHz linear array with a wide slice thickness at the depth of the tube causing echoes displayed within the tube. **B,** Image obtained using a 5-MHz linear array having a narrow slice thickness at the depth of the tube.

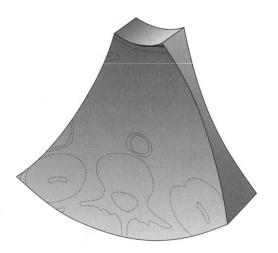

Figure 7-31. Representation of scan section that is depicted on an ultrasound B-mode image. Although an ultrasound image is thought of as viewing a thin plane in the body, actually all reflectors within a section of tissue *(left)* contribute to the echoes that are displayed. This can cause obliteration of small focal objects located in the scan plane.

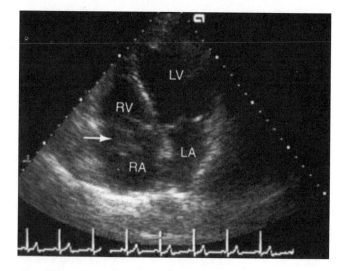

Figure 7-32. Two-dimensional image of the heart, where artifactual echoes are seen in the left ventricle because of slice thickness effects. (From Otto CM, Perlman AS: *Textbook of Clinical Echocardiography,* Philadelphia, 1994, WB Saunders.)

ial. An ultrasound beam traversing this mass undergoes greater attenuation than beams traveling over the same distance but in the background material. Consequently echoes from the background material distal to the mass are weaker than adjacent echoes along the uniform path. "Partial shadowing" is said to occur. Clinically, masses that have greater attenuation than the normal surrounding tissue are recognized in part by the presence of shadowing.

The opposite effect takes place when a low attenuating mass, such as a cyst, is encountered in a similar situation. Echo signal "enhancement" is said to take place because of the increased amplitude of the displayed signals beyond the cyst. Occasionally we say that the mass has good "through-transmission" properties. As the diagram suggests, echo enhancement is seen for all echoes detected distal to the low-attenuating mass.

The presence of either of these features provides clues regarding the nature of masses visualized on an ultrasound scan. The mass in the breast visualized on the ultrasound image in Figure 7-34 has "fluidlike" features. One tip-off is that the mass exhibits enhancement (or, as mentioned earlier, good through-transmission), meaning echoes are somewhat brighter distal to the mass compared to adjacent echoes. Of course, other characteristics of the image of the mass, including lack of echoes within the border and a relatively smooth wall, also provide clues to the nature of the lesion.

Figure 7-35 is an image of a more attenuating mass in the breast. In this case, the echo strength directly distal to the mass is somewhat subdued compared to echoes from the same depth but along paths that do not traverse the lesion. Partial shadowing has occurred.

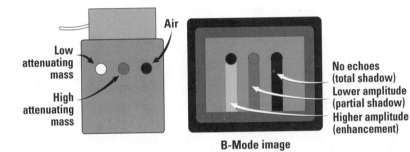

Figure 7-33. *(Left),* Schematic showing a linear array imaging a hypothetical tissue phantom containing uniform material. Several inclusions are present that provide different amounts of sound beam attenuation. *(Right),* Schematic drawing of the image produced showing shadowing and enhancement.

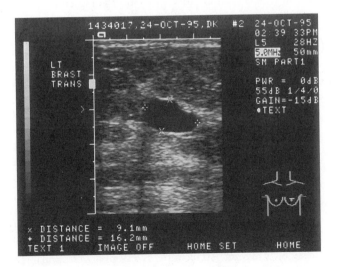

Figure 7-34. B-mode image of a breast containing a cyst. There is echo enhancement distal to the cyst.

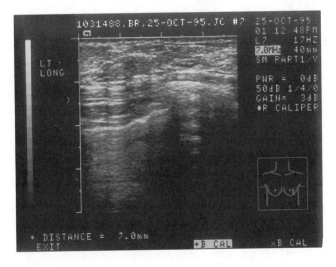

Figure 7-35. Attenuating mass *(crosses)* in the breast. Echo signals acquired from structures distal to the mass are weaker than signals acquired from the same depths but through beam paths that do not traverse the mass.

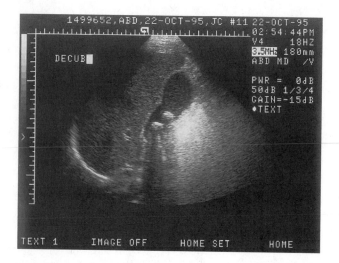

Figure 7-36. Image of a gallbladder with stones; the stones completely shadow the structures beneath.

Some interfaces in the body produce nearly complete acoustical shadowing on an image. Tissue-air interfaces (e.g., loops of gas-filled bowel or airways) are completely impenetrable because of the large impedance mismatch associated with them. Nearly complete shadowing is also obtained from gallstones and other calcified objects (Figure 7-36). Manifestation of such shadowing from small objects is somewhat dependent on the objects' positions in the ultrasound beam. If a small shadowing object is nearly in the focal region of the transducer, it stands a better chance of interrupting a significant fraction of the sound beam than if it is placed in other regions of the beam.

Refraction

Refraction of a sound beam takes place when the beam strikes an interface at an angle and the speed of sound is different on each side of the interface. The larger the difference in the speed of sound, the greater the refraction effect. The greatest speed-of-sound difference where refraction can occur is at a soft tissue–bone interface. However, refraction here is usually of little practical consequence because in most instances we do not image through bone interfaces. (In fact, the significant refraction effect contributes to the problem of transmission through bone.) The major exception of clinical interest is imaging and Doppler examining through the skull, where ultrasound is gaining in use.

Because of the relatively high speed of sound in the lens and the curvature of the tissue surfaces, it can significantly refract, distort, and deflect a sound beam. Excellent demonstrations of this effect using Schlieren photography have been published.[11] For this reason imaging the eye with ultrasound usually involves the use of windows that exclude the lens, unless the lens is of specific interest in the examination.

Fat can also result in substantial refraction artifacts. The speed of sound through fat is significantly lower than through most soft tissues. Moreover, fat is often found in abundance in planes throughout the body. These planes can be imaged with sharp angles of the incident sound beam. When refraction occurs, structures can appear on an image in locations that do not conform to reality. This is illustrated in Figure 7-37 for a sector scanner. Because of refraction, echoes are detected from the lower target, not when the beam is transmitted directly towards the object, but when it is aimed slightly to the left of it (Figure 7-37, B). Consequently the target is displaced slightly to the left on the two-dimensional gray scale image (Figure 7-37, C).

Refraction and beam deflection artifacts involving fat have been demonstrated by Madsen, Zagzebski, and Ghilardi-Netto[12] using an abdominal tissue phantom. The phantom contains various structures embedded in a liver-mimicking material. Included in this phantom is a simulated kidney with a surrounding fat pad, surrounded by liver-mimicking material. The speed of sound through the fat pad material is 1450 m/s, whereas through the simulated liver and kidney it is 1560 m/s; this is sufficient difference to produce refraction for the curvature of the interfaces involved.

Images through a section of this phantom, obtained with a manual (static) scanner, are shown in Figure 7-38, A and B. In A the structures seen to the right of the kidney and fat pad are images of a set of thin nylon fibers whose axes are perpendicular to the plane of the image. Several fibers forming a backward L make up the set. The scan in Figure 7-38, A was obtained with a simple scan technique, no compound scan motion being employed.

The image in Figure 7-38, B is from the same region of the phantom, and shows significant distortion of the fiber images due to transmission through the kidney and fat pad. It was produced by sectoring the transducer beam from several positions on the surface, including positions above the fat pad region. The effects on the fiber images are quite dramatic. With this simple phantom it was possible to account for the reflections and refraction that make up the distorted image. The case presented shows the effects that beam deflection and refraction can have on a B-scan image.

Under most clinical circumstances the geometry and complexity of the patient's anatomy make it difficult to recognize such artifacts, if indeed they exist, in clinical scans. Occasionally, however, effects as striking as that just presented are seen. An example is a double gestational sac sign early in pregnancy, giving the clinical impression of twins (Figure 7-39) even though other ultrasound images from different orientations prove that only a single fetus is present.[13] This artifact is seen occasionally when a trans-

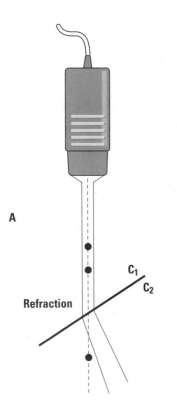

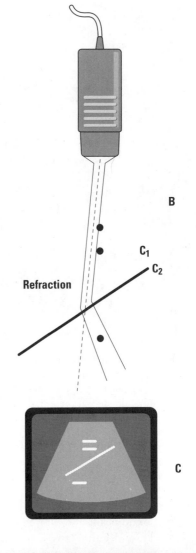

Figure 7-37. Lateral displacement of a target image, caused by refraction. **A,** Although the axis of this transmitted beam passes through the object, refraction causes the lower object to be missed. **B,** The target is insonified by the refracted beam when the transmitted beam axis is left of the lower target. **C,** Final image; note the lower target is displaced to the left.

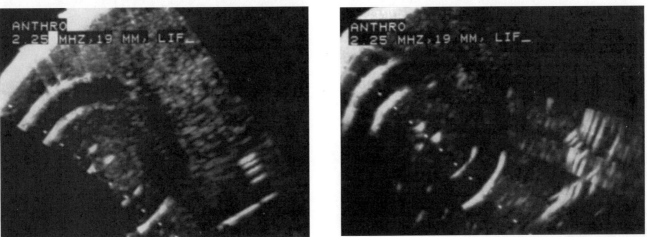

Figure 7-38. A, B-mode image of a section of tissue phantom meant to mimic a kidney and surrounding fat pad. These appear as circular objects in this simple phantom representation. The L-shaped dots are from a series of small resolution targets. **B,** Composite image of the kidney and fat pad obtained when different sound beam paths were used through the fat pad and kidney. Refraction and beam deflection contribute to misplacement of the objects. (From Madsen EL, Zagzebski JA, Ghilardi-Netto T: An anthropomorphic torso phantom for ultrasonic imaging, *Med Phys* 7:43, 1980.)

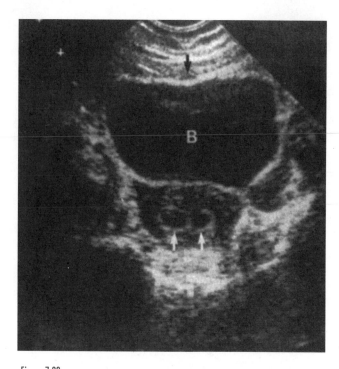

Figure 7-39. Ultrasound image of the bladder and uterus obtained using a transverse scanning plane. Although two gestational sacs are visualized (*arrows*), additional scanning confirmed that only one sac was present. Refraction artifacts are believed to have caused the apparent twin sac. (From Sauerbrei E: The split image artifact in pelvic ultrasonography: anatomy and physics, *J Ultrasound Med* 4:29, 1985.)

verse echogram is obtained through the lower abdomen.[14,15] Sound beams traveling through the underlying muscle, fat, and connective tissue layers may be deflected, resulting in the beam sweeping past the gestational sac from more than one beam axis position in the scan (Figure 7-40.)

An intriguing artifact is frequently observed distal to the lateral margins of some cysts and vessels, including the gallbladder (Figure 7-41; also see Figure 7-34). It is a shadowing effect below these areas. This also is a useful artifact since it sometimes aids in characterizing these structures. Depending on the characteristics of the medium, the artifact may be related to attenuation of the sound beam through beam deflection and refraction at the vessel interface[16]; it may also be partially due to attenuation in the vessel walls. If the speed of sound through a circular object is lower than through the surrounding material, a sound beam incident on the edge of the object will be deflected. Beam spreading of this type is accompanied by significant attenuation. Reflectors situated distal to regions where beam spreading occurs will yield lower level echo signals than if the beam is unperturbed. Thus, the apparent partial shadow occurs.

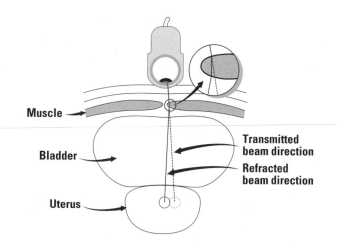

Figure 7-40. Origin of the twin gestational sac image in the previous figure. It is supposed that refraction, such as at the surface of the abdominal muscles, caused slightly laterally directed beams to be refracted towards the midline, where the sac was situated. In this drawing, the effect is shown for two different beam directions.

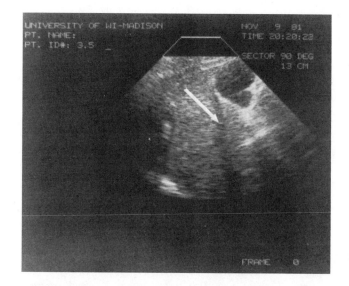

Figure 7-41. Edge shadow at the gallbladder, apparently related to beam deflection at the wall.

Another source of beam attenuation along the margins of cystic regions may be the walls of these structures. The thickness of the wall material that must be traversed by the beam is greater at the periphery of the structure. If the attenuation coefficient of the wall is greater than that of the surrounding tissues, the increased path length results in greater attenuation at the lateral margins than through the near and far walls of the structure.

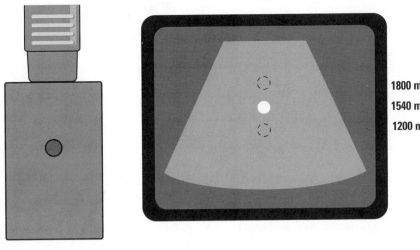

1800 m/sec
1540 m/sec
1200 m/sec

**Assumed speed of sound
= 1540 m/sec**

Figure 7-42. Effect of imaging an object at a fixed depth if the speed of sound in the medium were higher (or lower) than 1540 m/s. The object appears closer (farther) on the image than its actual distance.

In any case the edges of many cysts and vessels produce a so- called lateral shadow sign. A combination of the lateral shadow sign and the echo enhancement accompanying the transmission of sound through low-attenuating masses has come to be called the *tadpole tail sign*.

Speed of sound artifacts

The time versus distance relationship in an ultrasound instrument is based on a speed of sound of 1540 m/s. If the ultrasound beam travels through a region in which the speed of sound is greater than this, it takes less time for an echo to return than if the object were at the same depth but embedded within a medium whose speed of sound is 1540 m/s. Because 1540 m/s is still assumed, the object appears to be at a shallower depth than it actually is (Figure 7-42). Conversely, for an object in a medium that has a lower speed of sound, it takes longer for an echo to return from a given depth than when the speed of sound is 1540 m/s, so the object appears to be at a greater depth.

This effect is illustrated in Figure 7-43. This is a B-mode image of the liver containing a hyperechoic mass.[17] The speed of sound within the mass appears to be lower than the speed in the surrounding liver tissue. This is evident because of the distorted position of the diaphragm, as seen in Figure 7-43, indicating a longer echo transit time through the mass than through corresponding liver tissue. Fatty tissues with a lower speed of sound are believed to be present in this mass.

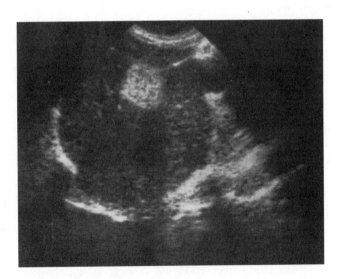

Figure 7-43. B-mode image of a hyperechoic mass in the liver. The displayed position of the diaphragm is displaced, apparently because of a lower speed of sound within the mass than within the liver.

Another common example of this artifact occurs when scanning a breast implant containing silicone, which has a lower speed of sound than does soft tissue. All structures distal to this material appear further away than they are because of this longer echo transit time.

DISTANCE, AREA, AND VOLUME COMPUTATIONS

Distance

Dimensions. Accurate measurements of organ and structure dimensions are possible in diagnostic ultrasound because the speed of sound in most soft tissues is known to within about 1%. By using an instrument's "digital calipers," which assume that the speed of sound is 1540 m/s, a measurement accuracy to within 1% or 2% is possible. Even greater measurement accuracy can be obtained in ophthalmological applications because of the use of high frequencies, careful scanning, and well-known speeds of sound in the media traversed.

Linear distance measurements are done routinely with ultrasound instruments. Examples shown in Figure 7-44 are simple length measurements and measurements of diameters. The units for length are millimeters (mm), centimeters (cm), and meters (m); millimeters and centimeters are most commonly used in ultrasonography.

Careful choice of measurement reference positions is necessary to achieve maximum accuracy with distance measurements. On a B-mode image the leading edge of the reflector echo signal, as viewed from the transducer position (Figures 7-45 and 7-46), is usually the best choice. This point is least affected by variations in echo signal amplitude, such as might occur for different output or gain settings of the instrument.

Distance measurements are usually more reliable when it is possible to align the measurement line along the beam axis (Figure 7-47). The reflector position can be pinpointed more accurately in this orientation. Beam width effects cause the image of a "point" reflector to spread out horizontally, contributing to the measurement uncertainty.[18] Incomplete outlining on B-mode images of surfaces that are not perpendicular to the ultrasound beam also contributes to uncertainty for horizontal measurements[19] (Figure 7-48).

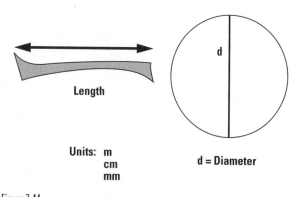

Figure 7-44. Linear measurements. Units most often used in ultrasound are cm or mm.

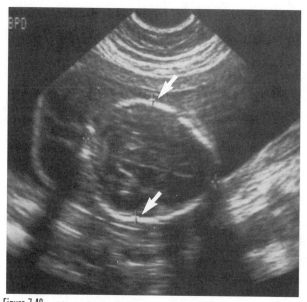

Figure 7-46. Clinical image showing caliper positioning *(white arrows)* for biparietal diameter measurements. (From Goldstein R, Filly R, Simpson G: Pitfalls in femur length measurements, *J Ultrasound Med* 6:203, 1987.)

Figure 7-45. Schematic showing proper caliper position for a biparietal diameter measurement. Calipers should be placed to measure from the "leading edge" of one surface to the "leading edge" of the second.

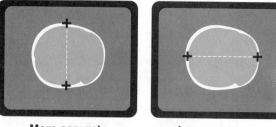

Figure 7-47. Distance measurements are usually more accurate along the beam direction than perpendicular to the beam direction.

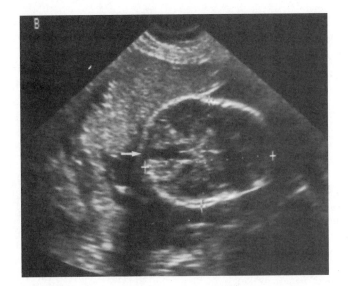

Figure 7-48. Distance measurements in the lateral direction can be uncertain, particularly when the object is not completely outlined, as in this example. (From Goldstein R, Filly R, Simpson G: Pitfalls in femur length measurements, *J Ultrasound Med* 6:203, 1987.)

Circumference. The distance around the perimeter of an object is the circumference, and this measure also is used in ultrasonography. Units for circumference are the same as for simple distances discussed in the previous section, millimeters or centimeters being most common. Sometimes the circumference is measured directly, by tracing around the structure. If the object has a simple geometric shape, such as a circle (Figure 7-49), standard formulas can be applied using distance measurements.

Area

In certain situations the cross-sectional area of a structure viewed on an ultrasound image provides diagnostic information. Areas are measured in "square" units, such as mm^2 (square mm) or cm^2 (square cm). Often the area can be estimated by assuming a shape and applying appropriate formulas to the area measurement. For circles and ellipses the areas are presented in Figures 7-50 and 7-51. Some instruments have built-in programs requiring operator input of structure axes from which the circumference and area are computed internally.

For complex shapes some instruments provide area analysis programs that require tracing the region of interest using a joy stick or cursor (Figure 7-52). Once this is done, the system can first count the number of pixels enclosed by the outlined region. Each pixel can be thought of as a tiny piece of the area of the entire contour. The number of pixels within the contour is then multiplied by the pixel area, yielding the area of the structure.

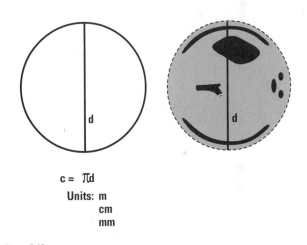

$$c = \pi d$$
Units: m
cm
mm

Figure 7-49. The circumference of a circle is given by $\pi \times d$, where d is the diameter and π is 3.14. In ultrasound the diameter is measured from 2-D images.

Volume

Ultrasound images can also be used to estimate the volumes of structures and organs. Such measurements may provide more sensitive indications of changes in structure dimensions than simple distance or area measurements. Volume calculations also form the basis for cardiac output estimates in ultrasonography.

Volumes are three-dimensional quantities, usually specified in mm^3 or cm^3. Volume also may be expressed in liters (L) or milliliters (ml). Estimates of volume are sometimes made by assuming a simple shape and using ultrasound scans to obtain the necessary dimensions to plug

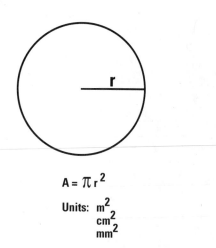

$$A = \pi\, r^2$$

Units: m^2
cm^2
mm^2

Figure 7-50. Measurement of the area of a circular structure. The area, A, is $\pi \times$ the square of the radius. (This can also be expressed as $\pi \times$ the diameter squared, divided by 4, or $\pi\,\frac{d^2}{4}$.)

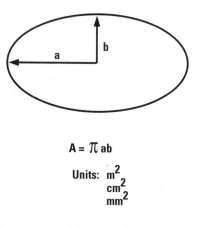

$$A = \pi\, ab$$

Units: m^2
cm^2
mm^2

Figure 7-51. Measurement of the area of an ellipse. Measurement a is called the *semi-major axis* and b the *semi-minor axis*.

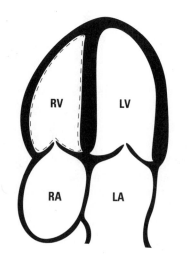

Figure 7-52. Tracing the outline of an irregular structure for computing the area.

into equations for the volumes. In certain cases, for example, it is reasonable to estimate the volume by assuming that the shape is a sphere (Figure 7-53) or a prolate spheroid (Figure 7-54). Computations of the volume using structure dimensions are illustrated in these figures.

For irregularly shaped structures in which a sphere or spheroid is not appropriate for estimating the volume, a serial scan approach can be followed. One implementation of this technique is outlined in Figure 7-55. A series of images from planes that are separated by a known distance, ΔL, are recorded. Then the area of the structure is estimated for each image. The area can be estimated by any of the methods just outlined. The area multiplied by the distance between image planes represents a section of the volume. Summing all the volume sections corresponding to each scan that cuts through the structure provides an estimate of the volume.

A similar approach, sometimes referred to as *Simpson's rule*, has been used for left ventricular volume estimates.

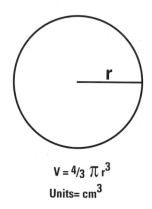

$$V = \tfrac{4}{3}\,\pi\, r^3$$
Units $= cm^3$

Figure 7-53. Measuring the volume by assuming the object is a sphere. The volume, V, is $\tfrac{4}{3}\,\pi \times$ the radius cubed.

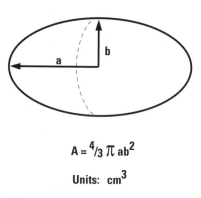

$$A = \tfrac{4}{3}\,\pi\, ab^2$$

Units: cm^3

Figure 7-54. Measuring the volume of an object by assuming the shape is a prolate spheroid. Measurement a is the semi-major axis and b the semi-minor axis. (A prolate spheroid is formed by rotating an ellipse about its major axis, $2a$.)

Similar to the technique just described, images are obtained that provide an estimate of the area of the structure for serial planes. The implementation for echo cardiography uses a single ultrasound image and assumes the ventricle can be approximated as a stack of circular disks as shown in Figure 7-56. The volume is the summed volume of all disk section volumes. For a disk section (a circular structure) the area is πr^2, where r is the radius of the section. The product of $\pi r^2 \times h$, the thickness of each section, equals the volume of the section. (Note, since the radius, r is $^1/_2$ the diameter, d, $r^2 = d^2/_4$). Adding all section volumes together gives the total volume.

One application of this technique is in echocardiography. In Figure 7-57, the ultrasound instrument has automatically determined the diameters of a set of disks that cover the left ventricle. Computation of the left ventricular volume, adding up the volumes of all the sections, is then also done automatically by this machine.

SUMMARY

Echo signal amplitudes from specular reflectors are dependent on the orientation of the reflector with respect to the ultrasound beam. Signals from diffuse reflectors and scatterers are much less dependent on orientation. Regional variations in ultrasound scattering are recognized on gray scale images and help delineate normal and abnormal structures.

The distribution of speckle dots on a 2-D gray scale image is often called "texture." Much of the gray-scale texture on ultrasound images is the result of interference of waves from small, unresolvable scatterers.

An artifact is any echo signal whose displayed position does not correspond to the position of a reflector in the body. Reverberations, beam width effects, mirror images, slice thickness effects, shadowing and enhancement were among the types of artifacts considered. Fat can result in noticeable refraction artifacts because its speed of sound is lower than that in most soft tissues. If the sound propagation path to a reflector is partially through a structure whose speed of sound differs from 1540 m/s (or the value assumed in the calibration of the instrument), echo "position registration" artifacts will be produced.

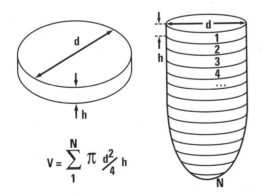

Figure 7-55. Method for estimating volumes by (1) scanning through several planes of the object, (2) estimating the area of the object as seen in each plane, and (3) adding all the areas multiplied by the distance between slices. To utilize this method it is necessary to control the distance between image planes, which may require three-dimensional scanning.

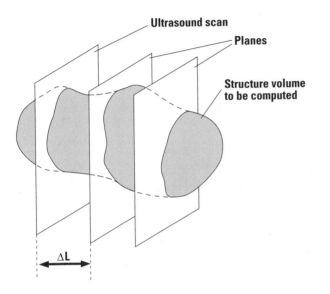

$$V = \sum_{1}^{N} \pi \, \frac{d^2}{4} \, h$$

Figure 7-56. Simpson's rule for estimating volumes in echo cardiography. Similar to Figure 7-55, the volume is considered to be made up of smaller increments, in this case circular disk sections with thickness h. The area of each section ($\pi \times \frac{d^2}{4}$) times its thickness (h) equals the volume of that section. The Σ sign means "add all the section volumes."

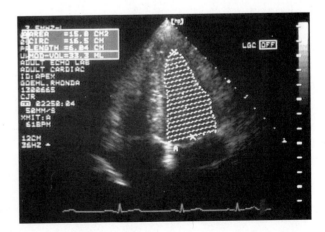

Figure 7-57. Using Simpson's rule to estimate the volume of the left ventricle. Each of the horizontal lines is a diameter of one of the disk sections shown in Figure 7-56.

References

1. Hagen-Ansert SL: *Textbook of diagnostic ultrasonography,* ed 4, St Louis, 1995, Mosby.
2. Schwartz D et al: The use of real-time ultrasound to enhance fetoscopic visualization, *J Clin Ultrasound* 11:161, 1983.
3. Wendell B, Athey P: Ultrasonic appearance of metallic foreign bodies in parenchymal organs, *J Clin Ultrasound* 9:133, 1981.
4. Lewandowski B, French, G, Winsberg F: The normal post-cholecystectomy sonogram; gas vs clips, *J Ultrasound Med* 4:7, 1985.
5. Scanlan KA, Hunt KR: *Ultrasound imaging: artifacts and medical devices.* In Hunter T, Bragg D, editors: *Radiologic guide to medical devices and foreign bodies.* St Louis, 1994, Mosby.
6. Ziskin M, et al: The comet-tail artifact, *J Ultrasound Med* 1:1, 1982.
7. Avruch L, Cooperberg P: The ring-down artifact, *J Ultrasound Med* 4:21, 1985.
8. Pozniak MA, Zagzebski JA, Scanlan KA: Spectral and color Doppler artifacts, *Radiographics* 12:35, 1992.
9. Otto CM, Pearlman AS: *Textbook of clinical echocardiography,* Philadelphia, 1994, Saunders.
10. Zagzebski JA, et al: A teaching phantom for ultrasonographers. Program and abstracts, Twenty-sixth annual meeting of the American Institute of Ultrasound in Medicine, San Francisco, August, 1981.
11. Lizzi F, Burt W, Coleman D: Effects of ocular structures in the eye, *Arch Ophthalmol* 84:6, 1970.
12. Madsen EL, Zagzebski JA, Ghilardi-Netto T: An anthropomorphic torso phantom for ultrasonic imaging, *Med Phys* 7:43, 1980.
13. Buttery B, Davison G: The ghost artifact, *J Ultrasound Med* 3:49, 1984.
14. Sauerbrei E: The split image artifact in pelvic ultrasonography: anatomy and physics, *J Ultrasound Med* 4:29, 1985.
15. Muller N, et al: Ultrasonic refraction by the rectus abdominus muscles: the double image artifact, *J Ultrasound Med* 3:515, 1984.
16. Robinson D, Wilson L, Kossoff G: Shadowing and enhancement in ultrasonic echograms by reflection and refraction, *J Clin Ultrasound* 9:181, 1981.
17. Richman T, Taylor K, Kremkau F: Propagation speed artifact in a fatty tumor (myelolipoma): significance for tissue differential diagnosis, *J Ultrasound Med* 2:45, 1983.
18. Goldstein R, Filly R, Simpson G: Pitfalls in femur length measurements, *J Ultrasound Med* 6:203, 1987.
19. Rumack CM, Wilson SR, Charboneau JW, editors: *Diagnostic ultrasound,* St Louis, 1991, Mosby.

Questions for Review

1. The amplitude of an echo from a specular reflector depends on each of the following *except:*

   A. Angle
   B. Attenuation
   C. Pulse repetition frequency
   D. Distance

2. Another name for an interface that reflects sound in all directions is a:
   A. Specular reflector
   B. Organ boundary
   C. Scatterer
   D. Attenuator

3. Echoes from scatterers sometimes appear brighter on the display than echoes from organ boundaries because:

   A. Scatterers exhibit angular effects
   B. Organ boundaries exhibit angular effects
   C. Scatterers are larger in diameter than boundary interfaces
   D. Scatterers are not accompanied by tissue attenuation

4. The term *hyperechoic* signifies a region that has

   A. Fewer sources of echoes than other regions
   B. Interfaces that have high impedance
   C. Elevated echogenicity
   D. No reflectors

5. The granular dot display of organ parenchyma on a two-dimensional B-scan image is also known as:

   A. Speckle
   B. Sparkle
   C. Points of light
   D. Points of scatter

6. Which of the following phenomenona is most closely related to the production of texture on a B-mode image of a uniform organ or a tissue phantom?

   A. Refraction
   B. Shadowing
   C. Interference
   D. Reverberation

7. "Structures and features on an image that do not have a one-to-one correspondence to the object being scanned" is a definition of:

   A. Reverberations
   B. Refraction
   C. Speckle
   D. Artifacts

8. When a two-dimensional B-mode image is constructed, echo dots are positioned:

   A. Anywhere on the image, but at a depth corresponding to the echo arrival time
   B. Along the transmitted beam axis
   C. At random locations in the beam
   D. Along a line corresponding to the lateral margins of the beam

9. Many echoes generated from the same interface describes:

   A. Refraction
   B. Speckle
   C. Reverberation
   D. Attenuation

10. An interface is located 2 cm from the transducer. If a single reverberation occurs, the reverberation echo would be found at a depth of:

   A 1 cm
   B. 2 cm
   C. 4 cm
   D. 8 cm

11. A series of echoes below the position of a metallic object on a B-mode image is most likely due to:

   A. Reverberations within the object
   B. Reaction of the tissue distal to the object
   C. Reaction of the tissue proximal to the object
   D. Enhancement caused by low attenuation by the object

12. Echoes appearing to arise distal to near-perfect reflectors such as the diaphragm can often be attributed to:

   A. Refraction of the beam beyond the reflector
   B. Mirror image artifacts
   C. Attenuation of the beam by structures distal to the reflector
   D. Echo enhancement by the reflector

13. Doppler spectral mirroring occurs for:

   A. Flow through an artery located at a large distance
   B. A Doppler angle of 90 degrees
   C. Venous flow only
   D. Arterial flow only

14. The lateral spreading of the image of a pointlike reflector is due to:

   A. Beam width effects
   B. Speed of sound artifacts
   C. The Doppler effect
   D. Refraction effects

15. Artifactual fill-in on images of anechoic tubes whose axes are perpendicular to the ultrasound beam may be attributed to:

   A. Beam width effects
   B. Slice thickness effects
   C. Echoes arriving from within the tubes
   D. Echoes arriving from distal to the tubes

16. Which of the following types of effects occur with a linear array transducer but not a single element transducer?

   A. Beam width effects
   B. Side lobe effects
   C. Grating lobes
   D. Reverberations

17. Artifactual fill-in on images of anechoic spheres may be attributed primarily to:

   A. Beam width effects
   B. Slice thickness effects
   C. Echoes arriving from within the spheres
   D. Echoes arriving from distal to the spheres

18. Echo enhancement most noticeably affects signals arising from _____ a low attenuating object.

   A. Within
   B. Proximal to
   C. Lateral to
   D. Distal to

19. The opposite of echo enhancement is:

   A. Detection
   B. Obliteration
   C. Shadowing
   D. Good through-transmission

20. If refraction occurs, the machine:

   A. Uses Snell's law to compute reflector positions
   B. Places echo dots along lines corresponding to refracted beams
   C. Places echo dots along lines corresponding to nonrefracted beams
   D. Cannot receive echo signals from the medium

21. A reflector is at a depth of 10 cm. The scanner displays an echo from this reflector as though it is at a depth of 9 cm. This most likely means:

   A. Refraction occurred
   B. There are reverberations
   C. The speed of sound is lower than 1540 m/s
   D. The speed of sound is greater than 1540 m/s

22. Units for circumference measurements are:

   A. mm
   B. mm^2
   C. mm^3
   D. cm^3

23. The area of a circle that is 2 cm in diameter is closest to:

   A. $3 \ cm^2$
   B. $12 \ cm^2$
   C. $36 \ cm^2$
   D. $72 \ cm^2$

24. Simpson's rule is often used in ultrasound to estimate:

   A. Speeds of sound
   B. Distances
   C. Volumes
   D. Whether artifacts are present

Chapter 8

Ultrasound Equipment Quality Assurance

QA testing provides confidence that image data, such as distance measurements and area estimations, are accurate and that image quality is the best possible from the instrument.

In diagnostic ultrasound, equipment **quality assurance** (QA) involves steps taken periodically to ensure that ultrasound instruments are operating consistently at their expected level of performance. During routine scanning every sonographer is vigilant for equipment changes that could lead to suboptimal imaging and might require service. Thus in some ways, equipment quality assurance is carried out every day, even when not identified as a process in itself. However, quality assurance steps to be discussed here go beyond judgments of imaging performance that are made during routine scanning. They involve prospective actions to identify problem situations, even before obvious equipment malfunctions occur. Quality assurance testing also provides confidence that image data, such as distance measurements and area estimations, are accurate and that image quality is the best possible from the imaging instrument.

SETTING UP A QUALITY ASSURANCE PROGRAM

Quality assurance and PM

Different approaches are followed by imaging facilities when setting up a quality assurance program for their scanners. Sometimes these programs include both "preventive maintenance" (PM) procedures done by trained equipment service personnel and "in-house" testing of scanners done using phantoms and test objects. Some facilities rely on only one of these measures. For PM, emphasis usually is given to electronic testing of system components, such as voltage measurements at test points on the scanner; sometimes PM also involves an assessment

of the imaging capability by scanning a normal subject or a phantom.

In-house scanner QA programs usually involve imaging phantoms or test objects and assessing the results. The in-house tests might be done by sonographers, physicians, medical physicists, clinical engineers, or equipment maintenance personnel. References 1 to 4 at the end of this chapter provide detailed recommendations from professional organizations on establishing an in-house QA program.

Tissue-mimicking phantoms

In-house scanner QA tests are most often done using tissue-mimicking phantoms. In medical ultrasound a phantom is a device that mimics soft tissues in its ultrasound transmission characteristics. Phantoms represent "constant patients," enabling images taken at different times to be closely compared. Penetration capabilities, for example, are readily evaluated for changes over time when images of a phantom are available for comparison. Phantoms also have targets in known positions, so images can be compared closely with the region scanned. Examples include simulated cysts, echogenic structures, and thin "line targets."

The tissue transmission characteristics that commercially available phantoms mimic are the speed of sound, the ultrasonic attenuation, and to some degree the echogenicity, that is, the ultrasonic scattering level. It should be mentioned that phantoms cannot replicate acoustical properties of soft tissues exactly. This is partially because of the complexity and variability of tissues. Instead, phantom manufacturers construct these objects to have average acoustical properties that are *representative* of tissues.

Sometimes the term *tissue-equivalent* is used when describing phantoms. However, this term should not be interpreted literally because most phantom materials are not acoustically "equivalent" to the tissues they represent.

Typical QA phantom design. Examples of general purpose ultrasound QA phantoms are shown in Figures 8-1 to 8-3. Each example shows the outside of the phantom as well as B-mode images that illustrate their contents.

Figure 8-3, *C* is a schematic showing details of the phantom in Figure 8-3, *A*. The objects in the three examples are similar, so this one will be used as an example.

The tissue-mimicking material in the phantom in Figure 8-3 consists of a water-based gelatin in which microscopic graphite particles are mixed uniformly throughout the volume.[5,6] The speed of sound within the

phantom material is about 1540 m/s, the same speed assumed in the calibration of ultrasound instruments. The ultrasonic attenuation coefficient versus frequency is one of two values: either 0.5 dB/cm-MHz or 0.7 dB/cm-MHz.* Some users prefer the lower attenuating material because they find it easier to image objects in the phantom. However, standards groups recommend the higher attenuation because it challenges machines more thor-

---

*Attenuation coefficients are in dB/cm. To include the dependence of attenuation on frequency, phantom manufacturers divide the attenuation coefficient by the frequency at which the measurement is done. This yields units of dB/cm-MHz. Strictly speaking, this approach should be used only when attenuation is directly proportional to the frequency, as we often assume for tissues.

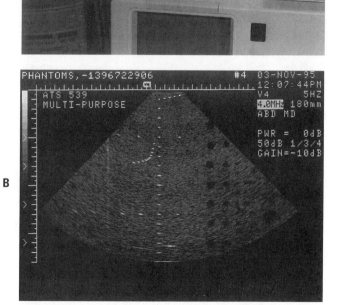

A

B

Figure 8-1. Photograph **(A)** and B-mode image **(B)** of a general purpose tissue-mimicking phantom, the ATS #539. (Courtesy ATS Laboratories, Bridgeport, CT.)

A

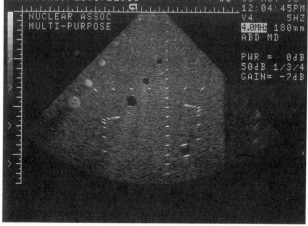

B

Figure 8-2. Photograph **(A)** and B-mode image **(B)** of a general purpose tissue-mimicking phantom, the Nuclear Associates 84-340JV. (Courtesy Nuclear Associates, Carle Place, NY.)

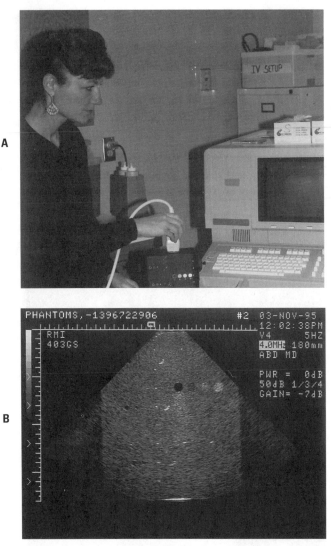

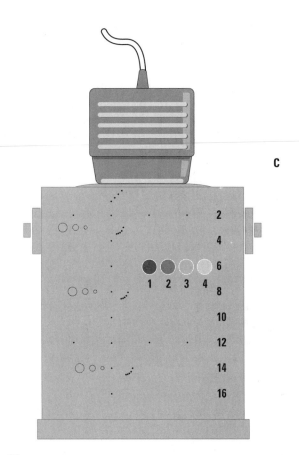

Figure 8-3. Photograph **(A)** and B-mode image **(B)** and sketch showing details of the interior **(C)** of a general purpose tissue mimicking phantom, the Gammex/RMI 403GS. (Courtesy Gammex-RMI, Middleton, WI.)

oughly.[3,4] For example, 0.7 dB/cm-MHz is representative of the attenuation coefficient in difficult to penetrate fatty liver.[7,8] The depth that structures can be visualized within tissue-mimicking material having this amount of attenuation more closely correlates with clinical penetration capabilities in challenging situations.

Attenuation in the gel-graphite material in the phantom is proportional to the ultrasound frequency, mimicking the behavior in tissues. Other types of materials have been used in phantoms, but water-based gels laced with powder are the only ones shown to have both speed of sound and attenuation with tissuelike properties.[5,6]

Small scatterers are distributed throughout the tissue-mimicking material. Therefore the phantoms appear echogenic when scanned with ultrasound imaging equipment (Figure 8-3). Many phantoms, including the one pictured in Figures 8-1 to 8-3, have simulated cysts, which are simply low-attenuating, nonechogenic cylinders. These should appear echo free on B-mode images and

should exhibit distal echo enhancement. Some tissue phantoms provide additional image contrast by having simulated masses of varying echogenicity. Such objects are evident in the image in Figures 8-2 and 8-3.

Discrete targets. Most QA phantoms also contain discrete reflectors, such as nylon-line targets, to be used mainly for evaluating the distance measurement accuracy of a scanner. Tests of the accuracy of distance measurements rely on the manufacturer of the phantom to have filled the device with a material whose sound propagation speed is 1540 m/s, or at least close enough to this speed that no appreciable errors are introduced in calibrations. They also rely on the manufacturer having defined the reflector positions accurately.

Phantoms often contain a column of reflectors, each separated by 1.0 cm or 2.0 cm, for vertical measurement accuracy tests. One or more horizontal rows of reflectors are used for assessing horizontal measurement accuracy. Additional sets of reflectors may be found for assessing axial resolution and lateral resolution of scanners.

BASIC QUALITY ASSURANCE TESTS

A typically recommended set of instrument QA tests[3] includes checks for consistency of instrument sensitivity; evaluation of image photography and image uniformity; and checks of both vertical and horizontal distance measurement accuracy. This group of tests can be done by a sonographer in 10 to 15 minutes, including time for recording the results on a worksheet or in a notebook.

Transducer choice

Results of some test procedures depend on which transducer assembly is used with the instrument. On systems where several transducer assemblies are available it may be inconvenient to do routine tests with more than one probe. If this is the case, choose a transducer assembly that will become a standard for all test procedures. A good choice is the transducer assembly used most frequently in clinical scanning. Be sure to record all necessary transducer assembly identification information, including the frequency, size, and serial number, so future tests will be conducted with the same probe.

System sensitivity

The sensitivity of an instrument refers to the weakest echo signal level that can be detected and displayed clearly enough to be discernible on an image. Most scanners have controls that vary the receiver amplification ("gain") and the transmit level (e.g., "output" or "power"). These are used to adjust the sensitivity during clinical examinations. When the controls are positioned for their maximum practical settings, we refer to the maximum sensitivity of the instrument. Often the **maximum sensitivity** is limited by electrical noise appearing on the display when the receiver gain is at maximum

levels (Figure 8-4). The noise may be generated externally, for example, by electronic communication networks or computer terminals. More commonly it arises from within the instrument itself, such as in the first preamplification stage of the receiver amplifier.

Concerns during quality assurance tests are usually centered around whether notable *variations in sensitivity* have occurred since the last QA test. Such variations might result from a variety of causes, such as damaged transducers, damaged transducer cables, or electronic drift in the pulser-receiver components of the scanner. Sometimes questions related to the sensitivity of a scanner occur during clinical imaging; a quick scan of the QA phantom and comparison with results of the most recent QA test help determine whether there is cause for concern.

A commonly used technique for detecting variations in maximum sensitivity is to measure the **maximum depth of visualization** for signals from scattered echoes in the tissue-mimicking phantom.[1-4, 10] Output power transmit levels and receiver sensitivity controls are adjusted so that echo signals are obtained from as deep as possible into the phantom. This means that the output power control is positioned for maximum output and the receiver gain adjusted for the highest values without excessive noise on the display. (Experience helps in establishing these control settings; they should be recorded in the quality control worksheet, described below.) The phantom is scanned and the maximum depth of visualization of texture echo signals estimated (Figures 8-5 and 8-6).

In the example in Figure 8-5, the maximum depth of visualization is 15.8 cm. In Figure 8-6 it is 6.3 cm, reflecting the higher attenuation experienced using a 7.5-MHz

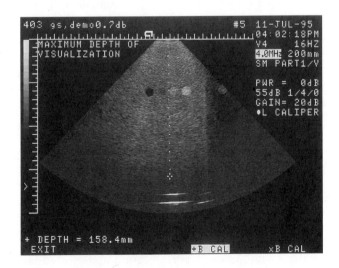

Figure 8-5. Determining the maximum depth of visualization for background echoes in a tissue-mimicking phantom. The maximum depth of visualization for this transducer operating at 4 MHz is 15.8 cm. (The attenuation in the phantom is 0.7 dB/cm-MHz.)

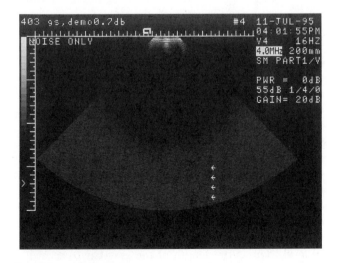

Figure 8-4. Electronic noise appearing on the display *(arrows)* of a B-mode imager.

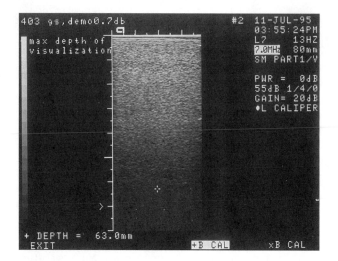

Figure 8-6. Maximum depth of visualization test for a 7.5-MHz transducer. In this example the maximum depth for visualizing background echo signals is 6.3 cm.

frequency probe. To interpret the results of the test, a comparison is made with maximum visualization results from a previous test, say 6 months earlier. Results should agree to within 1 cm. Normal trial-to-trial variations in scanning and interpretation prohibit making closer calls than this. These errors might be several millimeters, so penetration cannot be judged any better than this.

However, using hard copy images and records of maximum depth of visualization tests, it should be possible to ascertain whether a scanner/transducer combination has drifted significantly over time in echo detection capabilities.

In addition to doing this measurement using the standard transducer, it is useful to perform the test occasionally using different transducers. For example, the test can be done with all transducers that are available for each instrument when quality control tests are first established and semiannually thereafter. This helps to pinpoint the source of any decrease in the maximum sensitivity or at least determine whether the standard transducer is at fault.

Photography and gray scale hard copy

Perhaps the most frequent source of ultrasound instrument variability over time is related to image photography. All too often drift in the imaging instrument, in the hard copy cameras, or in film processing reduces image quality to the point that significant amounts of detail related to echo signal amplitude variations are lost on hard copy B-mode images. However, if image viewing and recording monitors are set up properly, and if sufficient attention is given to photography during routine quality control, these problems can be reduced.

Setting up monitors and recording devices. Most instruments provide both an image display monitor, which is viewed during scan build-up, and an image recording device. As a general rule the display monitor should be set up properly first, and then adjustments made, if necessary, to multiformat cameras or other hard copy recording devices to produce acceptable gray scale on hard copy images. It is expected that establishing proper settings is only done during installation of a scanner, during major upgrades, or when image problems are detected. Image display settings should not be shifted routinely. Many facilities go so far as to remove the control knobs on image monitors once the contrast and brightness are acceptable, removing the temptation to change settings casually.

An effective method for setting up both viewing and hard copy monitors has been described by Gray.[9] This author recommends that adjustments be done using an image containing a clinically representative sampling of gray shades. Attention is first directed to the display monitor viewed during scan build-up. With the contrast settings of the monitor initially set at minimum settings, the brightness is adjusted to a level that just allows TV raster lines to be discernible. Once this is done the monitor contrast is adjusted until a clinically acceptable image is obtained. After the viewing monitor is properly adjusted, provisions should be made to prevent casual changes in settings by department personnel.

The image recording device is then adjusted to obtain the same image gray shades as appear on the display monitor. This may require several iterations, varying the contrast and the overall brightness, until satisfactory results are obtained. The control settings are fixed once acceptable results are obtained.

Routine QA of image recording. Routine checks should be done of the quality of gray scale photography or other hard copy recording media. Photography and processing should always be such that all brightness variations in the viewing monitor image are successfully recorded on the hard copy image.

Images of a tissue-mimicking phantom, along with the gray bar pattern appearing on the edge of most image displays, can be used for routinely assessing photography settings. On an image of a tissue-mimicking phantom (or of a patient), check to see whether weak echo signal dots appearing on the viewing monitor are successfully recorded on film. Also determine whether the entire gray bar is visible and that all gray levels are distinguished. For example, for a scanner whose gray bar includes 15 levels of gray, along with the background, the hard copy image should portray distinctions between all levels. The entire length of the gray bar pattern displayed on the viewing monitor should be visible on the final image (Figure 8-7).

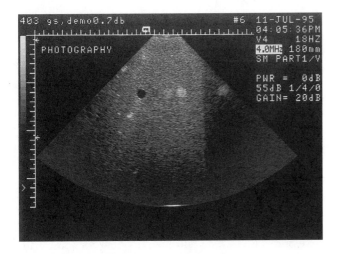

Figure 8-7. Photography test. Different gray levels over the entire gray bar should be visible on the hard copy image or record *(arrows)*. Weak echo dots from weak reflectors should also be successfully recorded.

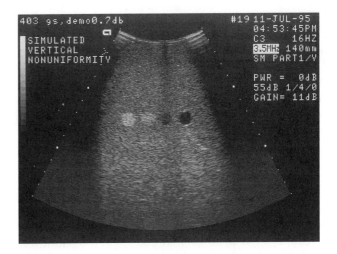

Figure 8-8. Simulation of nonuniformity caused by partial loss of signals from one or more elements in an array. The problem leads to vertical "shadows" emanating from the position of the transducer surface. (This simulation was done by placing a thin rubber strip over an element on the transducer.)

For multiple images on a single sheet of film or paper, all images should have the same background brightness and display the gray bar pattern the same. This may be verified from clinical images taken on the day of QA tests or from the QA films themselves.

Scan image uniformity

Ideally when a uniform region within a phantom is scanned, and the machine's gain settings are adjusted properly, the resultant image will have a uniform brightness throughout. Nonuniformities due to the ultrasound imager can occur from several sources:

1. Bad elements in a linear or curved array or loose connections in beam former board plug-ins can lead to vertically oriented nonuniformities (Figure 8-8) (boards can be loosened if the scanner is wheeled over bumps or if it is transported by van to other hospitals).
2. Inadequate side-to-side image compensation in the machine can lead to variations in brightness from one side of the image to another.
3. Inadequate blending of pixel data between transmit and receive focal zones can lead to horizontal or curved streaks parallel to the transducer surface (Figure 8-9).

QA testing is an ideal time to assess whether such faults are noticeable. An image is taken of a uniform region in the QA phantom, and the image inspected for these problems.

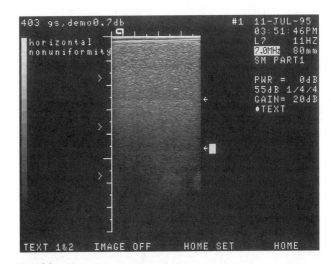

Figure 8-9. Subtle horizontal stripes, apparently related to focal zones. (These are well within an acceptable range; more severe discontinuities might warrant attention, however.)

Distance measurement accuracy

Instruments used for measuring structure dimensions, organ sizes, and areas should be tested periodically for accuracy of distance indicators. Distance indicators usually include 1-cm depth markers on M-mode and B-mode scanning displays, and digital calipers on B-mode scanning systems. Calipers on workstations that are part of computer archiving systems also should be checked for accuracy.

Our principal distance measurement tests are separated into two parts: one for measurements along the sound beam axis, referred to as the *vertical or axial distance measurement test,*★ and a second for measurements taken perpendicular to the sound beam axis, called a *horizontal distance measurement test.*

Vertical distance measurements. Vertical distance measurement accuracy is also called *depth calibration accuracy* in some texts. To evaluate a scanner's vertical distance measurement accuracy a scan of the phantom is obtained with a vertical column of reflectors in the phantom clearly imaged (Figure 8-10). The digital calipers are positioned to measure the distance between any two reflectors in this column. Correct caliper placement is from the top of the echo from the first reflector to the top of the echo from the second, or from any position on the first reflector to the corresponding position on the second. When testing general-purpose scanners, choose reflectors separated by at least 8 to 10 cm for this test. Most labs also measure a closer spacing, such as 4 cm. For small parts scanners and probes, use a distance of approximately 3 or 4 cm. The measured distance should agree with the actual distance given by the phantom manufacturer to within 1 mm or 1.5%, whichever is greater. If a larger discrepancy occurs, consult with the ultrasound scanner manufacturer for possible corrective measures.

Horizontal distance measurements. Horizontal measurement accuracy should be checked similarly. Measurements obtained in this direction (Figure 8-11) are frequently less accurate because of beam width effects and scanner inaccuracies. Nevertheless, results should agree with phantom

---

★Please do not confuse this test with *axial resolution.*

manufacturer's distances to within 3 mm or 3%, whichever is greater. Correct caliper placement for this test is from the center of one reflector to the center of the second. For the example in Figure 8-11, measurement results are within 1 mm of the actual distance between the reflectors examined. This is well within the expected level of accuracy.

Other important instrument QA tasks

During routine performance testing it is a good idea to perform other equipment-related chores that require occasional attention. These include cleaning air filters on instruments requiring this service (most do!); checking for loose and frayed electrical cables; looking for loose handles or control arms on the scanner; checking the wheels and wheel locks; and performing recommended preventive maintenance of photography equipment. The last may include dusting or cleaning of photographic monitors and maintenance chores on cameras.

DOCUMENTATION

Performance test worksheet

An important aspect of a QA program is keeping track of the results of tests. Most laboratories will want to adopt a standardized worksheet to write down the test results. The worksheet helps the user carry out the tests in a consistent manner by having enough information to facilitate recall of transducers, phantoms, and machine settings. It also includes blank spaces for recording the results. An example is given in the box on p. 155.

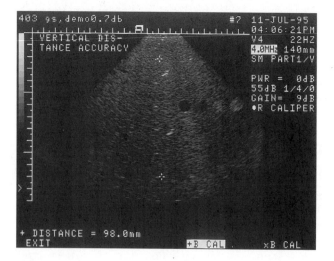

Figure 8-10. Vertical distance measurement accuracy test using a QA phantom. Calipers are positioned to measure the distance between two targets placed 10 cm apart. The indicated distance is 9.8 cm (98 mm).

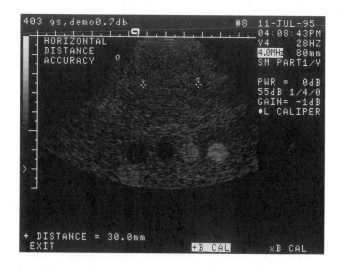

Figure 8-11. Horizontal distance measurement accuracy test. The cursors are positioned to measure the distance between two reflectors separated horizontally in the phantom by 3 cm. The indicated distance is also 3 cm.

Box 8-1. Ultrasound Quality Control Results

Machine: <u>Acuson 128</u>   Room: <u>E3 315</u>
Transducer assembly: I.D.: <u>L 382</u> Serial no: <u>555-1212</u>
Date: <u>1/18/88</u>   Phantom: <u>RMI 413/A—No</u>

Instrument settings: Power <u>0</u>   dB
                   Dynamic range <u>50</u>dB
                        Pre<u>1</u>/Persis<u>3</u>/Post<u>7</u>
                   Gain <u>4</u> dB
                   Transmit focus: <u>11 cm</u>
                   Image magnification: <u>16 cm</u>

1. Depth measurement accuracy
   Marker grids
      Measured distance . . . . <u>101</u> mm
      Actual distance . . . . <u>100</u> mm
      Error . . . . <u>1</u> mm
   Electronic calipers
      Measured distance . . . . <u>100.2</u> mm
      Actual distance . . . . <u>100</u> mm
      Error . . . . <u>0.2</u> mm

2. Horizontal measurement accuracy
   Electronic calipers
      Measured distance. . . . . . . <u>61</u> mm
      Actual distance. . . . . <u>60</u> mm
      Error . . . . <u>1</u> mm

3. Depth of penetration
      Measured distance. . . . . . . <u>133</u> mm
      Baseline distance . . . . <u>140</u> mm
      Variation from baseline . . . . <u>7</u> mm

4. Image uniformity
   Significant   Excellent
   *non*uniformity   uniformity
    1   2   3   4   5

5. Photography
   Gray bars
      Number of gray bars visible . . . . . . <u>14</u>
      Number of gray bars visible
        on baseline . . . . <u>15</u>
      Variation . . . . <u>1</u>
   Low-level echoes
      All echoes displayed on viewing monitor also
      seen on film: Yes <u>x</u> No __
   Contrast and brightness
      Level of agreement between contrast and
      brightness on viewing monitor and film:
      Poor   Excellent
       1   2   3   4   5

6. Filters
   Clean _____   Dusty _____

The quality assurance notebook

The quality assurance tests outlined above form a useful battery of procedures that can be done routinely and the results analyzed fairly quickly. To document the results of performance checks it is best to maintain a quality control notebook, in which a log of the test results written on the worksheets, along with relevant images, can be kept.

It is also recommended[2,3] to maintain a log of equipment malfunctions and equipment service calls in the quality control data book for each instrument. This information provides fairly complete documentation of the operating and performance characteristics of an instrument over time.

SPATIAL RESOLUTION TESTS

Some laboratories include spatial resolution in their QA testing. Measurements of spatial resolution generally require more exacting techniques to acquire results that allow intercomparisons of scanners. Therefore many centers do not do such performance tests routinely, but may do so only during equipment acceptance tests.[10,11] Common methods for determining axial resolution, lateral resolution, and slice thickness are discussed in this section.

Axial resolution

Axial resolution is a measure of how close two reflectors can be to one another along the axis of an ultrasound beam and still be resolved as separate reflectors. Axial resolution also is related to the "crispness" of the image of a reflector oriented approximately perpendicularly to the ultrasound beam.

Axial resolution may be estimated by measuring the thickness of the image of a line target in the QA phantom (Figure 8-12). Alternatively, some phantoms contain sets of reflectors for axial resolution testing. The axial separation between successive targets is 2 mm, 1 mm, 0.5 mm, and 0.25 mm. The closest spaced pair that can be distinguished is the axial resolution (Figure 8-13).

Lateral resolution

Lateral resolution is a measure of how close two reflectors can be to one another perpendicular to the beam axis and still be distinguished as separate reflectors on an image. One approach that is used for lateral resolution tests is to measure the width on the display of a pointlike target, such as a line target inside a phantom. For example, Figure 8-14 demonstrates such a measurement. The cursors indicate that the displayed width is 1.4 mm for this case. The displayed response width is related to the lateral resolution at the depth of the target. By imaging targets at different depths it is easy to see that the lateral resolution usually varies with depth for most transducers.

Cautions regarding resolution tests

Every sonographer knows that the size of an image of a pointlike target depends on the power setting and the gain setting on the machine. This is one of the difficulties of adopting such tests in routine testing. Read this section only if you are interested in doing more quantitative lateral and axial resolution measurements.

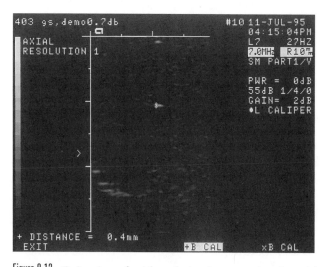

Figure 8-12. Estimation of axial resolution by measuring the axial thickness on the image of a very thin target. The thickness was estimated to be 0.4 mm for this 7-MHz system.

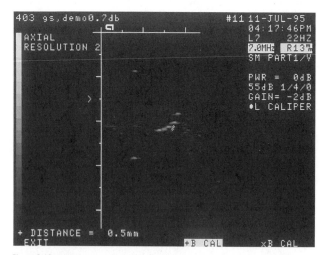

Figure 8-13. Estimation of axial resolution by scanning axial resolution group in the Gammex RMI 409 GS phantom. The vertical spacings between successive reflectors are 2 mm, 1 mm, 0.5 mm, and 0.25 mm. In this example, the 0.5 mm pair is just resolved, but the 0.25 mm pair is not because the axial range of the dots overlaps.

Quantitative results for any of the above methods can be obtained if we define the resolution with respect to a threshold level on the B-scan display.[8,10] One requirement for quantitative resolution tests is a calibrated sensitivity control on the instrument, one where someone has demonstrated that when you increase the setting by say, 20 dB, the change in sensitivity is indeed 20 dB. If this is not available, you should consult the instrument manufacturer or physicist or engineer who may be able to provide such a calibration. With a calibrated sensitivity control, reflectors are imaged at a sensitivity level for which they are just barely discernible on the display. This is called the display threshold for that reflector. Then the calibrated control is adjusted to increase the sensitivity by a fixed amount (e.g., 20 dB) and the scan is repeated. On the resultant image the reflector spacing that can be resolved or the displayed width of the pointlike object is measured using calipers. This is the axial or lateral resolution at the level below threshold corresponding to the sensitivity control increase above.

Slice thickness

The slice thickness usually is the worst measure of spatial resolution of ultrasound imagers. A phantom intended for detailed evaluation of slice thickness[12] is shown in Figure 8-15. It consists of a planar sheet of scatterers arranged so that the scanning plane intersects the sheet at a 45-degree angle. When an image is obtained using the orientation shown in Figure 8-15, the part of the plane imaged appears as a horizontal band. Though not so obvious without a close look at the angles involved, the axial length of this band equals the slice thickness.[10]

Engineers and physicists use the slice thickness phantom to make assessments of this parameter as a

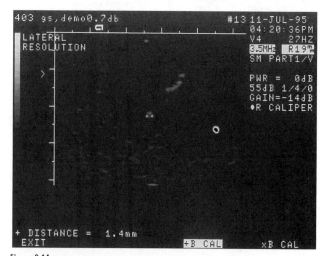

Figure 8-14. Estimation of lateral resolution by measuring the lateral width on the image of a very thin target in a QA phantom. The width is about 1.4 mm for this 3.5-MHz array.

function of distance from the transducer. Two images, each with the plane intersecting the scan plane at different depths, are presented in Figure 8-16. The slice thickness from this 4-MHz linear array is 9.3 mm at a depth of 2.5 cm and 4.2 mm at a depth of 10 cm. (Compare these results with lateral resolution for this transducer, in Figure 8-14.) The slice thickness phantom helps us understand the difficulty in imaging small masses with an array transducer, particularly at close distances and well beyond 10 cm from the transducer.

Spherical object phantom

Another type of phantom becoming increasingly popular for spatial resolution tests is one that has simulated focal lesions embedded within echogenic tissue-mimicking material.[2,10,13] Different simulated lesion sizes and object contrast levels (i.e., relative echogenicity) have been tried.[13] An example is presented in Figure 8-17, where the phantom imaged contained 5-mm diameter, low echo masses.

A test of the ultrasound imaging system is to determine the "imaging zone" for detection of masses of a given size and object contrast.[2] A 3.5-MHz linear array may allow detection of 5-mm low scatter masses from depths of 4 to 10 cm, for example, while a 5-MHz array may provide imaging from 2 to 8 cm for this size structure.

A very useful aspect of spherical mass phantoms is that they present realistic imaging tasks that readily demonstrate resolution capabilities in terms of resolution. For spherical targets the resolution is a combined, effective resolution, made up of axial and lateral as well as slice thickness. If cylindrical objects are used, as in Figure 8-3, then only two dimensions, usually axial and lateral, are involved in their visualization. Because slice thickness usually is the worst measure of spatial resolution with array transducers, cylindrical objects can be misleading in terms of translating minimum sizes resolved into resolution of actual focal masses. The spherical lesion phantom is superior in this regard.

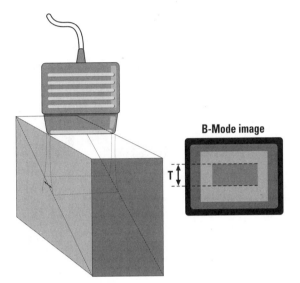

Figure 8-15. Schematic diagram showing the layout of the slice thickness phantom. The object viewed is a plane of scatterers oriented at an angle of 45 degrees with respect to the scanning plane. The transducer can be translated to view the scattering plane at various depths. The 45 degree angle makes it possible to estimate slice thickness directly from the vertical extent of the image of the plane.

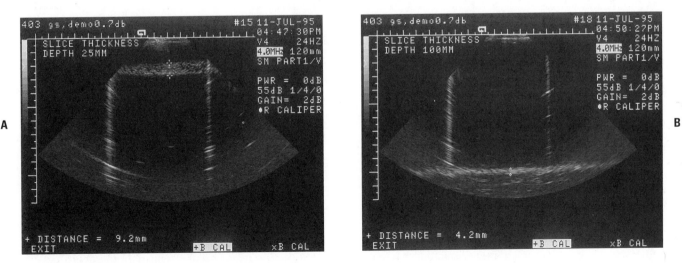

Figure 8-16. Images of slice thickness phantom. **A,** At a depth of 2.5 cm, where the slice thickness is 9.3 mm. **B,** At a depth of 10 cm, where the slice thickness is approximately 4.2 mm.

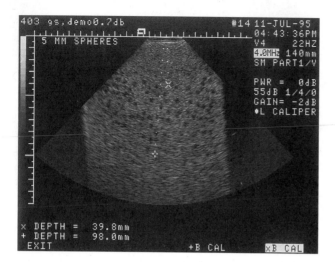

Figure 8-17. Image of spherical mass phantom. Masses with a diameter of 5 mm and echogenicity that is 15 dB lower than the background are seen. The masses are visualized most clearly between about 4 cm (cursor is at 39.8 mm) and 10 cm (the distal cursor is at 98 mm) with this 4-MHz array transducer.

DOPPLER TESTING

Limited evaluations of Doppler and color flow equipment also can be done in the clinic. A number of devices, including string test objects, flow velocity test objects, and flow phantoms are available to clinical users for carrying out tests of Doppler equipment.[14-16]

String test objects

String test objects (Figure 8-18) consist of a thin string wound around a pulley and motor-drive mechanism. The string is echogenic, so it produces echoes that are detected by an ultrasound instrument. The drive moves the string at precise velocities, either continuously or following a programmed waveform. This provides a way to evaluate the velocity measurement accuracy of Doppler devices. String test objects also may be used to evaluate the lateral and axial resolution in Doppler mode and can be used to determine the accuracy of gate registration on duplex Doppler systems.[15]

The advantage of the string test object is that it provides a small target moving at a precisely known velocity. The disadvantages are (1) the echogenic characteristics of the string are not the same as blood; and (2) actual blood flow, with its characteristic distribution of velocities across the vessel, is not mimicked.

During use, the target part of a string test object is immersed in water, and the ultrasound transducer is fixed with respect to the object. The record in Figure 8-19 was obtained while the string was moving at 100 cm/s. The

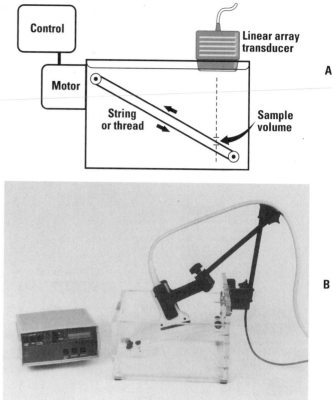

Figure 8-18. A, Schematic drawing of a string test object for evaluating some aspects of Doppler performance. B, Photograph of a Doppler string test object set to test an ultrasound system. (Courtesy Nuclear Associates, Carle Place, NY.)

spectral velocity trace appears to accurately display this velocity. Equipment testing using the string phantom generally includes running through a battery of string velocities and observing the displayed velocity on the spectral scale.

Doppler flow phantoms

Doppler flow phantoms (Figure 8-20) consist of one or more hollow tubes coursing through a block of tissue-mimicking material. A blood-mimicking fluid is pumped through the tube(s) to simulate blood flowing through vessels in the body. Usually the blood-mimicking fluid is made of a water-glycerol solution that has small plastic particles suspended in it. The blood-mimicking material should provide the same echogenicity as whole human blood at the ultrasound frequencies of the machine, and reasonable representative blood-mimicking materials now are available for use in these phantoms. If the tissue-mimicking material in the body of the phantom has a representative amount of beam attenuation, the depth-dependent echogenicity of the fluid within the phantom will be representative of signal levels from actual vessels in vivo.

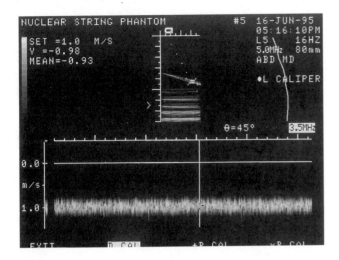

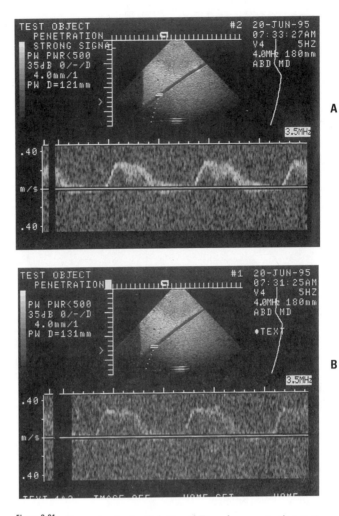

A

B

Figure 8-19. B-mode image and spectral Doppler record of the string test object. One test with the device is to compare the velocity of the string with the velocity indicated by the spectral display. The velocity of the string is 100 cm/s; the Doppler machine indicates the velocity is 99 cm/s, in perfect agreement.

Figure 8-21. Records obtained during a Doppler penetration test. **A,** The sample volume is at 12.1 cm; **B,** the sample volume is at 13.1 cm; the spectral trace is barely perceptible above the noise. This was called the *maximum depth of penetration.*

Figure 8-20. Photograph of a Doppler flow phantom. (Courtesy Gammex-RMI, Middleton, WI.)

Doppler flow phantoms are used for several types of tests of Doppler and flow imaging equipment [14-16]:

1. The maximum depth at which flow waveforms can be detected in the phantom has been used to assess whether the Doppler sensitivity has varied from one QA test to another.★ This is illustrated in Figure 8-21. Penetration in this case is 12.1 cm.

2. Alignment of the pulsed Doppler sample volume with the volume indicated on a duplex B-mode image.
3. Volume flow accuracy. Some Doppler flow phantoms have precise volume flow measuring equipment. A flow phantom can thus be used in assessments of the accuracy of flow measuring algorithms on Doppler devices.
4. Velocity accuracy. If the velocity of the fluid within the phantoms can be determined accurately, then this can be used to evaluate velocity displays on Doppler and color flow machines.

★This measurement may be useful for consistency checks, which are an essential part of QA, in attempting to verify that equipment is operating at least as well as when it was delivered or last upgraded. As an absolute measure of Doppler sensitivity, it is controversial, because many factors are involved in the concept of Doppler sensitivity. The reader is referred to reference 14.

5. Color flow penetration (Figure 8-22). System sensitivity settings are at their maximum levels without excessive electronic noise. The maximum depth at which color data can be recorded in the flow phantom is noted. Any changes over time, such as greater than 1 cm, indicate a change in the sensitivity of the instrument.

6. Alignment of color flow image with B-mode image (image congruency test). This test simply checks on whether the color flow image and B-mode image are aligned so that they agree spatially. Color images of vessels should be completely contained within the B-mode image of the vessel. Sometimes bleeding out occurs, and this can be corrected for very easily by equipment service personnel.

SUMMARY

Routine quality assurance tests help document gradual deterioration of instrument performance and provide a more objective means of assessing operating consistency than can be obtained from impressions of image quality on clinical scans.

Tissue-mimicking phantoms provide the capability of testing ultrasound equipment performance under conditions that simulate clinical scanning conditions. These devices mimic tissues in speed of sound propagation, in attenuation characteristics, and somewhat in ultrasound scatter (echogenicity).

The maximum sensitivity of an instrument refers to the weakest echo signal level that can be detected and displayed clearly enough to be discernible above noise. Quality assurance assessments of variations in sensitivity are done by noting changes in the maximum depth of visualization of background echoes in a tissue-mimicking phantom.

When photography controls are adjusted properly, weak echo signals will be visible above the background at the same time that brightness changes produced by variations of large-amplitude echoes are detectable. Geometric tests of scanners include depth calibration (also called *vertical measurement accuracy*) and horizontal measurement accuracy.

A quality control notebook, along with record sheets for documenting the results of tests, should be part of the quality control records for an instrument.

Doppler performance tests are becoming available, with several test objects or phantoms now commercially available. Velocity accuracy, gate alignment, and sensitivity tests are often described for Doppler equipment, while color flow equipment is evaluated using sensitivity tests and color flow image–B-mode image congruency tests.

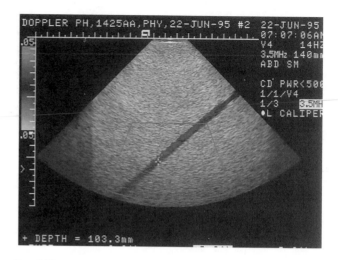

Figure 8-22. Color flow penetration test. The maximum depth of visualization for color signals in this case is 10.3 cm. (See Color Plate that follows p. 178.)

We can expect additional development of Doppler/flow imaging test procedures and devices in coming years.

References

1. *NCRP report 99: quality assurance for diagnostic imaging equipment,* Bethesda, MD, 1988, National Council on Radiation Protection and Measurements.
2. *AIUM quality assurance manual,* Laurel, MD, 1995, American Institute of Ultrasound in Medicine.
3. *AAPM quality assurance manual,* College Park, MD, 1995, American Association of Physicists in Medicine.
4. Carson P, Goodsitt MM: Acceptance testing of pulse-echo ultrasound equipment. In Goldman L, Fowlkes B, editors: *Medical CT and ultrasound: current technology and applications,* Madison, WI, 1995, Advanced Medical Publishers.
5. Madsen E et al: Tissue mimicking material for ultrasound phantoms, *Med Phys* 5:391, 1978.
6. Burlew M et al: A new ultrasound tissue-equivalent material with a high melting point and extended speed of sound range, *Radiology* 134:517, 1980.
7. Maklad N, Ophir J, Balara V: Attenuation of ultrasound in normal and diffuse liver disease in vivo, *Ultrasonic Imaging* 6:117, 1984.
8. Lu ZF, Lee FT, Zagzebski JA: Ultrasonic backscatter and attenuation in diffuse liver disease, Manuscript submitted for publication to *Academic Radiology.*
9. Gray J: Test pattern for video display and hard copy cameras, *Radiology* 154:519, 1985.
10. *AIUM standard methods for measuring performance of ultrasound pulse echo equipment,* Laurel, MD, 1990, American Institute of Ultrasound in Medicine.
11. Carson P, Zagzebski J: *Pulse echo ultrasound imaging systems: performance tests and criteria,* AAPM Report No 8, New York, 1980, American Institute of Physics.
12. Goldstein A: Slice thickness measurements, *J Ultrasound Med* 7:487, 1988.

13. Madsen EL et al: Ultrasound lesion detectability phantoms, *Med Physics* 18:1771, 1991.
14. *Performance criteria and measurements for Doppler ultrasound devices,* Laurel, MD, 1993, American Institute of Ultrasound in Medicine.
15. Hoskins PR, Sheriff SB, Evans JA, editors: *Testing of Doppler ultrasound equipment,* Rep No 70, York, YO1 2WR, UK, 1994, The Institute of Physical Sciences in Medicine.
16. Zagzebski J: Acceptance tests for Doppler ultrasound equipment. In Goldman L, Fowlkes B, editors: *Medical CT and ultrasound: current technology and applications,* Madison, WI, 1995, Advanced Medical Publishers.

Questions for Review

1. Routine tests done to determine that an ultrasound scanner is operating at its expected level of performance are referred to as:

   A. Equipment acceptance tests
   B. General equipment maintenance
   C. Quality assurance
   D. Instrument upgrades

2. Which one of the following statements is true regarding quality assurance tests of ultrasound scanners?

   A. They require expertise of a hospital engineer or physicist.
   B. QA for each scanner takes around 2 hours per week.
   C. Good record keeping is an essential component.
   D. Quantitative results are generally not necessary.

3. In-house QA programs usually involve all of the following except:

   A. Tests using phantoms
   B. Inspection and cleaning of air filters
   C. Records and worksheets showing test results
   D. Voltage measurements at specified test points

4. Material making up the body of a typical QA phantom is "tissuelike" in terms of its _____ properties.

   A. Attenuation and perfusion
   B. Sound speed and attenuation
   C. Sound speed and reflector location
   D. Echogenicity and reflector location

5. The maximum depth of visualization can indicate changes in:

   A. Vertical distance measurement accuracy
   B. Axial and lateral resolution
   C. Slice thickness
   D. Sensitivity

6. Maximum depth of visualization tests are done using:

   A. Minimum receiver gain and maximum transmit power
   B. Maximum receiver gain and minimum transmit power
   C. Maximum receiver gain and maximum transmit power
   D. Minimum receiver gain and minimum transmit power

7. Maximum depth of visualization is often limited by:

   A. Noise at high gain
   B. Poor axial resolution
   C. Too low a power setting
   D. Too low a transducer frequency

8. Suppose that the maximum depth of visualization using a 3.5-MHz transducer is 14.2 cm. On the previous two tests 3 months and 6 months earlier it was 14.4 cm and 14.1 cm, respectively. These variations should be interpreted as:

   A. Just barely tolerable performance
   B. Normal variations inherent in the machine
   C. Excessive variations, indicating the machine requires immediate service
   D. Normal variations inherent in the measurement process

9. A scan is done of a uniform section in a phantom, and a vertical shadow emanates from a position on the image corresponding to the transducer surface. This likely is caused by:

   A. Poor TGC control
   B. Poor lateral gain control
   C. Inadequate gray scale photography
   D. Loss of signal from one or more transducer elements

10. On the viewing monitor of a scanner a sonographer counts 16 shades of gray in the gray bar pattern. The hard copy B-mode image displays only the 13 brightest gray bars. This should be interpreted as:

    A. Normal performance
    B. Too low a receiver gain setting
    C. Inadequate photography and processing that need correction
    D. Poor contrast and brightness settings on the viewing monitor

11. To be used for tests of geometric accuracy, the _____ and _____ in a phantom must be precisely specified.

    A. Echogenicity and reflector location
    B. Sound speed and reflector location
    C. Attenuation and reflector location
    D. Echogenicity and attenuation

12. A measurement comparing the actual separation between two reflectors placed at different positions along the beam axis with the separation indicated on calipers is a test of:

    A. Axial resolution
    B. Ultrasound wavelength
    C. Vertical distance measurement accuracy
    D. Horizontal measurement accuracy

13. Where should the digital caliper cursors be placed for the above measurement?

    A. Top of the higher reflector, bottom of the other
    B. Top of one and top of the other
    C. Left side of one and right side of the other
    D. Bottom of the higher reflector, top of the other

14. If the actual distance between two reflectors in a phantom is 4.0 cm, but the digital caliper readout indicates it is 3.8 cm, the percentage error in the caliper readout is:

    A. less than 1%
    B. 1.5%
    C. 5%
    D. 10%

15. An image of a pointlike reflector results in a short line on the display. Horizontal measurement accuracy is done by placing the calipers to measure the distance between two such reflectors displaced laterally from each other. Where should the caliper-cursors be placed?

    A. From the inside of one to the inside of the other
    B. From the center of one to the center of the other
    C. From the outer margin of one to the center of the other
    D. From the left-most margin of one to the right-most margin of the other

16. For which of the following tests would it be okay if the results varied with the transducer frequency?

    A. Maximum depth of visualization
    B. Axial distance measurement accuracy
    C. Lateral distance measurement accuracy
    D. Scan uniformity

17. A measure of the minimum spacing along the beam axis that still allows two reflectors to be identified is called the:

    A. Lateral resolution
    B. Axial resolution
    C. Axial depth of visualization
    D. Axial distance measurement accuracy

18. The size of the displayed echo from a single, tiny reflector, measured along the direction of beam propagation, is related most closely to the:

    A. Depth measurement accuracy
    B. Axial resolution
    C. Lateral resolution
    D. Monitor distortion

19. Two reflectors are separated along a line perpendicular to the beam axis in the image plane. A measure of the minimum distance between the reflectors that still allows them to be distinguished is called the:

    A. Lateral resolution
    B. Axial resolution
    C. Axial depth of visualization
    D. Axial distance measurement accuracy

20. The width of the ultrasound beam, measured perpendicular to the scanning plane, determines the:

    A. Horizontal distance measurement accuracy
    B. Maximum depth of visualization
    C. Lateral resolution
    D. Slice thickness

21. On the slice thickness phantom the slice width is estimated from the _____ of the image of the scattering plane.

    A. Axial extent
    B. Lateral margins
    C. Brightness
    D. Amount of shadowing

22. Large slice thickness hinders visualization of:

    A. Small, low-contrast spherical masses
    B. Nylon fibers oriented perpendicular to the scan plane
    C. Narrow anechoic tubes oriented perpendicular to the scan plane
    D. Specular reflectors oriented perpendicular to the beam

23. A "string phantom" is useful for measuring:

    A. Maximum depth of Doppler signal detection
    B. Velocity accuracy in spectral Doppler
    C. Axial resolution in B-mode
    D. Vertical distance measurement accuracy

24. A useful feature of a Doppler string test object is:

    A. Its depth from the transducer can be specified precisely
    B. It presents a parabolic velocity profile like blood
    C. Its velocity can be precisely specified
    D. It has the same echogenicity as blood

25. Doppler flow phantoms are useful for determining:

    A. Maximum depth of Doppler signal detection
    B. Vertical distance measurement accuracy
    C. Acoustical output during color flow imaging
    D. Horizontal distance measurement accuracy

26. In order to produce echo signals that are of a similar magnitude as blood in the body, what two factors in a Doppler phantom must be comparable to human tissues?

    A. Phantom material attenuation and mimicking material blood echogenicity
    B. Phantom material density and mimicking material blood attenuation
    C. Mimicking material blood viscosity and attenuation
    D. Mimicking material blood velocity and acceleration

Chapter 9

Bioeffects and Safety Considerations

. . . No confirmed biological effects on patients or instrument operators caused by exposure at intensities typical of present diagnostic ultrasound instruments have ever been reported. Although the possibility exists that such biological effects may be identified in the future, current data indicate that the benefits to patients of the prudent use of diagnostic ultrasound outweigh the risks, if any, that may be present.

AIUM Statement on Clinical Safety[18]

The passage of sound through a medium involves acceleration and displacement of particles in the medium as well as localized forces and stresses. When sound wave transmission is through tissues, the possibilities of biological effects, no matter how remote, come into question. It is well known that ultrasound beams of sufficient intensity, such as those used in therapeutic ultrasound, can modify and even damage biological tissues. On the other hand, the vast experience that has been gained with clinical diagnostic ultrasound equipment has been accompanied by no known tissue damage and with no documented instance of a patient being injured from this diagnostic modality.[1] Thus we are led to believe that diagnostic ultrasound is "safe" or, at least, is accompanied by a low risk of producing biological effects. Unfortunately, insufficient experimental data exist at present to satisfactorily define this risk factor. Research laboratories continue, therefore, to investigate effects of low-level ultrasound on biological tissues.

In this chapter important acoustical exposure quantities for diagnostic instruments are outlined briefly, with discussion of the methods used to measure these parameters. New exposure indices that relate acoustical output levels to mechanisms for biological effects are described. The topic of ultrasound bioeffects also is considered, especially as it relates to the operation of clinical ultrasound scanning equipment.

ACOUSTICAL POWER, ACOUSTICAL INTENSITY, ACOUSTICAL PRESSURE

Acoustical power

An ultrasound source transmits energy into the medium with which it is in contact. To quantify the amount of acoustical energy transmitted and describe how this energy is distributed, physicists and engineers measure the acoustical power and the acoustical intensity in the beam. Other wave variables, such as the acoustical pressure amplitude, also are specified to more completely characterize the strength of the sound waves.

Power is the rate at which energy is transmitted from the transducer into the medium. Appropriate units for power are watts (W) or milliwatts (mW). (Notice that these are the same units used to specify the rate of energy consumption by electrical appliances, for example.) The acoustical power emitted by a diagnostic ultrasound transducer is typically on the order of 10 mW. Slightly lower powers are found with some M-mode applications. Higher power levels are seen with color flow imaging (Table 9-1).

Acoustical Intensity

Simply specifying the power results in a very incomplete description of the acoustical exposure situation, because

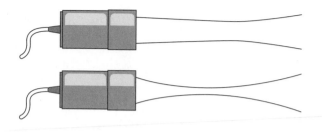

Figure 9-1. Two cases where the distribution of acoustical energy within the beam is different. For the same acoustical power, the two beams might produce very different biological effects because of focusing. Intensity is a parameter that distinguishes the two cases.

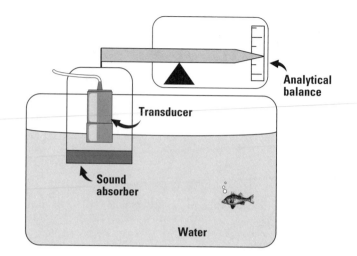

Figure 9-2. Measurement of the acoustical power for an ultrasound scanner. The apparatus measures the radiation force when the ultrasound beam is absorbed by a target. Because the force is very small, sensitive analytical balances are used.

the distribution of this ultrasonic energy in space also needs to be taken into account. For example, suppose the acoustical power for each of the two transducers shown in Figure 9-1 is the same. Our intuition tells us that the two cases shown could result in substantially different effects. In one case the ultrasonic energy is distributed over a fairly broad region, whereas in the other it is concentrated through focusing. Variations in the spatial distribution of the ultrasonic power are described by specifying the intensity at different points in a beam. Intensity is the ultrasonic power per unit area, given in watts per square meter (W/m²), or more commonly, milliwatts per square centimeter (mW/cm²).

Pressure amplitude

Sometimes it is useful to know the pressure amplitude in the acoustical field, either the peak positive pressure (peak compressional pressure) or the peak negative (rarefactional) pressure. Such discussions are relevant when assessing the risk of producing **cavitation,** discussed more fully later in this chapter.

Measurements of power

Radiation force balance. Practical measurements of the very low ultrasonic power levels produced by diagnostic instruments can be carried out by measuring the radiation force, a small steady force that is produced when a sound beam strikes a reflecting or an absorbing interface. It may be measured by a laboratory force balance (Figure 9-2). With a setup like that shown in Figure 9-2 the balance is "zeroed" with the ultrasound beam off. The beam is then turned on and a reading from the balance is taken. The force, indicated by the reading of the balance, is proportional to the acoustical power. To get an idea of the levels involved, if the acoustical power is 8 mW and the interface absorbs all of the incident ultrasound beam, the resultant force is approximately equal to the weight of a stationary drop of water 1 mm in diameter. Although of

very low magnitude, the force can be measured by using sensitive analytical balances. The ultrasonic power is directly related to the radiation force through a simple conversion factor.

Power by summing spot measurements across the beam. Another way acoustical power is measured for diagnostic beams is by determining the amount of power passing through spots throughout the beam and adding these together to get the total power in the beam. A device called a **hydrophone**, described below and in Figure 9-3, may be used to measure the acoustical pressure and then calculate the time average intensity at various points. Imagine the total beam area being divided into small increments of area, like squares on a miniature checkerboard, and the intensity determined within each square. If the time average intensity (in mW/cm²) passing through each increment (each square on the checkerboard) is multiplied by the area (in cm²) of the increment, we arrive at the power (in mW) passing through that increment. By summing up the power for all area increments in the beam, the total power is estimated.

Measurements of pressure amplitude

Hydrophones. The shape of the ultrasound beam and the acoustical pressure distributions within the beam are measured by a miniature hydrophone (Figure 9-3). A hydrophone is simply a small-diameter probe with a tiny piezoelectric element, usually about 0.5 mm in diameter, at one end. When placed in an ultrasound beam, the hydrophone produces an electrical signal whose amplitude is proportional to the acoustical pressure amplitude.

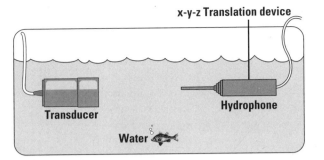

x-y-z Translation device

Transducer

Hydrophone

Water

Figure 9-3. Hydrophone positioned in water and located at the focal region of the transducer.

If this signal is squared, the resultant signal is proportional to the instantaneous intensity at the position of the hydrophone face. (Equation 1-5 in Chapter 1 helps here!) Thus the hydrophone may be used by engineers to measure the pressure signal at any spot in the beam. The acoustical pressure itself is an important ultrasound exposure quantity. Pressure also may be used to derive intensity quantities, as we shall see in the next section.

Hydrophones are *calibrated* by measuring their response in an acoustical beam whose pressure amplitude and intensity are known. When this is done, the hydrophone will measure the absolute acoustical pressure and allow determinations of absolute intensity at points in a sound beam.

Scanning tank. When ultrasound equipment manufacturers determine the acoustical output levels of their scanners, they use a measurement system such as illustrated in Figure 9-3. The ultrasound beam from the transducer is transmitted into water. A hydrophone is attached to a positioning device, which moves it about in the ultrasound beam. The hydrophone signal is recorded for various positions in the beam.

The pressure signal. If the hydrophone is placed at the spot where the maximum signal is found, it provides a measure of the maximum acoustical pressure. The signal is illustrated schematically in Figure 9-4, *A*. The pressure waveform in this figure corresponds to the signal detected when a hydrophone is positioned in the beam of a pulsed transducer. This waveform is a brief, steadily repeating signal. Reviewing concepts discussed previously, the number of signals produced in a second is the pulse repetition frequency (PRF). The interval from the beginning of one pulse to the beginning of the next is called the *pulse repetition period, PP*. The peak positive (or peak compressional) as well as the peak negative (or peak rarefactional) acoustical pressures are indicated in the waveform in Figure 9-4*A*. As mentioned in Chapter 1, pressure is given in pascals (Pa) or megapascals (MPa).

Specifying the acoustical intensity

Temporal peaks and temporal averages. Recall also from Chapter 1, the intensity at a point in the beam is proportional to the square of the pressure. Intensity is complicated because it varies over time. Occasionally we use temporal peak values of this quantity; more commonly, intensity is averaged over some period. Different parameters can be seen, depending on the time over which the averaging is done. For example, intensity might be averaged over a single half cycle in the wave (I-max), over the pulse duration (called the *pulse average intensity*), or over the time from one pulse to the next (called the *time average intensity*). These ideas are outlined in the next paragraphs.

The "intensity" waveform in Figure 9-4, *B* illustrates the instantaneous intensity, obtained by squaring the hydrophone signal and applying the appropriate calibration factor. For most of the time, the instantaneous intensity is zero because of the low duty factor in pulsed ultrasound. However, the instantaneous intensity is very high during the time of the ultrasound pulse.

The temporal peak intensity, I(TP), is shown in the diagram in Figure 9-4, *B*. Sometimes a quantity called *I-max* is reported. This is the maximum value that is obtained when the intensity is averaged over half-cycles. I-max is also shown in the diagram.

The *pulse average intensity*, I(PA), is the average intensity during the time of the acoustical pulse. This is shown by the second trace in Figure 9-4, *B*. The pulse average intensity is a little lower than the temporal peak and I-max, but still is representative of the high instantaneous intensity during the time of passage of the ultrasound pulse.

The lowest intensity value that is used is the *time average intensity*, I(TA). This quantity is found by averaging over the entire time the transducer is producing pulses, including the time between pulses. For a stationary beam the time average intensity is equal to the pulse average intensity multiplied by the duty factor:

$$I(TA) = I(PA) \times DF \qquad (9\text{-}1)$$

where DF is the duty factor.

From Table 3-2 in Chapter 3, typical duty factors are less than 1% for ultrasound machines. Therefore the time average intensity is always very small compared to the pulse average intensity. In fact, the intensity during the very brief time of the acoustical pulse, the pulse average intensity, I(PA), may exceed the time average intensity by a factor of 1000 or more!

What do you need to know about beam intensities? One important point is that in pulsed ultrasound the intensity measured during the pulse itself usually is quite high! The most important quantities describing the intensity during the pulse are the pulse average intensity and I-max. A second important point is that the temporal aver-

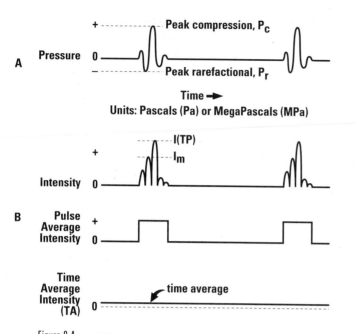

A, Pressure — Peak compression, P_c; Peak rarefactional, P_r; Time →; Units: Pascals (Pa) or MegaPascals (MPa)

B, Intensity — I(TP), I_m; Pulse Average Intensity; Time Average Intensity (TA) — time average

Figure 9-4 **A,** Waveforms measured using a hydrophone positioned in the focal region of the transducer. The peak rarefactional and peak compressional pressures are shown. **B,** Derived intensity values from the hydrophone pressure signal. The instantaneous intensity waveform is found by applying Equation 1-5, i.e., squaring the hydrophone pressure signal. I_m or I-max, is the intensity during the maximum 1/2 cycle in the waveform. The pulse average intensity is the average intensity during the time of the pulse itself. The time average intensity is found by averaging the intensity waveform over the time from the beginning of one pulse to the beginning of the next.

age intensity, I(TA), is much lower than the pulse average intensity because of the low duty factors in pulsed ultrasound.

Spatial peaks and spatial averages. Another reason the intensity is a complicated quantity is that it varies from point to point within the ultrasound beam. To avoid the need to describe the complete beam point by point, acceptable parameterization schemes for sound fields have been defined.

For diagnostic instruments the spatial average (SA) intensity is used occasionally; more commonly, the spatial peak (SP) intensity quantities are specified.

Putting the intensity designators together. So far, spatial and temporal aspects of the sound beam intensity have been considered separately. In fact, both designations must be provided *simultaneously* to indicate which measure of intensity is being referred to. Intensity values commonly measured for diagnostic instruments are as follows:

I(SATA): Spatial average–time average intensity; often it is specified at the transducer surface or at the surface of

a transducer assembly where the sound beam enters the patient.

I(SPTA): Spatial peak–time average intensity.

I(SPPA): Spatial peak–pulse average intensity.

I-max: Average intensity during the half cycle that gives the largest value. It is usually at the location in the beam where it is highest, that is, at the (SP) point.

I(SPTP): Spatial peak–temporal peak intensity.

The ranking from top to bottom is the same as ranking these intensities from low to high. Not all designators listed are relevant to every acoustical exposure situation. See, for example, the acoustical output parameters listed in Table 9-1.

There is a useful relationship between one of the parameters, I(SATA), and the acoustical power. The spatial average–time average intensity, I(SATA), is equal to the acoustical power, *W,* contained within the beam, divided by the beam area, *A:*

$$I(SATA) = \frac{W}{A} \tag{9-2}$$

Example: If the ultrasonic power emitted by a 2-cm diameter transducer is 10 mW, what is I(SATA) at the transducer surface?

Solution: The intensity averaged over the area of the sound beam at the transducer surface is equal to the acoustical power divided by the beam area. Very close to the transducer surface, take the beam area, *A,* as being equal to the area of the transducer.

$$A = \pi r^2$$

where *r* is the transducer radius and π is 3.14. Thus

$$A = 3.14 \times (1 \text{ cm})^2 = 3.14 \text{ cm}^2$$

Solving for the spatial average–time average intensity gives

$$I(SATA) = \frac{W}{A} = \frac{10 \text{mW}}{3.14 \text{ cm}^2} = 3 \text{mW/cm}^2$$

For this example, the spatial average–time average intensity is approximately equal to 3 mW/cm² at the transducer surface.

Acoustical output levels for scanners

Sources of information. Where can the acoustical output values for scanners be found? In the United States, all scanners must have certain acoustical output parameters listed in the *operator's manual* in a convenient location and in an easy-to-read format. Values are presented in tabular form for each transducer supplied with the instrument (Figure 9-5).

Example for a state-of-the art scanner. Typical values for the acoustical power and intensities measured for one type of diagnostic ultrasound instrument are presented in Table 9-1. The example is for a curved array scanner.[2] The system operates in four different modes—scan mode, M-mode, pulsed Doppler mode, and color flow imaging. Values are presented for each mode.

A number of observations are made for these data:

1. Many, though not all, acoustical output quantities are highly dependent on the operating mode. The most significant variations from one operating mode to another occur for the total acoustical power and the spatial peak–time average intensity.

2. Acoustical power is a measure of the rate at which the transducer delivers ultrasonic energy to the tissue. The lowest acoustical power in this example occurs for M-mode. Typically, this is because the PRF is only about 500/s for M-mode. The highest acoustical power is seen for color flow imaging.

3. Even though the acoustical power is much less for M-mode than for B-mode imaging, the time average intensity, I(SPTA), is actually greater in M-mode. This is because the beam is stationary in M-mode, always directed toward the measurement point, whereas it is always scanning in B-scan mode. Therefore we see that time average intensities measured at a point in the beam depend on whether the beam is stationary or whether it is scanning.

4. An operating mode in which the spatial peak–time average intensity, I(SPTA), is very high is pulsed Doppler (see Table 9-1). This is typical for Doppler systems intended mainly for vascular imaging. Pulsed Doppler involves a stationary ultrasound beam concentrating most if not all of its energy along the Doppler beam line. Also, the duty factor is often higher in this mode than in other modes, especially when high PRFs are used to record high Doppler-frequency signals. Consequently the time average intensity at the focal point of the beam may be very high in Doppler applications.

5. In all cases the pulse average intensity, I(SPPA), is much larger than the time average values in every mode. The units used in the table for pulse average intensity are W/cm^2, while those for time average intensities are mW/cm^2. Typically we see pulse average intensities that are more than 1000 times greater than time average intensities. The only exception noted in Table 9-1 is for pulsed Doppler mode, where we see only a factor of about 200 increase.

6. Although time average intensities are quite variable from one mode to the next, the pulse average intensities do not change too drastically among operating modes. Peak pressure values also seem comparable among the operating modes for this transducer and scanning system.

For any operating mode there is a large variation of output powers and intensities produced by different types of instruments, either different transducer assemblies from a given manufacturer or instruments from different manufacturers.[2,3] The values quoted in Table 9-1, therefore, only give an indication of the levels involved and the differences that might be encountered for different operating modes. Instruments are available whose powers and intensities are much lower than the values given in the table; some units are available that produce even greater intensities than those shown. (See further discussion of this topic in Appendix A.) As mentioned earlier, data for your own equipment should be available in the operator's manual.

Derated quantities. The acoustical output parameters are measured in water. They represent worst case situations because they are obtained with control settings, such as output power, adjusted for their maximum values.

One useful adjustment is to form "derated" intensity values taken from the water values. Derated quantities are obtained by a calculation, simply by mathematically applying a uniform attenuation rate to the water values. The intent is to estimate what the values would be in a tissuelike medium, where higher attenuation is present

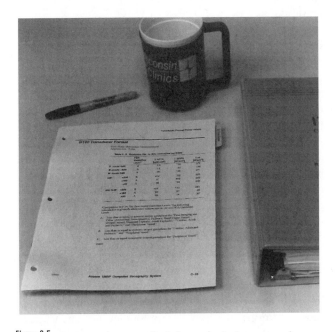

Figure 9-5. Sonographers can find the acoustical output values for their scanners in the operator's manual.

Table 9-1 Typical acoustical output values for ultrasound scanners

Operating mode	Pr	I(SPTA)	I(SPPA)	Power
B-Scan imaging	1.68 MPa	18.7 mW/cm^2	174 W/cm^2	18 mW
M-mode	1.68 MPa	73 mW/cm^2	174 W/cm^2	3.9 mW
Pulsed doppler	2.48 MPa	1140 mW/cm^2	288 W/cm^2	30.7 mW
Color flow	2.59 MPa	234 mW/cm2	325 W/cm2	80.5 mW

Acoustical output levels from diagnostic ultrasound equipment, American Institute of Ultrasound in Medicine, 14750 Sweitzer Lane, Suite 100, Laurel, MD, 20707-5906, 1992. (Primarily a compilation of data, but accompanied by some explanations of the data).

than in water. An ultrasound attenuation coefficient of 0.3 dB/cm-MHz is usually assumed. This is a very simple and basic model, and probably does not apply to most actual ultrasound exposures to people. However, it is useful because it allows for at least some estimate of the effects of attenuation of higher frequencies on acoustical output quantities.

REAL-TIME ACOUSTICAL OUTPUT LABELING

Higher power levels allow echoes from more weakly reflecting interfaces to be detected. With many scanners, ultrasonographers routinely adjust the transmit power during the course of an examination, trying to get maximum beam penetration. Until recently there have been no widely accepted methods for presenting the output levels to the operator. Depending on the manufacturer, the relative transmit level might be labeled as a percent (percent of what?), in dB (dB with respect to what?) or in a qualitative fashion as "low," "medium," or "high" (which also conveys very little meaning).

A consortium of professional and manufacturer's organizations, government bodies, and consumer groups developed a standard in 1992 that addresses this problem.[4] The standard calls for real-time labeling of two quantities related to acoustical output levels. The quantities are called a *Thermal Index, TI,* and a *Mechanical Index, MI.* The labeled quantities were carefully selected for their relevance to risks from biological effects. (See discussion on mechanisms later in this chapter.) One possibility for implementing the standard is shown in Figure 9-6, where the quantities appear on the display screen of the scanner.

Thermal index

Definition and relevance. One biologically relevant ultrasound exposure quantity is related to the possibility of tissue heating as ultrasound energy is absorbed by tissue. The standard defines and specifies a quantity called a **thermal**

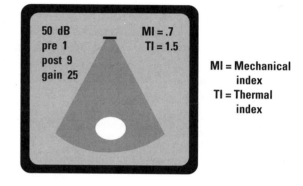

Figure 9-6. New acoustical output labeling, designating the mechanical index, MI, and the thermal index, TI. These parameters are computed internally in the scanner following standardized algorithms. The sonographer is in a better position to minimize acoustical exposures and practice the principle of ALARA given the presentation of these parameters than when arbitrary parameters, not tied to a bioeffect mechanism are provided.

index, TI. This is the ratio of the acoustical power produced by the transducer to the power required to raise the temperature in tissue 1 degree C. The TI is estimated by algorithms in the scanner, taking into account the acoustical power, the ultrasound frequency, and the beam area, making assumptions about the attenuation and absorption properties of the tissue and tissue's thermal properties, and assuming fairly long exposure times. A TI value of one means that under tissue conditions assumed in the algorithm, the output level is high enough that up to a 1-degree elevation in temperature could occur when the transducer assembly is held stationary. A TI of 5 means a 5-degree elevation is possible, etc.

Now this does not mean that if you see "TI=5" on the scanner screen, the temperature in the patient will immediately rise 5 degrees at some point in the ultrasound beam! The algorithm has to assume some worst-case conditions, such as a certain low level of beam attenuation and a stationary beam, in coming up with the TI value. The assumed conditions may or may not apply closely to the exposure condition you are encountering. Actual temperatures depend on the type of tissue in the beam, amount of perfusion, and exposure time, and at present it is impossible for a scanner to "know" all the relevant quantities. What the thermal index does for the sonographer is provide a rational means for implementing the principle of ALARA ("as low as reasonably achievable") during scanning. Obviously, equipment operators will want to scan using a minimum TI value consistent with obtaining useful clinical information.

TIS, TIB, TIC. There are several TI quantities that you might see on machines that implement this type of acoustical output reporting. TIS (S for soft tissue) assumes the tissue path is soft tissue. It is probably the thermal index quantity yo⸱ ⸱ill see most often on scanner console screens. A ⸱ ⸱ quantity, TIB (B for bone), applies if bone is a⸱ ⸱ne focus of the transducer and a non-scanning ⸱⸱g mode, such as pulsed Doppler, is selected b⸱ ⸱ ⸱as much greater acoustical absorption than soft tiss⸱ ⸱ if it is present in the scanned field, this can result i⸱ ⸱ n higher TI values. TIB is most appropriate whe⸱ ⸱ ⸱an includes fetal bone during a second- or third-trimester pregnancy. If the scanner "knows" that a second- or third-trimester pregnancy scan is being done, for example, if this choice of exam is selected by the operator from an application menu, then TIB is reported on the screen. Finally, TIC is a cranial bone thermal index. It applies if bone is at or near the skin surface, such as during a cranial examination. Regardless of which quantity is reported on the screen, the sonographer can apply the ALARA principle knowing the TI value.

Mechanical index

What is it? The second index quantity is called a **mechanical index,** which is related to the likelihood of cavitation produced with this energy. *Cavitation* refers to activity of tiny gas bubbles in the tissue in the presence of ultrasound waves (see next section). The MI value is computed from the peak rarefactional pressure and the frequency, using relations between these parameters and cavitation thresholds established by researchers.[3,5] In other words, MI is directly proportional to P_r, the peak rarefactional pressure in the medium, and inversely proportional to F, the square root of the ultrasound frequency (in MHz). Manufacturers assume the attenuation in the medium is 0.3 dB/cm-MHz in doing the calculation.

Because MI is proportional to P_r, if P_r doubles, MI doubles; if it halves, MI halves. As you increase the output setting on a scanner, usually the amplitude of the transmit pulse, hence the P_r value, increases, increasing the MI value.

The dependence on frequency is a little more subtle. MI is inversely proportional to the square root of the frequency, so as frequency increases, MI actually decreases (assuming the pressure amplitude stays the same). Because of the square root dependence, the frequency has to quadruple (e.g., increase from 2 MHz to 8 MHz) for the MI to halve.

Similar to the manner in which the thermal index should be regarded, sonographers will want to adopt the ALARA principle, to scan using a minimum MI value consistent with obtaining useful clinical information.

Advantages of the indices

The advantages provided by this new approach are numerous. Among these are the following:

1. Standardization of output specification information between manufacturers. For those scanners labeled according to the standard, the same algorithms are used to compute the MI and TI values.
2. Presentation of output quantities that are relevant from the standpoint of potential bioeffects from ultrasound. As pointed out in the next section, we generally are concerned with the possibility of tissue heating by the ultrasound beam and of mechanical effects of the pressure wave (mainly cavitation). It is nearly impossible for clinical users to ascertain risk factors from the older, established ultrasound field quantities, such as I(SPTA). A given value for the spatial peak–time average intensity, for example, could lead to a noticeable temperature elevation, to a negligible elevation, or any value in between, depending on other exposure parameters, such as beam area and frequency. With the TI quantity, these factors have already been taken into account. A similar statement is applicable for the mechanical index and temporal peak acoustical beam parameters, such as peak pressure.
3. Information is available for users to implement ALARA.

Do the indices ever underestimate the temperature or MI?

The MI and TI values are meant to represent worst-case situations as far as thermal effects are concerned. The calculations are explicitly conservative in this regard. For example, a reasonably low average ultrasound attenuation (0.3 dB/cm-MHz) is assumed in computing the intensity of the ultrasound beam at points in the insonified medium.

One situation where the indices could underestimate the exposure situation, however, is where a large fraction of the path between the transducer and insonified region contains fluid, such as through the bladder and/or through large amounts of amniotic fluid. For example, if a maternal body wall is very thin, and if the fetus is located a fairly long distance from the transducer and bone is insonified, the TI value can underestimate the actual temperature increase.

When the TI (or the MI) value is available, the sonographer should always consider what the actual tissue path is. If a large fraction of the path consists of attenuating soft tissue, it may not be unreasonable to use high TI and MI settings because much of the ultrasound beam is being attenuated. On the other hand, for a tissue path consisting of mostly fluid between the transducer and sensitive tissue the TI (and MI) values can underestimate the actual indices. Luckily these circumstances usually allow for lower transmit power settings on the scanner because of the low attenuation. The minimal power levels consistent with obtaining useful diagnostic information should always be used in an ultrasound examination.

MECHANISMS FOR PRODUCTION OF BIOLOGICAL EFFECTS

At sufficiently high intensities and long enough exposure times, ultrasound is capable of producing a measurable effect on tissues. The effect may be a small temperature elevation or complete destruction of tissue depending on the acoustical exposure. We shall consider briefly some of the modes whereby a sound beam can produce a biological effect. These have been documented *mainly* for acoustical exposure conditions that exceed those of diagnostic ultrasound.

Heating

As a sound beam propagates through tissue, it undergoes attenuation. A significant fraction of this attenuation is due to absorption or, essentially, conversion of the ultrasonic energy into heat. For very low ultrasonic power levels, any heat that is deposited by the sound beam is quickly dissipated. Therefore no measurable temperature increase occurs. On the other hand, ultrasound therapy devices producing beams with areas of several square centimeters and higher and operating at spatial average–time average intensities of 1000 mW/cm^2 or greater can cause significant temperature elevations in tissue. In fact, deep heating is one of the beneficial effects of this mode of therapy.[6]

Some concern is warranted with diagnostic ultrasound when certain operating modes are applied. In particular, pulsed Doppler equipment and color flow imaging equipment may have fairly high power levels and time average intensities, or may result in large values for the thermal index. The sonographer should keep in mind the TI value displayed on the instrument, particularly when this quantity exceeds one.

Mechanical effects: cavitation

Intense ultrasound beams in a fluid can generate tiny bubbles from dissolved gases in the fluid. This process, along with any associated gas bubble activity, is called *cavitation*.[5,6] In the presence of the sound beam the bubbles can grow in size and produce an effect on the medium. The cavitation bubbles expand and contract synchronously with pressure oscillations in the sound field. This, in turn, causes particle displacements and stresses in excess of those resulting from the sound beam alone. Some experimentally induced biological effects have been attributed to this cavitation process.

Two types of cavitation may exist.[6] **Stable cavitation** refers to the creation of bubbles that oscillate with the sound beam, as mentioned. In contrast, **transient** (also called inertial) **cavitation** is a process in which the oscillations grow so strong that the bubbles collapse, producing very intense, localized effects (Figure 9-7).

It may be possible to produce cavitation with some clinical instruments if the conditions in the medium are favorable; in fact, cavitation is believed to be responsible for some in vitro biological effects involving single-cell suspensions exposed to diagnostic ultrasound.[8] Cavitation also is believed to be responsible for damage to lungs of experimental animals exposed to 4-mHz pulsed Doppler and color Doppler beams.[9,10] A key ingredient to these latter exposures is the presence of preexisting gas bodies in the form of alveoli. Whether either form of cavitation is responsible for damage to tissues without gas bodies, exposed in vivo to diagnostic ultrasound beams, has not been demonstrated.

Thresholds for cavitation are believed to be closely related to the acoustical pressure amplitudes in the medium. Therefore instrument manufacturers measure and report peak rarefactional and peak compressional pressures in the field of their instruments. The newly

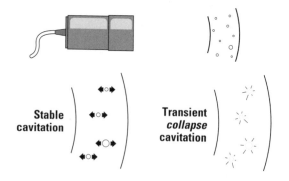

Figure 9-7. Cavitation mechanism. Cavitation is activity associated with tiny bubbles in the sound field. Two types of cavitation exist: stable and transient (or inertial). During stable cavitation, the bubbles grow and oscillate in the field. During transient (inertial) cavitation the bubbles collapse, with potential for localized damage.

adopted mechanical index is intended to provide information more clearly to the operator on potential for cavitation.

Noncavitation mechanical effects

Sound transmission is associated with displacements, accelerations, and stresses on particles in the medium. Thus it is possible that the perturbations caused by passage of sound waves will lead directly to bioeffects. Biological effects have been produced in some experimental studies on plants and cells in which no temperature rise could have occurred and cavitation was known to be absent. When these two mechanisms are ruled out as the cause of a biological effect accompanying exposure to ultrasound, direct mechanical effects of the ultrasound beam are usually thought to have occurred.

IS THERE A RISK?

Nearly every clinical study and therapeutic action involves some calculated risk to patients. In many of these cases the level of risk is well known. In making a decision to do a procedure on a patient, clinicians must weigh the risk against the expected benefit.

For diagnostic ultrasound we must presume that there is some element of risk to ultrasound exposure, no matter how low it may be. What researchers are attempting to obtain, and will probably be seeking for a long time, are data that will enable them to better quantify the risk level for different ultrasound exposure conditions. Out of perhaps hundreds of thousands of individuals already insonified during diagnostic ultrasound examinations, no known ill effects have been suffered from these exposures. This information, though certainly very comforting, also indicates that the task of determining a risk factor for diagnostic ultrasound is a difficult one.

Where does information on ultrasound bioeffects come from to help determine risk factors? We can identify at least three important sources: epidemiology; studies using in vitro exposure systems; and animal studies.

Epidemiology

A number of different approaches are being followed in these investigations. Epidemiological studies[11] are aimed at determining whether previous diagnostic ultrasound examinations of fetuses (in utero) may have resulted in any ill effects. Such investigations involve comparisons of medical records and present physical condition of groups of individuals insonified in utero and presumably identical groups of individuals who were not insonified. The idea is to attempt to determine whether factors such as abnormal size and weight, prevalence toward illness, and

others are more evident in the group that was exposed. The work is time consuming, because to obtain valid results investigators must study large numbers of patients.

Some epidemiology studies have suggested that there are differences between individuals exposed to ultrasound and those not exposed, reporting an increased incidence of low birth weight babies in the exposed group.[11] However, others analyzing the same data did not agree with this finding. Some professional organizations, with panels of experts in the biological effects field, provide guidance to help interpret these apparently conflicting reports. For example, the American Institute of Ultrasound in Medicine[12] evaluated epidemiological studies and concluded in 1987:

1. Widespread clinical use over 25 years has not established any adverse effect arising from exposure to diagnostic ultrasound.
2. Randomized clinical studies are the most rigorous method for assessing potential adverse effects of diagnostic ultrasound. Studies using this methodology show no evidence of an effect on birthweight in humans.
3. Other epidemiologic studies have shown no causal association of diagnostic ultrasound with any of the adverse fetal outcomes studies.

The Institute cautioned that the acoustical exposure levels in the studies referred to in (2) and (3) may not be representative of the full range of fetal exposures for current equipment. Nevertheless, the bottom line is these experts conclude that epidemiology studies have not shown adverse effects, including no evidence of low birth weights, from diagnostic ultrasound.

In vitro cell studies

In addition to epidemiological investigations, numerous studies have been and continue to be performed on animals in vivo and on mammalian cells in vitro. Excellent reviews of the recent literature on bioeffects[13] have been published.

In vitro studies generally expose macromolecules, membranous transport systems, cells, or clumps of cells suspended in liquid (Figure 9-8). Although the exposure conditions are quite different from conditions that any cells would be exposed to in vivo, the experiments do provide useful information. Their purpose is to investigate mechanisms for damage and to establish damage thresholds.

Although many negative studies have been reported, that is, no biological effects, even at intensities exceeding those produced by most diagnostic scanners, many positive results from these kinds of exposures also have been reported. For example, Liebeskind et al.[8] used a diagnostic instrument and found that ultrasound appeared to cause detectable effects on DNA and growth patterns of

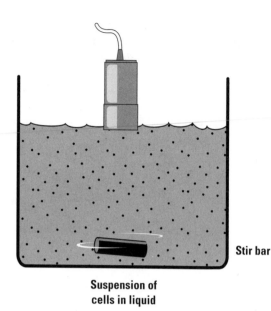

**Suspension of
cells in liquid**

Stir bar

Figure 9-8. Exposure arrangement for in vitro experiment on cells.

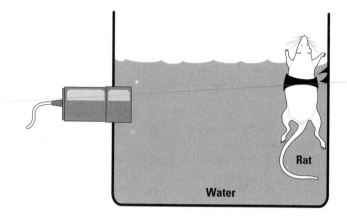

Rat

Water

Figure 9-9. Typical exposure arrangement to study effects of ultrasound on animals and animal models.

animal cells in vitro. Other research has reported sister chromatid breaks when cells were exposed to ultrasound in vitro.[14] Unfortunately, the results are very controversial, and it often happens that researchers in other laboratories are not able to reproduce the effects noted, particularly at the ultrasound exposure levels.[15,16] Therefore it appears that some effects of ultrasound on cells exposed in vitro have been detected but the meaning of these experimental findings is difficult to judge.

How should such studies be interpreted? Again, the American Institute of Ultrasound in Medicine experts provide guidance here.[12] Paraphrasing their in vitro bioeffects statement:

1. Although the interactions and mechanism may not be the same as in vivo situations, an in vitro effect must be regarded as a real effect of the ultrasound.
2. In vitro studies provide the capability to control experimental variables. This enables researchers to explore and evaluate mechanisms for damage.
3. Reports of in vitro studies that claim direct clinical significance should be viewed with caution.

Animal studies

Exposures that are higher than diagnostic levels. Definitive evidence for biological effects has been obtained in investigations in which small animals were insonified (Figure 9-9). Most, although not all, of these studies were done at spatial peak–time average intensities and exposure times

that exceed values for diagnostic equipment.[13] At high time average intensity levels fetal weight reductions in rats, death of rat fetuses, and altered mitotic rates were observed. For these effects to be produced, it was usually necessary to expose the animal to some minimal time average intensity for a given time. If the intensity was reduced, the exposure time had to be increased to compensate for the reduced acoustical energy.

This last statement is illustrated in Figure 9-10 for mammalian tissues exposed to high-intensity ultrasound. Curves such as the one shown have been produced by researchers in an attempt to place the vast amount of experimental data on bioeffects research into perspective. The line divides the data into a region where exposure conditions were sufficient to produce the effect investigated, such as fetal weight reduction (above the line), and a region where the effect being studied could not be found (below the line). In some experiments with high spatial peak intensities, only a brief exposure resulted in an effect. To produce the same effect at a lower intensity level, it was necessary to expose the animal for a longer time. For spatial peak–time average intensities greater than 100 mW/cm² the demarcation line follows a curve in which the product of the intensity, I, and the exposure time, T, is given by

$$I \times T = 50(\text{w/cm}^2)\text{s} = 50 \text{ joules/cm}^2$$

(A **joule** is a unit of energy; it is the product when watts are multiplied by seconds.)

Below 100 mW/cm² these data indicate that none of the effects for which the researchers were looking could be produced—no matter how long the exposure.

Most experiments leading to a 100 mW/cm² demarcation line at long exposure times were done by using large beams from unfocused transducers, and researchers

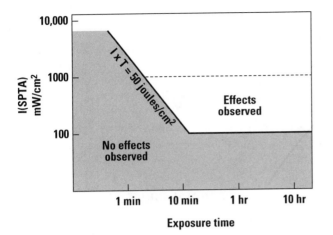

Figure 9-10. Intensity versus time curve relevant to production of biological effects in mammalian tissue. Exposure conditions that resulted in positive biological effects are separated from conditions for which no effects were observed for animal studies. (Date from *Bioeffects and safety of diagnostic ultrasound,* American Institute of Ultrasound in Medicine Bioeffects Committee, American Institute of Ultrasound in Medicine, 14750 Sweitzer Lane, Suite 100, Laurel, MD, 20707-5906, 1992.)

believe the bioeffects were due to heating of tissue. However, for focused transducers (the ones used in nearly all diagnostic procedures) greater time average intensities are tolerated because any heat deposited over a small focal area is dissipated easily to the surrounding, unexposed tissue. This has been shown both by thermal computational models and by experimental evidence.[3] Taking this into account and considering additional experimental results, the AIUM has extended the observations, claiming that intensities as high as 1 W/cm^2 have led to no observed effects in mammalian tissues exposed to highly focused sound beams.[3] The line 1 W/cm^2 is drawn also in Figure 9-10. Although all diagnostic beams are not as highly focused as those considered by the AIUM, it is comforting to know that time average intensities higher than 100 mW/cm^2 may be okay in some instances.

Positive bioeffects at diagnostic exposure levels. Most of the time when animals have been exposed to diagnostic ultrasound beams, no biological effects have been observed. The exception to this is when the exposure field includes the lung.[9,10,17] Mouse lung hemorrhage[17] and lesions on the surface of rat lungs[10] occurred recently when diagnostic beams were used to insonify animals in these studies. Hemorrhagic lesions in lungs of monkeys were also observed when this tissue was exposed to pulsed Doppler beams.[17] The biological effect was believed to be related to the presence of gas pockets in the alveoli. Cavitation effects are hypothesized to be the cause, although the study of Holland et al.[9] could not confirm that cavitation was definitely present.

Nevertheless, when gas bodies are present in the ultrasound beam, it appears that diagnostic ultrasound pulses, at least those at high levels and applied for fairly long exposure times, can cause an effect.

The lung usually is avoided with diagnostic ultrasound beams, for obvious reasons (NO PENETRATION). Therefore the clinical significance of these findings and the significance of the noted effects themselves are not completely clear. The bottom line is, ultrasound provides significant diagnostic information when applied to the body for medical purposes. However, this modality does apply energy to the patient being scanned, and users need to be aware of potential for adverse effects! They need to know how to acquire diagnostic ultrasound information from patients, while at the same time minimizing risks.

American Institute of Ultrasound in Medicine Statement on NonHuman Mammalian In Vivo Biological Effects, Approved October, 1992

To help clarify the vast amount of data on acoustical exposures, the AIUM Bioeffects Committee developed and the AIUM has approved statements summarizing these exposures. Unfortunately, the statements have become increasingly complex over the years; this primarily reflects the increasing amount of experimental evidence being obtained. Here is the statement:

Information from experiments utilizing laboratory mammals has contributed significantly to our understanding of ultrasonically induced biological effects and the mechanisms relative to specific ultrasound parameters and indices. . . .

In the low megahertz frequency range there have been no independently confirmed adverse biological effects in nonhuman mammalian tissues exposed in vivo under experimental ultrasound conditions, as follows.

a) When a thermal mechanism is involved, these conditions are unfocused beam SPTA intensities below 100 mW/cm^2, focused beam SPTA intensities below 1 W/cm^2, or thermal index values less than 2.

Furthermore, such effects have not been reported for higher values of thermal index when it is less than

$$6 - \frac{\log_{10} t}{0.6}$$

where t is the exposure duration (in minutes, ranging from 1-250).

b) When a nonthermal mechanism is involved, in tissues that contain well-defined gas bodies, these conditions are in situ peak rarefactional pressures below approximately 0.3 MPa or mechanical index (MI) values less than approximately 0.3.

Furthermore, for other tissues no such effects have been reported."[3]

Interpretation of part a. The statement is based on small animal exposures rather than human exposures to ultrasound. Nevertheless, it provides some information relative to the current knowledge of risk factors for diagnostic ultrasound. If the acoustical intensities (spatial peak–time average) can be kept substantially below 100 mW/cm², or if the TIS or TIB is significantly lower than two, it appears from the statement that the risk factor is low. For situations in which the spatial peak–time average intensity approaches or exceeds 100 mW/cm², or the TIS or TIB value begins to approach two (i.e., is one or more), we may be dealing with ultrasonic exposures that carry a higher risk of producing an adverse effect on tissues. Unfortunately, there are no absolute, numerical guidelines that can be applied; users must become informed on ways to minimize exposures while providing the needed diagnostic information.

It should come as no surprise that exposure time also is a factor in producing biological effects in mammals. Part a of the Statement quantifies the dependence of exposure time and intensity level (expressed as a TI value here) on observations of biological effects. In words, the equation states that for animal exposures to ultrasound, no effects have been reported with a thermal index as high as almost 6 when the exposure time is less than 1 minute. The equation also quantifies the degree to which longer exposure times reduce the value of the thermal index at which reported bioeffects in animals occurred. Computed results from that equation are presented in Table 9-2.

Interpretation of part b. Although not all scanners have MI (mechanical index) values displayed, Table 9-1 illustrates that it is not unlikely that an instrument might produce pressure amplitudes that exceed the 0.3 MPa value quoted in part b of the Statement. Users should always keep the transmit level as low as practical to keep the peak pressures in turn as low as attainable while producing useful diagnostic information. It appears that diagnostic instruments are capable of producing effects such as minor hemorrhage in the presence of gas bodies. Thus far the only mammalian results reported are associated with direct insonification of the lung. The statement indicates that effects related to a high mechanical index from diagnostic

Table 9-2 Calculations from AIUM Statement indicating relationship between TI (thermal index) values and exposure times for which no biological effects in nonhuman mammals have been reported.

Exposure time	Highest TI without an effect
1 minute	6
10 minutes	4.3
100 minutes	2.7

ultrasound machines have not been noted when gas bodies are not present.

The AIUM statement regarding nonhuman mammalian exposures does not offer absolute safe levels, or even state permissible levels; nor does it specify upper intensity limits for ultrasound equipment. It merely summarizes in words the conclusions of experts in the field of bioacoustics regarding the tremendous number of published experiments involving ultrasound biological effects.

A RATIONAL APPROACH, PRUDENT USE, AND ALARA

No matter what the outcome of bioeffects studies, prudence dictates that the lowest possible acoustical exposures be used during ultrasound examinations. The following points are offered in accordance with this philosophy:

1. Do not hesitate to use diagnostic ultrasound when the situation warrants. However, diagnostic ultrasound should be used only when there is a valid medical reason. For example, it seems difficult to justify ultrasound exposures of individuals during commercial demonstrations.

   Responsible individuals only use diagnostic ultrasound to obtain an anticipated benefit such as diagnostic information or research results.

2. Users should familiarize themselves with their equipment so they can recognize which operating modes and which control settings result in high or low acoustical intensities. Thus they can avoid using high acoustical intensities (or high MI and TI values) except when the examination warrants. They should avoid using an instrument for purposes for which it may not have been designed. They should avoid using instrument "presets" for uses other than those the manufacturer intends especially when scanning the fetus. Table 9-1 shows that the spatial peak–temporal average intensity for different classes of instruments and different operating modes may vary significantly.

   Information on acoustical exposure from ultrasound instruments is provided by ultrasound equipment manufacturers in the operator's manual accompanying the equipment. Some of these data has been compiled into single documents.[2]

3. Many instruments have controls that vary the acoustical power. Learn to recognize these controls. On such instruments as a general rule, *use a high receiver gain setting and a low power setting, not vice versa!*

   Start an examination with power settings initially adjusted for low power output. Increase the power only when adequate sensitivity cannot be attained with the receiver gains peaking out at their maximum values, or when there is insufficient penetration because of electronic noise on the display. You should be aware that a 10-dB reduction in the output power means a factor of 10 reduction in the acoustical intensity (see Table 1-6). A 20-dB reduction means a factor of 100 reduction in intensity!

4. *Reduce the exposure time* by avoiding repeat scans if possible and avoiding holding the transducer stationary in contact with the patient unless the examination warrants this.

5. Practice the principle of ALARA (as low as reasonably achievable) during ultrasound examinations. Points 2, 3, and 4 above are in tune with this principle. Sometimes it is difficult for the operator to know for sure which controls will help bring about ALARA, because, for example, many controls can affect the output besides the transmit power. Examples include the velocity setting in spectral Doppler, the depth (or field of view) setting, and even some of the "presets" for specific types of examinations. The mechanical and thermal indices displayed on the screen of a diagnostic ultrasound instrument, if available, can help significantly.

Ultrasound instrument manufacturers are expected to design their equipment so it will deliver the lowest possible acoustical exposure consistent with the diagnostic expectations of that equipment. However, as the above points indicate, user awareness and responsibility are major elements in ensuring patient safety during an ultrasound examination.

AMERICAN INSTITUTE OF ULTRASOUND IN MEDICINE SAFETY STATEMENT

This chapter borrows much information from the AIUM, especially from documents produced by experts within this organization who help interpret reports on ultrasound bioeffects. We will conclude this text with the AIUM's complete statement on clinical safety,[18] we hope putting the information in this chapter in the proper perspective.

Diagnostic ultrasound has been in use since the late 1950's. Given its known benefits and recognized efficacy for medical diagnosis, including use during human pregnancy, the American Institute of Ultrasound in Medicine herein addresses the clinical safety of such use:

No confirmed biological effects on patients or instrument operators caused by exposure at intensities typical of present diagnostic ultrasound instruments have ever been reported. Although the possibility exists that such biological effects may be identified in the future, current data indicate that the benefits to patients of the prudent use of diagnostic ultrasound outweigh the risks, if any, that may be present.

References

1. *Medical ultrasound safety, part 1: bioeffects and biophysics, part 2: prudent use, part 3: implementing ALARA,* Laurel, MD, 1994, American Institute of Ultrasound in Medicine. (Intended for Sonographers, and written with the sonographer in mind.)

2. *Acoustical output levels from diagnostic ultrasound equipment,* Laurel, MD, 1992, American Institute of Ultrasound in Medicine. (Primarily a compilation of data, but accompanied by some explanations of the data.)

3. AIUM Bioeffects Committee: *Bioeffects and safety of diagnostic ultrasound,* Laurel, MD, 1992, American Institute of Ultrasound in Medicine.

4. *Standard for real-time display of thermal and mechanical acoustical indices on diagnostic ultrasound equipment,* Laurel, MD, 1992, American Institute of Ultrasound in Medicine.

5. Apfel R, Holland C: Gauging the likelihood of cavitation from short pulse, low duty cycle diagnostic ultrasound, *Ultrasound Med Biol* 17:179, 1991.

6. Nyborg W: Mechanisms for biological effects of ultrasound. In Nyborg W, Ziskin M: *Clinics in diagnostic ultrasound,* vol 16, *Biological effects of ultrasound,* New York, 1985, Churchill Livingston.

7. Holland C: Ultrasound bioeffects: the mechanical and thermal indices. In Goldman L, Fowlkes B, editors: *Medical CT and ultrasound: current technology and applications,* Madison, WI, 1995, Advanced Medical Publishing.

8. Liebeskind D et al: Diagnostic ultrasound: effects on the DNA and growth patterns of animal cells, *Radiology* 131:177, 1979.

9. Holland C et al: Direct evidence of cavitation in vivo from diagnostic ultrasound, *Ultrasound Medicine Biol,* 1996 (in press).

10. Child SZ et al: Lung damage from exposure to pulsed ultrasound, *Ultrasound Med Biol* 16:817, 1990.

11. Ziskin M: Epidemiology and human exposure. In Nyborg W, Ziskin M: *Clinics in diagnostic ultrasound,* vol 16, *Biological effects of ultrasound,* New York, 1985, Churchill Livingston.

12. *Safety considerations for diagnostic ultrasound,* Laurel, MD, 1992, American Institute of Ultrasound in Medicine.

13. Tarantal AF, Obrien W: Safety of ultrasound. In Sabbagha R, editor: *Diagnostic ultrasound applied to obstetrics and gynecology,* ed 3, Philadelphia, 1993, Lippincott.

14. Ehlinger CA et al: Diagnostic ultrasound increases sister chromatid exchange: preliminary report, *Wis Med J* 80:21, 1981.

15. Barnett SB, Baker RS, Barnstable S: Is pulsed ultrasound mutagenic? Proceedings of the World Federation of Ultrasound in Medicine and Biology, Brighton, England, July, 1982.

16. Martin AO: Biologic effects. In Sabbagha R, editor: *Diagnostic ultrasound applied to obstetrics and gynecology,* ed 2, Philadelphia, 1987, Lippincott.

17. Tarantal AF, Canfield DR: Ultrasound induced lung hemorrage in the monkey, *Ultrasound Med Biol* 20:65, 1994.

18. *Safety considerations for diagnostic ultrasound,* Laurel, MD, 1991, American Institute of Ultrasound in Medicine.

Questions for Review

1. The rate at which acoustical energy is transmitted into the medium is the acoustical:

   A. Intensity
   B. Speed
   C. Power
   D. Frequency

2. Units for acoustical intensity are:

   A. Milliwatts
   B. mW/cm^2
   C. W/m
   D. mW-cm

3. Acoustical pressure is expressed in:

   A. Pascals
   B. Watts
   C. mW/cm^2
   D. Lbs

4. Acoustical power is given in:

   A. Pascals
   B. Milliwatts
   C. mW/cm^2
   D. Joules

5. Radiation force, where an absorber in water interrupts the whole ultrasound beam, may be used to measure:

   A. Pressure amplitude
   B. I(SPPA)
   C. Acoustical power
   D. Dynamic range

6. Ultrasound equipment manufacturers measure the acoustical output of their machines with the detector placed in:

   A. Air
   B. Water
   C. Tissue
   D. A liquid that has an attenuation of 0.3 dB/cm-MHz

7. Which of the following devices may be used for measuring acoustical pressure amplitudes and determining acoustical intensities in the field of a diagnostic ultrasound transducer?

   A. A wattmeter
   B. A tissue-mimicking phantom
   C. A sensitive balance
   D. A hydrophone

8. The intensity is related to the _____ of the pressure amplitude.

   A. Square root
   B. Cube root
   C. Square
   D. Third power

9. What is the duty factor if the PRF is 10,000 and the pulse duration is 1 μs?

   A. .1
   B. .01
   C. .001
   D. .0001

10. In pulsed ultrasound, the I(SPPA) is much greater than the I(SPTA) because:

    A. Wider sound beams are used for the I(SPPA)
    B. They are related by the duty factor, which is small
    C. Higher acoustical power settings are used to record I(SPPA)
    D. I(SPPA) is recorded in water; I(SPTA) is a derated value

11. If an unfocused transducer produces 10 mW of power, and the transducer has an area of 2 cm^2, the I(SATA) at the transducer surface is:

    A. 5 mW/cm^2
    B. 10 mW/cm^2
    C. 20 mW/cm^2
    D. 50 mW/cm^2

12. The following symbols represent intensities from a pulse-echo scanner. Which intensity value is the highest?

    A. I(SATA) (Spatial average–time average)
    B. I(SPTA) (Spatial peak–time average)
    C. I(SATP) (Spatial average–temporal peak)
    D. I(SPPA) (Spatial peak–pulse average)

13. The mechanical index (MI) is an indication of the likelihood for:

    A. Cavitation
    B. Heating
    C. A faulty transducer
    D. A transducer with a moving scan head

14. Where can a sonographer find a listing of power, intensity, and peak pressure values for the transducers and operating modes of a scanner in the lab?

    A. In the operator's manual
    B. In clinical ultrasound journals
    C. At seminars and scientific meetings
    D. By calling the Food and Drug Administration

15. The thermal index provides information related to possibilities of:

    A. Heating
    B. Cavitation
    C. Direct mechanical damage to cells
    D. In vitro bioeffects

16. The ultrasound operating mode producing the highest spatial peak time average intensity is:

    A. B-mode imaging
    B. M-mode
    C. Combined B-mode imaging and M-mode
    D. Pulsed Doppler

17. The following table gives values for ultrasound power, I(SPTA), and I(SPPA) for several operating modes. Mode 1, mode 2, and mode 3 most likely are, respectively:

MODE	Power (mW)	I(SPTA) (mW/cm²)	I(SPPA) (W/cm²)
1	10	10	50
2	10	200	50
3	75	2000	30

   A. Pulsed Doppler, continuous-wave Doppler, B-mode scanning
   B. B-mode scanning, M-mode, pulsed Doppler
   C. B-mode scanning, continuous-wave Doppler, pulsed Doppler
   D. Continuous-wave Doppler, pulsed Doppler, M-mode

18. Localized heating due to a pulsed Doppler unit might be of concern because of the relatively high _____ of these units.

   A. I(SPPA)
   B. I(SPTP)
   C. Frequency
   D. Power and I(SPTA)

19. The role of "derating models" is to:

   A. Reduce the transmit power when water is insonified
   B. Translate output values in water to values in an attenuating medium
   C. Correct for the difference in sound speed between water and tissue
   D. Correct for the difference in impedance between air and tissue

20. Mechanisms by which ultrasound energy could induce a biological effect include:

   A. Heating
   B. Cavitation
   C. Mechanical effects other than cavitation
   D. A, B, and C

21. The two types of cavitation are_____ and _____.

   A. Large bubble and small bubble
   B. Stable and oscillatory
   C. Stable and transient
   D. Total and partial

22. At present the best indication that there have been no ill-effects on the human fetus exposed to diagnostic ultrasound comes from:

   A. Cell survival studies
   B. Epidemiological studies
   C. Dose effect studies in small animals
   D. Fetal survival statistics

23. Exposure of cells in a fluid is an example of:

   A. An in vitro study
   B. An in vivo study
   C. An epidemiological study
   D. A study on effects of heating

24. A conclusion from in vitro studies is:

   A. They are not real studies
   B. They are valuable for studying mechanisms
   C. They overwhelmingly indicate existence of harmful effects
   D. They are valuable for simulating exposure conditions during diagnostic studies.

25. Animal studies in which positive bioeffects were observed in the fetus were insonified using:

   A. clinical ultrasound scanners
   B. high-intensity ultrasound equipment
   C. equipment producing lower intensities than clinical devices
   D. audible sound waves

26. The AIUM statement on bioeffects claims that there have been no known effects from exposures to mammalian tissue by unfocused transducers at spatial peak–temporal average intensities below:

   A. 100 mW/cm²
   B. 1000 mW/cm²
   C. 5 W/cm²
   D. 100 W/cm²

27. The AIUM statement on bioeffects claims that for very tightly focused sound beams there have been no known effects from exposures to mammalian tissue at spatial peak–temporal average intensities below:

   A. 100 mW/cm²
   B. 1000 mW/cm²
   C. 5 W/cm²
   D. 100 W/cm²

28. The AIUM statements mentioned in the two previous problems were based on exposures to:

   A. Small mammals, such as rats and mice
   B. Large animals, such as dogs
   C. Pregnant women
   D. Cell suspensions

29. The AIUM statement also says that for thermal effects, no know ill-effects occurred for a TI value less than:

   A. 2
   B. 4
   C. 20
   D. 40

30. Risk of cavitation is most closely associated with which of the following acoustical quantities or parameters?

   A. Peak compressional or rarefactional pressure
   B. I(SPTA)
   C. Attenuation and absorption coefficients
   D. Acoustical power

31. The real-time acoustic output labeling index that is most closely related to risk of cavitation is the:

    A. Mechanical index
    B. Index of refraction
    C. Thermal index
    D. Frequency index

32. To minimize exposures to ultrasound, sonographers should scan using:

    A. Any transmit power, low receiver gain setting
    B. Low transmit power, high receiver gain setting
    C. High transmit power, low receiver gain setting
    D. High transmit power, any receiver gain setting

33. The term *ALARA* stands for:

    A. Alarm for action
    B. As long as reason allows
    C. A lengthy and real action
    D. As low as reasonably achievable

34. Sufficient safety factors are built into the MI and TI calculations that they always represent worst-case situations.

    A. True
    B. False

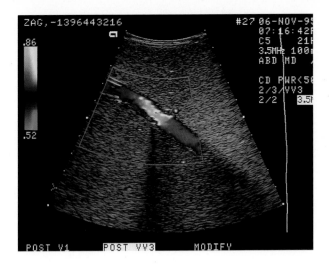

Fig. 6-9 Image of a Doppler phantom with a variance display map. The variance is shown in yellow.

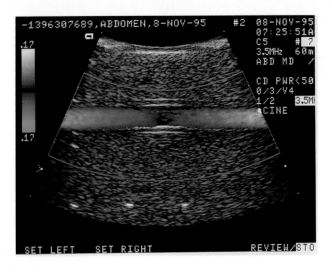

Fig. 6-11 B, Color flow image for the arrangement in A (p. 114).

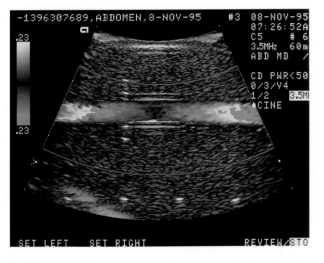

Fig. 6-14 Color flow image of horizontally oriented vessel, done with a sector probe. In this example, aliasing is present. Flow is from right to left.

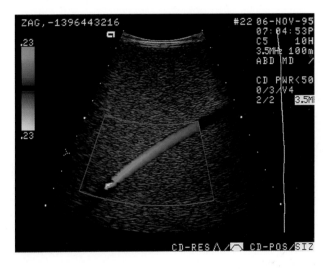

Fig. 6-15 Image of a flow phantom as in Fig. 6-15, with signal processing yielding a frame rate of 10 images per second.

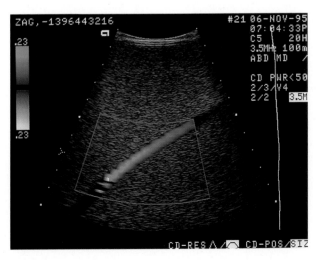

Fig. 6-16 Image of the same flow phantom, only now the signal processing in the scanner was adjusted, yielding a frame rate of 20 per second. This image is noticeable coarser than that of Fig. 6-15.

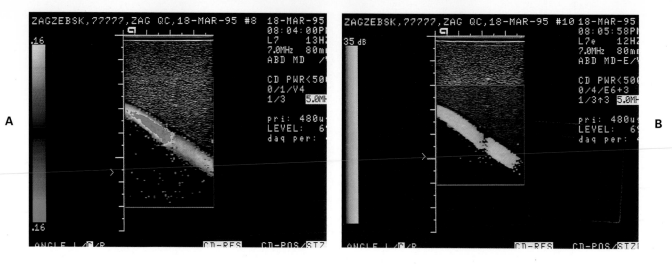

Fig. 6-19 **A,** Color flow image of a phantom containing a stenosis. Higher velocities are seen in the stenosis. **B,** Energy mode image of the same region in the phantom.

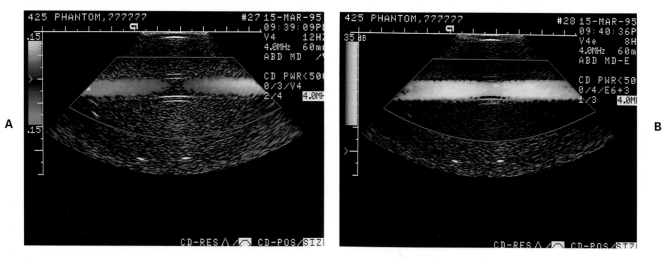

Fig. 6-20 **A,** Color flow image of a horizontal vessel in a phantom obtained using a sector transducer. **B,** Energy mode image of the same region in the phantom.

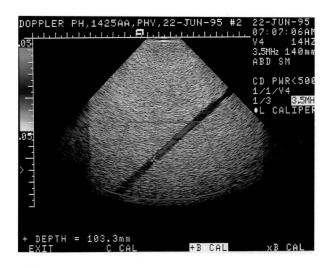

Fig. 8-22 Color flow penetration test. The maximum depth of visualization for color signals in this case is 10.3 cm.

Appendix A: Review of Math Concepts

Scientific notation

Although perhaps not necessary for a cursory understanding of the material, liberal use of exponentials is made in the examples worked out in the text. It is suggested that the student who wishes more than a brief review of this material consult a textbook on college mathematics.

A quantity is usually expressed in scientific notation as a number between 1 and 10 multiplied by 10 raised to the correct power.

$$25 = 2.5 \times 10^1$$
$$693 = 6.93 \times 10^2$$
$$3200 = 3.2 \times 10^3$$
$$6,000,000 = 6 \times 10^6$$
$$0.25 = 2.5 \times 10^{-1}$$
$$0.003 = 3 \times 10^{-3}$$
$$0.00042 = 4.2 \times 10^{-4}$$

In adding or subtracting two numbers expressed with this notation, it is necessary to express both numbers as the same power of 10 first and then carry on with the operation. Thus

$$1.75 \times 10^6 - 3 \times 10^5$$
$$= 1.75 \times 10^6 - 0.3 \times 10^6$$
$$= (1.75 - 0.3) \times 10^6$$
$$= 1.45 \times 10^6$$

$$0.23 + 4.1 \times 10^{-2}$$
$$= 23 \times 10^{-2} + 4.1 \times 10^{-2}$$
$$= (23 + 4.1) \times 10^{-2}$$
$$= 27.1 \times 10^{-2}$$
$$= 2.71 \times 10^{-1}$$

To multiply or divide numbers expressed as 10 to a power, use the formula

$$\frac{a \times 10^m}{b \times 10^n} = \frac{a}{b} \times 10^{m-n}$$

and

$$(a \times 10^m) \times (b \times 10^n) = (a \times b) \times 10^{m+n}$$

This means that exponential values are *subtracted* from each other when you divide and *added* to each other when you multiply.

Sine and cosine functions

The sine and cosine are trigonometric functions used quite often in acoustics and descriptions of wave phenomena. They are defined with the use of the right triangle shown in the following diagram. Let a, b, and c be the sides of this triangle, as shown. For angle B

$$\sin B = \frac{b}{c}$$

$$\cos B = \frac{a}{c}$$

(The notation $|$mp means "is defined as.") It is easy to see that when angle B is small, side b is also very small and sin B is nearly 0. If angle B is small, side a is almost equal to side c. It follows then that the cosine for a very small angle is nearly 1. Similarly, as angle B approaches 90 degrees, sin B goes to 1 and cos B goes to 0.

A graph of cos B and sin B when angle B is between 0 and 90 degrees is shown below:

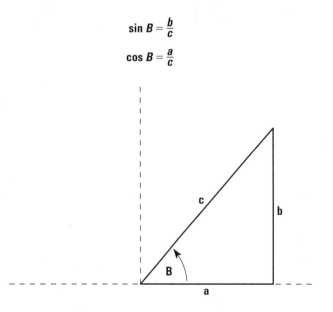

$$\sin B = \frac{b}{c}$$
$$\cos B = \frac{a}{c}$$

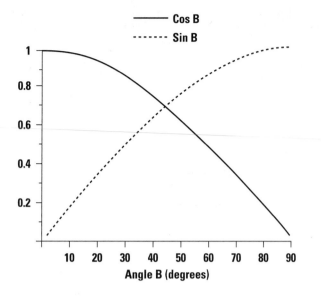

Following are the more commonly used metric system conversions:

Prefix	Meaning	Abbreviation
micro	10^{-6}	μ
milli	10^{-3}	m
centi	10^{-2}	c
deci	10^{-1}	d
kilo	10^{3}	k
Mega	10^{6}	M

Summary of important units

The units commonly used in ultrasound are as follows:

Quantity	Unit	Abbreviation
Length	meters	m
Mass	kilograms	kg
Time	seconds	s
Speed	meters/second	m/s
Period	inverse seconds	s^{-1}
Area	square meters or meters squared	m^2
Volume	cubic meters or meters cubed	m^3
Frequency	cycles per second (hertz)	cps(Hz)
Density	kilograms per cubic meter	kg/m^3
Impedance	kilograms per square meter per second	$kg/m^2/s$
Attenuation	decibels	dB
Attenuation coefficient	decibels per centimeter	dB/cm
Power	watts	W
Intensity	watts per square meter	W/m^2
Amplifier gain	decibels	dB

Appendix B: Answers to Review Questions

Chapter 1

1. B; this is a general definition applicable to any sound wave.
2. C; a vacuum has no molecules or "particles" to transmit sound waves.
3. B; the only property applicable to all sound sources is they vibrate and consequently produce vibrations in the medium.
4. C; sound speed depends on the density and stiffness of the medium.
5. C; regions of compression have a higher density and higher pressure. The opposite is regions of rarefaction.
6. B; only longitudinal sound waves travel through soft tissue; transverse waves (another name for shear waves) are severely attenuated; radio waves are, of course, not sound waves.
7. C; Pascals. Joules are units of energy and Newton are units of force.
8. B; period.
9. D; period is 1/frequency = 1/1,000,000 = 0.000001
10. C; deci = 1/10; centi = 1/100; milli = 1/1,000; micro = 1/1,000,000
11. D; air has the lowest and bone the highest; water has a lower speed than average soft tissue.
12. C; 1540 m/s = 1.54 mm/μs = .154 cm/s
13. B; the wavelength; wavelength also is sound speed divided by frequency and for soft tissue is 1.54 mm/F(MHz) where F(MHz) is the frequency given in MHz.
14. A; wavelength = 1.54 mm/F(MHz) = 1.54 mm/5 = .3 mm
15. B; wavelength is inversely proportional to frequency.
16. B; this is the definition for the characteristic impedance of a material.
17. C; impedance is directly proportional to the density, so if the latter increases by 10%, so does the impedance.
18. B; call the impedance of material 1 "1" and that of material 2 "2". Then R = (2 − 1)/(2 + 1) = 0.33. Any other number will work, as long as material 2's impedance is two times that of material 1.
19. B; which can be verified by using impedance values given in the text.
20. A.
21. C; essentially all the sound is reflected at a tissue-air interface.
22. D; for refraction to occur, the sound must be incident at an angle that is not perpendicular and the sound speeds must be different at the interface.
23. C; Snell's law relates the transmitted beam direction to the incident beam angle and the speeds of sound at the interface. Given any three of the four quantities lets you solve for the fourth.
24. B; the sine increases as the angle increases from 0 to 90 degrees.
25. A; scattering is the main source of echo signals in ultrasonography.
26. C; we usually say scatterers are smaller than the wavelength.
27. A; it reflects sound waves in all directions, so there is less of a dependence of the detected echo amplitude on the angle of the interface.
28. D; decibels are used to quantify the ratio of two amplitudes or intensities.
29. D is incorrect; at MHz frequencies, sound absorption is very low in fluid cavities in the body, such as the bladder, compared to absorption in soft tissues.
30. C; dB/cm is used to express the attenuation coefficient.
31. C; attenuation can be assumed to be proportional to frequency. You are given the attenuation coefficient at 1 MHz, so multiply by 5 to get the value at 5 MHz.
32. C; enhancement results from good through-transmission in a mass or fluid-filled cavity.
33. C; attenuation (in dB) is the attenuation coefficient (dB/cm) × distance (cm) = 1 dB/cm × 12 cm.
34. B; high-frequency (greater than 20 kHz) sound waves traveling through media besides water are still ultrasound; the waves can be other than longitudinal if the medium will support their transmission.

Chapter 2

1. B is incorrect. Most piezoelectric transducers have a resonance frequency that depends on the thickness of the element. They respond best at the resonance frequency.
2. D; the thickness of the element determines the resonance frequency.
3. C; scatter, attenuation, and resolution depend on frequency. Sound speed is essentially independent of frequency, depending mainly on the medium.

4. A; it is polarized by heating above the Curie temperature and then cooling with a strong electric field applied.

5. C; composite transducers have a lower impedance (making it easier to match the impedance to tissue) and wider bandwidth than standard piezoelectric ceramics.

6. C; after an electrical signal is applied, a piezoelectric transducer oscillates.

7. A; the backing material helps dampen the vibrations of the transducer.

8. D; by matching the impedance of the transducer to the tissue, the layer improves transmission of sound between the transducer and tissue, improving the sensitivity.

9. B; usually the matching layer has an impedance that is between the impedances of the two materials being matched.

10. D; wide frequency bandwidths.

11. D; axial resolution is determined by the pulse duration.

12. B; increasing the duration of the pulse produces a narrower range of frequencies in the pulse.

13. B; imaging transducers generally generate pulses as short as 3 cycles to optimize axial resolution.

14. C; gets worse.

15. A; improves. For the same number of cycles in the pulse, a higher frequency has a shorter pulse duration.

16. B; spatial burst length is synonymous with pulse duration.

17. C; beam width is the best response; beam width does depend on transducer size, but it also depends on frequency and focusing.

18. D; Huygen's principle.

19. A; the near field, or Fresnel zone.

20. D; the beam of an unfocused transducer diverges in the Fraunhofer zone or far field.

21. D; greater beam divergence results in a wider beam and poorer lateral resolution.

22. B; near field length = diameter squared/(4 × wavelength) = 32 mm.

23. A; if the frequency doubles, the wavelength halves. NFL is inversely proportional to wavelength, so it will double when the wavelength halves.

24. D; out of the list of performance factors presented, poor lateral resolution is most closely associated with erroneous fill-in of small echo-free structures.

25. D; focal distance.

26. A; this is another description of an array.

27. A; a phased array steers sound beams at an angle relative to the surface in order to sweep the beam during scanning.

28. C; the focus of a single-element transducer is fixed during the manufacturing of the transducer.

29. B; the linear array produces images by transmitting sound beams that are parallel to one another.

30. A; usually receive focus is done dynamically no matter what the transmit focal distance is. The transmitted beam can only be focused at one depth, but receive focus can change dynamically as echoes arrive from deeper and deeper reflectors.

31. D; the annular array's beam is symmetrical, having the same width in the slice thickness direction as in the lateral direction. When its focus is changed electronically, both lateral resolution and slice thickness are affected.

32. D; apodization is one trick the manufacturer can apply to help reduce side lobes.

33. B; dynamic aperture increases the number of elements used during reception as echoes are detected from deeper and deeper structures. This helps keep lateral resolution nearly constant with depth.

34. A; a fixed focal length lens. Some manufacturers are starting to use $1^1/_2$ D arrays, however.

35. C; small focal lesions.

Chapter 3

1. B; the range equation related reflector distance to echo arrival time.

2. B; the echo arrival time is directly proportional to the distance to a reflector.

3. B; 13 μs/cm times 10 cm is 130 μs.

4. A; 1.54 mm/μs is the same as .154 cm/s = 1540 m/s.

5. A; duty factor is the fraction of time the transducer emits sound.

6. B; pulse repetition period is the inverse of pulse repetition frequency.

7. B; pulse duration equals the time from the beginning to end of the same pulse.

8. A; duty factors are usually less than 1%; most of the time the transducer is waiting for echoes to arrive from tissue.

9. A; out of the choices, only increasing the number of pulses per second would increase the duty factor.

10. C; increasing (or decreasing) the power by 3 dB doubles (or halves) the transmit power.

11. B; usually the transmit control affects the amplitude of the pulse emitted by the transducer.

12. E; gain is the ratio of the output amplitude to the input amplitude.

13. A; clearly, use a low power and high receiver gain to minimize patient exposure.

14. B; TGC compensate for attenuation.

15. B; TGC is applied to the receiver.

16. B; reject eliminates low-level signals, we hope including electronic noise.

17. D; this definition is for the displayed echo dynamic range sometimes called local dynamic range.
18. E; the monitor.
19. A; the image will exhibit lower contrast with a high dynamic range setting.
20. B; demodulation.
21. B; the A-mode display presents echo amplitude (spike height) versus reflector depth (echo return time).
22. D; the A-mode does not provide two-dimensional cross-sectional information.
23. B; an M-mode display shows reflector depth along one axis and time on an orthogonal axis.
24. D; again, organ cross-sectional information is not seen on the M-mode display.
25. C; most manufacturers shoot at least 100 or more ultrasound beams in different directions to produce a single frame for a B-mode image.
26. D; fundamentally, the *B* is for brightness in this display mode.
27. D; all but D are assumed implicitly by the machine when constructing B-mode images.
28. A; the amplitude is related to dot brightness, but it is not involved in figuring out where to position the dot on the display. The other factors are.
29. B; these devices did offer large imaged fields.
30. A; by backing the transducer away from the skin surface using water path coupling, a single-element focused transducer could provide excellent detail of superficial structures.
31. D; an array is a transducer consisting of a number of small elements.
32. B; an array allows the focal distance to be changed electronically.
33. D; scanning speed is limited by sound travel time; the greater the imaged depth, the slower the scanning speed.
34. B; 13 μs/cm $\times$ 10 cm $\times$ 100 = 13 ms for one scan.
35. C; if the depth setting is halved, it takes half as long to collect the echo information for each beam line and the frame rate can double.
36. A; each transmit focal depth requires a separate transmit pulse. Consequently, multiple transmit focusing reduces the frame rate.
37. E; up to a point, more beam lines result in better spatial detail.
38. A; reducing the sector angle can reduce the number of beam lines used to form the image and increase the frame rate.

39. B; the smaller footprint of the phased array makes it desirable for cardiac imaging, where beams must be sent between the ribs.
40. C; the curvilinear array operates much like a linear array; however, its curved scan head results in a sectored image.

Chapter 4

1. C; the memory is also called the *scan converter.*
2. A; the scan converter accepts echo data as they are acquired from the scanner and reads data out to a video (*tv*) monitor; the write and read data formats are different.
3. C; better spatial resolution is not necessarily present in digital devices.
4. A; discrete levels; discrete times.
5. C; binary digit
6. B; binary numbers use two as the base.
7. A; pixel stands for picture element.
8. C; spatial resolution is associated with the number of pixels horizontally and vertically.
9. A; bits per pixel is related to the details of the amplitude differences that can be represented at any location.
10. A; read zoom; with read zoom, image data from only a fraction of the pixels are spread across the entire image display.
11. B; 2 to the eighth power (2 $\times$ 2 $\times$ 2 $\times$ 2 $\times$ 2 $\times$ 2 $\times$ 2 $\times$ 2) = 256.
12. B; echo signals are digitized in the A/D converter.
13. D; interpolation
14. C; amplitude resolution is related to the bits per pixel.
15. C; to view changes in preprocessing, you need a live image.
16. B is the best answer out of the choices given.
17. D; typically video monitors have 525 horizontal lines and are refreshed at a rate of 30/s.
18. B; by splitting the 525 line image into two 262^1/$_2$ line fields, each field is scanned at a rate of 60/s, eliminating the flicker that can be perceived by humans if a single 525 line field is scanned at 30/s.
19. A; the other choices are definite advantages of a laser camera.
20. C.
21. A.
22. B; users need to be aware of the other choices when using video tapes.

Chapter 5

1. D; the perceived frequency of a sound wave changes when there is relative motion between the source and listener or transducer and reflector.
2. A; there must be motion of the listener or source (or both) for a Doppler shift.
3. D; the Doppler equation relates the Doppler frequency to the velocity of the reflector; the relationship involves the speed of sound and the Doppler angle.
4. C; the echo signals themselves are still close to 5 MHz. The Doppler signal of course will be much lower.
5. A; for a given velocity, the Doppler shift will be directly proportional to the ultrasound frequency; halving the ultrasound frequency halves the Doppler frequency.
6. D; the Doppler angle is the flow direction relative to the ultrasound beam.
7. C; as the Doppler angle increases from 0 to 90 degrees, the cosine decreases. The Doppler frequency is proportional to the cosine of the Doppler angle.
8. D.
9. D; 85 degrees is closest to perpendicular to the vessel.
10. D; see Table 5-1.
11. D.
12. B; one is a transmitter, the other a receiver.
13. D; a sample gate adjustment is found on pulsed but not CW Doppler.
14. A; the wall filter is also called a *high pass filter* because it eliminates low frequencies but passes higher frequencies.
15. A.
16. C; laminar or parabolic flow has the greatest velocity at the center, but the velocity goes to zero at the walls.
17. D; out of the choices given, the strength is related to the number of red blood cells contributing to the Doppler signal; the strength also depends on beam attenuation.
18. C; the FFT algorithm does a spectral analysis of the Doppler signal.
19. C; zero crossing detectors provide an approximation of the frequency of the Doppler signal.
20. D; reflector velocity.
21. B; the gray level, or the brightness of the display.
22. C; pulsatility index is closely related to the distal resistance to flow.
23. C; gating is associated with pulsed Doppler.
24. A; aliasing is not present with CW Doppler.
25. D; the description is of aliasing.
26. D; the sampling frequency must be twice the frequency of the signal.
27. D.
28. A; the sampling rate (also the PRF) is 12,000 Hz; $^1/_2$ this frequency is 6000 Hz.
29. D; on most Doppler devices, when you change the spectral scale, the PRF changes.
30. D; 2 m/s.
31. D; again, 2 m/s.
32. A; the ambiguities result from several Doppler sample gates.

Chapter 6

1. D; color flow imaging presents a rougher estimate of the average Doppler frequency than pulsed Doppler, and it *is* subject to aliasing as well. But it does provide cross-sectional views.
2. B; Doppler processing is sensitive to the echo signal phase.
3. A; the packet is often thought of as just the series of transmit pulses, but strictly speaking it includes a series of pulse-echo sequences.
4. C.
5. A; it takes longer to acquire the echo data when more pulse echo sequences are used in a packet to acquire the Doppler data along each beam line.
6. D; phase shift autocorrelation provides estimates of Doppler frequency, and hence, reflector velocity.
7. B; the color processor estimates the mean Doppler frequency for each pixel location.
8. D; variance, which can be estimated from the Doppler processed signal.
9. A; to detect turbulence.
10. A.
11. B; red, blue, and green are primary colors.
12. B; the angle of the color beam line with flow in a horizontal vessel changes across the field for the orientation described.
13. C.
14. B; if the color threshold is lowered, this may help decrease the "bleeding." Increasing gain, decreasing velocity scale, or increasing gate size might all have the opposite effect.
15. A.
16. A; the color "wraps" around so that velocities exceeding the scale appear as though reversed.
17. C; all other actions may help reduce or eliminate aliasing.
18. C; CW Doppler will not exhibit aliasing, the other modes listed will.
19. A; velocities are greatest in the middle of the vessel when laminar flow is present.

20. A; if the gap between color beam lines is increased, fewer color beam lines are needed and the frame rate can increase.
21. B; it is difficult to start and stop the mechanical scanning action fast enough, so the mechanical transducer actually continues to move as Doppler data are collected along each beam line.
22. A; the display is most affected by Doppler signal strength.
23. C; power mode is said to have greater sensitivity particularly to low flow in very small vessels and for detecting perfusion.
24. D; reflector displacements from one pulse echo sequence to the next are measured using time domain correlation. Then the reflector velocity is computed.
25. B; velocity is displacement (cm) per unit time (s), or cm/s.
26. C; the pulses used are often the same as those used in B-mode imaging.
27. B.
28. C; volume flow rate is sometimes estimated with Doppler or color flow imaging systems. Flow rate is volume (milliliters or liters) per unit time (min or s) or liters/s.
29. B; CW Doppler is not as good as spectral Doppler to isolate a "selected location." Both, however, are better than color at providing a display of the velocities present. Power mode does not display velocity, but displays Doppler signal strength.
30. A; duty factors.

Chapter 7

1. C; echoes from a specular reflector are highly dependent on the beam angle with respect to the interface. Attenuation, which depends on frequency and distance, also influences the echo amplitude. PRF, however, should have no effect.
2. C; a scatterer.
3. B; the echo from a specular reflector often is not seen because of angle effects, as shown in Figure 7-1.
4. C; elevated echogenicity.
5. A; speckle.
6. C; interference. Speckle, or texture, results from echoes picked up simultaneously from many scatterers, and interference determines the exact amplitude.
7. D; artifacts.
8. B; along the transmitted beam axis (and at a depth corresponding to the echo arrival time). Notice that the first part of answer A is incorrect.
9. C; reverberations.

10. C; 4 cm, or twice the actual distance to the reflector.
11. A; reverberations within the metallic object.
12. B; mirror image artifacts.
13. B; a 90-degree Doppler angle.
14. A; beam width effects.
15. A; beam width effects as long as the tubes are perpendicular to the image plane.
16. C; grating lobes only occur for array transducers.
17. B; slice thickness is the best answer. Beam width effects also are likely to contribute, but for most array scanners the beam width is narrower than the slice thickness.
18. D; distal. Distal enhancement gives a clue that the attenuation in the object is lower than attenuation in the surrounding tissue.
19. C; shadowing.
20. C; the machine always places echo dots along the assumed ultrasound beam axis during scanning.
21. D; the echo would have to arrive "sooner" than expected for the scanner to display it at an apparent depth of 9 cm. This means the speed of sound is higher than 1540 m/s, the speed assumed in the range equation calibration of the scanner.
22. A; mm.
23. A; area is πr^2, where r is the radius (half the diameter, or 1 cm). π is 3.14, so the area is 3.14 cm^2.
24. C; volumes.

Chapter 8

1. C; acceptance tests are done when a scanner is purchased; quality assurance tests are those done routinely.
2. C.
3. D; these may be done by PM personnel, however.
4. B; sound speed and attenuation properties.
5. D; sensitivity
6. C; although some users do not like to use the absolute maximum receiver gain because there may be too much noise on the display.
7. A; electronic noise.
8. D; most likely.
9. D.
10. C; inadequate photography is a frequent source of image quality problems
11. B; sound speed and reflector location must be precisely known because these determine where the machine places the objects.
12. C; vertical measurement accuracy.
13. B; from "leading edge to leading edge."
14. C; (4 - 3.8)/4 = 0.05 = 5%.
15. B; from the center to the center for horizontal measurement accuracy.

16. A; we expect the results to vary with frequency because of different amounts of beam penetration at different frequencies.
17. B; the minimum resolvable spacing along the beam axis is axial resolution.
18. C.
19. A; (again).
20. D; slice thickness.
21. A.
22. A; this was demonstrated in the text.
23. B, velocity accuracy.
24. C.
25. A.
26. A.

Chapter 9

1. C; power is the rate at which energy is delivered. Units are watts or milliwatts.
2. B; think of intensity as power per unit area. Then apply the units and you get milliwatts/cm^2.
3. A; pascals
4. B; power is given in watts or milliwatts.
5. C; radiation force using a sensitive balance is used to measure acoustical power.
6. B; water. For reporting some output values the manufacturer does calculate an attenuation factor, assuming the attenuation is 0.3 dB/cm-MHz. However, the actual measurement is done in water.
7. D; the hydrophone, with its small sensitive element, is used to measure the pressure at points in the field.
8. C; the square of the pressure amplitude.
9. B; DF = 10,000/sec × 0.000001 sec = 0.01; notice, duty factor has no units, though it may be expressed as a percentage.
10. B; the I(SPTA) = I(SPPA) × DF, and DF is usually less than 0.01.
11. A; take the power (10 mW) and divide by the transducer area (2 cm^2) and you get 5 mW/cm^2.
12. D.
13. A; cavitation.
14. A; the fastest way is from the operator's manual that came with the scanner.

15. A; the thermal index is the ratio of the acoustical power to the power needed to raise tissue 1 degree C. (The needed power is, of course, estimated based on certain assumptions about beam attenuation and tissue thermal properties.)
16. D; because the beam dwells in one spot, and because the PRF may be high to avoid aliasing and the pulse duration is somewhat longer than the pulse duration in imaging.
17. B; the mode with the highest expected I(SPTA) is pulsed Doppler, eliminating A and D. CW Doppler is not pulsed, so you would not see an I(SPPA) that is 400 × greater than the I(SPTA), thus eliminating C. The correct answer is deduced to be B.
18. D.
19. B.
20. D; all are discussed in the text. Most books and documents now emphasize heating and cavitation.
21. C; stable and transient.
22. B.
23. A.
24. B.
25. B; the studies in which damage to the fetus were documented almost always used high I(SPTA) values and large ultrasound beams.
26. A; 100 mW/cm^2.
27. B; when tightly focused ultrasound beams are considered, a higher intensity is tolerated, apparently, because any heat generated can be more quickly dissipated than if a large beam area from an unfocused beam were involved.
28. A; small animal exposures.
29. A; 2.
30. A; the peak pressure level and the frequency.
31. A; the MI or mechanical index.
32. B; use a low transmit power and high gain.
33. D.
34. B; false; although researchers expect the index calculations to usually overestimate the exposure, the assumed attenuation of 0.3 dB/cm-MHz may predict too high an attenuation if most of the path between the transducer and sensitive tissue (such as the fetus) is fluid. In this case it is possible that the TI and MI would underestimate the exposure.

This is a comprehensive exam covering material in all nine chapters of this book. It is roughly the same length as typical board certification examinations, so readers might wish to use this section as a practice test. Questions are not in order of their appearance in the book.

(Please note, some of these questions are challenging, so don't be discouraged if you do not get them right on the first try.)

1. When you adjust the "focus" on the scanner, you vary:

   A. The focal depth of the transmitted beam
   B. The focal depth of the array during reception
   C. The focus of the scan converter memory
   D. The focus of the image monitor

2. Two targets in a phantom are separated vertically by exactly 10 cm. Which of the following properties of the phantom is most relevant in order to use these targets for vertical distance measurement accuracy tests?

   A. The attenuation is 0.5 dB/cm
   B. The speed of sound is 1540 m/s
   C. The echogenicity is equal to that of liver
   D. The density of the material in the phantom is 1 gm/cm^3

3. Mirror image artifacts are common distal to highly _____ interfaces.

   A. Reflective
   B. Refracting
   C. Shadowing
   D. Absorbing

4. The acoustical impedance is the product of the:

   A. Speed of sound and reflection coefficient
   B. Speed of sound and amplitude
   C. Density and wavelength
   D. Density and speed of sound

5. The two types of acoustical cavitation are:

   A. Prompt and delayed
   B. Stable and transient
   C. Experimental and theoretical
   D. Mechanical and electromagnetic

6. This image shows an anechoic tube oriented horizontally in a phantom. The echoes within the vessel most probably are caused by:

   A. Beam width effects
   B. Slice thickness effects
   C. Excessive shadowing
   D. Poor axial resolution

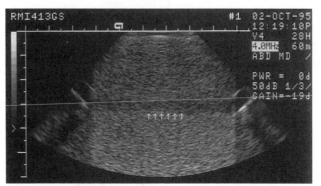

7. The type of transducer whose beam steering is done by element selection is:

   A. A single element
   B. A phased array
   C. A curved array
   D. An annular array

8. The column of targets is imaged using a linear array transducer. The calipers show us that at an 8 cm depth, the _____ is about 1.8 mm.

   A. Axial resolution
   B. Slice thickness
   C. Distance calibration accuracy
   D. Lateral resolution

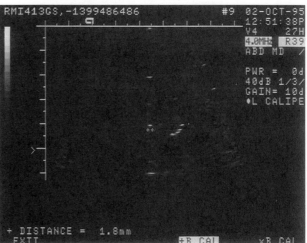

9. Reverberations might give the impression that:

   A. Beam penetration is lower than expected
   B. There is a greater amount of refraction than actually exists
   C. There are more reflectors than actually exist
   D. More structures are anechoic than actually are

10. Which one of the following can pulsed Doppler provide but continuous-wave (CW) Doppler cannot provide?

    A. Better sensitivity
    B. Narrower frequency bandwidths
    C. Selection of sample volume depth
    D. Detection of velocities greater than 2 m/s

11. Sound waves cannot travel through:

    A. Air
    B. Bone
    C. Lead
    D. Vacuum

12. Units for intensity in the field of an ultrasound transducer are:

    A. Decibels
    B. m/s
    C. Milliwatts
    D. mW/cm^2

13. If the impedance in the tissue on the distal side of an interface is 1.1 times the impedance of the tissue on the proximal side, the amplitude reflection coefficient is approximately:

    A. 0.05
    B. 0.25
    C. 0.5
    D. 0.95

14. An advantage of write zoom over read zoom on a B-mode imager is that:

    A. A larger number of pixels are used to store the zoomed image
    B. It can be done on the frozen image
    C. More gray levels are available than in read zoom
    D. A higher frequency is introduced during write zoom

15. The scan format of an ordinary video monitor is described most accurately as:

    A. 1000 lines; 60 images per second
    B. 10,000 lines; 600 images per second
    C. 51 lines; 300 images per second
    D. 525 lines; 30 images per second

16. Mechanisms by which ultrasound might induce biological effects are:

    A. Refraction and side lobe production
    B. Attenuation and absorption
    C. Reflection and scattering
    D. Heating and cavitation

17. Decibels are used to express all of the following EXCEPT:

    A. The peak rarefactional pressure amplitude from the transducer
    B. The ratio of two amplitudes or intensities
    C. The dynamic range of the receiver
    D. The gain of an amplifier

18. The number of cycles per second is the:

    A. Frequency
    B. Wavelength
    C. Wave period
    D. Pulse repetition period

19. The distance a sound wave travels during one period of vibration of the source is the:

    A. Frequency
    B. Wavelength
    C. Half value layer
    D. Depth of penetration

20. The method of separating and displaying the various frequencies in a Doppler signal is called:

    A. Range-gating
    B. Noise rejection
    C. Spectral analysis
    D. Signal demodulation

21. A highly reflective interface is located 4.2 cm from the transducer. A reverberation echo would appear to come from what depth?

    A. 2.1 cm
    B. 4.2 cm
    C. 6.3 cm
    D. 8.4 cm

22. Heating a transducer above _____ will cause depolarization.

    A. The Curie temperature
    B. The boiling point
    C. Room temperature
    D. The body temperature

23. The speed 1540 m/s is equivalent to:

    A. 1.54 cm/s
    B. 1.54 m/μs
    C. 1.54 mm/μs
    D. 154 cm/s

24. The wavelength for a 10-MHz sound wave in tissue is about:
    A. 0.15 mm
    B. 0.3 mm
    C. 1.5 mm
    D. 3 mm

25. Which statement is true about the use of decibels?
    A. Decibels represent absolute power levels
    B. Decibels are a way to express the ratio of two amplitudes
    C. Decibels only apply to signals at ultrasound frequencies
    D. Decibels cannot be used to quantify attenuation

26. The real-time acoustical output labeling index that is most closely related to risk of heating is the:
    A. Mechanical index
    B. Index of refraction
    C. Absorption index
    D. Thermal index

27. Which interface will reflect the highest percentage of the incident ultrasound beam power or intensity?
    A. An interface between any soft tissue and bone
    B. An interface between any soft tissue and water
    C. An interface between any two soft tissues
    D. An interface between any soft tissue and air

28. When we refer to digital devices, the term *bit* is an acronym for:
    A. Big type
    B. Binary text
    C. Binary digit
    D. Basic reject

29. Which of the following display modes depicts reflector depth versus time?
    A. A-mode
    B. B-mode
    C. C-mode
    D. M-mode

30. A piezoelectric transducer is caused to vibrate at ultrasonic frequencies by doing what?
    A. Striking it with a hammer
    B. Applying an electrical pulse
    C. Applying damping material
    D. Applying pressure pulses

31. Exposing human cells to ultrasound beams in an experimental chamber is an example of:
    A. In vivo bioeffects experiment
    B. Epidemiological study
    C. In vitro bioeffects experiment
    D. Small mammalian animal bioeffect study

32. The speed of sound depends on the:
    A. Wavelength and frequency
    B. Amplitude and intensity
    C. Density and stiffness
    D. Attenuation and scattering

33. These two waveforms differ in:
    A. Intensity
    B. Amplitude
    C. Frequency
    D. Phase

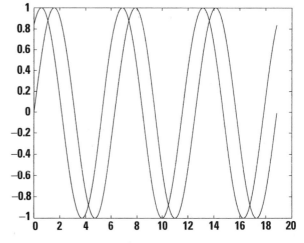

34. The width of the ultrasound beam in the image plane is most closely related to which of the following?
    A. Dynamic range
    B. Grating lobe width
    C. Lateral resolution
    D. Slice thickness

35. The angle of beam divergence in the far field of a 5-MHz, unfocused single-element transducer is _____ that of a 2.5-MHz transducer of the same diameter.
    A. Treater than
    B. About the same as
    C. Less than
    D. Nonexistent compared to

36. The near field length of a 5-MHz unfocused, single-element transducer will be _____ that of a 2.5-MHz transducer of the same diameter.
    A. Twice
    B. Equal to
    C. $1/2$
    D. $1/4$

37. A change in the direction of an ultrasound beam at an interface between two materials that have different speeds of sound is called:

    A. Focusing
    B. Reflection
    C. Scattering
    D. Refraction

38. If the frequency is 5 MHz, the period is:

    A. 0.1 μs
    B. 0.2 μs
    C. 1 μs
    D. 2 μs

39. If the attenuation coefficient of a tissue is 0.5 dB/cm at 1 MHz, how much will a 5-MHz beam be attenuated over a 5-cm distance?

    A. 5 dB
    B. 0.5 dB
    C. 2.5 dB
    D. 12.5 dB

40. Doppler processing used in some color flow imaging machines is sensitive both to the echo signal amplitude and to the:

    A. Reflector size
    B. Reflector lateral position
    C. Echo signal phase
    D. Echo signal display mode

41. Which ONE of the following types of transducers could produce grating lobes?

    A. Dual-crystal, CW Doppler
    B. Single element unfocused
    C. Single element focused
    D. Linear array

42. Which one of the following types of sound waves does not travel through soft tissue?

    A. Transverse
    B. Longitudinal
    C. High frequency
    D. Audible frequency

43. Echo data emerging from the transducer:

    A. Are in analog format
    B. Are in digital format
    C. Contain a mixture of analog and digital signals
    D. Are either analog or digital, depending on the type of transducer

44. The number of pixels horizontally and vertically in the scan converter determines:

    A. The number of amplitude levels stored at each location
    B. The scan converter's spatial resolution
    C. The amount of time an image can be frozen
    D. The dynamic range of the scan converter

45. A device used to measure the acoustic pressure waveform in the beam of an ultrasound transducer is:

    A. A watt meter
    B. A radiation balance
    C. An ammeter
    D. A hydrophone

46. Axial resolution is determined by the:

    A. Beam width
    B. Pulse duration
    C. Amount of beam focusing
    D. Position of the beam axis

47. Which of the following could cause artifactual lateral displacement of the image of an object?

    A. High speed of sound in the medium
    B. Reverberations
    C. Shadowing
    D. Refraction

48. The main advantage of an annular array over a standard curvilinear array is:

    A. It produces a sector image, while the curvilinear does not
    B. It can more easily combine B-mode imaging with color flow and Doppler operating modes
    C. Its electronic focusing controls beam width AND slice thickness
    D. It is more sensitive than the curvilinear

49. The number of ultrasound pulses per second emitted by an ultrasound machine is the:

    A. Transmit power
    B. Image frame rate (IFR)
    C. Pulse repetition frequency (PRF)
    D. Wave frequency

50. An advantage of a broad bandwidth pulse over a narrow bandwidth pulse is:

    A. Better lateral resolution
    B. Better axial resolution
    C. Greater dynamic range
    D. Allows higher PRFs

51. On a modern ultrasound scanner using array technology, the "beam former" is best described as being located:

    A. Between the transducer and patient
    B. Between the transducer and receiver
    C. Inside the scan converter
    D. Between the scan converter and image monitor

52. The prefixes mega, kilo, centi, and milli mean, respectively:

    A. 100,000, 1,000, 0.1, and 0.000001
    B. 1,000,000, 1,000, 10, and 0.0001
    C. 100,000, 1,000, 100, and 0.001
    D. 1,000,000, 1,000, 0.01, and 0.001

53. Which of the following has the highest speed of sound?

    A. Water
    B. Bone
    C. Tissue
    D. Air

54. Units for diameters, circumferences, and areas are, respectively:

    A. mm, mm^2, mm^3
    B. cm, cm, cm^2
    C. mm, cm^2, m
    D. cm, mm, μm

55. Which operating mode or condition tends to have the highest duty factor?

    A. B-mode gray scale imaging
    B. Combined M-mode and gray scale imaging
    C. Pulsed Doppler
    D. Image freeze

56. Suppose the acoustic power emitted by a scanner is measured to be 40 milliwatts. The sonographer increases the transmit power by 6 dB; this results in a power level of _____.

    A. 46 milliwatts
    B. 80 milliwatts
    C. 160 milliwatts
    D. 240 milliwatts

57. This image is poor because of inadequate:

    A. Overall gain
    B. TGC
    C. Acoustical power
    D. Log compression

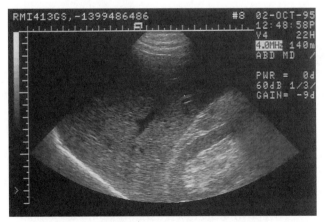

58. An advantage obtained when the sector field of a phased array B-mode scanner is reduced is a higher:

    A. Dynamic range
    B. Frame rate
    C. Output power
    D. Ultrasound frequency

59. Suppose a Doppler signal of 10 kHz is picked up for reflectors moving 1 m/s. For exactly the same conditions, what frequency Doppler signal is obtained for reflectors moving 50 cm/s?

    A. 50 Hz
    B. 500 Hz
    C. 1000 Hz
    D. 5000 Hz

60. Before analog echo signals are stored in the digital scan converter memory, they must pass through:

    A. The display monitor
    B. Postprocessing circuits
    C. An analog-to-digital converter
    D. An image processor

61. For a single-element transducer, focusing is most commonly done using:

    A. Electronic time delays only
    B. A curved element only
    C. A water path
    D. A curved element AND electronic time delays

62. Suppose an object appears to be circular on an ultrasound image. If the diameter is 4 cm, the area is closest to which of the following?

    A. 6.25 mm
    B. 12.5 cm^2
    C. 50 μm
    D. 50 cm^2

63. Suppose a Doppler signal of 5 kHz is obtained using a 5-MHz ultrasound transducer. For exactly the same conditions, what Doppler signal frequency will be obtained for a 10-MHz ultrasound transducer?

    A. 1 kHz
    B. 5 kHz
    C. 10 kHz
    D. 50 kHz

64. Echo signals from just distal to a mass are "brighter" (have greater amplitudes) than other echoes from the same depth. This is probably caused by a _____ in the mass.

    A. Lower impedance
    B. Higher attenuation
    C. Higher sound speed
    D. Lower attenuation

65. For a one-dimensional linear array, slice thickness focusing is done by which one of the following?

    A. Using very thin transducer elements
    B. Using a mirror
    C. The manufacturer applies an acoustic lens
    D. Electronic time delays are applied

66. A sonographer notices that the image frame rate is 30 frames per second when the depth setting is 14 cm. If the depth setting were changed to 7 cm, the image frame rate could be as high as:

    A. 15 frames per second
    B. 40 frames per second
    C. 60 frames per second
    D. 30 frames per second; frame rate does not change with depth setting

67. Which statement is true for single-element focused transducers?

    A. The focal distance may be varied electronically
    B. The beam is not affected by focusing
    C. The beam width is independent of frequency
    D. The focus cannot be varied by the sonographer

68. Some sector scanners provide the capability to reduce the imaged field sector angle. The main advantage of this operation is:

    A. It allows use of higher frequencies
    B. A smaller sector angle offers a higher frame rate
    C. A smaller sector improves the dynamic range
    D. It enables increased acoustical power in the patient

69. Studies indicate that ultrasound exposures to small animals have resulted in no biological effects as long as the spatial peak–temporal average intensity produced by an unfocused ultrasound beam is below:

    A. 100 mW/cm^2
    B. 1000 mW/cm^2
    C. 100 W/cm^2
    D. 1000 W/cm^2

70. A piezoelectric transducer serves as a detector by doing what?

    A. Producing an electrical signal from incoming sound waves
    B. Producing an electrical signal following shock excitation
    C. Focusing sound beams and sending them to the receiver
    D. Reflecting sound beams back into the medium

71. Suppose for a pulsed Doppler device, the maximum velocity that can be detected from a depth of 10 cm without aliasing is 1 m/s. If the depth is changed to 5 cm, but the ultrasound frequency and the beam angle remain the same, the maximum velocity that can be picked up without aliasing will be:

    A. 0.5 m/s
    B. 1 m/s
    C. 2 m/s
    D. 4 m/s

72. Which Doppler instrument control can be adjusted to eliminate high-amplitude, low-frequency signals from the spectral display while retaining high-frequency signals?

    A. Doppler gain
    B. Angle cursor
    C. Transmit power
    D. High pass filter

73. Which of the following is NOT an example of a CRT (cathode ray tube) device?

    A. Monitor on a personal computer
    B. Oscilloscope
    C. Video monitor
    D. Thermal printer

74. The number of bits per pixel in the scan converter memory is most closely related to:

    A. Axial resolution capabilities
    B. Lateral resolution capabilities
    C. Scan converter spatial resolution
    D. The number of amplitude levels stored

75. Which number COULD be a binary number?

    A. 101
    B. 212121
    C. 98
    D. 3.2 × 10^4

76. The duty factor would likely increase if which one of the following were done by the sonographer?

    A. Increase the receiver gain
    B. Decrease the transmit power
    C. Decrease the depth setting
    D. Increase the dynamic range

77. The ultrasound operating mode producing the highest spatial peak–time average intensity is:

    A. B-mode imaging
    B. M-mode
    C. Combined B-mode imaging and M-mode
    D. Pulsed Doppler

78. Which feature of a Doppler signal depends on the reflector speed?

    A. Amplitude
    B. Frequency
    C. Phase
    D. Depth of origin

79. These two images were taken using the same output power and receiver gain settings. The most likely control that was varied between the two scans is the:

    A. Depth setting
    B. Transmit focus
    C. Log compression
    D. TGC slope

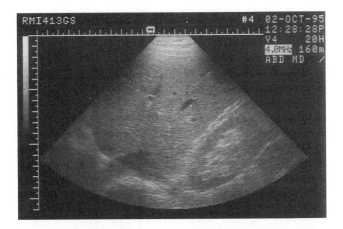

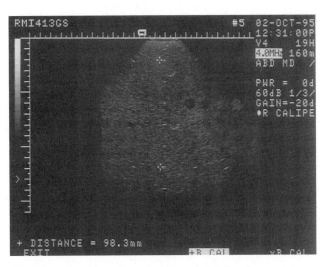

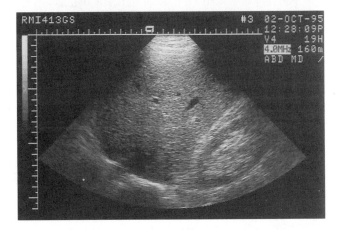

80. A standard VCR stores information in the form of:

    A. Digitized signals
    B. Darkened regions on tape
    C. Microscopic holes or pits
    D. Magnetized regions on tape

81. An advantage of time domain correlation over Doppler processing for color flow imaging is that for the same ultrasound frequency, time domain correlation has greater:

    A. Axial resolution
    B. Sensitivity and penetration
    C. Acoustical exposure
    D. Ease of use for the operator

82. This caliper setup and distance readout in this image indicates the:

    A. Axial resolution
    B. Maximum depth of visualization
    C. Vertical distance measurement accuracy
    D. Slice thickness

83. Doppler flow phantoms are useful for determining

    A. Maximum depth of Doppler signal detection
    B. Vertical distance measurement accuracy
    C. Acoustical output during color flow imaging
    D. Horizontal distance measurement accuracy

84. In pulse-echo ultrasound, the reflector depth is determined from:

    A. The echo amplitude before TGC
    B. The echo arrival time
    C. The echo frequency content
    D. The ultrasound beam axis

85. Which of the following DOES NOT OCCUR when the pulse power is INCREASED?

    A. The transducer oscillates at a higher amplitude
    B. The ultrasound wave amplitude in the tissue increases
    C. The acoustical exposure to the patient decreases
    D. Echoes detected by the transducer have greater amplitudes

86. The depth of the sample volume in a pulsed Doppler system is most closely determined by:

    A. The axial distance of an operator-positioned electronic gate
    B. The lateral position of an operator-positioned Doppler gate
    C. The axial resolution of the device in Doppler mode
    D. The vertical scale of the spectral display

87. A common technique for obtaining mean Doppler shift frequencies for color flow imagers is known as:

    A. Demodulation
    B. Autocorrelation
    C. Zero crossing detection
    D. Frame averaging

88. Acoustical shadowing indicates that the _____ of a proximal object is high.

    A. Sound propagation speed
    B. Attenuation level
    C. Interior scattering
    D. Mass density

89. Which ONE of the following statements is true about aliasing in color flow imaging?

    A. It cannot occur
    B. Image pixels appear as flow reversal
    C. It is independent of angle
    D. It is independent of pulse repetition frequency

90. Suppose the sonographer adjusts a control on the machine that doubles the pressure amplitude but does not change the pulse duration or the pulse repetition frequency. You can expect the time average intensity to:

    A. Halve
    B. Remain the same
    C. Double
    D. Quadruple

91. The average intensity during the very brief time the acoustical pulse passes a point in the field is known as the:

    A. Time average intensity
    B. Temporal peak intensity
    C. Pulse average intensity
    D. Point intensity

92. On a color flow image with blue indicating motion towards the transducer and red motion away, a vessel may appear as both blue and red on the same image because of:

    A. Angle effects
    B. Slice thickness effects
    C. Velocity errors in the machine
    D. Use of different frequency pulses for different regions

93. On this image of a test phantom, object *a* differs from the background because of its higher:

    A. Backscatter only
    B. Speed of sound only
    C. Backscatter and speed of sound
    D. Attenuation and backscatter

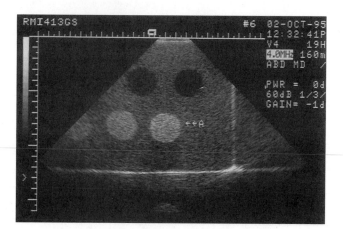

94. Aliasing in pulsed Doppler will occur when the Doppler signal _____ exceeds the Nyquist limit.

    A. Amplitude
    B. Power
    C. Frequency
    D. Phase

95. Structures and features on an image that do not correspond to the object being imaged are called _____.

    A. Texture or speckle marks
    B. False positives
    C. Artifacts
    D. Pixels

96. A pointlike target, such as a small calcification, appears elongated on an ultrasound B-mode image because of:

    A. Slice thickness effects
    B. Beam width effects
    C. Refraction effects
    D. Shadowing

97. A measurement comparing the actual separation between two reflectors placed at different positions perpendicular to the beam axis, with the separation indicated on calipers, is a test of:

    A. Axial resolution
    B. Ultrasound wavelength
    C. Vertical distance measurement accuracy
    D. Horizontal measurement accuracy

98. When you measure the width of the ultrasound beam in a direction PERPENDICULAR to the image plane, you are determining the:

    A. Axial resolution
    B. Grating lobe width
    C. Lateral resolution
    D. Slice thickness

99. The acoustical power from an ultrasound scanner is expressed in:

    A. Milliwatts

    B. Decibels

    C. Joules

    D. m/s

100. Increasing which of the following BOTH increases echo signal amplitude over the entire image AND increases the acoustical exposure to the patient.

    A. Receiver overall gain

    B. Dynamic range of the receiver

    C. Transmit power

    D. TGC slope

101. The peak rarefactional pressure is most likely to be given in:

    A. Decibels

    B. Megapascals

    C. Milliwatts

    D. Kilohertz

102. If the acoustical power of a transducer is 20 mW, and the transducer has an area of 4 cm², the I(SATA) at the transducer surface is:

    A. 5 mW/cm²

    B. 10 mW/cm²

    C. 24 mW/cm²

    D. 80 mW/cm²

103. In a sound wave, regions where the pressure is lower than the background pressure are called regions of:

    A. Rarefaction

    B. Scatter

    C. Compression

    D. Interference

104. If the sonographer adjusts a control on the machine that doubles the pulse repetition frequency, but does not change the pulse amplitude or the pulse duration, you can expect the time average intensity to:

    A. Halve

    B. Remain the same

    C. Double

    D. Quadruple

105. In general, ALL sound waves, including audible and ultrasonic, are produced by:

    A. A piezoelectric crystal

    B. An electromagnetic transducer

    C. A cathode ray tube

    D. A vibrating source

106. Which ONE of the following statements is true regarding the acoustical output levels of ultrasound scanners?

    A. Scanners from different manufacturers produce about the same output in B-mode imaging mode.

    B. The acoustical power and time average intensities are about the same for all operating modes.

    C. The operating mode producing the highest spatial peak–time average intensity is M-mode.

    D. Acoustical output levels reported in operator manuals are for maximum transmit levels rather than typical control settings.

107. No Doppler shift is detected when the Doppler angle is _____ degrees.

    A. 0

    B. 45

    C. 90

    D. 180

108. How is beam steering done by a phased array transducer?

    A. A single, separate channel is used for each beam

    B. All elements are excited; time delays control the beam direction

    C. A motor inside the transducer housing oscillates the array

    D. Groups of elements are excited separately; the active group position determines the beam direction

109. Matching layers on the transducer surface:

    A. Improve transmission from the piezoelectric element to tissue

    B. Protect the patient from high-amplitude pressure pulses

    C. Make the piezoelectric element less dense

    D. Focus the ultrasound beam

110. Frame rates are lower in color flow imaging than in B-mode imaging mainly because:

    A. The signal processing after echo data are detected is more time consuming in color mode

    B. Velocity computation requires several pulse-echo sequences for every beam line

    C. Lower ultrasound frequencies generally are used in color

    D. Lower frame rates reduce the acoustical exposure

111. Suppose the wavelength is 0.5 mm. If the frequency doubles, the new wavelength is:

    A. 1 mm
    B. 0.5 mm
    C. 0.25 mm
    D. 0.125 mm

112. How many discrete amplitude levels are available in a "6-bits per pixel" scan converter memory?

    A. 6
    B. 12
    C. 36
    D. 64

113. The extra image of a kidney (arrow) in this longitudinal image of the liver and right kidney most likely is a:

    A. Mirror image artifact
    B. Side lobe artifact
    C. Refraction artifact
    D. Reverberation

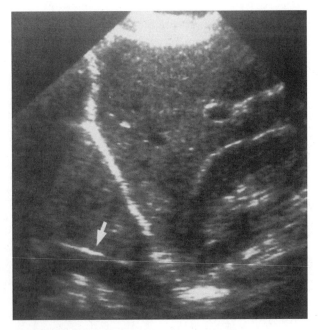

114. Units for energy are:

    A. Newtons
    B. Joules
    C. Watts
    D. Pascals

115. The number 1540 is expressed in scientific notation as:

    A. 1.54
    B. 1.54×10^3
    C. 1/1540
    D. 15.4×10^3

116. Which of the following actions would not lead to a DECREASE in the image frame rate of a phased array scanner?

    A. Increase the image depth setting
    B. Increase the number of transmit focal zones
    C. Increase the width of the image sector
    D. Increase the transmit power to the transducer

Answers to Test Yourself

1. A, the focal depth of the transmitted beam Most scanners focus the received echoes dynamically, regardless of the transmit focal position
2. B, the speed of sound
3. A, reflective interfaces, such as the diaphragm or bone
4. D, speed of sound and density
5. B, stable and transient
6. B, slice thickness effects. The tube is oriented horizontally, so the slice thickness causes echoes from out of the image plane to fill in the tube's image.
7. C, the curved array (A linear array works the same way.)
8. D, the calipers are set to measure the displayed width of the image of a point target. This is closely related to the beam width or the lateral resolution.
9. C, lots more reflectors
10. C, selection of the sample volume depth
11. D, vacuum, of course!
12. D, mW/cm^2
13. A, call Z_1 1 rayl, making Z_2 1.1 rayl. The amplitude reflection coefficient is then (1.1 - 1)/(1.1 + 1) = 0.1/2.1, or about 0.05.
14. A, in write zoom, the zoomed region occupies all the available pixels, whereas in read zoom the pixels corresponding to the region to be zoomed are enlarged on the monitor
15. D, 525 lines, 30/s
16. D, heating and cavitation
17. A, acoustical pressure is given in pascals. Although a *change* in pressure can be indicated by decibels, absolute values of pressure are expressed in pascals.
18. A, the frequency
19. B, wavelength
20. C, spectral analysis
21. D, twice the reflector distance, or 8.4 cm
22. A, Curie temperature
23. C, 1540 m/s = 1.54×10^6 mm/s = 1.54 mm/μs
24. A, $\lambda = c/f = (1.54$ mm/μs)/(10 cycles/μs) = 0.154 mm.
25. B, decibels are used to quantify the ratio of two amplitudes, intensities, or power levels
26. D, thermal index, abbreviated TI

27. D, a tissue-to-air interface will reflect nearly 100% of the incident beam energy. It is even more reflective than a soft tissue-to-bone interface.
28. C, binary digit
29. D, M-mode (A-mode is echo amplitude versus depth.)
30. B, applying an electrical pulse
31. C, an in vitro experiment
32. C, the medium's density and compressibility or "stiffness"
33. D
34. C, the lateral resolution
35. C, for the same transducer diameter, beam divergence decreases as frequency increases
36. A, NFL = a^2/wavelength; because the wavelength at 5 MHz is $1/2$ the wavelength of 2.5 MHz, the NFL doubles
37. D, refraction
38. B, period is equal to the inverse of the frequency $1/(5,000,000/s) = 0.0000002$ s $= 0.2$ μs.
39. D, the attenuation coefficient at 5 MHz will be 0.5 dB/cm $\times$ 5 $= 2.5$ dB/cm. The total attenuation will be 2.5 dB/cm $\times$ 5 cm $= 12.5$ dB.
40. C; as the phase of the echo from moving reflectors changes from one pulse echo sequence to the next, motion is detected
41. D, the linear array (Grating lobes may also be possible with phased arrays and curvilinear arrays; manufacturers use small, closely spaced elements to avoid or reduce them.)
42. A, transverse waves do not travel through soft tissue
43. A, analog format
44. B, its spatial resolution
45. D, a hydrophone
46. B, pulse duration
47. D, refraction
48. C
49. C, the pulse repetition frequency
50. B, shorter duration pulses and better axial resolution
51. B, between the transducer and patient
52. D
53. B, bone has the highest sound speed
54. B, diameters and circumferences have linear units; areas have square units
55. C, pulsed Doppler tends to have (1) longer duration pulses and (2) higher pulse repetition rates, leading to higher duty factors
56. C, using the "3-dB rule", divide the 6-dB increase into two 3-dB increments; each increment represents a doubling of the power
57. B, inadequate TGC
58. B, reducing the sector angle reduces the number of beam lines used to form the image and allows a higher frame rate

59. D, the Doppler frequency is proportional to the velocity, which was halved; 5000 Hz is $1/2$ of 10 kHz.
60. C, an analog-to-digital converter
61. B, a curved element
62. B, area is π $\times$ radius squared, $= 3.14 \times$ $(2$ cm$)^2$ $= 12.5$ cm^2
63. C, the Doppler frequency is proportional to the ultrasound frequency, which was doubled
64. D, the description is for acoustical enhancement, related to lower attenuation in overlying structures
65. C, currently, with one-dimensional arrays the elevational focusing is done using a lens or a curved element (A few newer arrays employ $1^1/2$ D technology, enabling electronic focusing in the elevational direction.)
66. C, changing the depth setting from 14 cm to 7 cm halves the time needed for each beam line
67. D, the focus of a single-element transducer cannot be changed by the sonographer
68. B, higher frame rates are allowed
69. A, this is part of the AIUM Statement on results of exposures to small mammals
70. A
71. C, it will double to 2 m/s because the PRF can be doubled
72. D, this is a description for the high pass filter, or wall filter
73. D, they are all based on CRTs except D
74. D, the number of amplitude levels stored
75. A, binary numbers use only 0s and 1s.
76. C, on many scanners, when the depth setting is reduced, the frame rate increases. This must mean that the pulse repetition frequency also increases
77. D, pulsed Doppler
78. B, the Doppler frequency depends on the reflector speed
79. C, the log compression. This is evident because of the higher contrast on image B.
80. D, magnetized regions on tape
81. A, time domain correlation, as implemented in the Philips system, can use short-duration pulses, providing better axial resolution
82. C, they are set to measure vertical measurement accuracy
83. A
84. B, the echo arrival time
85. C, the acoustical exposure would generally increase, not decrease, if the pulser power is increased
86. A
87. B, autocorrelation
88. B, attenuation level
89. B, just as with spectral Doppler, there appears to be flow reversal when aliasing occurs

90. D, generally, intensity is proportional to the square of the pressure amplitude
91. C, pulse average intensity
92. A, angle effects
93. D, the increased scatter leads to brighter echoes. The excess shadowing is due to increased attenuation.
94. C, frequency
95. C, artifacts
96. B, beam width effects
97. D, horizontal measurement accuracy is measured along a line perpendicular to a beam axis and in the image plane; vertical measurement accuracy is measured along a beam axis
98. D, the slice thickness
99. A, watts or milliwatts
100. C, both happen when the transmit power is increased
101. B, absolute values for the pressure are in pascals or in this case, megapascals
102. A, 20 mW/4 cm^2 = 5 mW/cm^2
103. A, rarefaction
104. C, double

105. D, all sound waves are produced by vibrating sources. A piezoelectric transducer is but one type of sound source.
106. D, this is the only true statement
107. C, 90 degrees, where flow is perpendicular to the ultrasound beam direction
108. B
109. A, they improve sound transmission from transducer to patient
110. B, the use of multiple pulse-echo sequences along each beam line slows the frame rate
111. C, doubling the frequency halves the wavelength
112. D, 64 levels, found by evaluating 2^6 ($2 \times 2 \times 2 \times 2 \times 2 \times 2$).
113. A, this is a mirror image artifact. The "mirror" in this case is the diaphragm.
114. B, joules.
115. B, 1.54×10^3. A number in scientific notation is most often expressed as the product of a number from 1-10 $\times$ 10 raised to the appropriate power. 2,521 = 2.521 $\times 10^3$; 0.002 = 2.0 $\times 10^{-3}$; etc.
116. D, an increase in the transmit power level will not affect the frame rate. Increases in all other parameters mentioned generally result in a decreased frame rate.

$1^1/_2$ Dimensional array: a linear, curvilinear, or phased array in which some elevational focus and beam forming is done electronically. In conventional arrays the elevational focusing is done only with a lens. By providing a limited degree of electronic focusing elevationally, the slice thickness can be made smaller over an extended range. The term $1^1/_2 D$ refers to the fact that whereas an array usually has over 128 elements laterally, it may have only 5 or so elements in the elevational plane.

3-dB rule: silly way to remember that when the output of a scanner increases (decreases) by 3 decibels, the power and the intensity double (halve). If the power is 20 mW and the sonographer reduces it by 9 dB (three 3-dB increments) repeated application of the 3-dB rule tells you that the reduced power is 20 mW $\times$ $^1/_2$ $\times$ $^1/_2$ $\times$ $^1/_2$ = 2.5 mW.

absorption: conversion of acoustical energy into heat. Absorption is one mechanism leading to ultrasound beam attenuation in tissue.

acoustical impedance (characteristic acoustical impedance): the speed of sound in a medium multiplied by its density. Part of the energy of an ultrasound beam is reflected at interfaces between materials that have unequal acoustical impedances.

acoustical power: quantity describing the rate at which acoustical energy is emitted by the ultrasound transducer of an ultrasound instrument.

acoustical pressure amplitude: the maximum cycle-to-cycle increase (or decrease) in the pressure due to a sound wave, relative to the background pressure.

acoustical wave: see **sound wave**

active aperture: the area of an array transducer that is actively transmitting or receiving; the active aperture is determined by whichever elements are transmitting or receiving.

address: a unique number associated with each memory location in a computer or other digital device.

aliasing: the production of artifactual, lower frequency components in a Doppler signal spectrum when the pulse repetition frequency of the Doppler instrument is less than two times the maximum frequency of the Doppler signal.

A-mode (amplitude mode) display: method of displaying pulse-echo ultrasound signals in which a trace presents the instantaneous echo signal amplitude versus time after transmission of an acoustical pulse. Since the time is proportional to reflector distance, this trace also is a record of echo signal amplitude versus reflector distance.

amplitude: maximum cyclical change in a quantity, such as the pressure in an ultrasound wave.

amplitude reflection coefficient: the ratio of the reflected pressure amplitude (p_r) to the incident pressure amplitude (p_i) at an interface.

analog-to-digital (A/D) converter: component or device that accepts analog signals, such as from a transducer or an amplifier, and converts these to a digital format for processing in a computer.

annular array: a transducer array consisting of a number of ring-shaped piezoelectric elements arranged concentrically, along with a central disk. An annular array can provide multiple transmit focal zones, dynamic receive focusing, and dynamic aperture. However, scanning must be done by mechanically sweeping the beam. (See also linear array, curvilinear array, and phased array.)

aperture: another name for the active radiating or receiving surface of a transducer assembly.

apodization: decreasing the relative excitation near the edges of the radiating surface of a transducer during transmission, or decreasing the relative sensitivity near the edge of the receiving surface of the transducer, in order to reduce side lobes. Apodization is used in most array transducer assemblies.

array transducer assembly: a group of piezoelectric elements, each one of which can be excited individually and whose echo signals can be detected and amplified separately.

artifact: (in an ultrasound image or record) any echo signal whose displayed position does not correspond to the actual position of a reflector in the body or whose displayed amplitude is not indicative of the reflecting or scattering properties of the region from which the echo originated.

attenuation: reduction in the amplitude and intensity of a sound wave as it propagates through a medium. Attenuation of ultrasound waves in tissue is caused by absorption and by scattering and reflection.

attenuation coefficient: the amount of attenuation per unit distance traveled by a wave; typical units are dB/cm.

autocorrelation: see **correlation detector**

auto scanner (automatic scanner): another name for a B-mode scanning instrument in which the sweep of the ultrasound beam is done, either mechanically or electronically, by the scan head. Real-time scanners are a type of auto scanner.

axial resolution: minimum reflector spacing along the axis of an ultrasound beam that results in separate, distinguishable echoes on the display. The shorter the pulse duration, the better the axial resolution, that is, the closer the reflectors can be and be distinguished.

bandwidth: see **frequency bandwidth**

base plus fog: a slight opacity of photographic or x-ray film, found upon developing without any exposure.

beam: the directed ultrasound field produced by an ultrasound transducer.

beam former: part of an imaging instrument that provides the pulse-delay sequences for transmit focusing and for dynamic receive focusing. The beam former also controls the beam direction for electronically scanned arrays.

binary number: a number consisting of a series of 0s and 1s to represent a quantity. Binary numbers are used in digital computers. They have 2 as a base, in contrast to the decimal number system, which has 10 as its base.

biplane imaging: simultaneously forming and displaying B-mode images of two different planes, usually perpendicular to one another.

bit: acronym for "binary digit." A bit is the fundamental unit of information in a computer or other digital system. It is formed by a device that can be in either of two states, "on" or "off."

B-mode (brightness mode) display: method of displaying pulse echo ultrasound signals in which echoes are displayed as intensity-modulated dots at a position corresponding either to the reflector location, as in B-mode scanning, or to the reflector depth, as in M-mode records. When gray scale processing is used, the brightness of the dot indicates the echo signal amplitude.

B-mode image: a two-dimensional image obtained with a pulse-echo scanner and depicting reflectors and scatterers in a region interrogated by a B-mode scan.

B-mode scan: process of generating a two-dimensional ultrasound B-mode image by scanning the sound beam over the region to be examined and displaying resultant echo signals at a position corresponding to the reflector location using the B-mode display. The term *B-mode scan* also is sometimes used to denote a B-mode image.

byte: group of bits in a computer or other digital system; it usually is used to refer to eight bits.

cavitation: formation of gas- or vapor-filled cavities within a medium due (in the case of ultrasound waves) to the large acoustical pressures accompanying an intense ultrasound beam. Cavitation also refers to gas bubble activity, such as growth and collapse in transient cavitation, in the presence of the sound field.

clutter (Doppler): interfering echoes from stationary or nearly stationary structures, which can overwhelm echoes from blood during Doppler detection of flow.

clutter (transducer): spurious echo signals originating from points outside the main beam of an array transducer assembly and caused by side lobes, grating lobes, and inadequate isolation between elements.

color angio mode: see **energy mode**

color flow imaging: operating mode available on some ultrasound instruments in which a two-dimensional image is generated that portrays moving reflectors in color. Most instruments that provide color flow images display gray scale B-mode images simultaneously.

comet-tail artifact echoes resulting from reverberation within (usually) a metallic object, such as gunshot material, metallic clips, etc.

compensation use of TGC or swept gain to correct echo signal amplitudes for attenuation effects.

composite piezoelectric element: transducer element material formed by dicing standard piezoelectric ceramic material and filling the grooves with an epoxy. Composite piezoelectric materials have greater sensitivity, lower acoustical impedance, and wider frequency bandwidths than standard piezoelectric materials.

compression (acoustical waves): elevations in the density at a location in a medium, accompanying the cyclic pressure elevations during the passage of a sound wave. (See also **rarefaction**)

compression (electrical signals): method for reducing the range of amplitudes among signals, while retaining information regarding the relative amplitude levels. Logarithmic compression is used frequently, enabling weak signals to be boosted above the display threshold at the same time that strong signals do not saturate the display.

confocal imaging: see **multiple transmit focal zones**

console: another name for the part of an ultrasound instrument to which the transducer assembly is attached through its interconnecting cable; the console contains the pulser, receiver, scan converter, and display.

continuous-wave (CW) Doppler: type of Doppler device and processing involving transmitting a constant amplitude sound wave continuously into the region to be examined and processing echo signals for Doppler-shifted frequencies. Because the transmitter transducer continuously flood the examined region, there is little or no discrimination of the depth of the moving reflectors.

contrast resolution: the smallest variation in echo level that can be distinguished as a shade of gray on a B-mode display. Also, the smallest variation in scattering level between an object and the surrounding material, which results in the object being just noticeable on a B-mode display.

convex array: see **curvilinear array**

correlation detector: scheme used to measure changes in a signal wave train from one time to another, such as from one transmit pulse to the next in a color flow instrument. Such devices are used in color flow imaging instruments to detect phase changes in echo signals from moving reflectors.

cosine (cos): for an angle A in a right triangle, the ratio of the adjacent side to the hypotenuse.

coupling: providing a transonic material between two media, such as the transducer assembly and the skin, to ensure that sound waves propagate from one to the other. Coupling gel or oil eliminates air between the transducer assembly and the patient's skin in an ultrasound examination.

critical angle: smallest angle of incidence of a sound beam at a refracting interface for which there is total reflection of the incident beam. A critical angle exists when the speed of sound in the material on the transmitted beam side of the interface is greater than that in the material on the incident beam side.

Curie temperature: temperature at which a piezoelectric transducer becomes depolarized.

curvilinear array: a type of sequential array transducer assembly used in B-mode imaging in which the array elements are arranged in an arc. A curvilinear array does B-mode scanning in a fashion similar to that of a **linear array,** by element selection.

damping: dissipation of energy in motion of any type; here it is the dissipation of vibrational energy of an ultrasonic transducer in order to reduce the pulse duration.

decibel (dB): unit used to quantitatively express the ratio of two amplitudes or intensities. Decibels are not absolute units, but express one sound level or intensity in terms of another or in terms of a reference. Example: The amplitude 10 cm from the transducer is 10 dB lower than the amplitude 5 cm from the transducer. The relation between two signal amplitudes, A_1 and A_2, is expressed in decibels as $20\log(A_2/A_1)$. The relation between two intensities, I_1 and I_2, is expressed in decibels as $10\log(I_2/I_1)$. (See the **3-dB rule.**)

demodulation: removal of the high frequency components of a modulated signal, yielding an A-mode display for pulse-echo ultrasound or the Doppler signal for Doppler mode.

density: mass per unit volume; units are grams/cm^3, kg/m^3, etc.

depth calibration accuracy: see **vertical distance measurement accuracy**

diffraction: sound beam pattern when waves from different regions of a source or the edges of an obstacle add up at different points in the field.

diffuse reflector: a reflecting interface that has an irregular rather than a smooth surface; the sizes of the irregularities are comparable to or greater than the wavelength. Reflected waves from such an interface spread out in all directions.

digital: of or relating to data that are stored, manipulated, or read out in discrete units or levels.

digital calipers: system for measuring the distance between reflectors displayed on a B-mode image or M-mode display. The operator positions electronic markers or cursors on the display, adjacent to the structures to be measured, and the instrument computes the distance between cursors.

directional discrimination: measure of the ability of a directional Doppler instrument to display flow signals in the proper direction only.

directional Doppler: Doppler signal processing in which both the reflector speed and direction of motion (i.e., towards the transducer or away from the transducer) are detected and displayed.

displayed beam width: the size of the B-mode image of a point or line target, measured perpendicular to the direction of the sound beam. The displayed beam width varies with the receiver gain, the reflector depth, the acoustical impedance change at the reflector interface, etc.

displayed dynamic range: see **local dynamic range**

Doppler amplitude mode: see **energy mode**

Doppler angle: angle between the direction of reflector motion and the direction of propagation of the ultrasound beam.

Doppler effect: phenomenon whereby there is a change in the perceived frequency of a sound source relative to the transmitted frequency when there is relative motion between a sound source and a listener.

Doppler energy mode: see **energy mode**

Doppler shift: in general, the change in the perceived frequency relative to the transmitted frequency when there is relative motion between a sound source and a listener; in ultrasound, the difference between the frequency of a transmitted pulse and that of an echo signal when there is motion of the reflector relative to the transducer.

Doppler shift frequency (f_D): the difference between the frequency of received echo signals and the frequency of the transmitted ultrasound beam in a Doppler study.

duplex scanners: real-time B-mode scanners with built-in Doppler reception, processing, and display capabilities.

duty factor: the fraction of time that the transducer is actively producing ultrasound energy. It is often expressed as a percentage and is usually less than 1% for pulse-echo systems. The duty factor is equal to the pulse repetition frequency times the pulse duration.

dynamic aperture: term used to identify a process whereby the number of receiving elements in a transducer array automatically increases (thereby increasing the size of the aperture) with increasing reflector depth. Increasing the receiving aperture size with increasing reflector depth keeps lateral resolution nearly constant over the entire useful range of a transducer.

dynamic focus: process of electronically changing the *receiving* focal distance of an array transducer assembly so that it tracks the acoustic pulse position and reflector depth in real time. Each time a sound pulse is transmitted, the instrument initially sets the receiving focal distance at a shallow depth. As the time duration after the transmitted pulse increases, the receiving focal distance increases automatically.

dynamic frequency tracking: varying the center frequency of the amplifier of a pulse-echo instrument so that it gradually changes with time following each transmit pulse. Dynamic frequency tracking sometimes is used to optimize the receiver's sensitivity so that it coincides best with the frequencies available in the echo signal pulses picked up from structures at different depths.

The latter frequencies change with increasing reflector distance because of preferential attenuation of higher frequency sound waves by tissues.

dynamic range: the ratio of the largest to smallest signals that an instrument or a component of an instrument can respond to without distortion. In diagnostic ultrasound the dynamic range frequently is expressed in decibels. (See also **local dynamic range.**)

echo signal enhancement: see **enhancement**

effective beam width: the displayed beam width that results from the combined shape of the transmitted beam and the receiving sensitivity pattern of a transducer assembly. In an array transducer assembly the transmitted beam pattern and receiving sensitivity pattern may be quite different.

electronically sectored array: see **phased array**

elevational resolution: the ability to distinguish between reflectors separated along a line that is perpendicular to the ultrasound image plane. (See also **slice thickness.**)

energy: the capacity to do work. (In this context work is formally defined as that which is done when a force acts on matter and moves it.) Units for energy are *joules*.

energy mode: method of color flow processing and display in which the Doppler signal amplitude or the signal intensity, averaged over a small time interval, is displayed rather than the average Doppler frequency. Velocity and flow direction are not displayed, and aliasing does not affect the image. This display mode also is called *power mode, Doppler amplitude mode,* and *color angio mode.*

enhancement: a manifestation of increased echo signal amplitudes returning from regions lying beyond an object in which the attenuation is lower than the average attenuation in adjacent overlying regions. (See also **partial shadowing.**)

epidemiology: The field of science dealing with the relationships of the various factors involved in the frequencies and distributions of an infectious process, a disease, or a physiological state. Epidemiology is sometimes used to study whether diagnostic ultrasound exposures of humans have led to a measurable effect of some kind.

far field (Fraunhofer zone): that part of the field of an ultrasound transducer that is a large distance from the probe. In the far field the beam diameter generally increases with increasing distance. For an unfocused circular, single-element transducer of radius a the far field is usually taken to extend beyond the distance a^2/λ, where λ is the wavelength.

FFT analyzer: (fast Fourier transform analyzer) device for doing frequency analysis of complex signals. FFT analyzers are often used in spectral Doppler instruments to obtain a display of the frequency characteristics of the signal.

focal distance: the distance from the transducer to the plane where the effective beam width is narrowest.

focal zone: the region over which the effective width of the sound beam is within some measure of (such as two times) its width at the focal distance.

focusing (receiver): process of controlling the receiving sensitivity pattern of a transducer in order to narrow the effective beam width and improve the lateral resolution over some depth range. The receiving focal distance of an array can change dynamically as echoes from along a given beam line are received.

focusing (transmit): process of controlling the convergence of a transmitted sound beam in order to narrow the beam and sometimes to increase the intensity over some axial range. Transmit focusing can be done with a concave transducer element, an acoustic lens, or an array of elements along with electronic time delays. The focal distance of the array may be varied electronically by changing the electronic delay sequence, and thus may be user selectable.

frame rate: the rate at which images are updated on the display of a real-time scanning instrument. Often used synonymously with scan repetition rate.

freeze: see **image freeze**

frequency: the number of cycles per second that a periodic event or function undergoes; the number of cycles completed per unit time. The frequency of a sound wave is determined by the number of oscillations per second of the vibrating source.

frequency bandwidth: a measure of the spread of frequencies in a pulsed waveform or the range of frequencies to which a device responds. The frequency bandwidth of a transducer can be determined by spectral analysis of an echo signal from a plane, smooth reflector. The shorter the pulse duration emitted by a transducer, the wider the frequency bandwidth, and vice versa.

frequency bandwidth of a receiver: the range of ultrasound signal frequencies that the receiver can amplify with maximum or nearly maximum gain.

gain: a measure of the amount of amplification of an amplifier. It is the ratio of the output signal amplitude to the input signal amplitude and can be expressed as a simple ratio or in decibels.

grating lobe: in the sound beam from an array, energy falling outside the main lobe or main beam as a result of the active transducer aperture being split into elements. Grating lobes are reduced or eliminated by using very small elements.

gray scale processing: signal processing used to modulate the brightness of dots on a B-mode display in accordance with the amplitude of individual echo signals.

hertz: unit for frequency, equal to 1 cycle per second and abbreviated Hz.

high PRF mode: pulsed Doppler instrument operating condition in which the PRF is so high that a transmit pulse is emitted by the transducer before echo signals corresponding to the previous transmit pulse arrive from the sample volume. Ambiguities in the range from which Doppler signals originate may result. High PRF mode is used to avoid aliasing in pulsed Doppler.

horizontal distance accuracy: a measure of the accuracy to which the distance between two point reflectors, separated along a line perpendicular to the direction of the central beam line forming a B-mode image, can be determined on the display.

hydrophone: a device consisting of a small piezoelectric element mounted on the end of a narrow tube or supported on a thin membrane, commonly used to measure the acoustic pressure and determine the intensity at points in an ultrasound field.

hyperechoic: adjective used to describe a region for which the average echo signal amplitude is greater that that in the material surrounding the region.

hypoechoic: adjective used to describe a region for which the average echo signal amplitude is lower than that in the surrounding region.

image freeze: condition in which B-mode image, M-mode, Doppler, and/or color flow image data are retained in a scan converter's memory for examination and/or photography as well as for video recording.

image texture: see **texture** and **speckle**

impedance matching layers: thin layers attached to the outer surface of a piezoelectric element in a transducer in order to provide efficient transmission of sound waves from the transducer element to soft tissue, and vice versa. Matching layers minimize reflections at the transducer–soft tissue interface, improving the sensitivity.

inertial cavitation: see **transient cavitation.**

intensity: a measure of the strength of a sound wave. It is equal to the power per unit area transmitted through a region and has units of milliwatts per square centimeter (mW/cm^2) or watts per square centimeter (W/cm^2). For many conditions in ultrasonics the intensity is proportional to the square of the pressure amplitude. The following are commonly used intensity terms:

spatial average (SA) intensity: the intensity averaged over the beam area for a stationary sound beam or over the scan crossed area for a scanning beam. With a stationary transducer it is equal to the acoustic power, P, contained within the beam, divided by the beam area A.

spatial peak (SP) intensity: the intensity at the point in the sound field where this value is the maximum. **temporal peak intensity:** the maximum instantaneous intensity attained during the pulse.

time average intensity: the relatively low value obtained when the intensity at any particular spot in the field, such as at the spatial peak location, is averaged over the time between pulses.

spatial peak–pulse average intensity I(SPPA): the average intensity in an acoustic pulse, measured at the location where this quantity is the largest.

spatial peak–time average intensity I(SPTA): the resultant measure of intensity, when averaged for a time equal to a scan repetition period in an automatic scanning mode or a pulse repetition period for a stationary beam, at the location in the field where this quantity is the largest.

spatial average–time average intensity I(SATA): the time average intensity, also averaged over the beam area for a stationary beam or the scan cross-sectional area for a scanning beam.

I_m: spatial peak intensity averaged over the largest half cycle of a pulse.

intensity reflection coefficient: the ratio of the reflected beam intensity to the incident beam intensity at an interface.

interface: surface forming the boundary between media having different properties.

interference: variation with distance or time of the amplitude of a wave, which results from the addition of two or more waves.

joule: unit of energy. (See also **watt, acoustical power,** and **energy.**)

kilohertz (kHz): 1000 hertz, or 10^3 cycles/s.

laminar flow: flow within a blood vessel in which most blood cells are moving with general uniformity of direction and velocity, and in which there is an organized distribution of velocities across the flow area.

lateral gain control: gain adjustment applied horizontally across the image to compensate for variations in transmission from one side of the image to the other. Controls are "TGC-like," only they are extended horizontally rather than vertically, reflective of their action on the image.

lateral resolution: minimum reflector spacing perpendicular to the axis of an ultrasound beam that results in separate, distinguishable echoes on the display. The narrower the ultrasound beam, the better the lateral resolution, that is, the closer the reflectors can be and be distinguished.

lead zirconate titanate: (abbreviated PZT) commonly used material for the piezoelectric element(s) in an ultrasound transducer.

linear array: an array transducer assembly used in B-mode imaging and color flow studies that has many, (usually) rectangularly shaped elements arranged side by side. Scanning is done by transmitting sound beams and receiving echo signals with clusters, or groups, of elements, the center of the element cluster defining the beam axis. It can be said that beam steering is done by element selection because of this process. A linear array sometimes is called a sequential array because of the method of beam steering. (See also **phased array, curvilinear array,** and **annular array.**)

linear scan: a type of scan used to generate a B-mode image in which motion of a transducer or ultrasound beam is along a straight line at right angles to the beam. (See also **sector scan.**)

local dynamic range: the echo signal level change causing the display in a pulse-echo instrument to vary from a just noticeable echo signal (e.g., the lowest gray level) to its maximum response (i.e., maximum brightness). This is also referred to as the *displayed dynamic range*.

logarithmic compression (log compression): a form of signal compression used in pulse-echo ultrasound. Logarithmic compression is especially useful for allowing amplitude variations between echo signals from weak scatterers to be evident on the display at the same time that changes in echo signal amplitude from strong reflectors are evident.

longitudinal sound wave: Sound wave for which the particle displacement is back-and-forth along a line parallel to the direction of wave propagation. Longitudinal ultrasound waves propagate through soft tissue.

manual scanner: type of ultrasound B-mode scanning instrument in which the sweep of the ultrasound beam in building up a single B-mode image is done by manually scanning a single element transducer over the region to be examined.

A scanning arm provides signals to track the position of the transducer and constrains the probe movement to the scanning plane. Also referred to as a *static scanner*. (See also **auto scanner**.)

maximum depth of visualization: the greatest distance in a tissue-mimicking phantom of specified properties at which parenchymal scatterers in the phantom can be visualized on the display.

maximum sensitivity: measure of the weakest echo signal level that can be detected and displayed clearly enough to be discernible above noise.

mechanical index (MI): a quantity derived from the peak rarefactional pressure and the frequency, indicating the likelihood of cavitation during an ultrasound scan.

mechanical scanner: transducer assembly that has one or more separate transducers and automatically scans the sound beam over the region of interest by physically moving the tranducers(s) or by oscillating a sound beam deflecting mirror.

megahertz (MHz): 1,000,000 hertz, or 10^6 cycles/s.

mirror image artifact: artifactual echoes and images appearing distal to a highly reflective interface, resulting when an echo from the interface is partially reflected by structures on its way back to the transducer.

M-mode (motion mode): method of recording and displaying pulse-echo ultrasound signals in which a B-mode trace is swept slowly across the display; generally, an M-mode display is formed using a stationary ultrasound beam, yielding distance/motion versus time information for reflectors along a single ultrasound beam line. Some instruments provide simultaneous M-mode records from two or more separate beam lines.

multiple transmit focal zones: focal zones established when two or more transmit focal distances are used simultaneously for each beam line in an ultrasound study. Each focal zone requires a separate transmit pulse, thereby increasing the scan time and reducing the frame rate. Also called *extended transmit focusing* and *confocal imaging*.

narrow-band amplifier: an amplifier that has a limited frequency range over which it responds to signals.

near field (Fresnel zone): that part of the field of an ultrasound transducer that is close to the face of the probe. In the near field the beam diameter generally decreases slightly with increasing distance from the transducer. For an unfocused circular, single element transducer of radius a, the near field is usually taken to extend to approximately a^2/λ, where λ is the wavelength.

near field length: a distance equal to a^2/λ from an unfocused transducer, where a is the transducer radius and λ is the wavelength.

newton: unit of force.

Nyquist sampling rate: the minimum rate that a signal can be "sampled" without aliasing. For a Doppler signal whose frequency is f_d, the Nyquist rate is $2f_d$. If the sampling rate is below the Nyquist rate, aliasing occurs. If it is above the Nyquist rate, the signal can be determined unambiguously.

operating mode: the distinct method used to acquire and display ultrasound echo signal information in an ultrasound instrument. Examples of discrete (separate) operating modes include B-mode imaging, pulse Doppler mode, and color flow imaging mode.

oscilloscope: electronic signal display device consisting of a cathode ray tube (CRT) and screen, with internal electron beam deflecting apparatus. The signal being displayed appears as a waveform on the screen of the device.

parabolic: adjective often applicable to flow conditions in blood vessels. Under parabolic flow, blood cells in the middle of the vessel move fastest, with a gradual decrease in flow velocity for points farther away from the center.

partial shadowing: a manifestation of decreased echo signal amplitudes returning from regions lying beyond an object in which the attenuation is higher than the average attenuation in adjacent overlying regions. (See also **shadowing** and **enhancement**.)

pascal: unit for expressing pressure amplitude.

peak compressional pressure: the temporal maximum positive pressure in the medium occurring during the passage of a pulsed sound wave. It is expressed in pascals or in megapascals.

peak rarefactional pressure: The temporal maximum negative pressure in the medium occurring during the passage of a pulsed ultrasound wave. It is expressed in pascals or in megapascals.

period: the duration of a single cycle of a periodic wave or event. It is equal to $1/f$, where f is the frequency.

phantom: see **tissue-mimicking phantom**

phase: the part of the cycle that a wave or a signal waveform happens to be in at some instant of time at the point considered.

phased array: an array transducer assembly that has very thin, (usually) rectangular elements arranged side by side. It relies upon electronic beam steering to sweep sound beams over a sector-shaped scanned region. Beam steering is done using electronic time delays in the transmitting and receiving circuits. (See also **linear array, curvilinear array,** and **annular array.**)

piezoelectric effect: generation of electrical signals as a result of, for example, an incident sound beam on a material that has piezoelectric properties. In the converse (or reverse) piezoelectric effect, the material expands or contracts when an electrical signal is applied.

pixel: (for picture element) separately addressable element in a digitally formatted image.

polarization: production of a relative displacement of positive and negative charges in a material.

polyvinylidene difluoride: (PVF_2) commonly used piezoelectric material in a hydrophone. PVF_2 sometimes is used in imaging transducers also.

postprocessing: manipulation and conditioning of signals and image data after they emerge from the scan converter memory and prior to display. Postprocessing is used to change the assignment of image brightness versus echo signal amplitude in memory.

power mode: see **energy mode**

preprocessing: conditioning and manipulation of echo signals prior to their storage in the scan converter memory.

pressure amplitude: see **acoustical pressure amplitude**

PRF: see **pulse repetition frequency**

proportional: term used to describe the relationship between two quantities when a fractional variation of one is always accompanied by the same fractional change in the other. For example, the wavelength is proportional to the speed of sound.

pulsatility index: a characteristic of the flow in a vessel, calculated by taking the difference between the peak systolic and the minimum diastolic velocities and dividing by the mean flow during the cardiac cycle.

pulsed Doppler: type of Doppler device involving transmitting a short-duration burst of sound into the region to be examined and processing the Doppler shifted signals from a limited depth range. The depth range is determined by a sample gate whose position and size usually can be selected by the instrument operator.

pulse duration: a measure of the time the transducer oscillates for each pulse. The shorter the pulse duration, the better the axial resolution.

pulse-echo response profile: a curve illustrating the amplitude of an echo from a small reflector versus the distance from the reflector to the transducer beam axis as the reflector is scanned perpendicular to the axis of an ultrasound transducer beam.

pulse-echo ultrasound: type of examination in which a short duration ultrasound pulse is transmitted into the region to be studied and echo signals resulting from scattering and reflection are detected and displayed. The reflector depth is inferred from the delay time between pulse transmission and echo reception.

pulser: component of an ultrasound instrument that provides signals for exciting the piezoelectric transducer in order to transmit an ultrasound beam.

pulse repetition frequency (PRF): number of acoustical pulses transmitted per second.

Q: see **quality factor**

quadrature detection: commonly used signal processing method to determine the flow direction in Doppler instruments. It is called *quadrature detection* because it involves splitting the received signal into two channels, one channel being mixed with the transmitted signal, the other mixed with the same signal only shifted in phase by 90 degrees.

quality assurance: steps taken, often including measurements with test objects and phantoms, to ensure that an instrument is operating consistently at its expected level of performance.

quality factor (Q): a measure of the frequency bandwidth, usually of a transducer. A high Q transducer has a narrower frequency bandwidth and poorer axial resolution than a low Q transducer.

quarter-wave matching layer: an impedance matching layer that is one quarter of a wavelength thick for waves of a given frequency. The acoustical impedance of this layer is between the impedance of the transducer and that of tissue. (See also **impedance matching layers.**)

radiation force: A small steady force that is produced when a sound beam strikes a reflecting or absorbing interface. The radiation force is proportional to the acoustical power.

radio frequency (rf): general term used to describe the frequency range into which medical ultrasound signals fall. (Note—the rf signal range generally is taken to be much broader than the frequency range used in medical ultrasound.)

radio frequency (rf) signal: an electrical signal whose frequency is in the rf frequency range. Signals within an ultrasound instrument between the transducer terminals and the components where rectification and filtering occur are referred to as *rf signals.*

range ambiguities: uncertainties in the actual range from which Doppler signals or echo signals originate. In pulsed Doppler instruments a high PRF can result in range ambiguities.

range equation: relationship between the distance to a reflector and the time it takes for a pulse of ultrasound to propagate to the reflector and return to the transducer.

rarefaction: reductions of the density at a location in a medium accompanying the cyclical pressure reductions during the passage of a sound wave. (See also **compression**.)

rayl: the unit for characteristic acoustical impedance; its fundamental units are $kg/m^2/s$.

Rayleigh scatterer: scattering object whose dimensions are much smaller than the ultrasonic wavelength. The scattered intensity from a volume of Rayleigh scatterers increases rapidly with increasing frequency, being related to frequency raised to the fourth power.

real-time scanner: an automatic scanner with sufficient scanning speed that images are updated frequently enough to allow positions of all reflectors of interest, including those that are moving, to be recorded.

receiving sensitivity pattern: the spatial response of a transducer as an echo detector. For a single-element transducer it is essentially the same as the transmitted beam. For transducer arrays it can be quite different from the transmitted beam.

rectification: step in echo signal processing in a pulse-echo ultrasound instrument in which rf signals, which oscillate both above and below zero volts, are converted to signals that oscillate in one direction only. An A-mode display is formed after rectification and filtering, that is, smoothing, the echo signal waveform.

reflection coefficient: see **amplitude reflection coefficient** and **intensity reflection coefficient**.

refraction: a change in the direction of propagation of a sound wave transmitted across an interface where the speed of sound varies. For refraction to take place the direction of the incident beam must not be perpendicular to the interface.

rejection: elimination of low-amplitude signals from the display, also known as *noise rejection.*

resolution: see **spatial resolution, contrast resolution, lateral resolution, axial resolution,** and **slice thickness.**

resonance frequency: (of an ultrasound transducer) the frequency for which the response of a transducer to an ultrasound beam is a maximum. Also, the frequency at which the transducer most efficiently converts electrical signals to mechanical vibrations.

reverberation: (in pulse-echo ultrasound) a back-and-forth reflection of part or all of a sound beam, usually between two strong reflectors, but sometimes between a scattering region and a strong reflector; reception of an echo signal from a reflector after a direct echo from this reflector has been received, due to multiple paths as above.

rf signal: see **radio frequency signal**

ring-down artifact: echo pattern caused by reverberation in a bubble or other soft tissue entity.

ring-down time: the time required for ringing (vibration of the transducer element at its resonance frequency) to decrease to a negligible level following excitation; also referred to as the *pulse duration.*

sample volume: the region in space from which Doppler data is collected in pulsed Doppler systems. The axial extent of the sample volume is determined by the duration of the transmitted pulse and the duration (length) of the sample gate. The width is determined by the lateral margins of the ultrasound beam.

scan convertor: component of an ultrasound scanning instrument that accepts echo signal data from the ultrasonic scanner, formats and stores these signals in an internal memory, and reads out the data to a TV monitor. In most instruments the data can be frozen, or retained in memory for a period of time, if so desired.

scanning speed: the rate at which the sound beam is swept across the scanned region in a B-mode scan and echo signal data are displayed. The maximum scanning speed is limited by the travel time of sound pulses in tissue.

scan plane thickness: same as **slice thickness.**

scan repetition rate: the number of times per second that a complete scan is done by an auto scanning instrument. It is sometimes referred to as the *frame rate* of the scanner.

scatter: reflection of a wave in various directions, caused by interfaces that are on the order of the size of the wavelength or smaller.

sector scan: a type of scan used to generate a B-mode image in which the transducer or the ultrasound beam is rotated or swept through an angle, the center of rotation being near or behind the surface of the transducer.

sensitivity: a measure of the weakest echo signal that an instrument is capable of detecting and displaying.

sequential (linear) array: see **linear array**

shadowing: loss of echo signals from distal structures due to attenuation of overlying structures. (See also **partial shadowing.**)

side lobes: energy in a sound beam that falls outside the main lobe or main beam.

simple harmonic motion: a periodic motion that is a sinusoidal function of time; it is characterized by a particular frequency.

sine (sin): for an angle A in a right triangle, the ratio of the opposite side to the hypotenuse.

sine wave: a waveform in which wave variables at a given location, such as the pressure or the particle displacement, vary in proportion to the sine of a constant times the time. Alternatively, at a fixed time the variable may vary in proportion to the sine of a constant times the distance.

slice thickness: the thickness of the section of tissue that contributes to echoes visualized on an image. Slice thickness depends on beam size, analogous to lateral resolution. However, it is the size of the beam **perpendicular** to the image plane—rather than in the image plane as in lateral resolution—that establishes slice thickness. Slice thickness is sometimes referred to as *elevational resolution* and as *scan plane thickness.*

Snell's law: expression that is used to predict the direction of the transmitted beam when refraction occurs. Stated mathematically, if θ_t is the angle of the transmitted wave and θ_i the angle of the incident wave, $\sin\theta_t = (c_2/c_1)\sin\theta_i$, where c_2 and c_1 are the speeds of sound on the transmitted and incident beam sides of the interface, respectively.

sound frequency: See **frequency**

sound wave: mechanical energy transmitted by pressure waves in a material medium; a mechanical disturbance that propagates progressively through a medium. This general definition encompasses all types of sound, including audible and ultrasound.

spatial resolution: the minimum distance between two reflectors such that they can be seen as separate echoes on the display. Spatial resolution is usually divided into lateral resolution, axial resolution, and slice thickness.

speckle: the granular random *texture* pattern produced in an ultrasound B-mode image of a macroscopically uniform region in tissue or a tissue-mimicking phantom.

spectral analysis: a process by which a complex signal is broken down or analyzed into simple frequency components; it is used, for example, to show the distribution of frequencies in a Doppler signal.

spectral display: (for a pulse or a complex signal) a plot of the fraction of signal within a given frequency interval versus the frequency.

spectrum analyzer: instrument used to measure the relative amount of signal at different frequencies in a pulsed waveform or in a complex signal consisting of many frequencies.

specular reflector: a large smooth interface with dimensions that are greater than the size of the incident ultrasound beam.

speed: the distance traveled per unit time.

stable cavitation: The creation of cavitation bubbles that oscillate with the sound beam but do not collapse violently, as in transient cavitation. See also **cavitation.**

static scanner: another name for a manual scanner.

swept gain: a process whereby the receiver amplification is increased with time following the transmit pulse so that echo signals originating from distant reflectors are amplified more than echo signals originating from reflectors close to the transducer. Swept gain compensates for attenuation in the medium. It is also referred to as **time gain compensation (TGC).**

tadpole tail sign: colloquial term used to describe the B-mode image pattern that results from scanning through and around a region, such as a walled cyst, where there is higher than average attenuation near the lateral margins of the region and lower than average attenuation across the middle of the region. On the image, the echo enhancement pattern, bordered laterally by patterns with partial or total shadowing, is said to resemble a tadpole's tail.

texture: in a B-mode ultrasound image, refers to the pixel-to-pixel variations in image brightness due to interference when echo signals are obtained simultaneously from many scatterers or due to properties of the tissue.

TGC: see **swept gain**

thermal index: (TI). the ratio of the acoustical power produced by the transducer to the power required to raise the temperature in tissue 1 degree C. The TI is estimated by algorithms in the scanner, taking into account the acoustical power, the ultrasound frequency, and the beam area, and making assumptions about the attenuation and absorption properties of the tissue. A TI value of one means that under tissue conditions assumed in the algorithm, the output level is high enough that up to a 1-degree elevation in temperature could occur.

time gain compensation: see **swept gain.**

tissue-mimicking phantom: a material, often configured in some specified shape, that mimics certain soft tissues in ultrasonic propagation and sometimes scattering and reflection properties.

transducer: any device that converts signals from one form to another. Examples include pressure sensing transducers, which yield an electrical signal proportional to the static pressure, and ultrasonic transducers. (See also **ultrasonic transducer.**)

transducer assembly: another name for the transducer in an ultrasound instrument; especially used for the transducer, associated housing, and any internal electronic circuitry attached to the console of real-time scanning instruments.

transient cavitation: A process in which cavitation oscillations grow so strong that the bubbles collapse, producing very intense localized effects. See also **cavitation.**

transmit focal distance: the distance from the transducer assembly to the plane where the transmitted beam width is narrowest for a given transmit focus setting.

transonic: adjective used to describe a region that is relatively unattenuating to sound waves.

transverse wave: sound wave for which the direction of displacement of particles in the medium is perpendicular to the direction of propagation of the wave. Transverse waves do not propagate effectively in soft tissues.

ultrasonic transducer: a device that converts electrical signals to mechanical vibrations and high-frequency pressure pulses to electrical signals.

variance: in Doppler signal processing, a measure of the variation (over a short time) of the mean Doppler signal from the volume corresponding to a single pixel in a color flow image or a single pulsed Doppler sample volume. The signal variance is used to detect turbulence.

vector: quantity defined with both an amplitude and a direction, such as velocity. The amplitude of the velocity is the same as the speed.

vertical distance measurement accuracy: a measure of the accuracy to which the distance between two point reflectors, separated along the direction of an acoustic beam line, can be determined on the display of a pulse-echo instrument.

wall filter: electronic filter applied to the audio output signal of a Doppler ultrasound instrument to reduce or eliminate low-frequency Doppler signals, such as those due to vessel wall movement. The lower cutoff frequency of the filter usually is operator adjustable.

watt: unit of power, equal to a joule per second. (See also **acoustical power** and **energy.**)

wave: see **sound wave**

wavelength: the distance over which a wave repeats itself; the distance in the line of advance of a wave from one point to the next point of corresponding phase. Also, the distance the wave travels during one period of oscillation of the source.

weakly focused transducers: transducers that have focusing properties such that beam patterns are very dependent upon the transducer diameter and frequency as well as the curvature of the element. In contrast, a strongly focused transducer's beam properties are more dependent on the curvature of the element and less so on the frequency and diameter of the transducer.

wide-band amplifier: an amplifier that responds to ultrasound echo signals that cover a large frequency range; usually it responds equally to all frequencies produced by the different transducer assemblies that can be used with the instrument.

REFERENCES

(Some of the technical definitions were obtained or modified from the following references.)

Dorland's illustrated medical dictionary, Philadelphia, 1965, Saunders.

Websters ninth new collegiate dictionary, Springfield, MA, 1985, Merriam-Webster.

Recommended ultrasound terminology, Laurel, MD, American Institute of Ultrasound in Medicine

McGraw-Hill dictionary of physics and mathematics, New York, 1978, McGraw-Hill.

Recommendations for terminology and display for Doppler echocardiology, American Society of Echocardiography.

Acoustic output measurement and labeling standard for diagnostic ultrasound equipment, Laurel, MD, 1992, American Institute of Ultrasound In Medicine.

Index